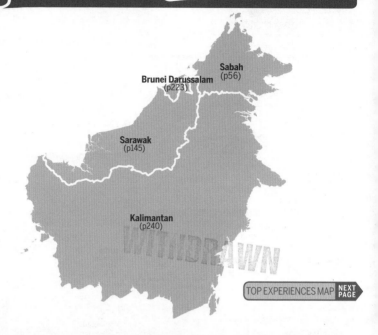

Sabah (p56)

Brunei Darussalam (p223)

Sarawak (p145)

Kalimantan (p240)

WITHDRAWN

TOP EXPERIENCES MAP | NEXT PAGE

PAGE 303

SURVIVAL GUIDE

VITAL PRACTICAL INFORMATION TO HELP YOU HAVE A SMOOTH TRIP

	Women
	Men
...ndas (M)	Toilets
Tutup	Closed
Wanita (f)	Women

Key Words

bottle	botol
breakfast	sarapan pagi
cold	dingin/sejuk (I/M)
cup	cangkir/cawan (I/M)
...ner	makan malam
	makanan
	garpu/garfu (I/M)

THIS EDITION WRITTEN AND RESEARCHED BY

**Daniel Robinson,
Adam Karlin, Richard Waters, Simon Richmond,
Iain Stewart, Joshua Samuel Brown**

Borneo

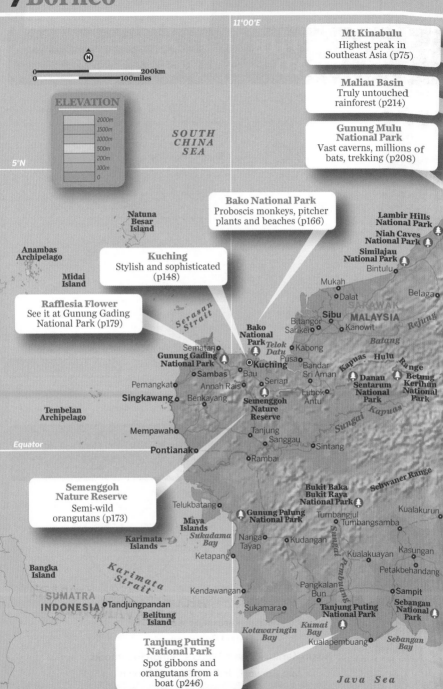

Mt Kinabulu
Highest peak in
Southeast Asia (p75)

Maliau Basin
Truly untouched
rainforest (p214)

**Gunung Mulu
National Park**
Vast caverns, millions of
bats, trekking (p208)

Bako National Park
Proboscis monkeys, pitcher
plants and beaches (p166)

Kuching
Stylish and sophisticated
(p148)

Rafflesia Flower
See it at Gunung Gading
National Park (p179)

**Semenggoh
Nature Reserve**
Semi-wild
orangutans (p173)

**Tanjung Puting
National Park**
Spot gibbons and
orangutans from a
boat (p246)

ELEVATION

2000m
1500m
1000m
500m
200m
100m
0

0   200km
0   100miles

SOUTH
CHINA
SEA

5°N

11°00'E

Natuna
Besar
Island

Anambas
Archipelago

Midai
Island

Lambir Hills
National Park
Niah Caves
National Park
Similajau
National Park
Bintulu
Belaga
Mukah
Dalat
SARAWAK
Bitangor
Sarikei
Sibu
Kanowit
MALAYSIA
Rejung
Batang

Serasan Strait

Sematan
Gunung Gading
National Park
Sambas
Annah Rais
Pemangkat
Singkawang
Benkayang
Bau
Serian
Kuching
Bako
National
Park
Telok
Datu
Kabong
Pusa
Bandar
Sri Aman
Lubok
Antu
Kapuas
Hulu
Danau
Sentarum
National
Park
Betung
Kerihun
National
Park
Semenggoh
Nature
Reserve
Sungai
Kapuas
Range

Tembelan
Archipelago

Mempawah
Tanjung
Sanggau
Sintang
Rambai

Equator

Pontianak

Telukbatang
Maya
Islands
Sukadama
Bay
Nanga
Tayap
Ketapang
Gunung Palung
National Park
Nanga
Kudangan
Bukit Baka
Bukit Raya
National Park
Tumbangjul
Tumbangsamba
Kualakuayan
Kasungan
Petakbehandang
Schwaner Range
Kualakurun

Karimata
Islands
Karimata
Strait

Bangka
Island

SUMATRA
INDONESIA
Tandjungpandan
Belitung
Island

Kendawangan
Sungai Pembuang
Pangkalan
Bun
Sukamara
Kumai
Bay
Kotawaringin
Bay
Kualapembuang
Tanjung Puting
National Park
Sampit
Sebangau
National
Park
Sebangan
Bay

Java Sea

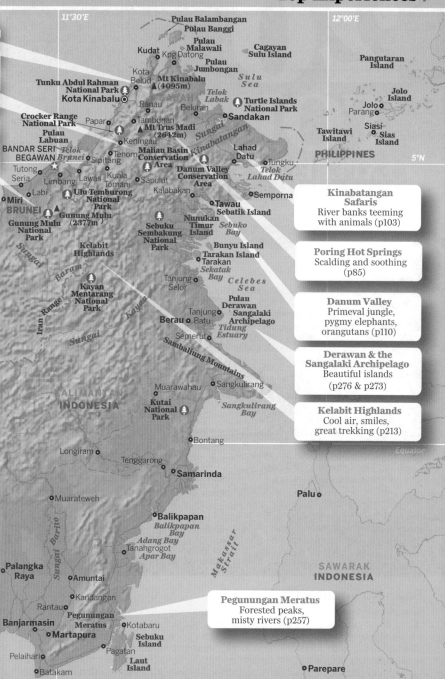

11°30'E

12°00'E

Pulau Balambangan
Pulau Banggi

Pulau Malawali

Cagayan Sulu Island

Pangutaran Island

Kudat
Kpg Datong

Pulau Jumbongan

Jolo Island

Kota Belud

Mt Kinabalu ▲(4095m)

Sulu Sea

Jolo
Parang

Tunku Abdul Rahman National Park
Kota Kinabalu

Ranau

Telok Labak

Turtle Islands National Park

Beluran

Tawitawi Island

Siasi
Sias Island

Crocker Range National Park

Papar

Tambunan

Mt Trus Madi ▲(2642m)

Sandakan

PHILIPPINES

5°N

Pulau Labuan

Keningau

Lahad Datu

BANDAR SERI BEGAWAN

Telok Brunei

Tenom

Maliau Basin Conservation Area

Tungku

Telok Lahad Datu

Sipitang

Tutong
Seria

Limbang

Lawas

Kuala Tomani

Sapulut

Danum Valley Conservation Area

Labi

Ulu Temburong National Park

Kalabakan

Semporna

BRUNEI

Miri

Gunung Mulu ▲(2377m)

Tawau
Sebatik Island

Kinabatangan Safaris
River banks teeming with animals (p103)

Gunung Mulu National Park

Sebuku Sembakung National Park

Nunukan Timur Island

Sebuko Bay

Poring Hot Springs
Scalding and soothing (p85)

Kelabit Highlands

Bunyu Island
Tarakan Island
Tarakan

Baram

Sekatak Bay
Celebes Sea

Danum Valley
Primeval jungle, pygmy elephants, orangutans (p110)

Iran Range

Kayan Mentarang National Park

Tanjung Selor

Pulau Derawan

Kayan

Sungai

Tanjung Batu

Sangalaki Archipelago

Derawan & the Sangalaki Archipelago
Beautiful islands (p276 & p273)

Berau

Semerut

Tidung Estuary

Sambaliung Mountains

KALIMANTAN
INDONESIA

Muarawahau

Sangkulirang

Kelabit Highlands
Cool air, smiles, great trekking (p213)

Kutai National Park

Sangkulirang Bay

Bontang

Equator

Longiram

Tenggarong

Samarinda

Palu

Muarateweh

Balikpapan

Sungai Barito

Balikpapan Bay
Adang Bay

Makassar Strait

Palangka Raya

Amuntai

Tanahgrogot
Apar Bay

SAWARAK
INDONESIA

Rantau
Kandangan

Pegunungan Meratus

Kotabaru

Pegunungan Meratus
Forested peaks, misty rivers (p257)

Banjarmasin
Martapura

Sebuku Island

Pelaihari

Pagatan

Laut Island

Batakam

Parepare

20 TOP EXPERENCES

Bako National Park

1 Wild jungle animals – think proboscis monkeys, bearded pigs and families of long-tailed macaques – are easier to spot on the rocky Bako peninsula than almost anywhere else in Borneo, although the park (p166) is just a short trip (by bus or car and then motorboat) from the bustle of Kuching. Over a dozen hiking trails take you to sandstone plateaus, waterfalls, secret bays and secluded beaches, passing through endangered lowland ecosystems – mangroves, heath forest, dipterocarp forest – that provide the ideal conditions for pitcher plants and terrestrial orchids.

Danum Valley

2 The last time we entered the Danum Valley (p110) it turned out it was not inhabited by dinosaurs and creatures of Jurassic lore. This seemed like false advertising – look at the Danum from every angle and it screams 'primeval jungle of time gone by'. But who could be disappointed? Between the shadowy, sheltering canopy, herds of pygmy elephants, wild orangutans and enough bird life to kick-start several thousand aviaries, this is Borneo at her most natural and enchanting.

Gunung Mulu National Park

3 If the only marvel at Mulu (p208) were the biggest cavern on earth, sprouting a phantasmagorical forest of stalactites and stalagmites, this park would be on any list of Borneo's best. If the only fauna were the twirling, spiraling clouds of bats that emerge each day at dusk, it would deserve Unesco World Heritage status. And if the only activity were spotting 20cm-long stick insects on a night walk, the flight from Miri would be worth it. But add in towering Gunung Mulu and the Pinnacles and you have one of Southeast Asia's wonders.

Kinabatangan River Safaris

4 Sungai Kinabatangan – the Kinabatangan River (p103) – deserves pride of place in a Joseph Conrad novel. Like a muddy brown python, Sabah's longest river constricts the jungle below Sandakan. The water is bracketed by riverine forest teeming with civet cats, orangutans, proboscis monkeys, saltwater crocodiles, monitor lizards, hornbills, kingfishers and hawks. Book yourself into one of several jungle camps in the villages of Sukau and Bilit, or stay in a local homestay, and set out on a river cruise for an excellent chance of spotting some of Borneo's most iconic animals.

Mt Kinabalu

5 Mt Kinabalu (p75) is so many things to so many people we don't know where to start. Highest mountain in Borneo and Malaysia, yet climbable by even novice trekkers? Check. Home of the spirits of local indigenous tribes? Check. Endemic cradle of some 6000 plant species and several unique-in-Borneo ecosystems? Check. On an island exploding with natural beauty, the sight of Mt Kinabalu's peak in the morning causes most folks to lose their breath. What poor words can we add to that experience?

ANDERS BLOMQVIST/LONELY PLANET IMAGES ©

Sarawak Longhouses

6 There's no better way to get a sense of indigenous tribal culture than to visit a longhouse – or, better yet, stay over. Essentially a whole village under a single roof, these dwellings can be longer than two football pitches and contain dozens of family units, each of which opens onto a covered common veranda used for economic activities, socialising and celebrations. All longhouses now enjoy at least some modern amenities, but most still have at least a few head-hunted skulls on display.

Iban girl at longhouse window, Sarawak Cultural Village (p170)

ANDERS BLOMQVIST/LONELY PLANET IMAGES ©

RICK RUDNICKI/LONELY PLANET IMAGES ©

Tunku Abdul Rahman National Park

7 Look out across the bay of Kota Kinabalu. Ah, turquoise water, white clouds, some soft humps of decidedly jungly-looking bliss burning under the sunset (plus a few large container ships. Ignore those). Those humps? The islands of Tunku Abdul Rahman National Park (p73). They're all eminently accessible by boat from the KK jetty, which means you can combine some urban adventures with a day trip to tropical serenity. These may not be the best islands off Borneo, but you can't beat them for convenience.

Kelabit Highlands

8 The air is clean and cool, the rice fields impossibly green, the local cuisine scrumptious and the trekking – from longhouse to longhouse – some of the best in Borneo, but the star attraction here is the people, justifiably famous for their ready smiles and easy way with visitors. Getting to Sarawak's remote northeastern corner (p213) is half the fun – you can either bust your butt on logging roads for 12 hours or take an exhilarating flight in a 19-seat Twin Otter turboprop.

KARL LEHMANN/LONELY PLANET IMAGES ©

Home Stays in Sabah

9 The Sabah sleeping situation generally divides between hostels, chalets and high-end hotels. Sadly, none of these experiences are dedicated to putting you in touch with locals. Home stays, on the other hand, are an excellent way of experiencing indigenous hospitality, enjoying home-cooked meals, being a cross-cultural ambassador and, while we're at it, getting a good bargain. They're particularly popular with families travelling with children, but anyone will find good home stays a refreshing change from the usual pace of Sabah lodging.

ANDERS BLOMQVIST/LONELY PLANET IMAGES ©

Kuching

10 Borneo's most sophisticated and stylish city (p148) brings together an atmospheric old town, a romantic waterfront, fine cuisine for all budgets, and chic night-spots that would be right at home in London. But the city's biggest draw is what's nearby: some of Sarawak's finest natural sites, easy to visit on day trips. You can spot semi-wild orangutans or search out a giant Rafflesia flower in the morning, look for proboscis monkeys and wild crocs on a sundown cruise in the South China Sea, and then dine on super-fresh seafood or crunchy midin fern tips.

Pegunungan Meratus (Meratus Mountains)

11 Before huge swaths of Borneo were aggressively carved up to make way for palm-oil plantations and voracious logging, the island looked something like the Meratus (p257). These mist-laced, river-crossed peaks are forested in thick jungle, steep valleys and jagged karst formations. They're also heavily Dayak, strong on religious custom with rituals lighting the night along with the shaman's drum. Home stay in a village that may have memories of head-hunting between river-rafting and trek-king in some of the most stunning scenery in Southeast Asia.

MARK DAFFEY/LONELY PLANET IMAGES ©

12 We'll forgive you for thinking the Poring Hot Springs (p85) are the overlooked add-on to Mt Kinabalu, because frankly, they're marketed that way. This is a shame, as the hot springs are more than a rushed extra. Located within a rather beautiful park, the springs are surrounded by a dark clump of jungle that's crisscrossed with small trekking paths, a swing bridge and a lovely canopy walkway. The springs themselves are basically artificial pools, but the water is pleasantly scalding and soothing for feet that have recently been up the mountain.

Rafflesia Flower

14 Up to 1m in diameter, the world's largest flower (p179) is a true wonder of the botanical world. Lacking roots, stems or leaves, this astonishing bloom – blotchy red and white with five fleshy petals – bursts forth from a cabbage-sized bud that takes nine months to mature and then lasts only five to seven days. Catching one in bloom is a matter of luck – keep your ears pricked for a hot tip in Kuching or Kota Kinabalu, both about two hours from prime Rafflesia territory.

KARL LEHMANN/LONELY PLANET IMAGES ©

Semenggoh Nature Reserve

15 Watching Homo sapiens encounter orangutans for the first time is almost as entertaining as watching our shaggy jungle cousins stuff half a dozen bananas into their mouths, grab a coconut and scramble back up into the jungle canopy. Both primate encounters are a twice-daily feature at Semenggoh Nature Reserve (p173) near Kuching, one of the best places in the world to see semi-wild orangutans swing from tree to tree, dangle nonchalantly from vines and take care of their adorable and very curious infants.

ANDERS BLOMQVIST/LONELY PLANET IMAGES ©

Temburong District

15 From a low-flying Twin Otter turboprop (or on Google Earth), Brunei's Temburong District (p236) looks like all of Borneo once did: an unbroken carpet of primary rainforest unblemished by roads, buildings or logging gashes. On the ground, most of the sultanate's eastern sliver is off-limits except to scientists, but you can get a taste of the primeval jungle at Ulu Temburong National Park (p238). The only way in is an exciting longboat ride. Once there you can climb into the jungle canopy and have wild fish nibble your feet in a cool stream.

DAVID KIRKLAND

Sepilok Orang-Utan Rehabilitation Centre

16 Most people find orangutans to be meltingly cute ambassadors of the Great Ape family. If you fit into this demographic, you'll love the Sepilok sanctuary (p99). You're likely not going to see orangutans gambolling as they would in the wild. That's because this is a dedicated research and rehabilitation facility, one of the better ones in Borneo. But it's still magical to watch these ginger giants during feeding times, when they bend their way over ropes and branches and turn their meal of bananas into so many scattered peels.

JOHN BANAGAN/LONELY PLANET IMAGES ©

PETER PTSCHELINZEW/LONELY PLANET IMAGES ©

Derawan & the Sangalaki Archipelago

17 There's a secret going round that a little group of islands in the Celebes Sea may be among the most beautiful and unspoilt in Indonesia. In the sleepy fishing island of Derawan (p276) it's par for the course you'll be having your morning dip with a giant green turtle and hiring a boat to take you to snorkel or scuba dive with manta rays in the coral blue waters of the Sangalaki Archipelago (p273). Barracuda, shark, rich coral reefs – all the treasures of the sea are waiting for you. Just don't tell anyone.

Tanjung Puting National Park

18 Arguably the best place in the world to experience close-up encounters with semi-wild orangutans, Tanjung Puting (p246) offers an unforgettable upriver journey on a chugging klotok boat (both your home and your lookout tower): the Milky Way glittering above you as you sleep alfresco on your top deck, the call of the gibbon waking you in the morning, and the emotional and fascinating experience of witnessing Borneo's critically endangered orangutans so close you're often rubbing shoulders with them.

CHRISTIAN ASLUND/LONELY PLANET IMAGES ©

Maliau Basin

19 You came to Borneo looking for something wild, right? The Maliau (p124) is as wild as it gets. The basin is a rock-rimmed depression filled with primary rainforest – that's untouched, uncut jungle, trees as old as civilisation. We asked a local ranger what he thought of the Maliau, and his Malay response was 'Adan da Hawa' – Adam and Eve. That's how fresh and perfect this forest feels, and while it may look expensive to enter, with a bit of initiative you too can experience the world as it once was.

Wildflowers, Maliau Basin

DANIEL ROBINSON

Sipadan

20 If the Danum Valley and Maliau Basin are the Platonic ideal of forests, then Sipadan (p115) is the same for coral reefs: the perfect incarnation of reef-dom. Maybe it's exaggerating to say all other reefs are but dreams of this reef, but more than a few publications place Sipadan next to the words 'World's Best Diving'. Between hammerheads and water monitors that resemble mini-Godzillas and gentle sea turtles and rays that could double as space ships, we dare you to enter these waters and walk away un-stunned by the sea.

welcome to
Borneo

It's a jungle out there! Borneo boasts some of the world's most species-rich equatorial rainforests – prime patches are easily accessible from multiethnic cities with great food.

Ancient Rainforests

If you love tropical greenhouses and can't wait to be enveloped by the humid fecundity of a real equatorial rainforest, Borneo will fulfil your wildest dreams. The island's jungles conjure up remoteness and peril, bringing to mind impenetrable foliage and river trips into the 'heart of darkness'. But look a little closer – on a nature walk with a park ranger, for instance – and nuances emerge: the pitcher plants, lianas and orchids of the lowland forest give way to conifers, rhododendrons and different kinds of orchids as you ascend the flanks of Mt Kinabalu. And the vegetation changes just as radically as you sail through the mangroves along the South China Sea. Deforestation makes for depressing headlines, but significant areas of the Bornean rainforest – among the most ancient ecosystems on earth – remain intact, protected by national parks and conservation projects whose viability depends in part on income from tourism.

Jungle Wildlife

For many visitors to Borneo, their most memorable moment is a personal encounter with a living creature: glimpsing a wild orangutan swinging through the jungle canopy, spotting an Irrawaddy dolphin in the shimmering waters of the South China Sea, or locking eyes with the reptilian gaze of a saltwater croc. Jungle animals are, by their nature, shy, but a good guide can help you tell the difference between a vine and vine snake (not as easy as you might think) and between a twig and a stick insect as long as an unsharpened pencil; they can also help you differentiate between the call of a gibbon and the cry of a hornbill, and identify a dominant male orangutan (hint: size counts but so do the cheeks). If you're keen to have close encounters of the animal kind, Borneo's jungles offer a unique combination of extraordinary biodiversity, unspoilt habitats and practical accessibility.

Cultural Riches

Borneo brings together an astonishing array of cultures, religions, languages and cuisines, and thanks to the age-old traditions of hospitality in the island communities, all these are easy to approach. The cities of Sarawak and Sabah have significant Chinese communities, while the picturesque coastal *kampung* (villages) are populated mainly by Muslim Malays, but head inland and the dominant culture is indigenous. Borneo's Dayak groups stopped nabbing noggins long ago, but many other ancient customs and ceremonies live on – in harmony with mod-cons – in longhouse communities. There's no better way to experience a slice of the Dayak way of life than to drop by for a visit – easy to arrange with a local guide.

need to know

Currency
» Malaysian ringgit (RM), Brunei dollar (B$), Indonesian rupiah (Rp)

Language
» Bahasa Malaysia, Bahasa Indonesia, Chinese dialects, indigenous languages

When to Go

Tropical climate, rain year-round

Kota Kinabalu
• GO year-round

Bandar Seri Begawan
GO year-round•

Kuching
•GO year-round

• Balikpapan
GO year-round

Banjarmasin
•GO year-round

» No good or bad season to visit

» Lowland areas always hot and humid

» Rain a real possibility every day all year (but without rain, as they say, it wouldn't be a rainforest)

» Indistinct wet season October to February, but conditions rarely interfere with travel, though can affect boat links to offshore islands and visibility for divers

» Accommodation and trekking guides most likely to be booked out July and August

Your Daily Budget

Budget less than
US$30

» Dorm bed: US$4–7

» Meals at food stalls, self-catering at fruit and vegie markets

» National park admission: US$3

» Almost all museums are free.

Midrange
US$30 –80

» Air-con double with bath: from US$20

» Meals at all but the priciest restaurants

» Taxis, chartered motorboats or tours to nature sites

Top end over
US$80

» Luxury double room: US$100

» Seafood dinner: $US8–20 per kilo

Money

» ATMs widely available in cities and larger towns. Credit cards usually accepted at top-end establishments.

Visas

» Generally not required for Malaysia and Brunei. Needed for Indonesia *except* if entering Kalimantan at Balikpapan, Pontianak or Tebedu-Entikong.

Mobile Phones

» Cheap international direct-dial calls can be made with a local SIM card in a 900/1800MHz phone. Settled areas have good coverage.

Transport

» Boats and planes go where roads don't. Buses link major cities in Sarawak, Brunei and Sabah.

Websites

» **Brunei Tourism** (www.bruneitourism. travel) Oodles of useful information.

» **Google Earth** (www. google.com/earth) Great town views.

» **Lonely Planet** (www. lonelyplanet.com) Information, bookings, forums and more.

» **Sabah Parks** (www. sabahparks.org) Sabah's national parks.

» **Sabah Tourism** (www.sabahtourism. com) Sabah Tourism Board.

» **Sarawak Forestry** (www.sarawakforestry. com) Sarawak's national parks.

» **Sarawak Tourism** (www.sarawaktourism. com) Sarawak's official tourism site.

Exchange Rates

		RM	B$	Rp
Australia	A$1	3.02	1.27	8930
Canada	C$1	3.05	1.28	9000
euro zone	€1	4.15	1.74	12,250
Japan	¥100	3.75	1.57	11,000
New Zealand	NZ$1	2.35	1.00	6950
Singapore	S$1	2.38	1.00	7020
UK	UK£1	4.85	2.04	14,300
USA	US$1	3.05	1.28	9025

For current exchange rates see www.xe.com.

Important Numbers

Country codes for Borneo.

Brunei	☏673
Indonesia	☏62
Malaysia	☏60

Arriving in Borneo

» **Malaysia**
Major airports such as Kuching, Kota Kinabalu and Miri have ATMs and orderly taxi queues with a voucher system and fixed prices.

» **Brunei**
Buses 23, 24, 36 and 38 link Brunei International Airport, which has ATMs, with the centre of Bandar Seri Begawan. Singapore dollars are universally accepted, with a conversion rate of one to one.

» **Kalimantan**
Taxis and other conveyances meet all incoming flights.

Wi-Fi & Internet Access

In Malaysian Borneo and Brunei, more and more guest houses and hotels – except some 'Chinese hotels' that focus on local custom – are wired for wi-fi, at least in the lobby, and many places also have internet computers.

Kalimantan is not quite as cyber-savvy, but as everywhere on the island, cities and large towns have cybercafes and, increasingly, cafes that offer wi-fi.

if you like...

Orangutans

You scan the canopy and wait, straining to hear the rustle of branches above the drone of cicadas. Suddenly, a fluttering of leaves and – a flash of orange-brown fur! It's a female orangutan, her baby hanging onto her long chest hair as the two of them swing through their native habitat, high in the rainforest canopy. Later, dangling in space, the mother crams bright yellow bananas into her mouth and casually hands fruit to her hungry infant.

Semenggoh Wildlife Sanctuary One of the best places in the world to see semi-wild orangutans (p173)

Sepilok Orang-utan Rehabilitation Centre Rescued orangutans, living free in the forest, drop by for fruit (p99)

Sungai Kinabatangan Home to lots of truly wild orangutans (p103)

Camp Leakey, Tanjung Puting National Park Great for sighting semi-wild orangutans at feeding times (p246)

Kutai National Park Guides work hard to spot wild orangutans in the canopy (p268)

Jungle Trekking

There's nothing quite like being a day or two's walk from the nearest road, entirely surrounded by old-growth rainforest as you tramp from one longhouse to the next. It's a challenging slog – the heat, the humidity and the leeches take their toll, and the trail itself sometimes disappears into a bog or, on muddy inclines, becomes as slippery as ice – but to be surrounded with such fecundity and botanical richness – the feeling is indescribable!

Maliau Basin Conservation Area Remote hikes through incomparable old-growth forest (p124)

Gunung Mulu National Park Options include the Headhunters' Trail (p211)

Bario to Ba Kelalan A classic trek through the Kelabit Highlands (p219)

Kinabalu National Park More than just the famous summit climb – also has great trekking (p75)

Pegunungan Meratus (Meratus Mountains) Trails criss-cross forested valleys, passing Dayak villages with a legacy of head-hunting (p258)

Diving & Snorkelling

Part of the 'Coral Triangle' (www.coraltrianglecenter.org), home to 600 coral species and over 3000 types of fish, Borneo boasts some of the most breathtaking dive sites anywhere on the planet. There's an abundance of healthy coral (sea fans can reach 3m across) and visibility is often 30m to 50m – and then there are the drop-offs, some an unimaginable 2000m! Reefs harbour an incredible variety of marine life, and divers regularly encounter sharks, dolphins, rays and green turtles.

Sipadan One of the world's greatest dive sites, legendary for coral walls, large pelagic species, turtles and deep wall dives (p115)

Layang Layang A remote island renowned for wall dives, pristine coral and real adventure (p92)

Pulau Mantanani Two little flecks of land ringed by a halo of colourful coral (p91)

Mabul Lots of small, colourful sea creatures (p118)

Pulau Derawan & Sangalaki Archipelago Has some brilliant pier, cave and wall dives (p276 and p273)

>> Clown fish in the reefs of the Sipadan region (p115)

TIM ROCK/LONELY PLANET IMAGES ©

PLAN YOUR TRIP IF YOU LIKE

Indigenous Culture

Borneo's Dayak groups – best known for the now-extinct practice of head-hunting – have lived in harmony with the rainforest for thousands of years, in remote communities based on mutual reliance and responsibility. Even a short longhouse visit (see p300) offers insights into their age-old traditions – and the ways they're adapting to modern life. Come during a festival and you may be asked to join in the merriment, liberally lubricated with *tuak* (rice wine).

Pegunungan Meratus Animist beliefs are strong and shamans have plenty of work in these remote hills (p259)

Kelabit Highlands One of the best places in Borneo to trek from longhouse to longhouse (p218)

Batang Ai Region Authentic, old-time Iban longhouses, many accessible only by boat (p183)

Batu Punggul Tribesmen still sport tattoos at the remote Murut longhouse of Tataluang (p129)

Penambawan A traditional village of the seafaring Bajau, with some old-style thatch houses (p87)

Classic Boat Trips

From time immemorial, rivers were the only transport arteries into Borneo's interior, and in some areas boats are still the only way to get around. Since river travel can be a blast, it makes sense to make a virtue of necessity by treating your transport as part of the adventure.

Kumai to Camp Leakey, Tanjung Puting National Park Takes you through rainforest teeming with macaques, wild orangutans, pythons and crocs (p247)

Sungai Mahakam The further upriver you go, the wilder the wildlife and the more authentic the longhouses (p269)

Wildlife River Cruise, Sungai Kinabatangan A boat is the ideal perch for spotting an ark's worth of animals, including orangutans and pygmy elephants (p105)

Batang Rejang The only way to get to Kapit and Belaga is by 'flying coffin' river express (p188 and p192)

Bandar Seri Begawan to Bangar You roar down Sungai Brunei, slap through palm-lined waterways and then tilt and weave among mangroves (p237)

Multicultural Cities

Nowhere is Borneo's extraordinary ethnic gumbo more colourful – and delicious – than in the cities. The minarets of Malay mosques tower over the streetscape a few blocks from bright red Chinese temples, and both are just a short walk from colonial-era shophouses and hawker centres with a tongue-boggling array of bubbling soups, barbecuing *satay* and fresh-squeezed juices. Many cities take special pride in their parks, promenades and festivals.

Kuching Fantastic for strolling and aimless exploration, with 19th-century forts, a picturesque Chinatown and excellent cuisine for every budget (p148)

Bangar Seri Begawan Blessed with picturesque water villages, two stunning mosques and some outstanding food stalls, BSB is as polite and unassuming as its people (p224)

Sibu The mostly Chinese 'Swan City' boasts a busy ferry port, 22 community parks, and a great night market (p184)

Kota Kinabalu Offers visitors a walkable centre, a lovely waterfront and a surprisingly happening nightlife scene (p57)

If you like...discovering new varieties of traditional music, plan your trip to coincide with the Rainforest World Music Festival, which features both international world musicians and longhouse-based Dayak bands (p155)

World-Record Flowers

In the sedate world of flowers, the Rafflesia is an unabashed mega-star, a bigger-than-life celebrity that turns mild-mannered amateur botanists into star-struck groupies and shameless paparazzi. Each Rafflesia patiently puts up with the hullabaloo, confident that its good looks and super-size charisma will last for its allotted few days until, Cinderella-like, it collapses into a black ring of limp, putrid flesh.

With flowers up to 1m across, there's nothing quite like this coquettish parasite anywhere in the botanical world, but not every visitor is lucky enough to be around when a bud bursts into bloom. In Kuching, stay alert for a hot Rafflesia tip – if one appears, drop everything and go!

Gunung Gading National Park Has 30 to 50 Rafflesia blooms a year within day-trip distance of Kuching (p179)

Tambunan Rafflesia Reserve Probably the best place in Sabah to see the world's largest flower (p127)

Exploring Caves

Borneo has an incredible variety of underground wonders. While some of the most breathtaking caves must be visited with a professional guide, others are easily accessible on plankwalks. Daily at dusk, millions of bats head out of Borneo's caves to hunt insects – an awesome sight!

Gunung Mulu National Park Some of the world's most spectacular caves, filled with fantastic stalactites, are home to millions of bats and swiftlets (p210)

Kuching Caving This small spelunking outfit mounts adventurous day-expeditions to Kuching-area caves (p177)

Gomantong Caves The cathedral-like grand chamber is speckled with rays of sunlight (p104)

Niah National Park Niah's enormous caverns, once home to prehistoric humans, are easy to explore on boardwalks (p198)

Wind Cave & Fairy Cave Pathways make it possible to visit unaccompanied (p177)

The Rainforest Canopy

Most jungle life lives high in the forest canopy, up where the light is. Unless you're a scientist, the only way to see this floating ecosystem, suspended between soil and sky, is from a gently swaying canopy walk, supported by towers or held aloft between trees. Wildlife is most plentiful after dawn and at dusk, but during the day you've got a good chance of glimpsing orchids, bird's-nest ferns, baby strangler figs and the flash of feathers as a bird swoops by.

Gunung Mulu National Park The 480m-long skywalk is one of the best in Southeast Asia (p209)

Ulu Temburong National Park A delicate aluminium walkway, secured by guy-wires, takes you 60m above the forest floor (p239)

Poring Hot Springs A series of walkways provides unmatched views of the forest (p111)

Danum Valley Swinging bridges traverse a 107m-long section of forest (p111)

Sepilok Rainforest Discovery Centre Eight canopy towers are under construction (p100)

month by month

1 **Gawai Dayak**, June

2 **Harvest Festival**, May

3 **Chinese New Year**, January

4 **Hari Raya Puasa**, August

5 **Rainforest World Music Festival**, July

Because the Islamic year has 12 lunar months (354 or 355 days), Muslim holidays move through the seasons, arriving 11 or 12 days earlier each year according to the Gregorian (Western) calendar. Listings below are based on holiday dates from 2012 to 2014. The Chinese calendar adds lunar leap months to keep it in line with the seasons but holiday dates vary from year to year.

January

The weather is hot and humid, with rain always likely. January is the wettest month of the year in Kuching, Sarawak and Banjarmasin, South Kalimantan. The sea off Sarawak can be rough.

⭐ Chinese New Year

Borneo's Chinese communities, especially large in Kuching and Sibu, welcome the New Year (late January or early February) with bright red lanterns, sweets, lion and dragon dances, drum performances, night markets and, often, a raucous (and illegal) display of firecrackers and fireworks.

April

The weather is hot and humid, with rain always likely, even in Sandakan, Sabah, where months don't get any drier than April.

⭐ Baleh-Kapit Raft Safari

This challenging race (see p191), spread over two days, recreates the experience of the Iban and Orang Ulu people who used to travel downstream by raft to bring their jungle produce to Kapit. Held in late spring, often in April.

⭐ Regatta Lepa

Bajau sea gypsy families deck out their *lepa* (boats) with streamers, bunting, flags, ceremonial umbrellas and gorgeously decorated sails. The mid-April festivities are further animated with violin, cymbal and drum music, duck-catching competitions and tug-of-war contests with boats (for details see p116).

May

The weather is hot and humid, with rain always likely. May is not the wettest month anywhere on the island, but neither is it the driest, so be prepared to get wet.

⭐ Miri International Jazz Festival

An eclectic assemblage of international artists from the US, France, the Netherlands, Brazil, Japan and China (that was the 2011 line-up) makes this festival, held on a weekend in mid-May, Borneo's premier jazz event. For details, see www.mirijazzfestival.com.

⭐ Harvest Festival

Rice is the basis of Sabah's indigenous way of life. To mark the annual harvest, native peoples gather in their home villages on 30 and 31 May for a colourful thanksgiving festival that's also known as Pesta Ka'amatan.

June

The weather is hot and humid, with rain always likely. June is the wettest month of the year in Balikpapan, West Kalimantan. Because of the northern-hemisphere summer, tourist numbers rise.

★ Gawai Dayak

Held on 1 and 2 June but beginning on the evening of 31 May, this Sarawak-wide Dayak festival (see p302) celebrates the end of the rice harvest season. City-dwelling Dayaks return to their longhouses to socialise, eat and down shots of *tuak* (rice wine).

July

The weather is hot and humid, with rain likely even in Kuching, where it's the driest month. Northern-hemisphere tourists flock to Borneo so consider booking treks, caving, guides and tours in advance.

★ Borneo Cultural Festival

The mostly Chinese city of Sibu, Sarawak, hosts music, dance and cultural performances representing the Chinese, Malay-Melanau and Dayak traditions. Usually takes place between the 1st and 2nd weekends of July. For details see www.borneoculturalfestival.com.

★ Rainforest World Music Festival

This three-day musical extravaganza (www.rainforestmusic-borneo.com), held in the Sarawak Cultural Village (near Kuching) on the 2nd weekend in July, brings together Dayak bands and international artists. Accommodation fills up well in advance.

★ Sultan of Brunei's Birthday

Colourful official ceremonies are held on 15 January to mark the birthday of Sultan Hassanal Bolkiah. In Bandar Seri Begawan, events include an elaborate military ceremony presided over by the supremo himself, smartly dressed in a medal-bedecked uniform.

★ Belaga Rainforest Challenge

Held around the remote river town of Belaga (p192), Sarawak, in July or August of even-numbered years, this three- or four-day festival combines a 12km jungle run with boat races and traditional music and dance. Intended for area tribes but tourists are welcome.

August

The weather is hot and humid, with rain likely even though August is the driest month in Banjarmasin, South Kalimantan. Northern-hemisphere tourists are numerous so consider booking treks, caving, guides and tours in advance.

★ Kuching Festival Fair

For three weeks in late July and August, scores of evening stalls serve the delicious dishes of Kuching's various Chinese communities, Nonya desserts and beer. Held about 2km southeast of the city centre next to Kuching South City Hall (MBKS Building; see p155).

★ Hungry Ghost Festival

On the 15th day of the seventh Chinese lunar month (mid-August or early September), when the spirits of the dead are free to roam the earth, offerings of food, prayer, incense and paper money are made to appease the spirits.

★ Ramadan

During the month of Ramadan (overlaps with July and August through 2014), Muslims are not allowed to eat, drink or have sexual relations from dawn to sunset. Celebratory breakfast meals are held after sundown. Many offices have shorter hours and some restaurants close during daylight.

★ Hari Raya Puasa

This festive, three-day Muslim holiday (in August or late July through 2014) marks the end of the fasting month of Ramadan. Many people travel to their hometowns, creating traffic jams and a shortage of air, boat and bus tickets.

September

The weather is hot and humid. September isn't the driest month anywhere on the island, so be prepared for rain.

⭐ Borneo International Kite Festival

Held on the runway of the old airport in Bintulu, Sarawak, this festival (www.borneokite.com) brings colourful, strange and marvellous kites to Borneo's natural-gas capital. Takes place over four days (Thursday to Sunday) in late September or early October.

⭐ Mooncake Festival

Colourful festivities, musical performances and stalls selling food, drink and, of course, mooncakes take over Jln Carpenter in Kuching's Chinatown for about a week in September or early October (see p155). Also celebrated in other towns with large Chinese communities.

⭐ Erau Festival

Held in very late September, this festival sees thousands of Dayaks from all over Kalimantan converging on Tenggarong (p269), on the mighty Sungai Mahakam (Mahakam River), in a whirl of tribal costumes, ceremony and dance.

itineraries

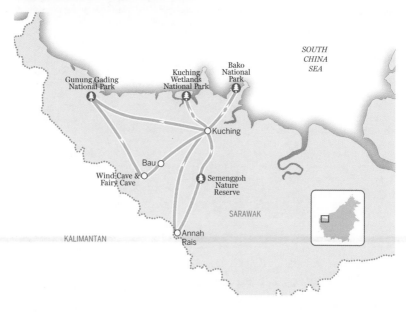

One Week
Kuching Excursions

> Spend your first day in **Kuching** picking up the vibe of the city's kaleidoscopic mix of cultures and cuisines. Explore the shophouses of **Chinatown**, ride a tiny passenger ferry to the English Renaissance-style **Fort Margherita**, and take a sunset stroll along the **Waterfront Promenade**. If it's Saturday, head to the **Weekend Market** in the afternoon; if it's Sunday, visit in the morning. And if a giant **Rafflesia flower** happens to be in bloom in **Gunung Gading National Park**, drop everything and rush over before it rots; on the way back explore the **Wind Cave** and the **Fairy Cave**. On other days, combine a daytime excursion with an evening enjoying Kuching's fine eateries and chic but laid-back nightlife. Spend a half-day spotting orangutans at **Semenggoh Nature Reserve**, then drive further inland to the longhouse of **Annah Rais**, where you can stay overnight. Take a boat to **Bako National Park**, keeping an eye out for proboscis monkeys, macaques and pitcher plants as you hike around the peninsula, or spend the sunset hour cruising around **Kuching Wetlands National Park**, alert for fireflies, crocs and proboscis monkeys.

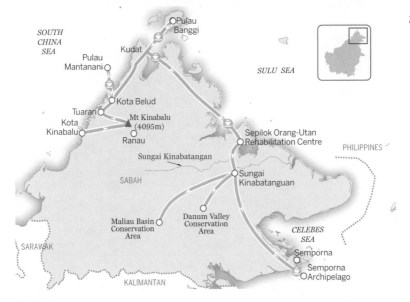

20 Days
Around Sabah

> Arrive in **Kota Kinabalu** (KK) and give yourself two days to pre-book accommodation in places like Sungai Kinabatangan, the Semporna Archipelago (if you plan on diving) and Mt Kinabalu – accommodation at the latter should ideally be booked before you get to Sabah. Whilst in KK, make sure to eat at the **Night Market**, take a trip to the **Mari Mari Cultural Village**, **Sabah Museum** and **Lok Kawi Wildlife Park** – you can get a taste of the cultures, landscapes and animal life you're about to encounter first hand! Party on the KK waterfront your first night in town, but try to keep your head clear the morning you leave Sabah's capital.

If you decide to climb **Mt Kinabalu**, it's easiest to leave from KK. You'll need to budget in two or three days for the mountain – there's the climb itself, and the day of rest you'll need afterwards! Whether you climb the highest mountain in Borneo or not, give yourself a few days to explore northwest Sabah. In **Tuaran**, you can see the lovely Penambawan water village, while in **Kota Belud** you can relax at Mañana Guest House and see, if you time things right, the famous Sunday *tamu* (market). Heading north are the hidden beaches of **Kudat**, and offshore, the isolated, off-the-tourist-trail islands of **Pulau Mantanani** (easier to get to from Kota Belud) and **Pulau Banggi**. This area is great for home stays.

Now a little over a week into your trip, head east to **Sepilok** and its famous orangutan sanctuary. After watching our arboreal cousins get fed in a wildlife reserve, try to spot them in the wild during a river cruise down the **Sungai Kinabatangan**. There are great lodges and home stays out this way. Relaxing in these two spots could easily fill four days to a week. Now decide – do you want to finish by diving in the **Semporna Archipelago**? Trekking in the **Danum Valley**, or the **Maliau Basin**? All of the above are possible, but to be practical and give these destinations the time they deserve, budget in five days for each. If you want to both dive and do the Danum or Maliau, cut out the days allotted for exploring northwest Sabah above.

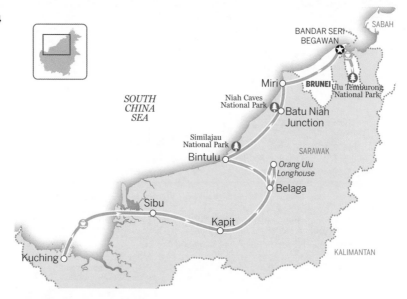

Two Weeks
Kuching to Brunei

> After exploring **Kuching** and nearby nature sites for a few days, hop on the express ferry to **Sibu**, a mostly Chinese river port that's long been the gateway to the mighty **Batang Rejang** (Rejang River), 'Borneo's Amazon'. Board an early-morning 'flying coffin' (express boat) upriver to **Kapit**, a bustling trading centre dating back to the days of the White Rajas. If the water is high enough, continue on to back-of-the-beyond **Belaga**, not far from several Orang Ulu **longhouses**. A bone-jarring 4WD will get you down to the coastal city of **Bintulu**; spend a day or two chilling out on the trails and beaches of oft-overlooked **Similajau National Park**. Then hop a bus to **Batu Niah Junction**, a short ride from the vast caves, bat colonies and prehistoric archaeology of **Niah Caves National Park**. Next stop is the petroleum city of **Miri**, now developing a guest-house scene to complement its lively dining options. After a day or two, take the daily bus – or the newspaper van – to **Bandar Seri Begawan**, the surprisingly laid-back capital of the tiny, oil-rich sultanate of Brunei. Finally, travel by speedboat, car and then longboat to the pristine jungles of **Ulu Temburong National Park**.

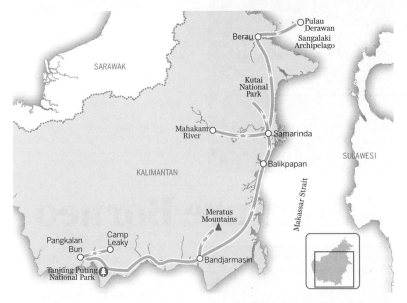

Three Weeks
Around Kalimantan

⟩ Fly to the town of **Pangkalan Bun** and then head upriver to **Camp Leakey** in **Tanjung Puting National Park** – this is the best place in the world to see semi-wild orangutans.
From there fly or bus it to **Banjarmasin**, a must for experiencing local river culture, including atmospheric floating markets. Nearby are the majestic **Meratus Mountains** – the area is perfect for trekking, river rafting and Dayak home stays surrounded by some of the best scenery in Borneo. Head north from Banjarmasin to oil-rich **Balikpapan** or straight on to **Samarinda**, the gateway city to the **Mahakam River**, ideal for the adventurer seeking out their own *Heart of Darkness* odyssey rich in shamans, longhouses and wildlife. From Samarinda, bus it to **Kutai National Park** to trek among wild orangutans, sun bears, monitor lizards, giant squirrels and 250 bird species, then return to Samarinda and fly straight to **Berau**, springboard for the beautiful coral-fringed desert island of **Pulau Derawan**, famed for its scuba diving, and the **Sangalaki Archipelago**.

Adventure Borneo

Best Rainforest Trekking

Maliau Basin (p124)
Kelabit Highlands (p218)
Gunung Mulu National Park (p208)
Pegunungan Meratus (Meratus Mountains; p258)

Best Mountain Climbing

Mt Kinabalu (p75)
Gunung Mulu (p211)

Best Caving

Gunung Mulu National Park (p208)
Niah National Park (p198)

Best Boat Trips

Sungai Mahakam (p269)
Sungai Padas (p129)
Sungai Kinabatangan (p105)
Batang Rejang (p187 and p192)
Ulu Temburong National Park (p239)

Borneo is one of Southeast Asia's premier adventure-sports destinations, with a spectacular mix of jungle, water and thrills that will wow both nature lovers and adrenalin junkies. If you like to experience a place by trekking it, climbing it, crawling through it or floating on it, you'll love Borneo.

Rainforest Trekking
When to Go

Borneo has some of the best jungle trekking anywhere in the world. While the island's forests are disappearing at an alarming rate, vast swaths of old-growth (primary) tropical rainforest still cover the middle of island and much of Brunei, and patches remain in parts of Sabah and Sarawak. If you've never walked through genuine tropical jungle, the experience is likely to be a revelation: you simply won't believe the biodiversity – or the leeches.

Borneo has wet months and less wet months – which depends on where you are – but precipitation varies so widely from year to year that a month that's usually dry can be very rainy, and vice versa. In short, no matter when you go you are likely to get wet.

What is seasonal, however, is the number of other travellers you'll be competing with for experienced guides and lodgings. For obvious reasons, northern hemisphere residents often come to Borneo during summer holidays in their home countries, so if you'd like to trek in July or August, book a guide or tour far in advance.

Guides

Many national parks have well-marked day trails and can be tramped unaccompanied. But for almost all overnights, only a fool would set out without a local guide. Remember, trail maps of any sort are completely unavailable and signage along remote trail networks non-existent.

Especially in Sabah, Brunei and Sarawak, the national parks are very strict about allowing only licensed guides. We've heard stories of groups being turned back when they arrived with an uncertified leader. Before you fork over any cash, compare notes with other travellers and ask to see the guide's national-park certification.

Guides for day walks can sometimes be hired at national park HQ, but for overnights you'll need to contact either a freelance guide or a tour agency.

Physical Demands

Hiking in the tropics is much more strenuous than in temperate zones. One kilometre in a place like Borneo is roughly equivalent to two in Europe or North America. Thanks to the combination of high temperatures and humidity, you will sweat enough to discover what eyebrows are for, so be sure to drink enough water. In *kerangas* (heath forests) and on mountains, prepare for intense sun by wearing a sun hat and sunscreen.

Borneo is hardly the Himalayas but even in the Kelabit Highlands (1500m) you may feel the altitude, at least for a few days.

Practical Preparations

Jungle trekking can be one of the highlights of a trip to Borneo. However, to the uninitiated, it can be something of a shock – like marching all day in a sauna with a pile of bricks strapped to your back. To make the experience as painless as possible, it's necessary to make some crucial preparations:

» On overnight trips, bring two sets of clothing, one for hiking and one to wear at the end of the day (keep your night kit dry in a plastic bag). Within minutes of starting, your hiking kit will be drenched and will stay that way throughout your trip. Never blur the distinction between your day and night kits, or you'll find that you have two sets of wet clothes.

» If you'll be travelling through dense vegetation, wear long trousers and a long-sleeved shirt. Otherwise, shorts and a T-shirt will suffice. Whatever you wear, make sure that it's loose-fitting.

» Bring fast-drying synthetic clothes. Once cotton gets wet, it won't dry until you bring it to the laundry back in town.

» It can be cool in the evening in Borneo, so bring a fleece top to keep warm.

» Unless you like a lot of support, consider hiking in running shoes with good traction.

» Buy a pair of light-coloured leech socks You won't find these in Borneo, so buy them online before coming. For more on leeches, see p29.

» Drink plenty of water. If you're going long distances, you'll have to bring either a water filter or a water-purification agent like iodine (most people opt for the latter to keep weight down).

» Get in shape long before coming to Borneo and start slowly. Try day hikes before longer treks.

» Always go with a guide unless you're on a well-marked, commonly travelled trail. Navigating in the jungle, where most of the time all you can see is the bottom of the canopy, is extremely difficult.

» Bring talcum powder to cope with the chafing caused by wet undergarments. Wearing loose underwear will also help prevent chafing.

» If you wear glasses, you might want to treat them with an antifog solution (ask at the shop where you buy your glasses). Otherwise, you may find yourself in a foggy white-out within minutes of setting out.

» Your sweat will soak through the back of your backpack. Consider putting something waterproof over the back padding to keep the sweat out of your pack. Otherwise, consider a waterproof stuff sack.

» Keep your camera in a Tupperware container, with a pouch of silica gel or other desiccant.

Guides & Agencies

A wide variety of tour agencies and guides can help you head for the hills.

Sabah

» Borneo Eco Tours (www.borneoecotours.com; p64)

» Borneo Nature Tours (www.borneonaturetours.com; p109)

» Borneo Adventure (www.borneoadventure.com; p63)

Sarawak

» Highlands Jungle Academy (www.borneojungleadventures.com; p216)

» Kelabit Highlands guides (p215)

» Borneo Tropical Adventure (www.borneotropicaladventure.com; p204)

LEECHES SUCK (BLOOD)

There's just no getting around it: if you want to experience Borneo's magnificent tropical rainforests, you're going to encounter leeches. If you do any jungle walking, at some point you'll find yourself getting up close and intimate with one of these slimy hemophages – or, more likely, with lots of them. If you can't stand the sight of blood, wear dark-coloured socks.

For some travellers, the spectre of leeches coming at them from every direction is – beyond being unspeakably disgusting – an outrageous reversal of roles: humans are supposed to eat, not be eaten! But look at things from the leech's point of view: the vibrations you produce as you walk are, literally, the opportunity of a lifetime.

There are two main varieties of leech in Borneo: the common ground-dwelling brown leech; and the striped yellow-reddish tiger leech, which often lives higher up on foliage. Leeches are probably the jungle's quietest creatures and since you can't feel the bite of the brown leech, you'll only realise when you actually spot him-and-her (leeches are hermaphrodites) – or when you notice blood seeping through your clothing. But you *can* feel the bite of a tiger leech – it's a bit like an ant sting – which means that if you're quick, you can take action before making an involuntary donation of protein to the jungle ecosystem.

While leeches are horrible creatures, they are almost completely harmless. They don't generally carry parasites, bacteria or viruses that can infect human beings. A bite may itch and bleed profusely for a few hours due to the anticoagulant juices the leech injects. The spot may itch for another week, and then it will scab over and resolve into a small dark spot that completely disappears after several weeks. The only danger is that the bite may get infected, which is why it's important to disinfect the bite and keep it dry.

Like hangover cures, everyone has a method of protecting themselves from leeches. Problem is, most don't work. Putting tobacco in your socks or on your shoes is a favourite method. We tried this one and it only seemed to encourage the little bastards. Many Kelabit

» Borneo Jungle Safari (www.borneojunglesafari.com; p204)

» Gunung Mulu National Park guides (www.mulupark.com; p208)

» Borneo Touch Ecotour (www.walk2mulu.com; p220)

» Borneo Adventure (www.borneoadventure.com; p165)

» Singgahsana Lodge (www.singgahsana.com; p156)

Brunei

» Borneo Guide (www.borneoguide.com; p229)

Kalimantan

» Banjarmasin-based guides (p253)

» Balikpapan-based guides (p262)

» Samarinda-based guides to Sungai Mahakam (p264)

» De'Gigant Tours (www.borneotourgigant.com; p267)

Mountain Climbing

Towering above the forests of Borneo are some brilliant mountains. Even non-climbers know about 4095m Mt Kinabalu, the highest peak between the Himalayas and the island of New Guinea. This craggy monster simply begs to be climbed, and there is something magical about starting the ascent in humid tropical jungle and emerging into a bare, rocky alpine zone so cold that snow has been known to fall. But beyond the transition from hot to cold, it's the weird world of the summit plateau that makes Mt Kinabalu among the world's most interesting peaks. It's got a dash of Yosemite and a pinch of Torres del Paine, but at the end of the day, it's pure Borneo.

Gunung Mulu (2377m) isn't quite as high but it's almost as famous, thanks in part to being a Unesco World Heritage Site. If you're a real glutton for punishment, you'll probably find the five-day return trek to the summit of this peak to your liking. Those who make the journey experience a variety of pristine natural environments, starting with lowland dipterocarp forest and ending with rhododendron and montane forest.

people swear that spraying your shoes with a powerful insecticide works (that's insecticide, not insect repellent). We didn't try this one for fear of 'complications'. There is only one really effective method of keeping leeches off: buy yourself a pair of leech socks before coming to Borneo. These are socks made from tightly knit fabric that reach to your knees. The best ones are light coloured so that you can see the leeches ascending your legs and pick them off. You can find these online from speciality shops.

If you do discover a leech on you, don't panic! Pulling off a leech can leave part of its jaws in the wound, and burning it can cause it to regurgitate its stomach contents. Slide your fingernail along your skin at the point where the leech is biting to break the suction. The leech will try to grab your finger with its other end so roll it around to prevent it from getting a grip and flick it away. If there are other people around, it's good form to chop the leech in half with your *parang* (Bornean machete). One more thing to remember: salt is to leeches as kryptonite is to Superman. Some people put a teaspoon of salt inside some thin cloth and tie it to the top of a stick – touch a leech with something salty and they'll fall right off. Don't squirt DEET directly on sucking leeches as the chemical may get in your wound.

If you find a few leech bites on your feet, console yourself with thoughts of what others have encountered in the Borneo forest:

'We woke periodically throughout the night to peel off leeches. In the light of the head torch, the ground was a sea of leeches – black, slithering, standing up on one end to sniff the air and heading inexorably our way to feed. Our exposed faces were the main problem, with leeches feeding off our cheeks and becoming entangled in our hair. I developed a fear of finding one feeding in my ear, and that it would become too large to slither out, causing permanent damage' (from Rich Mayfield's *Kinabalu Escape: The Soldiers' Story*).

If that doesn't put your suffering into perspective, then you can console yourself with the thought that you're playing an active role in the Borneo ecosystem!

Pre-Trip Preparations

Climbing one of Borneo's iconic mountains is like a jungle trek except more so – more exhausting, more psychologically challenging and especially more vertical. Be prepared for ascents that turn your legs to rubber and much colder weather. As with longer treks, book well ahead.

Guides & Agencies

Many of the agencies that handle trekking also offer mountain ascents. Some of the more experienced guides in Sarawak's Kelabit Highlands can take you to two rarely climbed peaks, Batu Lawi and Gunung Murud.

Caving

Slice one of Borneo's limestone hills in half and chances are you'll find that inside it looks like a Swiss cheese. Borneans have been living, harvesting birds' nests, planning insurgencies and burying their dead in these caves for tens of thousands of years. These days, the island's subterranean spaces – including some of the largest caverns anywhere on earth – are quiet, except for the flow of underground streams, the drip of stalactites and the whoosh of the wings of swiftlets and bats.

Sarawak's Gunung Mulu National Park is a place of spelunking superlatives. It's got the world's second-largest cave passage (the Deer Cave, 2km in length and 174m in height), the world's largest cave chamber (the Sarawak Chamber, which is 700m long, 400m wide and 70m high) and Asia's longest cave (the Clearwater Cave, 107km in length). Several of the park's caves are – like their counterparts in Niah National Park – accessible to non-spelunkers: you can walk through them on well-maintained walkways.

A pitch-black passageway deep in the bowels of the earth is not the ideal place to discover that you can't deal with narrow, confined spaces. Before heading underground, seriously consider your susceptibility to claustrophobia and fear of heights (some caves require scaling underground cliffs). If you have any concerns about a specific route, talk with your guide beforehand.

Be prepared to crawl through muck, including bat guano, and bring clothes you won't mind getting filthy in (some guides and agencies supply these).

AL'S JUNGLE KIT LIST *AL DAVIES*

General Kit
- ☐ rucksack
- ☐ rucksack liner
- ☐ waterproof bags
- ☐ daypack
- ☐ water bottles
- ☐ personal medical kit
- ☐ water purifier
- ☐ insect repellent (DEET)
- ☐ pocket knife
- ☐ head torch (flashlight)
- ☐ spare mini-torch
- ☐ small binoculars
- ☐ notepad and pencil

Clothing
- ☐ jungle boots
- ☐ breathable waterproof socks or boot liners
- ☐ sandals

- ☐ socks
- ☐ underwear
- ☐ Lycra bras
- ☐ long trousers (2)
- ☐ shorts
- ☐ long-sleeve shirts (2)
- ☐ lightweight waterproof jacket
- ☐ swimwear
- ☐ warm top
- ☐ sunhat
- ☐ sarong
- ☐ sweat rag

Sleeping
- ☐ basha (tarpaulin) sheet
- ☐ hammock
- ☐ mosquito net
- ☐ bungee cords
- ☐ sleeping mat

- ☐ sleeping bag
- ☐ sleeping-bag liner

Cooking & Eating
- ☐ mess tin
- ☐ spoon
- ☐ mug

Miscellaneous
- ☐ wash kit
- ☐ sunscreen
- ☐ towel
- ☐ toilet paper
- ☐ daily disposable contact lenses
- ☐ spare glasses
- ☐ tampons/sanitary napkins
- ☐ sewing kit
- ☐ waterproof freezer bags

When to Go

Rain can flood the interior of some caves. But since Borneo doesn't really have a dry season, this can happen year-round.

At places like Gunung Mulu National Park, which has a shortage of trained spelunking guides, make reservations well in advance. Some dates in July and August are already booked out by February.

Guides & Agencies

Gunung Mulu National Park (www.mulupark.com; p208)

Kuching Caving (www.kuchingcaving.com; p177)

Boat Trips

The mountains and jungles of Borneo are drained by some of Southeast Asia's longest rivers. Whether it's tearing up a mainline *batang* (Iban for 'large river') in a speedboat, rafting down a *sungai* (Bahasa Malaysia for 'river') or kayaking on a narrow *ai* (Iban for 'small river') in an *ulu* (upriver) part of the interior, you'll find that these watery highways are perhaps the best way to experience Borneo.

Many parts of Borneo's interior can be reached only by river, so hopping on a boat is a necessity. There's something magical about heading to a human settlement connected by road to absolutely nowhere, especially if you're in the safe hands of an experienced boatman and accompanied by locals.

On larger rivers, transport is by 'flying coffin' – long, narrow passenger boats with about 70 seats, not including the people sitting on the roof. Thanks to their powerful engines, these craft can power upriver against very strong currents.

Ferry safety is a major issue in Kalimantan, but even in Sarawak mishaps can happen. In October 2010 a 'flying coffin' lived up to its name by sinking on Sungai Anap, about 70km south of Bintulu, killing six passengers. Fortunately, pilots of larger craft are generally well trained.

In a smaller upriver craft, such as a *temuai* (shallow-draft Iban longboat), be prepared for you and your (hopefully waterproofed) kit to get dunked – and to get out and push if it hasn't rained for a while. Whatever the size of the vessel, be aware that rivers can suddenly rise by 2m or more after a downpour. If a boat looks unseaworthy or lacks basic safety equipment (especially life vests), don't

Borneo has occupied the world's imagination for centuries and there is no shortage of books about the island. Easily the best recent title is *Stranger in the Forest* by Eric Hansen, in which the author recounts his 1976 journey across the island in the company of Penan guides. It is not just the difficulty of the feat – Hansen is the only Westerner ever to cross Borneo on foot – it is the author's brilliant and sensitive storytelling that makes the book a classic. One cannot read it without a sense of sadness, for the world and the people described are now almost completely gone.

The most popular book about Borneo is Redmond O'Hanlon's *Into the Heart of Borneo*, a humorous account of the author's 1983 journey up a river in Sarawak to a mountain on the border with Kalimantan. While O'Hanlon makes a bit much of what was a fairly unremarkable journey, one cannot help but enjoy his colourful narrative.

Espresso with Headhunters: A Journey Through the Jungles of Borneo by John Wassner tells of a more extensive recent trip by an Australian traveller (and inveterate caffeine and nicotine addict). Not nearly as famous as O'Hanlon's book, this gives a more realistic account of what life is like in Sarawak. We only wish he had chosen a different title – it's time to let the whole Borneo headhunter thing die a quiet death.

If you climb Mt Kinabalu, you can't help but notice the gaping chasm of Low's Gully to your right as you climb the final summit pyramid. *Kinabalu Escape: The Soldiers' Story* by Rich Mayfield tells of the British Army's ill-fated 1994 attempt to descend the gully. The expedition, which was a textbook case in how not to run an expedition, led to an expensive rescue operation and the near deaths of several team members.

PLAN YOUR TRIP ADVENTURE BORNEO

be shy about asking your guide and/or boatman about it.

Sea-going craft for travel along the coast and out to islands have to deal with rougher waters than their inland counterparts. In Sarawak, this is especially true from November to March, when the northeast monsoon can bring choppy conditions.

Costs

Travel by boat does not come cheap, mainly because marine engines and outboards, which must shove aside prodigious quantities of water, really slurp up the petrol. For a small motorboat with a capacity of four to six people, count on paying about RM7 per kilometre, or roughly RM100 to RM150 per hour of actual sailing time. While the boat is moored somewhere – at an island or a remote beach, for instance – you'll have to remunerate the driver but, obviously, there are no fuel costs when the motor is off.

Tour Agencies

Below are some of the agencies that can organise rafting, kayaking and other waterborne adventures.

Sabah

» Borneo Authentic (www.borneo-authentic.com; p131)

» Borneo Eco Tours (www.borneoecotours.com; p64)

» Borneo Nature Tours (www.borneonaturetours.com; p109)

» Borneo Wavehunters (www.travelmateholidays.com; p129)

» GogoSabah (www.gogosabah.com; p63)

» Only in Borneo (www.oibtours.com; p131)

» Riverbug (www.riverbug.asia; p129)

» River Junkie (www.river-junkie.com; p130)

Sarawak

» Borneo Trek & Kayak Adventure (http://rainforestkayaking.com; p155)

» Gunung Mulu National Park (www.mulupark.com; p208)

Kalimantan

» Balikpapan-based guides (p262)

» Borneo Eco Adventures (www.borneoecotour.com; p243)

» Borneo Orangutan Adventure tour (www.orangutantravel.com; p243)

» De'Gigant Tours (www.borneotourgigant.com; p267)

» Kalimantan Tour Destinations (kevinmaulana@telkom.net; p249)

Regions at a Glance

Sabah, in Borneo's far north, brings together unspoilt rainforests – prime orangutan habitat – with some of the world's most phenomenal scuba diving. There's more excellent diving, and plenty of upriver jungle adventure, awaiting south of the Indonesian border on Kalimantan's east coast and, inland, along and between its rivers. On the north coast, Sarawak is home to the island's most accessible national parks – based in the sophisticated but laid-back city of Kuching, you can take day trips to see orangutans, hike in the jungle and visit longhouse communities. Tiny Brunei, with a tempo and culinary tradition all its own, offers visitors pristine habitats and a modernising take on Malay traditions.

Sabah

Hiking & Trekking ✓✓✓
Diving ✓✓✓
Jungle Wildlife ✓✓

Hiking & Trekking
Novice explorers can take a night trek near the Kinabatangan River or inch across a canopy walkway in Poring Hot Springs, while the fit can test their endurance at the limestone outcrops of Batu Punggul or on the icy peak of Mt Kinabalu.

Diving & Snorkelling
To say Sabah is known for its scuba scene is like saying France is known for its cuisine. The diving in spots like Pulau Mantanani, Layang Layang and of course, the famous Sipadan is – no hyperbole – some of the best in the world.

Jungle Wildlife
Hornbills shriek in trees inhabited by pot-bellied proboscis monkeys, and slow-swinging through the canopy comes the ginger mass of an orangutan – to see one of these primates in the wild is to be reduced to grinning awe.

p56

Sarawak

Hiking & Trekking ✓✓✓
Cave Exploration ✓✓✓
Jungle Wildlife ✓✓

Hiking & Trekking
Trekking from Bario to Ba Kelalan or assaulting the summit of Gunung Mulu will exhilarate experienced hikers, but even a relaxed stroll through one of Sarawak's Kuching-area national parks will envelop you in the wonders of the equatorial rainforest.

Cave Exploration
The Wind Cave, Fairy Cave and Niah National Park boast huge caverns with stalactites and bats, but for sheer size and spectacle you can't beat Gunung Mulu National Park, famed for the Deer Cave and the 700m-long Sarawak Chamber.

Jungle Wildlife
Wild proboscis monkeys munch leaves at Bako National Park, orangutans swing through the canopy at Semenggoh Nature Reserve, and estuarine crocodiles lurk in the muddy waters of Kuching Wetlands National Park.

p145

Brunei Darussalam

Culture ✓✓
Food ✓✓
Boat Rides ✓✓

Culture
Bandar Seri Begawan's two opulent 20th-century mosques feature eye-popping architecture and sumptuous interior decor, but many visitors find the traditional lifestyle and architecture of Kampung Ayer, a Malay stilt village, more engaging.

Food
Bruneian cuisine may not be well known, but we can guarantee you've never eaten anything like *ambuyat* (made from sago starch), and that the delicious *kuih* (baked sweets) available in night markets will perfectly complement a quick satay or curry chicken meal.

Boat Rides
The speedboat ride from Bandar Seri Begawan to Bangar is the biggest thrill B$6 can buy, but nothing beats starting the day heading upriver to Ulu Temburong National Park in a shallow-draft Iban longboat.

p223

Kalimantan

Hiking & Trekking ✓✓✓
Wildlife ✓✓✓
Diving ✓✓

Hiking & Trekking
The fit and adventurous can head to Kutai National Park or the Mahakam River, but the easiest area for a trek – with a wide range of guides available – is the stunning Meratus Mountains, using Loksado as base camp.

Wildlife
If you're an amateur naturalist, Kalimantan's rainforests will exceed even your wildest dreams. A good guide can help you spot orangutans, gibbons, macaques, flying squirrels, clouded leopards, crocodiles and giant butterflies.

Diving & Snorkelling
In the Sangalaki Archipelago and on Pulau Derawan in the Celebes Sea, you can swim in coral-blue water with giant green turtles, manta rays, myriad reef fish, sharks and whales. Borneo's best-kept secret!

p240

Look out for these icons:

 Our author's recommendation 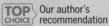 A green or sustainable option 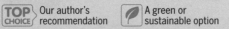 No payment required

On the Road

Gateway Kuala Lumpur

Best Places to Eat

» Jalan Alor (p40)

» Madras Lane hawkers (p40)

» Bijan (p40)

Best Places to Stay

» Sahabat Guest House (p39)

» Fraser Place Kuala Lumpur (p39)

» Rainforest Bed and Breakfast (p40)

Why Go?

Kuala Lumpur (KL) is the consummate Asian cyber-city: historic temples and mosques rub shoulders with space-age towers and shopping malls; traders' stalls are piled high with pungent durians and counterfeit handbags; and a monorail zips past lush parks and wi-fi–enabled cafes where locals sip cool drinks or feast on delicious hawker food. Malays, Chinese and Indian migrants and British colonials all helped shaped the city, leaving a fascinating assortment of cultural traditions. See Lonely Planet's *Malaysia, Singapore & Brunei* and *Kuala Lumpur, Melaka & Penang* guidebooks for more.

When to Go

KL's weather is constantly tropical with the most rainfall coming between October and March. If shopping is your aim, then visit during the general sales in March and the end of November through to early January. The end of March and early April is also a good time to take in events around the Malaysian Grand Prix. Foodies can dig into special treats at Ramadan markets and buffets across the city, usually in August and early September.

◉ Sights

KLCC & MENARA KL

The iconic **Petronas Towers** (www.petro nastwintowers.com.my; KLCC, Jln Ampang) are the focal point of the Kuala Lumpur City Centre (KLCC), a sprawling development that includes the impressive **Aquaria KLCC** (☑2333 1888; www.klaquaria.com; Concourse level, KL Convention Centre; adult/child aquarium RM45/35; aquarium & aquazone RM80/52; ☺11am-8pm), excellent kids' museum **Petrosains** (☑2331 8181; www.petrosains.com.my; Level 4, Suria KLCC; adult/child RM12/4; ☺9.30am-4pm Tue-Thu, 1.30-4pm Fri, 9.30am-5pm Sat, Sun & holidays), a world-class concert hall and the fine shopping mall **Suria KLCC** (www.suria klcc.com.my; ☺10am-10pm).

There are three packages for going up the towers, all of which can be purchased from the ticket counter in the basement. The cheapest deal only allows access to the 41st-floor **Skybridge** (☺9am-7pm Tue-Sun, closed 1-2.30pm Fri; tickets RM10) connecting the two towers, a modest 170m above ground. For RM40 you can continue up to the 88th-floor observation deck in Tower 2, while a premium package (including lunch/dinner RM200/350) also gains you access to the tower's exclusive members-only Malaysian Petroleum Club for a meal.

Only 1640 free tickets are issued daily: line up for one at the counter in the basement as soon as you can after it opens at 8.30am to ensure your place.

An equally good view of the city is available nearby at the **Menara KL** (KL Tower; ☑2020 5448; www.menarakl.com.my; 2 Jln Punchak). Sitting atop the Bukit Nanas Forest Reserve, the fourth-highest telecommunications tower in the world has a viewing deck at 276m and a good revolving restaurant.

These perpetually bustling areas are a salad bowl of KL's multi-culti citizens. Every night **Jln Petaling** in Chinatown becomes an atmospheric street market selling things such as 'authentic' Prada, Birkenstocks and Levis, while Saturday is the day to head to Little India for the *pasar malam* (night market) along Lg TAR.

Both areas are dotted with colourful places of worship including KL's principal Hindu temple, **Sri Mahamariamman Temple** (163 Jln Tun HS Lee; ☺6am-8.30pm, to 9pm Fri & Sat), the beautiful mosque **Masjid Jamek** (☺8.30am-12.30pm & 2.30-4pm, closed Fri 11am-2.30pm), the Taoist **Sze Ya Temple** (Jln Tun HS Lee; ☺7am-5pm) and the Buddhist **Guandi Temple** (Jln Tun HS Lee; ☺7am-5pm).

A prime hunting ground for Malaysian crafts and art is the **Central Market** (www.centralmarket.com.my; Jln Hang Kasturi; ☺10am-9pm), in a refurbished art deco building.

LAKE GARDENS

West of the centre, these spacious, hilly gardens – created during the colonial era as an urban retreat – feature the excellent **KL Bird Park** (☑2272 1010; www.klbirdpark.com; Jln Cenderawasih; adult/child RM45/35; ☺9am-6pm) and the gorgeous collection of the **Islamic Arts Museum** (☑2274 2020; www.iamm.org.my; Jln Lembah Perdana; adult/child RM12/6; ☺10am-6pm).

At the edge of the Lake Gardens, the **National Museum** (☑2282 6255; www. muziumnegara.gov.my; Jln Damansara; adult/ child RM2/free; ☺9am-6pm) boasts colourful displays on Malaysia's history, arts and culture.

🛏 Sleeping

Chinatown and Little India offer plenty of cheap crash pads, while the Golden Triangle

---

LOCAL KNOWLEDGE

ADLINE BINTI ABDUL GHANI: CURATOR

My personal highlights of the Islamic Arts Museum include:

» **Ottoman Room** A reconstruction of an 1820s decorative room from Syria.

» **Kiswah** A rare whole embroidered door panel from the holy Ka'aba in Mecca.

» **Chinese calligraphy scrolls** Only from the 1980s and '90s, but the use of reed brushes for the strokes is very expressive.

» **Limar** There's Islamic calligraphy in the pattern of this weft silk ikat fabric. The tradition of making these pieces has now died out.

» **Uzbek pectoral plates** Shatters the idea of jewellery being only delicate objects.

Kuala Lumpur

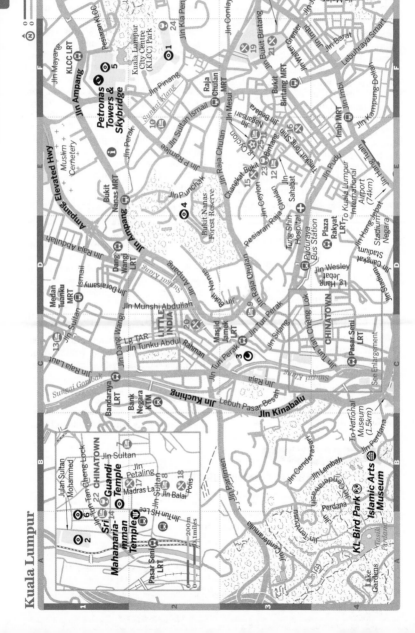

N

400 m
0.2 miles

has more upscale options as well as pricier but cleaner budget options.

CHINATOWN & LITTLE INDIA

BackHome HOSTEL $$
(☎2078 7188; www.backhome.com.my; 30 Jln Tun HS Lee; dm/d incl breakfast from RM42/100; ✳@⊛) This new hostel is a chic pit stop for flashpackers with its polished concrete finishes, fab rain showers and blissful central courtyard sprouting spindly trees.

5 Elements Hotel HOTEL $$
(☎2031 6888; www.the5elementshotel.com.my; Lot 243, Jln Sultan; s/d incl breakfast from RM170/200; ✳@) Offering a good range of rooms, some with views towards KL Tower, this hotel makes a credible stab at boutique stylings, with a sensuous design motif snaking its way across the corridor and bedroom walls.

Wheelers Guest House HOSTEL $
(☎2070 1386; www.backpackerskl.com/wheelers.htm; level 2, 131-133 Jln Tun HS Lee; dm/r with shared bathroom RM13/30, r with attached bathroom RM60; ✳@) One of KL's quirkier hostels, Wheelers has a mini-aquarium, gay-friendly staff and a great rooftop terrace where free Friday dinners are hosted.

Tune Hotel HOTEL $
(☎7962 5888; www.tunehotels.com; 316 Jln TAR; r from RM50; ✳@⊛) This innovative operation uses the low-cost approach of local budget airline AirAsia: book online six months in advance to snag a room with bathroom for under RM50 – walk-in rates are more likely to kick off at RM90.

GOLDEN TRIANGLE

TOP CHOICE Sahabat Guest House
GUEST HOUSE $$
(☎2142 0689; www.sahabatguesthouse.com; 41 Jln Sahabat; d incl breakfast from RM96; ✳@⊛) Rush to book this adorable blue-painted eight-room guest house. Small but comfy bedrooms, with small en suite bathrooms, are brightened up with a feature wall plastered in vivid patterned wallpaper. There's a small kitchen and a grassy front garden in which to relax.

TOP CHOICE Fraser Place Kuala Lumpur
SERVICED APARTMENTS $$$
(☎2118 6288; kualalumpurfrasershospitality.com; Lot 163, 10 Jln Perak; apt incl breakfast from RM350; ✳@⊛⊠) These super-stylish studios and apartments can be booked for as little as one night. The facilities, including an outdoor infinity pool, gym, sauna and games room, are topnotch.

DON'T MISS

JALAN ALOR

Hauling in everyone from society babes to backpackers are the roadside restaurants and stalls lining **Jln Alor**. From around 5pm till late every evening, the street transforms into a continuous open-air dining space where rival caterers compete for the passing trade (avoid the pushiest ones!).

Recommended options include the small complex **One Plus One** for 'drunken' chicken *mee* (noodles) with rice wine and good Hong Kong–style dim sum; **Wong Ah Wah** (⏲4pm-4am), unbeatable for addictive spicy chicken wings, as well as grilled seafood, tofu and satay; and the **frog porridge stall**: the choices are 'spicy' where the frogs legs are served separately or 'non-spicy' where they're mixed in with the tasty rice gruel (RM7 per bowl).

TOP CHOICE **Rainforest Bed & Breakfast** HOSTEL $$
(☎2145 3525; www.rainforestbnbhotel.com; 27 Jln Mesui; dm/d/tw incl breakfast RM35/105/130; ❄@🛜) The lush foliage sprouting around and tumbling off the tiered balconies of this high-quality guest house is eye-catching. Inside bright red walls and timber-lined rooms (some without windows) are also visually distinctive.

41 Berangan GUEST HOUSE $$
(☎2144 8691; www.41berangan.com; 41 Jln Berangan; d incl breakfast from R100; ❄@🛜) This property offers minimalist decor: two courtyard rooms have been built inside shipping crates, and they're planning to stack a couple more on top. There are a couple of cheaper rooms (RM80) with shared bathrooms.

Eating

KL is a non-stop feast. You can dine in incredible elegance or mingle with locals at thousands of street stalls. A meal at a night market, such as the ones in Little India and Kampung Baru every Saturday, is a must.

CHINATOWN & LITTLE INDIA

TOP CHOICE **Madras Lane hawkers** FOOD STALLS $
(Madras Lane; bowl of noodles RM5; ⏲closed Mon) Weave your way through Chinatown's wet market to this short alley of stalls. It's best visited for breakfast or lunch. Standout operators: the one offering 10 types of *yong tau fu* (stuffed tofu and vegies) in a broth of fish stock (stall open 9.30am to 3.30pm) and, at the far end of the strip, the one serving *asam* and curry laksa (stall open 8am to 2pm).

TOP CHOICE **Old China Café** MALAYSIAN & NONYA $$$
(☎2072 5915; www.oldchina.com.my; 11 Jln Balai Polis; mains RM40-50; ⏲11.30am-10pm) This atmospheric cafe captures some of the charm of old KL. Walls are covered with bric-a-brac, and the cook prepares Nonya dishes from Melaka and Penang, including a fine beef rendang (coconut and lime-leaf curry) with coconut rice and fiery Nonya laksa soup with seafood.

Saravanna Bhavan INDIAN VEGETARIAN $$
(☎2698 3293; ww.saravanabhavan.com; 1007 Selangor Mansion, Jln Masjid India; meals RM10-20; ⏲8am-10.30pm; ✎) Offers some of the best-quality Indian food you'll find in KL. The banana leaf and mini-tiffin feasts are supremely tasty, and you can you also sample southern Indian classics such as *masala dosa*.

GOLDEN TRIANGLE

Two major malls – **Pavilion KL** and **Starhill Gallery** – offer such a wide and top-quality range (from food courts to fine dining) that only the pickiest diner could find fault.

TOP CHOICE **Bijan** MALAYSIAN $$$
(☎2031 3575; www.bijanrestaurant.com; 3 Jln Ceylon; mains RM60-100; ⏲noon-2.30pm & 6.30-10.30pm Mon-Sat, 4.30-10.30pm Sun) Bijan offers skilfully cooked traditional Malaysian dishes in a sophisticated dining room that spills out into a tropical garden.

Little Penang Kafé MALAYSIAN & NONYA $$
(☎2163 0215; level 4, Suria KLCC; mains from RM15; ⏲11.30am-9.30pm) The line outside this mall joint attests to the authenticity of its Penang food, including specialities such as curry *mee* (spicy soup noodles with prawns), and spicy Siamese *lemak laksa* (curry laksa) only available Friday to Sunday.

Drinking & Entertainment

The cheapest places for a beer are Chinese eateries or open-air hawker stalls.

TOP CHOICE Palate Palette · CAFE, BAR

(www.palatepalette.com; 21 Jln Mesui; mains RM10-30; ☺noon-midnight Tue-Thu, to 2am Fri & Sat; ☜) Colourful, creative, quirky and super cool, this cafe-bar is our favourite place to eat, drink, play board games, and mingle with KL's boho crowd.

Reggae Bar · BAR

(www.reggaebarkl.com.my; 158 Jln Tun HS Lee; ☺10.30am-3am) Travellers gather in droves at this pumping bar in the thick of Chinatown – it has outdoor seats if you'd like to catch the passing parade. A fancier branch is at 31 Changat Bukit Bintang.

Sky Bar · BAR

(level 33, Traders Hotel, KLCC; ☺7pm-1am, to 3am Fri &Sat) Head to the roof-top pool area of this hotel for a grand view of the Petronas Towers – it's the perfect spot for sundowner cocktails or late-night flutes of bubbly.

No Black Tie · LIVE MUSIC

(☑2142 3737; www.noblacktie.com.my; 17 Jln Mesui; cover RM20-50; ☺5pm-2am Tue-Sun) This small, chic live-music venue, bar and Japanese bistro, hidden behind a grove of bamboo, hosts shows by talented singer-songwriters, jazz bands and classical-music ensembles.

ℹ Information

Emergency
Ambulance & Fire (☑994)
Police (☑999)
Tourist police (☑2166 8322)

Immigration Offices
Immigration office (☑2095 5077; Block I, Pusat Bandar Damansara; ☺8.30am-5pm Mon-Fri, closed 12.15-2.45pm Fri) Handles visa extensions; 2km west of Lake Gardens.

Internet Access
Internet cafes are everywhere; the going rate per hour is RM3. Free wi-fi is widely available; sign up for an account with **Wireless@KL** (www. wirelesskl.com).

Media
KLue (www.klue.com.my; RM5) Best local listings magazine, with many interesting features about what's going on in and around the city.
Time Out (www.timeoutkl.com; RM5) Monthly magazine in a globally familiar format.

Medical Services
Hospital Kuala Lumpur (☑2615 5555; www. hkl.gov.my; Jln Pahang) North of the centre.
Tung Shin Hospital (☑2072 1655; http:// tungshin.com.my; 102 Jln Pudu)

Post
The main **Pos Malaysia** (Jln Raja Laut; ☺8.30am-6pm Mon-Sat, closed first Sat of month) office is across the river from Central Market. Branch post offices are found all over KL.

Tourist Information
Malaysian Tourist Centre (MaTiC; ☑9235 4900; www.mtc.gov.my; 109 Jln Ampang; ☺8am-10pm)

Travel Agencies
MSL Travel (☑4042 4722; www.msltravel.com; 66 Jln Putra; ☺9am-5pm Mon-Fri, to 1pm Sat)
Sutra (☑2382 7575; www.sutra.my; level 3, Suria KLCC, Jln Ampang; ☺9am-9.30pm Mon-Fri, 10am-9.30pm Sat & Sun)

ℹ Getting There & Away
Air
Kuala Lumpur International Airport (KLIA; ☑8777 8888; www.klia.com.my) is 75km south of the city centre. All of Air Asia's flights are handled by the nearby **Low Cost Carrier-Terminal** (LCC-T; ☑8777 8888; http://lcct.klia. com.my).

WORTH A TRIP

BATU CAVES

Built by the Hindu community 120 years ago, the polychromatic temples of the **Batu Caves** (admission free, parking RM2; ☺8am-9pm) are found in a limestone outcrop 13km north of the capital. The main Temple Cave is guarded by an enormous golden statue of Muruga (aka Lord Subramaniam) and reached by a flight of 272 steps. Each year in late January or early February a million pilgrims converge here during Thaipusam, a three-day festival featuring surreal acts of self-mortification.

KTM Komuter trains terminate at Batu Caves station (RM1.30 from KL Sentral, 25 minutes). Alternatively, bus 11 (RM2, 45 minutes) leaves from where Jln Tun HS Lee meets Jln Petaling, just south of Medan Pasar in Chinatown. A taxi from KL costs around RM20.

Airlines with services to Borneo include:

AirAsia (www.airasia.com) To Kuching, Sibu, Bintulu and Miri in Sarawak; Kota Kinabalu, Sandakan and Tawau in Sabah; Pulau Labuan; Brunei; and Balikpapan in Kalimantan.

Malaysia Airlines (www.malaysiaairlines.com) To destinations all over Sarawak and Sabah.

MASwings (www.maswings.com.my) Bornean subsidiary of Malaysia Airlines; also flies to Sarawak and Sabah.

Royal Brunei (www.bruneiair.com) To Bandar Seri Begawan.

Bus

KL's primary long-distance bus station is **Puduraya** (Jln Pudu), with services to most destinations in peninsula Malaysia, plus Singapore and Thailand.

Train

KL Sentral station, just west of the centre, is the national hub of the **KTM** (Keretapi Tanah Melayu Berhad; ✆1300 88 5862; www.ktmb.com.my; ◷info office 9am-9pm, ticket office 7am-10pm) railway system. There are daily international departures for Thailand and Singapore.

❶ Getting Around
To/From the Airports

KLIA

Airport Coach (www.airportcoach.com.my) One way/return RM10/18, one hour. To KL Sentral.

KL Transit train Adult/child one way RM35/15, 35 minutes. To KL Sentral.

KLIA Ekspres (www.kliaekspres.com) Adult/child one way RM35/15, return RM70/30, 28 minutes, every 15 to 20 minutes, 5am to 1am. To KL Sentral.

Taxi Standard fare RM67.10 (up to three people); takes around one hour to the city.

Shuttle bus RM150, every 20 minutes, 6am to midnight. Connects KLIA and the LCC-T.

LCC-T

Aerobus One way RM8, at least every 15 minutes, 4.30am to 12.45am, one hour.

Taxi Prepaid fares RM62 to Chinatown or Jln Bukit Bintang (50% more midnight to 6am).

Shuttle bus To Salak Tinggi station, where you can pick up the KL Transit Train into the city.

Skybus (www.skybus.com.my) One way RM9, at least every 15 minutes, 4.30am to 12.45am, one hour.

Bus

Most buses are provided by either **Rapid KL** (✆7885 2585; www.rapidkl.com.my) or **Metrobus** (✆5635 3070). There's an **information booth** (◷7am-9pm) at the **Jln Sultan Mohammed bus stop** in Chinatown. A RM2 ticket is valid all day.

Taxi

Taxis have meters which drivers sometimes use. Trips around the city centre are about RM5 to RM10.

Monorail, Train & Light Rail Transit

Most useful is the **monorail** (www.klmonorail.com.my) linking many of the city's sightseeing areas. Fares are RM1.20 to RM2.50; the system runs 6am to midnight. There are two **KTM Komuter** (✆1300 88 5862; http://ktmkomuter.com.my) lines (tickets from RM1; system runs 6am to 11.45) and three **Light Rail Transit** (LRT) lines (tickets RM1 to RM2.80). You need a new ticket to change from one system to another.

Gateway Singapore

Best Places to Eat

» Café Le Caire (p46)
» Ocean Curry Fish Head (p46)
» Lau Pa Sat (p46)
» Maxwell Rd Hawker Centre (p46)

Best Places to Stay

» Gallery Hotel (p45)
» Inn Crowd (p46)
» Scarlet (p45)

Why Go?

Tidy and efficient, Singapore is a modern marvel in a region full of anachronisms. It's a perfect intersection of Western-style order in an Asian setting and intelligently cultivates culture, history and, most importantly, cuisine on a tiny spit of land. The island can be tackled in a few days thanks to the slick Mass Rapid Transit (MRT) train system, which delivers city explorers to glitzy Orchard Rd malls, antique buildings in the Colonial District, or the pungent lanes of Little India.

See Lonely Planet's *Malaysia, Singapore & Brunei* guidebook or *Singapore* city guide for more information, or head to **Lonely Planet** (www.lonelyplanet.com/singapore) for planning advice, author recommendations, traveller reviews and insider tips.

When to Go

Any time is a great time to visit Singapore, as the island-state is always buzzing. The Mosaic Music Festival (www.mosaicmusicfestival.com) is an annual 10-day feast of jazz, funk, hip-hop and world music that happens in March. In August you can catch the Hungry Ghost Festival in Chinatown and Geylang. If you come during the Formula One Grand Prix in September, you'd be well advised to book your room in advance (and be prepared to pay a premium).

GATEWAY SINGAPORE

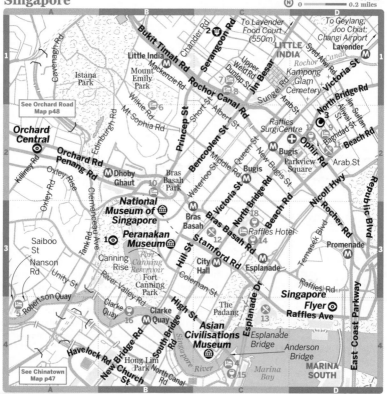

◉ Sights

COLONIAL DISTRICT

Architectural remnants of British rule are neatly arranged around the Padang, an old cricket pitch. The state-of-the-art **Asian Civilisations Museum** (Map p44; ☑6332 7789; www.acm.org.sg; 1 Empress Pl; adult/child & concession S$8/4; ⊙1-7pm Mon, 9am-7pm Tue-Thu, Sat & Sun, 9am-9pm Fri) has 10 thematic galleries dealing with Asian culture. The **Peranakan Museum** (Map p44; ☑6332 7591; 39 Armenian St; adult/child & concession S$6/3; ⊙1-7pm Mon, 9am-7pm Tue-Thu, Sat & Sun, 9am-9pm Fri) is a great place to experience the colour and beauty of Straits Chinese culture, and is very kid friendly. To visit both, buy a combined ticket (adult/child and concession S$11/5.50); there is also discounted admission between 7pm and 9pm on Friday. The architecturally stunning **National Museum of Singapore** (Map p44; ☑6332 3659; www.nationalmuseum.sg; 93 Stamford Rd; adult/child

$10/5; ⊙10am-9pm daily) includes a Singapore history gallery.

The **Singapore Flyer** (Map p44; ☑6333 3311; www.singaporeflyer.com.sg; Raffles Ave; adult/child $29.50/20.65; ⊙8.30am-10.30pm daily) is the world's largest observation wheel. The 30-minute ride is best done on a clear blue day, or on a clear night, when the lights of Indonesia and Malaysia frame the spectacular pan-Singapore views.

Fort Canning Park (Map p44) offers a peaceful and leafy retreat in Singapore's urban heart.

CHINATOWN

Bustling Chinatown is crammed with small shops, temples and eateries. The **Buddha Tooth Temple** (Map p47; ☑6222 0220; 288 South Bridge Rd; ⊙7am-7pm) houses the impressive Buddha Tooth Relic. Another highlight is the **Thian Hock Keng Temple** (Map p47; ☑6423 4626; 158 Telok Ayer St;

Singapore

◎ Top Sights

◎ Sights

🛏 Sleeping

✴ Eating

◎ Drinking

◎7.30am-5.30pm). For a peek into the past, the **Chinatown Heritage Centre** (Map p47; ✆6221 9556; www.chinatownheritage.com.sg; 48 Pagoda St; adult/child S$10/6; ◎9am-6.30pm) is crammed with interactive, imaginative displays.

ORCHARD RD

Orchard Rd is Singapore's major spot for retail therapy. Newest among its many malls is **Ion Orchard** (Map p48), a beautiful steel-and-glass monument to consumerism that's worth visiting as both a shopping and an architectural attraction. **Orchard Point Mall** (Map p48) is Singapore's tallest mall, and has a great glass elevator and a rooftop garden offering splendid views. Other great malls include **Wisma Atria Shopping Centre** (Map p48), **Ngee Ann City** (Map p48), **Lucky Plaza** (Map p48) and **Paragon** (Map p48). Rest from retail at the serene **Singapore Botanic**

Gardens (✆6471 7361; www.sbg.org.sg; 1 Cluny Rd; admission free; ◎5am-midnight).

🛏 Sleeping

Over the past few years Singapore has experienced an explosion of inexpensive hostels and guest houses. If it's more comfort you're after, there are plenty of boutique hotels to choose from. Most hostels offer free wi-fi, while pricier hotels charge a nominal fee.

COLONIAL DISTRICT & THE QUAYS

TOP CHOICE | **Gallery Hotel** — BOUTIQUE **$$$**
(Map p44; ✆6849 8686; www.galleryhotel.com.sg; 76 Robertson Quay; d from S$325; ✳@☀) Singapore's first boutique hotel is still totally hip. Rooms – each one with its own distinct theme, designed by different local artists – go retro with zanily coloured linen, frosted-glass bathroom walls and room numbers branded into the floorboards.

YMCA International House — YOUTH HOSTEL **$$**
(Map p44; ✆6336 6000; www.ymca.org.sg; 1 Orchard Rd; dm/tw S$35/180; ✳@☀) Even after you add on the $3.15 temporary membership, the Y's spacious dorms are a steal, with a pool, free breakfast and a central location that puts Orchard Rd, Chinatown and the CBD within walking distance.

Fullerton Hotel — HOTEL **$$$**
(Map p44; ✆6733 8388; www.fullertonhotel.com; 1 Fullerton Sq; d from S$400; ✳@☀) If you can afford it, this converted 1928 post office is considered one of *the* cool places to stay in Singapore.

CHINATOWN

A Beary Good Hostel — HOSTEL **$**
(Map p47; ✆6222 4955; www.abearygoodhostel.com; 66A & 66B Pagoda St; dm S$23; ✳@) For cuteness in the heart of Chinatown, this newly opened teddy-bear themed hostel takes the prize. Dorms are clean and comfortable, and the staff is predictably adorable.

Scarlet — BOUTIQUE HOTEL **$$$**
(Map p47; ✆6511 3333; www.thescarlethotel.com; 33 Erskine Rd; d/ste from S$320/780;✳@) Sexy Scarlet has seduced Singapore's boutique-hotel market with a string of gorgeous 1924 shophouses and bordello-decorated rooms. Even the website oozes sensuality.

Hotel 1929 — BOUTIQUE HOTEL **$$**
(Map p47; ✆6347 1929; www.hotel1929.com; 50 Keong Saik Rd; s/d from S$140/190; ✳@)

Another excellent boutique hotel, known for its quirky vibe and unique rooms.

LITTLE INDIA & KAMPUNG GLAM

Inn Crowd
HOSTEL $
(Map p44; ✆6296 9169; www.the-inncrowd.com; 73 Dunlop St; dm/d S$20/60; @) Extremely popular for its location, atmosphere and very cheap dorm beds, as well as its well-earned reputation as the backpacker party spot. Inn Crowd's communal chill-out spot features free internet, comfy pillows, and movies all day long.

Sleepy Sam's Guesthouse
HOSTEL $
(Map p44; ✆9277 4988; www.sleepysams.com; 55 Bussorah Rd; dm/s/d S$28/59/89; @) By far the most peaceful of the area's hostels, Sam's dorms and rooms are a bit cramped, but the location on this strip of restored heritage shophouses – not to mention the cool cafe – more than makes up for it.

Hangout@Mount Emily
HOSTEL $$
(Map p44; ✆6438 5588; www.hangouthotels.com; 10a Upper Wilkie Rd; dm S$40, d & tw S$150; ✳@) For state-of-the-art hostelling you can't beat this place.

Perak Hotel
HOSTEL $$
(Map p44; ✆6299 7733; www.peraklodge.net; 12 Perak Rd; d incl breakfast S$128-188; ✳@) Located in a renovated Peranakan-style building, the Perak is deservedly popular.

🍴 Eating

Singapore is easily one of the top food cities on the planet. Travellers looking for budget eats need look no further than the nearest neighbourhood hawker centre.

COLONIAL DISTRICT & THE QUAYS

My Humble House
SICHUAN $$
(Map p44; ✆6423 1881; 02-27/29 Esplanade Mall; mains S$20-25; ⊘lunch & dinner) With decor that's Alice in Wonderland-meets-Philippe Starck, this place is anything but humble.

Business groups dine from an elaborate Sichuan menu filled with delicacies. Dress snazzy; reservations essential.

Former convent **CHIJMES** (Map p44; 30 Victoria St) has been converted into a den of worldly pleasure housing more than 20 bars, restaurants and clubs.

CHINATOWN

Maxwell Rd Hawker Centre
HAWKER CENTRE $
(Map p47; cnr Maxwell Rd & South Bridge St; ⊘7am-10pm) Eternally busy and surprisingly untourted, this hawker centre has some fantastic Chinese and Malaysian food in an appropriately unkempt atmosphere and with wallet-friendly prices.

Ocean Curry Fish Head
SEAFOOD $$
(Map p47; ✆6324 9226; 181 Telok Ayer St; mains S$4-9; ⊘11am-8:30pm Mon-Fri, to 2pm Sat) This unpretentious buffet-style restaurant serves some of the best (and cheapest) seafood dishes in the area. The fish-head curry served here is different than the Indian-style curries typically found in Singapore. An absolute bargain.

Lau Pa Sat
HAWKER CENTRE $
(Map p47; 18 Raffles Quay; ⊘24hr) The most well known of Singapore's food courts, Lau Pa Sat is so big that it can get a bit bewildering, but don't let that stop you. If it's edible, chances are good that it can be found here. Note that most stalls close around 10pm.

Ci Yan Organic Vegetarian
VEGETARIAN $$
(Map p47; ✆6225 9026; 2 Smith St; mains S$6-10; ⊘noon-10pm; 🍴) Organic meals served 100% Buddhist style, meaning vegetarian, and no garlic, onions, or anything else that might disturb meditation.

LITTLE INDIA & KAMPUNG GLAM

TOP CHOICE | Café Le Caire
MIDDLE EASTERN $$
(Map p44; ✆6292 0797; 39 Arab St; meals from S$9; ⊘10am-late) A very popular spot in the evenings, for both its excellent Middle Eastern food and its shisha pipes (S$14 per

---

DON'T MISS

LITTLE INDIA & KAMPUNG GLAM

Little India is a sight in itself and one of its pleasures is wandering the side streets and soaking it all in. One must-see temple is **Sri Veeramakaliamman Temple** (Map p44; ✆6293 4634; 141 Serangoon Rd; ⊘8am-12.30pm & 4-8.30pm), dedicated to the goddess Kali.

Southeast of Little India is Kampung Glam, Singapore's Muslim quarter. Here, you'll find the golden-domed **Sultan Mosque** (Map p44; ✆6293 4405; 3 Muscat St; ⊘5am-8.30pm), the biggest mosque in Singapore. Nearby **Haji Lane** is a major evening chill-out spot.

Chinatown

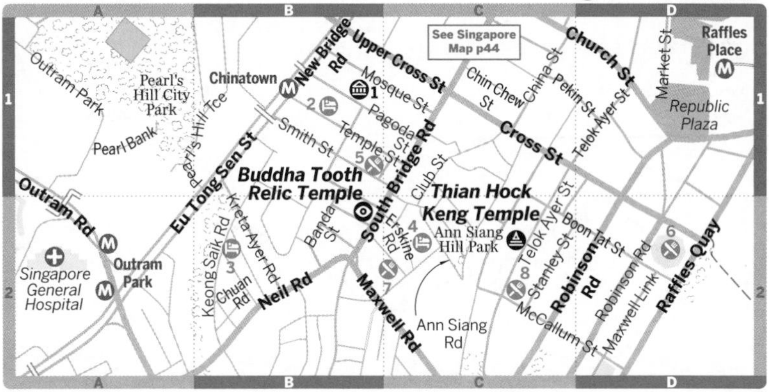

pipe). At S$15, the *mezza* platter, a selection of vegetarian appetisers, makes a great meal for one or late-night snack for several.

Lavender Food Court HAWKER CENTRE $
(cnr Jln Besar & Foch Rd; ⌚11am-3am) Much less touristy than most food centres, and stays open until the wee hours. The wonton noodles and dim sum are worth queuing for.

ELSEWHERE

Guan Hoe Soon SINGAPOREAN $$
(☎6344 2761; 38/40 Joo Chiat Pl; meals S$12-20; ⌚10am-8pm) The food at this restaurant alone makes the trip to Singapore's east side worth it. Try the *sotong sambal* (squid in sambal) or, our favourite Peranakan dish, *ayam buah keluak* (chicken cooked with black nut). Don't be surprised if you run into parliamentarians and other Singaporeans of note here.

Picotin FRENCH $$
(☎6877 1191; www.picotin.com.sg; 100 Turf Club Rd; dishes from S$15; ⌚8am-11am & noon-midnight) For excellent French cuisine and outstanding Western breakfasts in serene surroundings, you just can't beat this family-style bistro located in the converted rolling box of a former horse stable.

Samy's Curry Restaurant INDIAN $
(☎6472 2080; Civil Service Clubhouse, Dempsey Rd; dishes from S$4) A Singaporean institution, this banana-leaf curry joint housed in an old wooden army mess hall off Orchard Rd is a culinary pilgrimage.

Chinatown

Top Sights

Buddha Tooth Relic Temple	B2
Thian Hock Keng Temple	C2

Sights

1 Chinatown Heritage Centre	B1

Sleeping

2 A Beary Good Hostel	B1
3 Hotel 1929	B2
4 Scarlet	C2

Eating

5 Ci Yan Organic Vegetarian	B1
6 Lau Pa Sat	D2
7 Maxwell Rd Hawker Centre	C2
8 Ocean Curry Fish Head	C2

Drinking & Entertainment

The main party places include Mohamed Sultan Rd, Clarke and Boat Quays, and Emerald Hill Rd off Orchard Rd. Most bars open from 5pm daily until at least midnight Sunday to Thursday, and till 2am on Friday and Saturday. Cover charges at clubs range from S$15 to S$25. For frugal imbibers, the cheapest way to drink is in a hawker centre.

Long Bar BAR
(Map p44; ☎6337 1886; Raffles Hotel, 1 Beach Rd; ⌚11am-12.30am) It's a compulsory cliché to sink a Singapore Sling (S$16, or S$25 with a souvenir glass) in the Long Bar, but for a less touristy experience head for the snooker tables at the **Bar & Billiard Room** (Map p44).

GATEWAY SINGAPORE

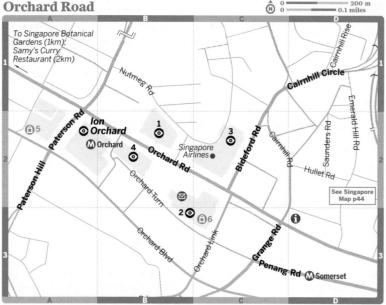

Crazy Elephant CLUB
(Map p44; ☑6337 1990; 01-07 Clarke Quay) One of Clarke Quay's oldest and best bars, the grungy Elephant has been bashing out live blues and rock forever.

Butter Factory CLUB
(Map p44; ☑6333 8243; www.thebutterfactory. com; 1 Fullerton Rd) Comfy-couched chill-out spots, dance floors and a good bar make this a decent night spot. Check website for hours and cover charges.

Going Om CAFE
(Map p44; ☑6297 9197; 63 Haji Lane) Part cafe, part chill-out space, Going Om has cocktails, coffees, teas, and even 'chakra drinks' of seven colours (one for each chakra). There's a space upstairs for yoga, tarot-card readings and even magic shows.

🛍 Shopping
See Sights for information about Singapore's department stores.

Borders BOOKS
(Map p48; ☑6235 7146; 01-00 Wheelock Pl, 501 Orchard Rd)

Kinokuniya BOOKS
(Map p48; ☑6737 5021; www.kinokuniya.com.sg; 03-10/15 Ngee Ann City, 391 Orchard Rd)

ℹ️ Information
Emergency
Ambulance (☑995)
Fire (☑995)
Police (☑999)

Internet Access
Internet cafes abound, especially in Little India. There are plenty of free wi-fi hotspots throughout the city.

Medical Services
Raffles SurgiCentre (Map p44; ☑6311 5555; www.raffleshospital.com; 585 North Bridge Rd)

Singapore General Hospital (Map p47; ☑6321 4311; Block 1, Outram Rd)

Money

Moneychangers can be found in every shopping centre and most do not charge fees on foreign money or travellers cheques.

Post

Changi Airport (024-39, terminal 2)

Lucky Plaza (Map p48; 02-09 Lucky Plaza, Orchard Rd)

Ngee Ann City (Map p48; 04-15 Takashimaya, 391 Orchard Rd)

Tourist Information

Most Singapore Tourism Board (STB) offices provide a wide range of services, including tour bookings and event ticketing.

STB head office (☑1800-736 2000; Tourism Ct, 1 Orchard Spring Lane; ☺8.30am-5pm Mon-Fri, to 1pm Sat); Orchard Rd (Map p48; ☑6336 7184; cnr Orchard & Cairnhill Rds; ☺9.30am-10.30pm); Little India (Map p44; ☑6296 9169; Inn Crowd, 73 Dunlop St; ☺10am-10pm)

Travel Agencies

Jetabout Holidays (☑6734 1818; www.jet about.com.sg; 06-05 Cairnhill Pl, 15 Cairnhill Rd)

Misa Travel (☑6538 0318; 03-106 Hong Lim Complex, 531A Upper Cross St)

STA Travel (☑6737 7188; www.statravel.com. sg; 07-02 Orchard Towers, 400 Orchard Rd)

Getting There & Away

Air

A major global hub, **Changi International Airport** (☑6541 2267; www.changi.airport.com.sg) is about 20km east of the city centre. SilkAir flies daily from Singapore to Balikpapan in Indonesia's Kalimantan province.

Among the airlines that fly to destinations in Borneo:

AirAsia (www.airasia.com) Cheap flights to Kuching, Miri and Kota Kinabalu.

Jetstar Asia (☑6822 2288; www.jetstarasia. com; Terminal 1, Changi airport) To Kota Kinabalu.

Malaysia Airlines (☑6336 6777; www. sg.malaysiaairlines.com; 02-09 Singapore Shopping Centre, 190 Clemenceau Ave) Flies via Kuala Lumpur to Malaysian Borneo.

Royal Brunei (www.bruneiair.com) To Bandar Seri Begawan.

Singapore Airlines (Map p48; ☑6223 8888; www.singaporeair.com; 04-05, Ion Orchard Mall) To Bandar Seri Begawan.

SilkAir (☑6223 8888; www.silkair.com; SIA Bldg, 77 Robinson Rd) To Kuching, Kota Kinabalu and Balikpapan.

Tiger Airways (☑1800-388 8888; www. tigerairways.com) To Kuching.

If you plan to fly to Malaysian Borneo, the airport in Johor Bahru, the city just across the causeway in Malaysia, often has cheaper flights on AirAsia and Malaysia Airlines.

Boat

Ferries connect Singapore to Indonesia's Riau archipelago. Departure points are the Harbourfront Centre (next to HarbourFront MRT station) for Pulau Batam, Tanjung Balai and Tanjung Batu; and Tanah Merah ferry terminal for Pulau Bintan and Batam. For Tanah Merah, take the MRT to Bedok, then bus 35. A taxi from the city is around S$15. One-way tickets are S$16 to Batam, S$24 to S$36 to Bintan, Balai or Batu.

WORTH A TRIP

ZOO, NIGHT SAFARI & JOO CHIAT

Nestled among the forest, the **zoo and night safari** (☑6269 3411; www.zoo.com.sg; 80 Mandai Lake Rd; adult/child zoo only $18/12, zoo tram $5/3, night safari $22/15, combined zoo & night safari $32/20, children on birthday free; ☺zoo 8.30am-6pm, night safari 7.30pm-midnight) are easily worth spending a day and night to fully experience. The forested parks offer the chance to see animals in their natural habitats. Visitors looking to do both parks in one trip can chill over dinner and drinks in the food court between the zoo's closing and safari's opening.

Travellers looking to escape the tourist crowd should head east to **Joo Chiat**, the heart of the city's Peranakan revival and a great place to wander around amidst colonial-style shophouses and restaurants serving Singapore's finest food. **East Coast Park** stretches along the southern coast and offers miles of beaches, bike trails, food courts and drinking venues.

Bus

If travelling across the causeway from Singapore to Johor Bahru in Malaysia, take bus 160 from Kranji MRT station (S$1.10). The buses stop at the border for immigration formalities and to pick up passengers on the other side. Keep your ticket so that you can reboard.

Agents at the Golden Mile Complex and Golden Mile Tower on Beach Rd selling long-distance-bus tickets to other peninsular Malaysian destinations are **Grassland Express** (☑6293 1166; www.grassland.com.sg; 01-26 Golden Mile Complex) and **Konsortium** (☑6392 3911; www.konsortium.com.sg; 01-52 Golden Mile Tower). Coaches typically use **Lavender St bus terminal** (cnr Lavender St & Kallang Bahru), a 500m walk north from Lavender MRT station, or depart from outside the Golden Mile Complex.

Train

Station is on Keppel Rd, south of the centre. **Keretapi Tanah Melayu Berhad** (☑6222 5165; www.ktmb.com.my) operates three air-conditioned express trains daily to Kuala Lumpur (2nd/3rd class S$34/19) with connections on to Thailand.

By 1 July 2011, the single-track railway from Singapore station to Woodlands will close, and the southern terminus of the Malaysian rail system will be relocated to the Woodlands Train Checkpoint, some 13 miles north of central Singapore.

Getting Around

To/From the Airport

Changi airport has connections by MRT to and from points within the city. Public bus 36 leaves for the city approximately every 10 minutes between 6am and midnight, and takes about 45 minutes. Taxis from the airport pay a supplementary charge (S$3 to S$5 depending on time) on top of the metered fare, which is around S$18 to the city centre.

REDUCED FARES

For frequent MRT train and/or bus trips, buy a S$15 EZ-link card (includes a refundable S$5 deposit and S$10 credit) from any MRT station. The card can be used on all public buses and trains and offers reduced fares (from S$0.66 to S$1.75).

Bus

Public buses are operated by **SBS Transit** (www.sbstransit.com.sg) and **SMRT** (www.smrt.com.sg). Fares start at S$0.80 and rise to a maximum of S$1.70. Most buses run between 6am and midnight.

The **SIA Hop-On** (☑9457 2896; http://siahopon.asiaone.com.sg/; 1-day ticket for SIA passengers S$3, adult/child non-passengers S$12/6) tourist bus does 19 loops of the city between 9am and 7.30pm, stopping at 21 points of interest.

MRT

The **MRT** (www.smrt.com.sg) subway system is the most comfortable way to get around. It operates from 6am to midnight, with trains running every three to six minutes. Single-trip tickets cost from S$0.90 to S$1.90 with a S$1 deposit for every ticket.

Taxi

The major taxi companies are **City Cab** (☑6552 2222), **Comfort** (☑6552 1111), **SMRT** (☑6555 8888) and **TransCab** (☑6553 3333).

Fares start at S$2.80 for the first kilometre, then it's S$0.20 for each additional 385m. There are various surcharges: peak-hour, late-night and public-holiday services, airport pick-ups and bookings. You can flag down a taxi any time or use a taxi rank.

Gateway Jakarta

🎵021 / POP 9.1 MILLION

Best Places to Eat

» Vietopia (p53)

» Lara Djonggrang (p53)

» KL Village (p53)

Best Places to Stay

» Hotel Formule 1 (p53)

» Alila Jakarta (p53)

» FM7 Resort Hotel (p53)

Why Go?

Dubbed the 'Big Durian', Jakarta – with more flights to Kalimantan than any other city – is a metropolitan mix of freeways, skyscrapers, slums, glitzy malls, crumbling colonial buildings and endless traffic jams. The acrid-smelling streets and polyglot citizens are a condensed version of Indonesia, and the city is loaded with cultural traits and culinary treats.

It can be a tough city to explore, lacking a coherent centre, but it presents a real workout for urban adventurers. Despite its chaotic appearance Jakarta is not a threatening place, and there's plenty to keep history buffs, culture vultures, clubbers and shopaholics entertained.

See Lonely Planet's *Indonesia* guidebook for more information.

When to Go

It's worth knowing that Jakarta often suffers from heavy flooding at the height of the rainy season (January and February are usually the worst months), when whole neighbourhoods can be under water and it's difficult to get around. In early March, the Jakarta Jazz Festival showcases international and emerging talent at the city's Convention Centre. Jln Jaksa hosts its annual street fair, featuring art exhibits, dance and music in August. JiFFest, the nation's premier film festival, takes place in early December, with over a hundred screenings per season.

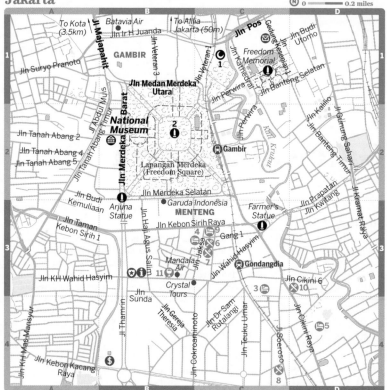

Sights

KOTA & SUNDA KELAPA

Jakarta's decaying historic heart is Kota, home to the remnants of the Dutch capital of Batavia. Take the Koridor 1 Busway to get here.

Taman Fatahillah, Kota's central square, is surrounded by imposing Dutch colonial buildings including the **Jakarta History Museum** (admission 2000Rp; ⊗9am-3pm) and elegant **Cafe Batavia** (p54) opposite.

A kilometre to the north is **Sunda Kelapa** (admission 2000Rp), the old Dutch port that's still used by graceful Bugis schooners. Tour the former warehouses of the VOC (Dutch East India Company), which now contain the **Museum Bahari** (www.museumbahari.org; Jln Pakin; admission 2000Rp; ⊗9am-3pm Tue-Sun), a good place to learn about Jakarta's maritime history.

Push-bike taxis (3000Rp) connect Kota and Sunda Kelapa.

CENTRAL & SOUTHERN JAKARTA

Soekarno attempted to tame Jakarta by giving it a central space, **Lapangan Merdeka** (Freedom Sq), and bestowing it with a gigantic **National Monument** (Monas; admission 5000Rp; ⊗8.30am-5pm, closed last Mon of every month). The 132m-high column, capped with a gilded flame, is irreverently called 'Soekarno's last erection' – whiz up the shaft for a shot of the city.

Northeast of here is the vast **Mesjid Istiqlal** (Jln Veteran 1), which can accommodate 200,000 worshippers and welcomes non-Muslim visitors (for a donation).

Sleeping

JLN JAKSA, CIKINI & MENTENG AREAS

Jakarta's backpacker enclave is Jln Jaksa, just south of Lapangan Merdeka and close to busy Jln Thamrin and the Transjakarta Busway, but be warned there are few decent cheap options. Nearby Cikini and Menteng are replete with midrange and luxury hotels.

Hotel Formule 1   HOTEL $$
(☑3190-8188; www.hotelformule1.com; Jln Cikini Raya 75; r 320,000Rp; family r 370,000Rp; ☻✼🛜) The winning formula here is a simple one: no-frills but comfortable modern rooms with zany colour schemes, private bathroom, flat-screen TV and wi-fi. Downstairs you'll find several restaurants, and there's a 50m public pool right behind the hotel.

Alila Jakarta   HOTEL $$$
(☑231-6008; www.alilahotels.com; Jln Pecenongan 7-17; r from US$70 plus 21% tax; ☻✼@🛜✼) A landmark tower close to Lapangan Merdeka, this very well-run place scores highly for both its facilities and modern design. You'll love the gorgeous outdoor pool, spa and gym. Service standards are sharp.

Hostel 35   HOSTEL $
(☑9824-1472; Jln Kebon Sirih Barat 1 35; r 70,000-90,000Rp, with air-con 140,000Rp; ✼) It looks slightly bizarre, with a tropical disco-style lobby, but this is one of the best budget deals in town. All rooms have brightly painted walls and fresh bed linen; most have en-suite bathrooms.

Istana Ratu Hotel   HOTEL $$
(☑314-2464; Jln Jaksa 7-9; r from 285,000Rp; ✼) A newish place, with large rooms, that offers style and comfort with great beds, bright duvets and soft pillows. Located close to the heart of the Jaksa action.

Gondia International Guesthouse
                                                  GUEST HOUSE $
(☑390-9221; gondia@rad.net.id; Jln Gondangdia Kecil 22; d from 200,000Rp; ✼) A friendly little guest house which occupies a leafy garden plot on a quiet street and has spacious tiled rooms with bathrooms.

AIRPORT

FM7 Resort Hotel   HOTEL $$
(☑5591-1777; www.fm7hotel.com; Jln Raya Perancis 67, Cengkareng; r from 549,000Rp; ☻✼@🛜✼) Just 2km from the airport, this excellent modern hotel is ideal for transit passengers. The stylish rooms boast contemporary furnishings, and there's a gym, indoor pool, sauna, and steam and massage rooms. Free airport transfers.

✖ Eating

JLN JAKSA AREA

Jln Jaksa's fine for no-nonsense Indonesian and Western grub. The night hawker stalls around the southern end of nearby Jln Haji Agus Salim are also good.

KL Village   MALAYSIAN $$
(Jln Jaksa 21-23; mains from 15,000Rp; ☉7am-11pm Sun-Wed, 24hr Thu-Sat; 🛜) Popular street-side place with pavement tables under a covered terrace. Feast on great curries or succulent noodle dishes and wash it down with a fresh juice.

Memories   INTERNATIONAL $$
(Jln Jaksa 17; mains 20,000Rp; ☉24hr) Long-running Jaksa backpacker hangout with filling breakfasts (from 19,000Rp), Chinese and Indonesian food, cold Bintang and a book exchange.

CIKINI

TOP CHOICE **Lara Djonggrang**   INDONESIAN $$$
(☑315-3252; Jln Teuku Cik Ditiro 4; mains 50,000-160,000Rp; ☉noon-10.30pm; 🛜) One of Jakarta's most atmospheric restaurants, this stunning place uses sensitive lighting to showcase tribal art and antique furnishings. The Indonesian cuisine is highly accomplished and beautifully presented and there's an excellent wine list.

Vietopia   VIETNAMESE $$
(☑391-5893; Jln Cikini Raya 33; mains 26,000-52,000Rp; ☉11.30am-10.30pm; 🛜) Authentic Vietnamese food, including steaming *pho*

NATIONAL MUSEUM

This **museum** (Jln Merdeka Barat 12; admission 750Rp; ⊗8.30am-2.30pm Tue-Sat) is easily the city's best and an essential visit. There's some stupendous statuary (including a 4.5m stone Bhairawa king shown trampling on human skulls) and fascinating textiles. In the impressive new wing you'll find golden treasures from Candi Brahu in Central Java. The **Indonesian Heritage Society** (☎572-5870; www.heritagejkt.org) organises free guided tours.

noodle broth, and plenty of delicious chicken, beef and seafood mains. All dishes are moderately priced and delicately spiced and the minimalist surroundings are a delight.

Drinking & Entertainment

Jakarta nights are fearsomely hedonistic. Clubs are concentrated in Glodok and Kota in the north of the city, while bars are scattered around town.

TOP CHOICE Melly's BAR
(Jln KH Wahid Hasyim 84; ⊗10.30am-12.30am; ☎) A bit like a neighbourhood pub, Melly's is the best bar in the Jaksa area, with a good mix of locals and Westerners, cheap snacks and cold beer. It's open-sided, so it doesn't get too smoky.

Red Square BAR
(Plaza Senayan Arcadia, Jln New Delhi 9, Senayan; ⊗noon-2am Mon-Fri, 6pm-4am Sat) Hip, lively vodka bar which even has a walk-in freezer for knocking back shots. DJs spin house mixes to a fashionable, moneyed crowd. It's about 5km southwest of Lapangan Merdeka.

Cafe Batavia BAR,-RESTAURANT
(Jln Pintu Besar Utara 14; ⊗8am-11pm) You have to stop by this wonderfully elegant colonial place, even if it's just for a coffee or beer, to soak up the classy art deco–inspired surroundings and refined ambience. The menu is perhaps a little grandiose for most tastes. Cafe Batavia is 4km north of Lapangan Merdeka.

Stadium NIGHTCLUB
(www.stadiumjakarta.com; Jln Hayum Waruk 111 FF-JJ; ⊗10pm Thu-11am Mon) Infamous club about 3km north of Lapangan Merdeka. Its fearsome tribal and trance sounds run

round the clock between Thursday and Monday. Only for the hardcore.

ℹ Information

BII Bank (Plaza Indonesia, Jln Thamrin) With ATM.

Crystal Tours (☎390-2929; Jl KH Wahid Hasyim 45) English-speaking staff and competitive flight prices.

Jakarta Visitor Information (☎315-4094; www.jakarta.go.id; Jakarta Theatre Bldg, Jln KH Wahid Hasyim 9; ⊗9.30am-7pm Mon-Sat, 9am-5pm Sun) Stocks an excellent colour map that shows the city's Busway routes.

Main post office (Jln Gedung Kesenian 1; ⊗8am-7pm Mon-Fri, to 1pm Sat)

SOS Medika Klinik (☎750-5980; www.internationalsos.com; Jln Puri Sakti 10, Kemang; ⊗24hr) Has English-speaking medical staff; 8km south of Lapangan Merdeka.

Tourist Police (☎566-000; Jln KH Wahid Hasyim) On the 2nd floor of the Jakarta Theatre.

ℹ Getting There & Away

Jakarta is the main travel hub for Indonesia.

Air

Soekarno-Hatta International Airport (www.jakartaairportonline.com) is 35km northwest of the city. Consult website for information and schedules. Airlines that link Jakarta with Borneo include:

AirAsia (☎5050-5088; www.airasia.com; Sukarno-Hatta airport) Flies to Kuala Lumpur, whence the company has flights to lots of cities in Sabah and Sarawak as well as Brunei and Balikpapan.

Batavia Air (☎3899-9888; www.batavia-air.co.id; Jln Ir H Juanda 15) Flies Jakarta–Banjarmasin.

Garuda Indonesia (☎0804-180-7807; www.garuda-indonesia.com; Garuda Bldg, Jln Merdeka Selatan 13) To Balikpapan and Banjarmasin.

Lion Air (☎632-6039; www.lionair.co.id; Jln Gajah Mada 7) Flies to both Balikpapan and Banjarmasin.

Malaysia Airlines (☎522-9690; www.malaysiaairlines.com; 14th fl, World Trade Center, Jln Sudirman 29-31) Flies to Kuala Lumpur, with onward flights to Sabah and Sarawak.

Mandala Air (☎0804-123-4567; www.mandalaair.com; Jln KH Wahid Hasyim 84-88) Connects Jakarta with Balikpapan and Tarakan.

Merpati (☎0800-101-2345; www.merpati.co.id; Jln Angkasa Blok B/15 Kav 2-3, Kemayoran) Links Jakarta with Banjarmasin.

Sriwijaya Airlines (☎640-5566; www.sriwi-jayaair-online.com; Jln Gunung Sahari Raya 13, Blok B8-10) Flights to Balikpapan, Banjarmasin and Tarakan.

Boat

Pelni (www.pelni.co.id) ferries to Kalimantan arrive at and depart from Tanjung Priok, 13km northeast of the city centre; take a Koridor 10 Transjakarta bus. The *Leuser* goes via Tanjung Pandan to Pontianak. Tickets (plus commission) can be bought from **Menara Buana Surya** (☎314-2464; Jln Menteng Raya 29), 500m east of Jln Jaksa.

Bus

Kalideres bus terminal, 15km northwest of the centre, has frequent buses to destinations west of Jakarta. Take a Koridor 3 Transjakarta bus to get there. **Kampung Rambutan**, 18km south of the city, primarily handles destinations south and southeast of Jakarta; Koridor 7 runs here. **Pulo Gadung**, 8km east of the centre, serves central and eastern Java, Sumatra and Bali; take a Koridor 4 or 2 Transjakarta bus. **Lebak Bulus**, 16km southwest of the centre, handles some deluxe buses to Yogyakarta and Surabaya.

Train

Jakarta has many train stations. **Gambir**, a 15-minute walk from Jln Jaksa, handles express trains to Bogor, Bandung, Yogyakarta, Solo, Semarang and Surabaya. If you are staying in Jln Jaksa, **Gondangdia**, just to the east, has some trains to Bogor and Kota.

Check timetables online at www.infoka.kereta-api.com.

ⓘ Getting Around

To/From the Airport

Soekarno-Hatta International Airport is about an hour from the centre via a toll road (up to two hours during rush hour).

There's a very useful Damri bus service (20,000Rp) every 30 minutes from 5am to 7pm between the airport and Gambir train station.

A metered taxi costs about 180,000Rp, including the airport service and toll road charges. These should be organised through the official booths.

Bus

Jakarta has a comprehensive city bus network. Stick to the very regular, air-conditioned **Transjakarta Busway** (☺5am-10pm) services which run on dedicated lanes and are by far the fastest way to get around the city. Tickets cost 3500Rp; buy before you board. The system operates like a metro with stations every kilometre or so.

Taxi

Metered taxis cost around 6000Rp for the first kilometre and 250Rp for each subsequent 100m. Make sure the *argo* (meter) is used. **Bluebird cabs** (☎794-1234; www.bluebirdgroup.com) can be booked ahead and have the best reputation; do *not* risk travelling with the less reputable firms.

Sabah

Best Places to Eat

» KK Night Market (p57)

» Sim Sim Seafood
Restaurant (p97)

» Grazie (p67)

» Mongolian Chicken Rice
(p123)

Best Places to Stay

» Paganakan Dii (p101)

» Mañana (p88)

» Labuan Homestay
Programme (p134)

» Mabul Water Bungalow
(p118)

Why Go?

Sabah is proof God didn't butter the earth's toast very evenly. How can such a relatively small area be blessed with so much beauty?

Let's look at the evidence in 'The Land Below the Wind'. Starting with the water: green, blue, teal and every shade of tropical cool between, inhabited by sea life so fantastical and surreal it feels like lost footage from the *Star Trek* cutting floor. This water laps on golden sand or filters into mangroves that shelter crocodiles and monitor lizards related to Godzilla, pygmy elephants, bearded pigs and of course the great ginger man himself: the orangutan. Hopping, grunting, hunting, squealing, squawking, preying and playing along the banks of the chocolate-brown Sungai Kinabatangan (Kinabatangan River), below the starlight fireflies of the Klias, amid the limestone daggers of Batu Pungull and in deep, ancient jungle. Topping it all is Mt Kinabalu, the tallest mountain in Borneo, home of spirits, snow, an 'iron road' and some of the most magnificent sunrises anywhere.

When to Go

» January and February are always good times to visit if you like loud noises and lots of gaudy red and gold: this is prime-time Chinese festival season, with the biggest celebrations going down in cities like Kota Kinabalu and Sandakan.

» Although the diving in Semporna is always excellent, the best time of year for scubaholics is supposed to be March through July, when the waters are calmer.

» If you want to climb Mt Kinabalu, February through April are the driest months on the mountain.

Getting There & Around

AIR

International flights connect Kota Kinabalu to the world via **AirAsia** (www.airasia.com), **Malaysia Air** (www.malaysiaairlines.com) and **JetStar** (www.jetstar.com). Between AirAsia and Malaysia Air's Borneo branch, **MASwings** (www.maswings.com), a web of flight routes connects Kota Kinabalu to every major city in Borneo, including Bandar Seri Begawan (Brunei).

BOAT

It is possible to travel into Sabah by boat from Kalimantan into Tawau (Indonesia; p123). From Brunei, there are car ferries to Menumbok and the Malaysian federal district of Pulau Labuan (p234), linked to KK by boat.

BUS

Buses link Brunei with destinations along Sabah's northwestern coast and KK (p234).
In Sabah, a paved road makes a frowning arc from KK to Tawau, passing Mt Kinabalu, Sepilok, Sandakan, Lahad Datu and Semporna (the gateway to Sipadan) along the way. It takes around 10 hours to complete the circuit.

KOTA KINABALU

POP 436,100

Kota Kinabalu – everyone calls it 'KK' – is probably a cooler city than you think. OK, it's probably not going to be the sleeper hit of your Borneo vacation, but as midsize Malaysian provincial capitals go, it's as good as the genre gets. The centre is compact and walkable, there's a lovely waterfront packed with atmospheric markets, some pretty good if garish malls, a surprisingly popping nightlife scene (relative to Malaysia) and some damn fine food. Right, we realise you almost certainly didn't come to Sabah for the urban scene, but you gotta book permits somewhere, you gotta sleep after climbing Mt Kinabalu/diving in Sipadan/exploring the jungle etc, and you need someplace to connect to onward travel. KK is a good place (sometimes the only place) to do all of the above. Grab a cold Tiger, a bowl of noodle soup and enjoy the karaoke bars. This is Southeast Asian city life on a small, manageable scale, which might be the appetiser you need before the main course of Sabah's natural wonders.

Sights

CITY CENTRE & WATERFRONT

KK Heritage Walk   WALKING TOUR
(012-802 8823; www.kkheritagewalk.com; admission RM200; walks 9am Tue & Thu) This

THE SOUTHSIDE CONNECTION

Getting from KK to Tawau via the northern half of the island, via a big frown, is easy. Doing the smile side of the loop (going back to KK through the south from Tawau): not so much. The road here is not entirely paved, but there's at least finely crushed gravel the whole way through, and a 2WD or even motorbike should be fine. An infrastructure of public buses does not yet exist here; at the time of research minivans occasionally ran this stretch of road, but only when needed by logging camps. If you can get a lift to Keningau, the rest of the journey to KK is a breeze.

two-hour tour, which can also be booked through several tour operators, explores colonial KK and its hidden delights. Stops include Chinese herbal shops, bulk produce stalls, a *kopitiam* (coffee shop), and Jln Gaya (known as Bond St when the British were in charge). There's also a quirky treasure hunt at the end leading tourists to the Jesselton Hotel. Guides speak English, Chinese and Bahasa Malaysia.

Night Market   MARKET
(Jln Tun Fuad Stephens; late afternoon-11pm) KK's main market is a place of delicious contrasts. Huddled beneath the imposing Le Meridien, the market is divided into two main sections: the southwest end is given over mostly to produce, while the northeast end (the area around the main entrance) is a huge hawker centre where you can eat your way right through the entire Malay gastronomy. A fish and food market extends to the waterfront; the closer you get to the ocean, the more the scent of salt water, death, blood and spices envelops you – an oddly intoxicating experience. If you've never seen a proper Southeast Asian market, this place will be a revelation.

Signal Hill   LANDMARK
There's a UFO-like observation pavilion on this hill at the eastern edge of the city centre. Come here to escape the traffic and get another take on the squatters' stilt village at Pulau Gaya (Gaya Island). The view is best as the sun sets over the islands. From the top, it's also possible to hike down to the

Sabah Highlights

1 Admiring the wild sea turtles among multicoloured reefs in the **Semporna Archipelago** (p115)

2 Hoofing it over pitcher plants and granite moonscapes for the ultimate Bornean sunrise atop **Mt Kinabalu** (p75)

3 Breathing in the air of an actual virgin rainforest in the **Maliau Basin** (p124)

4 Watching orangutans bend trees to their ginger will in **Sepilok** (p99)

5 Discovering the hidden beaches of northern Borneo near **Kudat** (p89)

Wetland Centre on the other side, but it's a longer way than it looks – don't try this if it's getting dark.

Sunday Market   MARKET
(Jln Gaya; ⊙7am-3pm) On Sundays, a lively Chinese street fair takes over the entire length of Jalan Gaya. If you're not digging the KK vibe, this market may change your mind – it's a combination of all of the above markets, intensely manic and a perfect spot for souvenir shopping.

Atkinson Clock Tower   LANDMARK
The modest timepiece at the foot of the hill is one of the only structures to survive the Allied bombing of Jesselton in 1945. It's a square, 15.7m-high wooden structure that was completed in 1905 and named after the first district officer of the town, FG Atkinson, who died of malaria aged 28.

Central Market   MARKET
(Jln Tun Fuad Stephens; ⊙6.30am-6pm) While it's not as interesting as the Night Market – this more of a 'useful things' bazaar – the Central Market is fun to wander about, and a nice spot for people watching as locals transact their daily business. Nearby, the Handicraft Market (Filipino Market; Jln Tun Fuad Stephens; ⊙10am-6pm) is a good place to shop for inexpensive souvenirs. Offerings include pearls, textiles, seashell crafts, jewellery and bamboo goods, some from the Philippines, some from Malaysia and some from other parts of Asia. Needless to say, bargaining is a must!

BEYOND THE CITY CENTRE
Some of KK's best attractions are located beyond the city centre, and it's well worth putting in the effort to check 'em out.

Sabah Museum   MUSEUM
(⌨088-253199; www.museum.sabah.gov.my; Jln Muzium; admission RM15; ⊙9am-5pm Sat-Thu) Centred on a modern four-storey structure inspired by the longhouses of the Rungus and Murut tribes, this is the best place to go in KK for an introduction to Sabah's ethnicities and environments. It's slightly south of the city centre, on the hilly corner of Jln Tunku Abdul Rahman and Jln Penampang.

In the main building there are good permanent collections of tribal and historical artefacts including ceramics. and exhibits of flora and fauna – some dusty, others well presented (including a centrepiece whale skeleton). The prehistory gallery has a rep-

lica limestone cave, in case you don't make it to any of the real ones. In the gardens, the Heritage Village offers the chance to wander round examples of traditional tribal dwellings, including Kadazan bamboo houses and a Chinese farmhouse, all nicely set on a lily-pad lake.

The adjoining Science & Education Centre has an informative exhibition on the petroleum industry, from drilling to refining and processing. The Sabah Art Gallery features regular shows and exhibitions by local artists. If you're heading east after KK, keep hold of your admission ticket – it will also allow you entry to Agnes Keith House (p93) in Sandakan.

Museum of Islamic Civilisation   MUSEUM
(⌨088-538234; admission incl in Sabah Museum ticket; ⊙9am-5pm Sat-Thu), with six galleries devoted to Muslim culture and history. The five domes represent the holy Five Pillars of Islam.

To get to the museum complex, catch a bus (RM1) along Jln Tunku Abdul Rahman and get off just before the mosque. Be warned: it's a short but steep walk uphill to the museum. Bus 13 also goes right round past the Queen Elizabeth hospital and stops near Jln Muzium. Taxi fare is RM10.

Kota Kinabalu Wetland Centre   MUSEUM
(⌨088-246955; www.sabahwetlands.org; Jln Bukit Bendera Upper; adult/child RM10/5; ⊙8am-6pm Tue-Sun) This lovely spot, across from the city mosque, encompasses the last 24 hectares of a mangrove swamp that once stretched across what was KK. A series of wooden walkways leads into a lovely wetland rife with fiddler crabs, mangrove crabs, mud lobsters, mudskippers, skinks, turtles and the adorably turd-like mangrove slug, among other swamp fauna. For many, the big attraction is a stunning variety of migratory birds, some from as far away as Siberia.

To get here, head north on Jln Fuad Stephens (the main road north out of town; in town it's also called Jln KK Bypass) and follow it as it curves around the coast. You'll then turn right at Jln Istidat and follow that for about 1km; the Wetland Centre will be on your right, just off a traffic roundabout.

Mari Mari Cultural Village   MUSEUM
(⌨019-820 4921; www.traversetours.com/cultural village.php, Jln Kiansom; adult/child RM150/130) When it comes to learning about local

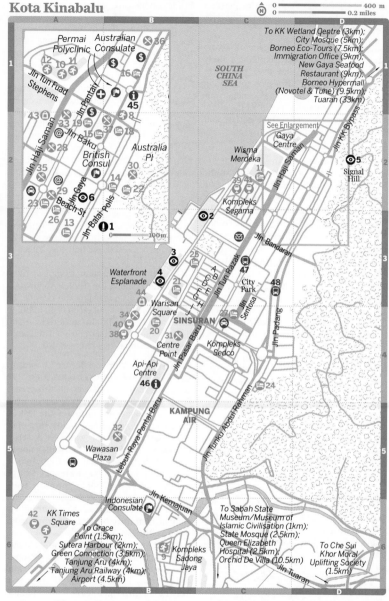

ethnic groups, this is the most interactive centre of its kind in the state. Visitors are taken on a three-hour show-tour (beginning at 10am, 3pm and 7pm), which winds through the jungle passing various tribal dwellings along the way. At each stop, tourists learn about indigenous folkways and can try their hand at bamboo cooking, rice-wine making (and drinking!), fire starting, tattooing, blowpipe shooting etc. A short dance recital and delicious meal (lunch or dinner depending on the time of visit) are included in the visit – the centre must be notified of any dietary restrictions in advance. A trip to the cultural village can be combined with a white-water rafting tour; contact **Riverbug** (p64) for more information.

There is also a small chute – **Kiansom Waterfall** (admission RM1; ⊙dawn-dusk) – about 400m beyond the cultural village, which is easily accessible by private transport or on foot. The area around the cascade lends itself well to swimming and it's a great place to cool off after a visit to Mari Mari.

Lok Kawi Wildlife Park   ZOO
(☑088-765710; www.lokkawiwildlifepark.com; Jln Penampang, Papar Lama; adult/child RM20/10; ⊙9.30am-5.30pm) If you'd like to check out the orangutans but won't make it out to Sepilok or the Kinabatangan, a visit to this wildlife park is highly recommended, especially for those with children in tow. There are plenty of other animals as well, from tarsiers to rhinos. Don't miss the giant aviary at the top of the hill, with its ominous warning sign 'beware of attacking birds'!

It's best to arrive by 9.50am at the latest – feedings take place throughout the park at

FIND YOUR WAY IN KK

Downtown KK is a dense grid of concrete buildings nestled between the waterfront and a range of low, forested hills to the east. It's compact, walkable and easy to navigate – most of the restaurants, markets, accommodation, tourist offices and tour operators are located here. Transport terminals bookend the city on either side.

10am. After the various feedings, an interactive show takes place at the stage around 11.15am everyday. After feeding time, most of the animals take their daily siesta – only the humans are silly enough to stay out in the scorching midday sun.

The 17B minibus goes to Lok Kawi (RM2). Visitors with a private vehicle can access the park via the Papar–Penampang road or the Putatan–Papar road. Travel agents offer half-day tours, or you can hire a taxi, which will cost around RM120, including a two-hour wait.

Monsopiad Cultural Village   MUSEUM
(☎088-761336; www.monsopiad.com; admission RM65; ☺9am-5pm) On the banks of Sungai Moyog, Monsopiad is named after a legendary warrior and head-hunter, whose direct descendants established this private heritage centre in 1996. The hefty entrance fee gives you a pretty similar experience to Mari Mari, with a bigger focus on specifically Kadazan-Dusun culture. The highlight is the House of Skulls, which supposedly contains the ancient crania of Monsopiad's unfortunate enemies, as well as artefacts illustrating native rituals from the time when the *bobolian* (priest) was the most important figure in the community.

Many tour companies include Monsopiad on local itineraries. To get here independently, take a bus from central KK to Donggongon (RM1.50), where you can catch a minivan to the cultural village (RM1). You can also take a taxi or charter a minivan direct from KK for around RM35-40.

Chinese Temples   TEMPLES
The main road north to Tuaran runs past some impressive Chinese temples.

Che Sui Khor Moral Uplifting Society
(Jln Tuaran) About four minutes north of KK, this complex is anchored by an 11-storey pagoda that shimmers in orange and green. Tourists can't enter the actual pagoda, but the friendly members of the society (they espouse believing in the best Christianity, Islam, Taoism, Buddhism and Christianity

have to offer) don't mind you poking around the rest of their library. You can get here via the bus terminal at Wawasan Plaza going north on the Jln Tuaran route (RM3). To get home, just stand outside the temple on the main road and a minibus or regular bus will pick you up. A return taxi should cost around RM20.

Puh Toh Tze Buddhist Temple
(Jln Tuaran) Also spelled Poh Toh Tse, this temple is about 20 minutes north of KK, at Mile (Batu) 5.5. It's quite impressive: a stone staircase-pavilion flanked by 10 Chinese deities leads up to a main temple complex dominated by Kwan Yin, Goddess of Mercy. A Chinese-style reclining Buddha rests inside. You're free to enter and wander around. The temple is on a small hill west of the main highway junction north; you can get here taking the Jln Tuaran bus again or, more easily, hire a taxi; a round-trip shouldn't be more than RM36.

Green Connection   AQUARIUM
(☎013-897 8005; www.aquaticakk.org/aquatica/index.htm; behind Wisma Wanita, Lorong Bunga Matahari 2; adult/child RM10/5; ☺10am-6pm daily). Run by a friendly staff of Malay and foreigners, KK's valiant attempt at an aquarium consists of several tanks of reptiles, freshwater fish, sea snakes and a pretty impressive megatank rife with rays that will inevitably make kids coo in pleasure. Environmental education programmes are run for children and adults on-site. This place seems to operate on a shoestring – when we visited, many of the exhibits were in need of some sprucing up – but we give it credit for making a sincere effort, and your support as a visitor will hopefully help the place improve in the future. To get here, either take a taxi (RM10) or find a south-bound minibus from the central station and ask to be let off at Wisma Wanita. The Green Connection is located on the path that curves behind the Wanita tower.

City Mosque   MOSQUE
(off Jln Tun Fuad Stephens) Overlooking the South China Sea, this mosque is built in classical style, and is far more attractive than the State Mosque in terms of setting

and design. Completed in 2000, it can hold up to 12,000 worshippers. It can be entered by non-Muslims outside regular prayer times, but dress modestly (long trousers and arms covered is a good rule of thumb, although you may get away with just shoulders covered) and remove your shoes before entering. To get here, take bus 5A from Wawasan Plaza going toward UMS (RM1.50). Just ask the conductor to drop you off outside the City Mosque after the Tanjung Lipat roundabout. Taxis are about RM20 each way.

State Mosque   MOSQUE
(Jln Tunku Abdul Rahman) Sabah's state mosque is a perfect example of contemporary Malay Muslim architecture: all modernist facade and geometric angles. Some will find it attractive, although we think it's a bit brutalistic. The building is south of the city centre past the Kampung Air stilt village, not far from the Sabah Museum; you'll see the striped minaret and chevronned dome on your way to or from the airport. Non-Muslim visitors are allowed inside, but again, dress appropriately.

Tanjung Aru   BEACH
This pleasant sweep of sand begins around the Shangri-La's Tanjung Aru Resort (p66) and stretches south to the airport. Tanjung Aru is a locals' beach, full of picnic spots, swoony-eyed couples and much familial goodwill. Food stalls are plentiful, most closing up a bit after dark, which reminds us: sunsets here are pretty perfect.

Orchid De Villa   FARM
(☑088-380611; www.orchid-de-villa.com.my; Jln Kiansom; ⊗8am-5pm) If you're just as crazy

about flora as fauna, head to this farm, located halfway between central KK and the cultural village (at Km 6). The farm specialises in rare Bornean orchids, hybrid orchids, cacti and herbal plants, and services all of the five-star hotels in the region with flower arrangements.

👉 Tours

KK has a huge number of tour companies, enough to suit every taste and budget. Head to Wisma Sabah – this office building is full of agents and operators. We've listed tour operators for relevant destinations throughout this chapter, so check each section to scout out the best company for you. The following options have an office in KK and offer a broad range of reputable tours.

TOP **CHOICE** **GogoSabah**   SIGHTS
(☑088-316385; www.gogosabah.com; Lot G-4, Ground fl, Wisma Sabah, Jln Tun Razak) Run by the friendly Joel, Gogo is a forward-thinking tour company that does a great job of booking just about anything, anywhere in Sabah while also helping independent travellers out with logistics, itineraries and information. Especially excellent for motorbike rentals – Joel will help map out some of the choicest areas for exploration in Sabah.

John Nair   GUIDE
(☑019-811 2117; borneotoursmalaysia@yahoo. com) Not technically a company – John is an award-winning freelance guide who helped the BBC produce the orangutan documentary shown regularly at Sepilok. He offers private guiding services and usually hangs out at Hunter's (p70) in the lobby of the Kinabalu Daya. Check his profile on Facebook: www.facebook.com/profile. php?id=100001411393459.

Borneo Adventure   ADVENTURE
(☑088-486800; www.borneoadventure.com; Block E-27-3A, Signature Office, KK Times Square) Award-winning Sarawak-based company with very professional staff, imaginative sightseeing and activity itineraries and a genuine interest in local people and the environment.

Borneo Authentic   BOAT
(☑088-773066; www.borneo-authentic.com) A friendly operation offering a variety of package tours including day-trip cruises on the Sungai Klias.

GAINING ENTRY TO THE WORLD'S BIGGEST THEME PARK

They call Sabah 'the world's largest theme park', and that analogy works in terms of how much fun you'll have here and, less positively, lines. Not for rides, but permits, while cutting through red tape etc. This isn't travel as you've experienced in the rest of Southeast Asia. Sabah rewards, and sometimes requires, prior planning and deeper pockets than the rest of the region. As we researched our way across the state, we encountered no fewt travellers lamenting booked beds, or bemoaning being barred from national parks. The best mantra is plan ahead, plan ahead, plan ahead. That said, yes, you can explore Sabah without any planning – just be prepared for a fair amount of little annoyances that might coalesce into one blindingly frustrating ball of hassle.

Here're our tips for some of Sabah's most visited sites:

Mt Kinabalu It's best to book as far in advance as possible – a month is ideal, but if you want your pick of lodging, six months is more like it. If you don't care where you sleep you can wait it out, but beds do get filled at the Laban Rata guest house, which you must sleep in on the summit route. Here's the drill: head directly to the Sutera Sanctuary Lodges office in KK (p83) if you did not organise your climb before leaving home – sitting in front of the booking agents will increase your chances of finding a cancellation (although you'll probably have to reshape your itinerary once they offer you an inconvenient ascent date). Most of the beds have been gobbled up by tour operators, so if you can't snag a bed with Sutera, chances are you can find a travel agency around town that can sell you one (at a much higher price, unfortunately; you're paying both Sutera and the agency's commission). Adventurers interested in tackling the mountain's *via ferrata* course should contact **Mountain Torq** (www.mountaintorq.com). You can just show up at Mt Kinabalu if you think you can manage the ascent and descent in a day, but you have to show up early (before 7am) and it's still wise to book accommodation beforehand. Trust us, you don't want to bother with finding a lodge after that climb!

Sipadan For a Sipadan scuba session, divers must obtain a permit, which usually comes with booking a dive package and/or accommodation in the Semporna archipelago. You'll want to book that lodging beforehand anyway, as no one wants to hang around Semporna

Borneo Divers   DIVING
(☑088-222226; www.borneodivers.info; 9th fl, Menara Jubili, 53 Jln Gaya) Longest-established Borneo dive outfit; can arrange courses and dives just about anywhere and has its own dive shop. It's possible to get discounted rates as a walk-in.

Borneo Eco Tours   SIGHTS
(☑088-438300; www.borneoecotours.com; Pusat Perindustrian Kolombong Jaya, Mile 5.5 Jln Kolombong) This is a place with a good reputation, arranging tours throughout Malaysian Borneo, including travel to the Kinabatangan area.

Borneo Nature Tours   NATURE
(☑088-267637; www.borneonaturetours.com; Block D, Lot 10 Kompleks Sadong Jaya) Professional and knowledgeable operation managing bookings for Danum Valley's beautiful Borneo Rainforest Lodge (p112). Its office building is on Ikan Juara 4, on the corner near a canal.

Scuba Junkie/River Junkie   DIVING, RAFTING
(☑019-601 2145, 088-266700; www.scuba -junkie.com; Lot G7, Ground fl, Wisma Sabah, Jln Haji Saman) Runs diving trips in the Semporna archipelago and white-water rafting trips in southwest Sabah aimed at the backpacker crowd.

Sutera Sanctuary Lodges   CLIMBING
(☑088-243629; www.suterasanctuarylodges. com; Lot G15, ground fl, Wisma Sabah, Jln Haji Saman; ◎9am-6.30pm Mon-Fri, 9am-4.30pm Sat, 9am-3pm Sun) Make this your first stop in KK if you're planning to climb Kinabalu and didn't book your bed in advance. Go now! Hurry!

Riverbug/Traverse Tours   SIGHTS
(☑088-260501; www.traversetours.com; Lot 227, Wisma Sabah, Jln Tun Fuad Stephens) An excellent and forward-thinking operator that has a wide variety of tours across Sabah.

town, so this isn't much of an issue. If you extend your stay in the islands your hotel/lodge should be able to get you extra days diving Sipadan. That said, only a limited number of Sipadan permits are granted per day, so if you're on a tight, inflexible schedule you should book well in advance (at least two weeks).

Sepilok The orangutan sanctuary does not require permits, just an entrance fee. The only booking you may need is for your lodging. Easy!

Sungai Kinabatangan (Kinabatangan River) If you want to stay at a meals-inclusive lodge on the river it's best to book at least a few days in advance. No permits are needed, but there are a limited number of chalets at each lodge. If you'd like to do a home stay you can probably just show up to Sukau or Bilit, but we'd strongly advise you to book ahead by at least a few days; it's both polite and practical.

Danum Valley/Tabin Wildlife Reserve You must book your lodging in advance if you want to enter the Danum Valley (see p110), one of the most beautiful rainforest preserves in Borneo. You can try just driving to Tabin, which is equally arresting; although technically frowned on, it's been done before, but we'd still advise prebooking in KK or Lahad Datu. You never know how strict the gate staff will be.

Maliau Basin The Maliau is usually only visited as part of an extremely expensive package tour, but we did run into travellers who were able to enter by negotiating with gate staff. For more information, see p124, and keep in mind that this is still a relatively expensive trip (but nowhere near as expensive as a package tour of the basin).

We hope we didn't put you off with all of the above information; it's just that a centimetre of preparation gives a kilometre of reward in Sabah. But you can – and should – discover this state under your own steam when you can. Swarms of travel agents in KK will try to convince you that Sabah can only be discovered while on a tour. This is simply not true. Rent a motorbike or a car and get out in that wild wonderland; you'll likely discover some treasure we missed, you lucky things.

🛏 Sleeping

A group of budget hotel and hostel owners have banded together to form the **Sabah Backpacker Operators Association** (SBA; www.sabahbackpackers.com) in an effort to help shoestring travellers in the region. Check out its website for discount deals on accommodation and tours. KK's midrange options seem to be sliding towards either end of the budget spectrum. Although backpacker hangouts and top-end treats are in great proliferation, there are still several spots around town suiting those Goldilockses out there.

TOP
CHOICE **Hotel Eden 54**   BOUTIQUE HOTEL **$$**
(☏088-266054; www.eden54.com; 54 Jln Gaya; r RM119-169; ❄🕸) This smart choice would likely cost five times what it does were it plopped in the West. Fortunately this Eden's contrasting solid dark and light colours, geometric design sensibility and immaculate furniture have turned up in Kota Kinabalu. A fine choice for flashpackers,

couples, even families, this is the rare real boutique in Borneo. Did we mention the staff are superlatively helpful with arranging tours? One warning: the cheapest rooms are windowless, and should be avoided.

Rainforest Lodge   HOTEL **$$**
(☏088-258228; www.rainforestlodgekk.com; Jln Pantai; dm/s/d/ste from RM30/98/128/148; ❄🕸) Located in the swinging centre of the 'Beach Street' complex, the Rainforest is the place to stay when you need to let loose, considering it is all of a stairward stumble from some of KK's best nightlife. More importantly: rooms are refreshingly chic, a nice mix of modern and Sabah-tribal style, and many have cool balconies that look onto the Beach St parade below. Just be warned: it gets loud at night.

Step-In Lodge   HOSTEL **$**
(☏088-233519; www.stepinlodge.com; Block L, Kompleks Sinsuran, Jln Tun Fuad Stephens; dm

with fan/air-con RM28/38, d with fan/air-con RM70/90; ✹🛜) This popular spot wins the award for KK's smartest hostel with larger-than-normal bunk beds, comfy mattresses, *real* coffee at breakfast, and excellent (not to mention knowledgeable) staff. These clever touches make Step-In feel much more homey than some of the factory-style operations nearby. Ask about special rates for families.

Le Meridien Kota Kinabalu   HOTEL **$$$**
(☑088-322222; www.starwoodhotels.com; Jln Tun Fuad Stephens; r from RM300; 🅿✹🛜≋) 'If you can't undercut 'em, outclass 'em' seems to be the motto at KK's most central five-star venture, which just reeks of luxury, from the incredible views from the pool deck to the flat-screen TVs and DVD players. The eye-watering prices come down a little in low season, and may even get as low as RM200 if you catch the right discounts.

Le Hotel   BOUTIQUE HOTEL **$$**
(☑088-319696; www.lehotel.com.my; 3rd fl, Block B, Warisan Square, Jln Tun Fuad Stephens; r RM120-198; ✹🛜) Head on down to the waterfront if you're hip enough not to have to prove it. The Le is bright colours and airy impressions, designed to look modern and cool without being pretentious. Located inside Warisan Square mall.

Summer Lodge   HOSTEL **$**
(☑088-244499; www.summerlodge.com.my; Lot 120, Jln Gaya; dm/d RM28/70; ✹🛜) Summer Lodge feels a bit like a bed factory, but it's got that social vibe backpackers adore – 'How long have you been travelling? Where did you come from/where are you going next? Isn't it funny when those foreigners do that thing they do? Gosh, diving/climbing/seeing those animals was amazing. Fancy a drink?' The answer to the last question is easily solved – the Beach Street bar complex is just below. Owners are very friendly and helpful.

Jesselton Hotel   HOTEL **$$$**
(☑088-223333; www.jesseltonhotel.com; 69 Jln Gaya; r/ste from RM 215/450; ✹🛜) The oldest hotel in KK doesn't need to manufacture character – it fairly drips it, in a dignified if dated way. Mock-colonial wood and marble make you want to don black-tie formal clothes, and the single suite even has its own fishpond! There's also a very good restaurant, coffee shop, business centre and red London cab to shuttle you to the airport.

Kinabalu Daya   BOUTIQUE HOTEL **$$**
(☑088-240000; www.kkdayahotel.com; Lot 3-4, Block 9, Jln Pantai; r/ste incl breakfast from RM135/260; ✹🛜) Oddly-angled hallways and strangely placed lifts give Kinabalu Daya a certain '10-year-old's-Lego-project' vibe. Nevertheless, tonnes of tourists swear by this midrange stalwart – and we can see why – it's in the centre of the action and the Best Western branding ensures a certain amount of familiar comfort. A newly renovated wing offers more stylish, boutique-chic rooms.

Lucy's Homestay   HOME STAY **$**
(Backpacker's Lodge; ☑088-261495; http://lucy-homestay.go-2.net; Lot 25, Lg Dewan, Australia Pl; dm/s/d incl breakfast RM20/45/50; 🛜) We have a soft spot for lovely Lucy and her homey home stay in Australia Place. There's loads of charm, with wooden walls smothered in stickers, business cards and crinkled photographs. It may not suit if you're a party person or want cushy extras – this is an old-school hostel – but if you're looking for a quaint home away from home, you'll find it here. Laundry service starts at RM15 per load.

Hyatt Regency Kota Kinabalu   HOTEL **$$$**
(☑088-221234; http://kinabalu.regency.hyatt.com; Jln Datuk Salleh Sulong; r from RM350; 🅿✹🛜≋) Located in the city centre, this branch of the Hyatt chain is all corporate glitz – a good spot to take a businessman for lunch while enjoying impressive views out of a top-storey suite. Rooms are done up in warm earth tones and packed with amenities, including quite possibly the best selection of cable-TV channels in the city.

Switz Paradise Hotel   HOTEL **$$**
(☑088-448177; www.switzparadisehotel.com; 3rd fl, Asia City, Jln Pantai; r RM88-108; 🅿✹🛜) The Switz, with its compact but comfy fantasy-in-white rooms, cheerful staff and penchant for odd spellings of landlocked European nations, is just a bundle of cuteness. In the low season room prices drop into the top of the budget range. Located in the Asia City mall.

Shangri-La's Tanjung Aru Resort & Spa
RESORT **$$$**
(STAR; ☑088-327888; www.shangri-la.com; Tanjung Aru; r from 590; 🅿✹🛜≋) The Shangri-La is a good choice for those who want to combine the attractions of Kota Kinabalu with the features of a tropical resort. It's a sprawl-

ing complex, dotted with swaying palms and metal gongs, located in the Tanjung Aru area about 3km south of the city centre. Dozens of uniformed staff are constantly on hand to respond to your every whim.

Akinabalu Youth Hostel
HOSTEL **$**

(☎088-272188; www.akinabaluy.com; Lot 133, Jln Gaya; dm/r incl breakfast from RM20/56; ❄☎) Friendly staff, fuchsia accent walls and trickling Zen fountains make this a solid option among KK's hostels, particularly if you find a quiet time to take advantage of the gratis internet and DVDs. Accommodation is mostly in basic four-bed rooms, with windows facing an interior hallway.

Sutera Harbour
RESORT **$$$**

(☎088-318888; www.suteraharbour.com; 1 Sutera Harbour Blvd; r from RM800; P❄☎☰) While not as 'old-world Asia' as the stunning Shangri-La, Sutera caters to big spenders with a cache of five-star amenities orbiting the vaulted lobby. Some of the rooms (especially those with carpeting) feel a bit tired, so don't hesitate to ask to see a couple of options. A second on-site tower, the Magellan, offers more options. Packages and discounts are available.

Borneo Gaya Lodge
HOSTEL **$**

(☎088-242477; www.borneogayalodge.com; 78 Jln Gaya; dm/d from RM25/69; ❄☎) A typical high-volume hostel. Staff are a peach, and will help organise nearly anything, and you're as centrally located in KK as can be.

Borneo Backpackers
HOSTEL **$**

(☎088-234009; www.borneobackpackers.com; 24 Lg Dewan, Australia Pl; dm/s/d incl breakfast from RM20/40/60; ❄☎) This long-running backpackers is a bit cramped, but it's very popular, especially with younger travellers.

A 'hypermall' complex, **1 Borneo**, located about 20 minutes north of the city centre, has a few chain-hotel options geared towards business travellers (there are roughly 900 hotel rooms on the grounds). A free shuttle bus connects the development to the city centre. Tourists who seek an international standard of comfort and don't mind being removed from the action should consider staying at one of the following options.

Novotel
HOTEL **$$**

(☎088-529888; www.novotel.com; 1 Borneo Hypermall, Jln UMS, d from RM200; ❄@☎) A stunner, but stunningly far from the city centre.

Tune
HOTEL **$$**

(☎03 7962 5888; www.tunehotels.com; 1 Borneo Hypermall, Jln UMS, d from RM200; ❄@☎) Also good for business travellers. A little plainer than the Novotel, but the high-powered showers are a treat!

✖ Eating

KK is one of the few cities in Borneo with an eating scene diverse enough to refresh the noodle-jaded palate. Besides the ubiquitous Chinese *kedai kopi* (coffee shops) and Malay halal restaurants, you'll find plenty of interesting options around the city centre – head to the suburbs if you're looking for some truly unique local fare.

CITY CENTRE

Ya Kee Bah Kut Teh
CHINESE **$**

(☎088-221192; 74 Jln Gaya; mains from RM5; ⏱4pm-11pm) Kosher and halal readers need not apply, because this spot is all about the pork. Pork pork pork, in herbal soup form (ie Bah Kut The). Fatty pork. Pork ribs. Pork belly. Pork with ginger and chillies. Pork offal. With all apologies to *Babe*, we gotta highly recommend this delicious option.

Grazie
ITALIAN **$$$**

(☎019-821 6936; Ground fl, Wawasan Plaza; mains from RM17; ⏱noon-3pm Fri-Sun, noon-6pm Mon-Thu) KK is chock-full of Italian places, but Grazie, run by Italian expat Salvatore Marcello (who, like a polar opposite of Ya Kee Bah Kut Teh, doesn't serve pork), tops them all handily. Many ingredients are imported (including a fine shot of grappa we finished our meal with); the pizza is thin crust and divine; the pasta and other mains sent from on high. Grazie, *grazie* indeed.

Borneo 1945 Museum Kopitiam
CAFE **$**

(☎088-272945; 24 Jln Dewan, Australia Pl; mains from RM3; ⏱7:30am-midnight) Odd name for a restaurant-cum-cafe? Yes, because this is a restaurant-cum-cafe-cum-museum, dedicated to the Allied fighting forces in Borneo during WWII. Perhaps the best iced coffee in KK is served here, alongside breakfast favourites like toast and *kaya* (coconut jam), indigenous fare like pandan chicken and rice and (why not?) reproductions of Anzac biscuits. Trust us, these ain't Tim Tams. The on-site minimuseum is worth a visit by itself.

Kohinoor
INDIAN $$$

(☎088-235160; Lot 4, Waterfront Esplanade; dinner about RM50; ☺11.30am-2.30pm & 5.30pm-11pm) There are several excellent restaurants along the Waterfront Esplanade, but this Indian place is an easy favourite. Take advantage of its authentic tandoori oven and don't forget to grab a side of pillowy garlic naan.

New Gaya Seafood Restaurant
SEAFOOD $$

(☎088 385020; Jln Bantayan, Kiansom Inanam; mains from RM10; ☺11am-11pm) When locals crave a fancy seafood experience, they often head to the New Gaya, located about 20 minutes out of the city centre next to the Gaya Sports Recreation Centre. Deep-fried crabs sizzle next to prawns cooked...well, perfectly. Perfectly cooked prawns. How can you go wrong?

Nagisa
JAPANESE $$$

(☎088-221234; Jln Datuk Salleh Sulong; sushi from RM15; ☺noon-10pm) For our money – and you'll spend a bit here – this is the best Japanese in KK. Why? Well, it's the sushi spot of choice for Japanese businessmen on return visits, which oughta tell you something. If they've got roe (caviar) on the menu, get it, and thank us later. Located in the Hyatt Regency (p66).

Beach Street
MALAY $$

(Beach Street Plaza, Jln Gaya; mains from RM10 ☺5pm-midnight) This outdoor restaurant sits at a natural junction between both Jln Gaya and the rest of the city and KK's eating, drinking and hotel scene. Plop into a seat, enjoy the live karaoke, order a cold Tiger and then get something off the Malaysian barbecue menu – we would murder you,

MAKAN: KK-STYLE

Kota Kinabalu may be light on sights, and its urban core isn't a stunner, but the city comes up trumps in the food category. KK's veritable melting pot of cultures has fostered a lively dining scene that differentiates itself from the rest of Malaysia with a host of recipes fusing foreign recipes and local ingredients.

KK's four essential eats:

» **Sayur Manis** – Also known as 'Sabah vegie', this bright-green jungle fern can be found at any Chinese restaurant worth its salt. It's best served fried with garlic, or mixed with fermented shrimp paste. The *sayur manis* plant is a perennial and can grow about 3m high. It is harvested year-round so there's a very good chance that your plateful of weeds was plucked from the jungle only a few days prior. Adventurous eaters might want to try other local produce like *tarap*, a fleshy fruit encased in a bristly skin, or *sukun*, a sweet-tasting tuber used to make fritters.

» **Filipino Barbecue** – Located at the north end of the KK Night Market, the Filipino Barbecue Market is the best place in town for grilled seafood at unbeatable prices. Hunker down at one of the crowded tables and point to your prey. Once the waitress has sent your order off to the grill, she'll hand you a cup (for drinking), a basin (to wash your hands) and a small plate to prepare your dipping sauce (mix up the chilli sauce, soy sauce, salt and fresh lime for your own special concoction). No cutlery here! Just dig in with your bare hands and enjoy steaming piles of fresher-than-fresh seafood. Figure around RM15 for a gut-busting meal.

» **Hinava** – Perhaps the most popular indigenous appetiser, colourful *hinava* is raw fish pickled with fresh lime juice, *chilli padi*, sliced shallots and grated ginger. The melange of tangy tastes masks the fishy smell quite well. The best place to try *hinava* is Grace Point, a posh local food court near Tanjung Aru. You'll find it at the 'Local Counter' for around RM2 per plate (the portions are small – the perfect size for a little nibble).

» **Roti Canai** – The ubiquitous *roti canai*, a flaky flat bread fried on a skillet, is served from dawn till dusk at any Indian Muslim *kedai kopi* around town. Although the dish may appear simple, there's actually a lot of skill that goes into preparing the perfect platter. The cook must carefully and continuously flip the dough (à la pizza chef) to create its signature flakiness. *Roti canai* is almost always served with sauce, usually dhal (lentil curry) or another curry made from either chicken or fish.

KK'S HAWKER CENTRES & FOOD COURTS

As in any Asian city, the best food in KK is the street food and hawker stalls. If you're worried about sanitation, you really shouldn't be, but assuage your fears by looking for popular stalls, especially those frequented by families.

» **Night Market** (off Jln Tun Fuad Stephens; meals from RM2; ⊙5pm-11pm) The night market is the best, cheapest and most interesting place in KK for dinner. Vegetarian options available. For details on the Night Market see p57.

» **Centre Point Basement Food Court** (Basement fl, Centre Point Shopping Centre, Jln Pasar Baru; mains RM3-10; ⊙11am-10pm) Your ringgit will go a long way at this popular and varied basement food court in the Centre Point mall. There are Malay, Chinese and Indian options, as well as drink and dessert specialists.

» **Grace Point** (Grace Point, Tanjung Aru; mains RM2-8; ⊙11am-3pm) Take bus 15 out near Tanjung Aru for some local grub at this KK mainstay. The development is actually quite chic compared to the smoke-swathed food courts in the city centre – KKers joke that the public bathrooms here are Borneo's nicest (and it's true!). Go for the Sabahan food stall (located in the far right corner when facing the row of counters) and try *hinava* – see p68 for more info.

dear reader (no offence!) for another crack at the chicken wings.

Port View Seafood Village　SEAFOOD $$$
(☎088-221753; Lot 18, Waterfront Esplanade; dinner from RM50; ⊙lunch & dinner) Do you hate fish? Not the taste – the animal species and all its aquatic kin: crabs, lobsters, squid. Have these beings wronged you? Because you can avenge yourself on the entire ocean at this cavernous Chinese seafood specialist. Eating here is like eating an aquarium. Seriously: walk amid the tanks, find some pretty undersea creature, tell the cooks how you want it prepared and bam: You Found Nemo (in spicy garlic sauce)! We'd feel a little bad about it, except it's so delicious.

Kedai Kopi Fatt Kee　CHINESE $
(28 Jln Bakau; mains from RM5; ⊙noon-10pm Mon-Sat) The woks are always sizzlin' at this popular Chinese place next to Ang's Hotel. Its *sayur manis* cooked in *belacan* (shrimp paste) is a classic, and the salt-and-pepper prawns are wonderfully tasty.

TANJUNG ARU

In the early evening, head to Tanjung Aru at the south end of town near the airport for sunset cocktails and light snacks along the ocean. The area has three beaches – First Beach offers up a few restaurants, Second Beach has steamy local stalls, and Third Beach is a great place to bring a picnic as there are no establishments along the sand. A taxi to Tanjung Aru costs RM20, or you can take public transport (RM1.80) – take bus 16, 16A or city bus 2.

First Beach Café　MALAY $$
(☎088-245158; Aru Drive, Tanjung Aru; drinks RM10, mains RM8-20; ⊙9am-2am) This restaurant boasts the best sunsets in KK and it's hard to argue: it's right on the beach at Tanjung Aru and you can literally step down from your table onto the sand. This is a good spot for light nibbles and beer in the evening.

Tanjung Aru Seafood Restaurant
　SEAFOOD $$$
(☎088-245158; Tanjung Aru; dinner from RM60; ⊙11am-2pm & 5-10pm) It's more about the sunset than the seafood here, but diners never complain (until they see the bill!). While locals prefer scruffy seafood markets around Sinsuran, this spot is a perennial expat fave. There's a cultural show on the weekends starting at 7pm.

Self-Catering

There are a variety of places to stock up on picnic items and hiking snacks, including the centrally located **Milimewa Superstore** (Jln Haji Saman) and **Tong Hing Supermarket** (Jln Gaya). **7-Eleven** (Jln Haji Saman; ⊙24hr) is conveniently open throughout the evening.

🍷 Drinking & Entertainment

Sabahans love a party. There's a relatively low number of Muslims about and a laid-back attitude towards life, and thus booze is a not uncommon social lubricant, to the general delight of travellers. If you're up for a quiet drink, you may best be served by grabbing a beer in a Chinese restaurant. Otherwise, get ready for loads of karaoke bars and big, booming nightclubs, clustered around the **Waterfront Esplanade** (Jln Tun Fuad Stephens), **KK Times Square** (Coastal Hwy), where the newest hot spots are congregating, and **Beach Street**, in the centre of town, a semipedestrian street cluttered with bars and eateries. Live music is the name of the game here; local bars and clubs provide employment for a whole flotilla of local and Filipino cover bands. The quality of the performances is often encouragingly high (you'd be surprised how little English some of these performers speak, considering how they *nail* those Lady Gaga covers), but drinks are quite pricey. Closing time across the board is 2am, but the aforementioned Chinese restaurants may stay open all night if you keep buying.

Bed
NIGHTCLUB

(088-251901; Waterfront Esplanade) It's big, it's crowded, it's cheesy – chances are you'll end up in Bed on one of your KK nights. Hahaha. Yes, get those bed puns ready, as well as your dancing shoes and patience for a *lot* of hip Chinese and locals in outfits that are alternatively slinky/shiny/skimpy. Bands play from 9pm, followed by DJs till closing.

White Room
NIGHTCLUB

(017-836 7718; KK Times Sq) The hot new thing with KK's hot young folks, the White Room is two levels of sweat, loud music, beautiful bodies and expensive drinks. You'll get jostled a lot but everyone looks gorgeous, so who's complaining?

Cocoon
KARAOKE

(088-211252; Jln Tun Razak Segama) Have you ever heard Ke$ha and Madonna sung in Bahasa Karaoke? Waaay better than you think, although a few beers helps the appreciation along. Plopped in a busy corner of town opposite the Hyatt, Cocoon is a smart bar-restaurant that goes all bar in the evening when the live bands emerge.

Shamrock
BAR

(088-249829; 6 Anjung Samudra, Waterfront Esplanade) This bar is as authentically Irish as, well, Borneo, but is an authentic Irish Bar, Model 1.0: green, Guinness, meat stew, luck o' the lass o' the laddish behaviour. Still

a nice place to shoot some stick and watch KK's monied elite get silly.

Hunter's
BAR

(016-825 7085; Kinabalu Daya Hotel) A favourite for local guides and expats, Hunter's offers up karaoke, sport on the plasma TV and balmy outdoor seating in the heart of the city.

Also worth a look:

Upperstar
BAR

(Jln Datuk Saleh Sulong) Opposite the Hilton, this pleasant semi-outdoor bar offers cheap booze and decent pub grub.

Rumba
BAR

(Le Meridien Kota Kinabalu, Jln Tun Fuad Stephens) Upbeat and danceable tunes are spun at this happenin' nightspot.

Loft
BAR

(Waterfront Esplanade) Yet another option along the pub-lined waterfront. Good place for sunset cocktails, but bypass at night if you want to avoid premature deafness.

Shopping

Like any Malaysian metropolis, KK is all about shopping. Malls seem to pop up every year; the **Centre Point** shopping complex, north of town, is the pride and joy of city fathers (in our opinion, it's just a mall). The city maps you get from the tourism board even mark city blocks off according to the mall or shopping arcade that dominates that particular part of town. The point is: whether you need essentials for a trekking trip or souvenirs before you head home, KK has got you covered.

Borneo Trading Post
CRAFTS

(088-232655; Lot 16, Waterfront Esplanade, Jln Tun Fuad Stephens) Upmarket tribal art and souvenirs.

Borneo Books
BOOKSHOP

(088-538077/241050; www.borneobooks.com; ground fl, Phase 1, Wisma Merdeka; 10am-7pm) A brilliant selection of Borneo-related books, maps and a small used-book section. Plenty of those useful Lonely Planet guides too. Wink.

Information

Free maps of central KK and Sabah are available at almost every hostel or hotel.

For details on the Indonesian consulate and the honorary consulates of the UK and Australia, see p307.

Emergency

Ambulance (☎999, 088-218166)

Fire (☎994 or 088-214822)

Police (☎999, 088-212092; Jln Dewan)

Internet Access

Every sleeping spot we list has some form of internet connection, be it dial-up or wi-fi.

Borneo Net (Jln Haji Saman; ⏰9am-midnight; per hr RM3) Twenty terminals, fast connections and loud headbanger music wafting through the air.

Net Access (Jln Pantai; ⏰9-2am; per hr RM3) Plenty of connections and less noise than other net places in KK. LAN connections are available for using your own laptop.

Immigration Office

Immigration office (☎088-488700; Kompleks Persekutuan Pentadbiran Kerajaan, Jln UMS; ⏰8am-1pm & 2-5pm Mon-Thu, 8-11.30am & 2-5pm Fri) In an office complex near the Universiti Malaysia Sabah (UMS), 9km north of town.

Medical Services

Permai Polyclinic (☎088-232100; 4 Jln Pantai) Excellent private outpatient clinic.

Queen Elizabeth Hospital (☎088-218166; Jln Penampang) Past the Sabah Museum.

Money

Central KK is chock-a-block with 24-hour ATMs.

HSBC (☎088-212622; 56 Jln Gaya; ⏰9am-4.30pm Mon-Thu, 9am-4pm Fri)

Maybank (☎088-254295; 9 Jln Pantai; ⏰9am-4.30pm Mon-Thu, 9am-4pm Fri)

Standard Chartered Bank (☎088-298111; 20 Jln Haji Saman; ⏰9.15am-3.45pm Mon-Fri)

Post

Main Post Office (☎088-210855; Jln Tun Razak; ⏰8am-5pm Mon-Fri) Western Union cheques and money orders can be cashed here.

Tourist Information

Borneo Images (☎088-270733; ste A33A, 3rd fl, Tanjung Aru Plaza; ⏰9am-5pm Mon-Fri, 9am-1pm Sat) A beautiful and informative gallery inspiring travel throughout the region. Definitely worth stopping by to get a photographer's perspective of Borneo.

Sabah Parks (☎088-486432, 486430; Lot 45 & 46, 1st-5th fl, Block H, Signature Office, KK Times Plaza; ⏰8am-1pm & 2-4.30pm Mon-Thu, 8-11.30am & 2-4.30pm Fri, 8am-12.50pm Sat) Good source of information on the state's parks.

Sabah Tourism Board (☎088-212121; www.sabahtourism.com; 51 Jln Gaya; ⏰8am-5pm Mon-Fri, 8am-4pm Sat, 9am-4pm Sun) Housed in the historic post office building, KK's main tourist office has helpful staff and a wide range of brochures, pamphlets and other information covering every aspect of independent and tour travel in Sabah. Ask about its home stay program.

Tourism Malaysia (☎088-248698; www.tourism.gov.my; ground fl, Api-Api Centre, Jln Pasar Baru; ⏰8am-4.30pm Mon-Thu, 8am-noon & 1.30-4.30pm Fri) This office is of limited use for travellers, but does offer a few interesting brochures on sights in Peninsular Malaysia.

Getting There & Away

Air

KK is well served by **Malaysia Airlines** (MAS; ☎1-300 883 000, 088-515555; www.malaysiaairlines.com; 1st fl, Departure Hall, KKIA; ⏰5.30am-7.30pm) and **AirAsia** (within Malaysia ☎03-2171 9333; www.airasia.com; ground fl, Wisma Sabah, Jln Gaya) offer the following international flights to/from KK: Brunei, Shenzhen, Jakarta, Manila, Singapore and Tapei. Within Malaysia, flights go to/from Johor Bahru, Kuala Lumpur and Penang in Peninsular Malaysia, and Kuching, Labuan, Miri, Sandakan, and Tawau in Borneo. **Jetstar** (www.jetstar.com) and **Tiger Airways** (www.tigerairways.com) both offer flights to Singapore.

Boat

All passengers must pay an RM3 terminal fee for ferries departing from Kota Kinabalu. Passenger boats connect KK to Pulau Labuan twice daily (first/economy class RM39/31), with onward service to Brunei (see p234) and to Tunku Abdul Rahman National Park (see p74). A schedule is in the works to link the state capital to Pulau Tiga.

Bus & Minivan

Several different stations around KK serve a variety of out-of-town destinations. For details on the bus to Brunei, see p234.

In general, land transport heading east departs from Inanam (Utara Terminal; 9km north of the city) while those heading north and south on the west coast leave from Padang Merdeka (Merdeka Field) Bus Station (also called Wawasan or 'old bus station'; at the south end of town). Local buses (RM1.80) from Wawasan can take tourists to Inanam if you don't want to splurge on the RM20 taxi. Have your hotel call ahead to the bus station to book your seat in advance. Same-day bookings are usually fine, although weekends are busier than weekdays. It's always good to ring ahead because sometimes

MAIN DESTINATIONS & FARES FROM KOTA KINABALU

The following bus and minivan transport information was provided to us by the Sabah Tourism Board and should be used as an estimate only: transport times can fluctuate due to weather, prices may change and the transport authority has been known to alter departure points.

DESTINATION	DURATION (HR)	PRICE (RM)	TERMINAL	DEPARTURES
Beaufort	2	10	Padang Merdeka	7am-5pm (frequent)
Keningau	2½	13	Padang Merdeka	7am-5pm (8 daily)
Kota Belud	1	10	Padang Merdeka	7am-5pm (frequent)
Kuala Penyu	2	18	Segama Bridge	8-11am (hourly)
Kudat	3	18	Padang Merdeka	7am-4pm (frequent)
Lahad Datu	8	40	Inanam	7am, 8.30am, 9am, 8pm
Lawas (Sarawak)	4	20	Padang Merdeka	8.30am & 1.30pm
Mt Kinabalu NP	2	15	Inanam & Padang Merdeka	7am-8pm (very frequent)
Ranau	2	15	Padang Merdeka	7am-5pm
Sandakan	6	33	Inanam	7.30am-2pm (frequent) & 8pm
Semporna	9	50	Inanam	7am, 8.30am, 9am, 8pm
Tawau	9	55	Inanam	7.30am, 2pm, 8pm
Tenom	3½	25	Padang Merdeka	8am, noon, 4pm

transport will be halted due to flooding caused by heavy rains.

Taxi

Share taxis operate from the Padang Merdeka Bus Station. Several share taxis do a daily run between KK and Ranau, passing the entrance road to the Kinabalu National Park office. The fare to Ranau or Kinabalu National Park is RM20 or you can charter a taxi for RM80 per car (note that a normal city taxi will charge RM150 to RM200 for a charter).

Train

The North Borneo rail line is currently closed and a reopening date has yet to be confirmed.

ⓘ Getting Around

To/From the Airport

The international airport is in Tanjung Aru, 7km south of central KK. Please note that the two terminals of Kota Kinabalu International Airport are not connected – they feel like two different airports. Most airlines operate out of Terminal 1, with the exception of AirAsia, Tiger Airways and charter flights, which depart from Terminal 2. City bus 2 and bus 16A (RM1) service Terminal 2 and can be boarded at City Park station downtown. Minibuses (RM3) leave from City Park

station for Terminal 1 (look for city bus 1 to access this terminal in the future). Public transport runs from 6am to 7pm daily. Taxis heading from terminals into town operate on a voucher system (RM30) sold at a taxi desk on the terminal's ground floor. Taxis heading to the airport should not charge over RM35 if you catch one in the city centre. From 9pm to 6am taxis to the airport cost RM40.

Car

Major car-rental agencies have counters on the 1st floor at KKIA and branch offices elsewhere in town. Manual cars start at RM100 per day and most agencies can arrange chauffeured vehicles as well.

Adaras Rent A Car (☏088-216671, 088-211866; adarasrac@hotmail.com; Lot G-03, Wisma Sabah)

Borneo Express (☏088-268009; G25, Wisma Sabah, Jln Tun Fuad Stephens)

Extra Rent A Car (☏088-218160, 088-251529; www.e-erac-online.com; 2nd fl, Beverly Hotel, Jln Kemajuan)

Kinabalu Rent A Car (☏088-232602; rentcar@po.jaring.my; Lot 2.47, 2nd fl, Kompleks Karamunsing)

Mayflower Car Rental (☎012-803 3020, 088-221244; D3-3A, 3rd fl, Block D, Plaza Tanjung Aru)

Minivans

Minivans operate from several stops, including Padang Merdeka Bus Station and the car park outside Milimewa Superstore. They circulate the town looking for passengers. Since most destinations in the city are within walking distance, it's unlikely that you'll need to catch a minivan, although they're handy for getting to the airport or to KK Times Square. Most destinations within the city cost RM1.

Taxi

Figure on around RM7 to RM10 for a ride in the city centre.

AROUND KOTA KINABALU

Tunku Abdul Rahman National Park

Whenever one enjoys a sunset off KK, the view tends to be improved by the five jungly humps of Manukan, Gaya, Sapi, Mamutik and Sulug islands. These swaths of sand, plus the reefs and cerulean waters in-between them, make up **Tunku Abdul Rahman National Park** (adult/child RM10/6), covering a total area of just over 49 sq km (two-thirds of which is water). Only a short boat ride from KK, the islands may not be much compared to Borneo's other offshore paradises, but hey: there's nice beaches and (usually clear) water and this is ideal day-trip material for anyone wanting an ex-urban unwind. Accommodation tends to be expensive, but most travellers come here for day trips anyway, and there are camping options.

PULAU MANUKAN

Manukan is the most popular destination for KK residents and has plenty of facilities. It is the second-largest island in the group, its 20 hectares largely covered in dense vegetation. There's a good beach with coral reefs off the southern and eastern shores, a walking trail around the perimeter and a network of nature trails – if you want to thoroughly explore all of the above it shouldn't take more than two hours, and you don't need to be particularly fit. There's quite a good range of tropical fish swimming around, many of which can be seen

simply by looking down from the jetty. When you depart the boat you'll likely be pointed towards a kiosk that hires equipment masks and snorkels (RM15), beach mats (RM5) and body boards (RM10).

Manukan Island Resort (☎088-477802; www.suterasanctuarylodges.com; villa RM1120; ❄❅), managed by Sutera Sanctuary Lodges, has the only accommodation on the island. It comprises a restaurant, swimming pool and tennis courts, and 20 dark-wood villas, all overlooking the South China Sea and decked out in tasteful Bali-chic style; the cool stone showers hemmed in by flowering plants are a nice touch.

PULAU MAMUTIK

Mamutik is the smallest island out here, a mere 300m from end to end. It also offers the best snorkelling, with a colourful coral garden and good beach that runs up and down the east coast of the island. There's no resort, but camping (RM5 per person, pay on arrival) is possible and there's a three-bedroom house for rent, although it was closed for renovation when we visited. There's a small store-restaurant-snorkel-rental place, but it's a good idea to bring supplies from the mainland. Mamutik gets busy with local tourists on weekends, but on weekdays you may well have it to yourself.

PULAU SAPI

Dwarfed by nearby Pulau Gaya, pin-sized Pulau Sapi (Cow Island) is another popular island that offers snorkelling and attractive beaches (although some tourists have complained that the water has been quite filthy). Sapi is separated from Gaya by a very shallow 200m channel that you can swim across if you feel up to it. Otherwise, the main activities include wading, relaxing on the beach around the jetty or exploring the trails through the forest. There's a decent coral garden around the southeast point of the island, but it's no match for the coral off Mamutik. There are changing rooms, toilets, barbecue pits, and a small snack kiosk, plus an outfitted campsite (RM5 per person), but you'll need to bring most supplies from the mainland.

PULAU GAYA

With an area of about 15 sq km, Pulau Gaya is the Goliath of KK's offshore islands, rising to an elevation of 300m. It's also the

SABAH AROUND KOTA KINABALU

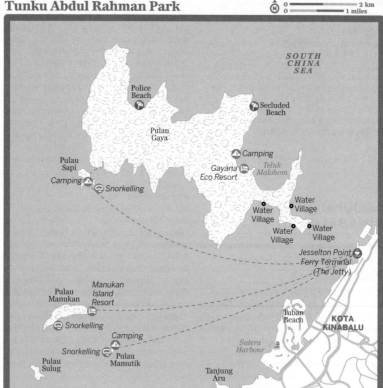

closest to KK and covered in virtually undisturbed tropical forest. The bays on the east end are filled with bustling water villages, inhabited by Filipino immigrants (legal and otherwise) who live in cramped houses built on stilts in the shallow water, with mosques, schools and simple shops, also built on stilts. Residents of KK warn against exploring these water villages, saying that incidences of theft and other crimes have occurred.

If you want to spend the night (and a lot of money), try **Gayana Eco Resort** (☎088-442233; www.gayana-eco-resort.com; villas from US$649; ❄), a stunning property with fresh-faced wooden bungalows on a fertile patch of beachfront.

PULAU SULUG

Shaped like a cartoon speech bubble, Sulug has an area of 8.1 hectares and is the least visited of the group, probably because it's the furthest away from KK. It only has one beach, on a spit of land extending from its eastern shore. Unfortunately, the snorkelling is pretty poor. If you want a quiet getaway, Sulug is a decent choice, but you'll have to charter a boat to get here; the normal ferries don't stop here. If you want a secluded beach and don't want to lay out for a charter (at least RM200), you'll do better by heading to Manukan and walking down the beach to escape the crowds.

ⓘ Getting There & Away
Boat

Boats leave from 7am to 6pm when full from KK's Jesselton Point Ferry Terminal (commonly known as 'The Jetty' by locals and taxi drivers). Inquire at the counter for the next available boat, sign up for your chosen destination and take a seat until there are enough passengers to depart. Catch a boat in the morning, as it's much harder to make up boat numbers in the afternoon. Boats also run from Sutera Harbour – more convenient for those staying near Tanjung

Aru (or for those wanting to reach Pulau Gaya). Return fares to Mamutik, Manukan and Sapi hover around RM30. You can also buy two-/ three-island passes for RM40/48.

The set fee for charter to one island is RM250, but this can be negotiated. Try to deal directly with a boatman if you do this – don't talk to the touts who prowl the area. And don't consider paying until you return to the dock.

A RM3 terminal fee is added to all boat journeys, and a RM10 entrance fee to the marine park, paid when you purchase your ticket (if you are chartering a boat this should be included).

NORTHWESTERN SABAH

The northern edge of Sabah manages to compact, into a relatively small space, much of the geographic and cultural minutiae that makes Borneo so special. The ocean? Lapping at miles of sandy beach, sky blue to stormy grey, and concealing superlative dive sites. The people? Kadazan–Dusun, Rungus, rice farmers, mountain hunters, ship builders and deep-sea fishermen. And then, of course, 'the' mountain: Gunung Kinabalu, or Mt Kinabalu, the focal point of the island's altitude, trekkers, folklore and spiritual energy. For generations, the people of Sabah have been drawn to the mountain; don't be surprised when you fall under its spell too.

Mt Kinabalu & Kinabalu National Park

Mt Kinabalu is called the Roof of Borneo in more than a few promotional materials distributed by Sabah Tourism, and honestly, the description fits. Of course, the mountain is the highest thing on the world's third largest island. But it's also a 'roof' in the sense it is, when in Sabah, always over your head. To the point you almost forget about the thing. Mt Kinabalu is a constant presence, catching the clouds and shading the valleys, shading the edge of your sight in KK. It is only when you give the mountain your full cognitive attention that you realise how special this peak, the region's biggest tourist attraction, truly is.

The goal? To climb. The 4095m peak of Mt Kinabalu may not be as wow-inducing as, say, a Himalayan sky-poker, but Malaysia's first Unesco World Heritage Site is by no means an easy jaunt. Around 60,000 visitors of every ilk make the gruelling trek up Borneo's ultimate Thighmaster each year, returning to the bottom with stories of triumph, pictures of sunlit moonscapes, and *really* sore legs. With that said, if you don't feel up to reaching the mountain top, its base has some worthy attractions, including a large network of nature trails.

Amazingly, the mountain is still growing: researchers have found it increases in height by about 5mm a year. On a clear day you can see the Philippines from the summit; usually, though, the mountain is thoroughly wreathed in fog by midmorning.

History
Although it is commonly believed that local tribesmen climbed Kinabalu many years earlier, it was Sir Hugh Low, the British colonial secretary on Pulau Labuan, who recorded the first official ascent of Mt Kinabalu in 1851. Today Kinabalu's tallest

---

DON'T MISS

KIVATU HEIGHTS HOMESTAY

In Penampang, about 15km south of Kota Kinabalu, is one of the quirkiest home stays in Sabah. **Kivatu Heights Homestay** (☎019-871 3935, 088-729107; http://kivatuheightshomestayborneo.blogspot.com; ❄🔊) is something...different. Most home stays in Sabah put you in a middle-class-style village home with bare if comfy amenities. Not Kivatu Heights. Here you're in an enormous, semi-Swiss-style chalet with chunky, funky wood furniture, an outdoor pool, on-site bullfrogs, a billiards room, a karaoke room, and a nearby tilapia fish farm (of course). Some rooms are tastefully decorated in Bali-tropi-chic, while some look like they could be Hugh Hefner's love den. Give Francis, the Canadian-educated Malay who runs the place, a call: he likes if you prebook and you'll need his directions to the place anyway. And make sure you take a day trip to see the Siga Monument, a statue honouring the native Sabahan... hat. No, really.

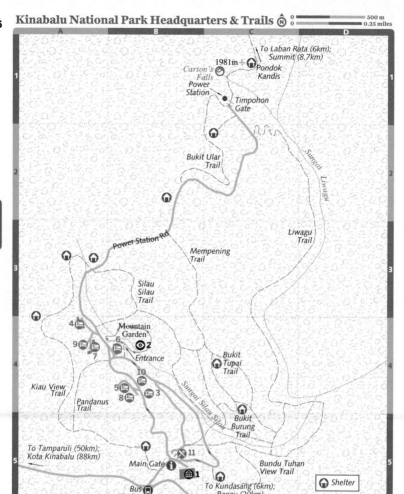

Kinabalu National Park Headquarters & Trails

Sights
1 Kinabalu Conservation Centre B5
2 Mountain Garden....................................B4

Sleeping
3 Grace Hostel B4
4 Hill Lodge..A4
5 Kinabalu Lodge......................................B4
6 Liwagu Suites...B4
7 Nepenthes Villa A4
8 Peak Lodge B4
9 Rajah Lodge A4
10 Rock Hostel B4

Eating
11 Restoran Kinabalu Balsam B5
Liwagu Restaurant..........................(see 6)

peak is named after him, thus Borneo's highest point is ironically known as Low's Peak.

In those days the difficulty of climbing Mt Kinabalu lay not in the ascent, but in getting through the jungle to the mountain's base. Finding willing local porters was another tricky matter – the tribesmen who accompanied Low believed the spirits of the dead inhabited the mountain. Low was therefore obliged to protect the party by supplying a large basket of quartz crystals and teeth, as was the custom back then. During the subsequent years, the spirit-appeasement ceremonies became more and more elaborate, so that by the 1920s they had come to include loud prayers, gunshots, and the sacrifice of seven eggs and seven white chickens. You have to wonder at what point explorers started thinking the locals might be taking the mickey...

Theses days, the elaborate chicken dances are no more, although climbing the mountain can still feel like a rite of passage.

Check out Mountain Torq's website (www.mountaintorq.com) for more fun facts about Kinabalu's history. It opened Asia's first *via ferrata* course in 2007 (see the boxed text p80 for details).

Geology

Many visitors to Borneo assume Mt Kinabalu is a volcano, but the mountain is actually a huge granite dome that rose from the depths below some nine million years ago. In geological terms, Mt Kinabalu is still young. Little erosion has occurred on the exposed granite rock faces around the summit, though the effects of glaciers that used to cover much of the mountain can be detected by striations on the rock. There's no longer a snowline and the glaciers have disappeared, but at times ice forms in the rock pools near the summit.

Orientation & Information

Kinabalu National Park HQ is 88km by road northeast of KK and set in gardens with a magnificent view of the mountain. At 1588m the climate is refreshingly cool compared to the coast; the average temperatures are 20°C in the day and 13°C at night. The hike to the summit is difficult – see p79 for detailed information about the climb.

On the morning of your arrival, pay your park entry fee, present your lodging reservation slip to the Sutera Sanctuary Lodges office

to receive your official room assignment, and check in with the Sabah Parks office to pay your registration and guide fees. See below for pricing details. Advance accommodation bookings are *essential* if you plan on climbing the mountain.

PERMITS, FEES & GUIDES

OK, this is where things appear to get tricky, but it's actually quite simple: a park fee, climbing permit, insurance and a guide fee are *mandatory* if you intend to climb Mt Kinabalu. All permits and guides must be arranged at the **Sabah Parks office** (☉7am-7pm), which is directly next door to the Sutera Sanctuary Lodges office, immediately on your right after you pass through the main gate of the park. Pay all fees at park HQ before you climb and don't ponder an 'unofficial' climb as permits (laminated cards worn on a string necklace) are scrupulously checked at two points you cannot avoid passing on the way up the mountain. Virtually every tour operator in KK can hook you up with a trip to the mountain, but some of these go for as much as RM1200. It's possible, and often cheaper, to do it on your own – just make sure you plan ahead. That said, there are a lot of tour outfits in KK; if one offers a package you find enticing, go for it.

All visitors entering the park are required to pay a **park entrance fee**: RM15 for adults and RM10 for children under 18 (Malaysians pay RM3 and RM1 respectively). A **climbing permit** costs RM100/RM40 for adults/children, while Malaysian nationals pay RM30/RM12. **Climbing insurance** costs a flat rate of RM7 per person. **Guide fees** for the summit trek cost RM100. Climbers ascending Kinabalu along the Mesilau trail will pay an extra RM10 (small group) or RM20 (large group) for their guide. Your guide will be assigned to you on the morning you begin your hike. If you ask, the park staff will try to attach individual travellers to a group so that guide fees can be shared. Couples can expect to be given their own guide. Guides are mostly Kadazan from a village nearby and many of them have travelled to the summit several hundred times. Try to ask for a guide who speaks English – he or she (usually he) might point out a few interesting specimens of plant life. The path up the mountain is pretty straightforward, and the guides walk behind the slowest

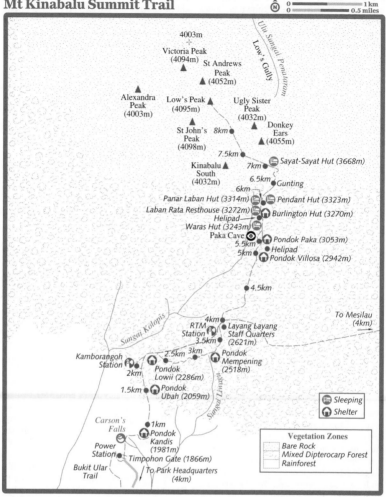

4003m
Victoria Peak (4094m)
St Andrews Peak (4052m)

Alexandra Peak (4003m)
Low's Peak (4095m)
Ugly Sister Peak (4032m)
Donkey Ears (4055m)

St John's Peak (4098m)

8km

7.5km

Kinabalu South (4032m)
7km
6.5km Gunting
Sayat-Sayat Hut (3668m)

6km
Panar Laban Hut (3314m)
Pendant Hut (3323m)
Laban Rata Resthouse (3272m)
Burlington Hut (3270m)
Helipad
Waras Hut (3243m)
Paka Cave
Pondok Paka (3053m)
5.5km
Helipad
5km
Pondok Villosa (2942m)

4.5km

To Mesilau (4km)

4km
RTM Station
Layang Layang Staff Quarters (2621m)
3.5km

Kamborangoh Station
2.5km
3km
Pondok Mempening (2518m)

2km
Pondok Lowii (2286m)

Sungai Kolopis

Sungai Liwagu

1.5km
Pondok Ubah (2059m)

Carson's Falls
1km
Pondok Kandis (1981m)
Power Station
Timpohon Gate (1866m)
Bukit Ular Trail
To Park Headquarters (4km)

Ulu Sungai Penataran
Low's Gully

Sleeping
Shelter

Vegetation Zones
Bare Rock
Mixed Dipterocarp Forest
Rainforest

member of the group, so think of them as safety supervisors rather than trailblazers.

All this does not include at least RM385 for room-and-board on the mountain at Laban Rata. With said lodging, plus buses or taxis to the park, you're looking at spending around RM700. That said, you *can* do a one-day hike if you show up at the park entrance when it opens (7am) and are judged physically fit by a ranger. This allows you to cut the cost of lodging, but when we say you need to be fit, we mean *fit*. A friend – one of those annoyingly healthy mountaineers who probably sleep-walks up Alps – attempted and managed the one-day hike. He made it back from the summit a little after 5pm, said it was the hardest thing he'd ever done and couldn't walk upstairs for two days. You've been warned.

Optional extra fees include a taxi ride from the park office to the Timpohon Gate (RM16.50 per vehicle, one-way, four-person maximum), a climbing certificate (RM10) and a porter (RM102 per trip to the summit

KINABALU PACKING LIST

» Headlamp (with spare batteries)
» Comfortable running shoes
» Wool socks and athletic socks
» Hiking shorts or breathable pants
» Three T-shirts (one made of lightweight synthetic material)
» Fleece jacket
» Lightweight shell jacket or rain jacket
» Fleece or wool hat
» Fleece gloves
» Long johns
» Hand towel
» Water bottle
» Light, high-energy snacks
» Camera
» Money
» Earplugs for dorms

The above items should easily fit into a small waterproof backpack. Apply a dab of sunscreen and insect repellent before you depart.

or RM84 to Laban Rata) who can be hired to carry a maximum load of 10kg.

If you need a helicopter lift off the mountain for emergency reasons, the going rate is RM2500.

EQUIPMENT & CLOTHING

No special equipment is required to successfully summit the mountain, however a headlamp is strongly advised for the pre-dawn jaunt to the top – you'll need your hands free to climb the ropes on the summit massif. Expect freezing temperatures near the summit, not to mention strong winds and the occasional rainstorm. Check out our tailor-made packing list (see above) for more information, and don't forget a water bottle, which can be refilled at unfiltered (but potable) tanks en route.

The Climb to the Summit

Climbing the great Mt Kinabalu is a heart-pounding two-day adventure that you won't soon forget. You'll want to check in at park headquarters at around 9am (8.45am at the latest for *via ferrata* participants; p80) to pay your park fees, grab your guide and start the ascent (four to six hours) to Laban Rata (3272m) where you'll spend the night before finishing the climb. On the following day you'll finish scrambling to the top at about 2.30am in order

to reach the summit for a breathtaking sunrise over Borneo.

Although you'll see hikers of all ages making the journey, a climb up Kinabalu is only advised for those in adequate physical condition. The trek is tough, and the ascent is unrelenting as almost every step you take will be uphill. You will negotiate several obstacles along the way, including slippery stones, blinding humidity, frigid winds and slow-paced Japanese 50-somethings in Chanel tracksuits.

There are two trail options leading up the mountain – the Timpohon Trail and the Mesilau Trail. If this is your first time climbing Kinabalu, we strongly advise taking the Timpohon Trail – it's shorter, easier (but by no means easy!) and more convenient from the park headquarters (an hour's walk or short park shuttle ride; RM16.50 one-way per vehicle, four-person maximum). If you are participating in Mountain Torq's *via ferrata,* you are required to take the Timpohon Trail in order to reach Laban Rata in time for your safety briefing at 4pm. The Mesilau Trail offers second-time climbers (or uberfit hikers) the opportunity to really enjoy some of the park's natural wonders. This trail is less trodden so the chances of seeing unique flora and fauna are higher.

As you journey up to the summit, you'll happen upon signboards showing your progress – there's a marker every 500m. There are also rest shelters (pondok) at regular intervals, with basic toilets and tanks of unfiltered (but potable) drinking water. The walking times that follow are conservative estimates – don't be surprised if you move at a slightly speedier pace, and certainly don't be discouraged if you take longer – everyone's quest for the summit is different.

TIMPOHON GATE TO LAYANG LAYANG
'Why am I sweating this much *already?*'

The trip to the summit officially starts at the Timpohon Gate (1866m) and from there it's an 8.72km march to the summit. There is a small bathroom outhouse located 700m before the Timpohon Gate, and a convenience shop at the gate itself for impulse snack and beverage purchases (get a 100-Plus!).

After a short, deceptive descent, the trail leads up steep stairs through the dense forest and continues winding up and up for the rest of the trip. There's a charming waterfall, **Carson's Falls**, beside the track

shortly after the start, and the forest can be alive with birds and squirrels in the morning. Five *pondok* (shelters) are spaced at intervals of 15 to 35 minutes between Timpohon Gate and Layang Layang and it's about three hours to the Layang Layang (2621m) rest stop. Near **Pondok Lowii** (2286m) the trail follows an open ridge giving great views over the valleys and up to the peaks.

LAYANG LAYANG TO PONDOK PAKA
'Why did I put all that extra crap in my rucksack?'

This part of the climb can be the most difficult for some – especially around the 4.5km marker. You've definitely made some headway but there's still a long trek to go – no light at the end of the jungly tunnel quite yet. It takes about 1¾ hours to reach **Pondok Paka** (3053m), the seventh shelter on the trail, 5.5km from the start.

PONDOK PAKA TO LABAN RATA
'Why did I pay all that money just to climb a freakin' mountain?!'

Also known as the 'can't I pay someone to finish this for me?' phase, this part of the climb is where beleaguered hikers get

VIA FERRATA

In 2007, Mountain Torq dramatically changed the Kinabalu climbing experience by creating an intricate system of rungs and rails crowning the mountain's summit. Known as *via ferrata* (literally 'iron road' in Italian), this alternative style of mountaineering has been a big hit in Europe for the last century and is just starting to take Asia by storm. In fact, Mountain Torq is Asia's first *via ferrata* system, and, according to the Guinness Book of World Records, it's the highest 'iron road' in the world!

After ascending Kinabalu in the traditional fashion, participants use the network of levers to return to the Laban Rata rest camp along the mountain's dramatic granite walls. Mountain Torq's star attraction, the **Low's Peak Circuit** (RM550; minimum age 17), is a four-to-five-hour scramble down metres upon metres of sheer rock face. This route starts at 3800m, passing a variety of obstacles before linking up to the Walk the Torq path for the last part of the journey. The route's threadlike tightrope walks and swinging planks will have you convinced that the course designers are sadistic, but that's what makes it so darn fun – testing your limits without putting your safety in jeopardy. Those who don't want to see their heart leaping out of their chest should try the **Walk the Torq** (RM400; minimum age 10) route. This two-to-three-hour escapade is an exciting initiation into the world of *via ferrata*, offering dramatic mountain vistas with a few less knee-shaking moments.

No matter which course you tackle, you'll undoubtedly think that the dramatic vertical drops are nothing short of exhilarating. But the best part about the whole adventure actually happens a few weeks later, when you're back home showing off your eye-popping photos to friends: 'Yeah, look at that shot of me dangling off the edge…I'm so hardcore…'

Via ferrata may be an Italian import, but Mountain Torq is pure Bornean fun. For more information about Mountain Torq, check out www.mountaintorq.com.

As your two-day Kinabalu adventure comes to an end and you limp across the Timpo-hon Gate a shrivelled bundle of aching muscles and bones, don't forget to glance at the climbing records chart. Every year the **Kinabalu International Climbathon** (http://climbathon.sabahtourism.com) attracts the fittest athletes from around the world for a competitive climb-off as dozens of hikers zoom up the mountain a la the Road Runner. In 2008, Agustí Roc Amador from Spain set the men's record by completing the round-trip (that's up to the summit and back to the gate – just to be clear) in two hours and 44 minutes. Corinne Favre from France set the women's record with a total time of three hours and 17 minutes.

And it's not just the clock-beaters who put casual trekkers to shame: the oldest person to reach the summit was a Japanese lady who battled her way to the top at the grand old age of 90. So just remember, when you're smugly slinking by slower hikers, there are pensioners out there who would leave you for dead...

a second wind as the treeline ends and the summit starts to feel closer. At the end of this leg you'll reach **Laban Rata** (3272m), your 'home sweet home' on the mountain. Take a good look at the slender signpost announcing your arrival – it's the propeller of the helicopter once used to hoist the construction materials to build the elaborate rest station. This leg takes around 45 minutes.

LABAN RATA TO SAYAT-SAYAT HUT

'Why am I waking up at the time I usually go to bed back home?'

It's 2am and your alarm just went off. Is this a dream? Nope. You're about to climb the last part of the mountain in order to reach the summit before sunrise. Most people set off at around 2.45am, and it's worth heading out at this time even if you're in great shape (don't forget your torch). The one-hour climb to **Sayat-Sayat** hut (3668m) involves a lot of hiker traffic and the crossing of the sheer Panar Laban rock face. There is little vegetation, except where overhangs provide some respite from the wind. It is one of the toughest parts of the climb, especially in the cold and dark of the predawn hours.

SAYAT-SAYAT HUT TO SUMMIT

'Why is it so darn cold out?! I'm standing near the equator for Pete's sake!'

After checking in at Sayat-Sayat, the crowd of hikers begins to thin as stronger walkers forge ahead and slower adventurers pause for sips from their water bottle. Despite the stunning surroundings, the last stretch of the summit ascent is, of course, the steepest and hardest part of the climb.

From just beyond Sayat-Sayat, the **summit** looks deceptively close and, though it's just over 1km, the last burst will take between one to three hours depending on your stamina. You might even see shattered climbers crawling on hands and knees as they reach out for the top of Borneo.

Once you're motionless at the top – waiting for the sun to rise – the coldness really starts to set in.

THE SUMMIT

[Speechless...]

This is it – the million-dollar moment (or the RM800+ moment for those who are keeping score...). Climbers crowd together while jockeying for the essential photograph of the summit sign. Flashbulbs go off like lightning waking up sleepy eyes, and everyone obsesses over trying to nab a seat at the official summit point, forgetting the sunrise can be glimpsed from anywhere on the mountain.

The summit warms up quickly as the sun starts its own ascent between 5.45am and 6.20am, and the weary suddenly smile; the climb up a distant memory, the trek down an afterthought.

True adventurers should sign up with Mountain Torq to climb back to Laban Rata along the world's highest *via ferrata*.

THE JOURNEY BACK TO THE BOTTOM

'Why didn't I believe anyone when they said that going down was just as hard as going up?!'

SABAH MT KINABALU & KINABALU NATIONAL PARK

FLORA & FAUNA OF MT KINABALU

Mt Kinabalu is a botanical paradise, designated a Centre of Plant Diversity as well as a Unesco-listed World Heritage Site. The wide range of habitats supports an even wider range of natural history, and over half the species growing above 900m are unique to the area.

Among the more spectacular flowers are orchids, rhododendrons and the insectivorous nepenthes (pitcher plant). Around park HQ, there's dipterocarp forest (rainforest); creepers, ferns and orchids festoon the canopy, while fungi grow on the forest floor. Between 900m and 1800m, there are oaks, laurels and chestnuts, while higher up there's dense rhododendron forest. On the windswept slopes above Laban Rata vegetation is stunted, with *sayat-sayat* a common shrub. The mountain's uppermost slopes are bare of plant life.

Deer and monkeys are no longer common around park HQ, but you can see squirrels, including the handsome Prevost's squirrel and the mountain ground squirrel. Tree shrews can sometimes be seen raiding rubbish bins. Common birds are Bornean treepies, fantails, bulbuls, sunbirds and laughing thrushes, while birds seen only at higher altitudes are the Kinabalu friendly warbler, the mountain blackeye and the mountain blackbird. Other wildlife includes colourful butterflies and the huge green moon moth.

You'll probably leave the summit at around 7.30am and you should aim to leave Laban Rata no later than 12.30pm. The gruelling descent back down to Timpohon Gate from Laban Rata takes between three and four hours (if you're returning to the bottom along the Mesilau Trail it will take more time than descending to the Timpohon Gate). The weather can close in very quickly and, although you probably won't get lost, the granite is slippery even when dry. During rainstorms the downward trek feels like walking through a river. Slower walkers often find that their legs hurt more the day after – quicker paces lighten the constant pounding as legs negotiate each descending step. If you participated in the exhilarating *via ferrata* you will be absolutely knackered during your descent and will stumble into Timpohon Gate just before sunset (around 6pm to 6.30pm).

A 1st-class certificate can be purchased for RM10 by those who complete the climb; 2nd-class certificates are issued for making it to Laban Rata. These can be collected at the park office.

Walks Around the Base

It's well worth spending a day exploring the marked trails around park headquarters; if you have time, it may be better to do it before you climb the mountain, as chances are you won't really feel like it afterwards. The various trails and lookouts are shown on the map on p76.

The base trails interconnect with one another like a tied shoelace, so you can spend the day, or indeed days, walking at a leisurely pace through the beautiful forest. Some interesting plants, plenty of birds and, if you're lucky, the occasional mammal can be seen along the **Liwagu Trail** (6km), which follows the river of the same name. When it rains, watch out for slippery paths and legions of leeches.

At 11am each day a **guided walk** (per person RM3) starts from the Sabah Parks office and lasts for one to two hours. The knowledgeable guide points out flowers, plants, birds and insects along the way. If you set out from KK early enough, it's possible to arrive at the park in time for the guided walk.

Many of the plants found on the mountain are cultivated in the **Mountain Garden** (admission RM5; ◷9am-1pm, 2:30-4pm) behind the visitors centre. Guided tours of the garden depart at 9am, noon and 3pm and cost RM5.

🛏 Sleeping

LABAN RATA (ON THE MOUNTAIN)

Organising your accommodation on the mountain can be the most difficult part of your Kinabalu adventure. Access to the summit is essentially limited by access to the huts on the mountain at Laban Rata (3272m) and this *must* be booked in advance (the earlier the better). In order to have any hope of clear weather when you reach the summit, you must arrive around dawn, and the only way to do this is by spending a night in one of the huts at

Laban Rata. Yes, Sabah Parks will let you attempt a one-day ascent, starting around 7am, but by the time you get to the summit in midafternoon, it will almost certainly be clouded over or raining. And just in case you're thinking about it: a) they won't allow a night climb and b) they will not allow an 'unofficial' climb (permits are carefully checked at several points on the mountain).

Sutera Sanctuary Lodges (☑088-303917; http://suterasanctuarylodges.com.my; Lot G15, ground fl, Wisma Sabah) in Kota Kinabalu operates almost all of the accommodation here, but space is limited. Many travellers report frustration with booking huts on the mountain – they complain that the booking system is disorganised and inefficient, the huts are often full or it's difficult to get a confirmed booking. Bookings can be made online, in person or over the phone – our experience was that it was best to try and book at Sutera's offices in KK (64).

The most common sleeping option is the heated dormitory (bedding included) in the Laban Rata Resthouse, which sells for RM435 per person. If you need privacy, twin shares are available for RM920. Three meals are included in the price. Non-heated facilities surrounding the Laban Rata building are also available for RM385 per person (meals included). Yes, the inflated prices feel monopolistic and are patently ridiculous, and to make matters worse, Sutera is trying to force climbers to stay in the park for two nights – one night at Laban Rata and one night at the base.

The other option at Laban Rata is to stay at **Pendant Hut** (p78), which is owned and operated by **Mountain Torq** (see the boxed text, p80; pricing is on par with Sutera). All guests sleeping at Pendant Hut take two of three meals at Sutera's cafeteria, and are required to participate in (or at least pay for) the *via ferrata* circuit. Pendant Hut is slightly more basic (no heat – although climbers sleep in uberwarm sleeping bags), however, there's a bit of a summer-camp vibe here while Laban Rata feels more like a Himalayan orphanage. Prices for Pendant Hut are comparable to Sutera.

See p77 for information about additional fees associated with climbing Kinabalu.

PARK HEADQUARTERS (AT THE BASE)
The following sleeping options are located at the base of the mountain and are all operated by Sutera Sanctuary Lodges. As per Sutera's monopolistic reputation, these options are overpriced when compared to the nonaffiliated sleeping spots outside the park.

Grace Hostel (Map p76; dm RM145) Clean, comfortable 20-bed dorm with fireplace and drink-making area.

Hill Lodge (Map p76; r RM470) These semi-detached cabins are a good option for those who can't face a night in the hostels. They're clean and comfortable, with private bathrooms.

Liwagu Suites (Map p76; r RM590) These hotel-like rooms (four in total) can be found in the Liwagu Building. While they sleep up to four people, they're best for couples as they contain only one bedroom and one living room.

Nepenthes Villa (Map p76; lodge RM915) These attached two-storey units fall somewhere between hotel rooms and private lodges. They have two bedrooms (one with a twin bed, one with a queen) and verandas offering limited mountain views.

Peak Lodge (Map p76; lodge RM795) These semi-detached units have two bedrooms (one with a bunk bed and one with two twin beds), pleasant sitting rooms, fireplaces and nice views from their verandas.

Rock Hostel (Map p76; dm RM145, tw RM420) Somewhat institutional 20-bed hostel with similar facilities to the Grace Hostel.

✖ Eating

LABAN RATA (ON THE MOUNTAIN)
At Laban Rata the cafeteria-style restaurant in the **Laban Rata Resthouse** (Map p78) has a simple menu and also offers buffet meals coordinated with the usual climbing times. Most hikers staying at Laban Rata (either in one of Sutera's huts or at Pendant Hut) have three meals (dinner, breakfast and lunch) included in their accommodation packages. It is possible to negotiate a price reduction if you plan on bringing your own food (boiling water can be purchased for RM1 if you bring dried noodles). Note: you will have to lug said food up to Laban Rata. Buffet meals can also be purchased individually – dinner costs RM45. A small counter in the dining area sells an assortment of items including soft drinks, chocolate, pain relievers and postcards.

BRINGING HOME A PIECE OF BORNEO

As you wend your way across the island, you'll happen upon thousands of potential souvenirs – masks, pearls, T-shirts, carpets, spices, tattoos – and sometimes it can be difficult to sort out the traditional crafts from the traditional crap.

In Sabah, the markets of KK are filled with little gems like irregular pearls, sold at record low prices. Items made from indigenous materials (like rattan) are generally authentic; however, the masks aren't very Bornean (in fact, the colourful ones are Balinese) and if some paintings look oddly Indigenous Australian – well, they are.

In Sarawak, Kuching has some great shops. Most longhouses also have handicrafts for purchase, but many of these objects were actually produced in Kuching and shipped into the jungle. There's no need to stress about debating the authenticity of that wicker basket – simply ask and the locals will be honest about the product's origin.

If you are looking to bring home something out of the ordinary, make sure you're aware of any relevant regulations affecting your purchase. Most outlets can organise the necessary fumigation of wooden artefacts, as well as shipping. Some antiques such as cannons and jars are difficult to export – you'll need to get permission from the Sarawak Museum before you make the purchase. In general, it is illegal to export any plants or seeds without a permit from the Department of Agriculture (Sarawak pepper is OK), and animal parts (like leopard teeth or hornbill feathers) are strictly off limits. Seashells are commonly sold around KK and Semporna – please do not purchase these as it will encourage local Sea Gypsies to pillage the ocean for more.

Some countries also restrict the importation of weapons as souvenirs. For example, Australian customs officials seem worried about the safety of suburban cats if blowpipes get in (they may have a point...). The machete-esque *parang*, once the head-hunting weapon of choice, is another trinket you may have trouble explaining to your postman back home (never mind trying to get past your local customs agent!).

PARK HEADQUARTERS (AT THE BASE)

There are two **restaurants** (⊘6am-10pm, to 11pm weekends) at park headquarters. Just outside of the park gates is a roadside restaurant, closed for renovations when we arrived but due to be open when you read this. Park staff told us it serves good Malaysian meals at good (ie cheap) Malaysian prices and is open for breakfast, lunch and dinner.

Restoran Kinabalu Balsam　　CAFETERIA $$
(Map p76; dishes RM5-15) The cheaper and more popular of the two options in the park is this canteen-style spot directly below the park HQ. It offers basic but decent Malaysian, Chinese and Western dishes at reasonable prices. There is also a small but well-stocked shop in Balsam selling tinned and dried foods, chocolate, beer, spirits, cigarettes, T-shirts, bread, eggs and margarine.

Liwagu Restaurant　　CAFETERIA $$$
(Map p76; dishes RM10-30) In the visitors centre, this is more expensive than the Balsam, but there's a huge range of dishes, including noodles, rice and seafood standards.

An 'American breakfast' is pretty ordinary here – the cheaper breakfast at the Balsam canteen is better value.

⊙ Getting There & Away

It is highly advised summit-seekers check in at the park headquarters by 9am, which means if you're coming from KK, you should plan to leave by 7am, or consider spending the night somewhere near the base of the mountain.

Bus

Express buses (RM25) leave KK from the city bus station every hour on the hour from 7am to 10am and at 12:30pm, 2pm and 3pm and leaves at the same times in the reverse directions. A shuttle bus (RM40) also runs from the Pacific Sutera (9am), the Magellan Sutera (9.10am) and Wisma Sabah (9.20am) to Kinabalu National Park HQ, arriving at 11.30am (RM40). In the reverse direction, it leaves Kinabalu National Park HQ at 3.30pm. There is also a shuttle bus from Kinabalu National Park HQ to Poring Hot Springs at noon (RM25) and another at 3.30pm (RM25) to Mesilau Nature Resort. Express buses and minivans travelling between KK and Ranau (and Sandakan) pass the park turn-off, 100m uphill from the park entrance. You can go to Sandakan (RM40) if the bus has room.

Taxi

Share taxis leave KK from Inanam and Wawasan (Padang Merdeka) stations (RM150).

Jeep

Share jeeps park just outside of the park gates and leave when full for KK (RM150) and Sandakan (RM400); each jeep can hold around five passengers, but they can be chartered by individuals.

Around Mt Kinabalu

Kinabalu National Park is home to Borneo's highest mountain and some of the island's best-preserved forest. Most travellers make a beeline for the mountain and the main park headquarters area, but the following spots are also worth exploring.

MESILAU NATURE RESORT

This lovely slice of country is the trailhead for an alternative approach up Mt Kinabalu, often favoured by trekkers as it's more challenging than the main route and much less crowded than park headquarters. The Mesilau route wanders up the mountain and links up with the Timpohon route to continue the ascent to Laban Rata. Arrange your trip with (who else?) Sutera Sanctuary Lodges (p83) and your guide will meet you at Mesilau. See p77for more information about permits and fees. See p86for information on lodging here.

KUNDASANG MEMORIAL

The junction for the Mesilau Nature Resort on the KK–Ranau Hwy is the site of the **Kundasang War Memorial** (Kundasang; admission RM10; ⊙8am-5.30pm), which commemorates the Australian and British prisoners who died on the infamous Sandakan Death Marches (p93). To be honest, we weren't expecting much when we came here – other memorials in Sabah have seemed neglected and forgotten – but the Kundasang gardens are remarkably touching. Four gardens, manicured in that bucolic yet tame fashion that is so very English, are separated by a series of marbled pavilions. In the Anzac Garden you can see a full list of the dead and at the back of the gardens is a viewpoint that offers a stunning view of Mt Kinabalu.

The memorial is in Kundasang, 10km east of Kinabalu National Park headquarters. You'll know you're in Kundasang when you see the market stalls on either side of the road. Take the turn on the left for Mesilau

Nature Resort. The memorial is on the right 150m after the turn-off. Look for the flags and the stone fort-like structure above the road. A taxi from Ranau will run you at least RM200 for a return trip.

RANAU

Ranau is a collection of concrete shop blocks on the road between KK and Sandakan. There's a busy Saturday **night market**, but otherwise this a good town for passing through: rampant construction is scarring the lovely valley it sits in. That said, there is a podiatry experience here you don't want to miss (we don't often write that sentence). After your epic Kinabalu climb, head to **Tagal Sungai Moroli** (admission RM10) in Kampung Luanti for a truly unique massage experience. The term *tagal* means 'no fishing' in the local Kadazan-Dusun language, as the fish in the river (a species known locally known as *ikan pelian*) are not to be captured – they are special massage fish. The townsfolk claim that they've trained the little swimmers to gently nibble at weary feet.

⊙ Sights

Sabah Tea Garden   TEA PLANTATION
(☑088-879220; www.sabahtea.com; factory tour RM12, 2-day, 1-night package from RM190) A pretty tea plantation that looks like a cluster of giant mossy tussocks huddles in the mountains near Ranau. Contact the tea garden to arrange tours of both the plantation and surrounding rainforests and river valleys. Overnight packages are available; you get to sleep in an on-site property in a tarted-up version of a traditional longhouse. Also offers tours of the facilities coupled with a trip to the fish foot massage (RM90).

PORING HOT SPRINGS

One of the few positive contributions the Japanese made to Borneo during WWII, **Poring Hot Springs** (adult/child RM15/10) has become a popular weekend retreat for locals. The complex is actually part of the Kinabalu National Park, but it's 43km away from the park headquarters, on the other side of Ranau.

The hot springs are located in a well-maintained forest park that does a very fine job of giving casual visitors a small slice of the jungle – there's various nature paths and the like that the elderly and children can enjoy. But the springs themselves are not natural puddles of hot water. Steaming, sulphurous water is channelled into man-made pools and tubs where visitors can relax their tired muscles after the trek to the summit of Mt Kinabalu. For some, it's a huge anticlimax, for others it's a perfect playground worth far more than the customary quick stop. Don't forget a towel and your swimming trunks.

For our ringitt, the highlight of the place is actually way above the springs: a **Canopy Walkway** (admission RM15; ⊙9am-4pm) that consists of a series of walkways suspended from trees, up to 40m above the jungle floor, providing unique views of the surrounding forest. Get there early if you want to see birds or other wildlife. A **tropical garden** (adult/child RM3/1.50; ⊙9am-4pm), **butterfly farm** (adult/child RM4/2; ⊙9am-4pm Tue-Sun) and **orchid garden** (adult/child RM10/5; ⊙9am-4pm) are also part of the Poring complex. Rafflesia sometimes bloom in the area; look out for signs in the visitors centre and along the road.

🛏 Sleeping & Eating

It's worth spending a night around the base of Kinabalu before your ascent, and there are plenty of accommodation options suiting everyone's budget. All of the following have attached restaurants.

The accommodation at Mesilau and Poring is run by Sutera Sanctuary Lodges (p83) with a notable exception (see below). At forested Mesilau, the **lodging** (dm/d RM145/380) is in functional dorms and doubles, but if you want to splurge there are some oddly-shaped chalets (they look like they were designed by Frank Gehry on a bad day) that go from RM1075 to RM1275.

Mesilau Nature Resort (p85) is 30 minutes beyond the entrance to Kinabalu (when driving towards Ranau from KK). The Sutera lodging in Poring is located within the hot-springs complex and is same-same, no difference, in terms of the room experience and the prices.

In Poring, Tom Hewitt, a British expat, is trying to upgrade the lodging situation, He's at work putting together a backpacker-midrange-focused **ecolodge** to be called 'Lupa Masa' (Malay: Forget Time) that will be green friendly, contribute money to local communities and offer a good range of treks into the jungle. Accommodation is in raised tents and traditional lodging made from local bamboo, roofed with palm leaves and kitted with stretcher hammocks and mosquito nets. The owners will offer guided treks with the local nomadic Penan tribe; see http://picnicwiththepenan.wordpress. com for details. Rates for beds at Lupa Masa will run for RM50-80, including breakfast. It's scheduled to be open by the time you read this; if you want to book, email Tom at lupamasaborneo@gmail. com. You can also follow him on Facebook at Lupa Masa.

There are also plenty of privately owned sleeping options looping around Kinabalu's base. Most of these are located along the road between the park headquarters and Kundasang (east of the park's entrance). We list these options in order of placement and proximity to the national park entrance.

SUPERSIZE ME

If Borneo were in the game of stealing slogans, it would probably choose 'supersize me'. And it wouldn't take long to figure out why. Everything about Borneo (from its biodiversity to its topography) is on a totally different scale from the rest of the world – it's like the island's taking steroids.

Here are a few examples:

» The biggest flower on the earth, a parasitic plant known as the Rafflesia, blossoms on Borneo to a whopping 1m in diameter (p127).

» The Sarawak Chamber (p210), the biggest cave chamber a tourist can visit, is located in Gunung Mulu National Park.

» The Kinabalu giant red leech can grow up to 30cm in length – that's longer than the average foot of an adult human male. (Luckily, it doesn't feed on humans!)

» Southeast Asia's highest point is Mt Kinabalu (p75), a stunning granite fortress rising 4095m.

And let's not forget, Borneo is the third-biggest island on the planet (only Greenland and New Guinea are larger).

Mountain Guest House
GUESTHOUSE **$**

(☏016-837 4040, 088-888632; dm/s/d incl breakfast from RM20/60/70) A good choice if you're on a tight budget, this guest house consists of bare but clean rooms (some with very feminine pink bedspreads) plopped into huts and chalets that seem to precariously lean out from the side of Mt Kinabalu.

D'Villa Rina Ria Lodge
LODGE **$$**

(☏088-889282; www.dvillalodge.com.my; dm/r RM30/120; @) This charming lodge is run by an exceptionally friendly staff that maintain cute, cosy rooms and a dining area that overlooks a lovely view over the mountain ranges/thick clouds of afternoon fog, depending on the mercy of the weather gods.

Strawberry Garden Hotel
HOTEL **$$**

(☏088-889309, 019-842 4015; bs_tours@ streamyx.com; Kundasang; r RM70-140) How can you not love a place with a name as cute as 'Strawberry Garden'? The building looks a bit institutional from the highway, but interior rooms are good value for money, with clean tile floors and comfy beds. The on-site restaurant cooks up some nice hot meals too.

Kinabalu Pine Resort
RESORT **$$$**

(☏088-889388; kinabalupineresort.com; Kundasang-Ranau Hwy; r from RM160) A paradigm of country club landscaping, this welcoming camp-style resort is extremely popular with Sabahans, who sit on the wooden balconies while enjoying the breezy sunsets. Ask for a room with hardwood floors – the carpeting seems a bit tattered.

❶ Getting There & Around
Bus & Van
KK round-trip buses stop in front of park headquarters and in Ranau (RM15, two hours) from 7am to 8pm. Minivans operate from a blueroofed shelter in Ranau servicing the nearby attractions (park HQ, Poring etc) for RM5. The national park operates a van service between the headquarters and Poring for RM25 – it leaves the park HQ at noon.

Northwest Coast
The A1 runs north from KK to Kudat and the tip of Borneo past wide headlands, sandy beaches, rice paddies and stretches of Sabah that are criminally overlooked by most tourists. This is a good area for renting a car or motorbike – the roads are pretty level, and public transportation links aren't reliable for getting off the main road.

TUARAN
Tuaran, 33km from KK, is a bustling little town with tree-lined boulevard-style streets and the distinctive nine-storey **Ling Sang Pagoda**, whose approaches are dominated by vividly painted guardian deities. There's little point stopping in the town itself unless you happen to pass through on a market day (Tuaran is likely named for the Malay word *tawaran*, or 'sale', reflecting its history as a trading post), but the surrounding area conceals two interesting stilt villages.

❍ Sights
Mengkabong Water Village is a stilt village of the Bajau people built over an estuary. It was once a picturesque spot, but encroaching development has diminished its rustic charms. The settlement at **Penambawan**, on the other hand, is probably the finest example of a traditional Bajau village on the west coast, with several houses built in the old thatch style. You can thank Penambawan's isolation; the only way out here is via a motorboat (RM50), which you must get to via a minivan to Serusup (RM1.50). The trip upriver takes about 15 minutes, and the boat will wait while you wander the plankwalks of the village. The villagers are friendly, but it can feel a bit intrusive just wandering around their backyards (or boards, as the case may be).

⌂ Sleeping & Eating
Given the town's proximity to KK (with its heaps of accommodation options), you probably won't need to stay in town. However, if for some reason you need a room, try **Orchid Hotel** (☏088-793789; 4 Jln Teo Teck Ong; r from RM80; ❄). It's somewhat overpriced but it'll do the trick for a night. Just a few doors away is **Tai Fatt** (Jln Teo Teck Ong; meals RM4; ☺7am-10pm), the best *kedai kopi* in Tuaran. It excels at *char mien/mee goreng*, the local, mouth-watering take on Chinese fried noodles, overflowing with vegetables, pork, oil, pork, egg, pork, wheat noodles and, yes, pork.

All buses north pass through Tuaran, and minivans shuttle regularly to and from KK (RM5 to RM10, 30 minutes). Minivans to Mengkabong are less frequent and cost RM1. Regular minivans go from Tuaran to Kota Belud (around RM12, 30 minutes).

THE KLIAS VALLEY & 4M CHALLENGE

At the roundabout situated just south of Tuaran, you'll see signs pointing to Tamparuli (it's the exit on the right side of the circle). The road blows past this small village; notice two bridges, a cement roadway and a high suspension walkway. The roadway is jokingly called 'underwater bridge' thanks to its habit of flooding; the suspension bridge (which stays dry) is for pedestrians. Past Tamparuli the hills and mountains begin to rise and you enter the Kiulu River Valley, a pretty stretch of water-smoothed rocks, gentle paddies, quiet kampungs (villages) and the occasional white egret and lounging water buffalo. Tour outfits in Kota Konabalu offer tubing and rafting trips on the Kiulu, which is calm enough for beginners and families – go with the ever-professional **Riverbug** (p64), which offers tubing, rafting and white-water kayaking tours.

This is deep Kadazan-Dusun country, and in October (usually; check with Sabah Tourism, as the event was held in December in 2010), the **Kiulu 4M Challenge** is the main, must-not-miss event. This is essentially the Kadazan–Dusun Olympics, but with more camaraderie and less billion-dollar opening ceremonies. The name '4M' refers to the four traditional Kadazan-Dusun sports: *memangkar* (bamboo rafting), *mamarampanau* (stilt walking), *managkus* (running) and *manampatau* (um...hard to explain. Like swimming. But with a bamboo pole). The event is open to outsiders, so why not come by, strap on a bamboo pole and some stilts and go for the gold.

KOTA BELUD

You might think Kota Belud isn't much to look at, but every Sunday a huge **tamu** takes place on the outskirts of this small, sleepy town. The market is a congested, colourful and dusty melee of vendors, hagglers, browsers, gawpers and hawkers, all brought together by a slew of everyday goods in a bustle that consumes the whole town every week (and a smaller version takes place on Wednesdays!). The most impressive site in Kota Belud is sadly an uncommon one these days: a procession of fully caparisoned Bajau horsemen from the nearby villages, decked out, along with their steeds, in vivid, multi-coloured satin 'armour' and embroidered barding.

A *tamu* is not simply a market where villagers gather to sell their farm produce and to buy manufactured goods from traders; it's also a social occasion where news and stories are exchanged. These days tourists now often outnumber buffalo, and the horsemen have mostly moved away from the car park, though some do put on a show for visitors.

Visitors looking for tribal handicrafts and traditional clothing may find a prize here, but it's cheaply made stuff for tourists. Ironically, the best way to experience this commercial event is to come not expecting to buy anything – soak up the convivial, occasionally manic atmosphere, enjoy a good meal at the lovely food stalls and just potter about like Grandma at a Sunday flea market. Sounds exciting? Honest, it is. The hilly views from the *padang* (grassy field) may also tempt you to stay awhile and do some walking away from the Sunday crowds.

🛏 Sleeping & Eating

Most people visit Kota Belud as a day trip from KK, since you can make it there and back with plenty of time for the market.

TOP CHOICE **Mañana**   GUEST HOUSE **$$**
(📱014-679 4679; www.manana-borneo. com; hammock/r/ste from RM50/70/150) This fantastic property is in the little village of Kampung Pituru Laut on the coast. The name comes from a Canadian guest, who was so enchanted with the resort he kept putting off leaving till mañana...then mañana...then mañana... Owners Yan and Nani have situated the property on a private beach that is basically a slice of heaven buttered with paradise. Simple chalets look out onto clear water, hammocks sway in the ocean breeze, an on-site restaurant-bar serves hot food and cold beer, and the sunsets will blow your mind. Ask about diving trips to see what may be the world's largest brain coral. The owners prefer you book ahead so transportation can be arranged; their suggested agent in KK is the excellent GogoSabah (p63).

Taginambur Homestay   HOME STAY **$**
(📱088-976595, 019-810 8753; www.taginambur. com.my; rikian@taginambur.com.my; 6 Plaza Kong

Guan; r RM40) This home stay has taken root in the nearby *kampung* (village) of Taginambur – you'll stay in very basic village accommodation and be given the chance to visit local schools, churches and go trekking along the nearby Kedamaian River. Email – you need to prebook.

Kota Belud Travelers' Lodge   LODGE **$**
(☎088-977228; http://mykbtl.com; 6 Plaza Kong Guan; dm RM25, r RM65-85; ❋) A simple affair in the centre of town, it's about 200m southwest of the mosque in a shopping block (it's well marked, so finding it shouldn't be a problem). It's got the whole concrete-block-with-surprisingly-cosy-rooms vibe going that is oddly typical of interior Sabah hotels.

Kota Belud is hardly a gastronome's delight, but plenty of tasty snacks can be picked up at the Sunday market. There are plenty of Chinese and halal coffee shops around the municipal offices.

❶ Getting There & Away

Minibus & Taxi
Minivans and share taxis gather in front of Pasar Besar, the old market. Most of these serve the Kota Belud–KK route, (RM5 to RM7, two hours) or Kudat (RM10 to RM12, two hours), departing from 7am to 5pm. To get to Kinabalu National Park, take any minibus going to KK and get off at Tamparuli, about halfway (RM5, 30 minutes). There are several minivans from Tamparuli to Ranau every day until about 2pm; all pass the park entrance (RM5, one hour). To go all the way to Ranau costs RM12 (the trip takes just over an hour).

USUKAN BAY
A lovely scallop of blue water scoops out Usukan Bay, which lies west of Kota Belud and has only recently been developed for tourism. Visiting here essentially means staying at the newly opened **Usukan Cove Lodge** (☎088-486168, 016-832-9193; http://sabahholidays.com/new/index.php/usukan-cove; r RM90-200; ❋). Which isn't such a bad thing – the lodge is a solid midrange choice, situated on a pretty, if small stretch of beach hemmed in by mangrove trees and dusty palms. The lodge can organise a host of activities such as fishing expeditions, boat trips up the nearby Kawa Kawa river (proboscis monkeys!), snorkelling and diving trips (we recommend snorkelling – the diving visibility here is often obstructed by rainwater from the mountains). Public-transport links out this way have not been regularly established, so contact the lodge

to arrange transport from either Kota Kinabalu or Kota Belud.

KUDAT
Despite being only a few hours from Kota Kinabalu, there's a dreamy, end-of-the-world feeling in Kudat. Maybe it's the drowsy quality of the air; Malaysian towns don't get much more laid-back and friendly than this. You can thank the local Rungus people. Filipinos too – there's loads of them around.

Kudat is a quiet port that rewards a bit of initiative. The town itself is fairly unremarkable; there is a large **Chinese temple** (admission free) by the main square and a **fish market** near the docks, but mainly this is a quiet place where it's nice to potter about, smile at people and be smiled at. It's the country that leads up to the tip of Borneo that you want to explore. There are miles and miles of beautiful beaches about, some of which are excellent for surfing, while others are good for watching lonely cattle and blood-red sunsets. The trick is finding these spots, as there's very little tourism infrastructure to speak of.

You can disappear down side roads that lead to the ocean and see what you find – we did and had a grand time, but we had our own wheels. We're purposely leaving this section a little DIY as there is such unreliable road signage here, yet not too many roads. Trust us when we say that with a little exploratory gusto you might find that mythical traveller pot of gold: the hidden, untouched beach. Swing by **New Way Car Rental & Souvenir Centre** (☎088-625868; 40 Jln Lo Thien Chok) if you want to explore the area under your own steam. Staff can also book your accommodation on Pulau Banggi (p91).

🛏 Sleeping & Eating

Howard Stanton (☎088-483519; Stanton_howard@yahoo.co.uk), a British expat who speaks fluent Malay, may well be the most popular man in Kudat with locals and travellers alike. He's a man of many stories (international rugby player, diver, first white man to play and referee top-level *cabbadi*, an Indian team tackle game) who runs a million projects: he's building his own eco-resort, sets up excellent home stays (around RM70) and can help arrange treks.

Hibiscus Riviera   VILLA **$$$**
(☎019-895 074; www.hibiscusvillaborneo.com; villas from US$1200, 3-night minimum stay; ❋ 🛜 ❋)

The Hibiscus looks like the place where Jay-Z and *GQ* magazine would throw the mother of all Southeast Asian parties. It's tasteful – dark-wood floors, indigenous art, scrubbed pebbles and an incredible infinity pool – yet unmistakably, impeccably upper class.

Kudat Riviera
VILLA **$$$**

(☎088-249276; www.oceanvillasgroup.com; Pantai Kulambu; villas incl breakfast from US$2000; ❄☏☒) Phew – this is a stunning attempt at luxury, and boy is it a success. There are several properties to choose from dotted around the Kudat peninsula. Lavish villas are constructed in a dreamy Balinese style – go for an ocean-facing Rice Barn Villa – the perfect incarnation of 'tribal chic'.

Ria Hotel
HOTEL **$$**

(☎088-622794; 3 Jln Marudu; r RM118-260; ❄@) The Ria hits all the right notes: clean, spacious, well-appointed rooms, nice bathrooms with hot showers, and little balconies (some with scenic views). It's a short walk southwest of the bus station.

Upper Deck
HOTEL **$$**

(☎088-622272; Jln Lintas; r R80-160; ❄) Above the Milimewa Superstore, this basic hotel has large, spartan rooms, and is perfectly serviceable, if not exactly cosy.

Meals are obviously included at the top-end villas, but otherwise your options are the usual assortment of cheapo Malay and Chinese *kedai kopi*, which all line Kudat's small centre.

❶ Getting There & Away

Bus

The bus station is in Kudat Plaza in the western part of town, very close to the Ria Hotel. Bus destinations include KK (RM25, three hours) and Kota Belud (RM15, 1½ hours). Minivans and jeeps also operate from here; a ride to KK in a full van will cost around RM40.

AROUND KUDAT

The area around Kudat is prime package-tour territory, although the area can easily be explored by private vehicle. You can attempt some of the side roads in a 2WD or motorbike, but be careful, especially if it's been raining (which doesn't happen often; this is the driest part of Sabah). Either way, make sure you take in one of the lovely tropical sunsets – Sabah's west coast is famous for 'em!

Rungus Longhouses

The indigenous people of the Kudat area are known as the Rungus, a subgroup of Sabah's Kadazan-Dusun peoples. The Rungus inhabit the Kudat Peninsula and the Pitas Peninsula, on the far side of Marudu Bay. While famous for their basketry and beadwork, what sets the Rungus apart is their fine longhouses, which house one extended family, rather than several unrelated families, as is the case with other groups in Borneo.

These days, as with many other indigenous people in Borneo, most of the Rungus have abandoned their longhouses in favour of Malay-style wooden or concrete-brick houses. However, the Rungus maintain two fine **longhouses** (Bavanggazo Rungus Longhouses/Maranjak Longhouse; ☎088-621673/612846; per person per night from RM70) in Kampung Bavanggazo that are meticulous recreations of their historical dwellings, and damn impressive to boot.

Make no mistake, these longhouses are primarily set up for display purposes and to attract tourists. But a night here still provides visitors with a good chance to interact with Rungus people and learn about their culture, and besides, the location is wonderful: in the dip of one of those impossibly green Borneo valleys that positively throbs with plant life. The rates include dinner and breakfast and simple cultural entertainment. You will sleep in a traditional room in one of the longhouses with insect netting above your bed. Most travellers like the experience, but some have complained about feeling like the whole affair was a bit too artificial.

Kampung Bavanggazo is 44km south of Kudat on the north–south highway (look for the mile post reading 'Kudat 44km'). There is a sign off the highway that reads 'Kg. Bavanggazo 'Rungus Longhouse'' (you may also see signs for Maranjak Longhouses; same destination, different marketing name). Follow this road (Jln Tinangol) down the hill for about 1.5km, cross a bridge and go uphill to the left. You will quickly come to the first longhouse, and the second one is at the top of the hill 800m further on. There is no public transport right to the longhouses. All KK–Kudat buses and minivans will stop at Kampung Bavanggazo if you ask the driver. A taxi from Kudat will cost around RM60.

Tip of Borneo

Sabah's northernmost headland, at the end of a wide bay some 40km from Kudat, is known as Tanjung Simpang Mengayu, or the Tip of Borneo. Magellan reputedly landed here for 42 days during his famous round-the-world voyage. Once a wild promontory, this windswept stretch where the cliffs meet the sea has been co-opted as a tourist attraction – there's a large, truncated globe monument dominating the viewpoint. A sign warns visitors not to climb down onto the rocks that form the mainland's actual tip, effectively guaranteeing that tourists will do exactly that – so watch out for crashing waves if you follow suit...

There's no public transport, so you'll need to negotiate a taxi from Kudat (around RM75, including waiting time upon arrival) or drive yourself (we suggest washing the dust off the car before returning it to the rental agency).

Offshore Islands

The real highlights of northwestern Sabah lie offshore. The first gem is Pulau Mantanani, perfect tropical islands lying about 40km northwest of Kota Belud. The second is Layang Layang, a diving mecca about 300km northwest of KK – it's basically just an airstrip built on a reef way out in the middle of the South China Sea. Famous for great visibility, seemingly endless wall dives and the occasional school of hammerheads, it's second only to Sipadan (p118) on Malaysia's list of top dive spots.

PULAU MANTANANI

Pulau Mantanani Besar (Big Mantanani Island) and **Pulau Mantanani Kecil** (Little Mantanani Island) are two little flecks of land fringed by bleach-blond sand and ringed by a halo of colourful coral, about 25km off the coast of northwest Sabah (about 40km northwest of Kota Belud).

Those on a budget – actually, anyone – should opt for the excellent **Mari Mari Backpackers Lodge** (☎088-260501; www.riverbug.asia; two-day, one-night all-incl dive packages from RM310), operated by Riverbug (p64). Guests are placed in raised stilt chalets pocked around a white-sand beach. The huts are a modern take on the thatch-longhouse theme, and a well executed one at that. Diving and snorkelling activities feature high on the itinerary list, but this

is also a lovely tropical escape if you just want to chill.

Borneo Sea Resort (☎088-230000; www.bornsea.com/mantanani; three-day, two-night all-incl dive packages from RM2100; ✱) sits on a private beach at the west end of the big island. The bungalows here are quite nice, with tile floors, hot-water showers and bathtubs, large double beds and verandas. Sea kayaks are available for rent and would allow you to explore the area, but be careful as there are strong currents offshore and you could easily get washed out to sea. KK operators offer day-trip diving packages for those who don't want to stay on the island.

PULAU BANGGI

If you want to fall off the map, get out to Pulau Banggi, which lies some 40km northeast of Kudat. The Banggi people, known locally for their unusual tribal tree-houses, are Sabah's smallest indigenous group, and speak a unique non-Bornean dialect. The island is a postcard-esque slice of sand, tropical trees and clear water, and frankly, we can't figure out why it hasn't become one of Sabah's big destinations. Oh well: more for you to discover, although we hope you don't mind isolation. The surrounding reef islands can also be visited on dive trips organised from KK, but at the time of research there were no local dive centres (but you could try Howard Stanton; see p89). There are supposed to be downed Japanese Zero planes in the waters off Banggi – if you do dive here, ask your operator about them.

Accommodation is provided by a small government **resthouse** (r RM40) and the modest **Banggi Resort** (☎019-587 8078; r fan/air-con RM50/65, huts RM70; ✱), which can arrange boat trips and other activities. The small huts have kitchens and twin beds – make sure you request the charming tree-house hut. This place can get fully booked on weekends, so reserve in advance. At either location, ask staff about the trails that lead into the small jungle interior of the island.

Kudat Express (☎088-328118; one-way RM15) runs a ferry between Kudat and the main settlement on Pulau Banggi. It departs the pier (near the Shell station) at 9am and 2pm daily. In the reverse direction, it leaves Pulau Banggi daily at around 3pm.

SABAH OFFSHORE ISLANDS

LAYANG LAYANG

Some 300km northwest of KK, Layang Layang is a tiny island surrounded by a coral atoll. It's an exclusive **dive location**, well known to scubaholics as part of the famous Borneo Banks. Thanks to its utter isolation, the reef here is healthy and diverse. Although it may not be quite as colourful as the reef at Sipadan, it's likely to be one of the most unspoilt bits of coral most divers have seen. And the best part is it just goes on and on and on.... The visibility here is usually excellent; 20m a norm, sometimes extending to 30m or more. While hammerheads are occasionally sighted, it might be better to consider them a bonus, and to concentrate on the reef fish, which are abundant and varied. There are also plenty of reef sharks in attendance, along with a healthy population of rays.

Please note: there is *no decompression chamber* at Layang Layang, so don't press your luck while underwater. The resort only provides air – no nitrox. Geography buffs may be pleased to know Layang Layang is the only one of the remote Spratly Islands that receives regular flights.

Layang Layang Island Resort (in Kuala Lumpur ☎03-2170 2185; www.avillionlayanglay ang.com; 6-day, 5-night all-inclusive package twin-share per person from US$1400; ✴✱) is the only game in town here and it's all about the diving. The five daily meals – that's right, five – are scheduled around the dive times. The standard rooms are very comfortable, with air-con, TV, private verandas and hot-water showers. The all-inclusive packages include accommodation, food, 12 boat dives and tank usage. Package rates for nondivers start at US$850. An extra night costs diver/nondiver $180/$125 . Be warned, nondivers: besides a little snorkelling, there's nothing for you to do here but sunbathe.

The resort operates its own Antanov 26 aircraft, which flies every Tuesday, Thursday, Friday and Sunday between KK and Layang Layang. The flight over from KK in this barebones Russian prop plane is a big part of the adventure: it feels more like a military transport than a commercial airliner. The return flight costs US$285, which is not included in the accommodation-food-dive package.

EASTERN SABAH

Eastern Sabah takes nearly everything that is wonderful about the rest of Borneo and condenses it into one hard-hitting brew of an outdoor shot consisting of equal parts adventure, wildlife, undersea exploration and flat-out fun. Let's tick off some of the natural wonders that are packed into this relatively tiny corner of the island: the great ginger men – ie the orangutans – of Sepilok; pot-bellied, flop-nosed proboscis monkeys in Labuk Bay; the looming vine tunnels and muddy crocodile highway of the Sungai Kinabatangan; pygmy elephants and treetop canopies that scratch in the sky in the Danum Valley and Tabin; plunging seawalls rainbow-spattered with tropical marine life in the Semporna Archipelago; a forest as old as human civilisation in the Maliau Basin.

Did we just pique your travel appetite? Yeah, we thought so. With easier transport links and improved infrastructure, it's easier than ever to hit up the east side of Sabah. You'll be told, when you're here, that the only way around is via package tours, but trust us – with a little prior planning and a bit of heart, you can explore this area independently and in-depth.

Sandakan

POP 450,400

Sandakan is not high on most people's Sabah itinerary. Sabah's second city lacks the small cosmopolitan pulse that keeps Kota Kinabalu throbbing; in contrast, Sandakan feels like a provincial city with provincial horizons, not to mention a pretty grubby city centre. But Sandakan was once a major port of call, and as such it has played an important role in Borneo's past, as attested by religious relics, haunting cemeteries and stunning colonial mansions. It is this history, rather than the present (an endless succession of construction cranes) that makes Sandakan worth some of your time. We take that back – the construction is a draw as well, in the sense it has made Sandakan into a midlevel hub with good transport links to both KK and KL.

◉ Sights

Central Sandakan is light on 'must-see' attractions, although history buffs will appreciate the *Sandakan Heritage Trail* brochure available at the tourist office. The centre, where you'll find most hotels, banks and local transport, consists of a few blocks squashed between the waterfront and a steep escarpment from where you can look out over the bay (Teluk Sandakan). Warning: don't go to the Sandakan Crocodile Park, highly touted in tourism brochures, unless you like watching abused reptiles.

Chinese Cemetery
CEMETERY

Sandakan's massive Chinese Cemetery essentially takes up all of a valley that runs into the hills east of Sandakan. Gravesites are studded into the slopes, many shaped by *feng shui* principles so that the back of the grave backs into the solid angle of the earth, while the front often features a small artificial pool, reflecting the traditional Chinese belief that an ideal home has a mountain behind it and running water in front. As you wander further along the cemetery, the graves become older and more decrepit – many have been claimed by the jungle. You will also see some charnel houses that accommodate the important members of Sandakan's major Chinese clans. Across

the road from the cemetery is a cremation ground for Hindus and Sikhs.

93

Japanese Cemetery
Located beyond the Chinese cemetery grounds, this is a poignant piece of Sandakan's ethnic puzzle. The gravesite was founded in the 1890s by Kinoshita Kuni, known to the English as Okuni of South Seas and to greater Sandakan as the successful madam-manager of the lucrative 'Brothel 8', once located on Lebuh Tiga. Today the cemetery is quite small, but at one time there were hundreds of buried dead, most of them prostitutes. A monument to the fallen Japanese soldiers of WWII was erected in the cemetery in 1989. To get here and to the Chinese cemetery, climb the shady Tangga Seribu (100 Steps) to Jln Residensi Drive and turn right; there will be signs pointing the rest of the way to the cemetery.

Agnes Keith House
MUSEUM

(Jln Istana; admission RM15; ☺9am-5pm) On the hill above town, overlooking Teluk Sandakan and the scruffy port itself, is Agnes Keith House, an old two-storey wooden villa now renovated as a museum. Keith

SABAH SANDAKAN

THE SANDAKAN DEATH MARCHES

Sandakan was the site of a Japanese prisoner-of-war camp during WWII, and in September 1944 there were 1800 Australian and 600 British troops interned here. What is not widely known is that more Australians died here than during the building of the infamous Burma Railway.

Early in the war, food and conditions were bearable and the death rate stood at around three per month. However, as the Allies closed in, it became clear to the officers in command that they didn't have enough staff to guard against a rebellion in the camps. They decided to cut the prisoners' rations to weaken them, causing disease to spread and the death rate to rise.

It was also decided to move the prisoners inland – 250km through the jungle to Ranau, on a route originally cut by locals to hamper the Japanese invaders, passing mainly through uninhabited, inhospitable terrain. On 28 January 1945, 470 prisoners set off; 313 made it to Ranau. On the second march, 570 started from Sandakan; just 118 reached Ranau. The 537 prisoners on the third march were the last men in the camp.

Conditions on the marches were deplorable: most men had no boots, rations were less than minimal and many men fell by the wayside. The Japanese brutally disposed of any prisoners who couldn't walk. Once in Ranau, the surviving prisoners were put to work carrying 20kg sacks of rice over hilly country to Paginatan, 40km away. Disease, starvation and executions took a horrendous toll, and by the end of July 1945 there were no prisoners left in Ranau. The only survivors from the 2400 at Sandakan were six Australians who escaped, either from Ranau or during the marches.

As a final bitter irony, it emerged postwar that a rescue attempt had been planned for early 1945, but intelligence at the time had suggested there were no prisoners left at the camp.

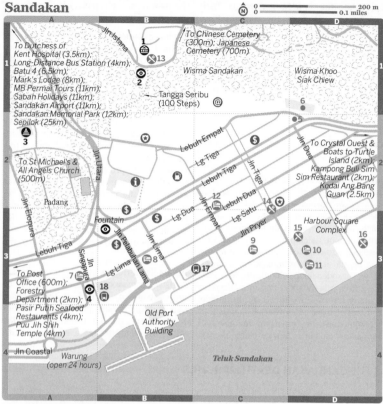

Sandakan

Sights
1 Agnes Keith House	B1
2 Observation Pavilion	B1
3 Sam Sing Kung	A2
4 Weesam Express	A3

Activities, Courses & Tours
Discovery Tours	(see 6)
5 Sepilok Tropical Wildlife Adventure	D2
6 SI Tours	D1
Wildlife Expeditions	(see 6)

Sleeping
7 Hotel Seafront	A3
8 Nak Hotel	B3
9 Sandakan Backpackers	C3
10 Sandakan Harbour Square B&B	D3
11 Swiss-Inn Waterfront Sandakan	D3
12 Winho Lodge	C2

Eating
13 English Tea House & Restaurant	B1
14 Habeeb Restaurant	C2
15 Harbour Square Complex	D3
Imperial Bayview	(see 16)
16 New Market	D3

Drinking
Balin	(see 8)

Transport
17 Local Bus Station	C3
18 Minibus & Minivan Stand	B3

was an American who came to Sandakan in the 1930s with her husband, then Conservator of Forests, and ended up writing several books about her experiences, including the famous *Land Below the Wind*. The house fell into disrepair during the 1990s, but Sabah Museum has since restored it as a faithful recreation of Keith's original abode.

The villa documents Sandakan in all its colonial splendour, with detailed displays on the lives of the Keiths. Most poignant are mementos of Agnes' imprisonment by the Japanese during WWII, when she had to try to care for her young son under gruelling conditions. There's some great vintage photographs, including a shot of Keith's husband standing with a shot elephant in full *Heart of Darkness* safari gear. The admission price includes entry to the various branches of the Sabah Museum in KK – now didn't we tell you to keep hold of your ticket? Also on the grounds is the English Tea House & Restaurant, conveniently ignoring Keith's American background and the fact that she found Sandakan to be 'too British' when she first arrived.

To reach the museum, follow Jln Singapura from the city centre and turn right up the hill, or head up the Tangga Seribu (100 Steps) to Jln Istana and turn left. Just below the museum gardens is an **observation pavilion** built by the local Rotary Club, which offers more fine views.

Sandakan Memorial Park HISTORICAL SITE
(Taman Peringatan; ⊘9am-5pm) This park marks the site of a Japanese POW camp and starting point for the infamous WWII 'death marches' to Ranau. Of the 1800 Australian and 600 British troops imprisoned here, the only survivors by July 1945 were six Australian escapees. Today the site of the POW camp has been converted into a quiet forest orchard and series of gardens.

Large, rusting machines testify to the camp's forced-labour programme, and a pavilion at the park's centre includes accounts from survivors and photographs from personnel, inmates and liberators. In 2006 the original march route was officially reopened as a memorial trail – see www.sandakan-deathmarch.com for details.

To reach the park, take any Batu 8 (or higher-numbered) bus from the local bus station in the city centre (RM1.80); get off at the 'Taman Rimba' signpost and walk down Jln Rimba. A taxi from downtown costs about RM20 one way.

Puu Jih Shih Temple TEMPLE
(Off Jln Leila) Architecturally, the Puu Jih Shih is one of the finer Chinese temples in Sabah: wrapped in the usual firework-colour display of reds, golds and twining dragons, festooned with lanterns that illuminate the grounds like a swarm of fat fireflies. As an added bonus, this large Buddhist temple is perched on a steep hill overlooking Teluk Sandakan, offering an extremely impressive view of the city. Take a bus to Tanah Merah and ask for directions; from where you depart the bus it's not a far walk, but it's a steep uphill one. A taxi here shouldn't cost more than RM6 one way, but don't be surprised if cabbies try to charge RM20 for a round-trip plus waiting at the temple.

St Michael's & All Angels Church CHURCH
(Off Jln Puncak) This incongruous slice of the Home Counties is one of the few all-stone buildings in Malaysian Borneo and the former locus of colonial worship. In 1893, prison labourers lugged said stones across the jungle during the church's construction (perhaps not the best example of Christian charity). Today, despite a little mouldering, the church very much looks like a displaced bit of the Cotswolds transplanted into the heart of Borneo. Although the church is officially off Jln Puncak, many people call the street 'Church Rd'.

Sam Sing Kung TEMPLE
(Jln Padang) The Sam Sing Kung temple (also pronounced 'Sam Sing Gong') dates from 1887, making it the oldest building in Sandakan. The name means 'three saints' temple – in this case saints for general righteousness, fishermen and students (easy to see how the latter two would be important to Sandakan's education-oriented, dependent-on-the-sea Chinese community). The temple itself is a smallish, if attractive affair – not as architecturally impressive as the Puu Jih Shih, but a lovely example of a house of worship dedicated to the traditional Chinese Taoist pantheon.

Kampong Buli Sim Sim VILLAGE
This traditional stilt village (*kampung* is Malay for village), located about 4km east of the town centre, is the original settlement Sandakan grew from. You'll likely be grinned at as you wander around the wooden boards built over the water, as much an

oddity to locals as their water village is to you. Have a stroll, be on the look for those budding entrepreneurs who have turned their homes into ad hoc souvenir shops, but please don't take pictures of people without asking permission. You can take a taxi here for no more than RM15.

👉 Tours

It is possible to visit many of the attractions around Sandakan independently, but if you want to stay at the river lodges on the Kinabatangan, you'll need to prebook accommodation. It's advisable to do so in Sandakan or in KK. Sandakan also has plenty of general tour operators offering packages to Sepilok, the Gomantong Caves and the Turtle Islands National Park. Hotels in Sandakan and Sepilok are all capable of booking tours as well.

Discovery Tours   SIGHTS
(☑089-274106; www.discoverytours.com.my; 9th fl, Wisma Khoo Siak Chiew, Lebuh Empat) Popular operator servicing the majority of Sabah's major attractions.

MB Permai Tours   SIGHTS
(☑/fax 089-671535, 089-673535; 1st fl, Sandakan Airport) Tours and car rental from RM150 per day (4WD from RM380).

Sabah Holidays   SIGHTS
(☑089-225718; www.sabahholidays.com; ground fl, Sandakan Airport) Rental cars and minivans, and can arrange tours and accommodation in Kota Belud, the Danum Valley and Maliau Basin.

Sepilok Tropical Wildlife Adventure
                                                      NATURE
(☑089-271077; www.stwadventure.com; 13 Jln Tiga) This midpriced tour specialist is connected to Sepilok Jungle Resort and Bilit Adventure Lodge on the Sungai Kinabatangan.

SI Tours   NATURE
(☑089-213502; www.sitoursborneo.com; 10th fl, Wisma Khoo Siak Chiew, Lebuh Empat) This full-service agency operates Abai Jungle Lodge and Kinabatangan River Lodge.

Uncle Tan   NATURE
(☑089-535784; www.uncletan.com; Batu 14) Tour menu includes its Sukau River Lodge on the Kinabatangan. Located in Sepilok.

Wildlife Expeditions   NATURE
(☑089-219616; www.wildlife-expeditions.com; 9th fl, Wisma Khoo Siak Chiew, Lebuh Empat) Tour menu includes its Sukau River Lodge on the Kinabatangan. Has a KK office.

🛏 Sleeping

Sandakan doesn't bowl folk over in the lodging department. Very few places feel worth their cost, and budget options are particularly sparse. That said, if you can shell out into RM80-and-above territory, there's some decent deals. If you're only passing through Sandakan to see the orangutans, it's better to stay at Sepilok itself, since the rehabilitation centre is about 25km from town.

Nak Hotel   HOTEL $$
(☑089-272988; www.nakhotel.com; Jln Pelabuhan Lama; s/d incl breakfast from RM85/118; 🌀🅰) The Nak is a solid midrange hotel that's a fair steal if you're travelling as a couple or with friends, and nice value even if you're by yourself. The oldest dedicated hotel in town has a somewhat Soviet-chic exterior, but once you get inside rooms are quite attractive: nice monochromatic colour schemes with hints of East Asian and Borneo-inspired design flairs. This well put-together spot, which is no surprise given the hotel's kick-ass roof lounge, Balin – a must even if you aren't staying here.

Mark's Lodge   HOTEL $$
(☑089-210055; www.markslodge.com; Lot 1-7, Block 36, Bandar Indah; r from RM154; 🌀🅰) The word 'boutique' is written in fogged glass across the front entrance – just in case you didn't get the memo. This business-class hotel, located at Batu 4 (Bandar Indah) is a solid option for a comfortable sleep. The rooms are all about the 'dark tropical wood floors plus white sheets' look, and it comes off quite well. It's a RM12 taxi ride into town.

Sandakan Harbour Square B&B   HOTEL $
(☑089-223582; www.shsbnb.com; HS10, Harbour Square Complex; dm/d RM20/40, d with bathroom RM45; 🌀🅰) This isn't a B&B as you may think of them – no cute lacy table settings and Devonshire teas. Think more of a modern, somewhat cookie-cutter Sabah budget spot for crashing out. Service is friendly and personable, and fan dorms are dirt cheap (but not dirty). Next to the KFC.

Sandakan Backpackers   HOSTEL $
(☑089-221104; www.sandakanbackpackers.com; Lot 108, Block SH-11, Harbour Square Complex; dm/s/d RM25/40/60; 🌀🅰) This place is one

of the most popular budget deals in town and a firm fixture on the Borneo backpacker trail besides. Clean, well-lit, affordable and a decent place to meet other citizens of Backpackistan.

Swiss-Inn Waterfront Sandakan   HOTEL $$
(☎089-240888; www.swissgarden.com; Harbour Square Complex; r from RM172; ✷🖥✸) If you're in the mood for an essentially Western style waterfront resort, the Swiss Garden is where you want to be. Big rooms, standard chain-style upper-class hotel decor, big windows that look out onto the water – there's no surprises here, and we mean that in a good way. A lovely pool, spa and workout facilities are all on-site at this business-class option. Try negotiating for discounts – it's rarely fully booked.

Hotel Seafront   HOTEL $$$
(☎089-221122; www.hotelsandakan.com.my; Lebuh Empat; r/ste incl breakfast RM240/310; ✷🖥) This is a solid three-star establishment offering comfortable if cookie-cutter Western-style rooms. It's just as luxurious as the Swiss Garden (which is to say, relatively – at the end if the day it's basically a business-man's big box sort of place), but it tends to get busier, this being more of a Sandakan institution. Book online for discounts. In Agnes Keith's time, staying here would have cost you $8...

Winho Lodge   HOSTEL $
(☎089-212310; www.winholodge.com/; Lot 8, Block 19, Jln Dua; dm/s/d incl breakfast from RM25/50/60; ✷@) While the rooms in this budget standby are painted a weird pinkish-tangerine colour that you'd do well to examine with sunglasses on, the Winho (we think it's pronounced 'Wino', but at least one traveller insisted it was 'Win-Ho', which would make sense given the Chinese management) is generally kept clean and fresh and the front desk is good at helping you arrange onward travel.

✗ Eating

For an authentic Malay meal, head to the KFC in the waterfront Harbour Square Complex (but don't eat there!) – the restaurants surrounding it are cheap and flavourful. Most are standard Malay *kedai kopi*, with prices that rarely top RM6 per mains; all are open from roughly 9am to 9pm. Habeeb Restaurant (Jln Tiga) is good for a cheap curry; it's actually part of a chain that serves good Indian Muslim food, so if you see other branches around town, consider them a solid bet.

New Market   FOOD STALLS $
(Jln Pryor; ⊘7am-2pm) Despite being located in what looks like a multistorey car park, this is the best spot in town for cheap eats and stall food. On the bottom floor you'll find the usual 'wet' and 'dry' markets, selling fish, sea cucumber, herbs, vegetables, meat and such. Farmers and fishermen rock up here from their fields and boats throughout the day, bringing fresh produce, bloody butchered meat and flopping denizens of the ocean. Upstairs you'll find strictly halal food stalls, with a mix of Chinese, Malay, Indonesian and Filipino stalls. Hours given for the food stalls above are a bit flexible, but by 3pm most are empty.

Sim Sim Seafood Restaurant   SEAFOOD $
(Sim Sim 8; dishes RM5; ⊘8am-2pm) Located in the heart of the Sim Sim stilt village, this 'restaurant' is more of a dockside fishery, where the daily catch is unloaded and sorted and prepared for the immediate consumption of travellers like you (and a lot of locals). A cluster of red plastic patio furniture huddles in the corner – just grab a seat and point to your prey! Or ask a friendly regular for help ordering; there are lots of off-menu specialities determined by what's caught that day. Ask a cab to drop you off at 'Sim Sim Bridge 8' (they'll very likely know where you're going).

English Tea House & Restaurant
                             TEAHOUSE $$$
(☎089-222544; www.englishteahouse.org; 2002 Jln Istana; mains RM24-40, cocktails RM26.50; ⊘breakfast, lunch & dinner) It seems every place that suffered under colonialism likes to recreate the atmosphere of being a rich colonialist, the English Tea House being Sabah's contribution to the genre. Don your safari suit, wax that moustache and butter that scone, *sahib*. The manicured gardens are a particular joy, with wicker furniture and a small croquet lawn overlooking the bay, perfect for afternoon tea (RM17.25), a round of sunset Pimms, some ice coffee or perhaps some snobbish guffawing as the staff totters around in ridiculously hot suits.

Imperial Bayview   SEAFOOD $$
(☎089-246888; Sandakan Harbor Sq; meals from RM15; ⊘9:30am-2pm & 6-10pm) The Imperial is an enormous emporium of everything related to China and things that comes

from the ocean, the Encyclopaedia Cuisinica of Chinese seafood. You can eat here on the barest budget while enjoying (quite excellent) dim sum and Chinese classics like duck rice and pork belly, or break the bank with RM100 platters of fresh lobster, spotted grouper, cockles, crabs, clams and the rest of the supporting cast of *The Little Mermaid*.

Drinking

If you're wondering where everyone goes when Sandakan shuts down in the evening, just hop in a taxi to Bandar Indah, commonly known as Mile 4 or Batu 4. This buzzing grid of two-storey shophouses is the playground of choice for locals and expats alike, packed with restaurants, bars, karaoke lounges and nightclubs. It comes alive at night in a way that makes central Sandakan seem deader than the morgue in a ghost town. Bars generally close around 1am or 2am, music venues slightly later.

TOP CHOICE **Balin** BAR
(☑089-272988; www.nakhotel.com; Nak Hotel, Jln Pelabuhan Lama; drinks from RM7, mains from RM15; ◷lunch & dinner) Bringing a certain LA rooftop sexiness to Sandakan, Balin is your best bet for nightlife in the city centre. The three tiers of uberchill lounge space are accented by a factory's worth of pillows and some genuinely classy cocktails that any boutique 'mixologist' bar in London or New York would be justifiably jealous of.

Information

Internet Access
Cyber Café (3rd fl, Wisma Sandakan, Lebuh Empat; per hr RM3; ◷9am-9pm)

Medical Services
Duchess of Kent Hospital (☑089-219460; Mile 2, Jln Utara)

Money
HSBC (Lebuh Tiga)

Maybank (Lebuh Tiga) In addition to a full-service bank and ATM, a sidewalk currency-exchange window is open 9am to 5pm daily for changing cash and travellers cheques.

Standard Chartered Bank (Lebuh Tiga)

Wang Liau Chun Mii Moneychanger (Tung Seng Huat, 23 Lebuh Tiga; ◷8.30am-4.30pm)

Post
Main post office (☑089-210594; Jln Leila)

Tourist Information
Tourist Information Centre (☑089-229751; Wisma Warisan; ◷8am-12.30pm & 1.30-4.30pm Mon-Thu, 8-11.30am & 2-4.30pm Friday) Located opposite the municipal offices (known as MPS) and up the stairs from Lebuh Tiga. The staff dispenses advice on everything from regional attractions to local restaurants and can link travellers together for group excursions. One of the more helpful TICs in Sabah.

Getting There & Away

Air
Malaysia Airlines (☑1-300-883000; cnr Jln Pelabuhan Lama & Lebuh Dua & 1st fl, airport) has daily flights to/from KK and KL; it's subsidiary, **MASwings**, located in the same office, offers one daily flight to/from Tawau and two to/from KK. **AirAsia** (☑089-222737; 1st & 2nd fl, Airport) operates two daily direct flights to/from KL and KK.

Boat
Weesam Express (☑089-212872; ground fl, Hotel New Sabah, Jln Singapura)goes to Zamboanga in the Philippines (RM260/280 1st/2nd class) on Tuesday and Friday, leaving Sandakan harbour at 6am and arriving in Zamboanga at 7.30pm the same day. Travellers we spoke to said you didn't need an onward ticket to enter the Philippines, but the Filipino government says otherwise; it may be wise to have one on you just in case.

Bus
Buses and minibuses to KK, Lahad Datu, Semporna and Tawau leave from the long-distance bus station in a large car park at Batu 2.5, 4km north of town (ie not particularly convenient). Most express buses to KK (RM33 to RM40, six hours) leave between 7am and 2pm, plus one evening departure around 8pm. All pass the turn-off to Kinabalu National Park headquarters.

Buses depart regularly for Lahad Datu (RM20, 2½ hours) and Tawau (RM35, 5½ hours) between 7am and 8am. There's also a bus to Semporna (RM30, 5½ hours) at 8am. If you miss it, head to Lahad Datu, then catch a frequent minivan to Semporna.

Minivans depart throughout the morning from Batu 2.5 for Ranau (RM26, four hours) and Lahad Datu (some of those continuing to Tawau). Minivans for Sukau (RM15) leave from a lot behind Centre Point Mall in town.

Getting Around

To/From the Airport
The airport is 11km from the city centre. Batu 7 Airport bus (RM1.80) stops on the main road about 500m from the terminal. A coupon taxi

The term 'orangutan' literally means 'man of the wild', or 'jungle man' – a testament to the local reverence for these great ginger apes. Traditionally, orangutans were never hunted like other creatures in the rainforest; in fact, Borneo's indigenous people used to worship their skulls in the same fashion as they did the heads taken from enemy tribesmen. Orangutans are the only species of great ape found outside Africa. A mature male is an impressive, not to mention hairy, creature with an arm span of 2.25m, and can weigh up to 144kg. Dominant males also have distinctive wide cheek pads to reinforce their alpha status. It was once said that an orangutan could swing from tree to tree from one side of Borneo to the other without touching the ground. Sadly this is no longer the case, and hunting and habitat destruction continue to take their toll; it's estimated fewer than 15,000 specimens now exist in the wild.

If you'd like to get involved with the work of the Sepilok Orang-utan Rehabilitation Centre, contact **Sepilok Orang-Utan Appeal UK** (www.orangutan-appeal.org.uk), a UK-based charity. The Appeal's orangutan adoption scheme is a particular hit with visitors: for UK£30 a year you can sponsor a ginger bundle of fun and receive updates on its progress; see the Appeal's website for details. If you're really taken with the place, Sepilok has one of the most popular overseas volunteer programs in Malaysia. Apply through **Travellers Worldwide** (www.travellersworldwide.com); the cost of an eight-week volunteer package, including accommodation, meals and a number of excursions, was UK£2995 at the time of research.

to the town centre costs RM30; going the other way, around RM25.

Bus & Minivan

Buses run from 6am to 6pm on the main road to the north, Jln Utara, designated by how far from town they go, ie Batu 8. Fares range from RM1 to RM4.

Local minivans wait behind Centre Point Mall; fares cost from RM2. Use for the Pasir Putih seafood restaurants and the harbour area.

To reach the long-distance bus station, catch a local bus (RM1.50) from the stand at the waterfront; it takes about 20 minutes. The same bus leaves when full from the bus station for the city centre.

Taxi

Short journeys around town should cost RM5; it's RM12 to Bandar Indah and RM40 to Sepilok. A taxi from the long-distance bus station to town (or vice versa) will probably run RM20; you may be able to argue drivers down to the local fare of RM10.

Sepilok

How does the wildlife of Borneo move? Pygmy elephants stomp; water monitors waddle; monkeys leap. The orangutan is most graceful of all: it bends the trees to do its bidding, and the most reliable place to see them do so is in the little hamlet of Sepilok, which sees almost as many visitors as the granite spires of Mt Kinabalu.

In fact, this is one of the most popular tourism destinations in Borneo. Sepilok's Orang-Utan Rehabilitation Centre (SORC) is the most popular place on earth to see Asia's great ginger ape in its native habitat. Those who have time to stick around will also uncover several scenic nature walks, a sanctuary for the elusive proboscis monkey and a couple of great places to call home for a night or two.

☉ Sights & Activities

Sepilok Orang-Utan Rehabilitation Centre (SORC)   SANCTUARY
(☎089-531180; soutan@po.jaring.my; admission RM30, camera fee RM10; ⊙9-11am & 2-3.30pm) One of only four orangutan sanctuaries in the world, SORC occupies a corner of the Kabili-Sepilok Forest Reserve about 25km north of Sandakan. The centre was established in 1964; it now covers 40 sq km and has become one of Sabah's top tourist attractions, second only to Mt Kinabalu.

Orphaned and injured orangutans are brought to Sepilok to be rehabilitated to return to forest life. We have to stress: while thousands of people see orangutans during feeding time at Sepilok, there is a chance you won't. These are, after all, wild animals. On the bright side, there are two major feeding times a day, so if you miss them in the morning, you can always try again in the afternoon (or the next day).

Feedings are at 10am and 3pm and last 30 to 50 minutes. Schedules are posted at the **visitor reception centre**. Tickets are valid for one day, although you can see two feedings in the same day. The morning feeding tends to be more tour-group heavy, so if you want a quieter experience, try the afternoon. Use the lockers provided for your valuables – orangutans and macaques have been known to relieve tourists of hats, bags, sunglasses, cameras, even clothing. It's especially important that you don't bring any containers of insect repellent into the reserve, as these are highly toxic to the apes and other wildlife. Spray yourself before entering.

Nature Education Centre

A worthwhile 20-minute video about Sepilok's work is shown five times daily (9am, 11am, noon, 2.10pm and 3.30pm) opposite reception in the auditorium here.

Walking trails

(⊙9am-4.15pm) If you want to explore the sanctuary further, several walking trails lead into the forest; register at the visitor reception centre to use them. Trails range in length from 250m to 4km, and different paths are open at different times of year. Guided night walks can be arranged through the centre or at the various lodges. There's also a 10km trail through mangrove forest to **Sepilok Bay**; this is quite a rewarding walk, and if you're especially fit you may be able to complete it between feeding times. A permit from the **Forestry Department** (☑089-213966; Jln Leila, Sandakan) is required in advance for this route. The department can also arrange basic overnight accommodation at the bay (RM100) or a boat back to Sandakan (RM170). Some travel or tour agencies can assist with the permit and other arrangements.

Rainforest Discovery Centre (RDC)

NATURE RESERVE

(☑089-533780; www.forest.sabah.gov.my/rdc; adult/child RM10/5; ⊙8am-5pm) The RDC, about 1.5km from SORC, offers an engaging graduate-level education in tropical flora and fauna. Outside the exhibit hall – itself filled with displays that are easily accessibly to children – a botanical garden presents varying samples of tropical plant life, the accompanying descriptions every bit as vibrant as the foliage. There's a gentle 1km lakeside walking trail, studded along the way with environmental education signage. A series of eight canopy towers is being built – at the time of research the project was about halfway done, and you can already walk a canopy walkway and peer into the green rooftops of the trees below, by far the most rewarding element of a trip here. Paddleboats (RM5) are available to ride around the inviting lake near the centre's entrance. You can also book night walks, which afford the chance to spot nocturnal animals like tarsiers and wild cats.

It's best to get there either at 8am or 4pm, as wildlife tends to hibernate during the sweltering hours in the middle of the day. A proper visit along the trails and towers takes around 1½ hours. This is a good spot to while away time between feedings at the SORC.

Labuk Bay Proboscis Monkey Sanctuary

RESERVE

(☑089-672133; www.proboscis.cc; admission RM60, camera/video RM10/20) Proboscis monkeys *(Nasalis larvatus)* are an even more exclusive attraction than orangutans. After all, you can see orangutans in Sumatra but the proboscis is found only on Borneo, although if you take a close look at them, you'd swear you've spotted one in the corner at a dodgy bar. Named for their long bulbous noses, proboscis monkeys are potbellied and red-faced, and males are constantly, unmistakably...aroused. With the arrival of Europeans, Malays nicknamed the proboscis *monyet belanda* (Dutch monkey). Because of their diets, proboscis monkeys tend to have severe flatulence, another attractive element of this already most graceful of species. Jokes aside, the proboscis are oddly compelling, and one of nine totally protected species in Sabah.

A local palm-plantation owner has created a private proboscis monkey sanctuary, attracting the floppy-conked locals with sugar-free pancakes at 11.40am and 4.30pm feedings. A third feeding at 2.30pm often occurs during a ranger-led hike deeper in the sanctuary. An estimated 300 wild monkeys live in the 6-sq-km reserve. Animals in the reserve generally steer clear of human contact, except for those mischievous macaques, who just love snacks and sunhats. This is clearly more of a commercial affair than the feedings at the SORC; the proboscis monkeys are enticed onto the main viewing platform so tourists can get better pictures, which may put you off if you're looking for a more ecologically minded experience.

The sanctuary offers package trips. A half-day visit costs RM160, including transfers from Sandakan (RM150 from Sepilok). Overnight trips with meals and a night walk start at RM250. Food and accommodation are provided at the **Nipah Lodge**, on the edge of the oil-palm plantations that surround the sanctuary; the lodge is quite comfortable, a collection of chalets that are simply adorned, airy and inviting in a tropical-chic way. Guests can also venture out on mangrove treks into the surrounding jungle, night treks with guides, and are often invited to give basic English lessons at a nearby village schoolhouse.

Independent travel here is difficult unless you have your own vehicle, as Teluk Labuk (Labuk Bay) sits 15km down a rough dirt track off the main highway. If you're staying here, Nipah Lodge will handle all transfers; otherwise your lodging in Sepilok will be able to arrange transport for around RM110. You can also look for minivans and taxis in the car park of SORC; travellers who want to go to Teluk Labuk should be able to negotiate shared taxis and vans to the proboscis feeding for around RM130 (round-trip from Teluk Labuk back to your Sepilok lodging).

🛏 Sleeping & Eating

If you came to Sandakan for the orangutans of Sepilok, do yourself a favour and stay near the apes. The lodging here tends to have more character than Sandakan spots. Most accommodation options are scattered along Jln Sepilok, the 2.5km-long access road to the rehabilitation centre.

TOP CHOICE **Paganakan Dii** BOUTIQUE HOTEL **$$**
(☎089-532005; www.paganakandii.com; dm/chalet RM30/150; ❄🕾) There are some places that reinvent what budget-to-midrange accommodation is capable of, and Paganakan Dii falls firmly into this vaunted category of hotel. This welcoming and quiet retreat sits deep within a deer preserve, just past a public park. Chic design details made from recycled materials, crisp white linens, smooth wooden chalets, views into a jungle seemingly sliced out of Eden and a ridiculously friendly staff will have you thinking the owners surely left a zero off the price tag. Overall, staying here is a great reason to get stuck in Sepilok...oh right, and don't forget to see the orangutans too...

Transfers to the Sepilok Rehabilitation Centre are included in the price. The ridge chalet are, in our opinion, the best value for money chalets in Sabah, especially seeing as they can be split between three to four people.

Sepilok Nature Resort RESORT **$$$**
(☎089-535001; http://sepilok.com; r RM250; ❄@) This is as luxurious as Sepilok gets – the full five-star tropical treatment. Run by very exclusive Pulau Sipadan Resort & Tours, these rattan-accented chalets are exquisitely decked out and have private verandas overlooking scrumptious gardens and a shaded lagoon. Breakfast (RM35) and dinner (RM55) are available at the on-site restaurant, which cooks the best Western food in Sepilok (not that there's a lot of competition).

Sepilok Forest Edge Resort RESORT **$$**
(☎089-533190, 089-533245; www.sepilokforestedge.com; dm/d/chalets from RM30/70/180; ❄🗗) This fine resort grew out of the excellent Labuk B&B, which is still technically part of the Forest Edge property. Serviceable dorm and double rooms are located in a pretty long house, but it's the chalets that are the property's pièce de résistance. The comfortable cabins are peppered across an obsessively maintained acreage (think golf course). There's a relaxing pool-like jacuzzi on the grounds as well, which is reserved for chalet guests (or backpackers willing to drop an extra RM8).

Sepilok B&B B&B **$**
(☎089-534050, 019-8330901; www.sepilokbednbreakfast.com; Jln Arboretum; dm/s/d RM23/40/60) The former head of Sabah's reforestation division manages this unpretentious option, which has a palpable summercamp vibe. That goes for the large crowds who stay here and the decor of the place, which runs towards stark, simple yet cosy. Crooked picnic tables and varnished lounge chairs offer backpackers plenty of room to chill out after a sweaty day of orangutanning under the equatorial sun. The B&B is opposite the forest research centre, about 250m off Jln Sepilok and 1km short of the SORC entrance.

Uncle Tan GUEST HOUSE **$**
(☎089-531639, 535784; www.uncletan.com; dm/tw incl all meals RM38/100; ❄@) The Uncle Tan empire is one of the oldest backpacker/adventure travel outfits in Sabah. Now he's set up shop right in the heart of Sepilok with a

couple of decent thatch-roofed gazebos and a stack of backpacker shacks.

Sepilok Jungle Resort　　RESORT $$
(☎089-533031; www.sepilokjungleresort.com; dm RM28, r 69-170; ❄@☎) Everyone seems to stay here but it's hard to see why. Well, no, it's not – this is a big stop on the package-tour path. Some rooms are a bit drab: cheap carpeting and bedspreads and musty windows. Renovated rooms are a better deal – the sort of clean, if institutional hotel room you'd expect at home (but in a jungle, so hey).

Most accommodation in the area serves breakfast, and some offer guests three-meal packages. The **SORC cafeteria** (meals from RM5; ☺7am-4pm) vends sandwiches, noodle bowls, rice plates, snacks and beverages, though they are known for running out of items during the tourist rush. **Mah Fung Enterprise** (☺Mon-Sat), across from the turnoff to the RDC, sells cold drinks, snacks, sunscreen and insect repellent. There's also a small hut with a blue fence at Batu 14 serving bread and cold drinks.

ℹ Information

Sepilok's located at 'Batu 14' – 14 miles (23km) from Sandakan. The street connecting the highway to the rehab centre is lined with the listed accommodation (except Pagnakan Dii, which is located on the other side of the road).

It's best to get **money** in Sandakan, but an ATM had been installed in a Petronas Station on the road between Sandakan and Sepilok at the time of research. The next-closest **ATM** is in Sandakan Airport. Money can be changed at upmarket sleeping spots for a hefty change fee.

ℹ Getting There & Away

Bus

Bus 14 from Sandakan (RM3) departs hourly from the city centre. If coming from KK, board a Sandakan-bound bus and ask the driver to let you off at 'Batu 14'. You will pay the full fare, even though Sandakan is 23km away.

Taxi

Taxi 'pirates', as they're known, wait at Batu 14 to give tourists a ride into Sepilok. It's RM3 per person for a lift. Travellers spending the night can arrange a lift with their accommodation if they book ahead of time. Walking to the SORC is also an option – it's only 2.5km down the road.

Van

You can usually organise a pick-up (in a shared van from the Kinabatangan operators) from Sepilok after the morning feeding if you are planning to head to Sungai Kinabatangan in the afternoon.

Sandakan Archipelago

You have to wonder who manages Sabah Tourism's public-affairs office. While everyone knows about the Semporna Archipelago, it seems hardly anyone wants to visit the Sandakan Archipelago, off the coast of its namesake port. What gives? You don't like fluffy specks of emerald that sprout like sandy, beautiful orchids out of the Sulu Sea? Or a lack of crowds? Or tales of POW derring-do? Because all of the above can be found in the Sandakan Archipelago – admittedly more expensive than Semporna, but equally beautiful, trust us.

PULAU LANKAYAN

Pulau Lankayan isn't just photogenic; it's your desktop screen saver. Water isn't supposed to get this clear, nor sand this squeaky clean. A spattering of jungle, a few swaying palms...sigh. No wonder so many lovers come here for their honeymoons, which are often (but not necessarily) accompanied by dive expeditions at **Lankayan Island Resort** (☎089-673999; www.sipadan-resort.com; Batu 6, Bandar Tyng, Sandakan; r RM3160/RM2544), the one accommodation option on Lankayan. There are 23 cabins dotted along the sand where the jungle meets the sea, decked out in flowing light linens and deep tropical hardwood accents, like a ballerina met the island of Bali and had a hotel baby. Transfers from Sandakan are included in your accommodation.

TURTLE ISLANDS NATIONAL PARK (SELINGAN)

Known as Pulau Penyu in Malay, this park 40km north of Sandakan is comprised of three small islands, Pulau Selingan, Pulau Bakungan Kecil and Pulau Gulisan, within swimming distance of nearby islands belonging to the Philippines.

Though numbers have fallen off, two species of marine turtles – the green and hawksbill – come ashore here to lay their eggs at certain times of the year, giving the islands their name. Since the laying seasons for each species are virtually complementary, it's possible to see one or the other at almost any time of year.

PULAU BERHALA

There's been plenty of talk of turning little Berhala island into Sabah's next visitor magnet. Well, proceed with caution, Sabahan government, because Berhala is already supremely serene, an exemplar of a rare genre: a lovely tropical island untouched by tourists. Sandstone cliffs rise above the Sulu Sea, hemming in quiet patches of dusty, sandy prettiness. The vibe is so sleepy it's narcoleptic, an atmosphere accentuated by a quiet water village inhabited by fishing families, loads of migrating birds (their presence is heaviest in October and November) and...well, OK. There's not a lot else, but who cares? Swim in the cerulean waters, have a picnic, smile at everyone, climb to the top of the cliffs and into the local lighthouse and enjoy the wonderful view. It's a good idea to bring some food and water with you

How do you get here? Good question. Pulau Berhala is about 30 minutes from Sandakan by boat, but there was no regular transport service here at the time of research. You're going to need to be savvy and a little aggressive: go to the Sandakan fishing jetties early in the morning and see if you can find a fisherman who will give you a ride (some may be returning home if they live on the island). There's no places to stay out here, so a bed may be part of your negotiations too – or try camping, as some adventurous travellers have done. Expect to pay around RM200 (at least) to charter a boat.

History lesson: Berhala was a leper colony during the colonial period, and the Japanese used the island as a civilian internment centre and POW camp during WWII. Agnes Newton Keith was kept here awhile, as was a group of Australian POWs who managed to escape the island by boat and sail to Tawi Tawi in the Philippines.

Turtle Island Park

Sea turtles are big, graceful, harmless vegetarians that spend most of their lives at sea. Green turtles commonly lay eggs on Pulau Selingan and Pulau Bakungan Kecil between July and October, while the smaller hawksbill turtle lays its eggs on Pulau Gulisan from February to April. The eggs are collected by permanent staff based on Pulau Selingan and transferred to fenced hatcheries, where they are safe from illegal collection by fishermen who eat or sell them.

The only way to visit the Turtle Islands is on an organised tour. While visitor income helps finance the conservation program, the Turtle Island tour is, at best, ill-managed, and at worst a circus. On any one night dozens of gawping tourists cluster round a single laying turtle; this seems to have the effect of scaring some of the reptiles off. Allowing visitors to handle baby turtles before releasing them is highly dubious – besides potential dangers to the turtle, it keeps visitors from regarding the animal as wildlife to be respected. Photography is allowed without flash, but there's *always* one idiot who can't work out how to adjust their camera, and accidental discharges will generally result in the ranger banning pictures altogether.

Many conservationists and nature lovers may find the experience unappealing.

If you decide to go, package prices start from RM220 per person (shared bathroom), going up to RM700 per night for full board, in pleasant air-conditioned chalets, with guide. Tours can be arranged directly through Sandakan travel agencies like **SI Tours** (089-213502; www.sitoursborneo.com; 10th fl, Wisma Khoo Siak Chiew, Lebuh Empat) and **Wildlife Expeditions** (089-219616; www.wildlife-expeditions.com; 9th fl, Wisma Khoo Siak Chiew, Lebuh Empat). These outfits can arrange air-con chalet accommodation on Pulau Selingan and speedboat transfers.

Most boats leave at 9.30am, so you'll have the whole day to hang around the tiny island before the evening turtle viewing. Swimming and snorkelling help pass the time, and there's a small **information centre** (6.30-9pm) above the cafeteria, but you might want to bring a book, as there's not a lot to do between arrival and egg-laying time.

Sungai Kinabatangan

The Kinabatangan River is Sabah's longest: 560km of water so chocolatey brown it would pose a serious safety risk to

THE BUSINESS OF BIRD NESTS

The Gomantong Caves are Sabah's most famous source of swiftlet nests, used for the most revered, rare, luck-and-'strength'-inducing dish of the traditional Chinese culinary oeuvre: the eponymous birds-nest soup. Wait, you ask, people *want* to eat bird nest? Well, it's not twigs and stones folk want to devour: swiftlets make their nests out of their own dried spit, which is the main ingredient in the soup. When added to soup broth, the swiftlet spit dissolves and becomes gelatinous. Wait, you ask, people *want* to eat bird vomit? Er, yes. Very much so.

There are two types of soupworthy bird nests: black and white. Black are a mix of twigs and spit, while the white nests are purely made from the birds' saliva. The white nests are significantly more valuable and Gomantong's got a relatively large amount of them. A kilogram of white swiftlet spit can bring in over US$4000 – that's a dollar sign, not ringitt, folks – making nest-grabbing a popular profession despite the perilous task of shimmying up bamboo poles.

In the last few years visiting has been restricted due to dwindling bird populations (cash-hungry locals were taking the nests before the newborn birds had enough time to mature). Today, the caves operate on a four-month cycle, with closings at the beginning of the term to discourage nest hunters. It's worth asking around before planning your visit – often the caves are empty or off-limits to visitors. The four-month cycles are strictly enforced to encourage a more sustainable practice of harvesting.

Augustus Gloop. It coils like the serpents that swim its length far into the Borneo interior. Riverine forest creeps alongside the water, swarming with wildlife that flee ever-encroaching palm-oil plantations. Lodges are set up all along the banks, while home stay programs pop up with the frequency of local monkeys. Dozens of tin boats putter along the shores offering tourists the opportunity to have a close encounter with a rhinoceros hornbill or perhaps a doe-eyed orangutan.

◉ Sights

Gomantong Caves　　　　　　　　CAVES
(🖉089-230189; www.sabah.gov.my/jhl; adult/child RM30/15, camera/video RM30/50; ⊗8am-noon & 2-4.30pm) Sarawak's Mulu and Niah caverns may be more famous, but for our ringitt, we think the Gomantong Caves give them a run for their money: a massive crack in a mountain, a cathedral-like grand inner chamber formed of limestone, spot-speckled with tubes of golden sunlight and a veritable small hill of bat shit, cockroaches and scorpions. The Gomantong Caves are disgusting, yes, but they're also magnificent.

The forested area around the caves conceals plenty of wildlife and a few good walks – we spotted a wild orangutan out here (best part of our Sabah trip? Yup), which local staff said was rare but not unheard of. The most accessible of the caves is a 10-minute walk along the main trail near the information centre. Head past the living quarters of the nest collectors to get to the main cave, **Simud Hitam** (Black Cave). Venture into the main chamber and keep walking counter-clockwise on the raised platform, which hovers over a steaming soup of bat crap and a chittering, chitinous armour of roaches, centipedes and scorpions. The same lovely mix coats the walkway's handrails, so try not to grip them when you (inevitably) slip on the river o' guano. A 45-minute uphill trek beyond the park office leads to **Simud Putih** (White Cave), containing a greater abundance of prized white nests. Both trails are steep and require some sweaty rock climbing.

The majority of visitors to Gomantong come as part of an add-on to their Kinabatangan tour package. It is possible to visit the caves under one's own steam, though, usually by private vehicle. The turn-off is located along the road connecting Sukau to the main highway and is quite well signposted. Minivans plying the route between Sandakan and Sukau (RM17) can drop you off at the junction, but you'll have to walk the additional 5km to the park office.

Bukit Belanda　　　　　　　　HILL
Bukit Belanda – Dutch Hill – is a 420m hill located behind the village of Bilit. The land is owned by the citizens of Bilit, who,

despite pressures from logging companies, have not opened the hill to the timber industry, preferring to maintain it as a haven for wildlife. You can hike to the top in an hour if you're fit, where you'll be rewarded by lovely views of Sungai Kinabatangan and, if you're lucky, glimpses of local wildlife (at the very least, you're sure to hear the shrieks of local primates). It's best to make this trek early in the morning for purposes of both catching the sunrise and avoiding the heat of the day. There's no official infrastructure when it comes to visiting the hill; just ask someone in your lodge or Bilit itself to guide you to the beginning of the ascent path.

Batu Tulug   CAVES
(☏089-565145; www.museum.sabah.gov.my/agoptulug/cyber_tulugmuseum.htm; admission RM15; ☺9am-5pm, closed Fri) On the road from Sandakan to Lahad Datu you can catch a glimpse of Agop Batu Tulug, a jutting knife of white limestone slicing out of the jungle. This hill, located above the village of Batu Putih, is studded with caves that house the ancestors of both local Chinese and the Orang Sungai (People of the River). Because the Kinabatangan has a habit of frequently flooding, the final resting place of the dead has traditionally been located in cave complexes (a practice that has eroded thanks to Christianity and Islam). Heavy wooden coffins – it must have been an awful effort lugging them up the sheer rocks – are interred in the Batu Tulug caves with spears, knives, gongs, bells and Chinese curios. Some coffins are carved with relatively simple geometric patterns, others in beautiful animal designs. This trove of artefacts makes the hill one of the most important archaeological sites in Sabah. **Sabah Museums** runs the site and has built wooden staircases that snake up the 40m hill. There are two main caves to explore, but if you climb the stairs to the top, you'll be rewarded with a nice view of the surrounding jungle and the Kinabatangan river. An interpretive information centre is also located on the site, but wasn't open to the public at time of research.

The easiest way to get here is to include the caves in your package tour of the Kinabatangan. If you've got your own vehicle, look for signs indicating the turn-off to Batuh Putih or Muzium Batu Tulug on the Sandakan–Lahad Datu road. The village is south of Sukau Junction, about 1½ hours

from Sandakan and 45 minutes from Lahad Datu.

Kinabatangan Orang-utan Conservation Project (KOCP)   RESEARCH CENTRE
(☏088-244502; www.hutan.org.my) Inside Sukau village is this conservation camp dedicated to studying and protecting Sabah's most iconic animal ambassador. The project is run in partnership with HUTAN, a French NGO, which also works with villagers to establish environmental-education programs, reforestation initiatives and an elephant-conservation project in the Sukau-Bilit area. The KOCP is not a tourist-oriented outfit like the Sepilok sanctuary, and as such is not open to casual visitors, but it may be worth contacting it as staff may be willing to hire out guides should you want to go searching for wild orangutans.

🏃 Activities

Wildlife River Cruises   BOAT
Wildlife is the number-one reason to visit Sabah, and a cruise down the Kinabatangan is invariably a highlight for visitors to the state. In the late afternoon and early morning, binocular-toting enthusiasts have a chance of spotting an ark's worth of wildlife – from nest-building orangutans and nosy proboscis monkeys to stealthy samba deer and timid pygmy elephants.

Mammals can be seen all year, moving around in small groups while travelling through plantations. Colourful birds are a huge draw: all eight varieties of Borneo's hornbills, plus brightly coloured pittas, kingfishers and, if you're lucky, a Storm's stork or the bizarre Oriental darter (also known as a snake-bird) all nest in the forests hugging the Kinabatangan. Avian wildlife is more numerous and varied during rainier months (usually October to late March), which coincides with northern-hemisphere migrations. Though friendly for birds, the rainy season isn't very accommodating for humans. Flooding has been a problem of late and a couple of lodges will sometimes shut their doors when conditions are severe.

The success rate of animal-spotting largely depends on luck and the local knowledge of your guide – don't be afraid to ask hard questions about the specifics of your trip before you sign up. Elephants and other larger animals come and go, as herds often break up to get through the palm plantations.

River tours should always be included in lodge package rates. If you prefer to explore independently, contact local home stay programs (see p108), which will be able to hook you up with a boat operator. Or ask about renting a boat in Sukau – everyone in the village is connected to the tourism industry either directly or through family and friends, and someone will be able to find you a captain. Another option: just before the entrance to Sukau village is a yellow sign that says 'Di sini ada boat servis' (Boat service here); different river pilots hang out here throughout the day. Whatever way you choose to find a boat and a guide, expect to pay RM60 to RM80 for a two-hour river cruise on a boat that can hold up to six people (ie you can split the cost with friends).

Trekking

Depending on the location of your lodge, some companies offer short treks (one to three hours) through the jungle. Night hikes are some of the best fun to be had on the Kinabatangan – there's something magical about being plunged into the intense, cavernlike darkness of the jungle at night. Headlamps should be carried in your hand, rather than worn on your head – bats tend to be attracted to light sources and may fly into them; they also secrete an enzyme causing localised paralysis (it's temporary but nonetheless uncomfortable).

Sleeping & Eating

River cruises are exceedingly popular and these days dozens of lodges are vying for your precious ringgit. You'll need to book at all the following places in advance.

In Kinabatangan lingo, a 'three-day, two-night' stint usually involves the following: arrive in the afternoon on day one for a cruise at dusk, two boat rides (or a boat-hike combo) on day two, and an early morning departure on day three after breakfast and a sunrise cruise. When booking a trip, ask about pick-up and drop-off prices – this is usually extra.

SUKAU

Sukau means 'tall tree' in the local dialect, and the name is quite fitting. The tiny town sits on the river among the skyscraping branches of a shaded thicket, across from massive stone cliffs that are quite attractive, seemingly lifted from a Chinese silk-scroll painting. For such a small town, Sukau seems quite blessed by the tourism industry given all the new model Protons being driven about. Today, it's still the most popular place to hang one's hat, but Bilit is also fast increasing in popularity. If you are planning to visit Sungai Kinabatangan on your own, then Sukau is your best option for lodging and river tours.

There is a small **internet cafe** (per hr RM1.50; ⊙9am-6pm) in the cream-tinged building along the main road (yes, the town is *that* small that buildings are referred to by their colour).

Last Frontier Resort   RESORT **$$$**
(☑016-676 5922; www.thelastfrontierresort.com; 3-day, 2-night package RM450; ✳@🛜) Getting to the Last Frontier is a good first step towards better cardiac health: the only hilltop lodge in the Kinabatangan region sits high, high up (538 steps!) on a hill overlooking the flood plains. Sadly a Sherpa is not included in the rates. What you do get is excellent fusion cuisine in the on-site **Monkey Cup cafe** (this place is owned by a Belgian-Malaysian couple – anyone want *frites mit/ avec nasi lemak*?), gorgeous views of the river, well-crafted, simple chalets and a host of trekking options.

Sukau Rainforest Lodge   LODGE **$$$**
(☑088-438300; www.sukau.com; 2-day, 1-night package RM1235; ✳🛜) The Rainforest Lodge has undergone a massive facelift aimed at upping its green credentials. It now participates in tree-planting projects aimed at reviving degraded portions of riverine forest, aims to reduce use of plastics and is pioneering the use of quiet electric motors on its river cruises (which utilise boats made of recycled materials). All this is well and good, but the sleeping experience is lovely as well: swish but unpretentious longhouses dotted into the jungle, situated around a lovely common space stuffed with gongs, tiki torches and *bubu* (local fish traps), welcome guests after their riverine adventures. Don't miss the 440m annotated boardwalk in the back that winds through the canopy.

Kinabatangan Riverside Lodge   LODGE **$$$**
(☑089-213502; www.sitours.com; 3-day, 2-night package RM550; ✳🛜) Come here to fall gently asleep in a series of luxury chalets, adrift in simple white sheets and polished wood floors, all connected by a series of shady raised walkways through the jungle. A looping nature trail is out the back and

an adorable dining area abounds with stuffed monkeys, faux foliage and traditional instruments. Pick-ups can be arranged at Sandakan Airport or at Sepilok Orang-Utan Rehabilitation Centre for an extra fee.

Barefoot Sukau Lodge
LODGE $

(✆089-235525; www.barefootsukau.com; r per person RM80, meals RM25) Take a peek out of Barefoot's cute waterfront cafe, then try to stuff your eyes back in your head: below you is the muddy river, above you a series of slate-grey cliffs mottled with jungle, creeper and vine. The smiley staff directs you to rooms that are small but covered with thick coats of white paint. This is pretty much the best budget option in Sukau outside of home stays.

Sukau Greenview B&B
B&B $

(✆013-869 6922, 089-565266; sukau_greenview@yahoo.com; s/tw RM45/60, meals RM10) A cheapie in central Sukau, this pleasant option offers nine rooms (all with twin-size beds) in a small cottage-style lodge. It's basic (the floors are made from particleboard) but comfy enough for the price. River cruises cost RM35, night rides are RM45 and trips to Oxbow Lake are RM45 (prices are per person). The friendly owners can organise a Sandakan-bound van (RM30 per person) when you depart – it leaves at 6.30am.

Sukau B&B
B&B $

(✆019-583 5580, 089-565269; dm/s/tw incl breakfast RM20/40/40) The road leading into Sukau ends here: a grassy knoll with longhouse-style accommodation and a small cottage out the back. The rooms here feel pretty cheap – you get what you pay for, right? – but this is as budget as the Kinabatangan gets; Two-hour cruises cost RM80 per boat (six person maximum), night cruises are RM100.

BILIT

Bilit is a teeny-weeny village that is primarily full of friendly locals and home stays. River lodges are located on both the Bilit side of the Kinabatangan and the opposite bank. There's a jetty from which boats depart to lodges on the other side of the river, and across the street is a small yard where you can park a car if you drove; the family that owns the house charges RM20 a day for the privilege. At the time of research, locals were planting a small banana orchard that was meant to act as a magnet for pygmy elephants, which are a) popular with tourists and b) have a bad habit of trampling and eating local crops.

Nature Lodge Kinabatangan
LODGE $$

(✆013 863 6263; www.naturelodgekinabatangan.com; 3-day, 2-night package dm/chalet RM320/355) Located just around the river bend from Bilit, this charming jungle retreat is a decent choice for backpacker budgets. The campus of bungalows is divided into two sections: the Civet Wing caters to penny-pinchers with dorm-style huts, while the spiffed-up Agamid Wing offers higher-end twin-bed chalets. Neither sleeping experience will blow you away: mattresses are thin and the rooms get dank after the rains, so don't expect luxury. The activity schedule, on the other hand, is fantastic: the three-day, two-night packages include three boat tours, three guided hikes *and* all meals, which is as good value for money as you'll find in these parts.

Bilit Rainforest Lodge
LODGE $$$

(✆089-202399; http://bilitrainforestlodge.com; 2-day, 1-night package from RM795, 3-day, 2-night package RM1210; ✳🛜) One of the more luxurious sleeping spots along the Kinabatangan, this snazzy option caters to an international clientele with huge bungalows, modern bathrooms and generous amounts of gushing air-con. Common areas are plucked from luxury travel magazine pictorial spreads, and the outdoor bar is especially lovely for night-time drinks. A huge array of package tours is available; see the website for more details.

Bilit Adventure Lodge
LODGE $$$

(✆089-271077; www.stwadventure.com; 2-day, 1-night package from RM620; ✳) This lodge allows you to adventure in style, or at least sleep as such, in a collection of 24 chalets, some fan-cooled and some with air-con, all tastefully decorated in safari style with wooden accents and big fluffy beds. Because the lodge is managed by Sepilok Tropical Wildlife Adventures, there is a great variety of packages on offer here, from one-day river cruises to five-day wildlife and trekking extravaganzas.

Myne Resort
RESORT $$$

(✆089-210837; www.myne.com.my; 2-day, 1-night package from RM855, 3-day, 2-night package RM1350; ✳🛜) The newest upmarket option on the river consists of over a dozen dark-toned chalets wedged into a dual ridgeline that overlooks a sweeping bend

HOME STAYS ON THE KINABATANGAN

If you talk to tourism information types in places like KK or Sandakan, it's easy to walk away with the impression that the only way to reach the Kinabatangan is via a package tour. This is hardly the case. Home stay programs are popping up with increasing frequency in Sukau, Bilit and other villages, giving tourists a chance to stay with local Orang Sungai and inject money almost directly into local economies. Please note the contacts we provide below are for local home stay program coordinators who will place you with individual families.

In Sukau, **Bali Kito Homestay** (☑013-869 9026; http://sukauhomestay.com; sukauhomestay@yahoo.com; r from RM50) can connect you with several different families and, for additional fees, hook you up with cultural programmes, fishing trips, opportunities to work on traditional farms (we're sure the villagers love it when foreigners head into the fields for their vacation), treks, wildlife cruises and other fun. A special walk-in rate of RM30 is also available if you just rock up to the village. A four-person three-day, two-night package that includes meals, four river cruises, transport to and from Sandakan and a visit to the Gomantong Caves runs to RM650 per person, but different packages can be arranged for smaller groups.

In tiny Bilit, we often wondered which houses *weren't* home stays. Contact the exceptionally helpful **Bilit Village Homestay** (☑013-891 3078, 019-537 0843, 019-853-4997; http://bilithomestay.wordpress.com; bilit2002@hotmail.com; r from RM55). This outfit offers package deals that are much the same experience as what you would find in Sukau. Three-day, two-night rates, which include river cruises and trekking, run RM360 per person.

Near Batu Pulih (the village adjacent to the Batu Tulug caves; see p105), **Mescot/Miso Walai Homestay** (☑089-551064, 551070; www.misowalaihomestay.com; r RM70) is one of the oldest, best-run community ecotourism initiatives in the area. By dint of its location, this home stay also happens to be outside the tourist crush in Sukau and Bilit, so your chances of spotting wildlife are a bit better.

When staying in a home stay, it is important to act as a guest in someone's home as opposed to a tourist on holiday. Privacy will be reduced, and you may be expected to help with chores, cooking, cleaning etc (this depends on the family you stay with). Men and women should dress modestly and couples will want to avoid overt displays of affection, which locals tend to frown on. English may not be widely spoken, especially at newer home stays, although you'll be impressed at the multilingual abilities of kids who have grown accustomed to meeting travellers from around the world! The experience is a different one, one which many visitors absolutely love, but it's certainly not everyone's cup of tea. That said, we strongly encourage giving home stays a shot if you haven't done so before.

---

of the Kinabatangan. With fresh smooth sheets, comfy air-con and an enormous deck area for snacking and drinking, this is a solid upper-tier choice that tends to be popular with tour groups from Europe and China.

Kinabatangan Jungle Camp LODGE $$
(☑089-533190; www.kinabatangan-jungle-camp.com; 2-day, 1-night package RM400) This earth-friendly retreat caters to a niche market of birders and serious nature junkies; facilities are functional, with the focus emphasising quality wildlife-spotting over soft, comfortable digs. Packages include three meals, two boat rides, guiding and transfers. The

owners also run the Labuk B&B in Sepilok, and four out of five travellers opt for a Kinabatangan-Sepilok combo tour.

Proboscis Lodge Bukit Melapi LODGE $$
(☑088-240584; http://proboscislodge.com; 2-day, 1-night package tw share per person RM330; ❀) The Proboscis is a study in subdued, simple luxury. The management has created a sociable ambience with its large bar area and comfy tree-stump seating. Wooden bungalows, strewn along a shrubby hill, have oxidised copper-top roofs that clink when it rains. The two-day, one-night packages include three meals, one river cruise and a pick-up from the Lapit jetty.

UPRIVER

Abai Jungle Lodge
LODGE $$$

(☑089-213502, 013-883 5841; www.sitoursborneo.com; 2-day, 1-night packages from US$260) Managed by SI Tours (the same company that runs Kinabatangan Riverside Lodge), Abai Jungle Lodge sits 37km upstream from Sukau just as the river emerges from the secondary forest. This is a great option for the adventurous – isolated and ecologically minded, Abai also manages to feel quite comfortably luxurious. The woodsy exterior pavilions are good for strolling after crashing in your cosy private room. Eco-conscious attempts are being made to increase sustainability: rainwater is collected in cisterns above the chalets, which run on low-emitting diesel engine generators. Tree-planting projects and a bird-observation tower will attract nature enthusiasts as well. The lodge also helps facilitate a local home stay program (RM50 per person per night, including meals).

Uncle Tan's Jungle Camp
LODGE $$

(☑531-639; www.uncletan.com; 2-day, 1-night packages from RM300) Uncle Tan was one of the earliest guides and environmentalists working along the Kinabatangan. Although he died in 2002, his legacy lives on in the form of this lodge, a descendant of his original backpacker mecca. All vaunted history aside, Uncle Tan's competition in the budget stakes is fierce these days, and its position as backpacker mecca feels undeserved. This camp isn't for everyone; some travellers may be put out by the spartan conditions, which are basic (running water is the concession to luxury). Others may embrace the roughing-it attitude, especially as the drop in creature comforts is offset by experienced staff members who are skilled at finding wildlife. The standard package costs RM380 for a three-day, two-night stay in the forest, including meals, boat safaris, jungle treks and transport from its office/B&B in Sepilok (see p101).

ⓘ Getting There & Away

Transfers are usually arranged with your lodging as part of your package, but you can save by arriving independently. Arrange transport from any of the drop-off points (see below) with your tour operator or with a local minivan. Don't get on Birantihanti buses – they stop anytime someone wants to get on or off, which could quadruple travelling time.

Bus & Minivan

From KK Board a Tawau- or Lahad Datu–bound bus (RM35) and ask the driver to let you off at 'Sukau Junction,' also known as 'Meeting Point' – the turn-off road to reach Sukau. If you are on a Sandakan-bound bus, make sure your driver remembers to stop at the Tawau-Sandakan junction – it's called 'Batu 32' or 'Checkpoint' (sometimes it's known as Sandakan Mile 32).

From Sepilok or Sandakan Expect to pay around RM15 to reach 'Batu 32', and around RM20 if you're on a Sandakan–Tawau bus and want to alight at 'Meeting Point'.

From Lahad Datu A minivan ride to 'Meeting Point' from Lahad Datu costs RM20. When buying your bus tickets remember to tell the vendor where you want to get off so you don't get overcharged.

Car

If you are driving, note that the Shell petrol station on the highway at Sukau Junction (at the turn-off to Sukau) is the last place to fill up before arriving at the river. The road to Sukau is pretty smooth, but as you get closer to Bilit you'll start running into some dirt patches. These may be paved by the time you read this, and even at the time of research we found it was possible to get to Bilit via 2WD – just drive carefully, especially if it's been raining.

Lahad Datu

POP 213,100

'Lahad Datu' literally means 'place of princes' in the Sulu dialect, but there's nothing particularly regal about it. In fact, the city would probably qualify as Sabah's most boring destination if it weren't for the rumours of seafaring pirates, who eschew Johnny Depp romanticism in favour of speedboats and machine guns.

There's no real reason to stop here except to arrange a visit to the Danum Valley or Tabin Wildlife Reserve. **Borneo Nature Tours** (☑089-880207; www.borneonaturetours.com; Lot 20, Block 3, Fajar Centre), which runs the Borneo Rainforest Lodge (BRL), and the **Danum Valley Field Centre** (☑089-881092, 881688; danumvalley@gmail.com; Block 3, Fajar Centre) have offices next to each other in the upper part of town – known as Taman Fajr, or Fajar Centre. See p112 for the difference between the two Danum options (and yes, these are your only two options). Most people are here to book a stay in the Danum Valley Field Centre, as those who can afford to stay with Borneo Nature Tours aren't likely to book at the last minute and will probably arrange lodging earlier (either in KK or overseas). Because the Field Centre is exactly that – a research centre that doesn't cater to tourists – its office doesn't tend to respond to emails or phone calls asking for lodging. Instead, you need to show up here, in person, and politely request to speak with someone about sleeping arrangements. We want to stress: you may get lucky with an email or phone call (we did not), but if these methods don't work, you'll need to appear in the flesh.

Around the block, you'll find the booking office of **Tabin Wildlife Holidays** (088-267266; www.tabinwildlife.com.my), a secondary forest sanctuary on the other side of Lahad Datu. As this office is a tourism outfit, it is much better about responding to emails; nonetheless, you'll likely pass through Lahad Datu on your way to Tabin.

Sleeping & Eating

Executive Hotel   HOTEL $$
(089-881333; 238-240 Jln Teratai; s/d/ste from RM130/295/340; ❄@❀) A big 'EH' welcomes guests to Lahad Datu's most upmarket sleeping option. Tuxedoed receptionists move at glacial speeds, but the rooms are good enough for your one-night layover. Go for a superior room – the 'standard' ones don't have windows. There's wi-fi in the lobby which is supposed to be extended throughout the entire property by the time you read this.

Full Wah   HOTEL $
(089-884100; Jln Anggerik; s/d from RM40/60; ❄) If you're on a tight budget, we recommend Full Wah. While located in a *very* dowdy building, the interior rooms are exceedingly mediocre, in a good way – clean, characterless carpets and bedding. This as opposed to mildew ceilings and mouldy bathrooms, which seems the unfortunate norm in Lahad Datu's cheaper accommodation.

MultiBake (cakes from RM1.80; ❀8am-10pm) Malaysia's franchised patisserie is located in Fajar Centre (it has free wi-fi too).

Dovist (mains from RM5; ❀lunch & dinner) Around the corner from the Danum booking offices; a respectable spot for a more substantial meal.

It's worth stopping by one of the convenience stores in Fajar Centre to stock up on a couple of snacks before your trip into the Danum Valley.

🛈 Getting There & Away

Air

MASwings (1800-88 3000, outside Malaysia 03-7843 3000) currently operates four daily flights to Lahad Datu from KK. The airport is in the upper part of town near Fajar Centre. You must take the first flight of the day (departing KK at 7am) if you don't want a one-day layover in town before heading to the Danum Valley.

Bus

Express buses on the KK–Tawau route stop at the Shell station (Taman Fajr) near the Danum Valley office in the upper part of town. Other buses and minivans leave from a vacant lot near Tabin Lodge in the lower part of town. There are frequent departures for Sandakan (RM35, 2½ hours), Sukau (RM20, two hours), Semporna (RM25 to RM30, two hours) and Tawau (RM25 to RM35, 2½ hours). Charter vehicles and 4WDs wait in an adjacent lot; these guys are difficult to hire after sunset.

Danum Valley Conservation Area

Flowing like a series of dark, mossy ripples over some 440 sq km of central Sabah, the Danum Valley is a humid, cackling, cawing mass of lowland dipterocarp arboreal amazement. The forest here is thick – so thick that is has never been (to the best knowledge of anyone living) settled permanently. By humans, that is. Oh, there's life here of another sort in abundance: orangutans, tarsier, sambar deer, bearded pigs, flying squirrel, proboscis monkeys, gibbons and the pygmy elephant (to name a few), watered by Sungai Segama and shaded by 70m-high (!) old-growth canopy and 1093m-high Mt Danum.

This pristine rainforest is currently under the protection of **Yayasan Sabah** (Sabah Foundation; www.ysnet.org.my), a semigovernmental organisation tasked with both protecting and utilising the forest resources of Sabah. They say that at any given time, there are over a hundred scientists doing research in the Danum Valley. Tourists are less frequent visitors, but they are here, and you should count yourself lucky if you join their ranks. That said, to come here you either need a lot of cash or persistence, as the only two places to stay are a very luxurious resort or a budget-priced research centre where the main priority is accommodating scientists as opposed to, well, you. See the website of the **South East Asia Rainforest Research**

Programme (www.searrp.org) for more information on research occurring in the valley.

⊙ Sights & Activities

Both the Borneo Rainforest Lodge (BRL) and the Danum Valley Field Centre offer a variety of jungle-related activities. Only the BRL has official nature guides, whereas the Field Centre offers park rangers.

Trekking

The main activities at the BRL and the Danum Valley Field Centre are walking on more than 50km of marked, meandering trails.

At the BRL, take advantage of the well-trained guides who can point out things you would have never seen on your own. The **Coffincliff Trail** is a good way to start your exploration and get your bearings. It climbs 3km to a cliff where the remains of some Kadazan–Dusun coffins can be seen (although the provenance of the coffins is unclear). After reaching a fairly eye-popping panoramic viewpoint 100m further up the way, you can either return the way you've come or detour around the back of the peak to descend via scenic **Fairy Falls** and **Serpent Falls**, a pair of 15m falls that are good for a quick dip.

The **Danum Trail**, **Elephant Trail** and **Segama Trails** all follow various sections of the Sungai Danum and are mostly flat trails offering good chances for wildlife spotting. All can be done in an hour or two. The **Hornbill Trail** and **East Trail** have a few hills, but are still relatively easy, with similarly good chances for wildlife sightings. Finally, if you just need a quick breath of fresh air after a meal, the **Nature Trail** is a short plankwalk near the lodge that allows you to walk into the forest unmolested by leeches.

There are heaps of fantastic trails weaving around the Field Centre – you must bring a ranger along if you aren't a scientist (note that a guide is better than a ranger though, as rangers are not trained to work with tourists). About a two-hour hike away are the **Tembaling Falls**, a cool slice of tropical Edenic beauty. A more strenuous, four-hour trek gets you to the immensely rewarding **Sungai Purut** falls, a series of seven-tiered pools that are fed by waters that drop down 20m from the nearby mountains.

Birdwatching

Danum Valley is very popular with birdwatchers from around the world, who come here to see a whole variety of Southeast Asian rainforest species, including the great argus pheasant, the crested fireback pheasant, the blue-headed pitta, the Bornean bristlehead and several species of hornbill, among many others. If you're serious about birding, it may be best to stay at the Borneo Rainforest Lodge. The canopy walkway here is ideal for birdwatching, and some of the guides are particularly knowledgeable about birds; attempts are made to match birders up with these pros. The access road to BRL is also a good spot for birding, as is, frankly, your porch.

Canopy Walkway

As you'll probably know, most of the action in a tropical rainforest happens up in the forest canopy, which can be frustrating for earthbound humans. The BRL's 107m-long, 27m-high canopy walkway gives mere mortals a means of transcending the surly bonds of Earth. The swinging bridges traverse a nice section of forest, with several fine *mengaris* and *majau* trees on either side. Birdwatchers often come here at dawn in hopes of checking a few species off their master list. Even if you're not a keen birder, it's worth rolling out of bed early to see the sun come up over the forest from the canopy walkway – when there's a bit of mist around, the effect is quite magical. It's located on the access road, a 10-minute walk from the lodge. You need to be a guest at the BRL to access the walkway.

Night Drives

This is one of the surest ways to see some of the valley's 'night shift', but driving in the forest hardly gets a gold star for eco-friendliness; sensitive souls might empathise with that 'caught-in-the-headlights' feeling. Expect to see one or two species of giant flying squirrels, sambar deer, civets, porcupines and possibly even leopard cats; lucky sightings could include elephants, slow loris and clouded leopards (if you spot those, boy are you ever lucky).

Night drives leave the BRL most evenings; the best trips are the extended night drives, which depart at about 8.30pm and return at 1am or 2am. Things you'll be glad you brought: light waterproof jacket, camera with flash, binoculars and a powerful torch. Drives can be arranged at the Field

Centre as well, although you'll probably have to arrange the vehicle one day in advance.

🍴 Sleeping & Eating

There are two lodging options in the Danum Valley, and you absolutely must have accommodation arranged with one of them before you visit – no dropping in. Each one of the following has its own set of pros and cons. If price is paramount go for the Field Centre. Wildlife fanatics who value professionally trained guides should pick the BRL. The people at Sabah Tourism will try to point you towards the BRL and are reluctant to recommend the Field Centre.

Borneo Rainforest Lodge   RESORT $$$
(BRL; ☎088-267637, 089-880207; www.borneo naturetours.com, www.borneorainforestlodge. com; standard/deluxe 3-day, 2-night full-board package RM1890/2750) is a class act deep within the buzzing haze of Sabah's remaining old-growth forest. Want the experience of staying in an uber-luxurious chalet while keeping an eye peeled for an adorable tarsier? You're in luck. Go for the deluxe if you can; they have private jacuzzis on the wooden verandas that overlook the quiet ravine – romantic as hell. Honeymooners should go for Kempas D11 – this room has a secluded jacuzzi in its own wooden pagoda. Meals are taken on a beautiful terrace also fronting the river. We were pretty impressed with the assortment of dishes at the buffet – especially since it all had to be lugged in by 4WD. The BRL's only downfall is its marketing strategy. Yes, the lodge is lovely and the outdoor jacuzzis in the superior rooms are undoubtedly lavish, but this isn't a five-star resort. And how could it be, surrounded by relentlessly encroaching jungle and steamy tropical mist? We're impressed, though, that this much luxury exists so deep in the rainforest. Guests who temper their expectations will adore the ambience and find plenty of creature comforts at their fingertips (no air-con though). It's best to book online or in KK.

Danum Valley Field Centre   LODGE $$
(DVFC; ☎089-8841100/1, 088-881688; resthouse r & board from RM160, camping RM30; 🌐) An outpost for scientists and researchers, the field centre also welcomes tourists. Accommodation at the centre is organised into four categories: hostel, resthouse, VIP and camping. We recommend the resthouse rooms, which are located at arm's length from the canteen (the only place to eat). These rooms are basic but clean, sporting ceiling fans and twin beds. Towels are provided for the cold-water showers. The simple hostel is about a seven-minute walk from the canteen, and the barracks-style rooms are separated by gender. If you want to camp, you can lay your sleeping kit (no tent needed) out on the walkways – bug spray recommended! All buildings at the field centre run on generated power, which shuts off between midnight and 7am. There are no professionally trained guides at the centre – only rangers who can show you the trails. You might luck out and find a friendly researcher who will point you in the direction of a few cool things, but some of the scientists (especially the birders) value their privacy (and can you blame them?). There is a kitchen on the campus, however it is reserved for the research assistants. Tourists take their meals in the cafeteria-style canteen (vegie-friendly). For booking here, see our section on Danum Valley accommodation in Lahad Datu (p110).

❶ Getting There & Away

Bus & Car

The Danum Valley is only accessible by authorised private vehicle. Borneo Rainforest Lodge guests depart from the lodge office in Lahad Datu at 9am, arriving by lunchtime. If you do not want to spend the night in Lahad Datu, it is recommended you take the morning MASwings flight from KK arriving in Lahad Datu at 7.55am. If you've prebooked, the driver will wait should your flight be delayed.

Tourists staying at the Danum Valley Field Centre must board one of two jungle-bound vans that leave the booking office in Lahad Datu at 3.30pm on Mondays, Wednesdays and Fridays. Transport is RM100 per person each way. Vans return to Lahad Datu from the Field Centre at 8.30am on the same days.

Chartering a private vehicle into the park costs at least RM300.

Tabin Wildlife Reserve

Tabin's patch of jungle is starting to emerge as an alternative to the Danum Valley. The 1205-sq-km reserve consists mainly of lowland dipterocarp forest with mangrove areas – most of it is technically secondary forest, but that doesn't seem to trouble the wildlife or visitors. The stars here are the elephants and primates – gibbons, red-leaf monkeys and macaques, plus a lot of orangutans. Rescued orangs from Sepilok are actually released here, so you've got a pretty good chance of spotting some hairy red primates in the wild. Birdlife is abundant, and there's a herd of the endangered Sumatran rhino, though you're unlikely to see them.

The park is managed by **Tabin Wildlife Holidays** (☎088-267266; www.tabinwildlife. my; Lot 11-1, Block A, Damai Point, Kota Kinabalu; 2-day, 1-night package from RM900), which runs the on-site Tabin Wildlife Resort, an attractive retreat with a clutch of upscale chalets. Five trails snake out into the jungle from in front of the resort. Try the Elephant Trail (800m) if you're interested in belching mud pits. The Gibbon Trail (2.8km) leads to the pretty Lipa Waterfall.

An all-inclusive day-trip package to the park (8am to 2.30pm) costs RM210 per person. The three-day, two-night 'Observation 'n' Nature' package will set you back RM1010.

Tabin can be accessed with a rental vehicle (4WD is a must). You can try just showing up to the gate with nothing booked on the inside; you may be cheerfully waved in or made to wait or turned back – it depends on the guard. There are several entrances to the reserve; the easiest one to navigate to is near the junction of Ladan Tungju and Ladang Premai (it's 15km from Lahad Datu airport to Ladang Kajai). Pay the RM5 entry fee at the park's second gate (there are six gates in total).

Semporna

POP 140,400

Most travellers, upon reaching Semporna, turn into little kids on a long car trip: 'But how much *longer* till we get there,' with 'there' being Sipadan. Semporna-the-town is the mainland stopping point before Semporna-the-archipelago and all your diving/snorkelling fantasies. Unless you're lucky enough to get here early in the morning, there's a good chance you'll be sticking around overnight. Usually, this is the part where we say, 'But there's more to Semporna than onward travel to the islands', but for the average traveller, there's not. In fact, thanks to large numbers of decidedly tough-looking unemployed young men, this is one of the few places in Sabah

where we felt a bit uncomfortable at night. Semporna's fine for an evening of carousing at a bar before donning your fins or checking out the many *pasar ikan* (fish markets; see, there *is* more than onward travel); past that, enjoy your sleep. Not much longer, kids.

◎ Sights & Activities

'Diving' or (rarer) 'snorkelling' is the answer every tourist gives when someone asks them why they're in Semporna. Scuba is the town's lifeline, and there's no shortage of places to sign up for it. Operators are clustered around the 'Semporna Seafront', while other companies have offices in KK. Due to the high volume of interest, it is best to do your homework and book ahead – diving at Sipadan is limited to 120 persons per day. If time isn't an issue, consider swinging through town to examine your options, book your dive package, and come back a few weeks later to hit the waves.

See p115 for everything you need to know about diving at Sipadan (and at the other sites in the Tun Sakaran Marine Park).

🛏 Sleeping

If you have to overnight in Semporna, your options are limited – but not dire. If you've already signed up with a scuba operator ask them about sleeping discounts (and don't be shy about trying to finagle a good deal, especially if you're sticking around for a while).

Seafest Hotel   HOTEL **$$**

(☎089-782333; www.seafesthotel.com; Jln Kastam; r RM90-260; ❄) If we must overnight in Semporna, we prefer doing so in the jauntily-dubbed Seafest: six storeys of bay-view, business-class comfort at the far end of the 'Semporna Seafront' neighbourhood. It's affiliated with Seafest fishery, so check the restaurant's catch of the day. Don't be shy about asking for discounts, and note suites aren't really worth the extra ringgit.

Dragon Inn   HOTEL **$**

(Rumah Rehat Naga; ☎089-781088; www.dragoninnfloating.com.my; 1 Jln Kastam; dm RM15-20, r incl breakfast RM70-99; ❄@) The owners of Dragon figured 'Tourists want stilt houses built over the water and tiki tropical decor' and ran with that theme several miles. It's a bit tacky, but in an endearing way. The water the Inn stands over is green slop, but

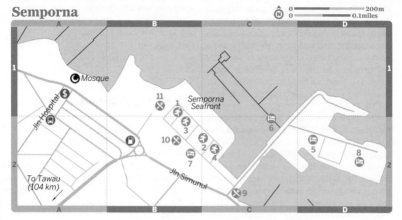

Semporna

Activities, Courses & Tours

Sleeping

Eating

Drinking

the staff is so friendly and eager to please we forgive this minor trespass.

Scuba Junkie Backpackers HOSTEL $
(☑089-785372; www.scuba-junkie.com; Lot 36, Block B, Semporna Seafront; dm/r RM40/100; ❋@) A sociable, clean and basic spot offering 50% discounts for divers who book through Scuba Junkie. There's an adjacent bar (open from 4pm till the last guest passes out) that gets kicking with the dive instructor set come night.

Borneo Global Sipadan BackPackers
HOSTEL $
(☑089-785088; borneogb@gmail.com; Jln Causeway; dm/tr incl breakfast RM22/90; ❋) Near the Seafest (on the seafront – say that three times fast), this dullish spot is cheap and cheerful, if without character. Although there are posters of fish, to remind you of why you came to Semporna, we guess.

✗ Eating

Just across the street from the Scuba Junkie hotel is a **street hawker** who claims he once cooked for the prime minister of Malaysia; he'll likely regale you with a sales pitch in the evening. We can't vouch for the truth of this, but he did cook us up a very tasty, screamingly fresh seafood meal for RM25, which went down a treat with a cold beer. Various *kedai kopi* line the 'Semporna Seafront', while restaurants at the Seafest Hotel complex offer Chinese seafood. If you wanna go native, sample the *nasi lemak* or *korchung* (rice dumplings) – Semporna is well known for these two dishes.

Anjung Paghalian Café SEAFOOD $
(Jln Kastam, mains RM3-5; ⊙5pm-10pm) Beside the Tun Sakaran Marine Park entrance sign, this indoor-outdoor place on a pier features fish, prawn, chicken, squid and venison sold by portions (for two or more people) and cooked in your choice of up to 12 different styles. It also has standard Malay hawker stalls and even one which serves burgers.

Mabul Steak House STEAKHOUSE **$$**

(☑089-781785; Semporna Seafront; mains from RM11; ⊙noon-11pm) This easygoing balcony restaurant's large and glacial 'ice-blended juices' are a soothing antidote for sucking bottled air. For further chilling, there's a leather couch and overstuffed chairs around a huge TV showing movies or sport. Malaysian standards are done well, and the signature steaks are a surprisingly mouth-watering treat after long days of diving.

❶ Information

If you're arriving in Semporna under your own steam, leave the bus and minivan drop-off area and head towards the mosque's spiking minaret. This is the way to the waterfront. Follow the grid of concrete streets to the right until you reach 'Semporna Seafront' – a collection of buildings decked out in primary colours that starkly contrast with the charmless pastels throughout the rest of town. This neighbourhood is home to the diving outfitters, each stacked one next to the other in a competitive clump. Sleeping and eating options, plus a host of internet cafes, crowd around here too.

Decompression Chamber (☑089-783100) The Semporna navy base has the closest decompression chamber .

Maybank (☑089-784852; Jln Jakarullah) Expect small lines and the occasional beggar, especially in the evening.

❶ Getting There & Away

Air

Flights to Tawau from KK and KL land at Tawau Airport, roughly 28km from town. A private taxi from Tawau airport to Semporna costs RM90, while Tawau–Semporna buses (RM15) will stop at the airport if you ask the driver nicely. Buses that do not stop at the airport will let you off at Mile 28, where you will have to walk a few (unshaded) kilometres to the terminal. Remember that flying less than 24 hours after diving can cause serious health issues, even death.

Bus

The 'terminal' hovers around the Milimewa supermarket not too far from the mosque's looming minaret. All buses run from early morning until 4pm (except Kota Kinabalu) and leave when full.

Kota Kinabalu (RM50, nine hours) leaves at around 7am or 7pm.

Lahad Datu (RM20 to RM25, 2½ hours)

Sandakan (RM35 to RM40, 5½ hours)

Tawau (RM15, 1½ hours)

Semporna Archipelago

Take the word 'blue' and mentally turn it over through all of its possibilities. From the deepest, richest shades to the light robin's egg shade of the sky to kelp-like aqua. This is the rippled waterscape of the Semporna Archipelago, broken up with pebbles of white sand and swaying palms and the rainbow-coloured boats of copper-skinned Sea Gypsies. But no one comes this way for islands, such as it were – rather it is the blue, the ocean and everything beneath it, that appeals, because this is first and foremost a diving destination, one of the best in the world. Sipadan's technicolour sea walls reach deep down – 2000m to the distant ocean floor – and act like an underwater beacon luring docile turtles, slippery sharks and waving mantas.

❂ Sights & Activities

Maybe the name Semporna doesn't ring a bell – that's because the key word here is 'Sipadan'. Located 36km off Sabah's southeast coast, **Sipadan** (also called 'Pulau Sipadan') is the shining star in the archipelago's constellation of shimmering islands. The elliptical islet sits like a clay-tinged crown atop a stunning submerged pinnacle with its world famous near-vertical walls. This underwater beacon is a veritable way station for virtually all types of sea life, from fluttering coral to school-bus-sized whale sharks. Sea turtles and reef sharks are a given during any dive, and luckier scubaholics may spot mantas, eagle rays, octopus, scalloped hammerheads and water monitors that could double as Godzilla.

Roughly a dozen delineated dive sites orbit the island – the most famous being the aptly named **Barracuda Point**, where streamers of barracuda collide to form impenetrable walls of undulating fish. Reef sharks seem attracted to the strong current here and almost always swing by to say hello. **South Point** sits at exactly the opposite end of the island from Barracuda Point and usually hosts the large pelagics (manta magnet!). The west side of the island features technicolour walls that tumble down to an impossibly deep 2000m – words can't do the sight of this justice. The walls are best appreciated from out in the blue on a clear afternoon. The east coast tends to be slightly less popular, but that's a relative statement – oodles of turtles and sharks are still inevitable.

Although Sipadan outshines the neighbouring sites, there are other reefs in the marine park that are well worth exploring. The macro-diving around **Mabul** (or 'Pulau Mabul') is world-famous. In fact, the term 'muck diving' was invented here. The submerged sites around **Kapalai**, **Mataking** and **Sibuan** are also of note.

While it is possible to rock up and chance upon an operator willing to take you to Sipadan the following day, we strongly suggest that you book in advance. There are travellers and operators who say we are being too cautious with this advice, but your holiday is likely limited, and frankly, better safe than sorry. The downside to prebooking, of course, is that you can't visit each dive centre's storefront to suss out which one you like best, but Johnny-come-latelies might be forced to wait a few weeks before something opens up.

The government issues 120 passes (RM40) to Sipadan each day (this number includes divers, snorkellers and day trippers). Bizarre rules and red tape, like having certain gender ratios, make the permit process even more frustrating. Each dive company is issued a predetermined number of passes per day depending on the size of its operation and the general demand for permits. Each operator has a unique way of 'awarding' tickets – some companies place their divers in a permit lottery, others promise a day at Sipadan after a day (or two) of diving at Mabul and Kapalai. No matter which operator you choose, you will likely be required to do a non-Sipadan intro dive unless you are a Divemaster who has logged a dive in the last six months. Permits to Sipadan are issued by day (and not by dive) so make sure you are getting at least three dives in your package.

A three-dive day trip costs between RM250 and RM500 (some operators include park fees, other do not – make sure to ask), and equipment rental (full gear) comes to about RM50 or RM60 per day. Cameras (around RM100 per day) and dive computers (around RM80 per day) are also available for rent at most dive centres. Top-end resorts on Mabul and Kapalai offer all-inclusive package holidays (plus a fee for equipment rental).

Although most of the diving in the area is 'fun diving', Open Water certifications are available, and advanced coursework is popular for those wanting to take things to the next level. The only problem with getting your Open Water certification here is that all other dive sites may pale in comparison! Diving at Sipadan is geared towards divers with an Advanced Open Water certificate (currents and thermoclines can be strong), but Open Water divers should not have any problems (they just can't go as deep as advanced divers). A three-day Open Water course will set you back between RM750 and RM850. Advanced Open Water courses (two days) cost around RM700 to RM850, and the Divemaster certification runs for around RM1900.

DON'T MISS

REGATTA LEPA

The big annual festival of local Bajau Sea Gypsies is the Regatta Lepa, held in mid-April. (A *lepa* is a type of small boat, so the title somewhat redundantly means 'Boat regatta'.) Traditionally, the Bajau only set foot on mainland Borneo once a year; for the rest of the time they live on small islets or their boats. Today the Bajau go to Semporna and other towns more frequently for supplies, but the old cycle of annual return is still celebrated and marked by the regatta *lepa* . For visitors, the highlight of the festival is the *lepa*-decorating contest held between Bajau families. Their already rainbow-coloured boats are further decked out in streamers, flags (known as *tapi*), bunting, ceremonial umbrellas (which symbolise protection from the omnipresent sun and rain that beats down on the ocean) and *sambulayang*, gorgeously decorated sails passed down within Bajau clans. On each boat you can see a smaller, rectangular *lamak kapis* sail and the larger *lamak bua'an* sail, shaped to resemble the maw of a fish. Violin, cymbal and drum music, plus 'sea sports' competitions like duck catching and boat tug-of-war, punctuate the entire affair. It's a hell of a show. The regatta occurs in mid-April; check www.etawau.com for details, and don't miss the show if you're in town at this time of year.

Many nondivers wonder if they should visit Semporna. We give a qualified 'yes'. The diving here is obviously the main draw, as there are no real beaches to speak of (besides some small patches of sand). But if you like snorkelling, there's some incentive to come out this way. Snorkelling is not the obsessive hobby that diving is – people don't plan their holidays around it the way they do with diving. But if you're travelling in a group or as a couple where some dive and some don't, the Semporna islands are a lot of fun; dive and snorkelling trips are timed so groups leave and come back at similar times, so you won't feel isolated from each other. If you're on your own and only want to snorkel, it's still pretty great, but not as world class as the diving experience, and a bit pricey relative to the rest of Malaysia – snorkel trips cost around RM100 to RM150, and you also have to factor in the relatively high cost of accommodation here and the price of getting out to the islands. Then again, you still have a good chance of seeing sting rays, sea turtles and all sorts of other macro-marine wildlife while in the midst of a tropical archipelago, so really, who's complaining?

The following dive operators are among the growing list of companies in the area. Several operators are based at their respective resorts, while others have shopfronts and offices in Semporna and/or KK. Please note we have listed the following alphabetically, not in order of preference – we simply didn't have the time to go diving with every outfitter in the islands. No matter where your desired operator is located, it is *highly* recommended you contact them in advance.

Billabong Scuba   DIVING
(☎089-781866; www.billabongscuba.com; Lot 28, Block E, Semporna Seafront) Semporna-based outfit with reasonable prices. Accommodation can be arranged at a rickety 'home stay' on Mabul.

Blue Sea Divers   DIVING
(☎089-781322; www.blueseadivers-sabah.com; Semporna Seafront) Reputable day-trip operator in Semporna. Request chicken curry for your postdive lunch.

Borneo Divers   DIVING
(☎088-222226; www.borneodivers.info; 9th fl, Menara Jubili, 53 Jalan Gaya, Kota Kinabalu) The original operators in the area, Borneo Divers unveiled Sipadan to an awestruck Jacques Cousteau. It has maintained its high standards throughout the years, offering knowledgeable guides and comfy quarters. The office is located in Kota Kinabalu. See p118 for information about its comely resort on Mabul. Recommended.

Scuba Junkie   DIVING
(☎089-785372; www.scuba-junkie.com; Lot 36, Block B, Semporna Seafront) Popular with the young backpacker crowd, Scuba Junkie invented the hard sell in Semporna. Prices are kept low and diving gear is well maintained. Ask about cheap sleeps – staff'll hook you up with a budget bed on Mabul or in the hostel across from its storefront in Semporna (p114). If you're sleepless in Semporna, stop by its restaurant in the wee hours for some greasy pizza.

Scuba Jeff   DIVING
(☎019-5855125, 017-8690218; www.scubajeffsipadan.com) Jeff, a friendly local bloke, runs his adventures out of the local fishing village in Mabul (p119). Good option for the budget crowd.

Seaventures   DIVING
(☎088-261669; www.seaventuresdive.com; 4th fl, Wisma Sabah, Kota Kinabalu) A professional, highly regarded outfit that will put you up in an ocean platform(!) off the coast of Mabul (p118). Offices in KK.

Sipadan Scuba   DIVING
(☎089-784788, 089-919128; www.sipadanscuba.com; Lot 23, Block D, Semporna Seafront) Twenty years of Borneo experience and an international staff makes Sipadan Scuba a reliable choice. This is the only PADI 5 Star Instructor Development Centre in Semporna. Recommended.

Sipadan Water Village   DIVING
(☎089-751777, 089-950023, 089-784100; www.swvresort.com; Jln Kastam) A private operator based at the Mabul resort with the same name (p119). Has offices in the Monaco Dynasty Hotel in Tawau and along the Semporna Seafront.

SMART DIVING

(☎088-486389; www.sipadan-mabul.com.my)
The dive centre operating at Sipadan-Mabul Resort and Mabul Water Bungalow; both are located on Mabul (p118). Also has offices in KK.

Uncle Chang's DIVING

(Borneo Jungle River Island Tours; ☎089-785372; 36 Semporna Seafront) Offers diving and snorkelling day trips, plus stays at its 'lodge' on Mabul (p119) (RM80 per person).

🛏 Sleeping & Eating

From opulent bungalows to ragtag sea shanties, the marine park offers a wide variety of accommodation catering to all budgets. Sleeping spots are sprinkled across the archipelago with the majority of options clustered on the peach-fringed island of Mabul (Sipadan's closest neighbour).

At almost all of the places listed below, you are tied to a set schedule of three to five meals broken up by roughly three diving (or snorkelling) trips per day. Meals are included; drinks are always extra, although tea and coffee are often gratis. If you feel the need to let loose at night, there are occasional parties at Uncle Tan's or Scuba Junkie on Mabul. High-end resorts have their own bars and restaurants; you may be able to eat and drink here if you're staying in a budget spot if the man at the gate is in a good mood, but you'll pay for it.

Divers and snorkellers can also opt to stay in the town of Semporna, which offers a slightly better bang for your buck, but you'll miss out on postdive chill sessions and fiery equatorial sunsets that plunge into the crystalline sea. Perhaps more pertinently, it takes at least 30 minutes, and usually a bit longer, to get to dive sites from Semporna town.

Every one of the accommodation options listed below can arrange diving trips, including certification courses and trips to Sipadan.

SIPADAN

Although it has been several years since the government banned Sipadan sleepovers, we just wanted to reiterate that it is not possible to stay here. The island is under the control of the Wildlife Department and is patrolled by rangers and local army personnel. Day trips to the island and its house reef are capped at 120 individuals.

SINGAMATA

Not an island at all, but rather a floating village built onto a sandbar about 30 minutes from Semporna, Singamata (☎089-784828, 019-8430550; www.singamata.com; dm RM50, d RM175 or RM130 per person for 2) is a ridiculously beautiful assemblage of stilt chalets and decks with its own pool full of giant fish (which you can snorkel amid). If you feel like dipping into the water, you can literally just step out of your room (annoyingly, rubbish from Semporna sometimes still floats into the vicinity). Rooms are basic but pretty and breezy. You may feel isolated out here, but if you need a budget escape from it all, this is a lovely option.

MABUL

Mabul is the main accommodation centre in the islands. This is a pretty little speck of land, blessed with one very small white-sand beach, fantastically blue waters and two small settlements: a camp of Bajau Sea Gypsies and a Malaysian water village of stilt houses built over the seashore, where most of the island's budget accommodation is clustered. Question: Do sea gypsies sell tourists tacky seashell souvenirs? Answer: Yes.

It's worth having a walk around the island, which should take you all of an hour or two. Behind the resorts are generators and barracks-style housing for resort staff. The locals are quite friendly and eager for your business; there's dozens of little shops in the villages that sell candy, crisps, cigarettes and other little incidentals. Plus watching the sunset bleed the ocean from red to orange to lavender to cool blue over stilt houses, as the Bajau set cooking fires in their houseboats, is mind-blowingly romantic, and a bit unexpected in a place that's so marketed towards diving.

Mabul Beach Resort RESORT $$

(☎089-785372; www.scuba-junkie.com; dm RM80, r RM150-270; ❄🛜) Owned and operated by Scuba Junkie, this spot is all the rage with the flashpacker crowd. Chalets with en suite bathrooms, porches and polished wood floors make for some posh digs priced (relatively) within the top of the budget range. Note the room prices are for single occupancy – rooms all have two beds, and are cheaper if rented out by two.

Mabul Water Bungalow RESORT $$$

(☎088-486389; www.mabulwaterbungalows. com; 3-day, 2-night dive package from RM3150, nondivers RM1910; ✴🛜) Um...wow. Two things travellers love about Asia: crystal-clear water and temples. These two concepts come together with a heaping dash of amazing at Mabul Water Bungalows, a gorgeously executed series of chalets-cum-Balinese shrines built over the Celebes Sea. This is easily the best upmarket option on Mabul. Rooms are effortlessly opulent, and the resort's only suite, the Bougain Villa (ha!), features a trickling waterfall in the bathroom, its own private dock and glass floors revealing the starfish-strewn sea floor.

Borneo Divers Mabul Resort   RESORT $$$
(☏088-222226; www.borneodivers.info; 3-day, 3-night dive packages from US$690, nondivers $549; ✴@🛜) The oldest dive centre in the region offers lodging in a horseshoe of semi-detached mahogany bungalows with bright-yellow window frames. Open-air pavilions with gauzy netting punctuate the perfectly manicured grounds. Wi-fi is available in the dining room.

Scuba Jeff   LODGE $
(☏019-5855125, 017-8690218; www.scubajeff sipadan.com; r RM60-80) Jeff is a very friendly dude, always up for a chat, a beer or a smoke, who maintains this large stilt house in the Malay fishing village. While his place is a little tatty, it reminds us of the fun of backpacking – staying in a flophouse and meeting random folk on a budget (including quite a few backpacking Malays).

Arung Hayat Resort   HOME STAY $
(☏089-782526; www.arunghayat.com; per person r/ste RM70/90) Also located in Mabul's fishing village, this is a friendly home stay with low-slung beds, baby-blue walls and plenty of smiles located in a stilt-house over the water. Staff'll help arrange dive trips for you and the owners cook up some mean fish.

Uncle Chang's   GUEST HOUSE $
(☏017-895002, 089-786988; www.ucsipadan.com; per person dm/s/d RM60/80/90, per person d with air-con & bathroom RM90; ✴) A Sipadan backpacking stalwart catering to the like-named dive operator, Chang's is a fun, sociable spot that periodically throws kicking little parties. The air-con rooms, clocking in at RM90, are good value for money.

Seaventures Dive Resort   RESORT $$$
(☏088-261669; www.seaventuresdive.com; 5-day, 4-night dive package from RM2720; ✴) This oil rig (no, really) sits just off Mabul's silky shoreline. There are two schools of thought on Seaventures' aesthetic impressions: a) 'A worthy attempt at giving tourists a unique accommodation option; and b) 'That thing? Forget it.' Honestly, we're not sure where we fall in this debate, but its diving staff comes well recommended at least.

Billabong   GUEST HOUSE $
(☏089-781866; www.billabongscuba.com; per person r RM70) Hey – *another* home stay built into the local water village. Chill with fishermen, watch the sunset over the plankboards and set out for some diving adventures with associated Billabong Scuba.

Lai's Homestay   HOME STAY $
(per person r RM70) Features a large, wood-planked veranda stretching over the sea. The rooms are clean and breezy; this is one of the newer home stays in the fishing village, although still shanty-esque (in a shanty-chic kinda way).

Sipadan-Mabul Resort   RESORT $$$
(SMART; ☏088-486389; www.sipadan-mabul. com.my; 3-day, 2-night dive package from US$762, nondivers US$503; ✴🛜♨) Even though the summer-camp styling suits the tropical landscape, the prices here are a bit out of whack. If you're gonna splurge why not go all the way and snag a room at SMART's sister property (see p118). Wi-fi is available in the dining area.

Sipadan Water Village Resort   RESORT $$$
(☏089-751777; www.swvresort.com; 4-day, 3-night package from RM3800; ✴@) Outmoded design details (although when were wooden tarantula ornaments ever in style?) quickly set the tone here – this resort-on-stilts doesn't pull off 'graceful elegance' quite like Mabul Water Bungalow next door, despite the idyllic location. If you decide that this is the spot for you, then go for the 'grand deluxe' bungalows.

KAPALAI
Although commonly referred to as an island, Kapalai is more like a large sandbar sitting slightly under the ocean surface. From afar, the one hotel, **Kapalai Resort** (☏088-238113; www.dive-malaysia.com; Block B, 1st fl, Plaza Tanjung Aru, Jln Mat Salleh, Kota Kinabalu; 4-day, 3-night package from RM2480; ✴@), looks like it's sitting on palm trunks in the middle of the sea. The resort designers went for a Sea Gypsy theme and tacked on an opulent

twist, making the sea cabins out of shiny lacquered wood.

MATAKING

Mataking is also essentially a sandbar, two little patches of green bookending a dusty tadpole tail of white sand. **Mataking Island Resort** (☑089-770022, 089-782080; www.matakingisland.com; Jln Kastam, Semporna; 3-day, 2-night package for divers/nondivers from RM2470/2110; ❀@) is the only accommodation here. This is an impeccably luxurious escape full of dark-wood chalets and gossamer sheets. This sandy escape has some beautiful diving – an artificial reef and sunken boats provide haven for plenty of sea life – and has set up a novel 'underwater post office' at a local shipwreck site.

POM POM

Pom Pom needs no cheerleading – this stunning, secluded haven sits deep within the Tun Sakaran Marine Park, about one hour by boat from Semporna. **Sipadan Pom Pom Island Resort** (☑089-781918; http://pompomisland.com; 3-day, 2-night package for divers/nondivers from RM1700/1200; ❀@) runs the only operation on the island. The poshest rooms are built over the water, while reed-and-thatch bungalows offer sea views from spacious balconies. The cheapest rooms are set back in a 'garden' area, but are still basically a hop from the ocean.

ROACH REEFS

This network of artificial reefs was once the private underwater playground for a wealthy businessman, but today **Roach Reefs Resort** (☑089-779332; www.roachreefsresort.com; 2-day, 1-night package for divers/nondivers from US$345/278; ❀@) has opened its doors to tourists. You'll stay in simple shacks (a little *too* simple, frankly; we wouldn't mind a little more flash at these prices) plunked in a man-made spit of sand, shaded under coconut trees. Keep in mind boat transfers here come from Tawau, as opposed to Semporna.

❶ Information

The Semporna Islands are loosely divided into two geographical sections: the northern islands (protected as **Tun Sakaran Marine Park**, gazetted in 2004) and the southern islands. Both areas have desirable diving – Sipadan is located in the southern region, as is Mabul and Kapalai. Mataking and Sibuan belong to the northern area. If you are based in Semporna you'll have

a greater chance of diving both areas, although most people are happy to stick with Sipadan and its neighbours.

Consider stocking up on supplies (sunscreen, mozzie repellent etc) before making your way into the archipelago. Top-end resorts have small convenience stores with inflated prices. ATMs are nonexistent, but all resorts accept credit cards (Visa and MasterCard). Mabul has a small police station near the village mosque, as well as shack shops selling basic foodstuffs and a small pharmacy. Internet is of the wi-fi variety; most resorts now offer it, but service tends to be spotty.

The closest **decompression chamber** (☑089-783100) is at the Semporna Naval Base.

❶ Getting There & Around

Boat

With the exception of Roach Reefs, all transport to the marine park goes through Semporna. See p115 for detailed information on how to reach Semporna. Your accommodation will arrange any transport needs from Semporna or Tawau airport (usually for an extra fee), which will most likely depart in the morning (meaning that if you arrive in Semporna in the afternoon, you will be required to spend the night in town before setting off into the park). Chartered boats from Semporna can be scouted – the going rate is currently RM200 (this may well go up by the time you read this), which can be split between around eight people, depending on the size of the boat.

Tawau

POP 402,400

Ever been to an after-work happy hour and met a co-worker who is nice, courteous, polite, pleasant and agonisingly boring? Then you've met Tawau. There's nothing particularly *bad* we can write about this town, but (forgive us the pun) there's not a lot of 'wow' in Tawau either. This may be one of Sabah's larger cities, and it's the state's major border crossing to Indonesia – Kalimantan is just to the south (for more on border crossings, see p319). But apart from that? Not much. But if you're heading to Semporna or the Maliau Basin, there's a good chance you'll be passing through here for either transport links or pre-arranging. And hey – the people *are* friendly, the food is decent and the lodging is a pretty good deal. Just don't expect much past this and you'll likely leave satisfied after eating the great scoop of vanilla ice cream that is Tawau.

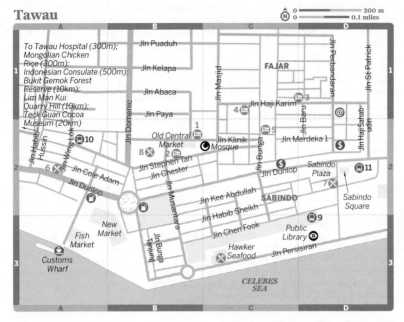

⊙ Sights

Tawau is light on sights; even the local markets seem understated compared to what's on offer in other towns.

Bukit Gemok Forest Reserve NATURE RESERVE (adult/child RM5/1) Located 10km from Tawau town centre, this reserve is a gem, and the best option for those who need to while away a day here. Developed in the early 1990s, the jungle is filled with chattering monkeys, and has become popular with trekkers, Hash House Harriers runners and tour groups – many consider it to be far better than the trails around Poring Hot Springs. The most popular trail is a demanding one-hour (if you're fit!) jaunt up **Lim Man Kui Quarry Hill**, a slate-grey knife of rock. It's a huff to make it to the top, but the stunning views from the top are worth it, as is your casual disbelief at the middle-aged Chinese fitness nuts who *jog* up this track on a regular basis.

Within the reserve, a 231m **canopy walkway** offers lovely views of the surrounding countryside and Tawau itself. Be on the lookout for the relatively enormous (15cm) seeds of the gourd *Alsomitra macrocarpa*; the seeds are flattened into aerodynamic pancakes and regularly

glide hundreds of metres through the forest; they're fairly breathtaking to watch in flight. A taxi to the park costs RM25 – make sure your driver either sticks around to wait for you or is willing to come back and pick you up, as there's little public transport out this way.

Teck Guan Cocoa Museum MUSEUM
(☎089-775566; 5-person guided tour RM100; ⏱8-11.30am & 1.30-4pm Mon-Fri, 8am-1pm Sat) This place markets itself as 'The only cocoa museum in Asia,' which we can't really verify. We can say for certain: you will likely learn more about cocoa then you ever, ever thought possible, and we were frankly charmed by the tour (also, a guide told us about a totally only-in-Asia creation, chocolate-covered prawns, which seems just diabolical enough to be delicious). A taxi from Tawau town to the museum (40 minutes away) costs RM40 to RM50 each way – the taxi should wait at no extra charge while you tour the grounds (two hours maximum).

🛏 Sleeping

Splurge for a midranger if you're stopping through Tawau. They cater to local businessmen and are excellent bang for your buck – miles beyond anything you can get in KK for a similar price. Jalan Bunga and Haji Karim are packed with good-value accommodation.

Kingston Executive Hotel HOTEL $$
(☎089-702288, 4581-4590 Jln Haji Karim; d RM80-100; ✳@) The title of this hotel may seem ambitious, but this 'executive' is nonetheless quite excellent value-for-money. It's a cheering attempt at emulating boutique quirk, an odd experience in sedate Tawau. Some rooms have duvets made from *kain songket* (traditional Malay hand-woven fabric with gold threads).

Shervinton Executive Hotel HOTEL $$
(☎089-770000; info@shervintonhotel.com; Jln Bunga; r from RM130; ✳🛜) We know – another 'executive' hotel, sorry. The Shervinton was brand new at the time of research – the brightest, most well-lit and freshest option in the city centre. An on-site spa, salon and gym facility (there's even a bakery!) make this a surprisingly luxurious option.

Belmont Marco Polo HOTEL $$$
(☎089-777988; www.sabahhotels.net; Jln Klinik; s/d from RM220/250; ✳) Forestry executives will feel at home with mahogany shutters and other elegant wooden accents at Tawau's luxury leader, which feels charmingly modest compared with some of the high-rise corporate style places outside the city centre.

Hotel Soon Yee HOTEL $
(☎089-772447; 1362 Jln Stephen Tan; r RM30-35; ✳) Those on a strict budget should head here. There's no phones, no hot water (except in shared bathrooms), but lots of camaraderie and character. Cheaper fan-cooled rooms have shared bathrooms.

TAWAU TREATS

Thanks to Tawau's proximity to Indonesia and large population of Indonesians, Filipinos, Bajau and Hakka Chinese, the town has developed some worthwhile culinary specialities. All of the following can be found in almost any of Tawau's *kedai kopi* and in the Sabindo Hawker Centre (p123).

» **Mee Jawa** – Javanese-style noodles, the Javanese take on Asia's ubiquitous noodle soup. This version comes with a yellowish broth swimming with bean sprouts, groundnuts, bean curd, fish balls, the occasional prawn and sometimes (interestingly), sweet potato, plus the usual garlic, shallots, chillies and shrimp paste.

» **Gado gado** – A deliciously simple Indonesian speciality: vegetable salad with prawn crackers and peanut sauce. The glory of *gado* is the variations of the standard recipe every cook and hawker puts a different spin on it.

» **Nasi Kuning** – Rice cooked with coconut milk and turmeric, hence the English translation of the name: 'yellow rice'. In Tawau, it is often wrapped and served in a banana leaf with deep-fried fish and eaten on special occasions.

» **Soto Makassar** – Oh yes! Soto (also spelled 'coto' and pronounced cho-to) Makassar is buffalo/beef soup from Southern Sulawesi, Indonesia. The dark broth is made incredibly rich by the addition of buffalo/cow blood, and enriched by a plethora of some 40 spices, plus beef heart, liver, tripe and brain. If you have a weak stomach, ignore those ingredients and trust us: this stuff is *delicious*, like liquid essence of beef spiced with all the wonderful herbs and spices of Southeast Asia.

Most travellers come to Tawau to either travel onwards to Semporna or cross into Indonesia. Tawau is the only crossing point with Kalimantan where foreigners can get a visa to enter Indonesia. The **consulate** (☏089-772052; 089-752969; Jln Sinn Onn; ☺9am-noon, 1-3pm) is known for being fast and efficient – many travellers are in and out in an hour. You technically need to either provide proof of onward travel or a credit card, which consulate staff will make a copy of. A 60-day tourist visa will run to RM170 and require two passport photos. Just note: you should bank on spending at least one night in town before shipping off to Indonesia, given the ferry departure schedule.

To get to the consulate, you can flag down a taxi (RM8) or take a bus from the central bus station (RM0.80). These buses leave every 30 minutes – as the touts swarm around you, just say 'Indonesia consulate' and they'll point you to the right vehicle. Ask the driver to drop you off in front of the consulate; to get back, just stand by the road and flag a bus or minibus down to return to the city centre for a similar fare.

The ferries **Tawindo Express** (☏089-774277) and **Indomaya Express** (☏089-772559) make the three- to four-hour trip to Tarakan (RM130; ☺11.30am Monday, Wednesday and Friday, 10.30am Tuesday, Thursday and Saturday) and the one-hour trip to Nunukan (RM65; ☺10am and 3pm daily except Sunday). We recommend showing up at least 60 minutes before departure to get a ticket; less than that is cutting it fine. A taxi ride to the ferry terminal costs RM5.

Monaco Hotel   HOTEL **$$**
(☏089-769911; hotelmayblossom@yahoo.com; Jln Haji Karim; r from RM80; ❄) It's not the Riviera – there's no oversized sunglasses, no slinky ladies in red dresses or suave men in tuxedos playing baccarat in this version of Monaco. Instead: an exterior painted a shade of yellow that may make your eyes bleed, offset by quite lovely interior rooms done up like the Holiday Inn, Malaysia-style.

✖ Eating

Locals love splurging on the buffet lunch at the **Belmont Marco Polo** which, for RM18 (RM33 on weekends), is a steal considering the variety of tasty bites. The interior courtyard around the Kingston Hotel has a few local haunts serving up tasty dishes, and there's cheap Chinese *kedai kopi* along Jalan Bunga; most open around 7am and close around 10pm. You may notice severe posters around town with pictures of mutilated fish that say *Bom ikan*. *Bom ikan* means 'bomb(ed) fish,' a reference to fish that have been harvested from dynamited coral reefs. The posters warn of the illegality of possessing or selling 'bombed fish'.

TOP CHOICE **Mongolian Chicken Rice**
    FOOD STALL **$**
(Jln Chester) A refreshingly new and delicious take on Malaysia's favourite comfort food.

The chicken, which is sweeter than normal (who knew: Mongols like caramelising their meat) is served with seafood soup, a take on the chicken-rice theme that is unique, delicious and appropriate given Tawau's proximity to the ocean. Locals tell us the place opens and closes on the whim of the owner, but that the lunch rush (noon to 2pm) is a reliable time to come by.

Restoran Azura   INDIAN **$**
(☏012-863 9934; Jln Dunlop; dishes RM3-6; ☺8am-9pm) Recommended for its tasty South Indian food and snicker-worthy menu, Azura serves up a killer fish-head curry and sundry 'tits-bits'. The noodles are pretty good too. There's another branch in Sabindo Sq.

Sabindo Hawker Centre   HAWKER CENTRE **$**
(Jln Waterfront; dishes from RM5; ☺11am-10pm) Located along the Tawau waterfront, Sabindo is the place to come for impeccably fresh street stall food, which, as is often the case in Asia, is the tastiest stuff around. Prices run the gamut from cheap-as-chips soup stalls to Chinese seafood emporiums.

Self-caterers should try the **Servay Department Store** (Jln Musantara), across from the Old Central Market, for everything from picnic lunches to DVDs of dubious authenticity.

> For tips, recommendations and reviews, head to shop.lonelyplanet.com to purchase downloadable PDFs of the Indonesia chapter from Lonely Planet's *Southeast Asia on a Shoestring* guide or the Malaysia chapter from Lonely Planet's *Southeast Asia on a Shoestring* guide.

❶ Information

Internet Access
City Internet Zone (☑089-760016; 37 Kompleks Fajar, Jln Perbandaran; per hr RM2-3; ⊘9am-midnight)

Banks
HSBC (Jln Perbandaran)
Maybank (☑089-762333; Jln Dunlop)

Tourist Information
Maliau Basin Conservation Area Authority (☑089-759214; maliaubasin@gmail.com; 2nd Floor, UMNO Building; Jln Dunlop) Can provide information on and help arrange visits to the Maliau Basin (p124).

❶ Getting There & Away
Air
Malaysia Airlines (☑089-761293; Jln Haji Sahabudin) and **AirAsia** (☑089-761946; Jln Bunga) have daily direct flights to KK and KL. **MASwings** (☑1300-883000) flies to Sandakan twice daily, the afternoon flight continuing to KK.

Bus
Kota Kinabalu Daily express buses for KK (RM75, nine hours) leave from behind the Sabindo area in a large dusty lot at 8am and 8pm (*not* in between).

Sandakan Departs hourly from Sabindo Sq (RM30, five hours, 7am to 2pm), one block on a diagonal from the KK terminus, behind the purple Yassin Curry House sign. That's also the spot for frequent minivans to the following:

Semporna (RM10 to RM15, two hours)
Lahad Datu (RM17 to RM20, three hours)

❶ Getting Around
To/From the Airport
The airport is 28km from town along the main highway to Semporna and Sandakan. A shuttle bus (RM10) to the local bus station in Tawau's centre leaves six times daily. A taxi costs RM45.

Tawau Hills Park

Hemmed in by agriculture and human habitation, this small reserve has forested hills rising dramatically from the surrounding plain. The **park** (admission RM10) was gazetted in 1979 to protect the water catchment for settlements in the area, but not before most of the accessible rainforest had been logged. Much of the remaining forest clings to steep-sided ridges that rise to 1310m Gunung Magdalena.

If getting into the Maliau Basin or Danum Valley feels like too much of an effort, consider Tawau Hills a user-friendly alternative. The forest here may not be as primevally awesome, but it's still impressively thick jungle, and the trails are quite easy on your feet. On a clear day the Tawau Hills Park's peaks make a fine sight.

The first trail leads along the Sungai Tawau (chattering with birds like a Disney movie when we attempted it) for 2.5km to **Bukit Gelas Falls** that, when not swarmed with school groups and tourists, is perfectly picturesque. Another track leads 3.2km to a group of 11 **hot springs** that are frankly as impressive as anything you'll see in Poring; locals believe the *ubat kulit* (skin medication) water has medicinal properties. If the above doesn't appeal, you can always take a quick 30-minute walk to **Bombalai Hill** (530m) to the south – the views from here are also quite rewarding.

There's accommodation at **Tawau Hills Park headquarters** (Taman Bukit Tawau; ☑089-918827/768719, 019-8009607; camping/dm/chalet RM5/20/200). Rates are lower on weekdays. Both dorms and chalets are utilitarian, and there's not much reason to stay here unless you can't stomach a night somewhere else. If you want to camp, you'll need to bring all of your own equipment.

Tawau Hills is 28km northwest of Tawau. A taxi will cost about RM30 to RM40.

Maliau Basin Conservation Area

In the minds of most travellers, and certainly the entire marketing division of Malaysia's tourism board, Sabah is associated with wild adventure. But while there are many wild stretches of Sabah, this state has also been heavily impacted by logging, oil palm and, on a smaller scale, suburban sprawl. Yet one pocket of truly untouched, Eden-as-God-made-it wilderness remains. Hemmed in by mountains, separated by distance and altitude and expense, the Maliau Basin Conservation Area (MBCA), known very appropriately as 'Sabah's Lost World', is...well, something special.

The basin is exactly that – a bowl-shaped depression of rainforest that was unnoticed by the world until a pilot almost crashed into the walls that hem it off in 1947. Run by the Sabah Foundation, this is the single best place in Borneo to experience the wonders of an old-growth tropical rainforest. More than that, it is one of the world's great reserves of biodiversity, a dense knot of almost unbelievable genetic richness. As such, it deserves to rank high on the itinerary of anyone interested in the natural world, as well as deserving the strongest protections afforded by the Malaysian government and world environmental bodies. And a visit to the basin is always a poignant affair, as you'll share the road with a parade of logging trucks hauling trees out of the forest at an astonishing rate.

Unbelievably, there is no known record of human beings entering the basin until the early 1980s (although it is possible that indigenous peoples entered the basin before that time). It is only recently that the area has been opened up to a limited number of adventurous travellers. Getting here requires time and resources, and officially a lot of money, although there may be ways around the latter.

Sights & Activities

Trekking

The trek through the Maliau Basin will undoubtedly be the most memorable hike of your Borneo experience. The density of the old-growth forest is striking, and as it is more remote than the Danum Valley, the preserved wildlife is even better.

Several treks are possible in the basin, ranging from short nature walks around Agathis Camp to the multiday slog to the rim of the basin via Strike Ridge Camp. The vast majority of visitors to the basin undertake a three-day, two-night loop through the southern section of the basin

that we'll call the Maliau Loop. This brilliant route takes in wide swaths of diverse rainforest and four of the basin's waterfalls: Takob Falls, Giluk Falls, Maliau Falls and Ginseng Falls. Do not attempt the trek unless you are in excellent shape (in fact, Borneo Nature Tours will require a letter from a doctor testifying to your ability to undertake the trek). Your tour operator will supply a guide and porters to carry your food. You'll be in charge of your day pack, camera, leech socks, walking clothes and dry kit for the evening.

A **canopy walkway** stretches near the Basin study centre, and it is pretty astounding to walk its length amid rainforest canopy that has never felt a human cut.

Sleeping

Accommodation in the Maliau is in the form of simple camps, which range from basic bunkhouses to wood-frame two-storey huts with private bedrooms. None of the camps are luxurious, but after a day on the trail fighting leeches, they'll seem like paradise.

There are two ways to get here. Borneo Nature Tours (✆088-267637; www.borneo naturetours.com; Lot 10, ground fl, Block D, Kompleks Sadong Jaya, Kota Kinabalu) and affiliated agents offer a five-day, four-night all-inclusive tour of the Maliau for RM4357 per person for two to three people (this can go as low as RM3780 per person for a group of 10 to 15). The package is purposefully cost prohibitive to eliminate those who aren't the most die-hard nature fans.

The other way is via your own steam and initiative. This method is not anywhere as easy as booking a tour, and it's not dirt cheap either, but it's a bit more affordable. For more information, see p126.

Information

The Maliau Basin is located in the southern part of central Sabah, just north of the logging road that connects Tawau with Keningau. The basin is part of the Yayasan Sabah Forest Management Area, a vast swath of forest in southeastern Sabah under the management of **Yayasan Sabah** (www.ysnet.org.my), a semigovernmental body tasked with both developing and protecting the natural resources of Sabah.

The **MBCA security gate** is just off the Tawau–Keningau Rd. From the gate, it's a very rough 25km journey to the **Maliau Basin Studies Centre**, for researchers, and about 20km to

INDEPENDENT EXPEDITIONS TO THE MALIAU BASIN

During our research, no private tour operators or employees of Sabah Tourism said it was possible to visit the basin without a prior tour arrangement, but we have found this is not necessarily true. With that said, you'll probably need at least RM1000 (and a fair bit of elbow grease) to make the following plan work, so this isn't an entirely budget proposal.

It's best to first contact the **Maliau Basin Conservation Area Authority** (☎089-759214; maliaubasin@gmail.com; 2nd Floor, UMNO Building; Jln Dunlop) in Tawau. You may need to show up to the office in person, as this is not a tourism body accustomed to dealing with visitors. You can also try driving to the park entrance from Tawau (2½ hours) or KK (at least five hours); a 2WD Proton can make the trip with cautious driving, while a motorbike would be dodgy but doable.

To get into the park you need to pay an administration fee (RM60), a vehicle entry fee (RM5 per vehicle), and if you stay overnight, a conservation fee (RM50). If you plan to hike (and what else are you going to do?) you *must* hire a guide, which costs RM200 per day. The different camps in the basin cost RM180 to RM205 per person per night for a room; some offer dorm beds for RM70, and you can camp in your own tent for RM30. Meals can be taken in the guest houses for RM40/50/60 per person for breakfast/lunch/dinner. You can also arrange meals while trekking; this requires a porter and costs RM70/100/130 for breakfast/lunch/dinner.

We have talked with travellers who were able to arrange all of the above at the park entrance without even stopping by the Tawau office. Our sense is this scenario will not be possible if a flood of travellers starts pounding on the basin's gates, so you may still want to check with the Tawau office before coming all the way out here (although hey, the drive is pretty).

Agathis Camp, the base camp for most visitors to the basin.

❶ Getting There & Away

There is no reliable public transport to the park, so you either need to drive yourself or arrange transport. Borneo Nature Tours will handle all transport if you book through them.

Minibus

Minibuses occasionally ply the route bringing loggers to their camps, but this isn't a regular service and cannot be relied upon.

Self-drive

Although the road here is not paved, there is gravel all along the route, and the basin can even be reached by motorbike. Drive carefully and take some jerry cans of petrol. A small shop at Batu 41, 15km from the park entrance, sells expensive petrol, but we can't guarantee its hours. Once at the security gate to the park, you'll have to take a dirt track to Agathis Camp. Rangers may transfer you if you're worried about driving your car.

Van

If you've prearranged with the Maliau Basin Conservation Area Authority in Tawau, that office may get a van to take you to the park entrance for RM600. In the park, rangers can arrange

vans to take you back to Tawau or Keningau (closer to KK; see p128) for a similar price.

SOUTHWESTERN SABAH

The Crocker Range is the backbone of southwestern Sabah, separating coastal lowlands from the wild tracts of jungle in the east. Honey-tinged beaches scallop the shores from KK down to the border, passing the turbid rivers of the Beaufort Division. Offshore you'll find Pulau Tiga, forever etched in the collective consciousness as the genesis site for the eponymous reality show *Survivor,* and Pulau Labuan, centre of the region's oil industry and the transfer point for ferries heading onto Sarawak and Brunei.

The Interior

The southwest interior of Sabah is dominated by the **Crocker Range**, which rises near Tenom in the south and runs north to Mt Kinabalu. The range forms a formidable barrier to the interior of the state and dominates the eastern skyline from

Kota Kinabalu down to Sipitang. Once across the Crocker Range, you descend into the green valley of the Sungai Pegalan that runs from Keningau in the south and to Ranau in the north. The heart of the **Pegalan Valley** is the small town of **Tambunan**, around which you'll find a few low-key attractions.

While much of the Crocker Range has been gazetted as **Crocker Range National Park**, there are few facilities for visitors. Likewise, the Pegalan Valley has no real must-see attractions. However, the Crocker Range and the Pegalan Valley make a nice jaunt into rural Sabah and are particularly suited for those with rental cars. As you make your way over the range between KK and Tambunan, you'll be treated to brilliant views back to the South China Sea and onward to Mt Trus Madi. The road itself is a lot of fun to drive, and you might find yourself craving a sports car instead of the Proton rental you're likely to be driving.

TAMBUNAN

Nestled among the green curves of the Crocker hills, Tambunan, a small agricultural service town about 81km from KK, is the first settlement you'll come to in the range. The region was the last stronghold of Mat Salleh, who became a folk hero for rebelling against the British in the late 19th century. Sadly Salleh later blew his reputation by negotiating a truce, which so outraged his own people that he was forced to flee to the Tambunan plain, where he was eventually besieged and killed.

⊙ Sights

Tambunan Rafflesia Reserve NATURE RESERVE
(☎088-898500; admission RM5; ⊙8am-3pm) Near the top of the Crocker Range, next to the main highway 20km from Tambunan, is this park devoted to the world's largest flower. The Rafflesia (see p179) is a parasitic plant that grows hidden within the stems of jungle vines until it bursts into bloom, at which point it eerily resembles the monster plant from *Little Shop of Horrors*. The large bulbous flowers can be up to 1m in diameter. The 12 or so species of Rafflesia here are found only in Borneo and Sumatra; several species are unique to Sabah, but as they only bloom for a few days it's hard to predict when you'll be able to see one. Rangers can guide into the jungle reserve for the day for RM100. Keningau-bound buses will

stop here if you ask the driver to let you off, but getting back to Tambunan will require hitching on the highway. A round-trip taxi from Tambunan costs RM100, which includes waiting time.

⊨ Sleeping

Tambunan Village Resort Centre

RESORT **$$**

(TVRC; ☎087-774076; http://tvrc.tripod.com; 24 Jln TVRC, Kampung Keranaan; r & chalets RM50-90; ☀) The main accommodation game is this quirky resort, located some 2km from the tiny town centre. The staff at the centre can help arrange trips up Mt Trus Madi. If you're driving here from KK, the centre is just south of the Shell station on the main road.

ⓘ Getting There & Away

Bus & Minivan

Regular minivans ply the roads between Tambunan and KK (RM15, 1½ hours), Ranau (RM15, two hours), Keningau (RM8, one hour) and Tenom (RM15, two hours). KK–Tenom express buses also pass through, though you may have to ask them to stop. The minivan shelter is in the middle of Tambunan town. Minivans to KK pass the entrance to the Rafflesia reserve; you'll usually be charged for the whole trip to KK.

MT TRUS MADI

About 20km southeast of Tambunan town is the dramatic **Mt Trus Madi**, Sabah's second-highest peak, rising to 2642m. Although logging concessions encircle the mount, the upper slopes and peak are wild and jungle-clad and classified as forest reserve. Ascents are possible, however it's more challenging than Mt Kinabalu, and more difficult to arrange. Independent trekkers must be well equipped and bring their own provisions up the mountain. It is possible to go by 4WD (RM400) up to about 1500m, from where it is a five- to seven-hour climb to the top. There are places to camp halfway up the mountain and on the summit. Before setting off, you are strongly advised to hire a guide (RM200) or at least get maps and assistance from the Tambunan Village Resort Centre (p127) or **Forestry Department** (Jabatan Perhutanan; ☎087-774691) in Tambunan. Trekking packages can also be booked at agencies in KK, many of which are located in Wisma Sabah.

KENINGAU

If you have a bent for the bucolic, you'll probably want to skip Keningau – this busy service town has a touch of urban sprawl about it, and most visitors only pass through to pick up transport, use an ATM or stock up on supplies. As far as attractions go, you might check out **Taipaekgung**, a colourful Chinese temple in the middle of town, or the large **tamu** (market) held every Thursday.

For a sleepover, try **Hotel Juta** (☎087-337888; www.sabah.com.my/juta; Lg Milimewa 2; standard/superior d from RM175; ❋), which towers over the busy town centre. It's convenient to transport, banking and shopping needs, and rooms are nicely appointed in the Western-businessman style. There is a restaurant on the premises. Shabbier options include the nearby forgettable **Crown Hotel** (☎087-338555; Lg Milimewa; standard/superior d from RM40).

There are eight daily express buses to/from KK (RM15, 2½ hours) and four to/from Tenom (RM7, one hour). These buses stop at the Bumiputra Express stop on the main road across from the Shell station. Minivans and share taxis operate from several places in town, including a stop just north of the express bus stop; they all leave when full. There are services to/from KK (RM40, 2½ hours), Ranau (RM25, three hours) and Tenom (RM8, one hour).

TENOM

This sleepy little town at the southern end of the Crocker Range has seen better days but still manages to be more attractive than traffic-choked Keningau. Tenom was closely involved in uprisings against the British in 1915, led by the famous Murut chief Ontoros Antonom, and there's a **memorial** to the tribe's fallen warriors off the main road. Most people pass through Tenom on their way to the nearby Sabah Agricultural Park.

If you somehow get stuck in town, spend the night at **Orchid Hotel** (☎087-737600; Jln Tun Mustapha; s/d RM40/50; ❋). Rooms are clean and well kept and good value for money. There are cheaper hotels in the vicinity, but they're all a bit musty.

Minivans operate from the *padang* (field) in front of the Hotel Sri Perdana. Destinations include Keningau (RM8, one hour) and KK (RM25, two to four hours depending on stops). There are also regular services to Tambunan (RM15, two hours).

RIDING THE BORNEO RAIL

The **North Borneo Railway** line (☎088 263933; www.northborneorailway. com.my) departs from Tanjung Aru Station in KK and chugs for about three hours to Tenom. This is more of a tourist activity than a utilitarian transportation method; the rail line is owned and operated by Sutera Resorts. Trains are renovated classic cars, and passengers will be able to lounge on open observation decks whilst watching the paddies flash by. Fares are yet to be determined as of research.

Taxis congregate at a rank on the west side of the *padang*.

SABAH AGRICULTURAL PARK

Heaven on earth for horticulturalists: the vast **Sabah Agricultural Park** (Taman Pertanian Sabah; ☎087-737952; www.sabah.net.my/agripark; adult/child RM25/10; ⊙9am-4.30pm Tue-Sun), about 15km northeast of Tenom, is run by the Department of Agriculture and covers about 6 sq km. Originally set up as an orchid centre, the park has expanded to become a major research facility, tourist attraction and offbeat camp site (RM10), building up superb collections of rare plants such as hoyas, and developing new techniques for use in agriculture, agroforestry and domestic cultivation.

Museums and exhibits scattered throughout delve deeply into the realms of animal husbandry, fisheries, beekeeping and orchids (we found all of these oddly charming). Flower gardens and nature paths abound and a minizoo lets you get up close and personal with some farm animals and deer, but due to the size of the place a fair bit of walking in the hot sun is involved (bring sunscreen, sunhats and sufficient clothing). Exploring by bicycle would be a good idea, but the fleet of rental bikes here has just about rusted to the point of immobility; if they've replaced them by the time you arrive, rentals cost RM3. There is a free 'train' (it's actually more like a bus) that does a 1½-hour loop of the park, leaving from outside the reception hourly from 9.30am to 3.30pm. If you're truly taken with the park, there's a bare bones on-site **hostel** (dm RM25), which is sometimes taken up by visiting school groups.

Take a minivan from Tenom heading to Lagud Seberang (RM5). Services run throughout the morning, but dry up in the late afternoon. Tell the driver you're going to Taman Pertanian. The park entrance is about 1km off the main road. A taxi from Tenom will cost around RM80.

BATU PUNGGUL

Perhaps even more so than the Maliau Basin, this is as remote as it gets in Sabah. Not far from the Kalimantan border, **Batu Punggul** is a jungle-topped limestone outcrop riddled with caves, towering nearly 200m above Sungai Sapulut. This is deep in Murut country and the stone formation was one of several sites sacred to these people. Batu Punggul and the adjacent Batu Tinahas are traditionally believed to be longhouses that gradually transformed into stone. The view from the upper reaches of Batu Punggul may be the best in Sabah – in every direction is deep jungle, knifelike limestone outcrops and, if you are lucky, swinging orangutans. It can be difficult and expensive to get here, but this is a beautiful part of Sabah that few tourists visit, and it offers a chance to rub shoulders with the jungle Murut.

You'll have to arrange a guide to get to Batu Punggul – the way up is too treacherous to attempt on your own. And there's no tourism infrastructure here either, which means no public places to stay or eat. The easiest way of getting here is arranging a trip through the **Keningau District Office** (☏087-301509; www.sabah.gov.my/pd.kgu, in Malay), located in Keningau town centre. You need to bank on spending at least RM400 to charter a jeep for the three-hour drive to Tataluang, a Murut longhouse community, and the 10-minute motorboat ride from there to Batu Punggul. On top of that, a guide will cost around RM200. Sleeping arrangements – some form of home stay – can also be arranged in Keningau; meals and a room will likely add about RM100 to the trip.

Beaufort Division

This shield-shaped peninsula, popping out from Sabah's southwestern coast, is a marshy plain marked with curling rivers and fringed by golden dunes. Tourists with tight travel schedules should consider doing a wildlife river cruise at Klias or Garama

if they don't have time to reach Sungai Kinabatangan. Yes, the Kinabatangan is better, but packs of proboscis monkeys can still be spotted here and it's only a day trip from KK. You can book trips to Beaufort, Weston and the Klias and Garama rivers in any of the travel agencies on the ground floor of Wisma Sabah in KK, or through any KK guest house (if you go with the latter choice, you'll obviously be charged a little more since your guest house will act as a middleman).

BEAUFORT

Born as a timber town, Beaufort has reinvented itself with the proliferation of palm-oil plantations. A suitable pit stop for tourists travelling between Sabah and Sarawak, this sleepy township is the gateway to whitewater rapids on the **Sungai Padas** and the monkey-filled Klias and Garama areas. The Sungai Padas divides Beaufort into two sections: the aptly named Old Town with its weathered structures, and New Town, a collection of modern shophouses on floodphobic stilts.

◉ Sights & Activities

Memorial stone   MEMORIAL
(Jln Tugu) There's a small monument to Private Thomas Leslie Starcevich, an Australian WWII veteran. In 1945, Starcevich single-handedly overwhelmed a Japanese machine-gun position, for which he received the Victoria Cross, the British military's highest decoration. The stone is at the bottom of a small embankment that can be a bit tricky to find; this website has a good map: http://duchessaffairs.blogspot.com/2009/09/private-l-t-starcevich-monument.html. If you don't have internet access, ask at the local police station or go southeast of the old railway station and look for the brown sign that points to the memorial.

RAFTING
White-water rafting enthusiasts can book a river trip with **Riverbug** (☏088-260501; www.riverbug.asia; Wisma Sabah, Jln Fuad Stephen, Kota Kinabalu), the premier operator in the area. **Borneo Wavehunters** (☏088-432967; www.travelmateholidays.com; Lot 27, Block D, Riverside Plaza, Kuala Inanam, Kota Kinabalu) is another reputable outfitter with a band of cheery guides. Scuba Junkie, which runs a very popular dive centre in Semporna (p117) has an affiliated river-rafting outfit here called, appropriately,

River Junkie (☑019-6012145; www.river-junkie.com; Wisma Sabah, Jln Fuad Stephen, Kota Kinabalu), which comes highly recommended by travellers. Day trips organised out of KK cost around RM200 to RM400 per person, depending on what package you choose. The cheapest options involve leisurely boat tours and proboscis monkey spotting; more expensive tours include white-water rafting expeditions and side trips to sites like the Mari Mari Cultural Village (p59). All trips include transfers by van, and normally require 24 hours' advance notice. Tourists who seek more serene waters can ride the rapids of Sungai Kiulu (bookable through the aforementioned operators), which is located near Mt Kinabalu and calm enough to be popular with families.

🛏 Sleeping

There's really no need to spend the night in Beaufort, but if you must, then try the **MelDe Hotel** (☑087-222266; 19-20 Lo Chung Park, Jln Lo Chung; s/d/ste RM60/80/90; ❄). The rooms are a bit crusty in the corners, but it's passable for a night's sleep while in transit. Go for a room on one of the upper floors – they have windows. The Chinese restaurant under the inn is very popular with locals. MelDe is located in Old Town. If you're stopping in town for a bite, make sure you try a pomelo (football-sized citrus fruit) and local *mee Beaufort* (Beaufort noodles) – both are locally famous.

❶ Getting There & Away

Bus

Express buses operate from near the old train station at the south end of Jln Masjid (the ticket booth is opposite the station). There are departures at 9am, 1pm, 2.15pm and 5pm for KK (RM10, 1½ hours). There are departures at 9.10am, 10.30am, 1.45pm and 6.20pm for Sipitang (RM4.50, 1½ hours). The KK to Lawas express bus passes through Beaufort at around 3pm; the trip from Beaufort to Lawas costs RM13 and takes 1¾ hours.

Minivans

Operate from a stop across from the mosque, at the north end of Jln Masjid. There are frequent departures for KK (RM10, two hours), and less-frequent departures for Sipitang (RM12, 1½ hours), Lawas (RM15, 1¾ hours) and Kuala Penyu (RM8, until around 2.30pm, one hour). To Menumbok (for Labuan) there are plenty of minivans until early afternoon (RM8, one hour).

Taxis

Depart from the stand outside the old train station, at the south end of Jln Masjid. Charter rates include: KK (RM70), Kuala Penyu (RM55), Sipitang (RM32), Menumbok (RM50) and Lawas (RM100).

KUALA PENYU

Tiny Kuala Penyu, at the northern tip of the peninsula, is the jumping-off point for Pulau Tiga if you are not accessing 'Survivor Island' via the new boat service from KK. From KK, minivans leave from behind Wawasan Plaza (RM10 to RM15, two hours). From Beaufort minivans to Kuala Penyu (RM5 to RM10) leave throughout the morning, but return services tail off very early in the afternoon, so you may have to negotiate a taxi or local lift back. A minivan to/from Menumbok costs RM65 per vehicle.

TEMPURUNG

Tempurung Seaside Lodge (☑088-773066; 3 Putatan Point; www.borneo-authentic.com; 3-day, 2-night package from RM450), set along the quiet coastal waters of the South China Sea, is the perfect place for hermits who seek a pinch of style. The main lodge was originally built as a vacation home, but friends convinced the owners that it would be a crime not to share the lovely property with the world. Rooms are scattered between several chalet-style bungalows accented with patches of jungle thatch. The packages include fantastic meals. Nightly rates are also available.

Borneo Express (☑012-830 7722) runs buses from KK (departing from Wawasan) at 6.45am, 10am and 12.30pm daily. Ask the driver to let you off at the junction with the large Kuala Penyu sign. The bus will turn left (south) to head towards Menumbok; you want to go right (north) in the direction of Kuala Penyu. If you arranged accommodation in advance, the lodge van can pick you up here (it's too far to walk). Buses pass the junction at 9.30am and 3.30pm heading back to KK. If you're driving, take a right at the junction and keep an eye out for the turn-off on the left side of the road just before Kuala Penyu. We suggest calling the lodge for directions. A charter taxi from Beaufort will cost about RM50.

KLIAS

The tea-brown Sungai Klias looks somewhat similar to the mighty Kinabatangan, offering short-stay visitors a chance to spend an evening in the jungle cavorting with saucy primates. There are several companies offering two-hour river cruises. We recommend **Borneo Authentic** (☎088-773066; www.borneo-authentic.com; package trip RM150), the first operator to set up shop in the region. Trips include a large buffet dinner and a short night walk to view the swarms of fireflies that light up the evening sky like Christmas lights. Cruises start at dusk (around 5pm), when the sweltering heat starts to burn off and animals emerge for some post-siesta prowling.

There is no accommodation in Klias, although Borneo Authentic can set you up with one of its comfy rooms at the Tempurung Seaside Lodge nearby. Tourists can make their own way to the row of private jetties 20km west of Beaufort, however, most trip-takers usually sign-up for a hassle-free day trip from KK (which ends up being cheaper since you're sharing transport).

GARAMA

Narrower than the river in Klias, the Sungai Garama is another popular spot for the popular river-cruise day trips from KK. Chances of seeing fireflies are slim, but Garama is just as good as Klias (if not better) when it comes to primate life. Gangs of proboscis monkeys and long-tailed macaques scurry around the surrounding floodplain offering eager tourists plenty of photo fodder.

Like Klias, the tours here start at around 5pm (with KK departures at 2pm), and after a couple of hours along the river, guests chat about the evening's sightings over a buffet dinner before returning to KK. There are several operators offering Garama river tours; we prefer **Only In Borneo** (☎088-260506; www.oibtours.com; package tour RM190), an offshoot of Traverse Tours. It has a well-maintained facility along the shores of Sungai Garama and offers an overnight option in prim dorms or double rooms.

It is technically possible to reach Garama with one's own vehicle, but the network of unmarked roads can be tricky and frustrating, especially at night when nothing is lit (and water buffalo start to wander the roads). We recommend leaving early in the morning from KK if you want to get here on your own steam.

WESTON

The little village of Weston – a couple of shacks clustered around a gold-domed mosque – is the jumping-off point for a gentle yet jungly patch of wetlands that is equal parts serene and overgrown. The area was bombed beyond recognition during WWII, but recent conservation efforts have welcomed groups of curious proboscis monkeys into the tidal marshlands, which are shaded by towering nipa palms and copses of spiderlike mangroves. As the tide rolls in and out, entire swaths of jungle are submerged and revealed. Monkeys, monitor lizards, otters and mud skippers flash through the aquatic undergrowth, and as the sun sets, clouds of flying foxes (ie *big* bats) flap in with the darkness.

Weston Wetland Paradise, in conjunction with **Borneo Eco Stay** (☎019-821 8038, 088-239476; www.westonwetland.com; Lot 12, 3rd fl, Block B, Damai Plaza, Jln Damai, Kota Kinabalu), operates a variety of package tours including river-cruise day trips and sleepovers at its swamp-side longhouse (all-inclusive two-day, one-night package RM230). The dorm facilities are rustic at best. We can charitably say this adds to the romantic, roughing-it appeal of the place, but if you caught us in a bad mood, we'd say the place feels kind of cheap. That said, while the digs aren't top of the line and there are a few mosquitoes around, there's also bursts of fireflies that will melt your heart during the long evenings. Note that the folk at Weston Wetland insist you prebook before visiting.

While you're here, you can ask folk at the lodge to take you to **Che Hwa Schoolhouse**, the oldest wooden school building in Borneo and a fine example of antiquarian Chinese architecture.

MENUMBOK

The tiny hamlet of Menumbok is where you can car catch ferries to the Serasa Ferry Terminal in Muara (see p234), 25km northeast of Bandar Seri Begawan (Brunei), and to Pulau Labuan (adult/car RM5/40, departures at 10.30am and 4.30pm).

On land, a charter taxi from Beaufort costs RM60, minivans from Kuala Penyu cost RM50 per vehicle. There is a direct bus service connecting Menumbok to KK (see p71).

Pulau Tiga National Park

Outwit, outplay and outlast your fellow travellers on what is known throughout the world as 'Survivor Island'. The name Pulau Tiga actually means 'three islands' – the scrubby islet is part of a small chain created during an eruption of mud volcanoes in the late 1890s. Over 100 years later, in 2001, the island had its 15 minutes of fame when it played host to the smash-hit reality TV series *Survivor*. TV junkies still stop by for a look-see, although the 'tribal council' was destroyed in a storm and the debris was cleared after it turned into a home for venomous snakes. Whatever your viewing preferences, it's still a great place for relaxing on the beach, hiking in the forest and taking a cooling dip in burping mud pits at the centre of the island.

◉ Sights & Activities

Pulau Kalampunian Damit ('day-mit,' not 'dammit, I'm on snake island) is little more than a large rock covered in dense vegetation but is famous for the sea snakes that come ashore to mate, hence the island's nickname, **Snake Island**. Sounds like the tourism destination of the 21st century, right? On any one day up to 150 snakes can be present, curled up under boulders, among roots and in tree hollows. It's a fascinating phenomenon, made doubly enigmatic by the fact that the snakes are never seen on nearby Pulau Tiga. Pulau Tiga Resort runs boat trips to the island (RM40 per person), with a stop en route for snorkelling for RM30 extra. You can also dive off the island for RM100 per dive, or RM150 for a fun dive for those with no scuba experience; it's not the best diving in Borneo, but then again, you're in Borneo, so there's plenty of rainbow-coloured fish to peep at.

⌨ Sleeping & Eating

Pulau Tiga Resort   RESORT $$
(☎088-240584; www.pulau-tiga.com; per person RM175-350; ❄) Built to house the production crew for the *Survivor* series (Jeff Probst stayed in cabin E), this compound has been turned into a lovely seaside resort. Accommodation is available in dorm-style 'longhouse' rooms (three beds in each), while more luxurious private cabins have double beds and plenty of air-con. The beach-facing grounds offer amazing views of the sunset, while a detailed map is available for those that want to track down the beach where the Pagong Tribe lived (called Pagong Pagong Beach). There's currently only one staff member who was working here when *Survivor* was being

filmed, but the most unpopular guest at the resort is still sent to Snake Island after dinner (joke!).

Sabah Parks   CAMPING $
(☎088-211881; www.sabahparks.org.my; Lot 1-3, Block K, Kompleks Sinsuran, Jln Tun Fuad Stephens, Kota Kinabalu; r from RM60) Sabah Parks runs more basic lodging (ie block houses) on the island for less affluent survivalists. It's right next door to Pulau Tiga Resort, about 10m from where 'Tribal Council' was once held (sadly, tiki torches no longer line the way). Facilities here are limited and there's no restaurant, though a cooking area is provided.

❶ Getting There & Away

Boat
From Kuala Penyu the boat ride takes about 20 minutes. Boats leave at 10am and 3pm. Most visitors to Pulau Tiga come as part of a package, in which case transport is included in the price. You can try showing up in Kuala Penyu and asking if you can board one of the day's boats out to the island (we don't recommend this option as priority is given to resort guests with bookings). For Sabah Parks' lodgings try to hop a ride with the Pulau Tiga Resort boat – chartering your own craft costs RM400 at least.

Pulau Labuan

POP 95,500

If you've ever wondered what a cross between a duty-free airport mall and a tropical island would look like, may we recommend turning off your imagination and visiting the federal district of Pulau Labuan. Some call this Sabah's version of Vegas, but we beg to disagree – Labuan is clean cut, family friendly, tacky...come to think of it, maybe this *is* Sabah's version of Vegas. By the way, everything here is actually duty free, because politically, Labuan is governed directly by KL. As such, a lot of the booze you consume and cigarettes you smoke in Sabah and Sarawak are illegally smuggled from Labuan.

The sultan of Brunei ceded Labuan to the British in 1846 and it remained part of the Empire for 115 years. The only interruption came during WWII, when the Japanese held the island for three years. Significantly, it was on Labuan that the Japanese forces in North Borneo surrendered at the end of the war, and the officers responsible for the death marches from Sandakan were tried on the island.

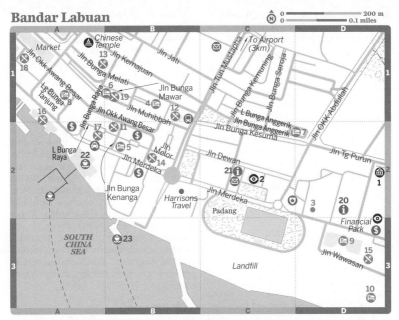

Bandar Labuan

Bandar Labuan is the main town and the transit point for ferries linking Kota Kinabalu and Brunei.

⊙ Sights & Activities

BANDAR LABUAN

Labuan's uncharismatic main settlement is light on character but has a couple of passable attractions.

FREE **Labuan Museum** MUSEUM
(☏087-414135; 364 Jln Dewan; ☺9am-5pm) This museum on Jln Dewan takes a glossy, if slightly superficial, look at the island's history and culture, from colonial days, through WWII, to the establishment of Labuan as an independent federal territory. The most interesting displays are those on the different ethnic groups here,

including a diorama of a traditional Chinese tea ceremony (the participants, however, look strangely Western).

FREE **Labuan Marine Museum** MUSEUM (☎087-425927/414462; Jln Tanjung Purun; ☺9am-6pm) On the coast just east of the centre, the Labuan International Sea Sports Complex houses a decent little museum with a good shell collection and displays of marine life found in the area. Don't forget to head upstairs where you'll find a 42ft-long skeleton of an Indian fin whale. The real highlight, however, and a guaranteed hit with the kids, is the 'touch pool' opposite reception. This has to be the only shark-petting zoo we've ever seen (fret not: the sharks are less than a metre long).

AROUND PULAU LABUAN

WWII Memorial (Labuan War Cemetery)
CEMETERY
A dignified expanse of lawn with row upon row of headstones dedicated to the nearly 4000 Commonwealth servicemen, mostly Australian and British, who lost their lives in Borneo during WWII. The cemetery is near the golf course, about 2km east of town along Jln OKK Abdullah. A **Peace Park** on the west of the island at Layang Layangan commemorates the place of Japanese surrender and has a Japanese war memorial.

Labuan Bird Park WILDLIFE RESERVE (☎087-463544) This pretty park offers refuge to a wide range of species in three geodesic domes, and a swath of rainforest – the birds look a little bored, but healthy.

Chimney LANDMARK
Believed to be part of an old coal-mining station (though strangely it was never actually used as a chimney), this is the only historical monument of its kind in Malaysia, and has good views along the coast. It's at the northeast tip of the island.

Labuan Marine Park PARK
Pulau Kuraman, Pulau Rusukan Kecil and Pulau Rusukan Besar are uninhabited islands lying southwest of Labuan that are now protected by the federal government. The beaches are pristine, but dynamite fishing has destroyed much of the coral. You can hire boats from the jetty at the Labuan International Sea Sports Complex to explore the marine park. A day's charter costs around RM500 to RM600 per group of six people.

Thanks to financial deregulation Labuan is now the home of some major offshore bank accounts, so you may also want to be on the lookout for men in sunglasses with big briefcases, although we suggest not taking pictures of them.

Diving
Labuan is famous for its **wreck diving**, with no fewer than four major shipwrecks off the coast (two from WWII and two from the 1980s). The only dive outfit operating here is **Borneo Star Dives** (☎087-429278; stardivers2005@yahoo.com; International Seasports Complex; dive packages from RM438), which does island-hopping tours and can take you out to all four sites. Note that only the 'Cement Wreck' is suitable for novice divers; the 'Blue Water Wreck' (in our opinion, the most impressive of the bunch) requires advanced open-water certification, and the 'American' and 'Australian' wrecks are only recommended for certified wreck divers.

🛏 Sleeping

TOP CHOICE **Labuan Homestay Programme**
HOME STAY $
(☎087-422622; www.labuantourism.com; 1/2 days incl full board RM65/140) This excellent service matches visitors with a friendly local in one of three villages around the island: Patau Patau 2, Kampong Sungai Labu and Kampong Bukit Kuda. Some of the homes are just as grand as one of the international-class hotels on the waterfront! If you want to be near Bandar Labuan, ask for accommodation at Patau Patau 2 – it's a charming stilt village out on the bay. Stay a bit longer and learn how to make *ambuyat*, also known as 'gluey sago porridge' and Brunei's favourite dish.

Grand Dorsett Labuan HOTEL $$$ (☎087-422000; www.granddorsett.com/labuan; 462 Jln Merdeka; r from RM475; ✳@☇☇) The Grand Dorsett (once a link in the Sheraton chain) has everything you would expect from an international hotel, with five-star rooms, good restaurants and a pub hosting live bands. Weekend rates go down to as low as RM230.

Waterfront Labuan Financial Hotel
HOTEL $$
(☎087-418111; leslbn@tm.net.my; 1 Jln Wawasan; r RM250-580, ste RM580-2150; ✳☇) Not just for merchant bankers – this is a large, luxurious leisure hotel which practically feels like

a mall, with full facilities and a small marina attached. The rooms are spacious and have a corporate appeal, and some have great sea views. There's a huge outdoor pool and a restaurant.

Mariner Hotel
HOTEL **$$**
(☏087-418822; mhlabuan@streamyx.com; 468 Jln Tanjung Purun; r from RM110; ❄@) Pitched at the low-end business-class market, this smart block offers good facilities for the price. Rooms come with fridges, laminate floors and neat, spacious bathrooms.

ASV Backpackers
HOSTEL **$**
(☏087-413728; asvjau@yahoo.com; Lot U0101, Jln Merdeka; r with shared bathroom RM35; ❄) As backpacker spots go, ASV is in a respectable league – it manages to be cheap while more functionally clean and comfortable than most of the dingy midrangers around town. Shame there's not more, y'know, backpackers in Labuan.

✖ Eating

Choice Restaurant
INDIAN **$$**
(☏087-418086; 104 Jln OKK Awang Besar; dishes RM3-10; ☺8am-10pm) Forget false modesty, the Choice simply proclaims 'We are the best', and this seems to be corroborated by the popularity of the authentic Indian meals with the authentic Indian residents who turn out for *roti*, fish-head curry and *sambal*.

Port View Restaurant
SEAFOOD **$$**
(☏087-422999; Jln Merdeka; dishes RM15-30; ☺lunch & dinner) An outpost of the successful Chinese seafood franchise in KK, this waterfront restaurant has air-con indoor seating and outdoor seating that affords a nice view over Labuan's busy harbour. It's one of the few proper sit-down restaurants in town (that is, something nicer than a *kedai kopi*).

There's lots of cheap *kedai kopi* about:
Kedai Kopi Fah Fah (cnr Jln Bunga Raya & Jln Bunga Melati; meals RM3-10; ☺8am-9pm) With indoor and outdoor seating, an English menu, tasty fresh juice and cheap beer, this simple Chinese restaurant is a good choice. We particularly liked its *kway teow goreng* (fried flat rice noodles).

Kedai Kopi Nam Thong (Jln Merdeka; meals from RM3; ☺8am-2pm) Has good chicken-rice and fried-noodle stalls.

Restaurant Ngee Hing (Jln Merdeka; meals from RM3; ☺7am-3pm) has a stall that does a good bowl of laksa (it's directly opposite the ferry terminal and serves as a good place to wait for a ferry).

Restoran Selera Farizah (Lg Bunga Tanjung; meals from RM3; ☺8am-10pm) If you prefer a Muslim *kedai kopi*, you could try this place, which serves *roti*, curries and *nasi campur*, accompanied by pro-wrestling videos.

In addition, you'll find outdoor **food stalls** at the east end of Jln Bunga Mawar and in the **Medan Selera Complex** near the Grand Dorsett. Self-caterers can do their grocery shopping at **Syarikat Teck Siong** (Jln Bunga Mawar).

ℹ Information

Banks
HSBC (☏087-422610; 189 Jln Merdeka)
Maybank (☏087-443888; Financial Park)

Tourist Information
Labuan Tourism Action Council (☏087-422622; ground fl, Labuan International Sea Sports Complex; 8am-1pm & 2-5pm Mon-Fri) Located about 1km east of the town centre, this is the most useful information office in town. It stocks the excellent *Fly Drive Labuan Island & Town Map of Labuan.*

Tourist Information Centre (☏087-423445; www.labuantourism.com.my; cnr Jln Dewan & Jln Berjaya; ☺8am-5pm Mon-Fri, 9am-3pm Sat) Tourism Malaysia office. Less useful than Labuan Tourism Action Council.

Travel Agencies
Harrisons Travel (☏087-408096; www.harrisonstravel.com.my; 1 Jln Merdeka) Handy and reputable travel agency.

ℹ Getting There & Away

Air
Malaysia Airlines (☏1300-883000; www.malaysiaairlines.com.my; airport) has flights to/from KK (45 minutes) and KL (2½ hours), which are usually booked full of oil prospectors. **AirAsia** (☏087-480401; www.airasia.com; airport) currently flies to KL only.

Boat
Kota Kinabalu Passenger ferries (1st/economy class RM39/31, 3¼ hours) depart KK for Labuan from Monday to Saturday at 8am and 1.30pm (3pm Sunday). In the opposite direction, they depart Labuan for KK from Monday to Saturday at 8am and 1pm, while on Sunday they depart at 10.30am and 3pm.

Brunei For details on car ferries to/from the Serasa Ferry Terminal in Muara, see p234. At

WANT MORE?

For in-depth information, reviews and recommendations at your fingertips, head to the Apple App Store to purchase Lonely Planet's *Malaysia* iPhone app.

Alternatively, head to Lonely Planet (www.lonelyplanet.com/malaysia, or www.lonelyplanet.com/asia) for planning advice, author recommendations, traveller reviews and insider tips.

press time, passenger-only ferries were in a state of disarray as Brunei had barred vessels operated by the Labuan-based ISRO Shipping Company from docking in Brunei, ostensibly for safety reasons.

Sarawak For information on the somewhat irregular speedboats to Limbang and Lawas in Sarawak's Limbang Division, see p221 and p222.

 Getting Around

Minibus

Labuan has a good minibus network based on a six-zone system. Minibuses leave regularly from the parking lot off Jln Tun Mustapha. Their numbers are clearly painted on the front, and fares range from 50 sen for a short trip to RM2.50 for a trip to the top of the island.

Taxi

Taxis are plentiful and there's a stand opposite the local ferry terminal. The base rate is RM8 for short journeys, or RM10 to the airport.

Borneo

Wildlife »
Diving »
Culture »

Iban warrior, Sarawak

Wildlife

Borneo's lush rainforests teem with mammals, birds, amphibians, reptiles and insects, many of them found nowhere else on earth. Most fauna wisely shun the limelight, but in certain places, at the right time of day or in the right season, visitors can glimpse jungle animals in their natural habitats.

Borneo's most charismatic creature is the orangutan, the world's largest tree-dwelling animal, whose human-like form and eerily familiar habits captivate their distant, guidebook-toting cousins. Another primate with extraordinary treetop agility is the proboscis monkey, instantly recognisable by one of evolution's more unexpected adaptations, the male's long, floppy nose. Sabah is home to about a thousand pygmy elephants.

The island's many colourful birds include eight species of hornbill, but to see them you'll probably have to get up at dawn or linger in the jungle at dusk. The most spectacular is the rhinoceros hornbill, instantly identifiable by some truly impressive avian bling, a red and yellow casque.

TOP WILDLIFE SPOTS

» **Sungai Kinabatangan** (p103) Home to an astonishing variety of wildlife, including wild orangutans and pygmy elephants.

» **Semenggoh Nature Reserve** (p173) Semi-wild orangutans frolic in the jungle canopy just 20 minutes from Kuching.

» **Bako National Park** (p166) The park's coves and trails are one of the best places to spot proboscis monkeys.

» **Sepilok Orang-utan Rehabilitation Centre** (p99) Semi-wild orangutans swing by to dine on fruit.

» **Gunung Mulu National Park** (p208) Discover astonishing stick insects on a ranger-led nightwalk.

Clockwise from top left
1. Orchid, Rainforest Discovery Centre (p100) 2. Male wread hornbill, Lok Kawi Wildlife Park (p61) 3. Young orangutan, Tanjung Puting National Park (p246) 4. Pitcher plant, Maliau Basin (p124)

FRANS LANTING/CORBIS

Diving

The waters off northeastern Borneo are as rich in weird and wonderful species as the island's terrestrial habitats. Somewhat wetter and considerably saltier than Borneo's rainforests, these celebrated reefs shelter a mind-boggling variety of corals, fish and marine mammals, offering some of the finest scuba diving in the world.

Borneo's most spectacular reefs fringe a number of tiny islands off the northeast coast. Amid thriving coral – sea fans can grow to 3km – and a wealth of sponges, divers often encounter shimmering schools of jacks, bumphead parrotfish and barracudas, and find themselves making the acquaintance of green turtles, dolphins, manta rays and several species of shark. Visibility can reach an incredible 30m to 50m, making the area's famed drop-offs - up to 2000m deep! - a truly breathtaking sight. If you've dreamed of experiencing the extraordinary biodiversity and astonishingly vivid hues of the 'Coral Triangle', Borneo offers some great options for your next underwater adventure.

TIM ROCK/LONELY PLANET IMAGES ©

1

WATERFRAME / ALAMY

4

TOP DIVE SITES

» **Sipadan** (p115) Legendary for its deep wall dives, Sipadan is a favoured hang-out of turtles, sharks and open-ocean fish.

» **Layang Layang** (p92) A deep-ocean island famed for its pristine coral and 2000m drop-off.

» **Pulau Mantanani** (p91) These isolated, coral-ringed islands are prime habitat for dugongs (sea cows).

» **Mabul** (p118) 'Muck dives' often turn up eels, crabs, squid, octopus and frogfish.

» **Pulau Derawan & Sangalaki Archipelago** (p276 and p273) The area boasts a fantastic assortment of colourful reef fish.

Clockwise from top left
1. Snorkelling at the beach, Sipadan–Mabul region
2. Colourful mandarinfish 3. Spectacular coral reef, Sipadan 4. Diving in the reefs, Sipadan–Mabul region

Culture

Cultural diversity comes naturally to Borneo, where civilisations, languages, religions and culinary traditions have been meeting and mixing for thousands of years. From sophisticated cities with chic urban amenities to remote Dayak longhouses on the upland tributaries of mighty rivers, the island's cultural vibrancy never fails to amaze.

Borneo's indigenous peoples, often known as Dayaks, still joke about their head-hunting past, but today many are working to integrate ancient lifestyles based on sustainability and mutual responsibility with the demands and opportunities of modern life. The best way to experience a slice of Dayak traditions is to visit a longhouse.

Many Muslim Malays live in picturesque *kampung* (villages) built on stilts over a river or estuary. Halal meals, including a delicious selection of BBQ meat, grilled fish and scrumptious rice and noodle dishes, are available in open-air markets.

Significant Chinese communities are found in many cities and towns. Each dialect group has its own dragon-adorned temples, community festivities and distinctive culinary traditions.

CHARLES O'REAR/CORBIS

TOM COCKREM/LONELY PLANET IMAGES ©

TOP CULTURAL ATTRACTIONS

» **Kuching** (p148) Borneo's most stylish city is a 'salad bowl' of Chinese, Malay, Dayak, Indian and Western culture.

» **Kelabit Highlands** (p213) The area's famously welcoming people are happy to share their traditions – and their delicious cuisine.

» **Batang Ai Region** (p183) Home to some of Sarawak's most traditional Iban longhouses.

» **Pegunungan Meratus** (Meratus Mountains; p259) Shamans still play an important role in this remote area.

» **Bandar Seri Begawan** (p224) Brunei's Malay traditions live on in the sultanate's water villages and markets.

Clockwise from top left
1. Dayak woman in traditional dress, Kalimantan 2. Omar Ali Saifuddien Mosque, Bandar Seri Begawan (p224) 3. Indonesian women at a mosque 4. Tua Pek Kong Temple, Sibu (p185)

Satok Weekend Market, Kuching (p154)
Vegetables and chillies at Kuching's biggest and liveliest market.

Sarawak

Best Places to Eat

» Top Spot Food Court (p157)

» Junk (p158)

» Café Tauh (p205)

Best Places to Stay

» Singgahsana Lodge (p156)

» Li Hua Hotel (p186)

» Minda Guesthouse (p204)

Why Go?

Sarawak makes access to Borneo's natural wonders and cultural riches a breeze. From Kuching, Borneo's most sophisticated and dynamic city, pristine rainforests – where you can spot orangutans, proboscis monkeys, killer crocodiles and the world's largest flower, the Rafflesia – can be visited on day trips, with plenty of time in the evening for a delicious meal and a drink in a chic bar. More adventurous travellers can take a 'flying coffin' riverboat up the Batang Rejang, 'the Amazon of Borneo', to seek out remote longhouses, or fly to the spectacular bat caves and extraordinary rock formations of Gunung Mulu National Park, a Unesco World Heritage Site. Everywhere you go, you'll encounter the warmth, unforced friendliness and sense of humour that make the people of Sarawak such delightful hosts.

When to Go

There's no good or bad season to visit Sarawak. January is the wettest month, but there's huge variability from year to year so you're likely to get sprinkled on whenever you come!

The average daily high in Kuching ranges from 29°C in January to 33°C in July; the average daily low is 22°C or 23°C every day of the year.

Because of the northern-hemisphere summer, adventure treks, caving trips and some accommodation gets booked out early in July and August.

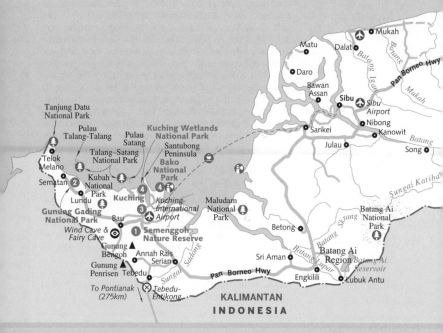

Sarawak Highlights

① Watching semi-wild orangutans swing through the canopy at **Semenggoh Nature Reserve** (p173)

② Seeing the elusive Rafflesia, the world's largest flower, at **Gunung Gading National Park** (p179)

③ Strolling the Waterfront Promenade in **Kuching** (p148)

④ Spotting endangered proboscis monkeys in **Bako**

National Park (p166) or **Kuching Wetlands National Park** (p172)

⑤ Watching the jungle glide by as you make your way into the very heart of Borneo along

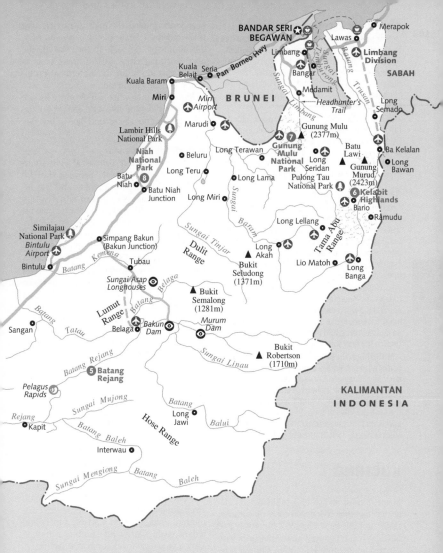

the **Batang Rejang**, 'Borneo's Amazon' (p188)

6 Experiencing longhouse life and Kelabit hospitality in the **Kelabit Highlands** (p213)

7 Ascending to the summit of Gunung Mulu, the highest peak in Borneo's best nature park, or going spelunking in **Gunung Mulu National Park** (p208)

8 Entering a netherworld of stalactites and bats in the caves of **Niah National Park** (p198)

ⓘ Getting There & Away

Unless you come overland from Kalimantan (via the Tebedu–Entikong crossing), Brunei (linked by bus with Miri, Limbang and Lawas) or Sabah, or take one of the boats that link Bandar Seri Begawan (BSB; Brunei) and Pulau Labuan with Limbang and Lawas, the only way to get to Sarawak is by air.

Kuching is Sarawak's main entry point – for details on flights to/from Singapore, Kuala Lumpur (KL) and other places, see p316. Miri has air links to Singapore, KL, Johor Bahru (Peninsular Malaysia), Kota Kinabalu (KK) and Pulau Labuan, while from Sibu you can fly to KK, KL and Johor Bahru.

ⓘ Getting Around

Coastal Sarawak is traversed by a decent network of mostly paved roads, along which you can travel by bus, taxi and private car. A web of 4WD-only logging roads has been slashed through the interior but, except from Bintulu to Belaga and from Miri to Bario (Kelabit Highlands), there's no public transport.

Ferries link Kuching with Sibu, Sibu with Belaga and Kapit (along the Batang Rejang), and Belaga with nearby longhouses. Motorised longboats are in use on virtually all of Sarawak's navigable rivers, and in many remote areas they're the only way to get around.

MASwings (Rural Air Service; www.maswings.com.my), a subsidiary of Malaysia Airlines, is basically Malaysian Borneo's very own domestic airline. Flights link its hubs in Miri and Kuching with 14 destinations around Sarawak, including the lowland cities of Sibu, Bintulu, Limbang and Lawas and the upland destinations of Gunung Mulu National Park, Bario and Ba Kelalan.

KUCHING

🕿 082 / POP 600,000

Borneo's most stylish and sophisticated city brings together a kaleidoscope of cultures, crafts and cuisines. The old Chinatown and bustling markets amply reward visitors with a penchant for aimless ambling. Chinese temples decorated with dragons abut shophouses from the time of the White Rajahs, a South Indian mosque is a five-minute walk from stalls selling half a dozen Asian cuisines, and a landscaped riverfront park attracts families out for a stroll and a quick bite.

Kuching's other huge asset is its day-trip proximity to a dozen first-rate nature sites (see p166).

◉ Sights

While Kuching has some great museums, colourful temples and a few historic sites to keep you occupied, the main attraction here is the city itself. Leave plenty of time to wander aimlessly and soak up the relaxed vibe and charming cityscapes of areas such as Chinatown, Jln India, the Waterfront Promenade and Jln Padungan.

Sarawak's museums, which are free, are open every day of the year, *except* on the first day (but not the second day) of two-day public holidays.

Waterfront Promenade PARK

(along Main Bazaar & Jln Gambier; ⊕) The south bank of Sungai Sarawak, between the Hotel Grand Margherita Kuching and the Indian Mosque, has been turned into a watery promenade, with paved walkways, lawns, flowerbeds, a children's playground, cafes and food stalls. It's a fine place for a stroll any time a cool breeze blows off the river, especially at sunset. In the evening the waterfront is ablaze with colourful fairy lights and full of couples and families eating snacks as *tambang* (small passenger ferries) glide past with their glowing lanterns. The loveliest views are from the bend in the river across from the Hilton; this is also where the best food stalls can be found. The water level is kept constant by a downstream barrage.

The promenade affords great views across the river to the white, crenellated towers and manicured gardens of the Astana; hilltop Fort Margherita, also white and crenellated; and, between the two, the Sarawak State Assembly, with its dramatic, golden pointy roof.

Just past the western end of Main Bazaar stands the **Square Tower** (interior closed), built in 1879. Along with Fort Margherita, it once guarded the lazy river against marauders. Over the past century, the tower – still emblazoned with Sarawak's Brooke-era coat-of-arms – has served as a prison, a mess and a dance hall. Nearby **Jln Gambier** is named after a vine used for tanning and dyeing.

Across the street from the Square Tower stands the **Brooke Memorial**, erected in 1924 to honour Charles Brooke, and the **Old Court House** (btwn Jln Tun Abang Haji Openg & Jln Barrack), built in the late 1800s to serve as the city's administrative centre. Today, this ensemble of airy, colonial-era structures – well worth a wander – is home to the very helpful Visitors Information Centre and the National Park Booking Office (see p163).

Jalan Carpenter CHINATOWN

Lined with evocative, colonial-era shophouses and home to several colourful Chinese temples, Jln Carpenter – Kuching's old-time Chinatown – stretches from ornamental **Harmony Arch** (cnr Jln Tun Abang Haji Openg & Jln Carpenter) eastward to **Hong San Si Temple** (cnr Jln Wayang & Jln Carpenter), also known by its Hokkien name, Say Ong Kong.

Jln Carpenter is also known as Attap St. *Attap* is the Malay word for roofs made from *nipa* palm fronds – the street was once lined with *attap*-topped timber structures, all of which were incinerated in the Great Fire of 1884. According to legend, as the flames roared down Jln Carpenter, onlookers spotted a mysterious boy waving a black banner. Suddenly, the wind changed direction and the fire stopped just short of Hong San Si Temple, which is thought to date to around 1840 (it was extensively restored in 2004). There is a big celebration here in April, with a long procession of floats, lion and dragon dancers, and other groups winding their way through town following the altar of Kong Teck Choon Ong (the deity at the temple).

Not far from Harmony Arch, **Hiang Thian Siang Temple** (Sang Ti Miao Temple; btwn 12 & 14 Jln Carpenter) was rebuilt shortly after the fire of 1884. It serves the Teochew congregation as a shrine to Shang Di (the Emperor of Heaven). The temple's most interesting celebration is the Hungry Ghost Festival, held on the 15th day of the seventh lunar month (mid-August or early September). The Chinese believe that the gates of hell swing open for the entirety of the month and the spirits of the dead are free to roam the earth. On the 15th day, offerings of food, prayer, incense and paper money are made to appease the spirits. A priest blesses the offerings and promptly burns an enormous effigy to the Hell King in a dramatic bonfire. In the evening, parcels of food are doled out in a chaotic lottery.

Directly across Jln Carpenter from the temple, you can get excellent Teochew Chinese dishes at Yang Choon Tai Hawker Centre.

One of Kuching's hidden gems is tucked away on the roof of the **Kuching Hainan Association** (36 Jln Carpenter). Mount the staircase (there are clean bathrooms on the 1st floor) and you soon get to a vivid little Chinese shrine, **Hin Ho Bio** (Temple of the Queen of Heaven; ⊙7am-about 5pm).

Jalan India   PEDESTRIAN STREET
(Jln India) Once Kuching's main shopping district for imported textiles, brassware and household goods, pedestrianised Jln

India – essentially the western continuation of Jln Carpenter – is still an exuberant commercial thoroughfare. The shops along the eastern section are mostly Chinese-owned; those to the west are run by Indian Muslims with roots in Tamil Nadu. This is *the* place in Kuching for cheap clothing.

Indian Mosque   MOSQUE
(Indian Mosque Lane; ⊙6am-8.30pm except during prayers) Turn off Jln India (between Nos 37 and 39A) or Jln Gambier (between Nos 24 and 25A) onto tiny **Indian Mosque Lane** (Jln Sempit) and you enter another world. At the Jln Gambier end, shops sell spices in bulk – orange-yellow turmeric, greenish-yellow coriander, reddish-orange chilli powder – and the aromas are both exhilarating and overwhelming! Further along, a hole-in-the-wall **hat shop** sells white crocheted caps (RM10) for men who have performed the hajj to Mecca and *songkok* (RM25), the black velvet hats worn by Malay men on formal occasions.

About midway between the two thoroughfares, entirely surrounded by houses and shops, stands Kuching's oldest mosque, built of *belian* (ironwood) in 1863 by Muslim traders from Tamil Nadu. Painted turquoise and notable for its simplicity, it is an island of peace in the middle of Kuching's bustling commerce.

FREE Sarawak Museum   MUSEUM
(☑244-232; www.museum.sarawak.gov.my; Jln Tun Abang Haji Openg; ⊙9am-4.30pm) Established in 1891, the excellent Sarawak Museum has a first-rate collection of cultural artefacts and is a must-visit for anyone interested in Borneo's peoples and habitats.

Old Building
At the top of the hill, on the western side of Jln Tun Abang Haji Openg, the Old Building has an ethnography section upstairs with superb exhibits on: Indigenous crafts, including masks, spears, basketry, musical instruments and a Bidayuh door charm for keeping evil spirits at bay; native customs such as tattooing and the infamous *palang* (see p161 and p182); and longhouses, including a full-size Iban longhouse and scale models for other groups.

Downstairs is an old-fashioned natural-history museum whose highlight – remembered with horror by generations of Kuching children – is a hairball taken from the stomach of a man-eating crocodile, accompanied by the following explanation: 'human dental plate found attached to hairball'. And if this

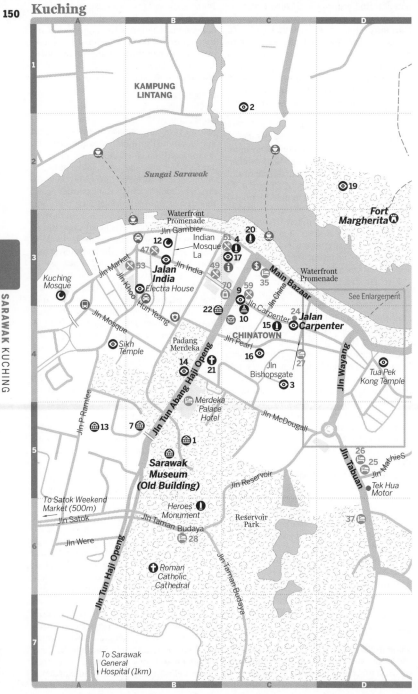

SARAWAK KUCHING

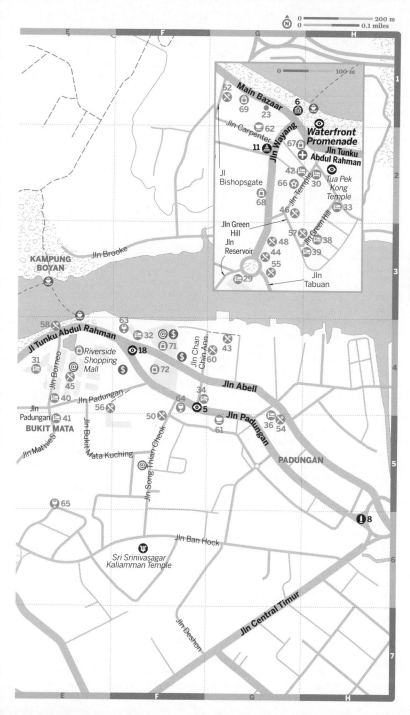

KUCHING

Kuching

Top Sights	
Fort Margherita	D3
Jalan Carpenter	C4
Jalan India	B3
Sarawak Museum (Old Building)	B5
Waterfront Promenade	H1
Sights	
1 Art Museum	B5
2 Astana	C1
3 Bishop's House	C4
4 Brooke Memorial	C3
5 Cats Column	F4
6 Chinese History Museum	G1
7 Dewan Tun Abdul Razak	B5
8 Great Cat of Kuching	H6
9 Harmony Arch	C3
10 Hiang Thian Siang Temple	C4
Hin Bio Temple	(see 15)
11 Hong San Si Temple	G2
12 Indian Mosque	B3
13 Islamic Museum	A5
14 Kapok Tree	B4
15 Kuching Hainan Association	C4
16 Old Anglican Cemetery	C4
17 Old Court House	C3
18 Polychrome Cats	F4
19 Sarawak State Assembly	D2
20 Square Tower	C3
21 St Thomas's Cathedral	B4
22 Textile Museum	B4
Activities, Courses & Tours	
23 Borneo Adventure	G1
Borneo Fairyland	(see 35)
Borneo Interland Travel	(see 23)
24 Bumbu Cooking School	C4
CPH Travel	(see 61)
Singgahsana Lodge	(see 42)
Sleeping	
25 B&B Inn	D5
26 Borneo Hotel	D5
27 Diocesan Centre	C4
28 Fairview Guesthouse	B6
29 Fata Hotel	G3
30 Harbour View Hotel	H2
31 Hilton Kuching Hotel	E4
32 Hotel Grand Margherita Kuching	F4
33 John's Place	H2
34 Kapit Hotel	F4
35 Kuching Waterfront Lodge	C3
36 Lime Tree Hotel	G5
37 Lodge 121	D6
38 Mandarin Hotel	H3
39 Nomad Borneo B&B	H3
40 Pinnacles	E4
41 Pullman Kuching	E5
42 Singgahsana Lodge	G2

isn't enough to put you off taking a dip in a muddy estuary, the 'watch found inside stomach' (a croc's stomach, of course) surely will – unless you'd like your cell phone to feature in some future exhibit!

Akuarium
(8.30am-5.30pm) In an outdoor pavilion behind the Old Building, the Akuarium is run by the city, on a shoestring budget, for educational purposes. It houses fish tanks (it's nice to see local fish that aren't laid out on ice, ready to be grilled, fried or baked) as well as turtles and crocodiles. To the south, a landscaped **public garden** leads past flowers and fountains to the **Heroes' Monument**.

Art Museum
Down the driveway from the Old Building, the Art Museum (Muzium Seni) features sculpture and paintings inspired by Dayak motifs and traditions and by Borneo's flora, fauna and landscapes.

Dewan Tun Abdul Razak
On the western side of Jln Tun Abang Haji Openg, Dewan Tun Abdul Razak (New Building) is linked by a footbridge to the Old Building. It has fine permanent exhibits on: Sarawak's fascinating history from the Brunei sultanate through the Brooke era; prehistoric archaeology, including objects from the Niah Caves; Chinese ceramics; and colourful Dayak crafts and costumes.

Islamic Museum
(Jln P Ramlee) Directly behind Dewan Tun Abdul Razak, this museum displays a little bit of everything related to Muslim material culture in Sarawak, including an astrolabe of the sort that helped Arab mariners travel this far east.

FREE **Chinese History Museum** MUSEUM
(cnr Main Bazaar & Jln Wayang; 9am-4.30pm) Housed in the century-old Chinese Court building, the Chinese History Museum provides an excellent introduction to the nine Chinese communities – each with its

own dialect, cuisine and temples – who began settling in Sarawak around 1830. Highlights include ceramics, musical instruments and some fearsome dragon- and lion-dance costumes. Paul never tires of sharing his enthusiasm and knowledge with visitors. The entrance is on the river side of the building.

FREE **Textile Museum** MUSEUM
(Jln Tun Abang Haji Openg; ⊙9am-4.30pm) Housed in a 'colonial Baroque'–style building constructed in 1909, this museum displays some superb examples of traditional Sarawakian textiles, including Malay *songket* (gold brocade cloth), as well as the hats, mats, belts, basketwork, beadwork, silverwork, barkwork, bangles and ceremonial headdresses created by Dayak groups such as the Iban, Bidayuh and Penan. Dioramas recreate the sartorial exuberance of Orang Ulu, Malay, Chinese and Indian weddings. Explanatory panels shed light on materials and techniques.

Fort Margherita HISTORIC FORT
(north bank of Sungai Sarawak, Kampung Boyan; ⊙9am-4.30pm) Built by Charles Brooke in 1879 and named after his wife, Ranee Margaret, this hilltop fortress long protected Kuching against surprise attack by pirates. It did so exclusively as a remarkably successful deterrent: troops stationed here never fired a shot in anger.

Inspired by an English Renaissance castle, whitewashed Fort Margherita manages to feel both medieval-European and tropical. A steep spiral staircase leads up three flights of stairs to the crenellated roof, a great place to take in panoramic views of the river and get a feel for the lie of the city.

To get there, take a *tambang* (50 sen) from the Waterfront Promenade to Kampung Boyan and then follow the signs up through the flowery village for 500m.

Astana GOVERNOR'S RESIDENCE
(north bank of Sungai Sarawak, Petra Jaya; closed to public) Built by Charles Brooke in 1869, the

Astana (Bahasa Sarawak for 'palace') and its manicured gardens still serve as the home of the governor of Sarawak. The best views are actually from the south (city centre) bank of the river, so it's not really worth taking a *tambang* across.

To walk from the Astana to Fort Margherita, you have to circle a long way north, around the Sarawak State Assembly.

Sarawak State Assembly STATE PARLIAMENT
(Dewan Undangan Negeri; north bank of Sungai Sarawak, Petra Jaya; closed to public) Inaugurated in 2009, the iconic home of Sarawak's State Assembly is an imposing structure whose soaring golden roof is said to resemble either a *payung* (umbrella) or a *terendak* (Melanau sunhat). The best views are from Jln Bishopsgate and the Waterfront Promenade.

St Thomas's Cathedral CHURCH
(http://kuching.anglican.org; ⊙6am-4.30pm Mon-Sat, to 6pm or 7pm Sun) Facing **Padang Merdeka** (Independence Sq), with its huge and ancient **kapok tree**, Kuching's Anglican cathedral (1954) has a mid-20th-century look and, inside, a bright red barrel-vaulted ceiling. The main gate is usually closed, so enter from Jln McDougall – it's named after Kuching's first Anglican bishop, who arrived here in 1848.

At the top of the hill is the **Bishop's House**, Kuching's oldest building. It was constructed in 1849 – with admirable solidness – by a German shipwright.

Tucked away in a corner of the Anglican compound, behind the Verger's Quarters, is the **Old Anglican Cemetery**, a number of whose tombs – there are just a few dozen – go back to the 1840s. Some are finely carved in granite while others are just weathered wooden planks; several belong to infants.

Cat Statues PUBLIC ART
It's just a coincidence that in Bahasa Malaysia, Kuching (now spelled *kucing*) means 'cat', but the city fathers have milked the homonym for everything it's worth, branding Sarawak's capital as the 'Cat City' and erecting a number of marvellously kitschy cat statues to beautify the urban landscape.

Perched at the eastern end of Jln Padungan, the large white pussycat with the blue eyes, burgundy bow tie and wire whiskers is known as the **Great Cat of Kuching**. An ensemble of polychrome cats stands on Jln Tunku Abdul Rahman opposite the Hotel Grand Margherita Kuching. And on the roundabout at the corner of Jln Padungan and Jln Chan Chin Ann, there's a column

featuring four cats around the bottom and four Rafflesia flowers near the top – the latter are just below the cat-adorned shield of the South Kuching municipality.

Cat Museum MUSEUM
(⌨446-688, ext 805; www.dbku.gov.my/cat museum.htm; Bukit Siol, Jln Semariang; admission free, camera/video RM3/5; ⊙9am-5pm) A veritable shrine to feline kitsch, this homage to the city's name features hundreds of *kucing* figurines – some the size of a cow, others über-cute and very Japanese – alongside learned presentations on 'Cats in Malay Society' and 'Cats in Chinese Art'. It's situated 4km northwest of the Astana but, by road, 8km from the city centre (via Jln Satok) in the hilltop Kuching North City Hall (known by its Malay abbreviation, DBKU), a landmark prestige project – some say it looks like a UFO – inaugurated in 1993. A taxi from the centre costs RM20 to RM25. If you're going to the Santubong Peninsula by cab, you can stop here on the way.

🏃 Activities

Satok Weekend Market MARKET
(Pasar Minggu; Jln Satok; ⊙about noon-10pm Sat & 6am-1pm or 2pm Sun) Kuching's biggest and liveliest market begins around midday on Saturday, when rural folk, some from area longhouses, arrive with their fruits, vegies, fish and spices. The air is heady with the aromas of fresh coriander, ginger, herbs and jungle ferns, which are displayed among piles of bananas (10 kinds!), mangoes, custard apples and obscure jungle fruits. If you smell something overpoweringly sweet and sickly from November to February, chances are it's a durian. Vendors are friendly and many are happy to tell you about their wares, which are often divided into quantities worth RM1 or RM2.

The market is about 1km west of the Sarawak Museum. To get there from the centre, walk south on Jln Tun Abang Haji Openg and turn east at Jln Satok (under the flyover).

Hash House Harriers FUN RUNS
Kuching's various HHH chapters hold about half-a-dozen one- to two-hour runs, over meadow and dale (and through thick jungle), each Tuesday (for men only), Wednesday, Saturday and Sunday. For details, ask around or visit www.kuching cityhash.com, the website of the Saturday run. Visitors are welcome.

Kuching Bike Hash CYCLING
(www.kbh.doturf.com) Bashers gather every second Sunday afternoon to ride 13km to 25km. Visitors are welcome.

🏊 Courses

Bumbu Cooking School DAYAK COOKING
(☑019-879-1050, 012-897-2297; http://bumbu cookingclass.weebly.com; 57 Jln Carpenter; per person RM150, without market visit RM120; ⊗8.30am-12.30pm or 2.30-6.30pm daily) Raised in a Bidayuh village, Joseph teams up with his auntie and sister to teach the secrets of Sarawakstyle (ie Dayak) cooking. At the market you'll learn to spot top-quality, jungle-harvested *midin* ferns; back in the kitchen you'll learn to prepare this crunchy delicacy, along with a marinated meat dish and a coconut milk dessert, served in a *pandan*-leaf basket you weave yourself. A bit pricey but gets great reviews. Maximum six participants.

🧭 Tours

Some of the agencies below offer walking tours of Kuching.

You can visit all of the sites in our Western Sarawak section on your own but, except in a few cases (Bako National Park, Semenggoh Nature Reserve, the Santubong Peninsula and the Sarawak Cultural Village), you'll need your own wheels. Since renting a car or hiring a taxi can be pricey, it often makes more sense to link up with a tour operator.

Most of the hotels, hostels and guest houses we list either offer their own tours or have a tour operator they like working with. The Visitors Information Centre can supply you with a list of well-established operators and, while they can't steer business to a specific company, they can point you in the right direction based on your preferences.

Operators:

Borneo Adventure WILDLIFE, TREKKING
(☑245-175; www.borneoadventure.com; 55 Main Bazaar) Award-winning company that sets the standard for Borneo tours and is the leader in cooperative projects benefiting Sarawak's indigenous peoples. Excellent guides.

Borneo Fairyland CULTURE, WILDLIFE
(☑420-194, 420-195; http://borneofairyland.tripod.com; 18 Main Bazaar)

Borneo Interland Travel CULTURE, PARKS
(☑413-595; www.bitravel.com.my; 1st fl, 63 Main Bazaar)

Borneo Trek & Kayak Adventure KAYAKING
(Rainforest Kayaking; ☑240-571; http://rainforest kayaking.com) Specialises in river trips.

Sarawak is the most culturally diverse state in Malaysia. The largest ethnic groups are the Iban (29%), Chinese (25%), Malay (22%), Bidayuh (8%) and Melanau (6%); other Dayak groups make up a further 5%. Virtually all Malays and about half of the Melanau are Muslim; the vast majority of other Dayaks and many Chinese belong to various Christian denominations.

CPH Travel BOATING, WILDLIFE
(www.cphtravel.com.my) Jln Padungan (☑243-708, 414-921; 70 Jln Padungan); Damai Puri Resort & Spa (☑846-618; Santubong Peninsula) A long-established and respected agency.

Singgahsana Lodge WALKING, TREKKING
(☑429-277; www.singgahsana.com; 1 Jln Temple) Runs Kuching walking tours and gets excellent reviews for its treks.

🎊 Festivals & Events

Rainforest World Music Festival MUSIC
(www.rainforestmusic-borneo.com; 1-/3-day pass RM110/300; ⊗2nd weekend in Jul) This three-day musical extravaganza brings together Dayak bands with international artists. Held in the Sarawak Cultural Village. Accommodation gets booked out well in advance.

Kuching Festival Fair FOOD
(Jln Padungan; ⊗5-11pm for 3 weeks late Jul-Aug) Scores of food stalls serve the dishes of various Chinese communities, Nyonya desserts and beer. Held next to Kuching South City Hall (MBKS Building), about 2km southeast of the Hilton.

Chinese New Year CELEBRATION
(⊗late Jan or early Feb) The main festivities are along Jln Padungan.

Mooncake Festival STREET FAIR
(⊗Sep or early Oct) Musical performances and food stalls selling food, drink and, of course, mooncakes take over Jln Carpenter.

🛏 Sleeping

Kuching's accommodation options range from international-standard suites with high-rise views to windowless, musty cells deep inside converted Chinese shophouses. Most of the budget places are in or near Chinatown, while the top-end spots are a bit to the east in Kuching's high-rise district, on or near Jln Tunku Abdul Rahman. There's a cluster of small, cheap hotels in the ugly commercial blocks on L-shaped Jln Green Hill. In most budget guest houses, the majority of the rooms – especially those under RM50 – have shared bathrooms. Prices at some guest houses rise in July, or from June to September.

Most hotels have pricey laundry services with per-piece rates and some guest houses have washing machines. Or you can head to **Mr Clean** (☏246-424; Jln Green Hill; per kg RM7, 4hr service RM10.50; ◷8am-6pm Mon-Sat, to 4pm Sun & holidays), a reliable laundrette on a commercial backstreet a block northeast of the Mandarin Hotel.

TOP CHOICE **Singgahsana Lodge** GUEST HOUSE **$$**
(☏429-277; www.singgahsana.com; 1 Jln Temple; dm RM30, d with shared/private bathroom RM88/98; ❊@⏾) Setting the Kuching standard for backpacker digs, this hugely popular guest house, decked out with stylish Dayak crafts, has an unbeatable location, a great chill-out lobby and a tropical rooftop bar. Prices aren't low and the rooms are far from luxurious, but breakfast is included. The shared bathrooms are spotless. Laundry costs RM5 per kilo. Organises group trips to Kuching-area nature sites.

Lime Tree Hotel HOTEL **$$**
(☏414-600; www.limetreehotel.com.my; Lot 317, Jln Abell; d/family ste RM160/390; ❊@⏾) Dashes of lime green – a pillow, a bar of soap, a staff member's tie, a cocktail sipped in the lobby's Cafe Sublime – accent every room of this semi-boutique hotel, opened in 2009. The 56 rooms are sleek and minimalist and offer good value. Lift-equipped. Situated at the eastern edge of the lively main tourist zone.

Hilton Kuching Hotel HOTEL **$$$**
(☏248-200; www.hilton.com; Jln Tunku Abdul Rahman; s/d RM364/399; ❊@⏾❄) Dominating the waterfront even from across the street, the Hilton has 350 spacious, international-standard rooms – newly renovated in shades of cream, beige and maroon – with flat-screen consoles, LED reading lights and glass-topped work desks. Amenities include two business centres, a spa, a fitness centre and a lobby cafe with scrumptious cakes.

Hotel Grand Margherita Kuching HOTEL **$$$**
(☏423-111; www.grandmargherita.com; Jln Tunku Abdul Rahman; d incl breakfast RM327; ❊@⏾❄) On a fine piece of riverfront real estate smack dab in the middle of town, this place will spoil you with a bright, modern lobby,

288 well-kept, very comfortable rooms and amenities such as a fitness centre and river-view pool.

Mandarin Hotel HOTEL **$**
(☏418-269; 6 Jln Green Hill; d from RM55; ❊) This old-time Chinese hotel – so traditional it lacks not only a website but even an email address – is head and shoulders above half-a-dozen similarly priced joints nearby. Has 20 clean, no-frills rooms with windows (no mustiness!) and '70s-style air-con. Central.

Lodge 121 HOSTEL **$**
(☏428-121; www.lodge121.com; Lot 121, Jln Tabuan, 1st fl; dm/s/d/tr/q with shared bathroom RM24/49/69/89/119, d/tr RM99/129; ❊@⏾) Polished concrete abounds at this mod charmer, whose owners have transformed a commercial space into a sleek, spotless and low-key hang-out for flashpackers. The carpeted dorm room, with mattresses on the floor, is in the garret, up the stairs from the bathroom. All 20 rooms have windows, either to the outside or a hallway. Prices include a simple breakfast. Coffee and tea are free.

Diocesan Centre GUEST HOUSE **$**
(☏381-442, 016-525-0468; bishopk@streamyx.com; Jln McDougall; s/d with shared bathroom RM20/25, apt with bathroom & kitchen RM30-50; ◷office 8.30am-approx 5pm Mon-Fri; ❊) In a century-old building behind the Anglican Cathedral, this very basic guest house has 36 gloriously ventilated rooms – no musty smell! – with cheap pressboard walls, twin beds, high ceilings and big windows. Has a bathroom on the ground floor and a night toilet on the 2nd floor. Enter from Jln McDougall; guests can request a key to the back gate, situated just a block south of Jln Carpenter. On weekdays after 5pm and on the weekend, call ☏016-525-0468. The best ultra-budget deal in town.

Harbour View Hotel HOTEL **$$**
(☏274-666; www.harbourview.com.my; Jln Temple; s/d RM130/155; ❊@⏾) If it's modern comforts you're after, this 243-room tower, 13 storeys high, is one of Kuching's best bargains – it offers full Western facilities for a thoroughly Southeast Asian price. The Malay, Chinese and Western buffet breakfast (RM25) is a lavish affair.

Pullman Kuching HOTEL **$$**
(☏222-888; www.pullmankuching.com; 1A Jln Mathies, Bukit Mata; d from RM265; ❊@⏾❄) Inaugurated in 2010, the Accor-affiliated Pullman

has 389 rooms – in subdued tones of aquamarine, brown, white and green – spread over 23 floors. The focus is on business travellers, but the hotel offers pretty good value (except that internet use costs a fortune).

Fairview Guesthouse GUEST HOUSE **$**
(☎240-017, 016-870-2005; www.fairview.my; 6 Jln Taman Budaya; dm/s/d/f incl breakfast RM25/50/70/150; ❄@) An oldie but a goodie, this garden villa, a bit out of the centre, scores big points for its unpretentious atmosphere and friendly owners who run great tailor-made tours. Room rates rise a bit from June to September.

Nomad Borneo B&B HOSTEL **$**
(☎237-831; www.borneobnb.com; 3 Jln Green Hill; dm/s/d/f RM18/40/50/90; ❄@wi-fi) There's a buzzing backpacker vibe at this Iban-run favourite. Bright patches of paint enliven the rooms, and guests congregate in the common area to hang out with the friendly management. The dorm rooms have windows, but the cell-like singles and doubles make do with exhaust fans. Laundry costs RM6 per load.

Tracks B&B HOSTEL **$**
(☎019-640-7372; www.tracksbnb.com; 5 Jln Green Hill; dm/d incl breakfast RM15/40; ❄@wi-fi) Run by the same people as neighbouring Nomad, this establishment, opened in 2010, has a laid-back local ambience, plenty of primary colours, graffiti testimonials on the stairwell walls, a washing machine and all-you-can-drink tea and coffee. Each floor is equipped with a bathroom, a kitchen and a communal room with cable TV. All but two rooms have windows; none have private bathrooms.

Pinnacles HOSTEL **$**
(☎419-100; www.pinnacleskuching.com; Lot 21, Block G, Jln Borneo, 1st fl; dm/d with shared bathroom RM30/80, d/q RM110/135; ❄@wi-fi) A bright orange lobby leads to 10 well-kept but unromantic rooms, all of them clean, some with airwell-view windows. Prices include breakfast.

B&B Inn HOSTEL **$**
(☎237-366; bnbswk@streamyx.com; 30-I Jln Tabuan; dm RM16, s/d/tr with shared bathroom RM25/35/45, d RM70; ❄@wi-fi) Clean, simple and low-key, this 12-room establishment has a lived-in, old-fashioned feel. Air-con costs RM5 extra per room per day. Women and men have separate dorm rooms. A few rooms lack windows.

John's Place GUEST HOUSE **$**
(☎258-329; 5 Jln Green Hill; d RM55-60, tr RM80; ❄@wi-fi) Hidden away in a commercial building, John's is a neat but rather unexciting spot to lay your head. Has 13 simple, practical rooms of medium size with spring mattresses and subdued colours – and without musty odours. The cheaper doubles look out onto the hallway.

Kuching Waterfront Lodge GUEST HOUSE **$$**
(☎231-111; www.kuchingwaterfrontlodge.com; 15 Main Bazaar; dm incl breakfast RM35-40, d RM115; ❄@wi-fi) The airy lobby, looking out on Main Bazaar, is stacked with traditional Chinese woodwork. Unfortunately, the public spaces have a lot more charm than the 22 rooms, which feel worn and, since most lack windows, tend to be musty.

Borneo Hotel HOTEL **$$**
(☎244-122; borneokg@tm.net.my; 30C Jln Tabuan; s/tw/tr RM120/135/155; ❄wi-fi) Kuching's first tourist-class hotel, built in the 1950s, is now a bit dowdy, but the marble lobby still gleams and the 65 rooms are clean and fairly spacious. Rooms without windows are cheaper but may be musty. Lift-equipped.

Kapit Hotel HOTEL **$**
(☎244-179, 420-091; kapithotelkuching@hotmail.com; 59 Jln Padungan; d/tr/q RM55/75/85; ❄wi-fi) This old Chinese hotel offers clean, utilitarian accommodation, spiced up with a bit of traffic noise. Not all 16 rooms have windows. In the heart of Kuching's nightlife district.

Fata Hotel HOTEL **$**
(☎248-111; fatahotel@hotmail.com; Jln McDougall, 1st fl; s/d/tr from RM61/68/88; ❄@wi-fi) A staircase decorated with tiny coloured tiles leads to 57 simple rooms that are slightly timeworn but clean. Has two wings, one standard, the other deluxe. Views are quintessentially Kuching: shophouses and traffic.

Eating

Kuching is a great place to work your way through the entire range of Sarawak-style Malay cooking and the cuisines of the city's nine Chinese dialect groups. At hawker centres, you can pick and choose from a variety of stalls, each specialising in a particular culinary tradition or dish. Jln Padungan is undergoing something of a restaurant, cafe and bar boom. For good Western fare try the upmarket hotels.

TOP CHOICE **Top Spot Food Court** SEAFOOD **$$**
(Jln Padungan; fish per kg RM35-70, vegetable dishes RM8-12; ⏲noon-11pm) A perennial favourite among locals and visitors alike, this lively, neon-lit courtyard and its half-a-dozen

seafooderies sits, rather improbably, on the roof of a concrete parking garage – look for the giant backlit lobster. Order anything from abalone and banana prawns to numerous varieties of fish (grilled white pomfret is a particular delicacy), chasing down your meal with a cold bottle of Tiger beer. Locals speak highly of Ling Loong Seafood (store No 6).

TOP CHOICE **Junk** WESTERN **$$$**
(☎082-259450; 80 Jln Wayang; mains RM20-50; ☺6-11pm, closed Tue) Filled to the brim with antiques, this chic complex of dining rooms (three) and bars (two) – housed in three 1920s shophouses – is a favourite among Malaysian celebs, who also love the lounge, amply supplied with pillows and provocatively decorated with pop art. The food is Western and fusion, with an Italian bias. Pasta costs RM24 to RM32, pizzas are RM20 to RM38.

TOP CHOICE **Jambu** FRENCH-INSPIRED **$$$**
(☎235-292; www.jamburestaurant.com; 32 Jln Crookshank; mains RM26-50; ☺5-11pm or midnight, closed Mon) Once the venue for elegant colonial parties (check out the photos on the walls) this 1920s mansion - with teak floors and soaring ceilings - is the best place in town for an elegant, French-accented meal. While enjoying a New Zealand steak with peppercorn sauce, you can decide whether to order profiteroles or crème brûlée for dessert. Has a stylish garden bar featuring tapas. Named for the *jambu air* (water apple) tree in the yard. Situated 1.5km south of the centre along Jln Tabuan and then Jln Crookshank.

Bla Bla Bla CHINESE, FUSION **$$$**
(☎233-944; 27 Jln Tabuan; most mains RM22-40; ☺6pm-midnight, closed Tue) Innovative, chic and stylish, Bla Bla Bla serves Chinese-inspired dishes that – like the decor, the koi ponds and the Balinese Buddha – range from traditional to far-out. Specialities include *midin* salad, cashew-nut prawns, ostrich meat stuffed with mozzarella, 'coffee chicken' and homemade cheesecake. The generous portions are designed to be shared.

Popular Vegetarian VEGETARIAN **$**
(Lot 105, Section 50, Jln Abell; 3-course lunch RM5; ☺9.30am-2pm & 5.30-9.30pm; ☑) Serves superb vegie versions of Chinese, Malay and assorted Asian dishes made with soy, mushrooms and oats instead of meat. Specialities include homemade bean curd, *cangkok Sabah* (a leafy local vegetable stir-fried with ginger), crunchy, stir-fried *midin* (a Sarawak classic) and refreshing *kedongdong* (umbra) juice. Situated four buildings south of the Lime Tree Hotel.

Open-Air Market HAWKER CENTRE **$**
(Jln Khoo Hun Yeang; mains from RM2.50-4; ☺6am or 7am-evening, some stalls to 9pm) The best hawker centre in town, with Malay and Chinese sections separated by a parking area. Dishes to look for include superb *laksa*, Chinese-style *mee sapi* (beef noodle soup), red *kolo mee* (noodles with sweet barbecue sauce), tomato *kway teow* (another fried rice-noodle dish) and shaved ice desserts (ask for 'ABC'). Perfect for breakfast before boarding the bus to Bako National Park.

Yang Choon Tai Hawker Centre
HAWKER CENTRE **$**
(23 Jln Carpenter; mains RM3.50-6; ☺6am-1am) There are some brilliant food stalls, run by members of the Teochew Chinese community, directly across the street from Hiang Thian Siang Temple. The stalls in this open-air food court serve up an eclectic assortment of native bites – *kolo mee* (flash-boiled egg noodles) with seafood and *cha siaw*

KEK LAPIS – COLOURFUL LAYER CAKES

The people of Kuching love to add a dash of colour to festivities, so it comes as no surprise to see stalls selling *kek lapis* (striped layer cakes) sprouting up around town (eg along Main Bazaar and the Waterfront Promenade) during festivals, including Hari Raya (Ramadan).

Kek lapis is made with wheat flour, egg, prodigious quantities of butter or margarine, and flavourings such as melon, blueberry or – a local favourite – *pandan* leaves. Since *kek lapis* are prepared one layer at a time and each layer – there can be 30 or more – takes five or six minutes to bake, a single cake can take up to five hours from start to finish.

Some 65 flavours of *kek lapis*, including *pandan*, mango, mint, green tea, durian and watermelon, are available year-round – to satisfy demand from Peninsular Malaysians – at **Maria Kek Lapis** (☎252-734; http://22.com.my/mariakeklapissarawak; 4 Jln Bishopsgate; ☺9am-6.30pm). Free tastes are on offer. Cakes stay fresh for about two weeks at room temperature and a month in the fridge.

LAKSA LUCK

Borneo's luckiest visitors start the day with a breakfast of Sarawak-style *laksa*, noodle soup made with coconut milk, lemon grass, sour tamarind and fiery *sambal belacan* (shrimp-paste sauce), with fresh calamansi lime juice squeezed on top. Unbelievably *lazat* ('delicious' in Bahasa Malaysia)!

(BBQ pork) and, in the morning, rice porridge with pork and *laksa* (RM4).

Waterfront Promenade   FOOD STALLS **$**
(Jln Tunku Abdul Rahman, opposite Hilton Kuching Hotel; meals from RM5; ☺evening) What could be better than an evening stroll along the river followed by fresh fruit juice and a few sticks of *satay*?

Magna Carta   ITALIAN **$$**
(Sarawak Tourism Complex, Jln Tun Abang Haji Openg; mains from RM12; ☺10am-midnight) For great Brooke-era atmosphere, you can choose between the breezy veranda, with garden views, and the interior, whose decor is a mash-up of medieval England and 19th-century Straits Chinese. Good options include pasta, pizza with exquisitely thin crust, homemade bread and freshly squeezed orange juice. Faces the river.

Rumah Hijau Cafe   MALAY **$$**
(✆016-589-1947; 24A & 24B Jln Rubber; mains RM5-7; ☺8am-5pm, closed Fri) Locals with a hankering for authentic Malay dishes, served in informal surrounds, often head to an old, wooden *rumah* (house), painted *hijau* (green), a few blocks west of the Satok Weekend Market. Specialities include *nasi ayam penyet* (breaded chicken thighs with rice and gravy; RM7) and, on Thursday, Saturday and Sunday, Indian biryani rice dishes. You can dine alfresco in the garden or à la air-con inside.

Vegetarian Food   VEGETARIAN **$**
(Jln Green Hill; mains RM3.50-5; ☺6am-3.30pm; ✍) Situated at the outside corner of Viva Cafe, a mini-hawkers centre, this stall does cheap, tasty vegie versions of all the local favourites.

Green Hill Corner   HAWKER CENTRE **$**
(cnr Jln Temple & Jln Green Hill; meals RM2.50-6; ☺7am-11pm) Several stalls here crank out porridge, *laksa*, chicken rice and noodle

dishes. Nestlé Milo adverts surround diners from every angle.

Lyn's Thandoori Restaurant   INDIAN **$$**
(Lot 267, Jln Song Thian Cheok; mains RM16-22; ☺9am-10pm Mon-Sat, 5-10pm Sun; ✍) Situated 300m due north of Kuching's Hindu temple, this upmarket North Indian place specialises in tandoori chicken, as you'd expect, but also serves delicious mutton, fish and almost 50 vegie options, including 18 types of *paneer*. The *naan* arrive crispy hot from the oven.

Little Lebanon   LEBANESE **$$**
(✆247-523; Japanese Bldg, Jln Barrack; mains RM5-15; ☺8.30am-10.30pm) Borneo's only Levantine restaurant sits in an elegant archway overlooking the eastern end of colourful Jln India. Arabic pop music wafts through the air as diners dip their pita pillows into freshly mashed hummus of a type entirely unknown in the Middle East. Also has a few Malay and Western dishes. Swing by after 6pm for flavourful puffs on a *sheesha* pipe (RM12 to RM21) – there's vanilla and pineapple, but mint is the best.

Benson Seafood   SEAFOOD **$$**
(Jln Chan Chin Ann; 'small' mains RM12-18; ☺5-11pm Mon, 9am-11pm Tue-Sun) In a gritty riverfront area that may become chic in five or 10 years, this informal, open-air pavilion is a big hit with Chinese families. Fresh Chinese-style fish and seafood and Sarawak classics such as *midin* stir-fried with *belacan* (shrimp paste) are brought steaming to big round tables covered with red tablecloths and surrounded by red plastic chairs. From the northern end of Jln Chan Chin Ann, turn right along the riverfront for half a block.

Zhun San Yen Vegetarian Food Centre
             VEGETARIAN **$**
(Jln Chan Chin Ann; meals from RM10; ☺8.30am-2pm & 5-8.30pm; ✍) A fine choice for a buffet-style Chinese vegie meal.

Jubilee Restaurant   INDIAN **$$**
(49 Jln India; ☺6.30am-6pm) A veteran halal Indian restaurant in the heart of Kuching's Indian Muslim district. Specialities include *nasi biryani* (rice with chicken, beef or lamb; RM6 to RM7), *roti canai* (flatbread; RM1) and *vaji* (deep-fried savoury breaded banana). The cook hails from Madras.

Dawn Cafe   HAWKER CENTRE **$**
(off Jln Borneo; mains RM2.50-4.50; ☺6am-8pm) The cheapest eats east of the Hilton. Hidden away a bit east of Jln Borneo, behind the

Tune Hotel, on the ground floor of two old cement office blocks.

Self-Catering

Ting & Ting
SUPERMARKET $

(30A Jln Tabuan; ⊙9am-9pm, closed Sun & holidays) An excellent source of wines (from Australia, California and France), Western-style snack food, chocolate, toiletries and diapers.

 Drinking

In most of Sarawak, an evening out on the town usually focuses on a meal, but cosmopolitan Kuching has a clutch of spirited drinking spots as well. Just for the record, Fort Margherita does not serve cocktails.

Jln Padungan mixes Chinese-owned businesses and a growing selection of cool cafes, pubs and nightspots that would not look out of place in Melbourne, London or San Francisco.

Junk
BAR

(80 Jln Wayang; mains RM20-50; ⊙4pm-1.30am, closed Tue) Kuching's chicest, most atmospheric hang-out is more than an Italian-inspired restaurant – it also has two bars: Junk Bar, tucked away in the back, and the Backstage Bar, chock full of old radios and musical instruments. The signature drink here is the 555 Sour, concocted with dried fruits.

Living Room
WINE BAR

(☑426-608; 23 Jln Wayang; ⊙6pm-midnight, closed Tue) At this soothing and impossibly cool cafe and wine bar, run by the same folks as Junk, you may find yourself wondering where you are: is this Borneo, Bali or Barcelona? Seated in the beer garden at the low, Japanese-style tables, you can choose from three types of mojito, one made with *tuak* (rice wine), or munch on finger food (eg fish and chicken nuggets).

Ruai
BAR

(off Persiaran An Hock; ⊙4pm-1am or 2am) An informal and welcoming Iban-owned open-air bar with a laid-back cool all its own. Serves as an urban *ruai* (the covered veranda of an Iban longhouse) for aficionados – local and expat – of vigorous outdoor activities such as caving, trekking and Hash runs. Situated behind the Telang Usan Hotel and 100m across a field (there's a path) downhill from the south side of the Pullman Kuching hotel. Gets very popular after about 10.30pm.

Funky Gibbon
BAR

(Jln Tunku Abdul Rahman, Riverbank Suites, ground fl; ⊙5pm-2am) A favourite with locals and expats alike. The veranda has superb river views. Got a soundtrack on your iPod you'd like to share? Ask to plug it into the sound system.

Black Bean Coffee & Tea Company
COFFEE SHOP

(Jln Carpenter; drinks RM2.50-4.20; ⊙9am-6pm Mon-Sat) Freshly ground coffee aromas assault the senses at this tiny shop, whose specialities – wholesale or fresh-brewed – include Arabica, Liberica and Robusta coffees grown in Java, Sumatra and, of course, Sarawak. Also serves oolong and green teas from Taiwan. Has just three tiny, round tables.

Coffee Bean & Tea Leaf
COFFEE SHOP

(Sarawak Plaza, Jln Tunku Abdul Rahman, ground fl; espresso RM6; ⊙8.30am-11.30pm Sun-Thu, to 12.30am Fri & Sat; ✴@🛜) The Kuching branch of this international chain, furnished with couches and wing chairs, serves muffins, Chicago cheesecake and sandwiches (RM10 to RM17). Internet computers cost RM3 per hour.

Ipanema
BAR

(62 Jln Padungan; ⊙4pm-1am Mon-Thu, to 2.30am Fri & Sat, closed Sun) The soundtrack here is sometimes Brazilian, but otherwise this sophisticated bar, its dark wood wall niches harbouring bottles of wine, makes you feel like you're somewhere in Europe. Beers on tap include Guinness (RM18 a pint) and Kilkenny (RM22). Also has a wine shop and serves Chinese and Western edibles.

Deli Cafe Patisseries
CAFE

(www.mydelicafe.com; 88 Main Bazaar; ⊙9am-5.30pm, closed Mon; @🛜) Arty photos, tiny round tables and a chill-out area at the back make this a stylish spot to relax with a cappuccino, latte or shake (RM7 to RM9). Got the munchies? Try a muffin, cupcake, French pastry or Western-style sandwich (RM8). Has free internet computers. Across from the Chinese History Museum.

Bing
COFFEE SHOP

(84 Jln Padungan; espresso RM5.50; ⊙10am-midnight; 🛜) This stylish, dimly lit coffee shop, in the heart of the Jln Padungan nightlife zone, serves a dozen varieties of hot and iced Illy coffee.

★ Entertainment

Kuching's charms are rather sedate, so other than eating well, hanging out in a cafe, pub or bar, and strolling along the Waterfront Promenade, there's not all that much happening after dark, ie after about 6.30pm year-round.

Star Cineplex
CINEMA

(www.starcineplex.com.my; 9th fl, parking garage, Jln Temple; tickets RM5-9; ⊙1st screening 11.30am, last screening 12.45am) For a couple of hours of escapism courtesy of Hollywood or the cinema industries of East Asia, head to Star Cineplex's five screens. Most movies are English; the rest have English subtitles. Situated across the back alley from the Singgahsana Lodge.

🔒 Shopping

If it's traditional Borneo arts and crafts you're after, then you've come to the right place – Kuching is the best spot in Borneo for collectors and cultural enthusiasts. Don't expect many bargains, but don't be afraid to negotiate either – there's plenty to choose from, and the quality varies as much as the price. Overpricing and dubiously 'aged' items are common, so be sure to spend some time browsing to familiarise yourself with prices and range.

For insights into Sarawak's varied and rich handicrafts traditions, stop by the Sarawak Museum and the Textile Museum and check out the website of the Kuching-based NGO **Crafthub** (www.crafthub.com.my), where you can download copies of *Crafts*, a quarterly magazine published for the Sarawak Craft Council.

The aptly named Main Bazaar, which stretches along the Waterfront Promenade from Jln Wayang west to Jln Tun Abang Haji Openg, is lined with souvenir shops, some outfitted like art galleries, others with more of a 'garage sale' appeal. Jln Carpenter, a block behind Main Bazaar, has a few shops as well (eg at 57 Jln Carpenter, home of the Bumbu Cooking School).

Main Bazaar
DAYAK CRAFTS

(Main Bazaar; ⊙approx 10am-6.30pm, some shops closed Sun) Along the block of Main Bazaar nearest Jln Wayang, you can admire and purchase a wide selection of handmade Dayak crafts from the highlands of Sarawak and Kalimantan. Items worth seeing, if not purchasing, include hand-woven textiles and baskets, masks, drums, brass gongs, statues (up to 2m high!), beaded headdresses, swords, spears, painted shields and cannons from Brunei. Some shops also carry pungent, locally grown pepper. At many places, staff enjoy explaining the origin and use of each item.

Sarawak Craft Council
DAYAK CRAFTS

(☎245-652; cnr Jln Tun Abang Haji Openg & Jln India; ⊙9am-4.30pm Mon-Fri) This state-run shop has a decent collection of Malay, Bidayuh, Iban and Orang Ulu handicrafts, including cowboy hats made entirely of bark. Prices are often lower at longhouses. Housed in the Round Tower, it was constructed in 1886 and used by the dreaded Kempeitai (Japanese military police) during the Occupation – that's why many locals believe it's haunted.

ARTrageously Ramsey Ong
ART GALLERY

(☎424-346; www.artrageouslyasia.com; 94 Main Bazaar; ⊙9am-6pm) Features vibrantly colourful contemporary paintings on tree bark, handmade paper and silk, many inspired by Sarawak's flora and fauna and traditional Dayak motifs. Also sells creative modern jewellery.

Fabriko
SARAWAK COUTURE

(☎422-333; 56 Main Bazaar; ⊙8.30am-5pm, closed Sun) This fine little boutique has a well-chosen selection of made-in-Sarawak fabrics and clothing in both traditional and modern designs, including silk sarongs and men's batik shirts.

Mohamed Yahia & Sons
BOOKS

(☎416-928; http://sites.google.com/site/mohdyahiasons; Basement, Sarawak Plaza, Jln Tunku Abdul Rahman; ⊙10am-9pm) Specialises in English-language books on Borneo. Also carries Sarawak maps, fiction, newspapers, magazines and plastic-wrapped LP guides (no peeking!).

Popular Book Co
BOOKS

(Level 3, Tun Jugah Shopping Centre, Jln Tunku Abdul Rahman; ⊙9am-7pm) A modern bookshop with a good selection of international titles.

Borneo Headhunters Tattoo & Piercing Studio
TATTOOING

(☎019-856-6317; www.borneoheadhunter.com; 47 Jln Wayang, 1st fl) International tattoo all-star Ernesto Umpie inks customers with a variety of intriguing Iban designs. Check out p162 for the full story on Borneo's traditional body art.

Tun Jugah Shopping Centre
SHOPPING MALL

(Jln Tunku Abdul Rahman; ⊙10am-9.30pm) A shiny place with stylish shops.

Sarawak Plaza
SHOPPING MALL

(Jln Tunku Abdul Rahman; ⊙10am-10pm)

BEJALAI BODY ART *BRANDON PRESSER*

Ernesto was the man to see around town for the best tattoos in all of Borneo. We talked with the artist about the cultural significance of his art, and the meaning behind his tribal tattoos.

The *bejalai*, he explained, can loosely be defined as a journey, or a voyage of discovery. After leaving the safety of the village, a warrior-to-be would head out into unfamiliar lands. Lessons were learned and skills were taught, like boat building, hunting, shamanism and even traditional dancing. With each task mastered, the traveller would add a tattoo to their body, creating a biographical constellation of swirling designs.

Traditionally, an Iban would get their first tattoo around the age of 10 or 11. The initiating tattoo was the eggplant flower, or the *bungai terung*, drawn on each shoulder. The design commemorated the beginning of one's journey as a man (women were known to get them as well). The squiggly centre of the flower symbolised new life and represented the intestines of a tadpole, visible through their translucent skin. The plant's petals were a reminder that patience is a virtue, and that only a patient man can truly learn life's lessons.

After receiving the eggplant ornaments, the Iban was ready to leave home. Scores of tattoos followed, including the popular crab design, usually inked on a man's arm. The design symbolised strength, and evoked the strong legs and hard shell of the crafty sideways walkers. When animism was more widely embraced, the Iban believed that the design, when drawn with magical ink, could act like the shell of a crab, protecting bearers from the blade of a machete. For women, tattoos on the arm meant that they were skilled at craft making.

Later on, the bravest travellers received the coveted throat tattoo as they evolved into a *bujang berani* (literally, 'brave bachelor'). The design – a fish body that morphs into a double-headed dragon – wanders up from the soft spot at the centre of the human clavicle, known as the 'life point' to the Iban.

In addition to the intricate rules of design, there were also several tattoo taboos surrounding the *bejalai* tradition. The most important faux pas to avoid was getting a tattoo on the top of one's hands – this area of the body was strictly reserved for those who had taken heads. Also, every animal inked facing inward must have something to eat – dragons were always depicted with a small lizard near their mouths – because if the design was left hungry it would feed on the bearer's soul.

Technically the *bejalai* never stopped during a warrior's life, although when they returned to their village, the tattoos acted like the stamps in a passport: visual aids when recounting stories of adventure. It is only through the *bejalai* that one could collect these veritable merit badges, and the number of tattoos acquired greatly increased one's desirability as a bachelor. It was also believed that a large number of tattoos enabled a soul to shine brightly in the afterlife.

Over the last century the tattooing materials have greatly changed. Traditionally, the ink was made from soot mixed with fermented sugarcane juice, and needles were made from bone or bamboo. Then brass needles were introduced, followed by steel, and in the 1970s household sewing needles were quite popular. Standard surgical steel needles are commonly used today.

In recent years, fewer Iban are getting inked, and those who do generally get designs commemorating trips to other countries, or military service. Although it is by no means a lost art, the tradition of *bejalai* body art is beginning to fade.

Ernesto K Umpie, 39, is a renowned Iban tattoo artist with a studio in downtown Kuching (p161). Visit www.borneoheadhunter.com to check out his work.

ⓘ Information

For details on the Indonesian consulate and the honorary consulates of the UK and Australia, see p307.

Dangers & Annoyances

There have recently been incidents of bag snatching from tourists (mainly women) by motorbike-mounted miscreants. Exercise reasonable caution when walking along deserted stretches of road (eg Jln Reservoir and Jln Tabuan), especially after dark. The British honorary consul advises visitors to avoid carrying vital documents in handbags and to secrete them instead in a money belt or hotel safe.

Emergency
Police, Ambulance & Fire (☏999)

Internet Access
Coffee Bean & Tea Leaf (ground fl, Sarawak Plaza, Jln Tunku Abdul Rahman; per hr RM3; ☺8.30am-11.30pm Sun-Thu, to 12.30am Fri & Sat) A Starbucks-style cafe with internet computers.

Cyber City (ground fl, Block D, Taman Sri Sarawak; 1st/2nd fl RM4/3; ☺10am-11pm Mon-Sat, 11am-11pm Sun & holidays) Hidden away behind the Riverside Shopping Mall (Jln Tunku Abdul Rahman) – to get there, exit the mall on the '2nd floor' and walk up the hill.

Daily Moo (8 Jln Song Thian Cheok; per hr RM3; ☺9am-11pm) An attractive little cafe with smoothies, coffee, cakes, breakfast and, in back, nine internet computers.

Maridon Treks (96 Main Bazaar, 1st fl; ☺10am-5.30pm) Free internet computers, wi-fi, tea and coffee.

Medical Services
Kuching has some first-rate but affordable medical facilities – some of the doctors are UK- and US-certified – so it's no surprise that 'medical tourism', especially from Indonesia, is on the rise. For minor ailments, guest houses and hotels can refer you to a general practitioner, who may be willing to make a house call.

Klinik Chan (☏240-307; 98 Main Bazaar; ☺8am-noon & 2-5pm Mon-Fri, 9am-noon Sat, Sun & holidays) Conveniently central. Great for minor ailments.

Kuching Specialist Hospital (☏365-777, emergency 365-030; www.kcsh.kpjhealth.com.my; Lot 10420, Block 11, Tabuan Stutong Commercial Centre, Jln Setia Raja; ☺emergency 24hr, clinics 8.30am-5pm Mon-Fri, to 12.30pm Sat, closed Sun & holidays) A private hospital with good facilities for tourists and English-speaking staff. Situated 9km southeast of the centre.

Normah Medical Specialist Centre (☏440-055, emergency 311-999; www.normah.com.my; Jln Tun Abdul Rahman, Petra Jaya; ☺emergency 24hr, clinic 8.30am-4.30pm Mon-Fri, to 1pm Sat) Considered Kuching's best private hospital by many expats. Has a 24-hour ambulance. Situated north of the river, about 6km by road (via Jln Satok and the Satok bridge) from the centre. Served by the same buses as Bako National Park.

Sarawak General Hospital (Hospital Umum Sarawak; ☏276-666; http://hus.moh.gov.my/v3, in Malay; Jln Hospital; ☺24hr) Kuching's large public hospital has good facilities and reasonable rates but is often overcrowded. Situated about 2km south of the centre along

Jln Tun Abang Haji Openg. To get there, take bus K6, K8, K9 or K18.

Timberland Medical Centre (☏234-466, emergency 234-991; www.timberlandmedical.com; Mile 3, Jln Rock; ☺emergency 24hr) Private hospital with highly qualified staff. Has a 24-hour ambulance. Situated 5km south of the centre along Jln Tun Abang Haji Openg and then Jln Rock.

Money
Most of Kuching's banks and ATMs are on or near Jln Tunku Abdul Rahman. If you need to change cash or travellers cheques, money changers are a better bet than banks, which often aren't keen on handling cash (especially banknotes with certain serial numbers – go figure! – and US$1 bills). Exchange rates are pretty standard; rip-offs are vanishingly rare.

Airport Exchange Counter (RHB Bank; ☺8.30am-7.30pm) Cash only.

KK Abdul Majid & Sons (45 Jln India; ☺9am-6pm Mon-Sat, 9am-3pm Sun) A licensed money changer dealing in cash only.

Maybank (Jln Tunku Abdul Rahman; ☺9.15am-4.30pm Mon-Thu, to 4pm Fri) Has ATMs open 6am to midnight; there's a 24-hour ATM 20m to the west.

Mohamed Yahia & Sons (Basement, Sarawak Plaza, Jln Tunku Abdul Rahman; ☺10am-9pm) No commission, good rates, accepts US$100 bills and travellers cheques in six currencies. Inside the bookshop.

Standard Chartered Bank (Jln Padungan; ☺9.15am-3.45pm Mon-Fri) Has a 24-hour ATM.

United Overseas Bank (2 Main Bazaar; ☺9.30am-4.30pm Mon-Fri) Has a 24-hour ATM around the corner on Jln Tun Abang Haji Obeng.

Police
Police Hotline (☏244-444; ☺24hr)

Post
Main post office (Jln Tun Abang Haji Openg; ☺8am-4.30pm Mon-Sat, closed 1st Sat of month) A Corinthian column–adorned structure built in 1931.

Tourist Information
Maridon Treks (☏421-346; 96 Main Bazaar, 1st fl; ☺10am-5.30pm; @☎) Run by the owners of Singgahsana Lodge, Marina and Donald, this lounge is a great place to relax, meet other travellers, assemble groups for tours or treks, and get the latest low-down on local travel options. Has an informative bulletin board, internet computers, free wi-fi, free tea and coffee and a clean toilet.

National Park Booking Office (☏248-088; www.sarawakforestry.com; Sarawak Tourism Complex, Jln Tun Abang Haji Openg; ☺8am-

5pm Mon-Fri) Next door to the Visitors Information Centre, this is *the* place to come to book overnight stays at Kuching-area national parks. Staff sell brochures on each of Sarawak's national parks and have the latest news flashes on Rafflesia sightings, which they post in the window for 24-hour viewing (the unlucky can check out a pathetic plastic Rafflesia replica inside). Telephone enquiries are not only welcomed but patiently answered. Bookings for accommodation at Bako, Gunung Gading and Kubah National Parks and the Matang Wildlife Centre can also be made via http://ebooking.com.my.

Visa Department (Bahagian Visa; ✆245-661; www.imi.gov.my; 2nd fl, Bangunan Sultan Iskandar, Kompleks Pejabat Persekutuan, cnr Jln Tun Razak & Jln Simpang Tiga; ☺8am-5pm Mon-Thu, 8-11.45am & 2.15-5pm Fri) Situated in a 17-storey federal office building about 3km south of the centre (along Jln Tabuan). From the Saujana Bus Station, take City Public Link bus K8 or K11, which run every half-hour or so, or Sarawak Transport Company buses 8G1, 8G2 and 8G3 (all RM1). A taxi from the centre costs RM15.

Visitors Information Centre (✆410-944/2; www.sarawaktourism.com; Sarawak Tourism Complex, Jln Tun Abang Haji Openg; ☺8am-6pm Mon-Fri, 9am-3pm Sat, Sun & public holidays) Located in the atmospheric old courthouse complex (built 1887), this office has helpful and well-informed staff, free maps and brochures (eg the useful *Official Kuching Guide*), and oodles of travel information, much of it on bulletin boards.

Travel Agencies

Some operators listed on p155 are also travel agents.

❶ Getting There & Away

As more and more Sarawakians have acquired their own wheels, bus transport – especially short-haul routes in the Kuching area – has been slashed. For complicated political reasons, some services have been 'replaced' by unregulated and chaotic minibuses, which have irregular times, lack fixed stops and are basically useless.

The only way to get to many nature sites in Western Sarawak is to hire a taxi or join a tour group. The exceptions are Bako National Park and Semenggoh Nature Reserve and, somewhat less conveniently, the Wind Cave and the Fairy Cave.

Air

Kuching International Airport is 12km south of the centre. There is a **Tourist Information Centre** (☺9am-5pm) in the arrivals area just outside customs; ATMs are situated in front of McDonald's. For details on flights serving Kuching, see p316 and p317.

Boat

For details on the ferry to Sibu – much faster and a lot more fun than the bus – see p187. Ferries depart from the **Express Wharf**, situated 6km east of the centre. A taxi from town costs RM25.

Bus

Long-distance buses depart from the **Regional Express Bus Terminal** (Third Mile Bus Terminal; Jln Penrissen), which is about 5km south of the centre. A taxi from the centre costs RM20 or RM25. Every half-hour or so from about 6am to 6.30pm, various buses run by City Public Link (eg K9) and the STC (eg 3A, 4B, 6 and 2) link central Kuching's Saujana Bus Station with the Regional Express Bus Terminal. Saujana's ticket windows can point you to the next departure.

A dozen different companies send buses along Sarawak's northern coast to Miri (RM90, 15 hours), with stops at Sibu (RM50, eight hours), Bintulu (RM70, 12 hours), Batu Niah Junction (jumping-off point for Niah National Park) and Lambir Hills National Park. **Bus Asia** (✆082-411-111), for instance, has 11 departures a day, the first at 7.30am, the last at 10pm. To get to Brunei or Sabah, you have to change buses in Miri.

For details on buses to Lundu, see p179. Buses to Bau leave from central Kuching's Saujana Bus Station.

A variety of companies, including Bus Asia and SJS, have services to Pontianak (economy RM55, 1st class RM80, eight to nine hours) in West Kalimantan. They cross the border at the Tebedu–Entikong crossing, where travellers from 64 countries can get an Indonesian visa-on-arrival.

Reservations and tickets for travel on Bus Asia, Rapid Kuching, Biaramas and Petra Jaya – all run by the same company – can be arranged at the in-town office of **Bus Asia** (✆411-111; cnr Jln Abell & Jln Chan Chin Ann; ☺7am-10pm).

A **new long-distance bus terminal** (Sixth Mile Bus Terminal; cnr Jln Penrissen & Jln Airport) is being built 10km due south of the city centre. Near the airport at a spot popularly known as Mile 6, it is likely to come on line during the life of this guide.

Taxi

For some destinations, the only transport option – other than taking a tour – is going by taxi. Hiring a cab for the whole day should cost about RM160. If you'd like your driver to wait at your destination and then take you back to town, count on paying about RM20 per hour of wait time.

Sample one-way taxi fares from Kuching (prices are 50% higher at night):

» Annah Rais Longhouse – RM80

» Bako Bazaar (Bako National Park) – RM40

» Express Wharf (ferry to Sibu) – RM25

- » Fairy Cave – RM40
- » Kubah National Park – RM50
- » Matang Wildlife Centre – RM50
- » Santubong Peninsula Resorts – RM50
- » Sarawak Cultural Village – RM50
- » Semenggoh Nature Reserve – RM40
- » Wind Cave – RM40

Getting Around

Almost all of Kuching's attractions are within easy walking distance of each other. Public buses or taxis are only really needed to reach the airport (about 12km away), the Regional Express Bus Terminal (5km), the Express Wharf for the ferry to Sibu (6km) and the Cat Museum (8km by road).

To/From the Airport

The price of a taxi into Kuching is fixed at RM26. Coupons are sold inside the terminal next to the car-rental counters and outside at the head of the orderly taxi rank.

Buses no longer serve the airport but it may be possible to find a local bus on a nearby highway – exit the terminal, turn left, walk to the T-junction, turn right and the bus station should be on your left. Rumour has it that Rapid Kuching is looking into adding a bus line to the airport.

Boat

Tambang shuttle passengers back and forth across Sungai Sarawak, linking several jetties along the Waterfront Promenade with destinations such as Fort Margherita and the Astana. The fare for Sarawak's cheapest cruise is 40 sen, 50 sen or RM1 (more from 10pm to 6am), depending on whether you go straight across the river or sail at an angle; pay as you disembark. If a *tambang* isn't waiting when you arrive, just wait and one will usually materialise fairly soon.

Bicycle

Three Bikes (☑233-835, 429-277; 1 Jln Temple), based at Singgahsana Lodge, rents out bicycles for RM25 per day, mainly to Singgahsana guests. **Borneo Adventure** (☑245-175; 55 Main Bazaar) may also begin renting out mountain bikes.

On Jln Carpenter, basic bicycle shops can be found at Nos 83, 88 and 96.

Bus

Central Kuching's underdeveloped and somewhat chaotic local bus terminal, **Saujana Bus Station** (Jln Mosque), is situated on the dead-end street that links Jln Market with the Kuching Mosque. It is served by three bus companies:

Bau Transport Company Bus 2 goes to Bau (RM2, hourly).

City Public Link (☑239-178) A new company whose line numbers start with K (eg K6). Has a proper ticket counter with posted schedules. Urban lines, including to the Regional Express Bus Terminal, run from 6.30am to about 6pm. Also goes to the Semenggoh Wildlife Centre.

Sarawak Transport Company (STC; ☑016-886-0855) Has buses to the Regional Express Bus Terminal. The ticket window is in an old shipping container.

Car

Several car-rental agencies have desks, usually open from about 8am to 9pm, in the arrivals hall of Kuching airport. These include:

Ami Car Rental (☑579-679, 886-8889; www.amicarrental.com)

Golden System (☑611-359, 333-609, 016-888-3359; www.goldencar.com.my)

Hertz (☑450-740; www.hertz.com)

In the city centre, **Tek Hua Motor** (☑233-957, 019-887-6848; 68B Jln Tabuan; ⊗8am-6pm Mon-Sat) rents cars for RM100 a day, plus a deposit of RM200.

For details on the pitfalls of renting a car in Borneo, see p320.

Motorbike

Two motorbike repair shops on Jln Tabuan hire out motorbikes (including a helmet) for RM25 to RM40, plus a deposit of RM100. Insurance covers the bike but not the driver and may be valid only within a 60km radius of Kuching, so check before you head to Sematan, Lundu or Annah Rais.

An Hui Motor (☑412-419, 016-886-3328; 29 Jln Tabuan; ⊗8am-6pm Mon-Sat, to noon Sun) Charges RM30 per day for a Vespa-like Suzuki RG (110cc) or RGV (120cc). Next to Ting & Ting supermarket.

Tek Hua Motor (☑233-957, 019-887-6848; 68B Jln Tabuan; ⊗8am-6pm Mon-Sat) Has both manuals and automatics. Charges RM25 for a Suzuki V100 (100cc) or RM40 for a Suzuki VS125 (125cc). Call ahead for pick up or return on Sunday.

Taxi

Taxis can be hailed on the street. The larger hotels have taxi queues; other **taxi ranks** can be found on Jln Khoo Hun Yeang (near the Saujana Bus Station) and Jln Gambier (near the western end of Jln India).

As of July 2010, all Kuching taxis – except those on the flat-fare run to/from the airport (RM26) – are required to use meters; flag fall is RM10. There is no extra charge to summon a cab by phone.

One-way taxi fares from central Kuching:

- » Cat Museum (North Kuching) – RM20 to RM25

» Indonesian consulate – RM25

» Regional Express Bus Terminal – RM25

» Visa Department – RM15

WESTERN SARAWAK

From Tanjung Datu National Park at Sarawak's far western tip to Bako National Park northeast of Kuching, and inland to Annah Rais Longhouse and the Batang Ai Region, western Sarawak offers a dazzling array of natural sights. Most are within day-trip or overnight distance of Kuching.

Bako National Park

Occupying a jagged peninsula that juts out into the South China Sea, Sarawak's oldest national park (☑082-478-011; www.sarawakforestry.com; admission RM10) is just 37km northeast of downtown Kuching but feels like worlds and eons away. Many visitors cite this park as one of their favourite Borneo experiences.

The coast of the 27-sq-km peninsula consists of lovely pocket beaches tucked into secret bays, interspersed with wind-sculpted cliffs, forested bluffs and stretches of brilliant mangrove swamp. The interior of the park is home to streams, waterfalls and a range of distinct ecosystems, including classic lowland rainforest (mixed dipterocarp forest) and *kerangas* (heath forest). Hiking trails cross the sandstone plateau that forms the peninsula's backbone and connect with some of the main beaches, all of which can be reached by boat from park HQ.

The park is notable for its incredible biodiversity, which includes almost every vegetation type in Borneo and encompasses everything from terrestrial orchids and pitcher plants to long-tailed macaques and bearded pigs. Of course, the stars of the show are the proboscis monkeys, and Bako is one of the best places in Borneo to observe these endemics up close.

Bako is an easy day trip from Kuching, but it would be a shame to rush it – we recommend staying a night or two to really enjoy the wild beauty of the place. Getting to Bako by public transport is cheap and easy.

Dangers & Annoyances

The muddy, tannin-stained waters of Bako's rivers shelter crocodiles, so forget about swimming in them. A few years ago a schoolboy was eaten by a croc a bit upriver from Bako Bazaar; his body was never found.

Stinging jellyfish sometimes hang out near Bako's beaches, especially in April and May. Also to be avoided, especially around Telok Paku: stingrays, whose stabs can be quite painful.

To keep away the sandflies, use mozzie repellent.

◉ Sights & Activities

Interpretation Centre   MUSEUM

The visitors centre has informative, if old-fashioned, displays on various aspects of the park's ecology, including an introduction to the park's seven distinct ecosystems and an exposé of the co-dependent relationship between nepenthes (pitcher plants) and ants. An entertaining video on the proboscis monkey is shown at regular times and also on request – ask at the office. There are plans to move the centre to a new building.

Wildlife Watching   ANIMALS

Bako is one of the best places in Sarawak to see wild animals in their native habitat. The best times to spot jungle creatures is right after sunrise and right before sunset, so for the best wildlife watching you'll have to stay over.

Bako provides a protected home for incredible natural diversity. Scientists estimate that the park is home to about 190 kinds of bird, some of them migratory; 24 reptile species, including the common water monitor, which can reach 2m; and 37 species of mammal, including silver-leaf monkeys, palm squirrels and, at night, mouse deer, civets and colugos (flying lemurs).

Surprisingly, the area around park HQ is one of the best places to spot wildlife. Reddish-brown proboscis monkeys, the males' pendulous noses flopping as they chew on tender young leaves, can often be found around the mangrove boardwalk between the jetty and park HQ, in the trees along the Telok Assam beach near park HQ, along the Telok Paku Trail where they forage in the trees lining the cliff, and along the Telok Delima Trail.

Walk very quietly and listen for the primates as they crash through the trees. Proboscis monkeys show little fear of humans, but neither are they much interested in us. Their pot-bellied stomachs are filled with bacteria that help them derive nutrients from almost-indigestible leaves.

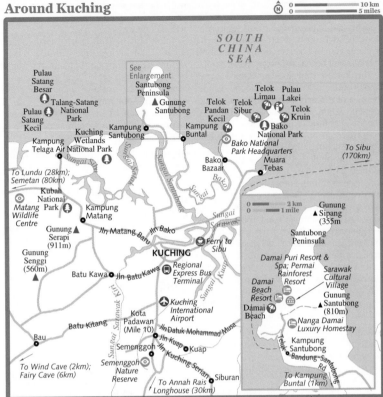

Some of the best bird-watching is near park HQ, especially in and around the mangroves at Telok Assam.

Mangrove forests are home to an assortment of peculiar creatures, including hermit crabs, fiddler crabs and mudskippers (fish that spend much of their time skipping around the tidal mud under mangrove trees). The Bornean bearded pigs that hang around near the cafeteria with their piglets are a big hit with kids. The largest of the creatures, who is truly massive, is a minor celebrity. A tourist guide was recently overheard saying, 'at the longhouse they would be on the grill already'.

Jungle Walks · HIKING

Bako's 17 trails are suitable for all levels of fitness and motivation, with routes ranging from short walks around park HQ to strenuous all-day treks to the far (ie eastern) end of the peninsula. It's easy to find your way around because trails are colour-coded and clearly marked with stripes of paint. Plan your route before starting out and aim to be back at Telok Assam before dark, ie by about 6pm at the latest. It's possible to hire a boat to one of the far beaches and then hike back, or to hike to one of the beaches and arrange for a boat to meet you there.

Park staff are happy to help you plan your visit, provide updates on trail conditions and tides, arrange boat hire and provision you with an excellent brochure (RM1.50) that has details on each of the park's hiking options. A billboard near the Education Centre lists all trails and conservative time estimates. Even if you know your route, let staff know where you'll be going so that they can inscribe you in the Guest Movement Register Book; sign back in when you return.

If you have only one day in Bako, try to get here early and attempt the **Lintang Trail** (5.8km, 3½ to four hours). It traverses a range of vegetation and climbs the sandstone escarpment up to the *kerangas,* where you'll find some grand views over the nearby rocky plateaus and many pitcher plants (especially along the trail's northeastern segment). Pitcher plants can also be seen on the trail down to Bako's best beach, at **Telok Pandan Kecil**.

The longest trail goes to **Telok Limau**, 13.2km from park HQ (eight hours), where there's a nice beach. Consider hoofing it one way and taking a boat the other (RM164). The area has little or no cell-phone coverage so don't count on being able to coordinate with your boatman by mobile.

Keep in mind that hiking in the tropics is much harder than in temperate zones. A good rule of thumb is that 1km in the tropics is equivalent to 2km in temperate zones. Take adequate water or purification tabs and be prepared for intense sun (with a sun hat and sunscreen) as it gets particularly hot in the *kerangas* and there's no shade for long stretches. Sun-sensitive folks might consider lightweight long-sleeve shirts and trousers. Mozzie repellent is a good idea as well.

A note on trail names: *tanjung* means point, *telok* means bay, *bukit* means hill, and *ulu* means upriver or interior.

Beaches
BEACHES

At Bako, it's easy to combine rainforest tramping, which quickly gets hot and sweaty, with a refreshing dip in the South China Sea.

Swimming is allowed at **Telok Assam**, near park HQ, but the water can be muddy. In the distance (to the west) you can see the Santubong Peninsula.

The gorgeous beach at **Telok Pandan Kecil**, a 2.5km walk from park HQ, is surrounded by spectacular sandstone rock formations. Around the point (to the northwest) is the famous **Bako Sea Stack**, an islet that looks like a cobra rearing its head. To get close enough for a photo, though, you'll have to hire a boat.

As you move east, the next beach you come to is **Telok Pandan Besar**, a quiet, attractive stretch of sand accessible only by boat (the trail that descends from the cliff top is closed). Hiring a boat at park HQ costs RM40/80 one way/return.

The beach at **Telok Sibur**, rarely visited by travellers, is accessible on foot (it's 5.3km from park HQ) but hard to reach as the descent is steep and you have to make your way through a mangrove swamp. Before heading out, check the tidal schedule with park staff to make sure the river

won't be too deep to cross, either going or returning. A boat from park HQ costs RM105 one way.

Telok Limau, at the park's northeastern tip, is 13.2km on foot from park HQ. A boat to/from Telok Limau and the nearby island of **Pulau Lakei**, which has a white-sand beach and the grave of a Malay warrior, costs RM164 one way.

Telok Kruin, at the peninsula's far eastern tip, is 12km on foot from park HQ; a boat ride costs RM250 one way.

Nightwalk
WILDLIFE WATCHING

(per person RM10; ◷1½-2hr) The creatures that are out and about at night are entirely different from those active during the day. The best way to see them – we're talking spiders, fireflies, cicadas, frogs, anemones, owls and the like – is to take a night-time walk led by a park ranger trained in spotting creatures that city slickers would walk right by. Reviewed by one traveller as 'awesome', Bako's night treks, when available, are not to be missed. Bring a torch (flashlight).

☞ Tours

Park HQ does not have enough permanent staff to accompany individual visitors, so if you'd like to hike with a guide, enquire at the boat terminal in Bako Bazaar or, better yet, ask the National Park Booking Office in Kuching for the phone numbers of approved guides. The park is very strict about allowing only certified guides (unlicensed guides and the groups they're with are forced to leave).

🛏 Sleeping

In-park accommodation often fills up, especially from June to August, so if you'd like to stay over book ahead:

» Online via http://ebooking.com.my
» At the National Park Booking Office in Kuching
» By phoning the park

Bako has developed a reputation for less-than-adequate accommodation but by the time you read this, the new hostel should be open and the six Type 5 chalets upgraded. There's a RM10 key deposit. Unlocked storage cubicles are available at park reception free of charge.

Forest Hostel
HOSTEL $

(4-bed r RM42) The brand-new hostel will have a private bathroom in each room; fees are likely to rise. Bring your own towel. Sheets are provided; blankets should be available on request.

That sign at Bako National Park's registration desk – 'Beware of Macaques' – is not a joke. The long-tailed macaques that hang about the park HQ are great to watch, but they are mischievous and cunning – an attitude fostered by tourists who insist on offering them food. The monkeys (and some tourists) are opportunists and will make running leaps at anything potentially edible they think they can carry off. Lock all your doors, close your bags and do not leave valuables, food or drink – or anything in a plastic bag – unattended, especially on the beaches or on the chalet verandas.

It's wise to leave the monkeys in peace – the males can be aggressive, and once you've seen a macaque tear open a drink can with its teeth you'll be happy that you didn't mess with them. Rangers advise against looking a macaque in the eye (he'll think you're about to attack) or screaming (if he knows you're scared, he'll be more aggressive). Recently, especially aggressive large males have been tranquilised, captured and released far, far away. Monkeys are not a problem after dark.

Forest Lodge Type 5   CHALET $$
(3-bed r RM105, 2-room chalets RM157.50) Each two-room (six-bed) chalet has one bathroom and one fridge. Fan-equipped.

Forest Lodge Type 6   CHALET $
(d RM52.50, 2-room chalets RM78.75) Each rustic, two-bed room has a wood-plank floor, private bathroom, fridge and fan.

Camping   CAMPING $
(per person RM5) The HQ's designated camping zone has only three spots. You can also pitch a tent in the park's far eastern reaches on Pulau Lakei (by boat RM164 one way) and at Telok Kruin (by boat RM250 one way).

✖ Eating

Cooking is not allowed in park accommodation, but the canteen can supply boiling water for instant noodles. If you bring your own coals and food, you can barbecue at the campground. Tap water at park HQ should be drinkable by the time you read this. The nearest grocery is in Bako Bazaar.

Canteen   CAFETERIA $
(buffet meals RM6-7; ⊙7.30am-10.30pm) The new macaque-proof cafeteria serves an unsurprising selection of fried rice, chicken, fish and hot dogs. A lunch buffet is served from 11.30am to 3pm, a dinner buffet from 6.30pm to 8pm or 9pm.

❶ Information

Park HQ and some other parts of the park have (low-power) mobile-phone coverage, ideal for coordinating your boat ride back to Bako Bazaar.

Cybercafe There are plans to set one up at park HQ.

Park HQ The helpful staff of the registration desk can advise you on hiking routes, boat hire and tidal conditions, and they sell an excellent brochure (RM1.50). The new HQ complex is made of concrete, which isn't as pretty as wood but is more ecologically sustainable and much longer-lasting.

❶ Getting There & Away

Bako National Park is accessible only by boat, but getting there by public transport is a cinch. First take one of the hourly buses from Kuching to Bako Bazaar, then hop on a motorboat to the park's Telok Assam jetty, about 400m along a wooden boardwalk from HQ.

Boat

Motorboat hire from Bako Bazaar dock, where visitors pay their park entry fee, to park HQ costs RM47; the journey takes 25 minutes. Each vessel can carry up to five people; assemble a quintet to optimise cost-sharing.

Late November to February or March, the sea is often rough. When the tide is low, boats may not be able to approach the jetty at Telok Assam because of a sand bar so you may have to wade ashore. Be aware that boatmen may insist on an early afternoon return time to beat the tides.

Take note of the boat's number (or ask for the boatman's mobile phone number) and be sincere when you agree to a pick-up time. If you prefer to share a different boat back, give park HQ your boat number – staff are happy to call and cancel your original boat. Boats generally operate between 8am and 5pm, though this is weather and tide dependent. Most day visitors try to get back to Bako Bazaar by 4pm so they can catch the 4.30pm bus to Kuching (the 5.30pm bus is not 100% reliable).

Bus

Bright red bus 1 (RM3), run by **Rapid Kuching** (☎012-883-3866; www.rapidkuching.com.my), leaves from 6 Jln Khoo Hun Yeang, Kuching, in front of buffet restaurant Toko Minuman Jumbo (and across the street from the Open-Air Market). Departures from Kuching are every hour on the hour 7am to 5pm, from Bako Bazaar every hour on the half-hour from 6.30am to (usually) 5.30pm or 6pm; confirm return times with your driver on the ride out. If you miss the last bus, ask around the village for a minibus or car heading to Kuching.

In Kuching, the bus also picks up passengers along the waterfront (motion to the driver to stop):

» At the bus shelter on Jln Gambier 50m east of the Square Tower

» On Main Bazaar next to the Chinese Museum

» On Jln Tunku Abdul Rahman next to the Riverside Suites

» On Jln Abell in front of Alliance Bank (a block northwest of the Lime Tree Hotel)

Taxi

A cab from Kuching to Bako Bazaar (45 minutes) costs RM40.

Santubong \Peninsula

☑082

Like Bako National Park 8km to the east, the Santubong Peninsula (also known as Damai) is a 10km-long finger of land jutting out into the South China Sea. The main drawcards are the longhouses of the Sarawak Cultural Village, some beaches, two short jungle walks, a golf course and a clutch of seafood restaurants in the small fishing village of Kampung Buntal. Santubong is the best place in Sarawak for a lazy, pampered beach holiday.

⊙ Sights & Activities

Sarawak Cultural Village   ECO-MUSEUM
(SCV; ☎846-411; www.scv.com.my; adult/child 6-12yr RM60/30; ☉9am-5.15pm, last entry 4pm) This living museum is centred on seven traditional dwellings: four Dayak longhouses (including a Bidayuh headhouse with three skulls and the only Melanau longhouse left in Sarawak), a Penan hut, a Malay townhouse (the only place you have to remove your shoes) and a Chinese farmhouse. It sounds hokey but the intent is sincere and even travellers who have been to Borneo's interior are generally impressed by the opportunity to see truly traditional longhouses (for obvious reasons, all real ones have been at least partly modernised).

The dwellings are (supposed to be) staffed by members of the ethnic group they represent – except the Penan dwelling, that is, whose emissaries, true to their nomadic tradition, went walkabout. Although staff quarters are provided, two of the ethnic representatives have chosen to live in their ersatz longhouses – saves on the commute, in any case! Signage, however, is poor, so if you don't ask questions of the 'locals' the subtle differences in architecture, cuisine, dress and music between the various groups may not be apparent.

Crafts demonstrations include making an Iban *pua kumbu* (cotton men's loincloth). In some houses you can buy traditional sweets made on the spot, such as Melanau biscuits made of sago, Iban *kuih jala* (rice cookies; 10 for RM3), Orang Ulu–style tapioca cookies (five for RM2) and Malay *kuih sepit* ('love letter cookies'; RM3). At the Penan hut you can try a blowpipe (RM1 for three darts), while the Malay house offers top spinning (three spins for RM1).

A twice-daily **cultural show** (45 minutes; ☺11.30am & 4pm) showcases the traditional music and dances of the various tribes. It's all quite touristy, of course, but most visitors – 60% of whom are Sarawakians, including school groups – generally enjoy the performances.

It may be possible to book workshops (RM5 per person per hour) in handicrafts (eg beads), music and dance – contact the SCV in advance. If you're planning to get married, you can choose to tie the knot here with a colourful Iban, Bidayuh, Orang Ulu or Malay ceremony.

Across the parking lot from the entrance, the **Damai Bay Bazaar**, a commercial development with a hawker centre and two restaurants, is supposed to open in early 2011.

Hotels and tour agencies in Kuching offer packages, but it's easy enough to get out here – just take one of the Kuching–Santubong shuttles (see p172). Shuttles to Kuching leave the SCV at 1.15pm, 3.15pm and 5.15pm. The SCV is a five-minute walk from the Damai Beach Resort and the Damai Puri Resort & Spa.

Jungle Walks   HIKING

Two trails – seriously upgraded in 2010 – take you into the jungle interior of the peninsula. One, with red trail markings, ascends **Gunung Santubong** (880m); the last bit is pretty steep, with steps and rope ladders, so it takes about three hours up and two hours down. The peak features in a variety of local ghost stories related to a princess captured by a prince. The other trail, an easy-to-moderate circular walk (2km) with blue markings, passes by a pretty **waterfall**.

Both trails start at the Green Paradise Cafe, on the east side of the highway about 1km south of the SCV. Parking costs RM5; the admission fee is RM1. A visitors centre is planned. Guides can be hired for the jungle trail (per person RM20, minimum two) and the summit (per person RM60).

Permai Rainforest Resort OUTDOOR ACTIVITIES
(☑082-846-490; www.permairainforest.com; Damai Beach; adult/child RM5/2; ▣) In addition to a safe beach with changing facilities – the day rate is a real bargain – this place offers a variety of leisure and adventure activities, including a high-ropes course (per person RM65), a climbing wall (with an instructor), sea kayaking (with or without a guide), mountain bikes (RM20 per hour), an obstacle course, abseiling and boat cruises. Great if you're travelling with kids.

Damai Beach Resort BEACH
(www.damaibeachresort.com; Teluk Bandung, Santubong) The day-use fee for the resort's great beach is just RM3. For RM185 two adults and two children have daytime room access and can use the resort's various facilities from 9am to 6pm.

☞ Tours

Coastal areas west and east of the Santubong Peninsula are home to a wide variety of wildlife. Oft-spotted species include endangered Irrawaddy dolphins (known locally as *pesut*), proboscis monkeys, estuarine crocodiles and all manner of birds.

Resorts on the peninsula and guest houses and tour agencies in Kuching can make arrangements, or you can contact:

CPH Travel BOAT
(☑082-846-618, in Kuching 24hr 082-243-708; www.cphtravel.com.my; Damai Puri Resort & Spa) The only tour agency with an office on the Santubong Peninsula. Offers well-regarded cruises through the Kuching Wetlands National Park.

Mr Ehwan bin Ibrahim BOAT
(☑019-826-5680; Kampung Buntal) A local boatman who offers a three-hour dolphin-and-mangrove tour, either at 9am or in the late afternoon (around 5pm). The cost for two/four people is RM180/155 per person. Also offers four- or five-hour fishing trips that include stopping at a

remote beach for a swim. Offers pick up at any Santubong hotel for RM30 (for up to six people).

🛏 Sleeping

Many resorts allow children to stay in parents' rooms for no extra charge. Kampung Santubong has several home stays. It's possible to camp at the Permai Rainforest Resort and the Green Paradise Cafe.

Permai Rainforest Resort BUNGALOWS $$
(☑082-846-487/90; www.permairainforest.com; Damai Beach; campsites RM14, 6-bed longhouses RM220, 6-bed cabins RM250, 2-bed tree houses RM260; @🛜▣) Set on a lushly forested hillside with sea views that's home to macaques and silver-leaf monkeys. Accommodation here ranges from rustic, simply furnished cabins to air-con wooden bungalows built 6m off the ground. There's a small jungle pool a few hundred metres past the tree houses. Prices include breakfast.

Damai Beach Resort RESORT $$$
(☑082-846-999; www.damaibeachresort.com; Teluk Bandung, Santubong; d from RM380; ❄🛜🏊▣) A great getaway for families, this 224-room resort has two separate sections, one right on the beach (wheelchair accessible) and the other – including luxurious in-the-round suites – on the hill above. There are enough activities and amenities to make you feel like you're on a cruise ship (in a good way), including a fine beach, two adult pools, two kiddie pools, beach volleyball, boat trips (RM550 for three hours), night fishing, sea kayaking (RM15 to RM20 per hour) and even an 18-hole golf course (www.damaigolf.com) designed by Arnold Palmer. Has a play room for the little ones and child minders.

Nanga Damai Luxury Homestay B&B $$
(☑019-887-1017; www.nangadamai.com; Jln Sultan Tengah, Santubong; d incl breakfast RM100-160; ❄@🏊) The lovely glass-enclosed living room, cosy chill-out veranda, 8m kidney-shaped pool and bright, comfortable rooms (six in total) make it easy to meet the two-night minimum stay. Run by a welcoming Anglo-Sarawakian couple. The minimum age is 16. The Kuching–Santubong shuttles pass by here, or you can take a taxi (RM50 from Kuching).

Damai Puri Resort & Spa RESORT $$$
(☑082-846-900; www.damaipuriresort.com; r from about RM300; ❄@🛜🏊) A classic tropical seaside resort with its own beach and two swimming pools. The 207 attractive, modern

rooms have wooden floors and sea views. Other amenities include an elegant, open-air lobby and a Balinese-style spa. Wheelchair accessible. Home to a branch of CPH Travel.

Eating

All the resorts have restaurants.

Lim Hock Ann Seafood SEAFOOD **$$**
(☑082-846-405/533; Kampung Buntal; mains RM6-32, fish per kg RM24-70; ☉10am-10pm or 11pm) A sprawling, open-air shed on stilts with a wide-plank floor and a tin roof, this is the biggest and best of the Chinese-style seafood restaurants in Kampung Buntal, a fishers' village 11km southeast of the SCV (on the east coast of the base of the peninsula). The fresh, locally landed fish is superb; lobster is RM78 a kilo, scrumptious white pomfret is RM70.

Green Paradise Cafe SEAFOOD **$$**
(☑013-824-2426; mains RM9-21; ☉noon-midnight) On the main road about 1km south of the SCV, at the base of the trail up to Gunung Santubong. Specialities include seafood, ginger chicken fillet (RM14) and beer (RM8).

❶ Getting There & Away

Minibus

Yellow-roofed 11-seaters link Kuching (near the Saujana Bus Terminal) with Kampung Buntal (RM10 per person; approx 7am to 5pm). No public transport from Kampung Buntal to the rest of the peninsula. Kuching to Santubong Peninsula is 45 minutes; minibuses are operated by two companies:

Damai Beach Resort (☑082-846-999, 082-380-970; adult/child under 12yr one way RM12/6, return RM20/10) Departures from Kuching's Grand Margherita Hotel and Riverside Majestic Hotel every two hours 7.15am to 10pm. Departures from Damai Beach Resort (five minutes on foot from the SCV) every hour or two 9.10am to 9pm.

Setia Kawan (☑019-825-1619; adult/child under 12yr RM10/5) Departures from Kuching's waterfront (the Singgahsana Lodge, the Harbour View Hotel and the Hilton) every two or three hours 7.15am to 10pm. Departures from the peninsula's Damai Puri Resort & Spa and Permai Rainforest Resort from 9.10am to 9pm.

Taxi

Kuching to SCV or resorts is RM50, to Kampung Buntal RM45.

Kuching Wetlands National Park

The only way to see the superb mangroves of 66-sq-km Kuching Wetlands National Park, recognised under the Ramsar Convention (www.ramsar.org) as 'wetlands of international importance', is – as you would expect – by boat. The park, situated about 15km northwest of Kuching (as the crow flies), don't have a park HQ complex and there aren't even any rangers, just low-lying islands and saline waterways lined with salt-resistant trees that provide food and shelter to proboscis monkeys, silver-leaf monkeys and fireflies (above the water line); estuarine crocodiles and amphibious fish called mudskippers (at the water line); and dozens of kinds of fish and prawns (below the water line). Nearby open water is one of the best places in Sarawak to spot snub-nosed Irrawaddy dolphins.

The morning (about 9am) is the best time to see the dolphins, while late-afternoon cruises are optimal for sighting a flash of reddish-brown fur as proboscis monkeys leap from tree to tree in search of the tenderest, tastiest young leaves. Sunset on the water is magical – and unbelievably romantic, especially if your guide points out an *api-api* tree (a 'firefly tree', surrounded by swirling green points of light). After dark, by holding a torch up at eye level, you can often spot the reflections of animalian eyes, including – if you're lucky – a crocodile, its reptilian brain wholly focused on biting, drowning and then devouring its next warm-blooded victim.

☞ Tours

A variety of Kuching tour agencies offer cruises through the park, both during the day, and during and after sunset. Packages include transfers from and to your hotel; boats usually set sail from the Santubong Peninsula (eg Kampung Santubong) or Telaga Air.

CPH Travel BOAT
(☑at Damai Puri Resort & Spa 082-846-618, in Kuching 24hr 082-243-708; www.cphtravel.com.my) Well-regarded; the only agency with an office on the Santubong Peninsula. Has a mangrove and Irrawaddy dolphin sighting cruise (RM140 per person) at 8.30am and a wildlife cruise (RM160) at 4.30pm.

Fairview Guesthouse BOAT
(☑082-240-017; www.fairview.my; Kuching) Eric Yap can arrange a cruise (RM160 per

person, departures from Kuching at 4pm) piloted by a local boatman.

Semenggoh Nature Reserve

One of the best places in the world to see semi-wild orangutans in their natural jungle habitat, swinging from trees and scurrying up vines, the **Semenggoh Wildlife Centre** (☑082-618-325; www.sarawakforestry.com; admission RM3; ◷8am-5pm), is easily accessible on a half-day trip from Kuching.

Situated within the 6.8-sq-km Semenggoh Nature Reserve, the centre is home to 27 orangutans: 11 who were rescued from captivity or orphaned; and their 16 Semenggoh-born offspring, some mere babes-in-arms who spend their days hanging onto their mother's shaggy chests. Five of the tree-dwelling creatures are completely wild (ie find all their own food), but the rest often swing by (literally) park HQ to dine on bananas, coconuts, eggs and – though they don't know it – medications. There's no guarantee that any orangutans, the world's largest tree-dwelling animal, will show up, but even in fruiting season (December to February or March) the chances are excellent. Semenggoh is noticeably less touristy (and much, much cheaper) than the widely publicised Sepilok Orang-utan Rehabilitation Centre in Sabah.

Hour-long feedings, in the rainforest a few hundred metres from park HQ, begin at 9am and 3pm. When the feeding session looks like it's over, rangers sometimes try to shoo away visitors (especially groups, whose guides are in any case eager to get back to Kuching), but orangutans often turn up at park HQ, so don't rush off straightaway if everything seems quiet. Other animals, such as brightly coloured squirrels, often put in an appearance to sneak a nibble at the buckets of fruit.

For safety reasons, visitors are asked to stay at least 5m from the orangutans – the animals can be unpredictable – and are advised to keep a tight grip on their backpacks, water bottles and cameras because orangutans know that humans often carry edibles and have been known to snatch things in search of something yummy. Flash photography, which annoys the orangutans, is forbidden.

Semenggoh Nature Reserve has two beautiful rainforest trails: the **Masing Trail** (Main Trail; red trail markings; 30 minutes), which links the HQ with the highway; and the **Brooke's Pool Trail** (yellow and red trail markings), a 2km loop from HQ. A guide can be hired at the Information Centre for RM20 (for up to five people). Most visitors rush back to Kuching rather than hiking, which is a shame as the trails pass through superb primary rainforest. Your entry ticket is valid for the whole day so it's possible to come for the morning feeding, take a hike, and then see the afternoon feeding as well. There's nowhere to buy food so bring lunch.

For more information on orangutans, see p248.

ℹ Getting There & Away

From Kuching's Saujana Bus Station, take City Public Link bus K6 (RM2.50; 7am, 9.30am, 1pm, 3pm and 5pm). At Semenggoh, the stop is 1.3km down the hill from park HQ. Back to Kuching, buses pass by at about 8.10am, 10.40am, 2pm, 4pm and 5.50pm. Sarawak Transport Company bus 6 (RM2.50) leaves Saujana Bus Station at about 7.20am and 1.20pm; buses back pass by Semenggoh at about 10am and 4pm.

A taxi from Kuching costs RM40 one way or RM90 return, including wait time.

Tours (per person RM35) are organised by Kuching guest houses and tour agencies.

Annah Rais Longhouse

Although this Bidayuh longhouse has been on the tourist circuit for decades, it's still an excellent place to get a sense of what a longhouse is and what longhouse life is like.

The 600 residents of **Annah Rais** (adult/student RM8/4) are as keen as the rest of us to enjoy the comforts of modern life – they love their mobile phones and can't wait to be connected to the internet – but they've made a conscious decision to preserve their traditional architecture and the social interaction it engenders. They've also decided that welcoming modern tourists is a good way to earn a living without moving to the city, something most young people end up doing.

The longhouse at **Kampung Benuk**, towards Kuching from Annah Rais, is no longer occupied except during celebrations but has a worthwhile museum.

◉ Sights & Activities

Longhouse Veranda   LONGHOUSE

Once you pay your entry fee (in an eight-sided wooden pavilion next to the parking lot), you're free to explore Annah Rais' three longhouses, with a guide or on your own. The most important feature is the *awah*, a long, covered common veranda – with a springy bamboo floor – that's used for economic activities, socialising and celebrations. Along one side, a long row of doors – Annah Rais has a total of 97 – leads to each family's private *bilik* (apartment). Paralleling the *awah*, opposite the long row of doors, is the *tanju*, an open-air veranda.

Headhouse   SKULLS

Whereas the Iban traditionally hung head-hunted heads outside each family's *bilik*, the Bidayuh grouped theirs together in the community's *baruk* (headhouse), which also served as a communal meeting hall. The heads are no longer believed to protect the village – these days the people of Annah Rais are almost all Anglican (the Bidayuh of Kalimantan are mainly Catholic) – but about a dozen smoke-blackened human skulls still have pride of place in the headhouse, suspended over an 18th-century Dutch cannon. It is said that in some longhouses, a few old people still remember the name of each of the heads.

Visitors – especially overnight ones – can go **trekking**, **rafting** and **fishing**, try (mock) **blowgun hunting**, visit a **natural hot springs** and even help bring in the rice harvest.

🛏 Sleeping

Annah Rais is a peaceful, verdant spot to chill out. Several families run home stays, either in the longhouse or in an adjacent detached house. It's usually possible to show up without reservations.

Edward Mining   HOME STAY **$$**
(www.longhouseadventure.com; 2 days & 1 night per person RM98, incl activities RM298) Offers a wide range of outdoor activities.

Macheree's Homestay   HOME STAY **$$**
(www.mdrlonghousehomestay.com; 2 days & 1 night per person RM298)

Akam Janga   HOME STAY **$$**
(☑016-882-4524; r RM60, per person per day incl meals & activities RM120) In a comfortable detached house right next to the longhouse, on the bank of the river.

Joseph Reis Anak Enang   HOME STAY **$$**
(☑082-462-642, 016-866-3277; annahrais_home stay@yahoo.com)

Emily & John Awang   HOME STAY **$$**
(☑016-855-2195, 016-824-9384; http://22.com. my/homestay)

Jenny Anak Dudu   HOME STAY **$$**
(☑016-862-9215) Jenny works in the longhouse committee's welcome pavilion.

🍴 Eating

If you opt to stay over or arrange to have a meal here, you'll get to taste classic Bidayuh cuisine made with fresh jungle ingredients.

The locally brewed *tuak* comes in two versions: a deliciously sweet elixir 'for the ladies' that has 5% or 6% alcohol, and a men's liqueur with an alcohol content of 45%.

🛍 Shopping

Local Bidayuh women make and sell intricate beadwork – much of it in the colours of the Sarawak flag – and items made of bamboo and rattan.

ℹ Getting There & Away

The only way to get to Annah Rais is by taxi. From Kuching, expect to pay RM80 one-way or RM160 return, including wait time.

In Kuching, a variety of tour agencies and guest houses offer four-hour group tours to Annah Rais for RM80 per person.

Gunung Penrissen & Vicinity

Although it's actually located in Kalimantan, Indonesia, 1329m-high **Gunung Penrissen** is usually approached from the Sarawak side. Because of its strategic location, it was a hot spot during the Konfrontasi period and was the site of a few border skirmishes. The military outpost near the peak now serves as a scenic lookout with spectacular views into Kalimantan as well as back into Sarawak. Experienced, well-equipped climbers can climb the mountain in a one-day burn or a more relaxed trek lasting two or three days. It's rough going and a guide is essential so the most practical way to do the trek is to contact a tour agency in Kuching.

🛏 Sleeping

Borneo Highlands Resort   LUXURY RESORT **$$$**
(☑082-577-930, 082-573-980; www.borneohigh lands.com.my; Jln Borneo Heights, Padawan; d incl

breakfast from RM388) Almost on the Kalimantan border at an altitude of 1000m, this 'exclusive' resort boasts a cool upland climate, an 18-hole golf course and a spa. Situated 60km southwest of Kuching, off the road to Anna Rais Longhouse.

Kubah National Park

A super destination for true lovers of the rainforest, this 22-sq-km national park (☎082-845-033; www.sarawakforestry.com; admission incl Matang Wildlife Centre RM10) is a haven for mixed dipterocarp forest, among the lushest and most threatened habitats in Borneo. It more than lives up to its clunky motto, 'the home of palms and frogs' – scientists have found here an amazing 98 species of palm (out of a total of 213 species in all of Sarawak) and 56 species of frog (out of Borneo's more than 150 species). Kubah's jungles are also home to a wide variety of orchids – and 11 semi-wild orangutans.

Kubah's trails are more shaded than those at Bako National Park, ideal for the sun-averse. When you're hot and sweaty from walking, you can cool off under a crystal-clear waterfall.

◉ Sights & Activities

The park's Interpretation Centre (visitors centre) is being completely rebuilt.

Rainforest Trails   HIKING
When you pay your entry fee, you'll receive a schematic map of the park's six trails, all of which are interconnected (except the Belian Trail). They're well-marked so a guide isn't necessary. The park has about half-a-dozen **rain shelters** – keep an eye out for them so you'll know where to run in case of a downpour.

The easy **Belian Trail** (1.5km or 40 minutes one way; trail-marked in red) showcases its namesake tree, otherwise known as 'ironwood' (*Eusideroxylon zwageri*). This incredibly durable – and valuable, and thus endangered – tropical hardwood was traditionally used in longhouse construction. Fruit trees you'll pass include wild jackfruit, durian and rambutan.

The **Selang Trail** (40 minutes; trail-marked in yellow), linking the **Main Trail** (trail-marked in white) with the Rayu Trail, passes by the **Selang Viewpoint**. Offshore you can see the turtle sanctuary of Pulau Satang.

The paved entrance road, known as the **Summit Road** (Gunung Serapi Summit Trail), runs along the park's southeastern edge right up to the top of Kubah's highest peak, **Gunung Serapi** (911m), which holds aloft a TV and telecom tower; on foot, it's 3½ hours up and a bit less coming down. As you ascend, notice that the mix of trees and plants (including pitcher plants and ferns) changes with the elevation. The summit is often shrouded in mist but near the top there's a **viewing platform** – when it's clear, there are stupendous views all the way from Tanjung Datu National Park on the Indonesian border (to the northwest) to Gunung Santubong and Kuching (to the east).

The **Waterfall Trail** (3km or 1½ hours one way; trail-marked in blue) passes wild durian trees and ends, as you would expect, at a waterfall and a natural swimming pool.

The **Rayu Trail** (3.8km or three hours one way; trail-marked in orange), known for its Bintangor trees, links Kubah with the Matang Wildlife Centre. Most visitors start at Kubah because it's a downhill walk to Matang.

Wildlife   ANIMALS
Bako National Park definitely has the edge for wildlife. Kubah's mammals are very shy, though you might see the aptly named giant squirrel, which can be up to 38cm long, with the tail adding another 44cm.

Natural Frog Pond   FROGS
Actually artificial, this pond, 300m above sea level and about a half-hour's walk from HQ, provides a breeding ground for seven species of frog, including the file-eared tree frog. Frogs are especially active an hour or so after sunset and on moonless nights – during the day most prefer to hide in a hole in a tree – so the only way to see them is to overnight at the park. Bring a good flashlight. It may be possible to hire a ranger as a guide.

Palmetum   GARDEN
A labelled palm garden near park HQ.

🛏 Sleeping

Kubah's attractive chalets can be booked online through http://ebooking.com.my, through the National Park Booking Office in Kuching, or by calling the park. There's usually space, even on weekends, except on major holidays.

Forest Lodge Type 5   CHALETS **$$**
(6-bed chalets RM225; ❄) These bi-level, all-wood chalets come with a balcony, a sitting

room, a shower with enough room for two, a two-bed room and a four-bed room.

Forest Lodge Type 4 CHALETS $
(10-bed chalets RM150) Has a living room with a couch and chairs, a dining table with a lazy Susan, and three bedrooms with a total of 10 beds. Fan-cooled.

Forest Hostel HOSTEL $
(dm RM15.75, entire hostel RM180) Has 12 beds. Fan-cooled.

✖ Eating

All accommodation options come with fully equipped kitchens, including fridge, toaster and burners. There's nowhere to buy food so bring all you'll need – unless you've got wheels, in which case you can drive to the local *kampung*.

❶ Getting There & Away

A taxi from Kuching costs RM50 one way or RM100 return, including wait time. If you'd like to see both Kubah and the Matang Wildlife Centre, you can arrange to be dropped off at one and picked up at the other.

Matang Wildlife Centre

A 15km drive beyond Kubah National Park, the **Matang Wildlife Centre** (☎082-374-869, 082-375-163; www.sarawakforestry.com; admission incl Kubah National Park RM10; ⊙8am-5pm, last entry 3.30pm) has had remarkable success rehabilitating jungle animals rescued from captivity, especially orangutans and sun bears. The highly professional staff do their best to provide their abused charges with natural living conditions on a limited budget, but there's no denying that the centre looks like a low-budget zoo plopped down in the jungle. Because of the centre's unique role, there are endangered animals here that you cannot see anywhere else in Sarawak.

◉ Sights & Activities

Rescued Animals ANIMALS
Some of the creatures here were orphaned, some were confiscated and others were surrendered by the public. Unless they're needed as evidence in court, all are released as soon as possible – unless they lack survival skills, in which case returning them to the wild would be a death sentence, either because they'll starve or because, having lost their fear of humans, they're liable to wander into a village and get eaten.

A baby orangutan can be worth US$50,000 in Taiwan, Japan or the Middle East; poachers in Kalimantan, though, are usually paid just US$100, so the profits from smuggling can be enormous. For every baby orangutan taken into captivity, it's estimated that five orangutans are killed, including the baby's mother. Captive orangutans are cute until they're about five years old, at which point they stop being cuddly – and start becoming dangerous – and are usually killed. The centre's orangutans are among those that survived. Orangutans with sufficient jungle survival skills spend at least part of their time in the jungle.

Among the most celebrated residents of Matang is Aman, one of the largest male orangutans in the world. Known for his truly massive cheek pads, he hit the headlines in 2007 when he became the first of his species to undergo phacoemulsification (cataract) surgery. The procedure worked, ending 10 years of blindness. His tongue had to be removed after he bit through an electric cable.

Matang is home to two female bearcats (binturongs) that are too old to release. This extraordinary tree-dwelling carnivore, whose closest genetic relative is the seal or walrus, can tuck away a fertilised egg for months and perhaps years, delaying pregnancy until sufficient fruit is available (the trick is called embryonic diapause).

Other animals that live here include nine of the happiest captive sun bears in the world. In terrible condition when brought here, they are undergoing a rehabilitation program that's the first of its kind anywhere.

One of the rarest creatures here is the false gharial, the most endangered of the 16 species of crocodile. Easily identifiable thanks to its long, thin snout, only 1000 are left in the wild.

Rare birds that live here include the black eagle, lesser adjutant stork, brahminy kite and white-bellied sea eagle.

Many of the animals at the centre are fed around 9am.

Trails HIKING
The **Animal Enclosure Trail** (⊙8.30am to 3.30pm) takes visitors through the jungle past animals' enclosures and cages. Tours by staff are planned.

The **Pitcher Nature Trail** (2½ hours), which loops around the centre, lives up to its name by heading through prime nepenthes (pitcher plant) territory. It was comprehensively upgraded in 2010.

The 15-minute **Special Trail**, also being rebuilt, is wheelchair accessible.

The **Rayu Trail** goes to Kubah National Park (three hours).

Volunteering

(2/4 weeks incl food & lodging UK£1000/1700) For details on paid volunteering – nothing glamorous: we're talking hard physical labour – see www.orangutanproject.com or contact Leo Biddle at the park. In keeping with best practice, volunteers have zero direct contact with orangutans because proximity to people (except trained staff) will set back their rehabilitation by habituating them to humans.

🛏 Sleeping

Matang has a longhouse-style **forest hostel** (4-bed r RM40) with fan and attached bathroom, two Type 5 **forest lodges** (RM150; ❄) that sleep eight, and a **campground** (per person RM5). Book accommodation by phone, online via http://ebooking.com.my or at the National Park Booking Office in Kuching.

✕ Eating

Cooking is forbidden in park accommodation but an electric kettle is available on request. At research time there was no place to buy food but by the time you read this the park should have a canteen (cafeteria).

❶ Getting There & Away

Yellow Nissan vans (four times a day from 8am, last van back to Kuching at 5pm) that take students from Kuching's **Satok Market** (Jln Satok) to the Politeknik Kuching Sarawak (RM5) pass by Matang – ask to get off at the entrance road. Heading to Kuching, you could try flagging one down but they're often full.

A taxi from Kuching costs RM50 one-way or RM100 return, including wait time.

Along the Rayu Trail (three hours), it's a three-hour walk up to Kubah National Park. If you've hired a taxi for the day, you could arrange to get dropped off at Matang and picked up at Kubah, or vice versa (most people prefer starting at Kubah because from there it's downhill).

Bau & Environs

About 26km southwest of Kuching, the one-time gold-mining town of **Bau** is the access point to two interesting cave systems and some Bidayuh villages.

WIND CAVE NATURE RESERVE

About 5km southwest of Bau, the **Wind Cave** (Gua Angin; ☏082-765-472; admission RM3; ⊙8am-12.30pm & 1.30-5pm, last entry 4.30pm, often open at noon) is a network of underground streams. Slippery, unlit boardwalks in the form of a figure eight run through the caves, allowing you to wander along the three main passages (total length: 560m) with chittering bats (both fruit- and insect-eating) swooping over your head. Sections of the walkway go through the forest outside. The cave's new entrance is 300m towards the main road from park HQ.

Near HQ, you can cool off with a refreshing swim in the waters of Sungai Sarawak Kanan; changing rooms are available.

The torches available for rent (RM3) are feeble so it's a good idea to bring your own.

No food is sold at the reserve itself, though there is a drinks stand.

FAIRY CAVE

About 5km further south (ie 9km southwest of Bau), the **Fairy Cave** (Gua Pari Pari; admission free; ⊙24hr) – almost the size of a football pitch and as high as it is wide – is an extraordinary chamber whose entrance is 30m above the ground in the side of a cliff; access is by staircase. Outside, trees grow out of the sheer rock face at impossible angles. Inside, fanciful rock formations, covered with moss,

---

SEEING MOUNTAINS FROM THE INSIDE

Many of Sarawak's limestone hills are as filled with holes as a Swiss cheese. Boardwalks let you stroll around in the Wind Cave, the Fairy Cave and the caverns of Niah National Park and Gunung Mulu National Park, but to get off the beaten track you need an experienced guide – someone just like UK-born James, who runs **Kuching Caving** (☏012-886-2347; www.kuchingcaving.com). He knows more than almost anyone about the 467 cave entrances that have been found within two hours of Kuching, the longest of which is 11km. For an all-day caving trip (9am to 8pm), he charges RM210 per person (minimum four), plus transport (RM50 per person).

To meet local cave-exploration enthusiasts and link up with a caving group that heads underground each Sunday, stop by Kuching's Ruai bar.

give the cavern an otherworldly aspect, as do thickets of ferns straining to suck in every photon they can.

TRINGGUS & GUNUNG BENGOH

Inland from Bau, most of the population is Bidayuh. Unlike their distant relations on the eastern side of the Bengoh (Bungo) Range – that is, in the area around Annah Rais – the Bau Bidayuh have never lived in longhouses. The area's Bidayuh speak a number of distinct dialects.

Tour agencies in Kuching can arrange treks into the valleys around **Gunung Bengoh** (966m) – including the fabled **Hidden Valley** (aka Lost World) – either from the Bau side or the Annah Rais side. Kuching's **Singgahsana Lodge** (082-429-277; www.singgahsana.com) runs treks to the remote and very traditional Bidayuh longhouse community of **Semban**, where a few old ladies still sport brass ankle bracelets. A three-day, two-night trip, including transport, food and a guide, costs RM570/380 per person in a group of two/seven.

The furthest-inland of the three Bidayuh hamlets known collectively as Tringgus, **Tringgus Bong**, has a delightful **home stay** (per person incl food RM60) in House 392; for details, call **Baon** (012-882-9489). At the confluence of two burbling streams, facing a hillside pineapple patch and reached by a traditional wood-and-bamboo bridge, this paradisiacal corner of Borneo is a great place to get away from it all. The nearest village across the border in Kalimantan is just 1½ hours away on foot.

❶ Getting There & Away

Two bus companies link central Kuching's Saujana Bus Station with Bau (RM4), which is 43km southwest of Kuching: **Bau Transport Company** (BTC), whose bus 2 runs eight times a day from 5.30am to 4.30pm; and **Sarawak Transport Company** (STC; 016-886-0855), whose last bus back to Kuching leaves Bau at 6pm.

To get from Bau to the Wind Cave turn-off (a 1km walk from the cave), take BTC bus 3 or 3A (RM1) – one or the other departs about hourly from 7.40am to 1pm, then at 3pm and 5pm.

To get from Bau to the Fairy Cave turn-off (a 1.5km walk from the cave), take BTC bus 3 (RM1), which has departures at 7.40am, 9am, 10.30am, 11.45am, 3pm and 5pm. Coming back, the last bus starts its run at 5.30pm.

From Kuching, a taxi to the Fairy Cave costs RM40 one way or RM80 return, including wait time. Visiting both caves costs about RM120, including an hour of wait time at each.

Two vans link Bau with Tringgus (RM4) four times a day until the early afternoon – for details, call **Baon** (012-882-9489) or **Bayin** (014-579-7814).

Lundu
082

About 55km west of Kuching, the quiet town of Lundu is the gateway to Gunung Gading National Park.

The road north out of town leads not only to Gunung Gading National Park but also to two beaches that are popular with Kuchingites on weekends and holidays but pretty dead the rest of the time. **Pantai Pandan**, 11km north of Lundu, fringed with coconut palms, has a gentle gradient that's perfect for kids. If so moved, you can arrange with folk from the picturesque seaside *kampung* to go out fishing with them. A few beachfront huts sell eats and drinks. Camping is possible. **Pantai Siar**, 8km north of Lundu, is home to several modest resorts that appeal mainly to the domestic market.

🛏 Sleeping

Retreat HOTEL $$
(453-027; www.sbeu.org.my; Pantai Siar; Sun-Fri/Sat bungalows from RM148/238, 10-bed dm RM198/298; ❄❄) Owned by the Sarawak Bank Employees Union, this is the ideal place to mix chilling on the beach with workers' solidarity. Set right on a clean beach, the grassy campus includes 21 neat, spotless bungalows with decor that's best described as '1990s modern'. Day use of the pool and beach volleyball court costs RM15 (RM5 for children). The restaurant stays open until 10pm. Situated 8km from Lundu; call to arrange transport (RM5 per person).

Lundu Gading Hotel HOTEL $
(735-199; 174 Lundu Bazaar; d RM58; ❄) Few hotels have less flair and pizzazz than this place, whose 10 rooms sport ageing carpets, colourful towels, big windows and, in some cases, more than a hint of mustiness. Situated 150m northeast (across the roundabout) from the market, across the street from the Lundu Chinese Association building.

🍴 Eating

Across the grassy triangular square from the bus station, up the stairs at the **fruit and vegie market**, there's a daytime Chinese and Malay **food court** (mains RM4). In the evening, a **Malay night market** opens in the roofed space across the street. Chinese *kopi-tiam* (coffee shops that also serve food) can be found around the grassy town square.

ⓘ Getting There & Away

Buses run by the Sarawak Transport Company (STC) link Kuching's Regional Express Bus Terminal with Lundu (RM10, 1½ hours); departures in both directions are at 8.15am, 11am, 2pm and 4pm.

Around the bus station, it should be possible to hire a private car to take you to Gunung Gading National Park or Sematan (RM30).

Gunung Gading National Park

The best place in Sarawak to see the world's largest flower, the renowned Rafflesia, **Gunung Gading National Park** (☎082-735-144;

www.sarawakforestry.com; adult/child RM10/5; ⊘8am-5pm or later) makes a fine day trip from Kuching. Its old-growth rainforest covers the slopes of four mountains *(gunung)* – Gading, Lundu, Perigi and Sebuloh – traversed by well-marked **walking trails** that are great for day hikes. The park is an excellent spot to experience the incredible biodiversity of 'lowland mixed dipterocarp forest', so named because it is dominated by a family of trees, the Dipterocarpaceae, whose members are particularly valuable for timber and thus especially vulnerable to clear-cutting.

The star attraction at 41-sq-km Gunung Gading is the *Rafflesia tuan-mudae* (see p179), a species that's endemic to Sarawak. Up to 75cm in diameter, they bloom pretty much year-round but unpredictably, so to see one you'll need some luck. To find out if

POWER FLOWER

One of the wonders of the botanical world, the Rafflesia flower is astonishing not only because of its world-record size – up to 1m in diameter – but also because of its extraordinary and mysterious lifestyle.

Rafflesias are parasites that lack roots, stems or leaves. In fact, they consist of just two parts: tiny filaments that burrow into the host vine – a member of the grape family called Tetrastigma – to extract nutrients; and the flower itself, which often erupts directly from the forest floor, bursting forth from a cabbage-sized bud that takes nine to 12 months to mature. Few buds survive that long as many are munched by small mammals, including civets and moon rats.

Scientists have yet to figure out the Rafflesia's sex life. The red flowers, whose five fleshy petals are covered with bumps and blotches, are either male or female – their reproductive organs are hidden under the spiky disk in the middle – but it's not clear how they manage to effect pollination given that two flowers rarely bloom anywhere near each other at the same time. The transfer of pollen is carried out by carrion flies, which are attracted by the flowers' revolting odour, said to resemble that of rotten meat. After the fruit ripens, about half a year after flowering, the seeds are distributed by small rodents such as tree shrews and squirrels, but precisely how the plants manage to attach themselves to their host vines, and why they grow only on Tetrastigmas, remains a mystery.

There are approximately 17 species of Rafflesia (estimates vary). Some are thought to be extinct and all – including the three species that live in Sarawak – are threatened to some degree, mainly by loss of habitat but also by bud poaching for medicinal use.

Featured over the years on Malaysian stamps and coins and ubiquitous on tourist brochures, the Rafflesia is named after Sir Stamford Raffles, who – at the head of an expedition to the Sumatran rainforest – 'discovered' the flower in 1818, the year before he founded Singapore.

The good news is that Borneo is one of the best places in the world to see Rafflesias. The bad news is that they bloom for just three to five days before turning into a ring of black slime. So it takes a fair bit of luck to see one. Rafflesias blossom pretty much all year round but irregularly – for the latest low-down on when and where, ask at your guest house or hotel. In Sarawak, you can call **Gunung Gading National Park** (☎082-735-144), 70km northwest of Kuching, or Kuching's **National Park Booking Office** (☎248-088; www.sarawakforestry.com). In Sabah, contact the **Tambunan Rafflesia Reserve Park** (☎088-898500), just southeast of KK, or look for signs around Poring Hot Springs.

a Rafflesia is in bloom – something that happens only 30 to 50 times a year here – and how long it will stay that way (never more than five days), call the park or the National Park Booking Office in Kuching.

The **Rafflesia Loop Trail** (620m), which begins 50m down the slope from park HQ, goes through a stretch of forest that Rafflesias find especially convivial. Since most of the blooms are off the path, finding them requires hiring a ranger (RM20 per hour per group).

A variety of well-marked, often steep trails lead through the lush jungle. Easily accessible (follow the red-and-white stripes painted on trees) are three cascades – great for cooling your toes – known as **Waterfall 1**, **Waterfall 3** (situated near a rain shelter) and **Waterfall 7** (1.5km from park HQ).

For views of the South China Sea, try the **Lintang View Point Trail** (three hours return; marked in red and yellow), which splits off from the Rafflesia Loop Trail.

Trekking up **Gunung Gading** (906m; trail-marked in red and yellow) takes seven to eight hours return, but don't expect panoramic views – the summit is thickly forested so you'll see mainly the bottom of the forest canopy. Somewhere atop the mountain are the ruins of a British army camp used during the Konfrontasi. At **Batu Berkubu** (10 hours return; trail-marked in red and blue), you can see a communist hideout from the same period. Since these hikes must be done in one day (camping is permitted only at park HQ), you might want to arrive the day before to facilitate an early start.

If you stay overnight, you can take a fascinating **night walk** – with or without a ranger – along the Rafflesia Loop Trail, where you may catch a glimpse of the house cat-sized leopard cat *(Prionailurus bengalensis)*, whose spots make it look like a miniature leopard. Some 23 small mammals and 51 species of bird have been spotted in the park – along with 15 types of dragonfly – but don't count on seeing many as the creatures are mainly nocturnal and wisely prefer the park's upper reaches, safely away from nearby villages.

Note that park signs give *one-way* hike times. Keep to the trails to avoid crushing Rafflesia buds underfoot.

Bathing is possible at Waterfall 7 and in the **swimming hole** – fed by a crystal-clear mountain stream – at the beginning of the Rafflesia Loop Trail.

Park HQ has an **Interpretation Centre** (under renovation) with displays on the Rafflesia, wildlife and local culture.

🛏 Sleeping & Eating

Accommodation can fill quickly when a flower is blooming. The busiest times are weekdays and school holidays. Bookings can be made online via http://ebooking.com.my, through the National Park Booking Office in Kuching, or by phoning the park. If spots in the park are full, it's always possible to stay in Lundu.

The **hostel** (dm/r RM15/40) has four fan rooms with a shared bathroom. The two three-bedroom **chalets** (chalet RM150; ✸) sleep up to six people. **Camping** (per person RM5) is possible at the park HQ, at a bathroom-equipped site.

A **canteen** serving meals is being constructed. When it's done, self-cooking in the chalets and at the hostel may be banned. Another culinary option: driving or strolling 3km to Lundu.

❶ Getting There & Away

Four public buses a day link Kuching's Regional Express Bus Terminal with Lundu, but from there you'll either have to walk north 3km to the park, or hire an unofficial taxi (RM5 per person).

Sematan

🖉082

The quiet fishing town of Sematan, 107km northwest of Kuching by road, sits at the mouth of the Sematan River. A grassy north–south promenade lines the waterfront and a long concrete pier affords wonderful views of the mouth of the river, its sand banks and the very blue, very clear South China Sea. This is the best place to hire a boat to Tanjung Datu National Park.

◉ Sights & Activities

In the northern end of the row of stores facing the waterfront promenade, notice the shop called **Teck Huat** (shops 1, 2 & 3), which hasn't changed in over a century. Built of *belian*, it still has wooden shutters instead of windows.

Shallow **Telok Sematan**, clean and lined with coconut palms, stretches along the coast northwest of town. It is home to several resorts that fill up with Kuchingites on the weekends; the rest of the week you'll have the sand to yourself. Jln Seacom parallels the beach a few hundred metres inland.

Telok Pugug, just across the mouth of the Sematan River from Sematan's jetty, can be reached by boat (RM30 return).

Sleeping

Sematan Palm Beach Resort BUNGALOWS $$
(082-712-388, www.spbresort.com; Lot 295, Jln Seacom, Kampung Sungai Kilong; bungalows for 2/4/6 RM168/320/365, weekends & holidays RM198/380/430; ❄❈❄) The cheerfully painted beachfront chalets (39 rooms in all) and the infinity pool are a great place to chill out with family or friends. Rents out bicycles (per hour RM8), eg for cycling to town, and sea kayaks (per hour RM15 to RM20) and arranges expensive boat trips. Usually booked out on weekends and holidays. Prices include dinner and breakfast. Day use of the facilities costs RM5. Situated 3km northwest of the Sematan jetty.

Sematan Hotel HOTEL $
(162 Sematan Bazaar; d RM50; ❈) This two-storey place, painted yellow and orange, has simple tiled rooms. Situated 150m inland from the town shield on the waterfront, which is held aloft by six columns. If no one's around, look for the owner in the cafe across the street.

Eating

Facing the riverfront promenade, there are several small **Chinese cafes** (mains RM2.50-3) serving chicken, rice and noodle dishes.

ℹ Getting There & Away

Buses link Kuching's Regional Express Bus Terminal with Lundu, 25km southeast of Sematan, but from there you'll have to catch a ride with locals or hire an unofficial taxi (about RM30 one way) at the bus station.

The only way to get to Telok Melano (one hour) or Tanjung Datu National Park (one hour) is by sea. Access is easiest from March or April to September; the rest of the year, the sea can get rough, so much so that on some days boats don't run at all.

Motorboats that can carry five to eight people, either for a day trip or an overnight, can be hired at the Sematan jetty for about RM450 return either to the park or Telok Melano. To find a boatman, ask around the jetty or contact:

Fairview Guesthouse (082-240-017; www.fairview.my; Kuching) Ask for Eric Yap.

Fisheries Development Authority (Persatuan Nelayan Kawasan Sematan/Lundu; 082-711-152; Jln Bauxite, Sematan) From the jetty, walk 100m south and a bit inland; the office is upstairs. Call during office hours Monday to Friday to book a boat.

Suaidi (019-876-5482) A boatman based in a light green house 150m south along the coast from the Sematan jetty. He can also arrange overnight fishing trips (2pm to 8am) for RM600. Suaidi doesn't speak much English.

Telok Melano
POP 300
This Malay fishing village, a 2.7km walk from Tanjung Datu National Park HQ, is about 30km northwest along the coast from Sematan. Offering pristine beaches and clear blue water against the backdrop of Gunung Melano, it can serve as a base for activities such as nature walks, boat trips and fishing. The National Park Booking Office in Kuching can supply details on **home stays** (per person incl board RM70) – or you can ask around at the Sematan jetty. A shop sells basic supplies.

The nearby Kalimantan border is not open to tourists.

ℹ Getting There & Away

Telok Melano is accessible only by boat. Sea conditions permitting, locals often (but not necessarily every day) pile into a motorboat and head to Sematan early in the morning, returning in the early afternoon (about 2pm or 3pm). If you join them, expect to pay RM30 per person one way.

It's usually possible to hire motorboats at Sematan's jetty for the trip to Telok Melano. Count on paying about RM450 for a day trip return (the earlier you head out, the better) and RM500 if you stay overnight.

Tanjung Datu National Park

Occupying a remote, rugged ridge on the peninsula that marks Sarawak's far western tip, this 14-sq-km park (no telephone; www.sarawakforestry.com; adult RM10) features endangered mixed dipterocarp rainforest, jungle trails that hear few footfalls, crystal-clear seas, unspoilt coral reefs and near-pristine white-sand beaches on which endangered turtles occasionally lay their eggs. Few visitors make the effort and brave the expense to come out here, but those who do come away enchanted.

The park has four trails, including the **Telok Melano Trail** from the fishing village of Telok Melano (2.7km), which is linked to Sematan by boat; and the **Belian Trail**, which goes to the summit of 542m-high **Gunung Melano** (2km, one hour) – just 200m from the border – and affords breathtaking views of the coastlines of Indonesia and Malaysia.

Snorkelling (but not scuba diving) is allowed in certain areas; details are available at park HQ. Bring your own equipment.

Cell-phone signals can be picked up about 15 minutes' walk from park HQ, on the beach.

Sleeping & Eating

The only places in the park to overnight are two open-sided **eco-huts** (per person RM10), for which bedding (a blanket, a sheet and a mozzie net; RM15) is available. Booking ahead is not possible – just show up.

Another option is to stay in a **home stay** (per person incl board RM70) in Telok Melano, a steep, 2½-hour walk from park HQ.

At press time, new park offices were being constructed and there was a plan to turn the old offices into **guest rooms**. Details should be available at the National Park Booking Office in Kuching.

Visitors must bring their own food. Cooking utensils can be rented for RM10.

Getting There & Away

Between October and March, the sea can be rough, making access difficult or impossible. For details on getting to the park by boat from Sematan, see p181.

From Telok Melano, park HQ is a demanding 2.7km walk or a short boat ride.

Talang-Satang National Park

Sarawak's first **marine park** (www.sarawak forestry.com), established in 1999 to protect four species of marine turtle, consists of the coastline and waters around four islands: the two **Pulau Satang**, known as *besar* (big) and *kecil* (small), which are 16km west of the Santubong Peninsula; and, 45km to the northwest, the two **Pulau Talang-Talang**, also *besar* and *kecil*, situated 8km due north of Sematan Beach.

Once every four or five years, female marine turtles swim vast distances – sometimes thousands of kilometres – to lay their eggs on the exact same beach where they hatched. Of every 20 turtles that come ashore in Sarawak to lay eggs, 19 do so on a beach in 19.4-sq-km Talang-Satang National Park. Of the 10,000 eggs a female turtle may lay over the course of her life, which can last 100 years, only one in a thousand is likely to survive into adulthood. To increase these odds, park staff patrol the beaches every night during the egg-laying season (mainly June and July, with fewer in August and a handful in April, May and September) and either transfer the eggs to guarded hatcheries or post guards to watch over them in situ.

Snorkelling and diving are permitted but only within certain designated areas, and divers must be accompanied by an approved guide. For details, contact the National Park Booking Office in Kuching.

PULAU SATANG

While the national park's conservation area is managed by Sarawak Forestry, the islands themselves are the property of a family from Telaga Air – their 999-year lease, granted by the last White Rajah, Charles Vyner Brooke, expires in the year 2945. About 100 cousins now share ownership, but day-to-day management has devolved to **Abol Hassan Johari** (☎010-974-9774, 016-850-0774), a retired accountant who lives in Telaga Air and is much more interested in conservation and research than in tourists.

PALANG

If you thought that tribal body art stopped at tattoos, you are very, very wrong. However, unlike the ubiquitous skin ink, you probably won't come head to head, so to speak, with a *palang*. The *palang*, a long-standing Dayak tradition, is a horizontal rod of metal or bone that pierces the penis, mimicking the natural genitalia of the Sumatran rhino. As times change, this type of procedure is becoming less common, but many villages still have an appointed piercer, who uses the traditional method of a bamboo vice in a cold river. The real macho men opt for some seriously extreme adornments, from multiple *palang* to deliberate scarification of the penis. Most bizarrely, some men will even sew beads into their foreskins to make their nether regions resemble the giant Rafflesia flower. (Overcompensating? Maybe...)

Surprisingly, the impetus behind these self-inflicted 'works of art' is actually to enhance a woman's pleasure rather than personal adornment. Among some communities these radical procedures were once just as important as lopping off heads.

His family retains customary rights to the turtles' eggs but these are 'sold' to the state government and the money donated to an orphanage.

The larger of the two islands, 1-sq-km **Pulau Satang Besar**, has a fine **beach** and a small wooden shelter. Lucky overnight visitors can sometimes watch fragile eggs being moved from the beach to a hatchery and, possibly, witness baby turtles being released into the wild.

Abol's resolutely non-commercial approach to the island, and the exigencies of conservation, mean that while you can theoretically overnight on Pulau Satang Besar, which is 14km northwest of Telaga Air, you probably can't as green turtles, hawksbill turtles, olive ridley turtles, leatherback turtles, researchers and students (in that order) are given priority.

PULAU TALANG-TALANG

The two Pulau Talang-Talang, accessible from Sematan or as a stop on the boat trip from Sematan to Tanjung Datu National Park, can be visited only during the day. You're allowed to land but swimming is forbidden within the core protected zone (anywhere within a 2km radius of the islands' highest point).

With the park's **Sea Turtle Volunteer Programme** (4 days & 3 nights RM2500), in operation from May to late September, paying volunteers can stay on Pulau Talang-Talang Besar and help the staff of the Turtle Conservation Station patrol beaches, transfer eggs to the hatchery and even release hatchlings. For details, contact the National Park Booking Office in Kuching; booking is through Kuching-based tour agents.

❶ Getting There & Away

The easiest way to visit the islands is to book a tour with a Kuching-based agency or to contact Eric Yap at Kuching's **Fairview Guesthouse** (☑082-240-017; www.fairview.my), who has connections up and down the coast.

Day-trip charters (RM400 per person) to Pulau Satang can be arranged through tour agencies. Boats usually set out from the coastal villages of Telaga Air, 10km northeast (as the crow flies) from Kubah National Park.

If you hire a boat to get from Sematan to Telok Melano or Tanjung Datu National Park (RM450 return), you can arrange with the boatman to stop at Pulau Talang-Talang for an additional fee of RM10 per person. Hiring a boat for a day trip from Sematan costs RM250. For details on finding a boat in Sematan, see p181.

Batang Ai Region

Ask anyone in Kuching where to find authentic, old-time longhouses – ie those least impacted by modern life – and the answer is almost always the same: Batang Ai, many of whose settlements can only be reached by boat. This remote region, about 250km (4½ hours) southeast of Kuching, is not really visitable without a guide, but if you're genuinely interested in encountering Iban culture, the money and effort to get out here will be richly rewarded.

Managed with the help of an Iban community cooperative, the 240-sq-km **Batang Ai National Park** (www.sarawakforestry.com) is part of a vast contiguous area of protected rainforest that includes the Batang Ai Reservoir (24 sq km), Sarawak's Lanjak Entimau Wildlife Sanctuary (1688 sq km) and, across the border in West Kalimantan, Betung Kerihun National Park (8000 sq km). The park's dipterocarp rainforests have the highest density of wild orangutans in central Borneo (sightings are not guaranteed but are not rare either), and are also home to gibbons (more often heard than seen), langurs and hornbills.

Trips to the Batang Ai region can be booked in Kuching, either with a tour operator or with a freelance guide. See p298 for everything you need to know about planning a longhouse visit.

🛏 Sleeping

Batang Ai National Park does not offer accommodation (in fact, it has no facilities whatsoever).

Nanga Sumpa Longhouse LODGE **$$**
(www.borneoadventure.com) Lauded as one of the most impressive indigenous ecotourism efforts in Borneo. With help from Borneo Adventure (p155), local Iban have constructed a small courtyard of huts to accommodate visitors. You'll pay a little more, but you'll probably be the only traveller sipping rice wine with the friendly villagers.

Hilton Batang Ai Longhouse Resort
LUXURY RESORT **$$**
(☑083-584-338; www.batang.hilton.com; d from RM239; ❋❄) Overlooking the Batang Ai reservoir, this wood-built resort takes 'longhouse chic' to a new level. Activities include visits to genuine Iban longhouses, jungle treks, kayaking, pedal-boats and trips to the national park (two hours away by boat). A shuttle departs the Hilton Kuching Hotel daily at 8am (four hours).

CENTRAL SARAWAK

Stretching from Sibu, on the lower Batang Rejang, upriver to Kapit and northeastward along the coast to Bintulu and Miri, Sarawak's midsection offers some great river journeys, fine national parks on or near the coast, and urban conveniences.

Sibu

📞084 / POP 255,000

Gateway to the Batang Rejang, Sibu has been a busy centre for trade between the coast and the upriver hinterland since the time of James Brooke. These days, it's a major transit point for travellers, and while the 'swan city' is no rival to Kuching in terms of charm, it's not a bad place to spend a day or two before or after a water-borne trip to the interior.

Known as Maling before Charles Brooke renamed it Sibu after a local variety of rambutan, Sibu – 60km inland from the coast – is Sarawak's most Chinese city. Many of the two-thirds of locals who trace their roots to China are descendents of migrants who came from Foochow (Fujian or Fuzhou) province in the early years of the 20th century.

Sibu

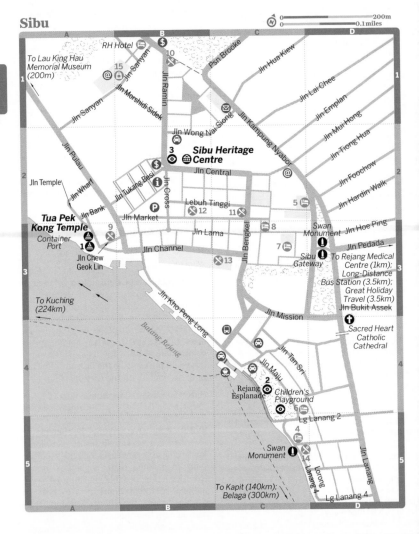

⊙ Sights

Strolling around the city centre (roughly, the area bounded by the pagoda, Wisma Sanyan, the Premier Hotel and the express ferry terminal) is a good way to get a feel for Sibu's commercial pulse.

Tua Pek Kong Temple   CHINESE TEMPLE
(Jln Temple; ⊙6am-8pm) This colourful temple was established in the early 1870s and damaged by bombs during WWII. Both the Taoist hall, on the ground floor, and the Chinese Buddhist sanctuary on the 1st floor will be explained – in lavish detail! – if you're lucky enough to drop by when Mr Tan Teck Chiang is in attendance (most days from 7am to 11am). For a brilliant view over the town and up and down the muddy Batang Rejang, climb the seven-storey **Kuan Yin Pagoda**, built in 1987; the best time is sunset, when a wheeling swirl of swiftlets buzzes the tower at eye level. Ask for a key to the pagoda at the ground-floor desk and, as you ascend, don't forget to lock the gate behind you.

Sibu Heritage Centre   MUSEUM
(Jln Central; ⊙9am-5pm, closed Mon) Opened in 2010 in a modernist complex built in 1960 (it used to be the municipal council building), the museum has well-presented exhibits – rich in evocative photographs – exploring the captivating history of Sarawak and Sibu. Panels cover the various Chinese dialect groups and the professions associated with each; Sarawak's communist insurgency (1965–90); Sibu's Christian traditions; and local opposition to Sarawak's inclusion in Malaysia in 1963. Don't miss the photo of a 1940s street dentist, which is painful just to look at.

Lau King Howe Memorial Museum   MUSEUM
(Jln Pulau; ⊙9am-5pm, closed Mon) The last remaining pavilion of a 1931 hospital, in which generations of Sibuans were born, has been turned into a seldom-visited museum showcasing Sarawak's medical history. One glance at the exhibits and you'll be glad saving your life never required the application of early-20th-century drills, saws and stainless-steel clamps – or the use of a ferocious gadget called a 'urological retractor'. Another highlight: an exhibit on the evolution of local nurses' uniforms that some visitors may find kinky. Situated about 500m northwest of Wisma Sanyan.

There's a cluster of old **shophouses** around the Visitors Information Centre, eg along Jln Tukang Besi. At the old **Rex Cinema** (Jln Ramin), art deco meets Chinese shophouse. The city has 22 **community parks**, most donated by Chinese clan associations. The **Rejang Esplanade** is a pleasant park with views of the wide, muddy river and its motley procession of fishing boats, tugs, timber-laden barges and 'flying coffin' express boats.

☞ Tours

Two well-regarded Sibu-based tour companies offer tours of the city and visits to sights both upriver and down.

Greatown Travel   CULTURAL, URBAN
(✆219-243, 211-243; www.greatown.com; No 6, 1st fl, Lg Chew Siik Hiong 1A) Offers longhouse visits (eg to Bawang Assan), visits to the 'Melanau heartland' around Mukah, and various other trips lasting three to six days. Can also tailor-make itineraries. Situated about 1km northeast of the centre along Jln Pedada.

Great Holiday Travel   WALKING, CULTURAL
(✆348-196; www.ghtborneo.com; No 23, 1st fl, Pusat Pedada, Jln Pedada) Based out near the long-distance bus station, this outfit can

organise half-day walking tours of Sibu, a day trip or longhouse overnight in Bawang Assan, and three-day trips up to the Kapit area. Reasonably priced.

Bawang Assan, an Iban village one hour downstream from Sibu (or 40 minutes by road), has eight 'hybrid' longhouses (ie longhouses that combine traditional and 21st-century elements). To stay in a longhouse without going through a tour company, contact **Bawang Assan Homestay Programme** (☑014-582-8105; http://ibanlonghouse stay.blogspot.com; per person RM70, students RM50). Ask for Marcathy Gindau. To arrange transport by van, call **Catherine Umban** (☑019-438-9749) or **Mr Broken** (☑019-836-1134).

✯✯ Festivals

Borneo Cultural Festival CULTURE
(www.borneoculturalfestival.com; ☺1st to 2nd weekend of Jul) Brings to town music, dance and cultural performances representing Central Sarawak's Chinese, Malay-Melanau and Dayak traditions.

🛏 Sleeping

Many of Sibu's midrange hotels – and better budget places – offer excellent value for money. However, some of the ultra-budget places (ie below RM30 a room) are of a very low standard – we recently heard of some Japanese tourists who were bitten by rats while staying in one local dive!

TOP **Li Hua Hotel** HOTEL $$
CHOICE (☑324-000; www.lihua.com.my; sibu@ lihua.com.my; Lg Lanang 2; s/d/ste from RM50/60/150; ✳🛜) Sibu's best-value hotel has 69 spotless, tile-floor rooms and a highly professional management. Lift-equipped. Especially convenient if you'll be arriving or leaving by ferry. The same company runs the new **Medan Hotel** (www.mymedan.com/ mh) next to the long-distance bus terminal.

Tanahmas Hotel HOTEL $$$
(☑333-188; www.tanahmas.com.my; Jln Kampung Nyabor; s/d RM281/304; ✳@🛜≋) Renovated in 2009, the Tanahmas is very central and has 114 comfortable, spacious rooms with writing desks. Amenities include a small fitness centre and, on the 3rd floor, an open-air pool.

Premier Hotel HOTEL $$
(☑323-222; www.premierh.com.my; Jln Kampung Nyabor; s/d from RM207/242; ✳@🛜) Offers a great downtown location, a business centre, and 189 crisp, spacious rooms, some

SWANS

While Kuching's mascot is, famously, the cat, Sibu's is the swan, an 'ancient Chinese symbol of good fortune and health, an auspicious omen for a community living in harmony, peace and goodwill'. Keep an eye out for swan statues as you wander around town.

with wi-fi. About what you'd expect for this price – think 3½ stars.

Victoria Inn HOTEL $
(☑320-099; 80 Jln Market; d RM55-75; ✳) Painted a peculiar shade of pink, this is a busy, business-oriented hotel with tile-floored rooms. Avoid the tiny, dark rooms for RM55. Lift-equipped. In the heart of Sibu's commercial centre.

River Park Hotel HOTEL $
(☑316-688, 016-578-2820; siewling1983@hot mail.com; 51-53 Jln Maju; d/q from RM50/100; ✳🛜) An unexceptional but well-run hotel, renovated in 2009, with friendly staff and a pleasant riverside location. All 30 rooms have windows (except the very cheapest), new tile floors, lowish ceilings and enclosed shower stalls, and some come with river views.

🍴 Eating

Sibu is a great spot for local eats, especially Foochow-style Chinese. Try *kam pua mee*, the city's signature dish, which is thin noodle strands soaked in pork fat and served with a side of roast pork.

Several open-air Chinese cafes can be found along Jln Maju, between the express ferry terminal and the Li Hua Hotel. In the morning, locals gather to dine on noodles, read Chinese newspapers and chat – a very local vibe.

Night Market FOOD STALLS $
(Pasar Malam; Jln Market; ☺5.30-11pm) Chinese stalls (selling pork and rice, steamed buns etc) are at the eastern end of the lot, while Malay stalls (with superb *satay* and scrumptious BBQ chicken) are to the west, on the other side of the clothing stalls. Also has a few Iban places.

Café Café FUSION $$
(☑328-101; 10 Jln Chew Geok Lin; mains from RM8.50-32; ☺noon-4pm & 6-11pm, closed Mon) At this chic local hotspot, fine fusion fare, including Nyonya-style pasta, is served

up amid flickering candles and decor that mixes Malay, Straits Chinese and Western elements.

Islamic Nyonya Kafé
PERANAKAN $$
(141 Jln Kampung Nyabor; mains RM10-13; ☺10am-11pm) Serves the deliciously spicy dishes of the Straits Chinese (as interpreted by the Indian chef), including *ayam halia* (ginger chicken) and *kari kambing* (mutton curry). 'Islamic' means it's halal. Has great lunch deals (11am to 2pm).

Victorious Cafe
HAWKER CENTRE $
(Lg Lanang 4; mains RM2.50-4; ☺6am-10pm) Dine under the hungry gaze of a gargantuan Sibu swan at this popular, breezy *kedai kopi*. The four stalls serve up dishes such as soup, *bubur* (porridge) and *mee sua* (stir-fried Chinese wheat noodles).

Fresh Vegetarian Cafe
VEGETARIAN $
(149 Jln Kampung Nyabor; mains RM2.50-5; ☺8am-9.30pm; 🖉) A simple cafe serving 100% vegie Chinese and Malay dishes, including *laksa*, 'chicken' and 'ham'. Even the *sambal* is vegetarian!

Self-Catering

Pasar Sentral Sibu
FOOD MARKET $
(PSS; ☺4am or 5am-7pm) One of Malaysia's largest fruit and vegie markets, with a fleet of helicopter fans overhead. Upstairs, Chinese, Malay and Iban food stalls serve food until 9pm.

Giant Supermarket
SUPERMARKET $
(ground fl, Wisma Sanyan, Jln Sanyan; ☺9am-10pm) Near McDonald's.

Drinking
Much of what passes for nightlife in Sibu involves cover versions of Western hits and scantily clad young women.

Queen
BAR
(12 Jln Chew Geok Lin; beer from RM10, cocktails RM22-38; ☺4pm-12.30am) Decked out like a Victorian sitting room, this chic, dimly lit bar features plush couches and overstuffed wing chairs in black and burgundy velvet. Stop by from 9pm to 11.30pm for live guitar and/or keyboard music. Food can be ordered from Café Café next door.

Shopping

Wisma Sanyan
MALL
A modern air-con mall owned by the Sanyan Group, a vast and exceedingly well-connected timber company.

Public Book Store
BOOKS
(4th fl, Wisma Sanyan, 1 Jln Sanyan; ☺9am-9pm or 9.30pm) The best bookstore in town, with a decent selection of English books and LP titles.

Information

Email Centre (ground fl, Sarawak House Complex, cnr Jln Central & Jln Kampung Nyabor; per hr RM3; ☺9am-9pm Mon-Sat, to 3pm Sun) Internet access near McDonald's.

HSBC Bank (131 Jln Kampung Nyabor; ☺9.30am-4pm Mon-Fri) Has ATMs.

ibrowse Netcafé (4th fl, Wisma Sanyan, 1 Jln Sanyan; per hr RM3; ☺9.30am-9.30pm) Internet access. Situated near the southwestern escalator bank.

Main post office (Jln Kampung Nyabor; ☺8am-4pm Mon-Fri, to 2.30pm Sat) Changes cash.

Rejang Medical Centre (☎330-733; www.rejang.com.my; 29 Jln Pedada) Used by most expats and tourists. Has 24-hour emergency services, including an ambulance. Situated about 1km northeast of the Sibu Gateway.

Sibu General Hospital (☎343-333; Jln Abdul Tunku Rahman) Situated 8km east of the centre, towards the airport.

Standard Chartered Bank (Jln Tukang Besi; ☺9.45am-3.45pm Mon-Fri) Changes cash and travellers cheques and has an ATM.

Visitors Information Centre (☎340-980; www.sarawaktourism.com; ☺8am-5pm Mon-Fri, closed public holidays) Well worth a stop. Has a friendly and informative staff (ask for Jessie) and plenty of maps, bus and ferry schedules, and brochures on Sibu's community parks and on travel around Sarawak. May move down the block to the Sibu Heritage Centre.

Yewon money changer (8 Jln Tukang Besi; ☺8am-5pm Mon-Fri, closed Sun) Changes cash. Look for the gold-on-red sign.

Getting There & Away

Air

MASwings (www.maswings.com.my) and **Air Asia** (www.airasia.com) link Sibu with Kuching (45 minutes) for as little as RM49, but these flights are often booked up well in advance. MASwings also offers direct flights to Bintulu, Miri and KK, while AirAsia has inexpensive flights to KL and Johor Bahru in Peninsular Malaysia.

Boat

At the entrance to the **express ferry terminal** (Terminal Penumpang Sibu; Jln Kho Peng Long), ferry company booths indicate departure times using large clocks, making it a snap to choose your boat. Tickets to Kuching are sold from 9am to 4pm.

'Flying coffins' run by six companies head up the broad, muddy Batang Rejang with goods and luggage strapped precariously to the roof. If you opt to ride up top for the view (not that we recommend it...), hang on tight! Good views are more safely available from the doors.

From Sibu, boats to Kapit (140km, 2¼ to three hours) leave once or twice an hour from 5.45am to 2.30pm; from Kapit, boats heading down to Sibu depart between 6.40am and 3.30pm. If you travel 2nd class (RM20), boarding is likely to involve inching your way along a narrow, rail-less exterior gangway; 1st class (RM30) and business class (RM25) passengers board near the prow.

Other upriver destinations include Kanowit and Song (RM17, 85km). If the water level at the Pelagus Rapids is high enough (verify that it is before you book), **one daily boat** (☑337-004, 013-806-1333) continues up to Belaga (about 300km from Sibu; RM55, 11 hours, 5.45am from Sibu, 7.30am from Belaga) and Bakun (RM65). It might also be possible to get off at longhouses between these towns – in any case, it never hurts to ask.

TO KUCHING

By far the quickest way to get from Sibu to Kuching is by boat. **Ekspress Bahagia** (☑in Sibu 319-228, 016-800-5891, in Kuching 082-412-246, 082-429-242, 016-889-3013) runs a daily express ferry to/from Kuching's Express Wharf (RM45, five hours, from Sibu 11.30am, from Kuching 8.30am) that passes through an Amazonian dystopia of abandoned sawmills and rust-bucket tramp steamers.

Bus

Sibu's **long-distance bus station** (Jln Pahlawan) is about 3.5km northeast of the centre along Jln Pedada. A variety of companies send buses to Kuching (RM40, eight hours, regular departures between 7am and 4am), Miri (RM40, 6½ hours, roughly hourly from 6am to 3.30am) and Bintulu (RM20, 3¼ hours, roughly hourly from 6am to 3.30am).

At the local bus terminal, **Lanang Bus** (Rajang Bus; ☑312-527; Jln Bengkel) has an office selling tickets to Bintulu (eight daily until 3pm) and Miri (four daily before noon).

🛈 Getting Around
To/From the Airport

The airport is 23km east of the centre. From the local bus station, the Panduan Hemat bus to Sibu Jaya passes by the airport junction (RM2.70, hourly 6am to 6pm), situated five minutes on foot from the terminal. It may also be possible to take a yellow-roof minibus. A taxi to/from the airport costs RM35.

Bus

To get from the local bus station (in front of the express ferry terminal) to the long-distance bus station, take Lanang Bus 20 or 21 (RM1, 10 minutes, once or twice an hour 6.30am to 5.15pm).

Taxi

There are three taxi stations right outside the express ferry terminal and another one 200m southwest of the main post office on Jln Wong Nai Siong. Or you can call ☑320-773 (24 hours). A cab to the long-distance bus station costs RM13.

Batang Rejang

A trip up the tan, churning waters of Batang Rejang (Rejang River) – the 'Amazon of Borneo' – is one of Southeast Asia's great river journeys. Though the area is no longer the jungle-lined wilderness it was in the days before Malaysian independence, it retains a frontier, *ulu-ulu* (upriver, ie back-of-the-beyond) vibe, especially in towns and longhouses accessible only by boat.

The 640km-long Rejang drains a huge swath of highland Sarawak. Much of this region used to be covered with pristine tropical rainforest but vast areas have been felled in the last few decades and replaced by secondary forest, tree plantations and row upon row of oil palms. Google Earth shows the river and its tributaries surrounded by a network of logging roads that seems to expand with each passing day. Adding to this environmental devastation is the controversial Bakun Dam (see p193), set for completion in 2011.

Longhouse Visits

Many of the indigenous people of the Batang Rejang basin, both Iban and members of Orang Ulu groups such as the Kenyah, Kayan, Lahanan, Punan and Sekapan, still live in longhouses. While most aren't as traditional as travellers may envision, visiting one is a great way to interact with some of Borneo's native people.

Based on geography, Kapit and Belaga *should* be good bases from which to set out to explore longhouses along the upper Batang Rejang and its tributaries. Unfortunately, we've been hearing about two sorts of difficulties faced by some recent travellers:

» Visiting longhouses without an invitation or a guide is becoming more complicated as traditional Dayak norms, according to which visitors are always welcome, are giving way to more 'modern' (ie commercial) ideas.

LOGJAM

In October 2010, the Batang Rejang was choked by an unprecedented logjam that turned the mighty river into a 50km-long jumble of wood and debris. The source of the logs is thought to have been massive landslides on a tributary of the Batang Baleh.

» Some area tour guides demand inflated prices and/or provide services that aren't up to standard. For instance, visitors may be dropped off at a longhouse with nothing to do and no way to communicate with the residents until they're picked up the next day.

In short, it can sometimes be difficult to find a guide who has good local knowledge and contacts, speaks English and charges reasonable prices. One option is to make arrangements through one of the tour agencies based in Sibu (see p185). For up-to-date feedback from other travellers, check out Lonely Planet's Thorn Tree forum (www.lonelyplanet.com).

Permits

Theoretically, a free, two-week permit, issued only at the Resident's Office in Kapit (see p192), is required for all travel:
» Along the Batang Rejang to points upriver from the Pelagus Rapids (32km upstream from Kapit).
» Up the Batang Baleh, which flows into the Batang Rejang 9km upriver from Kapit.

In fact, we've never heard of anyone having their permit checked, and the whole arrangement seems to be a bureaucratic holdover from the time when the government sought to control foreign activists' access to the communities around the controversial Bakun Dam. Permits are not required, even in theory, if you travel to Belaga overland from Bintulu.

❶ Getting Around

Pretty much the only transport arteries into and around the Batang Rejang region are rivers. A road from Sibu to Kapit is planned and a rough logging road already connects Bintulu with Belaga, so come now before easy land access changes the Batang Rejang forever.

Express boats link Sibu with Kanowit, Song, Kapit, Belaga and the Bakun Dam; for details, see Getting There & Away under Sibu, Kapit and Belaga. Boats can navigate the perilous Pelagus Rapids, 32km upriver from Kapit, only when the water level – determined by rainfall and the sluice gates of the Bakun Dam – is high enough.

KAPIT
☑084 / POP 14,000

The main upriver settlement on the Batang Rejang, Kapit is a bustling trading and transport centre dating back to the days of the White Rajas. A number of nearby longhouses can be visited by road or river but the pickings are thin when it comes to finding a good local guide.

Fans of Redmond O'Hanlon's *Into the Heart of Borneo* may remember Kapit as the starting point of the author's jungle adventures.

◎ Sights

Fort Sylvia   MUSEUM
(Jln Kubu; ☺10am-noon & 2-5pm, closed Mon & public holidays) Built by Charles Brooke in 1880 to keep the peace and gain control of the upper Rejang, this wooden fort – built of *belian* – was renamed in 1925 to honour Ranee Sylvia, wife of Charles Vyner Brooke. The exhibits offer a pretty good intro to the traditional lifestyles of the Batang Rejang Dayaks, alongside evocative photos of the colonial era – not a bad stop before you head to a longhouse. On the facade, lines mark the high-water marks of historic floods, one of which crested at an incredible 19m above normal.

Kapit Museum   MUSEUM
(Muzium Kapit; Jln Hospital; ☺8am-12.30pm & 2-5pm Mon-Thu, 8-11.45am & 2.15-5pm Fri, closed public holidays) Housed in the civic centre (Dewan Suarah), the somewhat tired exhibits include a relief map of area longhouses; displays on Orang Ulu groups, the Iban and the Chinese, and on their traditional crafts; badly stuffed jungle creatures; and an aerial photo of Kapit taken in 1977 (in the last room).

Waterfront   WATERFRONT
The waterfront is lined with ferries, barges, longboats and docks, all swarming with people. It's fascinating to watch the brisk riverine activity and to see porters shouldering (or sometimes 'heading') impossibly heavy or unwieldy loads – such as 15 egg crates stacked in a swaying pile – up the steep steps from the wharfs.

Pasar Teresang   MARKET
(☺5am-6pm) Some of the goods unloaded at the waterfront will end up in this colourful place. It's a chatty, noisy hive of grass-roots commerce, and the friendly vendors have a lot of fun trying to explain to tourists how to prepare and eat a galaxy of unfamiliar items

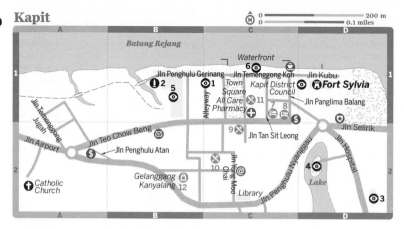

that grow in the jungle, including *uwie tut*, a kind of edible stalk. Orang Ulu people sell fried treats and steamed buns.

Chinese Pagoda   PAGODA
Half a block west of the market. Will shortly have its river view blocked by a new commercial building.

Lake   LAKE
(Jln Hospital) A few blocks southeast of the centre. Has a network of small pavilions and wooden bridges – fine for a watery wander or a picnic.

🏃 **Activities**

Streets worth a wander include a north–south **alleyway**, lined with shops and tiny cafes, situated midway between the Town Sq and the market. Enter through one of the **ceremonial gates** at each end.

👉 **Tours**
LONGHOUSE TOURS

Longhouses, many of them quite modern and some accessible by road (longboat travel is both slower and pricier than going by van), can be found along the Batang Baleh, which conflows with the Batang Rejang 9km upstream from Kapit, and the Sungai Sut, a tributary of the Batang Baleh. Longhouses along these rivers tend to be more traditional than their counterparts along the mainline Batang Rejang. At the time of research, Kapit had only two guides licensed by the **Sarawak Tourism Board** (www.sarawaktourism.com), **Alice Chua** (☎019-859-3126) and her partner **Christina Yek Leh Mee** (☎013-846-6133), who together constitute Kapit's only tour agency, **Alice Tours & Travel** (atta_kpt@yahoo.com; Lg 6, Jln Airport). A day trip to a nearby longhouse, including a simple jungle trek with an Iban guide and Iban-style food, costs RM280/330/380 for two/three/four people. A two-day, one-night trip is MR520/620 for two/four people, land transport included.

There have been reports that some other guides overcharge tourists – agree on a fair price before deciding which one to use.

VISITING LONGHOUSES ON YOUR OWN

These days, most travellers visit longhouses with a guide rather than showing up unannounced and making a beeline for the headman, but a few communities around Kapit are accustomed to independent travellers. Remember that there may not be much to do at a longhouse, especially if there aren't any English speakers around. For details on proper etiquette when visiting a longhouse, see p298.

Longhouses you may consider visiting:

Rumah Bundong One of the area's few remaining traditional Iban longhouses. Welcomes day-trippers and overnighters (RM60). Situated on Sungai Kapit a 45-minute (10km) drive from Kapit.

Rumah Jandok A traditional longhouse on Sungai Yong, which is down the Batang Rejang from Kapit.

Nanga Mujong This Iban longhouse, site of a school and a clinic, is now served by a road that ends on the opposite bank of the Batang Baleh.

Rumah Penghulu Jampi An Iban longhouse at the final express-boat stop on the Batang Baleh.

Rumah Lulut Tisa Has an official home stay. To get there, take the road to Rumah Masam, whence it's another 1½ hours by boat.

If you know which longhouse you'd like to visit, ask around the Town Sq for a van heading that way – or contact van driver **Maaruf Bin Abdullah** (✆013-895-5081). Alternatively, head to **Jeti RC Kubu** (Jln Temenggong Koh), a jetty facing Fort Sylvia, and negotiate for a longboat. These can be expensive – imagine how much fuel the outboard slurps as the boat powers its way upstream.

✯ Festivals & Events

Baleh-Kapit Raft Safari RACE
A challenging, two-day race recreating the experience of Iban and Orang Ulu people rafting downstream to bring their jungle produce to Kapit. Held sometime in late spring, often in April – for details, check with the Resident's Office in Kapit or Sibu's Visitors Information Centre.

Gawai Dayak HARVEST FESTIVAL
Beginning on the evening of 31 May, this Sarawak-wide Dayak festival celebrates the end of the harvest season. This is the best time to visit the region's longhouses, as Iban people cut loose in a mania of feasting, dancing and *tuak*-drenched celebrations.

🛏 Sleeping

New Rejang Inn HOTEL **$**
(✆796-600; 104 Jln Teo Chow Beng; d RM60; ✱) This well-run place has 15 clean, decent-sized rooms with tile floors, soft mattresses, hot water, TV, phone, fridge and Bibles marked – to avoid controversy – 'for Christians only'. The best-value accommodation in town.

Greenland Inn HOTEL **$**
(✆796-388; Jln Teo Chow Beng; d from RM90; ✱⊛) Think 'green land', not glaciers and icebergs. The 19 rooms, all but three with windows, are a respectable step up from budget class. The lobby is cheerily bedecked with fake flowers.

Regency Pelagus Resort RUSTIC RESORT **$$$**
(✆799-051; www.theregency.com.my; full board s/d RM419/560; ✱⊛) This Iban-longhouse-style rainforest resort, a 45-minute boat ride upriver from Kapit, is within earshot of the roaring Pelagus Rapids. The two-tiered wooden design blends beautifully into the jungle but the 40-room resort also boasts some very modern conveniences, such as a helipad. Serves Iban and Western cuisine.

✗ Eating

Night Market FOOD STALLS **$**
(Taman Selera Empaurau; mains from RM2.50; ⊗5pm-midnight) In contrast with the rest of Kapit's dining scene, which is overwhelmingly Chinese, this market is Malay so the emphasis is on *satay* and other *halal* dishes. Situated half a block up the slope from the Town Sq.

Soon Kit Café CHINESE **$**
(13 Jln Tan Sit Liong; mains RM4.50-6; ⊗5.30am-5.30pm) Does a mean chicken rice.

Famous Bakery BAKERY **$**
(22 Jln Teo Chow Beng; pastries from RM1; ⊗6am-6.30pm) Fresh Chinese and (approximately) Western-style pastries, cakes, mini-pizzas and other easy-to-pack day-trip fare.

🛍 Shopping

Sula Perengka Kapit HANDICRAFTS
(off Jln Penghulu Nyanggau; ⊗8am-4.30pm Mon-Sat, to noon Sun) One of several Iban handicrafts shops upstairs at Gelanggang Kenyalang, a triangular food court.

ℹ Information

All Care Pharmacy (✆798-382, 019-866-4962; 17 Jln Tan Sit Leong; ⊗8am-5.30pm Mon-Sat, 8am-1pm Sun) A good place to pick up all the meds you'll need in the jungle. Staffed by a Tasmania-trained pharmacist.

Good Time Cyber Centre (1st fl, 354 Jln Yong Moo Chai; per hr RM3; ⊙8.30am-10.30pm or 11pm) Internet access. Hugely popular with young gamers.

KL Ling Moneychanger (Jln Penghulu Gerinang; ⊙7am-5.30pm Mon-Sat, to 2pm Sun) Changes cash either upstairs or, often, in the ground-floor shop, Guan Seng Trading Company. The owner's daughter lives in Dorset, England.

Maybank (73C Jln Penghulu Atan; ⊙9.15am-4pm or 4.30pm Mon-Fri) Changes travellers cheques and has an ATM (open 6am to midnight).

Public Bank (64 Jln Panglima Balang; ⊙9am-4pm Mon-Fri) Changes travellers cheques and has an ATM (open 6am to midnight).

Resident's Office (☑796-230; www.kapitro.sar awak.gov.my; 9th fl, Kompleks Kerajaan Negeri Bahagian Kapit, Jln Bleteh; ⊙8am-1pm & 2-5pm Mon-Thu, 8-11.45am & 2.15-5pm Fri) A permit for upriver travel (see p189) takes just a few minutes to issue. Staff have a list of licensed guides but cannot provide information on visiting longhouses. The office, in a nine-storey building with green-tinted reflective windows, is 2km west of the centre; to get there, take a minibus (RM1.50) from the southeast corner of Pasar Teresang. To get back to town, ask the lobby guards for help catching a ride (offer to pay the driver).

❶ Getting There & Away

Boat

For details on 'flying coffin' boats that link the **Kapit Passenger Terminal** (Jln Panglima Balang) with Sibu, see p188.

When the water is high enough for the Pelagus Rapids (32km upriver from Kapit) to be navigable, one 77-seat express boat a day links the jetty at Kapit's Town Sq (two blocks west of the Kapit Passenger Terminal) with Belaga (RM35, 4½ hours). Boats set off from Kapit at about 9.30am and from Belaga at 7.30am or 8am. When the river is too low, the only way to get to Belaga is overland via Bintulu!

One express boat a day heads up the Batang Baleh, going as far as the Iban longhouse of Rumah Penghulu Jambi. It departs from Kapit at about 10am and from Rumah Penghulu Jambi at 12.30pm.

The express boat to Belaga does not stop at the Pelagus Rapids (45 minutes upriver from Kapit) so if you'd like to head that way for a day trip, ask around the wharf or at your hotel.

Van

A small road network around Kapit links the town to a number of longhouses. Vans that ply these byways congregate at the Town Sq.

BELAGA
☑086 / POP 2500

By the time you pull into Belaga after the long journey up the Batang Rejang, you may feel like you've arrived at the very heart of Borneo – in reality you're only about 100km (as the crow flies) from the coastal city of Bintulu. There's not much to do in the town itself except soak up the frontier vibe, but nearby rivers are home to quite a few Kayan/ Kenyah and Orang Ulu longhouses. We've received complaints about some local guides so network with other travellers and consult Lonely Planet's Thorn Tree forum (www.lone lyplanet.com) before you hand over any cash.

◉ Sights

To get a feel for the pace of local life, wander among the two-storey shophouses of the compact, mostly Chinese **town centre**, or stroll through the manicured **park** – equipped with basketball and tennis courts – between Main Bazaar and the river. Along the riverfront, the wooden bridge behind Kafeteria Mesra Murni leads downstream to **Kampung Melayu Belaga**, Belaga's Malay quarter, whose wooden homes are built on stilts.

⚡ Activities

Longhouse Visits   LONGHOUSE VISITS

The main reason travellers visit Belaga is to venture up a jungle stream in search of hidden longhouses and secret waterfalls. But before you can share shots of *tuak* with smiling locals, you'd do well to find a guide (there's a limit to what you can arrange on your own). Unfortunately, we have received reports of overcharging so network with other travellers and make sure you know what your trip does and does not take in. A good package should include jungle trekking, a waterfall swim, a night walk and activities such as cooking and fruit harvesting.

Possible destinations include a very traditional **Kejaman longhouse** across the river from Belaga; Kayan-Kenyah and Orang Ulu longhouses between Belaga and the Bakun Dam, such as **Sekapan** and **Sihan**; and the longhouses of the **Sungai Asap** (http://belaga homestaysarawak.com/; per night RM45), where Kayan/Kenyah people evicted from their land because of the Bakun Dam were resettled. The going rate for three days and two nights is about RM320 per person (minimum two people), including food and river transport.

Guides worth talking to:

Daniel Levoh (461-997, 013-848-6351; daniel levoh@hotmail.com; Jln Teh Ah Kiong) A Kayan former teacher and school headmaster, Daniel is friendly and knowledgeable. A three-day, two-night longhouse visit costs RM780 for a group of two or three.

Hamdani (019-886-5770) To find him, swing by the Belaga Hotel.

Hasbie (461-240; freeland_blg@yahoo.com; 4 Belaga Bazaar) If he's not in, check at the Belaga B&B.

Ah Soon (019-889-8286) A Kayan guide who lives in the longhouse of Rumah Kahei. Speaks just a little English but charges reasonable prices.

🎊 Events

Belaga Rainforest Challenge   TRIBAL EVENT
(☉ Jul or Aug of even-numbered years) The three- or four-day event combines a 12km jungle run with boat races and traditional music and dance performances. Intended for area tribes but tourists are welcome.

🛏 Sleeping

Belaga's accommodation is of the cheap and shabby variety.

Daniel Levoh's Guesthouse   GUEST HOUSE $
(461-997, 013-848-6351; daniellevoh@hotmail.com; Jln Teh Ah Kiong; dm RM10-15, d/tr RM25/35; 🛜) Run by one of Belaga's veteran guides, this new guest house – two blocks behind Main Bazaar – has four simple rooms, each named after one of the owners' children. Beds, a backpackers' chill-out balcony and bathrooms are all on the 2nd floor. The owners are happy to stage mock Kayan wedding festivities.

Hotel Belaga   HOTEL $
(461-244; 14 Main Bazaar; d RM30-35; ❄) A convenient location makes up for the less-than-perfect standards at this veteran doss house. The air-con works, which is more

---

BAKUN DAM: CLEAN ENERGY OR WHITE ELEPHANT?

The upper Batang Rejang basin will never be the same – on that point, at least, all sides are in agreement. In October 2010, after decades of bitter controversy, the huge Bakun Dam (www.bakundam.com), about 40km east of Belaga on the Batang Balui, began flooding a reservoir that will eventually submerge an area of once-virgin rainforest about the size of Singapore (690 sq km).

According to the Malaysian government, the 207m-high structure, 'the 2nd-highest concrete-faced rockfill dam in the world', will produce 2400MW of 'emission-free clean energy', giving a much-needed boost to Sarawak's economy.

But Malaysian and international watchdogs claim that the whole project – including contracts to clear the site of biomass, which involves logging the old-growth jungle – has been shot through with corrupt dealings designed to benefit the business associates of Malaysian and Sarawakian politicians. In 2005, Transparency International (www.transparency.org), in its *Global Corruption Report 2005*, declared the Bakun Dam a 'monument of corruption'.

Even the project's economic rationale is being called into question. The fact remains that Borneo does not need the power that the Bakun Dam will produce. Originally, 70% of the production was to be sent to Peninsular Malaysia through a 670km undersea cable – the world's longest – but that project has been shelved, leaving Sarawak with a huge over-capacity (when all the turbines are operating, the dam will produce 2½ times as many watts as Sarawak's current peak demand). Some of the slack may be taken up by energy-intensive industrial installations such as the massive aluminium smelter being built near Mukah.

Ten thousand Kayan/Kenyah people were displaced from their historic lands to protect the dam's catchment area, yet parts of the area are now being turned into oil-palm and tree plantations instead. Those displaced have not yet been compensated in full. And dam sceptics, including Sarawak's political opposition, are wondering whether plantations in the dam's supposedly protected watershed may increase erosion, and thus the river's sediment load, to such a degree that the reservoir – Malaysia's largest lake – will soon become clogged.

Now that the Bakun Dam is almost on line after a quarter-century of debate and delays, observers of all stripes are crunching the numbers in an effort to figure out whether the project will turn out to be a white elephant – a pertinent question, as a dozen more dams in highland Sarawak are in various stages of planning and execution. These include the 944MW Murum Dam, in a Penan area 60km upriver from Bakun.

than can be said of the plumbing. A free washing machine sweetens the deal.

Belaga B&B   HOTEL $
(461-512, 013-842-9767; Main Bazaar; r RM20-25; ❋) Has seven very basic but clean rooms. Run by Hasbie, a longtime longhouse guide.

Hotel Sing Soon Huat   HOTEL $
(☑461-307; 26-27 New Bazaar; r RM35-45; ❋) A bright yellow place whose 22 tiny rooms are a bit musty but in better shape than those at the Hotel Belaga, which is situated a block closer to the river. Reception is in a cage reminiscent of a 19th-century bank.

✕ Eating

A number of cafes and eateries serving simple Chinese and Malay dishes are sprinkled around the town centre, including Main Bazaar.

Kafeteria Mesra Murni   MALAY $
(Jln Temenggong Matu; dishes RM3-5; ◷7am-7pm) This family-run Malay restaurant can lay claim to having the only real riverfront dining in Belaga. Try the decent *mee goreng* or the exceptionally refreshing *limau ais* (iced lime juice). Situated 150m downriver from the ferry dock, at the entrance to Belaga's Malay quarter.

❶ Information

There nearest banks and ATMs are in Kapit and Bintulu.

Hasbee Enterprises (☑461-514, 013-842-9767; 4 Belaga Bazaar) Local travel services and internet.

Pusat Teknologi Maklumat & Komunikasi (◷8am-5pm Mon-Fri) Internet access up the stairs on the river side of the post office building, which is just upriver from the dock.

Teck Hua Chan Supermarket (Syarikat Ann; 8 Main Bazaar) Exchanges cash.

❶ Getting There & Away

When the express boat is running, it's possible to visit Belaga without backtracking, cruising the Batang Rejang in one direction and taking the bone-jarring logging road to Bintulu in the other. To find out if the Pelagus Rapids are open to navigation, you can ring the Belaga-based guides Daniel Levoh, Hamdani or Hasbie (see p193).

Boat

When the Batang Rejang is high enough for the Pelagus Rapids to be navigable, one daily express boat links Belaga with Kapit (155km) and Sibu – for details, see p192 and p188.

Land

A bone-jarring (and, in the rain, fiendishly slippery) logging road links Belaga with Bintulu (160km). Part of the way, you're on the 125km-long paved road that connects the Bakun Dam with Simpang Bakun (Bakun Junction), situated on the main (inland) Bintulu–Miri highway.

4WD Toyota Land Cruisers link Belaga with Bintulu (four hours) on most days, with departures from Belaga at about 7.30am and from Bintulu in the early afternoon (approximately 2pm). The charge is RM50 for one person or RM400 for the entire Land Cruiser, which – do the math! – usually travels stuffed to the gills with eight passengers.

In Belaga, 4WDs to Bintulu congregate in front of Belaga B&B at about 7am. Finding a vehicle in the bustle of Bintulu is a bit more complicated – ask around town and, chances are, no one will have a clue. One option is to stop by Wang Shieng Xing, a coffee and noodle shop near the New Ferry Terminal; another is to ring **Ah Kiat** (013-807-5598) or **Ah Kian** (☑461-392).

If you're coming from Miri or Niah Junction or heading up that way (ie northeast), you can arrange to be picked up or dropped off at Simpang Bakun, which is 53km northeast of Bintulu and 159km southwest of Miri.

UPRIVER FROM BELAGA
About 40km upstream from Belaga, the Batang Rejang divides into several rivers, including the mighty Batang Balui, which winds almost all the way up to the Kalimantan border. Just below this junction, the contentious Bakun Dam project is nearing completion. To visit areas upriver from the dam, it's a good idea to make arrangements with one of the guides based in Belaga.

One express boat a day links Belaga with the Bakun Dam area near Rumah Apan (RM20, one hour). Departures are at about noon from Belaga and 6.15am in the other direction.

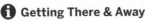

Bintulu
☑086 / POP 120,000

Bintulu is a bustling coastal town on the north bank of the Batang Kemena, roughly midway between Sibu and Miri (about 200km from each). Thanks to huge offshore natural gas fields, the town is Sarawak's most important centre for the production of LNG (liquefied natural gas) and fertiliser.

Bintulu makes an ideal staging post for visits to Similajau National Park and a convenient stopover on the way from Sibu to Niah National Park or Miri.

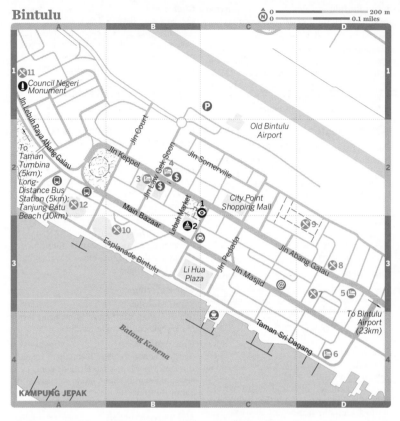

⊙ Sights & Activities

Tua Pek Kong TEMPLE

(Main Bazaar; ⊙dawn-dusk) Adding colour to the city centre is this Chinese temple. Follow the cock-a-doodle-doos to the park around back, where impressively plumed **fighting cocks** – kept tethered or in cages to avoid strife – strut and crow for aficionados.

Taman Tumbina ZOO, BOTANICAL GARDEN

(www.tumbina.com.my; Jln Tun Abdul Razak; adult RM2; ⊙9am-4.30pm) This is a pretty good place to get a glimpse of Borneo's unique flora and fauna. The 57-hectare park includes an orchid garden, a butterfly house and lots of flamingos. The name is a contraction of the first part of two Malay words, *TUMbuhan* (plant) and *BINAtang* (animal). Situated about 5km north of Bintulu Town.

Tamu Bintulu MARKET
(Bintulu Market; Main Bazaar; ⊘7am-6pm) A hive of small-scale commerce.

Tanjung Batu Beach BEACH
If you're in the mood to chill on the shore of the South China Sea, hire a taxi (RM15) for the 10km trip north to this beach (also called Temasya Beach), equipped with children's playground and gazebos.

✖⚹ Festivals

Borneo International Kite Festival KITES
(www.borneokite.com) An annual event, usually held sometime in the autumn that brings colourful kites from around the world to the old airport.

🛏 Sleeping

Bintulu's ultra-budget lodgings can be dodgy so you may be better off paying a bit more for peace of mind.

Kintown Inn HOTEL **$$**
(☑333-666; kintowninn@yahoo.com; 93 Jln Keppel; s/d RM80/86; ✿🕸) A proper hotel that delivers the best value for your buck in town. The 65 carpeted rooms are smallish but bright, with good views from the upper floors.

Riverfront Inn HOTEL **$$**
(☑333-111; riverf@tm.net.my; 256 Taman Sri Dagang; d from RM109; ✿🕸) A long-standing favourite with business and leisure visitors alike, the Riverfront is low-key but classy. Try to get a room overlooking the river – the view is pure Borneo.

Regency Plaza Hotel HOTEL **$$**
(☑335-111; fax 332-742; 116 Jln Abang Galau; r from RM170; ✿🕸🕸) The exterior is worn and service can be uneven but the 160 rooms are spacious and attractive, with big windows that let in plenty of light. Head to the upper floors for river views.

Bakun Inn HOTEL **$**
(☑311-111; 1st fl, 7 Jln Law Gek Soon; d RM50; ✿) The 15 simple, clean rooms come with windows, cramped bathrooms and carpets rich in life experience. The entrance is around the back, off the parking lot.

✗ Eating

Ban Kee Café SEAFOOD **$$**
(off Jln Abang Galau; seafood mains RM12; ⊘5.30am-midnight) An indoor-outdoor Chinese seafood specialist with fresh-as-can-be fish, crab, prawns, mussels, clams and squid. Vegie dishes are RM4 to RM8.

Chef BAKERY **$**
(92 Jln Abang Galau; cakes from RM1; ⊘8am-9.30pm) Makes Chinese-inflected halal baked goods, both sweet and savoury, that range from sugar doughnuts and raisin cookies to steamed buns and *satay* pizza (RM2.50). Perfect for a packed lunch.

Popular Corner Food Centre
HAWKER CENTRE **$**
(50 BDA Shahida Commercial Centre; mains RM3-8; ⊘5am-11pm) Eight stalls sell *laksa*, rice porridge and fresh Hong Kong–style seafood.

Night Market FOOD STALLS **$**
(off Jln Abang Galau; meals from RM2; ⊘5-10pm) A good place to snack track for Malay dishes and fresh fruit.

Pasar Utama FOOD STALLS **$**
(New Market; Main Bazaar; mains RM2.50-4; ⊘6am-5pm) Food stalls can be found on the upper floor of this blue, figure eight–shaped building.

Self-Catering

Tamu Bintulu MARKET **$**
(Bintulu Market; Main Bazaar; ⊘7am-6pm) Fresh fruit, vegies and jungle produce.

New World Mart SUPERMARKET **$**
(ParkCity, Commerce Sq; ⊘10am-10pm) Inside the ParkCity Mall, a modern, air-con shopping centre about 1.5km northwest of Tamu Bintulu.

ℹ Information

Fi Wee Internet Centre (1st fl, 133 Jln Masjid; per hr RM2.50; ⊘9am-1am) Has 30 internet computers.

Hospital Besar Bintulu (☑255-899; Jln Nyabau) A new government hospital 14km northeast of the centre.

HSBC (25 Jln Law Gek Soon; ⊘9.30am-4pm Mon-Fri) Has an ATM.

ℹ Getting There & Away

For details on travelling overland to Belaga, see p194.

Air

AirAsia (www.airasia.com) and **Malaysia Airlines** (www.malaysiaairlines.com) have direct flights to Kuching and KL. **MASwings** (www.maswings.com.my) can whisk you to KK, Miri, Sibu and Kuching.

Bus

The long-distance bus station is 5km northeast of the centre (aka Bintulu Town) at Medan Jaya.

A bunch of companies have buses approximately hourly to:

» Kuching (RM60 to RM70, 10 hours) via Sibu (RM20 to RM27, 3½ hours) from 6am to 1.30am.

» Miri (RM20 to RM27, 4½ hours) via Niah Junction from 6.30am to 1.30am.

ⓘ Getting Around

To/From the Airport

There is no public transport to/from the airport, which is 23km from the centre by road.

A taxi ride from Bintulu Town to the airport costs about RM30 or RM35. Coming *from* the airport, it's cheaper to take a cab to Kampung Jepak and then an ancient diesel ferry (RM0.50, 6am to 9pm) across the Batang Kemena to the Bintulu Town waterfront; in the other direction, you're likely to find it difficult or impossible to locate a taxi in Kampung Jepak.

Taxi

Taxis (☑332-009; ⊘4am-6pm or 7pm) congregate along the east side of Tua Pek Kong Temple (Lebuh Temple), and along with 10-seat minibuses, in front of Pasar Utama (Main Bazaar). Count on paying RM10 for a short ride in town, RM15 to/from the long-distance bus station, and RM50 to Similajau National Park.

Similajau National Park

An easy 30km northeast of Bintulu, **Similajau National Park** (☑086-327-284; www.sarawakforestry.com, http://friendsofsimilajau.blogspot.com; admission RM10; ⊘park office 8am-1pm & 2-5pm) is a fine little coastal park with golden-sand beaches, good walking trails and simple accommodation. Occupying a narrow, 30km-long strip along the South China Sea, its 90 sq km encompasses littoral habitats such as mangroves; *kerangas*; and mixed dipterocarp forest, ie classic lowland tropical rainforest (for more information, see p288).

One of the few true havens for wildlife in this part of the state, Similajau is home to 29 mammals, including gibbons, banded langurs and both short- and long-tailed macaques, and at least 187 species of bird. Various types of dolphin, including Irrawaddy dolphins, can occasionally be spotted out at sea, and marine turtles sometimes trundle ashore to lay their eggs along Turtle Beach I, Turtle Beach II and Golden Beach.

Park HQ is on the western (left) bank of the mouth of the Sungai Likau, while most of the park's territory is northeast across the river, spanned by a bouncy pedestrian suspension bridge.

Bintuluans flock to Similajau on weekends but the park is gloriously deserted on weekdays.

Dangers & Annoyances

Similajau's waterways are prime crocodile habitat so do not swim or wade in the rivers or near river mouths, and be careful when walking near riverbanks early or late in the day. An Iban man net fishing in Sungai Similajau was killed by a croc in 2008.

If you're stung by a jellyfish, the park HQ sells vinegar to reduce the pain.

Because of dangerous undertows, swimming is forbidden at the two Turtle Beaches and at Golden Beach.

Sights & Activities

Hiking Trails   HIKING

Similajau's gently undulating **Main Trail** (Coastal Trail) parallels the coast for 9.8km, starting across Sungai Likau from park HQ and ending at **Golden Beach** (four hours one-way). En route it passes by rocky headlands, small bays and **Turtle Beach I** and **Turtle Beach II** (7km or 8km, ie two or three hours, from park HQ). For a view back along the coast towards Bintulu and its natural gas installations, head to the **View Point** (1.3km from HQ).

As soon as you cross the suspension bridge, a plankwalk off to your right follows the river upstream. Both the 600m **Education Trail** and the 1.7km **Circular Trail** pass through brilliant estuarine mangroves and mixed dipterocarp forest.

Similajau's trails are easy to follow and are clearly marked (in the case of the Main Trail, in red) so a guide isn't necessary, though it's possible to hire one for RM30 per hour (RM40 per hour for a **night walk**). A simple but useful trail map is available at park HQ. Bring plenty of drinking water.

Boat Trips   BOAT TRIPS

HQ staff can arrange transport in a national park–owned boat with space for up to five passengers. Sea conditions are sometimes rough in the afternoon. Among your cruising options:

Night River Cruise (RM100; ⊘6-8pm or 7-9pm) A great way to see crocs.

Batu Mandi Tide Pools (RM100) The tidal pools around this low, rocky island can only be visited at low tide and when the sea is calm.

Turtle Beaches I and II (one-way/return RM100/150) Take the boat out there (it's a half-hour ride) and you can walk back.

Golden Beach (one-way/return RM150/200) Another option for a one-way walk.

The casuarina-lined beach at park HQ, strewn with driftwood but clean, is a great place to chill out and swim – but watch out for jellyfish.

📥 Sleeping

Similajau's simple but reasonably comfortable overnight options, at a lovely site just 100m from the beach, sometimes fill up on weekends and during school holidays. To book a room, contact park HQ. If you'll be arriving after 5pm, staff will leave your room key with security.

New chalets and additional hostel space are under construction. Current sleeping options include:

'Drive-In Chalets' CHALETS $
(1/2 r RM52.50/78.75) Each of the two rooms has two twin beds and an upright fan.

Rest House HOUSE $
(per night RM315) Sleeps four in air-con comfort.

Dormitory DORMITORY $
(per night RM42) Has four dorm beds and a wall fan. (Dorm beds are not available individually.)

Campground CAMPGROUND $
(sites per person RM5) Permitted only next to park HQ. Showers are provided.

✖️ Eating

The park's cafeteria (canteen; mains RM4.50-6; ⊙7.30am-9pm) serves noodle and rice dishes and can prepare packed lunches. Cooking is not allowed in the chalets or the hostel but there are designated sites for barbecuing. If you'd like to make packaged noodles, ask at the park office for an electric kettle.

❶ Getting There & Away

Similajau National Park is about 30km northeast of Bintulu along a paved road that forks off the old (coastal) road to Miri. Count on paying about RM50 one way to hire a taxi – or a 10-seat minibus – from Bintulu's Pasar Utama (Main Bazaar); from the airport, the cab ride is about RM70.

To get back to Bintulu, you can either have the driver wait for you for RM20 per hour; prearrange a pick-up time; or ask HQ staff to help you call for a taxi.

Niah National Park

The vast caverns of 31-sq-km Niah National Park (☑085-737-454/0; www.sarawak forestry.com; admission RM10; ⊙park office 8am-5pm) are among Borneo's most famous and impressive natural attractions. At the heart of the park is the Great Cave, one of the largest caverns in the world. The part of the park that gets daylight is dominated by a 394m-high limestone massif, Gunung Subis, and is covered in dense rainforest.

Niah's caves have provided groundbreaking insights into human life on Borneo way back when the island was still connected to mainland Southeast Asia. In 1958 archaeologists led by Tom Harrisson discovered the 40,000-year-old skull of an anatomically modern human, the oldest remains of a *Homo sapiens* discovered anywhere in Southeast Asia.

Rock paintings and several small canoe-like coffins ('death ships') indicate that much more recently the site was used as a burial ground. Some of the artefacts found at Niah are on display at the Sarawak Museum in Kuching; others (a handful) are in the park's own museum.

Niah's caves accommodate a staggering number of bats and are an important nesting site for swiftlets, some of whose species supply the vital ingredient for bird's-nest soup. Traditionally, the Penan are custodians and collectors of the nests, while the Iban have the rights to the caves' other commodity, bat and bird guano, which is highly valued as fertiliser (no prizes for guessing who got first pick). During the harvesting season (August to March), nest collectors can be seen on massive bamboo structures lashed together and wedged against the cave roof above.

We've heard travellers say that if you've been (or will be going) to Gunung Mulu National Park's Deer Cave, travelling to Niah might not be worth the effort – unless you're fascinated by human prehistory, of course.

Park HQ can supply a trail map (RM1.50). It may be possible to arrange a guided **night walk** and an excursion to spot crocodiles – for details, ask at HQ.

A new **visitors centre** is being built.

⊙ Sights & Activities

Niah Archaeology Museum MUSEUM
(⊙9am-4.30pm, closed Mon) Across the river from park HQ, the museum has rather old-fashioned displays on Niah Caves geology,

ecology and prehistoric archaeology, including an original burial canoe from at least 1200 years ago, a reproduction of the Painted Cave, a case featuring swiftlets' nests, and a replica of the 40,000-year-old 'Deep Skull'.

To get to the museum from HQ, cross the Sungai Niah by motor launch (per person RM1, 5.30pm-7.30pm RM1.50, after 7.30pm RM2 or RM3, 7am to 7.30pm, after 7.30pm by pre-arrangement).

If you don't have your own, torches (RM5; make sure the one you get is working) – extremely useful if you want to go any distance into the caves – can be hired at the ferry terminal and the museum.

Great Cave & Painted Cave   CAVES

From the museum, a raised boardwalk leads 3.1km through swampy, old-growth rainforest to the mouth of the Great Cave. The boards are loose in places and, when wet, can be slippery. Make sure to bring lots of water. To make it back by nightfall, start your walk by 1pm or 2pm.

As you walk, stop and stand silently every once in a while – you'll hear lots of birds and, if you're lucky, may hear or even see macaques.

Approaching the caves, the trail skirts jagged limestone outcrops festooned with giant vines and creepers. Just before the cave entrance the boardwalk forks; head right for the caves. The left fork goes to **Rumah Patrick Libau**, an Iban hamlet with a couple of longhouses. Villagers usually sit at the junction selling cold drinks and souvenirs.

The cave trail goes under the **Traders' Cave**, a large overhang with stout stalactites. As the name implies, this is where early bird's-nest and guano collectors carried on their business. The path then rounds a corner to enter the West Mouth of the **Great Cave**, a vast cavern approximately 2km long, up to 250m across and up to 60m high. Since you approach the cave from an angle, its enormous size may not be apparent straightaway.

Inside the cave, the boardwalk continues down to the right, but you'll need a torch to explore any distance. The stairs and handrails are usually covered with dirt or guano, and can get very slippery in places. The rock formations are spectacular and ominous by turns, and as you slip in and out of the gloom you may find yourself thinking of Jules Verne's *Journey to the Centre of the Earth*. When the sun hits certain overhead vents, the cave is penetrated by dramatic rays of other-worldly light.

Allow a good hour to explore the Great Cave. The trail splits to go around a massive central pillar, but both branches finish at the same point so it's impossible to get lost if you stick to the boardwalk.

A dark passage known as **Gan Kira** (Moon Cave) is not narrow enough to induce claustrophobia (unless you're severely affected) but it may make you wonder what would happen if your torch suddenly died. When you're halfway along, try turning off your flashlight to enjoy the experience of pure, soupy blackness.

After passing through Gan Kira, you emerge into the forest and traverse another section of boardwalk before arriving at the **Painted Cave**. It's easy to walk straight past the small fenced-off area by the cave entrance that protects the (now empty) 'death ships' – coffins shaped like boats made 1200 to 2000 years ago – and ancient drawings depicting jungle animals, human figures and the souls of the dead being taken to the afterlife by boat. A set of small travel binoculars are useful to make out the red hematite figures, as many have faded to little more than indistinct scrawls along a narrow 30m-strip at the back of the cave.

Bats & Swiftlets   FLYING CREATURES

At one time, some 470,000 bats and four million swiftlets called Niah home. There are no current figures, but the walls of the caves are no longer thick with bats and there are fewer bird's nests to harvest.

Several species of swiftlet nest on the cave walls. The most common by far is the glossy swiftlet, whose nest is made of vegetation and is therefore of no use in making soup. For obvious reasons, the species whose nests are edible (ie made up of delicious salivary excretions) are far less abundant and can only be seen in the remotest corners of the cavern. Several types of bat also roost in the cave, but not in dense colonies, as at Gunung Mulu National Park. Individuals can be picked out in the gloom, among the bird's nests, if you've got a powerful torch.

The best time to see the cave's winged wildlife is at dusk during the 'changeover', when the swiftlets stream back to their nests and the bats come swirling out for the night's feeding. If you do stick around, register at park HQ and make sure you either get back to the ferry by 7.30pm or coordinate a pick-up time with the boatman.

Bukit Kasut   TRAIL

This 45-minute trail, part of it a newly constructed boardwalk through freshwater swamp forest, goes from near the museum southward up to the summit of **Bukit Kasut** (205m). In the wet season, it can get muddy and treacherously slippery.

🛏 Sleeping & Eating

If you're not in a rush, Niah's forests, caves and hills can easily fill a couple of days.

NIAH NATIONAL PARK

Bookings for park-run accommodation can be made at park HQ or through one of the **National Park Booking Offices** (📞in Miri 085-434-184, in Kuching 082-248-088) – but *not* through Sarawak Forestry's website. Chalets and rooms often fill up on Chinese, Malay and public holidays.

Chalets   CHALETS $$
(1/2 r with fan RM105/157, with air-con RM236/157) The park has six reasonably comfortable two-room chalets; each room has four beds.

Rooms   GUEST ROOMS $
(r RM42) The park also has 20 four-bed rooms with shared bathroom. Dorm beds are available.

Campground   CAMPGROUND $
(sites per person RM5) Camping is permitted near park HQ.

Home Stay   HOME STAY $
(📞019-805-2415) In addition to the park-run options above, you can also stay near the Great Cave in the Iban longhouse village of **Rumah Patrick Libau**, which has an informal home stay program.

A new **canteen** (cafeteria) is under construction at park HQ. In the chalets and rooms, cooking is prohibited but you can boil water to make instant noodles.

BATU NIAH TOWN

Batu Niah town, 3km on foot from the park (4km by road), has two basic hotels.

Niah Cave Hotel   HOTEL $
(📞085-737-726; Lot 60, Batu Niah Bazaar; s/d/tr RM30/35/45; ❄) An old-fashioned Chinese cheapie whose six bare-bones rooms have spongy mattresses and spartan bath facilities. Mildly decrepit but good value for the price.

Niah Cave Inn   HOTEL $$
(📞085-737-333; fax 085-737-332; Lot 621, Batu Niah Bazaar; economy/standard r from RM64/75; ❄) The best hotel in Batu Niah, which isn't saying much. The windowless economy rooms recreate the dank odours of a cave with remarkable fidelity, but the standard

rooms, though worn and outmoded, are serviceable. Has 33 rooms. Lift-equipped.

BATU NIAH JUNCTION

If your bus arrives late or is leaving early, you might want to overnight at Batu Niah Junction, 15km south of park HQ.

TTL Motel   HOTEL $
(📞085-738-377; r with air-con & toilet RM65, with shared toilet RM35-40; ❄) A 43-room low-rise hotel that opened in 2010. Reception is open 24 hours. To get there, go out the back door of Batu Niah Food Court Centre and hang a diagonal left.

The junction's hangarlike **Batu Niah Food Court Centre** (🕐24hr) has lots of Chinese and Malay food stalls, a mini-post office and even 24-hour **internet access** (in the little grocery to the left as you enter the hall). Way in back, terrariums and aquariums hold snakes, iguanas, turtles and fish. There are more **food stalls** and a fruit and vegie **market** across the highway.

ℹ Getting There & Away

Niah National Park is about 115km southwest of Miri and 122km northeast of Bintulu. If you're pressed for time, the park can be visited as a day trip from either city.

Park HQ is not on the main (inland) Miri–Bintulu highway but rather 15km north of the highway's lively Batu Niah Junction. This makes getting to the park by public transport a bit tricky. All long-haul buses linking Miri with Bintulu, Sibu and Kuching pass by here, but the only way to get from the junction to Batu Niah Town (11km) or the park itself is to hire a private car. The price should be RM25 to RM30 but you'll have to nose around the market across the highway from the Batu Niah Food Court Centre to find one. National park staff (or, after hours, park security personnel) can help arrange a car (RM30) back to the junction.

Batu Niah Junction is a rest stop for virtually all buses travelling between Miri and points southwest. A **kiosk** (📞019-884-3662; 🕐7.30am-10.30pm) representing four bus companies – including Bintang Jaya and Suria – is a few metres to the right as you exit the Batu Niah Food Court Centre. Buses depart for Miri–Bintulu (RM10) from about 8am until late at night and for Bintulu (RM10) from about 8am to 10.30pm. Other well-served destinations include Sibu (RM30, five to six hours) and Kuching (RM70, 12 hours).

Batu Niah Town is 4km by road from park HQ, or 3km if you walk along the river's left bank (the trail starts near the red Chinese Temple). Hiring a private car costs RM10.

From Miri, a taxi to Niah costs RM150 one way or RM300 return, including three hours of wait time.

Lambir Hills National Park

The closest protected rainforest to Miri, the 69-sq-km **Lambir Hills National Park** (☎085-471-609; www.sarawakforestry.com; admission RM10; ☺park office 8am-5pm) offers dozens of jungle waterfalls, plenty of cool pools where you can take a dip, and a bunch of great walking trails through mixed dipterocarp and *kerangas* forests. A perennial favourite among locals and an important centre of scientific research, Lambir Hills makes a pleasant day or overnight trip out of the city.

The park encompasses a range of low sandstone hills with an extraordinary range of plants and animals – perhaps, say scientists, 'the greatest level of plant biodiversity on the planet'. Studies of a 52-hectare research plot (closed to visitors) have found an amazing 1200 tree species! Fauna includes clouded leopards, barking deer, pangolins, tarsiers, five varieties of civet, 10 bat species and 50 other kinds of mammals, though you are unlikely to see many of them around park HQ. Lambir Hills is also home to an unbelievable 237 species of bird, among them eight kinds of hornbill.

A new **visitors centre** is being built.

✺ Activities

Lambir Hills' colour-coded trails branch off four primary routes and lead to 14 destinations – rangers can supply you with a map and are happy to make suggestions. Make sure you get back to park HQ by 5pm – unless you're heading out for a **night walk**, that is, in which case you'll need to coordinate with park staff. Hiring a guide (optional) costs RM20 per hour.

From HQ, the **Main Trail** follows a small river, Sungai Liam, past two attractive waterfalls to the 25m-high **Latak Waterfall** (1km), which has a picnic area, changing rooms and a refreshing, sandy pool suitable for **swimming**. It can get pretty crowded on weekends.

You're likely to enjoy more natural tranquillity on the path to **Tengkorong Waterfall**, which is a somewhat strenuous 6km walk from park HQ. Another trail, steep in places, goes to the summit of **Bukit Lambir** (465m; 7km from HQ), where there are fine views. Keep an eye out for changes in the vegetation, including wild orchids, as the elevation rises.

🛏 Sleeping

It's possible to arrive at Lambir Hills in the morning, do a bit of walking and then head back to Miri or to Niah National Park, but this doesn't leave much time to appreciate the forest or its wildlife.

The park's reasonably comfortable **chalets** (d/q with fan RM50/75, with air-con RM100/150) have two bedrooms, each with two beds. **Camping** (per person RM5) is permitted near the park HQ.

Book by calling the park or through Miri's National Park Booking Office. Chalets are sometimes booked out on weekends and during school holidays. Dorm beds are not available.

✺ Eating

By the time you read this, park HQ should have a new **canteen** (cafeteria). Cooking facilities, except for places to barbecue, are not available.

❶ Getting There & Away

Park HQ is 32km south of Miri on the main highway. All the buses that link Miri's Pujut Bus Terminal with Bintulu pass by HQ (RM10 from Miri) – just ask the driver to stop. Buses from Miri to 'Lambir' go to the village of Lambir, not the park.

A taxi from Miri costs RM60 one way (RM120 return, including two hours of wait time).

Miri

☑085 / POP 295,000

An oil-rich boom town, Miri (www.mirire sortcity.com) serves as a major transport hub – if you're travelling to/from Brunei, Sabah, the Kelabit Highlands or the national parks of Gunung Mulu, Niah or Lambir Hills, chances are you'll pass this way. The city itself is busy and modern – not much about it is Borneo – but there's plenty of money sloshing around so the eating is good, the broad avenues are brightly lit and there's plenty to do when it's raining.

The population is about 40% Dayak (mainly Iban), 30% Chinese and 18% Malay. Foreign oil experts are gradually being replaced by Malaysian nationals so the city has fewer expats than a few years ago.

◉ Sights

Miri was never big on historical sites (most of the city is post-WWII) but a few years back the old Chinese shophouses around the southern end of Jln Brooke were levelled – and then, inexplicably, rebuilt from the ground up in a style that looks both fake and tasteless. However, Miri is not an unpleasant

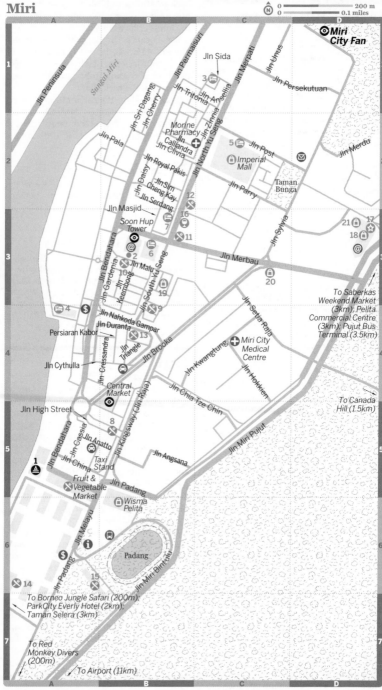

Miri City Fan

Sungai Miri

Jln Peninsula
Jln Pala
Jln Sri Dagang
Jln Cherry
Jln Royal Pakis
Jln Datsy
Jln Sim Cheng Kay
Jln Serdang
Jln Masjid
Soon Hup Tower
Jln Bendahara
Jln Gardenia
Jln Malu
Jln Kembong
Jln South Yu Seng
Jln Nahkoda Gampar
Jln Duranta
Jln Cressandra
Persiaran Kabor
Jln Triangle
Jln Cythulla
Jln Brooke

Jln Pernaisuri
Jln Tritonia
Jln Anselia
Jln Sida
Morine Pharmacy
Jln Callandra
Jln Clivia
Jln North Yu Seng
Jln Zinnia

Jln Merpati
Jln Unus
Jln Persekutuan
Jln Merdu

Jln Post
Imperial Mall
Jln Parry
Taman Bunga

Jln Sylvia
Jln Merbau

To Saberkas Weekend Market (3km); Pelita Commercial Centre (3km); Pujut Bus Terminal (3.5km)

Jln Serta Raja
Miri City Medical Centre
Jln Kwangtung
Jln Hokkien
Jln Chia Tze Chin

To Canada Hill (1.5km)

Central Market
Jln High Street
Jln Bendahara
Jln Cassia
Jln Anatto
Jln China
Jln Kingsway (Jln Raja)
Jln Angsana
Jln Miri Pujut
Taxi Stand
Fruit & Vegetable Market
Jln Padang
Wisma Pelita
Padang
Jln Melayu
Jln Padang
Jln Miri Bintulu

To Borneo Jungle Safari (200m); ParkCity Everly Hotel (2km); Taman Selera (3km)

To Red Monkey Divers (200m)

To Airport (11km)

0   200 m
0   0.1 miles

Miri

city, and a walk around the centre is a good way to get a feel for local commerce – streets worth a wander include (from north to south) Jln North Yu Seng, Jln South Yu Seng, Jln Malu and Jln High Street.

Miri City Fan   PARK

(Jln Kipas) A self-proclaimed 'resort city', greater Miri is studded with greenery and amenities. Nearest the city centre is the 10.4-hectare Miri City Fan, an expanse of nicely landscaped, themed gardens that boasts an indoor stadium and an Olympic-sized swimming pool (RM1). The area is popular with joggers.

Tua Pek Kong Temple   CHINESE TEMPLE

Miri's oldest Chinese temple – it was founded in 1913 – is a good spot to watch the river traffic float by. During the week-long celebration of the Chinese New Year, virtually the whole of this area, including Jln China, is taken over by a lively street fair with plenty of red lanterns and gold foil.

Canada Hill   MUSEUM

The low ridge 2km southeast of the town centre was the site of Malaysia's first oil well, the **Grand Old Lady**, drilled in 1910. Appropriately, the old derrick stands right outside the **Petroleum Museum** (Jln Canada Hill; ☺9am-4.30pm, closed Mon), whose interactive exhibits, some designed for kids, are a good introduction to the hugely lucrative industry that made Miri prosperous.

The hill itself is a popular exercise spot, and it's worth driving up here at sunset (it's too far to walk) for the views across town to the South China Sea.

Saberkas Weekend Market   MARKET

(☺3pm Fri-evening Saturday, daily during Ramadan) One of the most colourful and friendly markets in Sarawak. Vendors are more than happy to answer questions about their colourful products, which include tropical fruits and vegies, BBQ chicken, *satay*, grilled stingray and handicrafts. Situated about 3km northeast of the centre near the Boulevard Commercial Centre, Miri's newest shopping mall. Served by buses 1, 1A, 31, 42, 62, 63, 66 and 68.

San Ching Tian Temple   TAOIST TEMPLE

(Jln Bulan Sabit, Krokop) One of the largest Taoist temples in Southeast Asia. Built in 2000, the design features intricate dragon reliefs brought from China. Situated about 1km northwest of the Saberkas Weekend Market.

Taman Selera   BEACH

About 3km southwest of the centre, this park – near Miri's yacht marina – has a passable beach, a children's playground, and a hawker centre and pier that are great for romantic sunset views.

🏃 Activities

Red Monkey Divers   SCUBA DIVING

(☏014-699-8296; www.redmonkeydivers.com; Gymkhana Club, Jln Dato Abang Indeh; ☺10am-5pm Mon-Sat, closed Dec-Feb) Although the waters off Miri are better known for drilling than diving, the area has some excellent scuba sites, including old oil platforms teeming with fish and assorted trawler and freighter wrecks. Water visibility is at its best from March to

September. Red Monkey, based about 2km south of the Mega Hotel, is a professional outfit that offers PADI and BSAC courses.

Hash House Harriers   RUNNING

(www.mirihhh.com) Visitors are welcome to join locals and expats for runs at 4.30pm on Saturday (7.30pm on the fourth Saturday of the month) and 5.15pm on Tuesday. Club members are known to hang out at the Ming Cafe.

Megalanes East Bowling Alley   BOWLING

(upper level, Bintang Plaza, Jln Miri Pujut; per game RM3.80-5.90, shoes RM2; ☺10am-midnight) Offers 24 lanes of escape, great for a rainy day. To get there from the Star Cinema, walk past the ticket windows to the end and turn left.

King's Archery Sportscentre   ARCHERY

(☑419-500; lower fl, Bintang Plaza, Jln Miri Pujut; 40/100 arrows RM15/35, students RM10/28; ☺noon-10pm, closed Mon) You can pretend you're in the jungle hunting for dinner at this 8m archery range, hidden away on the 'lower roof' level of Bintang Plaza. To get there, turn left at the entrance to the Star Cinema and go up two flights of service stairs.

☞ Tours

Miri-based companies offering trekking in northeastern Sarawak include:

Borneo Jungle Safari   TREKKING

(☑422-595; www.borneojunglesafari.com; 1st fl, Centre Point Commercial Centre II, Jln Kubu)

Borneo Tropical Adventure   TREKKING

(☑419-337; www.borneotropicaladventure.com; ground fl, Soon Hup Tower, Jln Merbau)

✴✤ Festivals

Miri International Jazz Festival   JAZZ

(www.mirijazzfestival.com; Jln Temenggong Datuk Oyong Lawai; ☺weekend in mid-May) Features an eclectic assemblage of international artists. Held south of town next door to the ParkCity Everly Hotel.

🛏 Sleeping

Miri now has some excellent backpackers guest houses. If you're on a tight budget, choose your bed carefully – at the cheapie dives catering to oil-rig roustabouts, many of the dreary rooms are windowless and musty, and Miri's brothel business booms at some of the shadier bottom-end digs.

For laundry service, ask at your hotel or guest house or try **EcoLaundry** (☑414-266; 638 Jln North Yu Seng; per kg RM5; ☺7am-8pm Mon-Sat, to 6pm Sun). If you drop off your clothes before flying up to Gunung Mulu National Park or the Kelabit Highlands, you'll save checked baggage weight and have clean undies when you return!

TOP CHOICE Minda Guesthouse   GUEST HOUSE $

(☑411-422; www.mindaguesthouse.com; 1st & 2nd fl, Lot 637, Jln North Yu Seng; per person dm/d RM20/50; ❄@🅐) In the heart of Miri's liveliest dining and drinking district, this spotless, modern establishment offers 14 clean rooms with colourful bedclothes, a kitchen, a DVD lounge, unlimited tea and coffee and a rooftop sundeck where you can barbecue. Great value for money.

Dillenia Guesthouse   GUEST HOUSE $$

(☑434-204; dillenia.guesthouse@gmail.com; 1st fl, 846 Jln Sida; dm/s/d/q incl breakfast RM30/50/80/110; ❄@🅐) In the northwest corner of a commercial area, this super-welcoming hostel, with 11 rooms and cement floors, lives up to its motto, 'a home away from home'. Incredibly helpful Mrs Lee is an artesian well of useful travel information and tips.

Highlands Guesthouse   GUEST HOUSE $

(☑422-327; 3rd fl, 1271 Jln Sri Dagang; dm/d RM25/50; ❄@) Miri's original backpackers guest house, in a converted commercial building, still serves as a 'budget tourist and travel information centre'. The lounge, with satellite TV, is no longer overrun with cats. The affable owner, a Twin Otter pilot from New Zealand everyone calls Captain David, sometimes drops by.

Imperial Hotel   HOTEL $$

(☑431-133; www.imperialhotel.com.my; Jln Post; d from RM260; ❄❄) The city centre's poshest hotel boasts fitness centre, sauna and swimming pool. Significant discounts are available online.

Apollo Hotel   HOTEL $$

(☑433-077; fax 419-964; 4 Jln South Yu Seng; s/d/tr from RM60/65/85; ❄) For good midrange value, give us a well-maintained Chinese cheapie any time. This place is simple, clean and centrally located – and best of all, you can enjoy some of Miri's best seafood at the adjoining restaurant. Reception is around the back.

Mega Hotel   HOTEL $$

(☑432-432; www.megahotel.com.my; 907 Jln Merbau; r from RM195; ❄@🅐❄) Catering mainly to business travellers, this aptly named hotel dominates Miri's centre with its imposing blue and white bulk. Things improve once you get past the tacky lobby – the 288 rooms are

🏠**TreeTops Lodge** (📞085-472-172; www.treetops-borneo.com; Lot 210, Kampung Siwa Jaya; r incl breakfast per person RM30-60; ❄️🛜🏊), situated about 15km southwest of Miri along the coastal road, is a friendly, family-run 'eco-retreat' with a laid-back cluster of cabins and lots of tropical fruit trees. When you're not lounging on the nearby beach, you can fish for tilapia or go hiking.

From Miri's local bus terminal, take bus 13 (RM4, every hour or two from 5.50am to 6.30pm) to the end of the line. From the airport, a taxi costs about RM55. TreeTops is not far from the western reaches of Lambir Hills National Park but getting to park HQ involves a 40km drive.

comfortable and very spacious, though the decor is a bit old-fashioned. Amenities include a fitness centre (11th floor) and a 30m pool with a Jacuzzi and town views (4th floor).

Miri Trail Guesthouse　　AIRPORT HOTEL **$**
(📞017-850-3666, 016-807-1305; www.miritrailguesthouse.com; Airport Commercial Centre, Jln Airport; dm/d RM25/55, day use RM15/30; ❄️@) A basic crash pad with six rooms, most without windows, and shared bathrooms. Situated across the road from the airport (above the MASwings office), so if you're transiting through Miri you can rest here overnight or during the day. Several eateries are right downstairs.

🍴 Eating

If you won't be going up to the Kelabit Highlands, Miri may be your only chance to encounter the unique tastes and aromas of authentic Kelabit cuisine.

TOP CHOICE Café Tauh　　KELABIT **$$**
(Jln Airport; lunch buffet RM10; ⏰8am-4pm) Situated across the road from the airport (next to the new MASwings office), this family-run restaurant serves Kelabit specialities including *kikid* (rice porridge), *nubaq layaq* (vegies that are boiled and then mashed) and *labo laal sinutung* (chicken cooked with young tapioca leaves inside a length of bamboo). Many of the ingredients, including Bario pineapples that are out of this world, are flown in fresh from Bario. The name means 'our' or 'ours' in Kelabit.

TOP CHOICE Summit Cafe　　KELABIT **$**
(Centre Point Commercial Centre, Jln Melayu; mains from RM3; ⏰6am-3.30pm, closed Sun) If you've never tried Kelabit cuisine, this place will open up whole new worlds for your tastebuds. Try the colourful array of 'jungle food' – *canko manis* (forest ferns), *dure'* (fried jungle leaf), minced tapioca leaves, and – sometimes – wild boar. Come early for

lunch – once the food runs out they close! Next door to a place called Tian Tian. Not to be confused with the Summit Cafe across from the Apollo Seafood Centre.

Apollo Seafood Centre　　SEAFOOD **$$**
(4 Jln South Yu Seng; mains from RM6; ⏰10.30am-11.30pm) Hugely – and deservedly – popular among locals and expats alike. Just about anything you order will be delicious, but we recommend the fried *midin* with *belacan*, the crabs and the rather pricey lobster (February to July). Fish straight from the tank ranges from RM35 per kilo (for sole) to RM120 (for grouper). Enhance your meal with chilled Australian wine.

Khan's Restaurant Islamic　　INDIAN **$**
(229 Jln Malu; mains RM4-8; ⏰6.30am-8.30pm; 🍴) This simple canteen is one of Miri's best North Indian eateries, whipping up tasty treats like mouth-watering chicken vindaloo (RM12) and seven vegie mains (RM4).

Ming Café　　ASIAN & WESTERN **$$**
(www.mingcafe.com.my; cnr Jln North Yu Seng & Jln Merbau; mains RM5.50-25; ⏰7am-1am) Take your pick of Chinese, Malay, Indian and Western food at this ever-busy eating emporium. New for 2010: a bar. Happy hang out of the Hash House Harriers.

Muara Restoran　　INDONESIAN **$$**
(Jln North Yu Seng; mains RM8-12; ⏰10am-5am) Expat Indonesian oil workers in bright yellow overalls flock to this tin-roofed shed for *lalapan* (tofu, tempeh and raw vegies eaten with spicy *sambal belacan*). Great for a late-late meal.

There are several seafood places along Jln South Yu Seng and a row of chic, ultra-modern *kopitiam*, including **After 3** (Jln High Street).

Tamu Muhibbah　　MARKET
(Jln Padang; ⏰2am-7pm) Vegies, including *midin* ferns, are sold at stalls owned by Chinese, Malay, Iban and Orang Ulu.

Sin Liang Supermarket SUPERMARKET $
(Jln Duranta; ⊘8.30am-9pm) Well stocked with toiletries and Aussie wines.

Drinking

Jln North Yu Seng, brightly lit at night, has a row of tepee-covered cafes down the middle.

Barcelona BAR
(Jln North Yu Seng; draught beer RM8-12; ⊘4pm-2am, happy hour 4-8pm) More equatorial than Iberian but has a relaxed, upscale vibe and a big screen for footy. Seating is open-air at wooden tables. Liquid specialities range from Spanish and Australian wines to mojitos (RM15) and sex on the beach (RM20). Serves tapas and some Western dishes. Adjacent Soho hosts a live Filipino band from 9pm on Friday and Saturday.

Pelita Commercial Centre BAR DISTRICT
(cnr Jln Miri Pujut & Jln Sehati) Those keen on a pub crawl might consider catching a cab to this warren of small streets lined with pubs, cafes, restaurants and dodgy karaoke places 3km north of the centre. Don't mess with the local toughs.

☆ Entertainment

Star Cinema CINEMA
(☑417-610; www.starcineplex.com.my; upper level, Bintang Plaza, Jln Miri Pujut; tickets RM5-10; ⊘noon-11pm) Most films are in English. Perfect for rainy-day escapism.

🛍 Shopping

Miri Handicraft Centre HANDICRAFTS
(cnr Jln Brooke & Jln Merbau; ⊘8.30am-5.30pm) A dozen stalls, rented from the city, sell bags, baskets, sarongs, textiles etc made by Iban, Kelabit, Kenyah/Kayan, Lun Bawang, Chinese and Malay artisans. Stall No 5 has some fine beadwork from Bario.

Borneo Arts HANDICRAFTS
(Jln South Yu Seng; ⊘9am-9pm) Dayak handicrafts and souvenirs.

Popular Book Store BOOKS
(2nd fl, Bintang Plaza, Jln Miri Pujut; ⊘10am-10pm) A mega-bookshop with lots of fiction, non-fiction, biography and cookbooks, and a good selection of LP titles in English and Chinese.

Bintang Plaza SHOPPING MALL
(Jln Miri Pujut; ⊘10am-10pm daily) A modern, multi-storey, air-con mall that could be in Singapore.

Information

Internet Access
Internet Shop (1st fl, Soon Hup Tower, cnr Jln Bendahara & Jln Merbau; per hr RM2; ⊘8am-8pm) In the orange-pink building just west of the Mega Hotel. Popular with zombified teenage gamers.

IT Cyber Station (top fl, western end, Bintang Plaza, Jln Miri Pujut; per hr RM2.50; ⊘10am-10pm) Has 70 computers.

Medical Services
Colombia Asia Hospital (☑437-755; http://columbiaasia.com/miri; Jln Bulan Sabit; ⊘24hr) A 35-bed private hospital, used by many expats, with a 24-hour accident and emergency ward and a 24-hour ambulance. Situated 4km northeast of the Mega Hotel.

Miri City Medical Centre (☑426-622; www.mcmcmiri.com; 916-920 & 1203 Jln Hokkien) Has various private clinics and a 24-hour accident and emergency department. Accepts direct payment from certain insurance companies.

Morine Pharmacy (cnr Jln Callandra & Jln Merpati; ⊘8.15am-6.15pm Mon-Sat, to noon Sun & holidays) A good place to stock up on medicines and first-aid supplies before heading inland (there's no pharmacy at Gunung Mulu).

Money
ATMs can be found at Miri airport and are sprinkled all over town.

Maybank (Lot 112, Jln Bendahara; ⊘9.15am-4.30pm Mon-Thu, to 4pm Fri) The ATM, facing Jln Mereban, operates from 6am to midnight.

Maybank Bureau de Change (1271 Centre Point Commercial Centre; ⊘9am-5pm) Changes cash and travellers cheques and does cash advances. Has an ATM.

Post
Main post office (Jln Post; ⊘8am-4pm Mon-Fri, to 2.30pm Sat)

Tourist Information
National Park Booking Office (☑434-184; www.sarawakforestry.com; 452 Jln Melayu; ⊘8am-5pm Mon-Fri) Inside the Visitors Information Centre. Has details on Sarawak's national parks and can book beds and rooms at Niah and Lambir Hills (but not at Gunung Mulu or Similajau).

Visitors Information Centre (☑434-181; www.sarawaktourism.com; 452 Jln Melayu; ⊘8am-6pm Mon-Fri, 9am-3pm Sat & Sun) The helpful staff can provide city maps, information on accommodation and a list of guides. Publishes the useful, free *Miri & Northern Sarawak Guide* every couple of years. Situated in a little park. Has an airport branch that's theoretically open from 8am to 5pm, closed Saturday, Sunday and holidays.

Visas
Immigration Department (Jabatan Imigresen; ☑442-117; www.imi.gov.my; 2nd fl, Yulan Plaza, cnr Jln Kingsway & Jln Brooke; ☺8am-5pm Mon-Thu, 8-11.45am & 2.15-5pm Fri) For visa extensions.

❶ Getting There & Away

Miri is 212km northeast of Bintulu and 36km southwest of the Brunei border.

Air

Miri is the main hub of the Malaysia Airlines subsidiary **MASwings** (www.maswings.com.my), whose direct and often inexpensive flights go to Bario (Kelabit Highlands), Bintulu, Gunung Mulu National Park (Mulu), Labuan, Lawas, Limbang, Marudi, KK, Kuching and Sibu.

The discount airline **AirAsia** (www.airasia. com) can get you to Kuching, KK, KL, Johor Bahru and Singapore, while **Malaysia Airlines** (www.malaysiaairlines.com) flies to KL.

Miri's **airport** (Jln Airport) has a separate check-in area for MASwings' 'Rural Air Service' routes, eg to Gunung Mulu National Park and Bario. If you're flying on a Twin Otter, you'll be asked to stand on a giant scale while holding your carry-on.

The only place in the airport with wi-fi and internet access is the **Executive Lounge** (☑616-172; RM48) in the upstairs departure lounge.

Café Tauh serves superb Kelabit cuisine right across the road from the terminal.

For details on flying to Gunung Mulu National Park and Bario, see p213 and p218.

Boat

For details on getting to Gunung Mulu National Park via Marudi, see p213.

Bus

Long-distance buses use the Pujut Bus Terminal, about 4km northeast of the centre.

There are frequent buses to Kuching (RM90, 14 hours, departures from 6am to 10pm) via the inland Miri–Bintulu highway, Batu Niah Junction (15km south of Niah National Park), Bintulu (RM25, 3½ hours) and Sibu (RM50, eight hours). Companies include **Bintang Jaya** (☑438-301, 432-178), **Bus Asia** (Biaramas; ☑414-999, hotline 082-411-111; http://mybus.com.my) and **Miri Transport Company** (MTC; ☑438-161; www. mtcmiri.com).

Bintang Jaya also has services northeast to Limbang (RM45), Lawas (RM75) and KK (RM90). Buses leave Miri at 8am on Monday, Wednesday and Friday; departures from KK are at 7.30am on Tuesday, Thursday and Friday. The company

also runs a daily bus to Limbang at 1.30pm. Getting off in Brunei is not allowed.

For details on getting to destinations in Brunei, including BSB, see p233. At the time of research, short-haul bus service to Kuala Belait (Brunei) was suspended.

❶ Getting Around
To/From the Airport

A **taxi** (☺432-277) from the airport to the city centre takes about 15 minutes (25 minutes in traffic) and costs RM22 (RM33 after 11.45pm); in the other direction, the fare is RM20. Coupons are sold inside the airport terminal at the **taxi desk** (☺7am-11pm), which is just outside the baggage-claim area (next to the car-rental desks).

Bus 28 links the local bus station with the airport (RM2.80) seven or eight times a day from 7am to 4.45pm (until 6.30pm from the city to the airport). At the airport, the stop is on the Arrivals island in front of the terminal (look for an upright reading 'Bas').

Bus

Local bus transport is handled by three companies, Miri City Bus, Miri Transport Company (MTC) and Miri Belait Transport. The **local bus station** (Jln Padang), next to the Visitors Information Centre, has schedules posted. Fares start at RM1; most lines run from 7am to about 6pm.

MTC bus 33A links the local bus station with Pujut Bus Terminal (RM1.60, twice an hour until 6.30pm).

Car

Most of Miri's guest houses are happy to organise private transport to area destinations such as Lambir Hills National Park (RM85 return) and Niah National Park (RM180 return).

Companies with car-rental desks at Miri airport, just outside of baggage claim, include:

FT Car Rental (☑438-415; www.ftcarrental. com)

Golden System Car Rental (☑613-359; www. goldencar.com.my)

Hertz (☑614-740; www.hertz.com) Not always staffed.

Kong Teck Car Rental (☑617-767; www. kongteck.com.my)

Taxi

A short cab ride in the city centre is RM10, to the Pujut Bus Terminal it is RM15. Taxis run by the **Miri Taxi Association** (☑432-277; ☺24hr) can be found at:

Taxi rank (☺4am-7.30pm; cnr Jln Brooke & Jln Cythulla)

Taxi rank (Jln Anatto)

NORTHEASTERN SARAWAK

Gunung Mulu National Park

Also known as the **Gunung Mulu World Heritage Area** (☎085-792-300; www.mulupark.com; adult/child per day RM10/5; ☺park HQ 8am-5pm), this park may well be the single most impressive destination in all of Borneo. No wonder, then, that it was declared a Unesco World Heritage Site in 2005.

Few national parks anywhere in the world pack so many natural marvels into such a small area. From some of the world's most incredible (and accessible) **caves** (www.mulucaves.org), to brilliant old-growth tropical rainforest (the park has 17 different vegetation zones), to natural oddities such as the Pinnacles formation, this is truly one of the world's wonders.

Among the remarkable features in this 529-sq-km park are its two main mountain peaks, Gunung Mulu (2377m) and Gunung Api (1682m). In between are more rugged mountains, deep gorges with clear rivers, and a unique mosaic of habitats supporting fascinating and diverse species of wildlife. Mulu's most famous trekking attractions, though, are the Pinnacles, a forest of razor-sharp limestone spires, and the so-called Head-hunters' Trail, a trekking route that follows an old tribal war path down to Limbang.

Some cave tours (especially the more difficult ones) and treks (especially the longer ones) are booked out well in advance – for details on reservations, see the Guides, Fees & Reservations box below.

☉ Sights & Activities

When you register, park staff will give you a placemat-sized schematic map of the park on which you can plan out your daily activities. HQ staff are generally very helpful in planning itineraries.

Plankwalks are pressure cleaned every three months and swept every second day but still get very slippery.

The park's excellent website (www.mulupark.com) and brochures available at the park office have information on walks and **boat trips** not covered below.

Unguided Sights & Activities

Visitors are not allowed to go inside any of the caves without a guide but you can take a number of **jungle walks** unaccompanied so long as you inform the park office (or, when it's closed, someone across the path in the Park Security pavilion). You can walk unaccompanied through the rainforest to the entrance of the **Wind Cave** (3km one way) and to **Paku Waterfall** (3km one way), where it's possible to swim.

GUIDES, FEES & RESERVATIONS

Almost all of the caves and rainforest treks in **Gunung Mulu National Park** (☎085-792-300; www.mulupark.com) require that visitors be accompanied by a guide licensed by Sarawak Forestry, supplied either by the park or by an adventure tour agency (eg those based in Kuching, Miri or Limbang). Prices in this chapter are for tours booked directly through the park.

As these circuits are becoming more and more popular, advance reservations are a must, especially if you've got your heart set on adventure caving, or on trekking up to the Pinnacles or the summit of Gunung Mulu. Booking well ahead is especially important if you'll be coming in July and August, a period when some routes are booked out by February.

Gunung Mulu National Park's trekking and caving guides are well trained (by Sarawak Forestry) and speak good English but there are only 17 of them. As a result, multi-day treks are usually handled by freelance guides, many from nearby villages, whose training and knowledge (eg about flora, fauna and geology) ranges from excellent to barely sufficient. Park administrators have been working to improve the quality of the guides but this process has excluded – and thus angered – some locals who used to earn a living as (untrained) park guides.

A caving group must consist of at least four participants (including the guide) so that if someone is injured, one person can stay with them and the other two can head out of the cave to seek help.

Starting in late 2010, the park's prices for caving and treks are on a straight per-person basis.

Mulu Discovery Centre   MUSEUM

(☺7.30am-9pm) Has a pretty good introduction to the park as a 'biodiversity hotspot', including its extraordinary geology (eg the Pinnacles and cave formation), and a detailed map of the vast Clearwater Cave System. At research time, the centre was next to the Wild Mulu Café but was slated to move. Gloriously air-conditioned.

Tree Top Tower   BIRD-WATCHING

(admission free, key deposit RM50) Basically a 30m-high bird hide. The best time to spot our feathered friends is early in the morning (5am to 9am) or in the late afternoon (4pm to 8pm). Reserve a time slot and pick up the key at park HQ or, after 4.30pm, from Park Security (in the open-air pavilion across the boardwalk from the park office). Situated about 500m from park HQ.

Moonmilk Cave   JUNGLE WALK

'Moonmilk' – a fibrous mineral formation known to scientists as Lublinite – is created when bacteria break down calcite, the main component of limestone. Don't touch it – it's very fragile! This cave can be visited either on a two-hour walk from park HQ or on the way back from Wind Cave and Clearwater Cave. Bring a torch.

Guided Forest Walks

Nightwalk   FOREST WALK

(per person RM10; ☺7pm except if raining) The ideal first-night introduction to the park's nocturnal fauna, this 2km, two-hour walk follows a boardwalk through a swampy alluvial forest. Creatures you're very likely to see – but only after the guide points them out – include tree frogs hardly 1cm long, enormous spiders, vine snakes that are a dead ringer for a vine wrapped around a branch, and stick insects (phasmids), extraordinary creatures up to 20cm long that look like they've been assembled from pencils and toothpicks. If you put your torch (bring one!) up to eye level and shine it into the foliage, the eyes of spiders and other creatures will reflect brightly back.

Don't wear insect repellent or you risk repelling some of the insects you're trying to see. Mozzies are not a problem.

If you order dinner at the Wild Mulu Café before heading out, you can pick it up when you return (make sure you're back before 9.30pm).

You can take the nightwalk trail on your own, without a guide, either before 5pm (so that your scent, which scares away the wildlife, dissipates before the guided group comes through) or after 8pm. Make sure you inform either the park office or, when it's closed, someone in the Park Security pavilion.

Mulu Canopy Skywalk   CANOPY WALK

(per person RM30) Climbing up into the forest canopy is the only way to see what a tropical rainforest is all about, since most of the flora and fauna do their thing high up in the trees, not on the ground. This unforgettable, 480m-long skywalk is one of the best in Southeast Asia. There are departures every hour or two from 7am to 2pm. Tends to get booked out early so reserve as far ahead as possible.

Show Caves

Mulu's **'show caves'** (the park's name for caves that can be visited without special training or equipment) are its most popular attraction and for good reason: they are awesome. All are accessible on guided walks from park HQ. Bring a torch.

Deer Cave & Lang's Cave   CAVE TOURS

(per person RM20; ☺departures at 2pm & 2.30pm) A lovely 3km walk (40 to 60 minutes) through the rainforest along a plankwalk takes you to these adjacent caverns. The highlight here is not so much what's in the caves as what comes out of them every evening around dusk (unless it's raining): millions of bats in spiralling, twirling clouds that look a bit like swarms of cartoon bees. It's an awesome sight. The bats' corkscrew trajectory is designed to foil the dinner plans of bat hawks perched nearby on the cliffs. Count on getting back to park HQ at around 7pm.

The **Mulu Bat-Cam** (www.muluparkbatcam. com) – in fact, five infrared webcams – follows the lives of bats inside the Deer Cave. It's not internet live-streamed yet, but you can see the feed at the small **visitors centre**, next to the grassy bat-viewing amphitheatre.

The Deer Cave – over 2km in length and 174m in height – is the world's largest cave passage open to the public. (It was considered the world's largest cave passage, full stop, until an even larger one was discovered in Vietnam in 2009.) It is home to two million to three million bats belonging to 12 species (more than in any other cave in the world) who cling to the roof in a seething black mass as they gear up for their evening prowl. Baby wrinkle-lipped bats that have fallen from the ceiling can sometimes be seen near the path.

We're not sure who did the calculations or how, but it's said that the Deer Cave's bats devour 30 tonnes of mosquitoes every night.

That's why mosquito bites are almost unknown in the park.

If it's raining, the bats usually (but not always) stay home because echolocation (the way they find prey) is not very good at telling the difference between a flying insect and a raindrop.

Wind Cave & Clearwater Cave   CAVE TOURS
(per person incl boat ride RM40; ⊙departures at 8.45am & 9.15am) Zipping along an upland jungle river in a flat-bottomed longboat, wearing a fluorescent orange life vest, is not a bad way to start the day. This tour takes about four hours, leaving time for another cave visit in the afternoon.

Wind Cave, first on the tour, has several chambers – including the cathedral-like King's Chamber – filled with phantasmagorical forests of stalactites and stalagmites. It is named for the deliciously cool breezes that flow through a particular passage.

A 400m plankwalk takes you to Clearwater Cave, a 170km subterranean network of which only a tiny segment is open to casual visitors. As the name suggests, the highlight here is an underground river.

After visiting the caves, you can take a dip in the refreshingly cool water of a sandy swimming hole so don't forget your swimsuit; changing facilities are available. You don't need a guide to walk back to park HQ (1½ hours) via Moonmilk Cave.

Tours usually stop off at the riverside village of Batu Bungan, created by the government as part of a campaign to discourage the nomadic lifestyle of the Penan. Trinkets and handicrafts are for sale.

Lagang Cave   CAVE TOUR
(per person incl boat RM55; ⊙1pm) This cave route, nicknamed the 'Fast Lane', has gotten rave reviews since it opened in 2010, thanks to its extraordinary stalactites and stalagmites and to its state-of-the-art light show. Getting there requires a one-hour walk; the entire visit takes three or four hours. Groups are limited to eight people so book well ahead. An 'adventure cave' circuit through Lagang Cave is also available.

Adventure Caves
The limestone peaks of Mulu are riddled with some of the world's most incredible caves, so the park is one of the best places in the world to try the sport of adventure caving.

Routes that require special equipment and a degree of caving experience are known here as **'adventure caves'**. Rosters for the six half- or all-day options fill up early – the park has a shortage of qualified caving guides – so reserve well ahead. Groups are limited to eight participants. Heavy rains can cause caves to flood.

Caving routes are graded beginner, intermediate and advanced; guides determine each visitors' suitability based on their previous caving experience. If you have no background in spelunking, you will be encouraged to try an intermediate route (usually Racer Cave) before moving on to an advanced one. Minimum ages are 12 for intermediate and 16 for advanced. The park office has details on 'family adventure caving', ie adventure routes that are suitable for the entire family. Fees include a helmet and a headlamp; visitors need to bring closed shoes, a first-aid kit and clothes they won't mind getting dirty in.

Keep in mind that adventure caving is not for everyone, and halfway into a cave passage is not the best time to discover that you suffer from claustrophobia, fear of the dark or simply don't like slithering in the mud with all sorts of unknown creepy crawlies.

Sarawak Chamber   ADVANCED CAVING
(per person RM335; ⊙departures at 6.30am) Measuring an incredible 700m long, 400m wide and 70m high, this chamber – discovered in 1981 – has been called the world's largest enclosed space. Don't count on seeing much, though – ordinary lights are no match for the ocean of black emptiness, big enough to park 10 A380s lined up nose to tail. This circuit is very demanding – getting to the cave and back involves six hours of trekking (three hours each way) and getting around inside the cave requires some use of fixed ropes. The whole route takes 10 to 15 hours.

Clearwater Connection   ADVANCED CAVING
(per person RM170) This 4.8km, four- to six-hour circuit starts at Wind Cave and heads into the wilds of the vast Clearwater Cave system. There's a good bit of scrambling and the route includes a 1.5km river section.

Drunken Forest Cave   INTERMEDIATE CAVING
(per person RM125) This section of Clearwater Cave, famous for a forest of white stalagmites, is accessed from the Mulu Summit Trail. The route takes four to five hours.

Lagang Cave   INTERMEDIATE CAVING
(per person RM95) Lots of stalagmites, stalactites and boulders, plus an ancient river bed. No climbing. This cave also has a 'show cave' route; the adventure-caving route takes two to four hours.

Racer Cave INTERMEDIATE CAVING
(per person RM95) Has some rope-assisted sections that require a bit of upper-body strength. Named after the cave racer snake, which dines mainly on bats. Takes two to four hours.

Trekking & Climbing
The park offers some of the best and most accessible **jungle trekking** in Borneo. The forest here is in excellent condition and there are trails for every level of fitness and skill. For details see www.mulupark.com.

Expect rain, leeches, slippery and treacherous conditions, and a very hot workout – carry lots of water. Guides are required for overnights, except the Headhunters' Trail. Book well ahead. Don't even think of taking one of these treks if you've got asthma or knee problems.

The Pinnacles TREKKING
(per person RM325) The Pinnacles are an incredible formation of 45m-high stone spires protruding from the forested flanks of Gunung Api. Getting to a viewpoint overlooking the Pinnacles – undoubtedly the world's worst parachute drop zone – involves a boat ride (you can stop off at Wind Cave and Clearwater Cave) and, between two overnights at Camp 5, an unrelentingly steep 2.4km ascent; the final section involves some serious clambering and a bit of rope work. Coming down is just as taxing so when you stagger into Camp 5, a swim in the cool, clear river may look pretty enticing. The trail passes through some gorgeous jungle.

Bring shoes that will give you traction on sharp and slippery rocks, bedding (many people find that a sarong is warm enough at Camp 5), a first-aid kit, a torch and enough food for six meals. Cooking equipment and gas stoves are available at Camp 5. The trip takes three days and two nights.

Gunung Mulu Summit TREKKING
(per person RM405) The climb to the summit of Gunung Mulu (2376m) – described recently by one satisfied ascendee as 'gruelling' and, near the top, 'treacherous' – is a classic Borneo adventure. If you're very fit and looking for real adventure, this demanding 24km trek may be for you.

You will need to bring proper hiking shoes, a sleeping bag (Camp 4 can get quite chilly), a sleeping pad (unless you don't mind sleeping on wooden boards), rain gear (some groups end up having rain the whole way), a torch and a first-aid kit, as well as enough food for four days. The camps along the way have very basic cooking equipment, including a gas stove. Bring water-purification tablets if you're leery of drinking the rainwater collected at shelters en route. Near the summit you may spend much of your time inside clouds; a fleece jacket is the best way to ward off the damp and cold. Recent trekkers report having been visited by rats at Camp 3 and by squirrels who were 'keen on noodles' at Camp 4. The trip takes four days and three nights.

Headhunters' Trail TREKKING
The Headhunters' Trail is a backdoor route from Gunung Mulu National Park to Limbang and can be done in either direction, although most people start at the park. The route is named after the Kayan war parties that used to make their way up the Sungai Melinau from the Baram area to the Melinau Gorge, then dragged their canoes overland to the Sungai Terikan to raid the peoples of the Limbang region.

If you're heading from the park down to Limbang, you can walk unaccompanied to Camp 5 (per person RM30) – reserve in advance at the park office – and, the next morning, walk to Kuala Terikan (11km). From there (or from Lubang Cina), onward travel to Medamit (linked by road with Limbang) will be impossible unless you arrange to be met by a boatman or a guide. Park HQ can help arrange a longboat (RM565 for up to four people).

A simpler option is to take the Headhunters' Trail on a trek organised by the park (per person RM395, including the Pinnacles RM550).

Starting in Limbang, you can take the Headhunters' Trail up to the park without a guide, hiring boats as you go; or you can take a trek organised by Borneo Touch Ecotour – see p220. The trip takes two days and one night.

🛏 Sleeping
Accommodation options range from extremely basic to overpriced longhouse-style luxury. MASwings now uses larger aircraft for the Miri–Mulu route, so depending on how long people stay, there may end up being more seats on the planes than there are places to stay inside the park.

Camping is no longer permitted at park HQ but you can pitch a tent at some of the guest houses just outside the park (across the bridge from HQ). Elsewhere in the park, the only places you can camp – and then only if you have reservations (space is limited) – are Camp 5 and several camps along the Gunung Mulu Summit trail.

INSIDE THE NATIONAL PARK

All private rooms have attached bathroom. Park HQ has 24-hour electricity. Tap water is safe to drink. Prices (except for Camp 5) include a delicious breakfast.

It's a good idea to book at least a few days in advance, especially from June to August – just call ☎085-792-300 or visit www.mulupark.com. Reservations cannot be made through Sarawak Forestry.

Garden Bungalows   BUNGALOWS **$$**
(s/d/tr incl breakfast RM200/230/250; ❄)
These eight brand-new units replace the notorious 'rainforest rooms'.

Chalets   CHALETS **$$**
(s/d/tr/q incl breakfast RM170/180/215/250; ❄)
Each of the two chalets has two rooms.

Longhouse Rooms   ROOMS **$$**
(s/d/tr/q incl breakfast RM170/180/215/250; ❄)
There are 10 of these.

Hostel   HOSTEL **$**
(B&B RM40) All 19 beds are in a clean, spacious dormitory-style room with ceiling fans. Lockers are available for a RM10 deposit.

Camp 5   CAMPGROUND **$**
(per person RM30) An open-air sleeping platform with mats, cooking facilities (including cooking gas) and bathrooms. Space is limited (to 50 people) so only hikers who are heading up to the Pinnacles or down the Headhunters' Trail can stay here. Reserve and pay at the park office. It's warm enough to sleep here without a sleeping bag (a sarong will do).

OUTSIDE THE NATIONAL PARK

Several ultra-budget places are located just across the bridge from park HQ, along the banks of the river; the national-park office may neglect to mention this fact when they inform you they're booked out. Activities include hanging out with other budget travellers and swimming.

The Royal Mulu Resort is almost never full, the result of its size, its overpricing and the somewhat run-down state of the facilities (set for an upgrade).

Royal Mulu Resort   LUXURY RESORT **$$$**
(☎085-792-388; www.royalmuluresort.com, www.marriott.com; s/d incl breakfast & dinner from RM285/385; ❄☀) Situated 3km from park HQ, this 188-room behemoth feels worn and some of the hardwood rooms are musty.

This should soon change as the resort is supposed to be refurbished and 'reflagged' as the Mulu Marriott Resort & Spa. Tours booked here cost much more than those arranged online or at park HQ.

Benarat Inn   HOTEL **$$**
(☎in Miri 085-419-337; www.borneotropicaladventure.com; d/tr incl breakfast RM120/150) Run by Miri-based Borneo Tropical Adventure for its own tour groups, but open to the public if there's space. Has 18 simple, fan-equipped rooms with attached toilet, cold-water showers and electricity from 6pm to midnight. Reservations and payment must be made in advance, either through the Miri office or by email. Situated on a beautiful riverside site about 1.5km from park HQ, behind the Catholic church (the inn is not signposted from the main road but the church is). Transfer from the airport costs RM5 per person.

Mulu River Lodge   HOSTEL **$**
(Edward Nyipa Homestay; ☎012-852-7471; B&B RM35) Has 30 beds in a giant hall that's got spotless showers and toilets at one end. Electricity from 5pm to midnight. The only guest house outside the park with a proper septic system. Has a restaurant. Hot breakfast.

Gunung Mulu Homestay   GUESTHOUSE **$**
(☎012-875-3517; beds RM20, campsites per person RM5) Rooms are fanless but clean.

Mulu Homestay   GUEST HOUSE **$**
(☎for Anthony 017-895-9370; beds RM15, campsites per person RM5) Has 20 beds. Meals RM5 to RM8.

Melinau Canteen   GUEST HOUSE **$**
(MC; ☎for Diang 012-871-1372; beds RM20) Has two extremely basic rooms. This is the third guest house you come to if you follow the river bank from Mulu River Lodge – it's just past the oil drums.

✖ Eating

Only a handful of tiny shops – one in the Wild Mulu Café, another attached to the Stella Cafe and a third in the Penan village of Batu Bungan, out past the airport – sell a very limited selection of food items. Most food is flown in, which partly explains why prices are significantly higher than on the coast.

INSIDE THE NATIONAL PARK

Cooking is not allowed at any park accommodation except Camp 5.

Wild Mulu Café   ORANG ULU **$$**
(mains RM8-20; ☺7.30am-9.30pm, last orders 9pm) The Berawan women who work here

make excellent breakfasts (free if you're staying in the park, RM15 otherwise) and decent Western items, but the standouts are local dishes such as Mulu *laksa*. A beer or a glass of surprisingly good wine costs RM8. Staff are happy to prepare packed lunches.

OUTSIDE THE NATIONAL PARK
Some of the guest houses across the bridge from park HQ serve inexpensive curries, fried rice and noodle dishes.

Stella Cafe   RESTAURANT **$$**
(mains RM6-12; ⊙8am-3pm & 6-10.30pm, closed Sun) Situated just across the Bailey bridge from the Royal Mulu Resort (about 2.5km from park HQ), this popular riverside place serves some of the best-value food in the vicinity of the park. Offerings include fried noodles and chicken curry rice.

❶ Information
Gunung Mulu National Park is truly in the middle of nowhere. Consequently, there are no ATMs, no pharmacy and only a few poorly stocked shops.

For sums over RM100, the park accepts Visa and MasterCard (but not American Express). It may be possible to change money at the Royal Mulu Resort.

Internet computers are available at park HQ (RM10 per hour) and at the Royal Mulu Resort (RM35 per hour).

The **clinic** in Batu Bungan is staffed by a medic, not a doctor.

❶ Getting There & Away
Gunung Mulu National Park is accessible by air from Miri, Kuching and KK; by boat from Miri via Marudi; and by boat and on foot from Limbang (along the Headhunters' Trail). You can use the internet computers at the park office to book flights.

Air
MASwings (www.maswings.com.my) flies 68-seat ATR-72 turboprops from/to Miri. Departures from Miri are at 9.20am and 2.20pm and from Mulu at 10.25am and 3.20pm, with onward flights to KK and other destinations.

There's talk of adding an air link to Bario in the Kelabit Highlands, making it possible to do a Miri–Mulu–Bario–Miri loop.

Boat
It's possible (usually) to travel to Mulu from Miri by river, but it's a long, long trip and the journey actually costs more than flying.

First, take a taxi (RM35) – bus service doesn't start early enough to catch the first boat of the day – from Miri to the Kuala Baram Express

Wharf (at the Asean Bridge). From there, take the express boat to Marudi (RM20, first departure 7am or 8am), which takes about 2½ hours. If there are enough passengers, you'll be able to take an onward express boat to Long Terawan (RM20, departures around noon, three hours), but this service – which may end at Long Panai if the river is low – sometimes doesn't run for several days on end. In Long Terawan, you have to charter a long boat (RM330) for the final four-hour journey upriver to the park (RM330).

Car
Since a road to the park would bring in settlers and unwanted development, it's government policy never to build one.

The logging roads between Miri and Mulu are virtually impassable and, as one veteran put it, are 'bloody dangerous' because of dodgy bridges and careening logging trucks.

❶ Getting Around
Park HQ is about 1.5km from the airport and 3km from Royal Mulu Resort. An old rattletrap **van** (🚐for Diang 012-871-1372) usually meets incoming flights at the airport and takes passengers to park HQ and nearby guest houses (RM5 per person). Oversized tuk-tuks ferry guests between park HQ and the Royal Mulu Resort (RM6 per person).

It's possible to hire a longboat – most of the local boatmen are Penan from Batu Bungan – for excursions to destinations such as the Penan longhouse village of Long Iman (RM150 return), 40 minutes away by river.

Kelabit Highlands
🚐085
Nestled in Sarawak's northeastern corner, the upland rainforests of the Kelabit (keh-*lah*-bit) Highlands are sandwiched between Gunung Mulu National Park and the Indonesian state of East Kalimantan. The main activity here, other than enjoying the clean, cool air, is trekking from longhouse to longhouse on mountain trails. Unfortunately, logging roads – ostensibly for 'selective' logging – are encroaching and some of the Highlands' primary forests have already succumbed to the chainsaw.

The area is home to the Kelabits, who number only about 6500 worldwide, as well as the Penan, a semi-nomadic group whose members have fared much less well in modern Malaysia. For an excellent 'profile' of the Kelabits by Dr Poline Bala, a Bario-born anthropologist, see www.unimas.my/ebario/community.html.

Bario has produced some innovative leaders, including local councillor John Tarawe, CEO of the award-winning internet initiative eBario, who is much sought after around the world by groups (eg the UNDP) that are interested in 'community mobilisation' among indigenous groups. His efforts to plug the Highlands into the internet (even in remote villages he'd like the children to grow up 'IT savvy') and establish a community radio station have been so groundbreaking that NGOs on distant continents are copying the 'eBario model'. Bario and the Kelabits have some of Borneo's best websites, including www.ebario.org, www.bario.com and www.kelabit.net.

BARIO
POP 800

The 'capital' of the highlands, Bario consists of about a dozen 'villages' – each with its own church – spread over a beautiful valley, much of it given over to rice growing. Some of the appeal lies in the mountain climate (the valley is 1500m above sea level) and splendid isolation (the only access is by air and torturous 4WD track), but above all it's the unforced hospitality of the Kelabit people that will quickly win you over. An amazing number of travellers find themselves extending their stays in Bario by days, weeks or even years. Do yourself a favour and get stuck here for a while!

Before the Konfrontasi (see p283), Bario had only one small longhouse, but in 1963 residents of longhouses near the frontier fled raids by Indonesian troops and settled here for safety. The sleepy village also saw action during WWII, when Tom Harrisson parachuted in with a team of commandos.

Except for a few places powered by photovoltaic cells or small hydroelectric dam, Bario has electricity – provided by private generators – only in the evening. Bario has had cell-phone coverage only since 2009.

⊙ Sights & Activities

The forests around Bario are a great place to spot pitcher plants, butterflies and even hornbills – as well as tiger leeches. Most guest houses are happy to pack picnic lunches. The Bario area offers plenty of opportunities for jungle exploration even if you're not a hardcore trekker. Guides can arrange activities such as **fishing** and **bird-watching**.

Bario Asal Longhouse   LONGHOUSE

This friendly, 19-door longhouse, well worth a visit (you can also stay overnight), has the traditional Kelabit layout. On the *dapur* (enclosed front veranda) each family has a hearth, while on the other side of the family units is the *tawa'*, a wide back veranda – essentially an enclosed hall over 100m long – used for weddings, funerals and celebrations and decorated with historic family photos.

A few of the older residents still have earlobes that hang almost down to their shoulders, created by a lifetime of wearing heavy brass earrings. If you'd like a picture, it's good form to talk to them a bit (they may offer you something to drink) and only then to ask if they'd be willing to be photographed. Afterwards you might want to leave a small tip (RM5 or RM10).

Since 2009 24-hour electricity (night-time only during dry spells) has been provided by a micro-hydro project salvaged from a larger government-funded project that functioned for just 45 minutes after it was switched on in 1999.

Tom Harrisson Monument   MEMORIAL

This shiny stainless-steel monument, shaped like a *sapé* (a traditional stringed

---

THE PENAN

The Highlands are home not only to the Kelabits but also the Penan, a highland group that was nomadic – surviving exclusively on hunting and gathering – until quite recently and is often looked down upon (and discriminated against) by other Orang Ulu groups. Around Bario, if you see barefoot people wearing ragged clothes who look down when you approach, they are Penan. Kelabits have intermarried with Chinese, Westerners, Malays and other Orang Ulu groups for several generations but the first Kelabit-Penan marriage took place only recently.

The Sarawak government has often sold off traditional Penan lands to well-connected logging companies and then evicted the Penan with minimal or no compensation. The Swiss rainforest and human-rights advocate **Bruno Manser** (www.bmf.ch), who spent years living with the Penan and agitating to protect their rights, disappeared near Bario in May 2000. He is presumed dead and many people – in the Kelabit Highlands and abroad – suspect he was murdered.

With very few exceptions, the only way to explore the Kelabit Highlands is to hire a local guide. Fortunately, this could hardly be easier. Any of the guest houses in Bario can organise a wide variety of short walks and longer treks led by guides they know and rely on. If you link up with other travellers in Bario or Miri, the cost of a guide can be shared.

It's no problem to just turn up in Bario and make arrangements after you arrive, especially if you don't mind spending a day or two in Bario. If you're in a hurry, though, or your trip coincides with the prime tourism months of July and August, consider making arrangements with your guest house in advance by email or (preferably) phone.

The going rate for guides is RM80 per day (for either a Bario-based day trip or a longer trek), plus an additional RM20 per day if overnighting en route (except in Pa' Lungan) is involved. Some treks involve either river trips (highly recommended if the water is high enough) or travel by 4WD – naturally, these significantly increase the cost. Camping equipment (sleeping bag, mozzie net, bed roll) is not available in Bario but good guides should be able to supply it.

Guides recommend hiring a porter for treks that require lots of equipment (eg for camping), such as those to Gunung Murud and Batu Lawi. The standard fee is RM80 a day, plus a surcharge of RM2 for each kilo beyond 15kg.

If you are connecting the dots between rural longhouses, expect to pay RM40 per person (RM55 to RM70 in Pa' Lungan) for a night's sleep plus three meals (you can opt out of lunch and save RM10). Gifts are not obligatory but the people who live in remote longhouses are appreciative if, after you drink tea or coffee with them, you offer RM10 'to cover the costs' or 'to buy pens and paper for the children'.

If you're trekking in one direction only (eg Bario to Ba Kelalan), you will be asked to continue paying the guiding fee while your guide returns home through the jungle (in this scenario, it would take them two days to make the journey from Ba Kelalan back to Bario).

Detailed topographical maps of Sarawak exist but it's nearly impossible to get hold of them. The government's calculation seems to be that activists will find it harder to fight for native land rights if they lack proper maps.

instrument) and dedicated in March 2010, commemorates the March 1945 parachute drop into Bario by British and Australian commandos under the command of Major Tom Harrisson. Their goal – achieved with great success – was to enlist the help of locals to fight the Japanese, whose cruelty had made them hugely unpopular. For the life story of this colourful and controversial character, see *The Most Offending Soul Alive*, a biography by Judith M Heimann. Harrisson's widow still lives in Bario.

The monument is a short walk up the slope from the Bario Asal Longhouse, on the site of Tom's one-time garden (his house was about 100m from here, where the local cemetery now is).

Junglebluesdream Art Gallery ART GALLERY
(☏019-884 9892; junglebluesdream@gmail.com; ☉daylight hours) This gallery is where Kelabit artist Stephen Baya displays his renowned paintings, many of which have traditional Kelabit motifs. In 2011 his work will be featured at an exhibition in Cambridge, England, and in an illustrated children's book of Kelabit legends by Monica Janowski.

Prayer Mountain HALF-DAY TREK
From the Bario Asal Longhouse, it's a steep, slippery ascent (two hours) up to the summit of Prayer Mountain, which has a cross erected in 1973, lots of pitcher plants and amazing views of the Bario Valley and the hamlet of Arur Dalan, with its three defunct electric windmills. Two-thirds of the way up is what may be the world's least pretentious church.

Megalith Trails DAY TREKS
Hidden deep in the jungle around Bario are scores of mysterious megaliths and other 'cultural sites'. For more information, ask your guide for a copy of the booklet *Stone Culture of the Northern Highlands of Sarawak, Malaysia* (RM20).

Two day-trek routes, detailed below, are popular with visitors. At research time, trails for megalith treks lasting two, three and five days were being marked.

Pa' Umor Route From Bario head to **Pa' Umor** (1½ hours; longhouse accommodation

JUNGLE SURVIVAL SKILLS

Always wanted to learn how to survive in the rainforest? Bario-based **Highlands Jungle Academy** (☎019-891-2974; www.borneojungleadventures.com) offers three-/six-day introductory courses (from RM400/850 per person) as well as tailor-made itineraries. Longer sessions include overnights in the jungle.

available), passing a salt spring. From Pa' Umor, continue on (15 minutes) to Arur Bilit Farm, which is home to **Batu Navit**, an impressive stone carving featuring a human in the spread-eagled position among its designs; it was once used to tally each head that was taken. From the farm, use the log bridge to cross a small river (15 minutes) in order to reach **Batu Ipak**. According to local legend, this stone formation was created when an angry hunter named Upai Semering pulled out his machete and took a wrathful swing at the rock, cutting it in two. This route should take four or five hours – maybe a tad longer if your guide is a good storyteller.

Pa' Lungan Route The other option is to head from Bario towards **Pa' Lungan** (3½ or four hours) along a wide, muddy forest trail used by water buffalos to pull sleighs carrying goods and, on occasion, medical evacuees. About halfway you can stop at **Batu Arit**, a large stone featuring bird carvings and humanoid figures with heart-shaped faces. From Pa' Lungan it's a two-minute walk to **Batu Ritung**, a 2m stone table (probably a burial site), although no one is quite sure as the site was created outside of living memory. Also near Pa' Lungan (15 minutes away) is **Perupun**, a huge pile of stones. This type of rock pile was assembled to bury the valuables of the dead who had no descendants to receive their belongings.

If you've got a bit more time, you could consider basing yourself in Pa' Lungan, believed by many to produce the very best Bario rice, for a day or two to do jungle trekking. Longhouse **home stays** (per person incl board RM55 to RM70), including **Batu Ritung Lodge** (☎019-805-2119; baturitunglodge@yahoo.com), serve Kelabit-style dishes such as *pa'u* (fern) and *puluh* (bamboo shoots).

A scenic **boat ride** (up to 4 people RM250) can be arranged to take you from a spot an hour's hike from Pa' Lungan back to Pa' Umur.

🛏 Sleeping

Bario's various component villages have quite a few cosy guest houses where you can meet English-speaking locals and dine on delicious Kelabit cuisine (most places offer a per-person rate for bed plus board). Some of the most relaxing establishments are a bit out of town (up to 5km). Air-con is not necessary up in Bario but hot water – alas, rarely an option – is a nice treat. Very few places offer en-suite bathrooms. If you're on a very tight budget, enquire about renting a bed without board.

No need to book ahead – available rooms outstrip the space available on flights and guest-house owners meet incoming flights at the airport. Check out www.ebario.com (click 'Rooms') for a longer list of home stays and online booking. At press time three guest houses had experimental wi-fi. The places below are listed alphabetically.

Bario Airport Homestay   GUEST HOUSE $
(☎019-846-8482; barioairporthomestay@gmail.com; beds RM20, per person incl board RM70) Five rooms right across the road from the airport terminal. Run by Joanna, the airport's operations manager.

Bario Asal Lembaa   HOME STAY $
(☎014-590-7500; jenetteulun@yahoo.com; beds R20, per person incl board RM60) Four rooms in a bungalow right next to the Bario Asal Longhouse.

Bario Asal Longhouse   HOME STAY $
(☑for Peter 014-893-1139; paranmatu@yahoo.com; beds RM20, per person incl 3 meals RM86) A friendly spot with pictures of longhouse residents (past and present) on the walls and Bario's only 24-hour electricity.

De Plateau Lodge   GUEST HOUSE $
(☎019-855-9458; deplateau@gmail.com; beds RM20, incl full board RM70; ☜) Situated about 2km east of the centre (bear left at the fork), this two-storey wooden chalet has seven rooms (including one triple) and a homey living room. It is owned by Douglas, a friendly former guide who's a big fan of Liverpool FC. The 'plateau' in the name refers to the Highlands, the 'dee' (that's how it's pronounced) honours Douglas' family, most of whose members have names begin with the letter D.

Gem's Lodge   GUEST HOUSE $
(☎013-828-0507; gems_lodge@yahoo.com; dm RM25, per person incl 3 meals RM60) Situated 5km southeast of town (bear right at the fork) near the longhouse village of Pa' Umor. Managed by Jaman, one of Bario's nicest and

most experienced guides, this place is tranquillity incarnate, with five pleasant rooms, a two-room chalet (per person RM80), a cosy common area and solar power. Guests can swim in the river. Transport to/from the airport by 4WD costs RM25 per person.

Junglebluesdream GUEST HOUSE $
(☎019-884-9892; junglebluesdream@gmail.com; per person incl board RM70; 🛜) Owned by local artist (and one-time guide) Stephen Baya and his friendly Danish wife Tine, this lodge-gallery has four mural-decorated rooms, good-quality beds and quilts and fantastic Kelabit food. Bathrooms are in stalls on the ground floor. Guests can consult hand-drawn maps of the town and trekking routes.

Nancy & Harriss GUEST HOUSE $
(Hill View Lodge; ☎019-858-5850, 013-850-5850; nancyharriss@yahoo.com; per person incl board RM60) Seven guest rooms in a big house with a veranda, run by a former guide. Situated 250m south of the main road; the turn-off is just east of Kaludai. Prices include airport transfer.

Ngimat Ayu's Homestay GUEST HOUSE $
(☎013-840-6187; engimat_scott@yahoo.com; per person incl board RM70) This brown, two-storey place has 10 rooms and a chill-out veranda with rice-field views. Situated on a slope 200m east of the yellow public library.

Raja View Inn GUEST HOUSE
(☎Seluma 019-594-0039, Stuart 014-877-7322; rajaviewbario@gmail.com; per person incl board RM85) A very welcoming five-room place opened in 2010 and run by Bario's first Kelabit-Penan couple. The food is Penan-Kelabit fusion.

Tarawe's Lodge GUEST HOUSE $
(☎019-438-1777; jtarawe@bario.net; per person RM20; 🛜) Bario's oldest guest house, renovated in 2009, now has seven basic rooms (on the 2nd floor) with one to three single beds, wi-fi and 24-hour solar power. A 10-person chalet with bathroom and hot water is RM240 a night. Guests can cook their own meals. If you're willing to stick around for at least a month, John may be willing to provide food and lodging in exchange for help cleaning and running the place.

✗ Eating

Most guest houses offer full board – usually it's delicious Kelabit cuisine – but Bario also has several modest eateries. The yellow-painted commercial centre is home to three basic cafes.

BARIO SALT 217

If you're interested in the Kelabit's culinary traditions, you might want to walk out to Bario's **main tudtu** (literally 'salty sweet'; natural salt lick), on the way to Pa' Umor, where mineral-rich saline water is put in giant vats over a roaring fire until all that's left is high-iodine salt that goes perfectly with local specialities such as deer and wild boar. This traditional production technique is beginning to die out, but in Bario you can still purchase salt made the old way – look for something that resembles a 20cm-long green Tootsie roll wrapped in a leaf.

🍷 Drinking

Finding a bar or a beer in Bario can be hard. This is a very Evangelical town – you're as likely to hear Christian country as the sound of the *sapé* – so most establishments do not serve alcohol, and even those that do often keep it hidden. But what was it that Matthew once said? 'Ask, and it shall be given you; seek, and ye shall find.'

Y2K BAR
(⊙6am-midnight) Just up the road from the yellow commercial centre. Sells beer (RM4 to RM6) and has a pool table. Has karaoke in the evening.

Keludai BAR
(mains RM4; ⊙7am-midnight) Has a pool table.

Don't go through the swinging doors of the Bario Saloon, in the yellow commercial centre, looking for a stiff drink – it's a unisex beauty salon!

🛍 Shopping

Sinah Rang HANDICRAFTS
Sells lovely Kelabit beadwork, all locally made, from her living room in Bario Asal Longhouse. This is a good place to pick up a *kabo'* (RM80), a beadwork pendant shaped like a little beer barrel that's worn around the neck by Kelabit men.

Penan Handicrafts Shop HANDICRAFTS
(☎019-594-0039; jseluma@yahoo.com.my; ⊙7.30am-4.30pm Mon-Sat) Seluma (of Raja View Inn) sells Penan baskets, hats, blowpipes and other items from her shop in the yellow commercial centre, next to Bario General Trading.

RICE & PINEAPPLES

Bario is famous throughout Malaysia for two things: Bario rice, whose grains are smaller and more aromatic than lowland varieties; and sweeter-than-sweet pineapples that are free of the pucker-inducing acidity of their coastal cousins. Outside of the Kelabit Highlands, 1kg of Bario rice costs a whopping RM22 and Bario pineapples are usually unavailable at any price (except, perhaps, at Miri's two Kelabit restaurants).

Y2K GENERAL STORE

(☉6am-midnight) An old-fashioned, Old West–style general store that sells everything from SIM cards to something called Zam-Zam Hair Oil.

 Information

There are no banks, ATMs or credit-card facilities anywhere in the Kelabit Highlands so bring plenty of small-denomination banknotes for accommodation, food and guides, plus some extra in case you get stranded. There's no pharmacy, either, so bring any medications you might need. Commerce is limited to a few basic shops, some of them in the bright yellow commercial centre in the hamlet of Padang Pasir.

The best Malaysian cell-phone company to have up here is Celcom. The airport has wi-fi, as do three guest houses (more should be linked up by the time you read this).

eBario Telecentre (☎010-598-4170, 013-809-9583; www.ebario.com; per hr RM10; ☉10am-4pm Mon-Fri, to 2pm Sat) Solar-powered internet access.

Medical clinic (Airport Rd intersection) An ecologically sustainable clinic, powered by solar energy, should be open by the time you read this.

 Getting There & Around

Air

Bario is linked with Miri twice a day by **MASwings** (www.maswings.com.my) Twin Otters. Weather not infrequently causes delays and cancellations.

Twin Otters have strict weight limits so a heavy cargo load means that seats sometimes have to fly empty. Passengers are weighed when they check in and checked baggage is limited to 10kg. Enforcement is particularly strict on the way up because planes have to carry enough fuel to get back to Miri, and more cargo is flown into Bario than out. Consider leaving some of your belongings at your Miri guest house.

When you land in Bario, the first thing you should do is register for your flight out (RM10) at the counter – your name will be inscribed in a crumpled old ledger. A schematic map of the Bario area is posted on a nearby wall.

The airport is about a 30-minute walk south of the shophouses but you're bound to be offered a lift on arrival – as you'll notice, the people of Bario treat the air link to Miri almost like their own private airline and absolutely love dropping by the wi-fi-equipped airport terminal to meet flights.

There is talk of adding an air link to Gunung Mulu National Park, making possible a Miri–Gunung Mulu–Bario–Miri loop.

Bicycle

Junglebluesdream rents out mountain bikes for RM35 a day.

Car

Since 2009, it has been possible to travel overland to/from Miri along rough logging roads. The trip, possible only by 4WD, takes 12 to 14 hours, depending on road conditions. Expect to pay about RM150 per person (RM200 coming up from Miri).

In Bario, 4WD vehicles can be hired for RM250 or RM300 a day including a driver and petrol; guest houses can make arrangements.

Ba Kelalan

Known for its organic vegetables, apples and annual apple festival, the Lun Bawang town of Ba Kelalan is a popular destination for treks from Bario.

Guesthouse options include the nice **Ba Kelalan Apple Lodge Homestay** (per person RM65), run by **Borneo Jungle Safari** (☎013-286-5656, in Miri 085-422-595; www.borneojunglesafari.com); the Ba Kelalan Inn, which serves beer; and the **Green Valley Guesthouse** (per bed RM20).

 Getting There & Away

The only way to get here from Bario is on foot. A rough 125km logging road links Ba Kelalan with Lawas.

It's possible to get to from Ba Kelalan to Long Bawan in Kalimantan by motorbike.

MASwings (www.maswings.com.my) flies Twin Otters from Ba Kelalan to Lawas or Miri four times a week. Occasionally there are flights to Bario.

Trekking in the Kelabit Highlands

The temperate highlands around the Indonesian border offer some of the best jungle trekking in Borneo, taking in farming villages, rugged peaks and supremely remote Kenyah, Penan and Kelabit settlements. Most trails traverse a variety of primary and secondary forest, as well as – sadly – an increasing number of deforested areas. Treks from Bario range from easy overnight excursions to nearby longhouses to one-week slogs over the border into the wilds of Kalimantan.

While the Highlands are certainly cooler than Borneo's coastal regions, it's still hard work trekking up here (don't forget the altitude) and you should be in pretty good shape to consider a multi-day trek. Bring extra cell-phone and camera batteries as charging may not be possible. For details on what to bring, see the boxed text, p30.

The routes we list are intended just as a starting point. With so many trails in the area, there is ample scope for custom routes and creative route planning. The region's forest cover and even topography are constantly in flux due to marauding loggers so flexibility is the order of the day. Be prepared to encounter leeches – the trails are literally crawling with them.

If you're interested in the Highlands' military history, ask a guide to take you to the old British bunkers and trenches near **Pa' Main** (four hours' walk from Bario). There are plans to open up three long-distance **Commando Trails** that trace important WWII events.

Handicrafts, such as beadwork and woven rattan baskets, are available for purchase at many longhouses.

BARIO TO BA KELALAN

The three-day trek from Bario to Ba Kelalan covers a variety of mostly gentle terrain – some of it inside Kalimantan – and gives a good overview of the Kelabit Highlands. An alternative route, which takes five to seven days, goes deeper into Kalimantan, passing by Lembudud.

To avoid doubling back, you can trek from Bario to Ba Kelalan and then fly down to Miri or Lawas. If you do this, you'll have to pay the guide for the two days it will take to walk back to Bario.

BATU LAWI

If you were sitting on the left side of the plane from Miri to Bario, you probably caught a glimpse of the two massive limestone spires known as Batu Lawi, the taller of which soars to 2040m. During WWII, the peaks were used as a landmark for parachute drops.

While an ascent of the higher of the two rock formations, known as the 'male peak', is only for expert technical rock climbers, ascending the lower 'female peak' – described by one veteran trekker as 'awe-inspiring' – is possible for fit trekkers without special skills. It's a tough, five-day return trip from Bario. Be prepared to spend the second day passing through areas that have recently been devastated by logging.

GUNUNG MURUD

Sarawak's highest mountain (2423m), part of 598-sq-km **Pulong Tau National Park** (www.itto-pulongtau.com), is just begging to be climbed, but very few visitors make the effort to put the trip together. This adventure is only for the fittest of the fit.

The mountain is linked by trails with both Ba Kelalan and Bario. From Bario, the more common starting point, a typical return trip takes six days. You can also do a loop from Bario via Gunung Murud to Ba Kelalan (five days) but as you approach Ba Kelalan you'll have to walk along a depressing logging road through land recently devastated by loggers.

Opening up more options is the fact that a rough logging road links the base of Gunung Murud with the lowland town of Lawas (five to eight hours by 4WD).

Limbang Division

Shaped like a crab claw, the Limbang Division slices Brunei in two and separates the diminutive sultanate from Sabah. The area, snatched from the sultan of Brunei by Charles Brooke in 1890, is still claimed by Brunei.

For information on Brunei visas, see p314.

LIMBANG

A prosperous and bustling river port, Limbang is the main town in the Limbang Division. Tourism is underdeveloped in these parts but you may find yourself passing through en route between Brunei and Sabah, or after coming off the Headhunters' Trail from Gunung Mulu National Park. Bruneians flock here to find shopping bargains, including cheap beer (RM2.50 per can) smuggled in from duty-free Pulau Labuan. As one local put it with just a hint of exaggeration, 'Los Angeles has Tijuana, BSB has Limbang'.

Limbang sits along the east (right) bank of Sungai Limbang. It's 15km upriver from Brunei Bay so there aren't any beaches.

◉ Sights & Activities

The four city blocks south of the 12-storey Purnama Hotel, inland from Jln Wong Tsap En (formerly Main Bazaar), constitute Limbang's old town.

Limbang Regional Museum   MUSEUM
(www.museum.sarawak.gov.my; Jln Kubu; ⊙9am-4.30pm, closed Mon) Upstairs in one of Charles Brooke's forts, built in 1897 and rebuilt (after a fire) in 1991. The collection is well presented and features exhibits on the Limbang Division's archaeology, culture and crafts (eg musical instruments, fish traps, vests made of tree bark). From the Purnama Hotel, follow the riverbank upstream (south) for 1km (ie about 500m beyond the Limbang Raid Memorial).

Limbang Raid Memorial   MEMORIAL
(Jln Wong Tsap En) Commemorates four members of the Sarawak Constabulary and five members of the 42 Commando Royal Marines killed before and during the famous Limbang Raid of 12 December 1962, whose 50th anniversary will be marked in 2012. A trailer for a documentary about the raid, *Return to Limbang*, can be found on YouTube. On the riverfront 400m south of the Purnama Hotel, across the street from the police station.

Weekly Tamu   MARKET
(Jln Talap; ⊙Fri) Bisayah villagers, many of whom speak the Brunei Malay dialect, come in from all around the district to attend, as do Bruneians. From the Purnama Hotel, go one long block inland and then two blocks south.

Public Library   LIBRARY
(4th fl, Limbang Plaza; ⊙9am-5pm) Has an excellent collection of books on Sarawak and Brunei – a great place to do research before an upcountry trek, especially on a rainy day. In the shopping mall next to the Purnama Hotel.

Malay Kampung   VILLAGE
Directly across the river; little ferries connect it with the city centre.

ⓒ Tours

The following run wetlands canoe trips to see proboscis monkeys. They can also take you to the salty **Maritam Mud Spring** (aka 'the Volcano'), 34km towards BSB, and to the crash site of a **B-34 Liberator** shot down by the Japanese in 1944.

Chua Eng Hin   SIGHTSEEING, CANOEING
(☑019-814-5355; chualbg@streamyx.com) A well-known local personality with a passion for Limbang District's largely unknown charms.

Borneo Touch Ecotour   CANOEING, TREKKING
(☑085-212-849, 019-814-5355; www.walk2mulu.com; 1st fl, 2061 Rickett Commercial) Runs excursions around the Limbang District and well-regarded treks *up* the Headhunters' Trail to Gunung Mulu National Park (RM900 per person for four days).

⊨ Sleeping

Being a port town, most of Limbang's cheaper places are a little sleazy.

Continental Hotel   HOTEL **$**
(☑085-215-600; cnr Jln Wong Tsap En & Jln Wayang; d old/new RM45/68; ✳) A very central hostelry with 29 clean and comfy rooms, some with river views; seven were nicely remodelled in 2010. Situated four short blocks south of the Purnama Hotel.

Purnama Hotel   HOTEL **$**
(☑085-216-700; www.purnamalimbang.com; Jln Buangsiol; s/d from RM92/102; ✳⊛) Occupying Limbang's tallest building (12 storeys), this uninspiring hotel – ornamented with multicoloured balconies – has 218 spacious but aesthetically challenged rooms that come with small bathrooms and big views.

✕ Eating

Thien Hsing   VEGETARIAN **$**
(☑013-849-9111; mains RM2.50-4; ⊙6am-2pm; ☑) Serves delicious vegan Chinese dishes. On an alley 3½ short blocks south of

---

CROSSING INTO INDONESIA

Thanks to long-standing cultural and personal ties across the Sarawak–Kalimantan frontier, drawn in colonial times by the British and the Dutch, a local trans-border initiative has made it possible for both Highland residents and tourists to cross from Ba Kelalan into Kalimantan to visit nearby settlements such as Long Bawan, Lembudud and Long Layu. All you need is a *pas lintas batas* (transboundary pass), issued locally according to an agreement signed between the Malaysian and Indonesian foreign ministries. Passports are not stamped and you must return to Sarawak within 14 days. To make arrangements, contact John Tarawe in Bario.

Malaysian ringgits are very popular in this remote part of Kalimantan but US dollars are not.

For tips, recommendations and reviews, head to shop.lonelyplanet.com to purchase downloadable PDFs of the Indonesia chapter from Lonely Planet's *Southeast Asia on a Shoestring* guide or the Malaysia chapter from Lonely Planet's *Southeast Asia on a Shoestring* guide.

the Purnama Hotel and one short block inland from Jln Wong Tsap En.

Tamu Limbang HAWKER CENTRE $
(Jln Wong Tsap En; mains RM3.50-5; ☺6.30am-5.30pm) Limbang's main market has an upstairs hawker centre. Diagonally opposite the Purnama Hotel.

Night Markets FOOD STALLS $
After Tamu Limbang closes, food-stall action shifts to the Malay night market, on the riverfront 300m northwest of the Purnama Hotel (near the Lawas ferry dock); and to the Chinese night market, a block northeast of the Purnama Hotel.

ⓘ Information

Golden Cyber World (Jln Pandaruan; per hr RM2.50; ☺9am-11pm) Has eight internet computers. One long block east of the Purnama Hotel.

Maybank ATM (ground fl, Limbang Plaza Shopping Mall) One of several international ATMs in town. Next to the Purnama Hotel.

Public Library (4th fl, Limbang Plaza Shopping Mall; ☺9am-4.20pm) Free internet for up to an hour. Downstairs, Limbang Plaza also has a number of internet shops. Situated next to the Purnama Hotel.

ⓘ Getting There & Around

Air

MASwings (www.maswings.com.my) links Limbang's airport, 7km south of the centre, with Miri. A taxi costs RM20.

Boat

The fastest way to get to BSB is to take a 12-seat **speedboat** (Lumba Lumba; ☑in Limbang 012-852-2050, in Brunei +673-861-6192, +673-891-9192) from Limbang's immigration hall (just south of the Purnama Hotel) to downtown BSB (at research time, ferries docked next to the Yayasan Complex) – from Limbang MR20, from BSB B$10, from Limbang 11.30am, from BSB 8am, 30 minutes. Only sails when there are customers (there usually are on Friday); call to check schedules and let them know you're coming. You can charter the whole boat for RM200 one way.

Ferries to Pulau Labuan (RM30, two hours, 8am) are run by two companies on alternate days,

Lim Pertama (☑019-805-1260, 019-823-8337) and **Royal Limbang** (☑013-882-3736). Boats depart from Limbang's immigration hall daily.

For details on the ferry to Lawas, which docks 300m northwest of the Purnama Hotel, see p222.

Bicycle

Borneo Touch Ecotour (see Tours, p220) rents out mountain bikes.

Bus

Bus tickets are sold at various shops along north–south Jln Pandaruan, a long block inland (east) from the Purnama Hotel.

Jesselton Express (☑in Limbang 085-212-990, 016-855-0222, in Brunei +673-718-3838, 717-7755, 719-3835, in KK 016-836-0009) has a bus to BSB at 2pm or 3pm and to Bangar, Lawas (RM30), various towns in Sabah and KK (RM50) at 9.30am. Tickets are sold at **Wan Wan Cafe & Restaurant** (Jln Pandaruan).

Several companies have service *through* Brunei but without stops there (ie you'll be in Brunei but won't be able to get off the bus, at least not officially). From Brunei's Kuala Lurah border crossing, local buses 42, 44 and 48 go to BSB's bus station (B$1).

Biaramas (☑012-828-2042) Has a bus to Brunei's Kuala Lurah border crossing (RM10) and Miri (RM45, four to five hours) at 9am; in the other direction, the bus leaves Miri at 2pm. Tickets are sold in the **Cayaha Delima Cafe** (Jln Pandaruan).

Bintang Jaya (☑085-438-301, 085-432-178) Sends a bus to Brunei's Kuala Lurah border crossing and Miri (RM45) daily at 8am. Also serves Sabah and KK.

Borneo Express (☑in Limbang 085-211-384, in KK 012-830-7722, in Miri 012-823-7722) Has a bus to Brunei's Kuala Lurah border crossing (RM15) and Miri (RM45, four or five hours) at 2pm, and a bus to KK (RM50) at 1.30pm. Tickets are sold at **Hock Chuong Hin Cafe** (Jln Pandaruan).

Taxi & Minibus

Taxis and yellow-roofed minibuses hang out at the **stesyen teksi** (☑085-213-781; Jln Wong Tsap En; ☺5am-9pm), on the waterfront a block south of the Purnama Hotel.

Local taxis and minibuses won't usually agree to take you to destinations *inside* Brunei (ie BSB or Bangar) but they are happy to ferry you to one of Brunei's borders.

SARAWAK LIMBANG DIVISION

WANT MORE?

For in-depth information, reviews and recommendations at your fingertips, head to the Apple App Store to purchase Lonely Planet's *Malaysia* iPhone app.

Alternatively, head to Lonely Planet (www.lonelyplanet.com/malaysia, or www.lonely planet.com/asia) for planning advice, author recommendations, traveller reviews and insider tips.

If you're heading towards BSB, one-way travel to the Kuala Lurah crossing costs RM40 to RM60 (more from 6pm to 9pm); local buses can take you from there to BSB. If you're coming from BSB, taxis wait on the Malaysian side of the Kuala Lurah crossing.

If you're going east towards Brunei's Temburong District and Lawas, the fare to the Bangar crossing is RM20 to RM25 (more from 6pm to 9pm). Taxis for onward transport do not wait on either side of the border so if you're heading to Limbang, phone Limbang's *stesyen teksi*; and if you're heading towards the Temburong District, ask around on the Bruneian side of the frontier for someone who can summon a vehicle from Bangar.

LAWAS

w is a transit point in the slice of Sarawak sandwiched between Brunei's Temburong District and Sabah. A rough logging road heads from here up to Gunung Murud (five hours by 4WD) and Ba Kelalan.

🛏 Sleeping

Borneo Hotel   HOTEL **$$**
(☏085-285-700; 1st fl, Lot 437, Jln Masjid Baru; s/d RM58/77; 🕸🛜) The best accommodation in town, hands down. Opened in 2009, this spiffy place has 23 comfortable rooms with gloriously spacious bathrooms. From the bus station, cross Jln Punang and go half a block west, into the commercial zone.

Merarap Hotspring Lodge   LODGE **$$**
(☏019-819-5200; http://meraraphotspring.com; tr/q incl breakfast RM250-280) Rustic, family-owned accommodation next to a 45°C natural hot spring. Way off in the boonies, 65km towards Ba Kelalan along a 4WD-only logging road.

ℹ Information

Star Net (1st fl, Lot 117, Jln Datuk Taie; per hr RM2; ⊗8am-11pm) Internet access in an orange and pink corner building across the square from KFC and the Million Hotel.

ℹ Getting There & Around

Air

MASwings (www.maswings.com.my) flies Twin Otters from Lawas' airport, 2km by road from the centre, to Miri and Ba Kelalan. Taxis are in short supply so when you land, get out of the terminal quickly and be prepared to share (RM5 per person).

Boat

The ferry wharf and its immigration office are 500m northeast of the bus station.

The fastest way to get to BSB (to the Serasa Ferry Terminal in Muara) is to take the daily **express boat** (☏013-572-1413, in Brunei 875-7813): from Lawas RM25, BSB B$22, one hour.

The road to Limbang, via Brunei's Temburong District, will get appreciably faster when the bridge over Sungai Terusan is finished. In the meantime, you can still get to Limbang by **ferry** (☏019-874-8234) – RM30, 2½ hours, 9am – provided there are enough passengers.

You can also take a **ferry** (☏019-814-6868, at Bee Hiong Restaurant 085-285-137) to Pulau Labuan (RM30, 2½ hours, from Lawas 7.30am, from Labuan 12.30pm) daily except Tuesday and Thursday, if there are enough passengers.

Bus

Jesselton Express (☏in Lawas 016-832-6722, in Brunei +673-718-3838, in KK 016-836-0009) has a 12.30pm bus to Bangar (RM20, one hour), Limbang (RM30, two hours) and BSB (RM50, four hours). Its daily bus to Sabah, including KK (RM20, four hours), also leaves at about 12.30pm.

Bintang Jaya (☏085-283-178) has a bus to Sabah and KK (RM20) at 2.45pm on Monday, Wednesday and Friday, and to Limbang (RM30, two hours) and Miri (RM75) at 11.30am on Tuesday, Thursday and Saturday. Several other companies also go to Miri (without stops in Brunei) and KK.

Taxi

Taxis can be found across the street from the market, Pasar Besar Lawas, and behind the Ocean (Seven Seas) supermarket. Destinations served by taxi include Labu (on the Brunei border; RM60), Bangar (in Brunei's Temburong District; RM100) and Limbang (1¼ hours).

Brunei Darussalam

POP: 395,000 / AREA: 5765 SQ KM

Best Places to Eat

» Aminah Arif (p230)

» Tamu Kianggeh (p231)

» Taman Selera (p231)

Best Places to Stay

» Ulu-Ulu Resort (p239)

» Empire Hotel & Country Club (p229)

» Pusat Belia (p230)

Why Go?

The tiny sultanate of Brunei, the last remnant of a naval empire that once ruled all of Borneo and much of the Philippines, is known for its unimaginable riches – it has some of the largest oilfields in Southeast Asia – but should be no less famous for having had the foresight and wisdom to preserve its rainforests. Today the country is blessed with some of the most pristine jungle habitats in all of Borneo – you can get a sense of their verdant vastness at Ulu Temburong National Park. If you take the time to slow down and talk with the locals, in the capital Bandar Seri Begawan (BSB) and outlying towns and longhouses, you may find that there's more than first meets the eye in this quiet, verdant *darussalam* (Arabic for 'abode of peace').

When to Go

BSB gets more rain than Kota Kinabalu but less than Kuching. Totals vary greatly from year to year so even the rainiest months (October to December) are sometimes quite dry, and the driest months (February and March) can turn out as rainy as the wettest.

National Day (23 February) is celebrated with many official ceremonies. The sultan's birthday (15 July) is marked with festivities around the country. During Hari Raya Aidil Fitri (August in 2011 and 2012), the sultan's palace is open to the public for three days.

BANDAR SERI BEGAWAN

POP 100,000

If you're expecting some kind of lavish mini-Dubai, think again – Brunei may be a super-rich oil state, but BSB (as the capital is known) has little nouveau-riche ostentation. In fact, it's remarkably quiet and relaxed, with picturesque water villages, two opulent mosques (two-thirds of Bruneians are Muslims), some great food stalls (if you know where to find them) and a vibe as polite and unassuming as its people. Despite the almost total lack of nightlife, there's something quite alluring about BSB, whose mellow pace can definitely grow on you.

BSB's city centre is on the north bank of Sungai Brunei at a spot – 12km upriver from Brunei Bay – that's easy to defend against seaborne attack and sheltered from both storms and tsunamis. During the Japanese occupation, the city centre – known until 1970 as Brunei Town – was severely damaged by Allied bombing.

◉ Sights & Activities

All of central BSB is within easy walking or sailing distance of the Yayasan Complex, but unless you don't mind walking for hours in the tropical sun, you'll have to make do with buses and taxis to get to sights east, north and west of downtown.

CENTRAL BSB

Kampung Ayer   WATER VILLAGES

Home to an estimated 20,000 people, Kampung Ayer consists of 28 contiguous stilt villages – named after the crafts and occupations traditionally practiced there – built along both (but especially the southern) banks of Sungai Brunei. A century ago, fully half of Brunei's population lived here, and even today many Bruneians – despite government inducements – still prefer the lifestyle of the water village to residency on dry land. When the Venetian scholar Antonio Pigafetta, who accompanied Ferdinand Magellan on his last voyage, visited Kampung Ayer in 1521, he dubbed it the 'Venice of the East' and the moniker has stuck (there's really no resemblance, though – other than the turbid water part).

Founded at least a thousand years ago, Kampung Ayer is considered the largest stilt settlement in the world and has its own schools, mosques, police stations and fire brigade. The houses, painted sun-bleached shades of green, blue, pink and yellow, have not been cutesified for tourists, so while it's far from squalid, be prepared for the trash that, at low tide, carpets the intertidal mud under the banister-less boardwalks, some with missing planks.

A good place to start a visit – and get acquainted with Brunei's pre-oil culture – is the new **Kampung Ayer Cultural & Tourism Gallery** (◉9am-5pm Sat-Thu, 9-11.30am & 2.30-5pm Fri), directly across the river from Sungai Kiangggeh (the stream at the eastern edge of the city centre). Opened in 2009, this spiffy new riverfront complex focuses on the history, lifestyle and crafts of the Kampung Ayer people and usually has a live handicrafts demonstration. Like many of the sultanate's public institutions, this one is overstaffed, leading to lots of people who spend much of their time just standing around. A square, glass-enclosed **viewing tower** offers panoramic views of the bustling scene below.

Some of Kampung Ayer's most interesting villages are along the walkways – said to measure 29km in total – that lead west from the museum.

Getting across the river from the city centre (ie the area next to and east of the Yayasan Complex) or the Venetian-style eastern bank of Sungai Kiangggeh is a breeze. Just stand somewhere a water taxi – BSB's souped-up version of the gondola – can dock and flag an empty one down.

To visit to the villages on the river's **north bank** (the same side as the city centre), follow the plankwalks that head southwest from Omar Ali Saifuddien Mosque, or those leading west (parallel to the river) from the Yayasan Complex, itself built on the site of a one-time water village.

Water-Taxi Cruise   BOAT RIDE

The best way to see BSB's water villages and the sultan's fabled palace, Istana Nurul Iman, is from a water taxi, which can be chartered along the waterfront for about B$30 (a bit of negotiating on the price and time frame is a must). Finding a boat won't be a problem, as the boatmen will have spotted you before you spot them.

After you admire the palace's backyard, your boatman can take you further upriver to **Pulau Ranggu**, an island that's home to a large colony of proboscis monkeys. The best time to head out is late afternoon, as the monkeys are easiest to spot around sunset.

Omar Ali Saifuddien Mosque   MOSQUE

(Jln Stoney; ◉interior 8.30am-noon, 1.30-3pm & 4.30-5.30pm Sat-Wed, 4.30-5pm Fri, closed Thu,

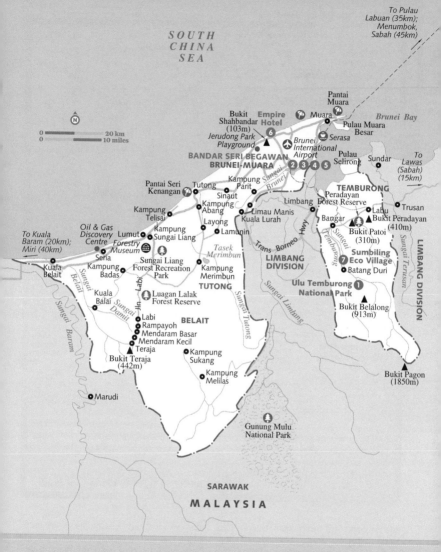

Brunei Darussalam Highlights

1 Climbing high into the rainforest canopy and swimming in a cool jungle river at **Ulu Temburong National Park** (p238)

2 Tearing along mangrove-lined waterways on a **speedboat** from BSB to Bangar (p237)

3 Taking a water taxi to the water village of **Kampung Ayer** (p224) and then a boardwalk stroll

4 Walking along BSB's newly refurbished **waterfront promenade** (p229)

5 Visiting BSB's opulent **mosques** (p224)

6 Marvelling at the over-the-top luxury of the **Empire Hotel & Country Club** (p229), a sparkling monument to world-class profligacy

7 Relaxing amid rural greenery at **Sumbiling Eco Village** (p238) in Temburong District

Bandar Seri Begawan

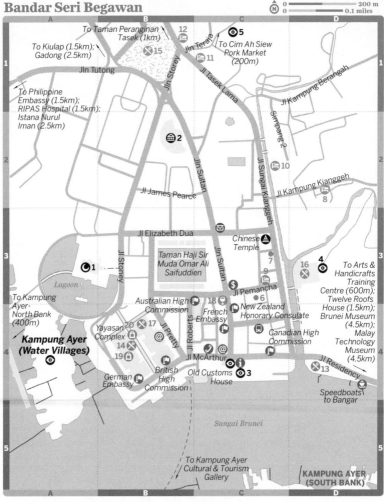

exterior compound 8am-8.30pm except prayer times) Built from 1954 to 1958, Masjid Omar Ali Saifuddien – named after the 28th sultan of Brunei (the late father of the current sultan) – is surrounded by an artificial lagoon that serves as a reflecting pool. The 44m minaret makes it the tallest building in central BSB, and woe betide anyone who tries to outdo it – apparently the nearby Islamic Bank of Brunei building originally exceeded this height and so had its top storey removed by order of the sultan.

Inside, the floor and walls are made from the finest Italian marble, the stained-glass windows and chandeliers were crafted in England, and the luxurious carpets were flown in from Saudi Arabia and Belgium. Jigsaw enthusiasts can admire the 3.5-million-piece Venetian mosaic inside the main dome.

The ceremonial stone boat sitting in the lagoon is a replica of a 16th-century *mahligai* (royal barge).

As you'll notice, the muezzin gently caresses the words as he issues the call to prayer. The more quietly he pronounces them, the more force they seem to carry.

Bandar Seri Begawan

FREE **Royal Regalia Museum** MUSEUM
(Jln Sultan; ◎9am-5pm Sun-Thu, 9-11.30am & 2.30-5pm Fri, 9.45am-5pm Sat, last entry 4.30pm) A celebration of the sultan and all the trappings of Bruneian royalty. The ground floor is dominated by a recreation of the sultan's coronation day parade, while other sections feature medals bestowed upon the sultan and a selection of gifts he has received.

When you are called upon to present a gift to the sultan of Brunei, you must inevitably confront the question: what do you give a man who has everything? Here you'll see how various heads of state and royalty have solved this conundrum (hint: you'll never go wrong with priceless gold and jewels). We particularly like the mother of all beer mugs, given by Queen Elizabeth.

Before entering, visitors must check cameras, mobile phones and bags and remove their shoes.

EAST OF CENTRAL BSB

Brunei Museum MUSEUM
(Jln Kota Batu; ◎9am-5pm Sat-Thu, 9-11.30am & 2.30-5pm Fri, last entry 30min before closing) Brunei's national museum was officially opened by Queen Elizabeth in 1972.

The oldest pieces in the **Islamic Art Gallery** – ceramics from Iran and Central Asia and blown glass from Egypt and the Levant – date from the 9th and 10th centuries. Other highlights include some wonderful illuminated manuscripts of the Koran, tiny Korans the size of a matchbox, and gold jewellery.

The **Brunei Traditional Culture Gallery** spotlights Brunei's role in Southeast Asia's history, cultures and commerce and has a section on Western trade and intervention in Brunei, starting with the arrival of the Spanish and Portuguese in the 1500s. It also has life-size scenes of a Malay wedding and a collection of Brunei's famous ceremonial cannons, some with barrels shaped like dragon heads.

The **Natural History Gallery**, though old-fashioned, provides an excellent introduction to Borneo's extraordinary biodiversity. Signs are clear, concise and informative – this is a worthwhile stop if you'll be trekking anywhere in Borneo.

The **Independence Gallery**, opened in 2010, has a display featuring the words of Brunei's national anthem, 'Allah Save the King' (sound familiar?). A **maritime museum** is supposed to open just down the slope.

The Brunei Museum is 4.5km east of central BSB along the coastal road, on a bluff overlooking Sungai Brunei. To get there, take bus 39 or a taxi (B$10 from the bus station).

Malay Technology Museum MUSEUM
(Jln Kota Batu; ◎9am-5pm Sun-Thu, 9-11.30am & 2.30-5pm Fri, 9.45am-5pm Sat, last entry 30min before closing) Linked to the Brunei Museum by a short path down the hill, this museum has somewhat outdated displays on life in a Malay water village (stilt architecture, boatmaking, fishing techniques, handicrafts) and a Murut (Lun Bawang) longhouse.

MOSQUE ETIQUETTE

If you intend to visit a mosque, it's good form to dress modestly – long pants for men, covered shoulders, elbows and knees for women. At mosque entrances, women – regardless of what they're wearing – are asked to put on a full-length gown and headscarf; men are asked to don a robe only if they arrive in shorts. Shoes, of course, must be removed.

Mosques are not open to visitors during prayer times and are closed all day Thursday and for all but an hour or so in the late afternoon on Friday.

Twelve Roofs House MUSEUM
(Bubungan Dua Belas; Jln Residency; ⊘9am-4.30pm Mon-Thu & Sat, 9-11.30am & 2.30-4.30pm Fri) The one-time residence of Britain's colonial-era high commissioners, said to be the sultanate's oldest extant building, is now a museum dedicated to the longstanding 'special relationship' between Brunei and the UK. The evocative photos include views of Brunei as it looked a century ago and many fine shots of Queen Elizabeth. The swimming pool out the back is rumoured to be haunted – during WWII the Japanese executed people there.

The building is 1.5km southeast of Sungai Kianggeh, towards the Brunei Museum, on a hilltop dominating the river. To get there from the city centre, take bus 39, a cab or a water taxi.

NORTH & WEST OF THE CENTRE

Jame'Asr Hassanil Bolkiah Mosque MOSQUE
(Sultan Hassanal Bolkiah Hwy, Kampung Kiarong; ⊘8am-noon, 2-3pm & 5-6pm Mon-Wed & Sat, 5-6pm Fri, 10.30am-noon, 2-3pm & 5-6pm Sun, closed Thu) Built in 1992 to celebrate the 25th year of the current sultan's reign, Brunei's largest mosque and its four terrazzo-tiled minarets are a fantastic sight, especially when illuminated in the evening. Because the sultan is his dynasty's 29th ruler, the complex is adorned with 29 golden domes big and small.

The interior is best described as jaw-dropping. The sheer volume in itself is amazing, not to mention the myriad woven rugs scattered across the men's prayer hall.

The mosque is about 3km northwest of the city centre towards Gadong. To get there, take buses 1 or 22.

Istana Nurul Iman PALACE
(Jln Tutong) The best way to measure the grandeur of any residential structure is by counting the bathrooms. Istana Nurul Iman, the official residence of the sultan, has 257! This 1788-room, 200,000-sq-metre behemoth – the largest habitation of any sort in the world – is, if you can believe it,

more than four times the size of the Palace of Versailles and three times larger than Buckingham Palace.

Designed by Filipino architect Leandro Locsin, the palace – 3km southwest of the centre of town – mixes Malay and Islamic elements with the sweep and oversized grandeur of an airport terminal. Nonetheless, it's relatively attractive from a distance or when illuminated in the evening.

Istana Nurul Iman ('palace of the light of the faith') is open to the public only during the three-day Hari Raya Aidil Fitri festivities at the end of Ramadan. The best way to check it out the other 362 days of the year, is to take a water-taxi cruise (see p224) or to stop by the riverside pavilion at **Taman Persiaran Damuan**, a landscaped park 1.2km beyond the palace (when travelling from the city centre).

Taman Peranginan Tasek PARK
(Tasek Recreational Park; Jln Tasek Lama) BSB's version of Central Park, with greenery, picnic areas and peaceful walks to a small waterfall and a large reservoir. Locals come here to do tai chi (6am to 9am), jog (in the evening), use the exercise apparatus and admire the view. Situated about 2km north of the city centre; to get there, turn east (right) 400m north of the Terrace Hotel.

JERUDONG

Jerudong Park Playground AMUSEMENT PARK
(Jerudong; admission free, 5/8 rides B$8/10; ⊘5-10.30pm Wed, Thu & Sun, 5pm-midnight Fri & Sat, closed Mon & Tue except during school holidays) In its heyday, this B$1 billion amusement park, a Prince Jefri project opened in 1994, was hugely popular with local young people – as one Bruneian in his mid-20s put it, 'this was the highlight of our childhood'. The concert hall hosted free shows by the likes of Whitney Houston and Michael Jackson, the latter to celebrate the sultan's 50th birthday, and the many rides included a giant roller coaster. That attraction, along with most of the others, was sold off to repay debts, but

10 rides still operate, including a merry-go-round and junior bumper cars. Other family-friendly features include formal landscaping (though the grounds keeping is no longer postcard-perfect), a clown show at 8pm and a musical fountain that does its thing at 8.30pm and 9.30pm.

There is no bus service to the park, which is near the coast about 20km northwest of BSB, so the only way to get there is by taxi (about B$35 from the centre) or private car.

MUARA

Muara Beaches   BEACHES

Not many people come to Brunei for a sun 'n' sand experience, but if you have some spare time to stretch out on the seashore, there are a couple of options about 25km northeast of BSB around the cargo, ferry and naval port of Muara, site of an Australian amphibious landing in April 1945.

Pantai Muara (Muara Beach), near the tip of the peninsula, is a popular weekend retreat. The white sand is clean, but like many beaches in Borneo it's littered with driftwood and other flotsam that comes in with the tide. Quiet during the week, it has food stalls, picnic tables and a children's playground.

About 4km west of Muara along the Muara–Tutong Hwy, **Pantai Meragang** (Crocodile Beach) is another stretch of pleasant seaside sand that's not quite as crowded as the others on weekends. There are a couple of food stalls that make this a good place for a picnic.

Muara's town centre is served by buses 37, 38 and 39 (B$1); bus 33 will take you from there to Pantai Muara. Pantai Meragang is difficult to get to without your own transport.

☞ Tours

A number of local agencies offer tours of BSB and trips to nature sites around the sultanate, including Ulu Temburong National Park and the mangroves of Pulau Selirong, 45 minutes by boat from the city. Some also offer night safaris on which you can spot proboscis monkeys, crocs and fireflies.

Borneo Guide   NATURE

(☑876-6796; www.borneoguide.com; unit B1, 1st fl, Warisan Mata-Mata, Gadong) Excellent service, good prices and a variety of eco-programs around Brunei and Borneo. A day trip to Ulu Temburong National Park costs B$98 from Bangar (9am to 3.30pm or 4pm) or B$110 from BSB (7.30am to 4.30 or 5pm). Two days and one night at the park, including food and activities, costs B$185 from BSB.

Intrepid Tours   NATURE

(☑222-1685/6; www.bruneibay.net; Unit 105, 1st fl, PGGMB Bldg, Jln Sungai Kianggeh) Has its own lodge near Batang Duri (on the way to Ulu Temburong National Park).

Mona Florafauna Tours   OUTDOOR, WILDLIFE

(☑223-0761, 24hr 884-9110; mft.brunei@gmail.com; 209 1st fl, Kiaw Lian Bldg, 140 Jln Pemancha; ⊙8.30am-5pm) Specialises in outdoor and wildlife tours. Destinations include the lowland rainforests of the Andulau Forest Reserve (B$298 per person for two days and one night) and the peat swamps of the Mendaram Forest Reserve (B$338 per person for two days and one night). Situated a floor below KH Soon Rest House.

Freme Travel Services   SIGHTSEEING

(☑223-4280; www.freme.com; 4th fl, office 4.03B, Wisma Jaya, Jln Pemancha) Also one of Brunei's largest travel agencies.

🛏 Sleeping

Budget options are thin on the ground. Upscale places often offer big discounts online.

We've heard murmurs about home stays and B&B establishments starting up in Kampung Ayer – the Kampung Ayer Cultural & Tourism Gallery should have the latest lowdown.

TOP CHOICE **Empire Hotel & Country Club**

RESORT **$$$**

(☑241-8888; www.theempirehotel.com; Muara-Tutong Hwy, Kampung Jerudong; r incl breakfast from

WATERFRONT PROMENADE

By the time you read this, the flash new promenade along Jln McArthur, at the foot of Jln Sultan facing Kampung Ayer, should have cafes under tepees, restaurants, a Brunei Tourism information kiosk and colourful lighting in the evening. If all goes according to plan, the old customs house will eventually house an art gallery.

B$400, villas B$1300-2900; ❋ @ ⊛ 🖳) Pharaonic (or perhaps Dubaian) in its proportions and opulence, this 523-room extravaganza was commissioned by Prince Jefri as lodging for guests of the royal family. To recoup some of the US$1.1 billion investment, the property was quickly transformed into an upscale resort, so now anyone with a thing for Las Vegas–style bling can hang out in the lobby and enjoy one of the US$500,000 lamps made of gold and Baccarat crystal (the other one lives in the Emperor Suite and can be appreciated privately for B$16,600 per night). Even the cheapest rooms (except the recently opened Ocean rooms) have remote-control everything, hand-woven carpets, gold-plated power points and enormous bathrooms with marble floors. Fun for an over-the-top honeymoon! Worth a visit just to take in the gilded spectacle; tea in the Lobby Lounge costs a mere B$5 a pot. To get there, take bus 57 from the city centre or Gadong (runs two or three times a day; on the way back, book at the Transport desk) or a taxi (B$30 to B$35).

Terrace Hotel   HOTEL **$$**
(☎224-3554/5/6/7; www.terracebrunei.com; Jln Tasek Lama; d B$65-75; ❋ @ ⊛ 🖳) A classic tourist-class hotel whose 84 rooms are dowdy (think 1980s) but clean, and come with marble bathrooms. Has a great little swimming pool. In a super location just 800m north of the waterfront, near a hawker centre. Excellent value.

Pusat Belia   HOSTEL **$**
(Youth Centre; ☎222-2900; Jln Sungai Kianggeh; dm B$10; ❋ 🖳) Gets rave reviews from backpackers despite the fact that couples can't stay together. The 28 spacious, strictly sex-segregated rooms, with four or 10 beds (all bunks), have functional furnishings, big windows, red cement floors and passable bathrooms. Situated at the southern end of the Youth Centre complex (behind the cylindrical staircase). Reception is supposed to be open from 7.45am to noon and 1.30pm to 4.30pm or later (often until 6pm or 6.30pm), but midday closure is longer on Friday and staffing can be intermittent on Sunday, in the evening and at night. If the office is locked, hang around and someone should find you. The adjacent swimming pool costs B$1. May fill up with government guests on holidays and for sports events.

Radisson Hotel   HOTEL **$$$**
(☎224-4272; www.radisson.com/brunei; Jln Tasek Lama; r from B$170; ❋ @ ⊛ 🖳) Brunei's only Western chain hotel, on the edge of the town centre, flies the flag for international standards. The sparkling lobby exudes comfort and wealth, as do the 142 newly renovated rooms. Amenities include two pools (one for kids), a fitness centre, a spa and two restaurants. Free shuttle service to Gadong and downtown three times a day.

Jubilee Hotel   HOTEL **$$**
(☎222-8070; www.jubileehotelbrunei.com; Jln Kampung Kianggeh; d B$70-95, f B$145; ❋ @) Not quite as appealing as the Terrace, the Jubilee offers rooms that aren't hip – they may remind you of your old aunt's seldom-used guest bedroom – but are liveable and clean. 'Superior' rooms come with kitchenettes. Has a tour agency and a mini-mart on the ground floor. Rates include airport pick-up and breakfast.

KH Soon Resthouse   GUEST HOUSE **$**
(☎222-2052; http://khsoon-resthouse.tripod.com; 2nd fl, 140 Jln Pemancha; s/d B$35/39, with shared bathroom B$30/35; ❋) This matter-of-fact guest house, in a converted commercial space with floors the colour of a man-o-war's decks, offers a unique combination for Brunei: budget rates, huge but spartan rooms, and a super-central location. An extra bed costs B$17; a room for five is B$85. Can supply details on public transport to Miri (in Sarawak) and Kota Kinabalu (KK).

🍴 Eating

If there's one word you should learn during a visit to Brunei, it's *makan* (food). *Makan* isn't just a word; it's a way of life (because, the locals joke, there's nothing to do other than eat!) This micro-nation really knows how to chow down.

In the city centre, restaurants can be found along the waterfront and on Jln Sultan (south of Jln Pemancha). The big shopping malls, including those out in Gadong, have **food courts** – at the Yayasan Complex, go to the 2nd floor of the northern end of the eastern building.

Aminah Arif   AMBUYAT **$$**
[TOP CHOICE] (☎223-6198; Unit 2-3, Block B, Rahman Bldg, Spg 88, Kiulap; ambuyat for 2 B$16; ⊙9am-10pm) Aminah Arif is synonymous with *ambuyat* (p232), Brunei's signature dish. If you're up for trying a generous serving of wiggly white goo, then this is a very good place. Also serves rice and noodle dishes. Meals can be washed down with iced *kasturi ping* (calamansi lime juice; B$1.80).

DON'T MISS

MONKEY BUSINESS

Long-tailed macaques and their adorable offspring often frolic in the trees along the road that heads up the hill (towards the radio tower) from the intersection between the Terrace and Radisson Hotels – listen for the telltale rustle of branches as they prance from tree to tree. The primates are somewhere nearby all day long – sneaking into someone's kitchen through an open window, perhaps – but are easiest to spot very early in the morning and in the late afternoon and around dusk.

A troupe of about 20 macaques, including babies, lives in the forested area behind (east of) Tamu Kianggeh and frequently comes down to the edge of the market, behind stall 49, in the morning (often from 6am to 8am) and in the afternoon (from about 2pm to 5pm).

TOP CHOICE **Tamu Kianggeh** FOOD STALLS **$**
(Jln Sungai Kianggeh; mains from B$1; ⊙5am-5pm) The food stalls here serve Brunei's cheapest meals, including *nasi katok* (plain rice, a piece of fried or curried chicken and sambal; B$1) and *nasi lemak* (rice cooked in coconut milk and served with chicken, beef or prawn, egg and cucumber slices; also B$1). In the market's northeast corner, a vegetarian-Chinese stall called **Tamu Chakoi** (stalls 49-51; ⊙8.30am-noon, closed Mon; 🖋) serves a variety of inexpensive fried pastries and noodle dishes. For dessert, stop by **Hajjah Hasnah** (stall 214) for *kelupis* (glutinous rice steamed in a leaf; five pieces for B$1), *wajid* (rice flavoured with coconut milk and wrapped in a leaf) and *tapai nasi* (half-fermented rice) – the latter dish, fermented for about three days, packs a gentle but perceptible punch. It's easy to spend hours wandering around and sampling delicious titbits.

Taman Selera HAWKER CENTRE **$**
(cnr Jln Tasek Lama & Jln Stoney; mains B$1-3.50; ⊙4pm-midnight) At this old-fashioned hawker centre, set in a shady park, diners eat excellent, cheap Malaysian dishes under colourful tarps and ceiling fans. Options include satay (four skewers for B$1), fried chicken, seafood, rice and noodle dishes, and iced drinks (B$1). Situated 1km north of the waterfront, across from the Terrace Hotel.

Pasar Malam Gadong NIGHT MARKET **$**
(Jln Pasar Gadong, Gadong; ⊙4-10pm) Thanks to its authentic Brunei-style snacks and dishes, this is Brunei's most popular and beloved night market. Unfortunately, it's geared to car-driving locals who take the food away so there are almost no places to sit. Situated 3km northwest of the centre and 200m across the river from The Mall shopping centre. Served by buses 1 and 22, but after about 7pm the only way back to town is by taxi (B$10 to B$15, more after 8pm).

Gerai Makan Jalan Residency FOOD STALLS **$**
(Jalan Residency Food Court; Jln Residency; mains B$2-5.50; ⊙24hr) Along the riverbank facing Kampung Ayer, this grouping of food stalls features satay (B$1 for four chicken or three lamb skewers), dozens of kinds of *mee goreng* and *nasi goreng*, and soups such as *soto* (noodle soup). Most places are open from 4pm to midnight, but one will take care of the munchies round the clock.

Nyonya Restaurant NONYA, THAI **$$**
(central courtyard, Yayasan Complex, Jln Pretty; mains B$3.80-5.80; ⊙11am-9pm) Serves up Nyonya (Peranakan), Thai and a few European dishes, including three kinds of pasta (from B$4.80), in an atmosphere of bistro-style air-con chic.

Cim Ah Siew Pork Market HAWKER CENTRE **$$**
(Jln Teraja; mains B$3.50-5; ⊙7am-10pm) It's forbidden to raise pigs in Brunei, but porcine delicacies can be found if you know where to look. Hidden away in an isolated white building 300m behind the Terrace Hotel, this market is the place to go for Chinese delicacies such as pork buns, pork dumplings and noodles with pig's trotters. Menus (on the wall) are in Chinese only.

Self-Catering

TOP CHOICE **Hua Ho Supermarket** SUPERMARKET **$**
(western Bldg, Yayasan Complex, Jln Pretty; ⊙10am-10pm) Dozens of kinds of absolutely scrumptious Bruneian cookies and snacks (B$3 to B$5) can be found in this four-storey department store's basement supermarket, in a case next to the fruit section. Some of the sweets are dusted with powdered sugar; many simply melt in your mouth. Among the highlights: *kuih lenggang*, a green, coconut-filled crepe.

AMBUYAT – GUMMY, GLUEY & GLUTINOUS

If Brunei had a national dish, it would be *ambuyat*. Remember that kid in kindergarten who used to eat paste? Well, this comes pretty darn close. Made from the pith of the sago tree, which is ground to a powder and mixed with water, the gelatinous goo was popularised during WWII, when the Japanese invaded Borneo and cut off the rice supply.

To eat *ambuyat*, you'll be given a special pair of chopsticks that's attached at the top (don't snap them in two!) to make it easier to twirl up the tenacious mucous. Once you've scooped up a bite-sized quantity, dunk it into a flavourful sauce. *Ambuyat* itself doesn't have a taste – it's the sauce that gives it its zing. Shrimp-and-chilli mixes are the most popular, although you can technically dip the dish in anything you'd like (we've heard of people using vanilla ice cream!). After your *ambuyat* is sufficiently drenched, place the glob of dripping, quivering, translucent mucilage in your mouth and swallow – don't chew, just let it glide down your throat...

The easiest way to try *ambuyat* is to stop by one of the nine branches of Aminah Arif in BSB.

Tamu Kianggeh　　　　　　　MARKET $
(Jln Sungai Kianggeh; ☺6am-6pm or 7pm; 🖉)
Stalls in the northern part of the market sell fruit and vegies, including wild durians (thinner and with longer thorns than the commercial variety). Especially busy on Friday and Sunday mornings.

 Drinking

The sale and public consumption of alcohol is officially banned in Brunei, but expats may know of places that discreetly serve beer to regulars or establishments that let you bring your own.

Locals are fond of *air batu campur* ('ice mix'), usually called ABC, which brings together ice, little green noodles, grass jelly, sago pearls and red beans.

Coffee Bean & Tea Leaf　　　　CAFE
(Mayapuri Bldg, 36 Jln Sultan; ☺8am-midnight Sun-Wed, to 1.30am Thu-Sat; 🛜) The hangout of choice for Western road warriors. Serves hot and 'ice blended' beverages, hearty breakfasts, pastries (muffins, cakes, scones), gourmet sandwiches (B$6 to B$8) and pasta (B$4.80 to B$7.50).

De Royalle Café　　　　　　　CAFE
(Mayapuri Bldg, 38 Jln Sultan; ☺24hr; 🛜) Organised into two mini-living rooms plus sidewalk tables, this always-open establishment has a supply of perusable English-language newspapers and serves up pastries, sandwiches (B$4 to B$11 – lox is the priciest) and, of course, fresh-brewed coffee. A fine place for a relaxed rendezvous with friends.

☆ Entertainment

Locals often head to Gadong for a night out, which in Brunei usually amounts to nothing more than dinner and perhaps a movie. Based on what you hear, you might conclude that the area is a seething nightlife zone or at least a fine collection of smart restaurants. Unfortunately, it's neither – just some air-con shopping malls and commercial streets.

🛍 Shopping

Shopping is Brunei's national sport. Locals bop through the shopping malls scouting out the best deals while bemoaning the fact that their micro-nation doesn't have as much variety as Singapore.

Arts & Handicrafts Training Centre　CRAFTS
(Jln Kota Batu; ☺8am-5pm Sat-Thu, 8.30-11.30am & 2.30-5pm Fri) Sells silverwork, carved wood items, ornamental brass cannons (from B$500) and ceremonial swords (about B$500), made by the centre's students and graduates, for much, much more than you'd pay in Sarawak or Kalimantan. Not bad for window-shopping, though – check out the *jong sarat*, hand-woven cloth made from gold and silver threads (B$400 to B$4000 for a 2m-long bolt). If you're serious about Bruneian artisanship, pick up the sultanate's *Directory of Handicraft Entrepreneurs* (B$4.80). The centre is on the river 600m east of Sungai Kianggeh.

Paul & Elizabeth Book Services　BOOKS
(📞222-0958; 2nd fl, eastern Bldg, Yayasan Complex, Jln Pretty; ☺9.30am-9pm) Stocks a few books on Brunei, a street map of the entire sultanate (B$14.90) and a small range

of English-language paperbacks, including some ancient LP guides!

Yayasan Complex MALL
(Kompleks Yayasan Sultan Haji Hassanal Bolkiah; Jln Pretty) Escape the oppressive heat at ritzy Yayasan, the city centre's main shopping mall, whose courtyard is aligned with Omar Ali Saifuddien Mosque.

Hua Ho Department Store DEPARTMENT STORE
(⊙10am-10pm) Don't miss four-level Hua Ho with its cache of traditional Bruneian sweets in the basement.

Tamu Kiangeh CRAFTS
(Jln Sungai Kianggeh) Woven crafts are sold along the river here, but prices are higher than in Malaysia.

Gadong SHOPPING DISTRICT
The country's only traffic jam occurs nightly in Gadong, about 3km northwest of the centre. The area features several air-conditioned bastions of commerce, including two huge malls, **Centrepoint** and **The Mall**.

❶ Information

Emergency
Ambulance (✆991)
Fire Brigade (✆995)
Police (✆993)

Internet Access
Amin & Sayeed Cyber Cafe (1st fl, cnr Jln Sultan & Jln McArthur; per hr B$1; ⊙9am-midnight)
Paul & Elizabeth Cyber Cafe (2nd fl, eastern Bldg, Yayasan Complex, Jln Pretty; per hr B$1; ⊙9am-9pm) Overlooking the central atrium in the eastern building of the complex. Decent connections, bad soundtrack.

Medical Services
RIPAS Hospital (✆224-2424; Jln Tutong; ⊙24hr) Brunei's main hospital, with fully equipped, modern facilities. Most of the senior staff are Western trained. Situated about 2km west of the centre (across the Edinburgh Bridge).

Money
Banks and international ATMs are sprinkled around the city centre, especially along Jln McArthur and Jln Sultan. The airport has ATMs too.

HSBC (cnr Jln Sultan & Jln Pemancha; ⊙8.45am-4pm Mon-Fri, to 11.30am Sat) Has a 24-hour ATM. You must have an HSBC account to change travellers cheques (B$25 fee).

Isman Money Changer (ground fl, eastern Bldg, Yayasan Complex, Jln Pretty; ⊙9.30am-7.30pm) Changes cash but not travellers cheques. Just off the central atrium.

For a mix of fresh news, business information and visitor tips about Brunei, check out www.brudirect.com.

Post
Main post office (cnr Jln Sultan & Jln Elizabeth Dua; ⊙8am-4.30pm Mon-Thu & Sat, 8-11am & 2-4pm Fri) Has a free internet computer. The Stamp Gallery displays some historic first-day covers and blow-ups of colonial-era stamps.

Telephone
International calling cards (for use in public phones) are sold at various shops around town, including several along Jln McArthur.

Amin & Sayeed Cyber Cafe (1st fl, cnr Jln Sultan & Jln McArthur; ⊙9am-midnight) Cheap overseas calls for B$0.25 to B$0.30 a minute.

Cheap Call (Jln McArthur; ⊙9am-6.45pm) Overseas calls for B$0.30 to B$0.50 a minute. Situated above Kong Guan Company, two shops east of the alley called Lorong Gerai Timur.

DST Communications (www.dst-group.com; ground fl, western Bldg, Yayasan Complex, Jln McArthur; ⊙9am-4pm Mon-Thu & Sat, 9am-11am & 2.30-4pm Fri, closed Sun) A cell-phone SIM card costs B$30, including B$5 worth of calls; registering (if you bought a SIM card elsewhere) is free. Bring your passport.

Tourist Information
Keep an eye out for the free **Borneo Insider's Guide** (BIG; http://bigmagazine.blogspot.com, www.borneoinsidersguide.com), a glossy magazine published four times a year.

Brunei Tourism (www.bruneitourism.travel), whose wonderful website has oodles of useful information, runs these tourist-information counters that can supply the only decent maps of the sultanate:

Airport (arrival hall; ⊙8am-noon & 1.30-5pm)

Kampung Ayer Cultural & Tourism Gallery (Kampung Ayer; ⊙9am-5pm Sat-Thu, 9-11am & 2.30-5pm Fri) Across the river from the city centre.

Old Customs House (Jln McArthur) Should be open by the time you read this.

❶ Getting There & Away

Border crossings generally are open from 6am to 10pm. Traffic at the Kuala Lurah crossing (BSB–Limbang) has been known to cause three-hour delays.

Air
Brunei International Airport (✆flight enquiries 233-6767, 233-1747; www.civil-aviation.gov.bn)

About 8km north of BSB centre. Short-haul flights, eg from Singapore, tend to be pricey. For details, see p316.

Boat

Travel by sea to the Temburong District, Sabah (either direct to Menumbok or via Pulau Labuan) and Sarawak's Limbang Division (Limbang and Lawas) is a good way to avoid the hassles and delays of land borders.

LIMBANG & LAWAS

The fastest way to get to Bangar (in Brunei's Temburong District) and Limbang and Lawas (both in Sarawak) is by speedboat – for details see p237, p221 and p222.

PULAU LABUAN & SABAH

Car ferries from Serasa Ferry Terminal in Muara, about 20km northeast of BSB, to the Malaysian federal territory of Pulau Labuan (1½ hours) are run by **PKL Jaya Sendirian** (☑in Muara 277-1771, in Labuan 087-415-777; www. pkljaya.com). Adults/cars B$10/30 from Brunei, RM25/60 from Pulau Labuan; departures at 8.45am from Muara, 11.30am from Pulau Labuan. If you've got a car, get there at least an hour before sailing. From Pulau Labuan, daily ferries go to Kota Kinabalu (115km by sea).

Passenger-only ferries usually ply the route between Serasa and Pulau Labuan several times a day, but at press time this service was in a state of disarray as Brunei had banned vessels operated by the Labuan-based ISRO Shipping Company from docking in Brunei, ostensibly for safety reasons.

PKL Jaya Sendirian also operates a car-ferry service from the Serasa Ferry Terminal to the Sabah port of Menumbok (2½ hours), which is 152km by road from KK. Adults/cars cost B$25/70 from Muara, MR60/168 from Menumbok; departures at 9.30am from Muara, 3pm from Menumbok.

To get to the Serasa Ferry Terminal by public transport, take bus 37, 38 or 39 to Muara town (B$1, at least twice an hour); from there it's a short ride on bus 33 to the ferry. Three express buses a day (B$2, 40 minutes) link BSB direct with the ferry; departures from BSB's bus terminal (from the berth for bus 39) are at 6.30am, 11.30am and 2.15pm.

TEMBURONG DISTRICT

The fastest way to get to Bangar is by speedboat – for details see p237.

Bus & Van

The only bus company authorised to take passengers to/from Malaysia is known by two names, Jesselton Express (towards KK) and PHLS (towards Miri). Employee **Danny** (☑880-1180), usually found assisting passengers to board, is very helpful.

For details on various bus and van options to Malaysia, contact KH Soon Resthouse in BSB, the Dillenia (Mrs Lee), Minda and Highlands Guesthouses in Miri, or Miri's Visitors Information Centre.

Jesselton Express (☑in BSB 718-3838, 717-7755, 719-3835, in KK 016-836-0009, 012-622-9722) sends a bus to KK (B$45, eight to nine hours) via Limbang (B$10 or MR20), Bangar, Lawas (B$25 or MR50) and various towns in Sabah daily at 8am. In the other direction, the bus leaves KK at 9.30am.

PHLS Express (☑in BSB 277-1668, 277-3818, 718-3838) links BSB with Miri (B$18 from BSB, RM40 from Miri, 3½ hours) via Seria and Kuala Belait (two hours) twice a day. Departures from BSB's PGGMB building (on Jln Sungai Kianggeh just south of the Chinese Temple) are at approximately 7am and 1pm and from Miri's Pujut Bus Terminal at about 8am and 4pm. Tickets are sold on board. Travel between Miri and Seria or Kuala Belait costs B$12 or RM25.

Another option for travel between BSB and Miri is a 'private transfer' (RM60 per person) by a **seven-seater van** (☑in Malaysia 013-833-2331, 016-807-2893) run by a father-son team. Departures from BSB are usually at 1pm or 2pm; departures from Miri are generally at 9am or 10am but may be earlier. It may also be possible to hitch a ride (RM50 per person, 3½ hours) with a **newspaper delivery van** (☑in BSB 876-0136, in Miri before 4pm 012-878-0136). Departure from Miri is at 5.30am; be prepared for an hour's delay at customs.

ⓘ Getting Around

To/From the Airport

The airport, about 8km north of central BSB, is linked to the city centre, including the bus terminal on Jln Cator, by buses 23, 24, 36 and 38.

A cab to/from the airport costs B$20 to B$25 (B$35 after 10pm); taxis are unmetered, so agree on a price before you get in. Some hotels offer airport pick-up.

Bus

BSB's carbon monoxide–choked **bus terminal** (Jln Cator) is on the ground floor of a multistorey parking complex two blocks north of the waterfront. It is used by domestic lines, including those to Muara, Seria, Tutong and Kuala Lurah, and services to Pontianak in Kalimantan, but *not* buses to Sabah or Sarawak. Schematic signs next to each numbered berth show the route of each line.

Brunei's public bus system, run by a variety of companies, is rather chaotic, at least to the uninitiated, so getting around by public transport takes a bit of effort. Buses (B$1) operate daily from 6.30am to about 6.30pm (7pm on some lines); after that, your options are taking a cab or hoofing it. If you're heading out of town and will need to catch a bus back, ask the driver if and when he's coming back and what time the last bus back is. Finding stops can be a challenge – some are marked by black-and-white-striped uprights or a shelter, others by a yellow triangle painted on the pavement, and yet others by no discernible symbol. Fortunately, numbers are prominently displayed on each 20- or 40-passenger bus.

The bus station lacks an information office or a ticket counter, and while the schematic wall map may make sense to BSB natives, it's a bit of a cipher to the uninitiated. Some tourist brochures include a schematic route map.

Car

Brunei has Southeast Asia's cheapest petrol – gasoline is just B$0.53 a litre and diesel goes for only B$0.30! If you're driving a car (eg a rental) with Malaysian plates and are not a Brunei resident, you'll be taken to a special pump to pay more (this is to prevent smuggling).

Hiring a car is a good way to explore Brunei's hinterland. Prices start at about B$80 a day. Surcharges may apply if the car is taken into Sarawak. Most agencies will bring the car to your hotel and pick it up when you've finished, and drivers can also be arranged, though this could add B$100 to the daily cost. The main roads are in good condition, but some back roads require a 4WD.

Among the rental companies (most of them local) with offices at the airport:

Avis (☑876-0642; www.avis.com)

Hertz (☑872-6000, 239-0300; www.hertz.com)

Taxi

Taxis are a convenient way of exploring BSB – if you can find one, that is: the entire country has less than 50 official cabs, all run by independent drivers. Unfortunately, there is no centralised taxi dispatcher and it's difficult or impossible to flag down a cab on the street. Hotels can provide drivers' cell-phone numbers. Most taxis have yellow tops; a few serving the airport are all white.

BSB's only proper taxi rank is two blocks north of the waterfront at the bus terminal.

Taxis do not have meters, so always agree on a price before getting in; fares go up by 50% after 10pm. The charge for an hour of wait time is B$30 to B$35. Sample daytime taxi fares from the city centre include the Brunei Museum (B$10), Gadong (B$10 to B$15), the airport (B$20 to B$25), the Serasa Ferry Terminal in Muara (B$30), the Empire Hotel & Country Club (B$30 to B$35) and the Jerudong Park Playground (B$35).

Water Taxi

If your destination is near the river, water taxis – the same little motorboats that ferry people to and from Kampung Ayer – are a good way of getting there. You can hail a water taxi anywhere on the waterfront a boat can dock, as well as along Venice-themed Sungai Kianggeh. Crossing straight across the river is supposed to cost B$0.50 per person; diagonal crossings cost more.

TUTONG & BELAIT DISTRICTS

Most travellers merely pass through the districts of Tutong and Belait, west of BSB, en route to Miri, but there are a few worthwhile attractions. Frequent buses link Kuala Belait, Seria and Tutong with BSB, but if you want to really see the sights the best way is to take a tour or rent a car.

Tutong

POP 19,200

About halfway between Seria and BSB, Tutong is the main town in central Brunei. The town itself is neat but unremarkable, but the area is famous in Brunei for two things: pitcher plants and sand. Tutong has six species of pitcher plants and the locals cook a variety of dishes in their insect-catching sacs. Some of the sand near Tutong is so white that Bruneians will often take pictures with it while pretending it's snow – you can see *pasir putih* (white sand) in patches along the side of the Pan Borneo Hwy.

There's a great beach, **Pantai Seri Kenangan**, also known as Pantai Tutong, a couple of kilometres west of town, on Jln Kuala Tutong. Set on a spit of land, with the ocean on one side and the Sungai Tutong on the other, the casuarina-lined beach is arguably the best in Brunei. The royal family clearly agrees, as they have a surprisingly modest palace here for discreet getaways.

❶ Getting There & Away

The buses that link BSB with Seria stop in Tutong (B$3, one hour, every 30 to 60 minutes until 5pm).

Jalan Labi

A few kilometres after you enter Belait district (coming from Tutong and BSB), a road branches inland (south) to Labi and beyond, taking you through some prime forest areas. The easiest way into the interior of western Brunei, Jalan Labi offers a chance to stop by Brunei's **Forestry Museum** (⊘closed Fri & Sun) and see a number of Iban longhouses, which in these parts come complete with mod-cons and parking lots.

About 40km south of the coastal road, Labi is a small Iban settlement with some fruit arbours. Further south, you come to the Iban longhouses of **Rampayoh**, **Mendaram Besar**, **Mendaram Kecil** and finally, at the end of the track, **Teraja**, where a local guide may be able to take you to a nearby waterfall.

Seria

POP 32,900

Spread out along the coast between Tutong and Kuala Belait, low-density Seria is home to many of Brunei Shell's major onshore installations. A Ghurkha infantry battalion of the British Army is stationed here, at the UK's last remaining military base in eastern Asia. A big market is held on Friday until about 3pm.

Sights

Oil & Gas Discovery Centre   MUSEUM
(☑337-7200; www.bsp.com.bn/ogdc; off Jln Tengah; adult/teenager/senior B$5/2/3; ☉9am-5pm Tue-Thu & Sat, 9am-noon & 2-5pm Fri, 10am-6pm Sun & holidays) Puts an 'edutainment' spin on the oil industry. Likely to appeal to young science buffs. About 700m northwest of the bus station.

Billionth Barrel Monument   MONUMENT
Commemorates (you guessed it) the billionth barrel of crude oil produced at the Seria field, a landmark reached in 1991. Out to sea, oil rigs producing the sultanate's second billion dot the horizon. Situated on the beach about 1km west of the Oil & Gas Discovery Centre.

Sleeping

Hotel Koperasi   HOTEL $$
(☑322-7586/89/92; hotel_seria@brunet.bn; Jln Sharif Ali; s/d B$68/78; ❋☏) Seria's only proper hotel, with 24 rooms. Situated 150m northwest of the bus station.

Getting There & Away

Frequent buses go southwest to Kuala Belait (B$1, three times an hour from 6.30am to 6.15pm) and northeast to BSB (B$6, 2½ hours, every 30 to 60 minutes until about 5pm) via Tutong.

Kuala Belait

POP 35,500

Almost on the Sarawak frontier, coastal KB is a modern, sprawling company town – the company is Brunei Shell – of one-storey suburban villas interspersed with grass-

hopper-like pump jacks. Although there's a reasonable beach, most travellers just hustle through on their way to or from Miri.

Sleeping & Eating

In the town centre, restaurants can be found along Jln McKerron and, two short blocks east, on parallel Jln Pretty, KB's main commercial avenue. Locals recommend the roast duck.

Hotel Sentosa   HOTEL $$
(☑333-1345/6/7; www.bruneisentosahotel.com; 92-93 Jln McKerron; s/d B$98/103; ❋@) Clean, well-run tourist-class accommodation right in the centre of town. Situated one block south of the bus station.

Information

HSBC Bank (cnr Jln McKerron & Jln Dato Shahbandar) Has an international ATM. Situated diagonally opposite the bus station.

Getting There & Away

The **bus station** (cnr Jlns McKerron & Dato Shahbandar) is smack in the town centre. At the time of research, short-haul bus services to/from Miri were suspended, leaving the two daily buses run by PHLS (see p234) as the only public-transit link with Miri. Purple minibuses go to Seria (B$1) three times an hour from 6.30am to 6.15pm.

TEMBURONG DISTRICT

Possibly the best-preserved tract of primary rainforest in all of Borneo covers much of Brunei's 1288-sq-km Temburong District (population 10,000), which is separated from the rest of the country by a strip of Malaysia's Limbang Division. The area's main draw is the brilliant Ulu Temburong National Park, accessible only by longboat.

The speedboat ride from BSB out to Bangar, the district capital, is the most fun you can possibly have for B$6. You roar down Sungai Brunei, slap through the *nipah*-lined waterways and then tilt and weave through mangroves into the mouth of Sungai Temburong.

If you fly over the area (or check out Google Earth), the outline of the Temburong District is easy to spot. At the Brunei frontier, Malaysia's logging roads – irregular gashes of eroded earth – and trashed hillsides give way to a smooth carpet of trackless, uninhabited virgin rainforest. Until not all that many years ago, almost all of Borneo looked like this.

Thanks to the Pan Borneo Hwy and some new bus links, it is now relatively easy, if time consuming, to travel from Sarawak to Sabah overland through Brunei. Make sure you've got empty pages in your passport – the traverse will add 10 chops. MASwings' Twin Otter flights from Miri to Lawas and Limbang – great fun! – owe much of their popularity to the hassle of border formalities.

All but one of the bus companies that can get you from Miri to Limbang and Lawas (both in Sarawak's Limbang Division) and onward to KK are not allowed to take passengers to or from destinations inside Brunei, eg BSB and Bangar. The exception is an outfit known as PHLS and Jesselton, whose daily buses link Miri with Kuala Belait, Seria and BSB and go from KK, Lawas and Limbang to Bangar and BSB (see p234).

For details on short-haul travel between Lawas, Bangar, Limbang and BSB by taxi, minibus, local bus and speedboat, see Getting There & Away in those sections. For information on visas to Brunei, see p314.

Bangar

Bangar, a three-street town on the banks of Sungai Temburong, is the gateway to (and administrative centre of) the Temburong District. It can be visited as a day trip from BSB if you catch an early speedboat, but you'll get more out of the town's easygoing pace if you stay over and explore the area, which has some fine primary rainforest and nine longhouses, not all of them very long.

🛏 Sleeping

The Temburong District has a number of home stays used mainly by tour operators and locals with cars.

Rumah Persinggahan Kerajaan Daerah Temburong GUEST HOUSE $
(☑522-1239; Jln Batang Duri; s/d/tr/q B$25 /30/40/50, 4-person chalets B$80; ✳🛜) Set around a grassy, L-shaped courtyard, this government-run guest house has friendly, helpful staff and six spacious but slightly fraying rooms with rather more bathtub rust and somewhat cooler hot water than many would deem ideal. Situated a few hundred metres west of the town centre, across the highway from the two mosques.

Youth Hostel HOSTEL $
(Pusat Belia; ☑522-1694; dm B$10; ⊘office staffed 7.30am-4.30pm, closed Fri & Sat) Part of a youth centre, this basic hostel sits in a fenced compound across the street from (west of) the Tourist Information Centre. Rooms, each with six beds (bunks), are clean and fan-cooled. If no one's around try phoning.

🍴 Eating

The **fruit and vegie market**, behind the row of shops next to the Tourist Information Centre, has an upstairs **food court** (⊘7am-10pm).

A handful of restaurants can be found around the market, along and just in from the riverfront.

ℹ Information

3 in 1 Services (per hr B$1; ⊘7.45am-9.30pm, closed Sun) Internet access on the first floor of the building next to the market (across the pedestrian bridge from the hawker centre). The shop number is A1-3.

Bank Islam Brunei Darussalam (⊘8.45am-3.45pm Mon-Thu, 8.45-11am & 2.30-4pm Fri, 8.45-11.15am Sat) The only bank in town. Changes US dollars and pounds sterling but not Malaysian ringgits. The ATM does not take international cards. On the river 150m north of the bridge.

Hock Guan Minimarket Exchanges Malaysian ringgits for Brunei dollars. In the second row of shops from the Tourist Information Centre.

Jayamuhibah Shopping Mart Carries some over-the-counter medicines (Temburong District does not have a proper pharmacy). In the second row of shops from the Tourist Information Centre.

Tourist Information Centre (☑876-6796) Run by Borneo Guide (www.borneoguide.com) but closed at the time of research. Has possibly useful signs in the window. Situated across the market access road from the youth hostel.

ℹ Getting There & Away
Boat

By far the fastest way to/from BSB is by speedboat (adult/senior B$6/5, 45 minutes, at least hourly from 6am to at least 4.30pm, until as late as 6pm on Sunday and holidays). Bangar's **ferry terminal**, Terminal Perahu Dan Penumpang, is on the western bank of the river just south of the red bridge. In BSB, the dock is on Jln Residency about 200m east of Sungai Kianggeh.

The crossing is handled by two companies that are known by their nicknames, **Ampuan** (☏522-1985), whose boats are usually red and white; and **Koperasi** (☏522-628), whose vessels are usually blue and yellow.

Boats depart at a scheduled time or when they're full, whichever comes first. When you get to the ticket counters, check which company's boat will be the next to leave and then pay and add your name to the passenger manifest. Peak-hour departures can be as frequent as every 15 minutes.

Bus

Buses run by **Jesselton** (☏in BSB 718-3838, 717-7755, 719-3835) pick up passengers heading towards Limbang and BSB in the early afternoon; its bus to KK (B$20) and Lawas passes through town at about 10am.

Taxi

Bangar doesn't have official taxis, but it's usually not too difficult to hire a car if you ask around under the rain awning in front of the ferry terminal. Drivers may not speak much English. Possible destinations include the Malaysian border towards Limbang (B$5), a distance of 4km; the town of Limbang (about B$40; the price is likely to drop once the ferry is replaced by a bridge); and the Peradayan Forest Reserve (Bukit Patoi; about B$25 return).

Taxis do not wait on the Malaysian side of the border towards Limbang – for information on summoning a taxi, see p221.

Pulau Selirong

At the northern tip of the Temburong District, this 25-sq-km island is a sanctuary for mangroves and the fauna that live in them, including proboscis monkeys. The only way to visit is with a boat tour – see p229 for a list of BSB-based tour companies. The trip across the open water of Brunei Bay takes about 45 minutes.

Batang Duri

Batang Duri, about 16km south of Bangar, is the jumping-off point for longboat rides to Ulu Temburong National Park. As you head south, the sealed road passes Malay settlements, then Murut (Lun Bawang) hamlets and finally a few partly modern Iban longhouses.

⛏ Sleeping

TOP CHOICE **Sumbiling Eco Village** GUEST HOUSE **$$** (☏876-6796; www.borneoguide.com/eco village; per person incl meals B$50) This rustic and very relaxing eco-friendly camp offers great Iban cuisine (served on simpur leaves) and a host of outdoor activities, including visits to nearby Ulu Temburong National Park, jungle overnights, inner-tubing and a forest trek. The basic rooms have glassless windows and a fan attached to the ceiling upside-down to make sure air circulates inside the mozzie nets. Also has a rain-protected camping area. Nearby is a five-door Iban longhouse with fierce, beautiful fighting cocks – each family's prized possessions – tethered outside. Prices do not include transport. Run by Borneo Guide in cooperation with the local community. Situated a few minutes downstream from Batang Duri.

Peradayan Forest Reserve

If you can't be bothered with the logistics or expense of a trip up to Ulu Temburong National Park, a good day trip alternative is the 5km (one-way) trek up to the jungle-cloaked peak of **Bukit Patoi** (310m); it may also be possible to continue on to **Bukit Peradayan** (410m). The trail, through pristine jungle, begins at the picnic tables and toilet block of **Taman Rekreasi Bukit Patoi** (Bukit Patoi Recreational Park), about 15km southeast of Bangar (towards Lawas). Bring lots of water and be prepared to turn back if the path, not always properly maintained along its entire length, becomes too overgrown to follow.

Getting out here from Bangar by unofficial taxi should cost about B$25 return.

Ulu Temburong National Park

One of the highlights of a visit to Brunei, **Ulu Temburong National Park** (admission B$5) is in the heart of a 500-sq-km area of pristine rainforest covering most of southern Temburong. It's so untouched that only about 1 sq km of the park is accessible to tourists; in order to protect it for future generations, the rest is off-limits to everyone except scientists, who flock here from around the world. Permitted activities include a canopy walk, some short jungle walks, and swimming in the cool mountain waters of Sungai Temburong – so don't forget your swimsuit.

The forests of Ulu Temburong are teeming with life, including as many as 400 kinds of butterfly, but don't count on seeing many vertebrates. The best times to spot birds and animals, in the rainforest and along river banks, are around sunrise and sunset, but you're much more likely to hear hornbills and Bornean gibbons than to see them.

Activities

Longboat Trip
BOAT RIDE

One of the charms of Ulu Temburong National Park is that the only way to get there is by *temuai* (shallow-draft Iban longboat). The exhilarating trip, which takes 25 to 40 minutes from Batang Duri, is tough on the boats, which last just a few years, and challenging even for experienced skippers, who need a variety of skills to shoot the rapids – going upriver – in a manner reminiscent of a salmon: submerged boulders and logs have to be dodged, hanging vines must be evaded and the outboard must be taken out of the water at exactly the right moment. When it rains, the water level can quickly rise by up to 2m, but if the river is low you might have to get out and push.

Aluminium Walkway
CANOPY WALK

The park's main attraction is a delicate aluminium walkway, secured by guy-wires, that takes you through (or, more accurately, near) the jungle canopy, up to 60m above the forest floor. In primary rainforests, only limited vegetation can grow on the ground because so little light penetrates, but up in the canopy all manner of life proliferates. Unfortunately, there are no explanatory signs here and some guides don't have the background to explain the importance of the canopy ecosystem and point out the huge variety of organisms that can live on a single tree: orchids, bird's-nest ferns and other epiphytes; ants and myriad other insects; amphibians and snakes; and a huge selection of birds.

The views of nearby hills and valleys from the walkway are breathtaking, if you can get over the vertigo – the tower, built by Shell using oil-rig-scaffolding technology, wobbles in the wind. Whatever you do, don't think of metal fatigue or lightning. If you'd

like to share the experience with friends or loved ones back home and have a Malaysian cell phone, the tops of the towers are a good place to catch a cross-border signal.

The trail up to the canopy walk begins near the confluence of Sungais Belalong and Temburong. It's a short, steep, sweaty walk. If you stay overnight at the resort, you can do the canopy walk at sunrise, when birds and animals are most likely to be around.

Rivers & Waterfalls
SWIMMING

Places to take a refreshing dip in the park's pure mountain waters include several rivers and waterfalls – your guide can point out the best spots.

At one small waterfall, just outside the boundaries of the national park, you can stand in a pool and 2cm- to 4cm-long fish that look like tiny sharks will come up and nibble on your feet, giving you a gentle, ticklish pedicure as they feast on the dry skin between your toes. To get there, head downriver from the resort for about 500m – your guide can help find the creek that you need to follow upstream for a few hundred metres.

Sleeping

Ulu-Ulu Resort
LODGE $$$

(www.uluuluresort.com; per person B$350; ❋) The park's only accommodation is an upscale riverside lodge, built entirely of hardwood, with 22 rooms, some in 1920s Malaysian-style chalets. It has a cinema for rainy evenings – after the canopy walk, Hitchcock's *Vertigo* might be an excellent choice. Prices include transport from BSB and board; activities tend to be expensive. In Malay, *ulu* (as in Ulu Temburong) means 'upriver' and *ulu-ulu* means, essentially, 'back of beyond'.

Getting There & Away

For all intents and purposes, the only way to visit the park is by booking a tour. For details on BSB-based tour agencies that organise park visits, see p229. The hour at which you need to be back in Bangar is determined by the departure time of the last speedboat to BSB (even if you're overnighting in Temburong District, your guide probably won't be).

WANT MORE?

For in-depth information, reviews and recommendations at your fingertips, head to the Apple App Store to purchase Lonely Planet's *Brunei* iPhone app.

Alternatively, head to Lonely Planet (www.lonelyplanet.com/brunei, or www.lonelyplanet.com/asia) for planning advice, author recommendations, traveller reviews and insider tips.

Kalimantan

POP 12,223,300 / AREA 558,266 SQ KM

Why Go?

With its dense jungles, hothouse biodiversity and indigenous peoples, Kalimantan is as mysterious as it is vast, covering some two thirds of Borneo and 30% of Indonesia's total land mass. But for the rivers that dissect its terrain of swampland and forest it would be almost impassable, and though decent air links and roads connect major cities, the best way to experience it really is by boat. Dramatically less developed than neighbouring Sabah and Brunei, its dark forests continue to reveal previously undiscovered mammals.

Formerly head-hunting country, this is a land of longhouses and superstitious Dayak villages where, despite incursions of 21st-century technology, the drum-roll of the shaman effortlessly coalesces with the trill of mobile phones. Given Kalimantan's ongoing environmental struggles, there has never been a more vital time to visit.

Best Places to Eat

» Pranaban Fish Restaurant (p244)
» Depot Kalimantan (p254)
» Ocean's Resto (p261)
» Bakso Surabaya (p266)

Best Places to Stay

» Nabucco Island Resort (see the boxed text, p277)
» Rimba Lodge (p248)
» Hotel Gran Senyiur (p260)

When to Go

February to April and August to September are great months to search for sweet-toothed wild orangutans in places like Kutai National Park, when the forests are in bloom with flowers and fruit. These months also represent the dry season, so there're slower rivers, less rainfall and fewer leeches!

In the last week of September, the Erau Festival sees thousands of Dayaks from all over Kalimantan converging on Tenggarong in a whirl of tribal costumes, ceremony and dance.

Map labels:

SOUTH CHINA SEA

Kota Kinabalu ◉
Sandakan
SABAH

BANDAR SERI BEGAWAN ✪
BRUNEI
Sebuku Sembakung National Park
Tawau ✕
Nunukan

Pulau Bunguran (Natuna Besar)

Pulau Lagong

Pulau Subi Besar

Apokayan Highlands

Long Bawan

Sulawesi Sea

MALAYSIA
Kayan Mentarang National Park
Tanjung Selor
Tarakan

Teluk Datu

Sibu

SARAWAK

Sungai Kayan

Tanjung Batu
Berau ④ Pulau Derawan & Sangalaki Archipelago

Kuching ◉
Sambas
Tebedu
Danau Sentarum National Park
Betung Kerihun National Park
Long Nawang
Muara Wahau
Sangkulirang
Kutai National Park ⑤

Singkawang
Entikong ✕
Putussibau
Nahabuan
Long Bagun
Datah Bilang
Sangatta

Mempawah

Sungai Kapuas
Long Pahangai
Sungai Mahakam
Sungai Belayan
Bontang
Samboja Lestari
Equator

Pontianak ◉
Sanggau
Sintang
Long Iram
Tering
Melak
Kersik Luwai Orchid Reserve
Tenggarong
Samarinda ◉

Nanga Pinoh
Sungai Mahakam ③
Mancong
Tanjung Isuy
Balikpapan ●

Bukit Baka (1617m) ▲
Bukit Raya (2278m) ▲
Tewah
Muara Teweh
Panajam

Pulau Padangtikar
Gunung Palung National Park
Bukit Baka–Bukit Raya National Park
Sungai Kahayan
Sungai Barito

Pulau Maya
Gunung Palung (1116m) ▲
Kasongan
Tanahgrogot

Teluk Sukadana
Ketapang
Palangka Raya
Sebangau National Park
Amuntai
Barabai
Loksado
Selat Makassar

Pulau Karimata
Riam
Negara
Kandangan
Pegunungan Meratus ②

Sukamara
Pangkalan Bun
Sampit
Kuala Kapuas
Banjarmasin ⑥
Martapura
Cempaka
Kota Baru
Pulau Sebuku

Tanjung Puting National Park ①
Banjarbaru
Pulau Laut
SULAWESI

N
0 — 200 km
0 — 100 miles

JAVA SEA

Kalimantan Highlights

① Close encounters with orangutans in **Tanjung Puting National Park** (p246)

② Trekking and rafting in the **Pegunungan Meratus** (Meratus Mountains; p257)

③ Travelling by boat up the mighty **Sungai Mahakam** (Mahakam River; p269) into Borneo's heart of darkness

④ Snorkelling with giant green turtles and manta rays off **Pulau Derawan** (p276) and the **Sangalaki archipelago** (p273)

⑤ Exploring the wonders of **Kutai National Park** while tracking wild orangutans in thick jungle (p268)

⑥ Catching a boat at dawn to see the **floating markets of Banjarmasin** (p253)

KALIMANTAN

How do you combat your country's desire to get rich at the expense of its forests? For the last 20 years, Yayorin, run by charismatic Togu Simorangkir (a former ranger at Camp Leakey), has been empowering villagers to retain their land; teaching them alternative, sustainable agricultural methods rather than a one-off sale to palm oil concessions. Slowly this grassroots movement has gained momentum, with loggers becoming farmers and villagers now wealthier and happier than before. This eco-driven tour de force also runs conservation clubs in schools and their mobile educational unit travels far and wide to engage adults and kids with the reality of their disappearing natural heritage. Yayorin walks the talk, living among communities to gain their trust and actively helping them set up eco-friendly initiatives.

History & Culture

Kalimantan's riches drew Chinese and Indian traders as far back as AD 400. Hinduism and, a millennium later, Islam arrived ahead of Europeans. Dutch and English imperialists began sparring over Kalimantan in the early 17th century; Holland won, while England took Sarawak and Sabah.

Dutch envoys signed treaties with local sultans, though Banjarmasin fought the imperialists in 1859, resisting until 1905. Global industrialisation and expanding wealth spurred demand for traditional commodities and new ones: coal and oil.

Petroleum drew Japan's attention during WWII, and a bitter chapter in the island's history ensued, with Europeans rounded up and summarily executed. It also spelled the end of the white man's rule, for the war's end brought independence to Indonesia. Over the past six decades, Kalimantan has struggled to find its place in Indonesia. Less homogeneous, it has three major ethnic groups: Malay Indonesians from other islands who tend to follow Islam and live along the coasts and rivers; Chinese, traders in Kalimantan for centuries; and Dayaks, Kalimantan's indigenous inhabitants. Each group holds a majority in parts of Kalimantan.

Population has grown through *transmigrasi* (transmigration), a government policy in which Indonesians from outside Kalimantan are given a plot of land here and a fresh start. Clashes between Dayaks and Maduranese, frequent transmigrants, erupt periodically. Economic opportunity increasingly attracts outsiders; with a cast of crusading missionaries and imams, loggers, planters and conservationists, government administrators and traditional leaders, the struggle for Kalimantan's soul continues. Joseph Conrad would be busy indeed.

ⓘ Getting There & Away

The only entry points to Kalimantan that issue visas-on-arrival (VOA) are Balikpapan's Sepinggan Airport, Pontianak's Supadio Airport and the Tebedu-Entikong land crossing between Kuching (Sarawak) and Pontianak. For details on visas to Kalimantan, see p315. All other entries from outside Indonesia – by land, sea or air – require that you have a visa issued in advance. For details on the Indonesian consulates in Kota Kinabalu and Tawau, both in Sabah, and in Kuching, see p307.

AIR Silk Air (www.silkair.net) flies between Balikpapan and Singapore. **Batavia Air** (www.batavia-air.co.id) flies between Pontianak and Kuching in Sarawak, plus Batam near Singapore. **Garuda** (www.garuda-indonesia.com) and Batavia fly the most routes to the rest of Indonesia.

Air schedules and carriers constantly change due to rapid growth and, following major accidents in 2007, heightened safety concerns. Rely on travel agents for the best information.

BOAT Boats depart daily (except Sunday) from Tarakan and more frequently from Nunukan in East Kalimantan to Tawau in Sabah.

Pelni (www.pelni.co.id) and other carriers connect to Jakarta, Semarang and Surabaya on Java and Makassar, Pare Pare, Mamuju and Toli Toli on Sulawesi.

BUS Air-con buses link Pontianak with Kuching (140,000Rp to 200,000Rp or RM35, nine hours), cities along Sarawak's central coast and even Brunei (B$80, 25 hours).

ⓘ Getting Around

Highways connecting major cities in Kalimantan range from reasonable to hopelessly pockmarked. Many connections feature basic buses (inflatable neck cushions most welcome!). Kijang, Kalimantan's ubiquitous taxi, can be chartered between cities. Short journeys can be taken in a Colt, a hop-on, hop-off minibus, usually blue, green and orange, which operates on given routes.

Kalimantan is immense – if time is against you, catching internal flights is the only way to see its scattered highlights. **Lion Air** (www2.lionair.co.id/), **Kal-Star** (www.kalstaronline.com), **Batavia air** (www.batavia-air.co.id) and **Garuda Air** (www.garuda-indonesia.com) are but a few of the many airlines competing for contracts between cities, all of which offer generally decent services.

A *kapal biasa* (river ferry) or *klotok* (wooden boat with covered passenger cabins converted into accommodation) is best for exploring the jungle. Scheduled and chartered speedboats and motorised *ces* (canoe) reach many small towns and tributaries.

WEST & CENTRAL KALIMANTAN

Enjoying fewer tourists than the rest of the country, West Kalimantan (KalBar) is dominated by Sungai Kapuas (Kapuas River) – at 1243km it's the country's longest. However, unlike the more dramatically satisfying Sungai Mahakam, much of the forests surrounding it have been heavily sacrificed to logging and rubber. If entering Kalimantan from Sarawak, your first destination will be Pontianak, which has plenty of accommodation and forward flights to the rest of the country (including Pangkalan Bun). In this chapter we've focused on major highlights, all of which are *outside* KalBar (West Kalimantan).

Formed in 1957 when it split from the south, Central Kalimantan (KalTeng) boasts a variety of landscapes ranging from coastal mangrove to peatland swamps and dipterocarp forest. The area between Pangkalan Bun and Sampit has fallen victim to palm oil plantations. Heavily Dayak, KalTeng is also home to one of the country's highlights: 4150-sq-km Tanjung Puting National Park, inside of which is Camp Leakey, the world's best place for close encounters with semi-wild orangutans.

Pangkalan Bun

🕿 0532 / POP 43,168

At first glance functional Pangkalan Bun doesn't win any glamour awards, but there's a handful of ATMs, hotels, tasty cafes and roadside *warung* (street-side food stalls). Serviced by a nearby airport, it's the easiest place to stay en route to Tanjung Puting National Park and is home to a number of environmental organisations such as Yayorin and two branches of The Orangutan Foundation.

Head to Sungai (river) Arot for more authentic charm, losing yourself among coloured wooden shacks and the romantic boardwalk. The back of the market is lined with *warung* hawking *bakso* (meatballs) and egg noodles; while the river buzzes with cargo-laden ships headed out of the interior.

☞ Tours

The following companies are based outside town and will happily visit you in your hotel to consult on your trip:

Borneo Eco Adventures   ADVENTURE
(🕿25631; www.borneoecotour.com) Headed up by Ari, a fluent English speaker, profits here are ploughed back into reforestation and fair treatment of guides. They organise trips to Tanjung Puting and beyond. Strongly recommended.

Borneo Orangutan Adventure Tour   ADVENTURE
(🕿0062-852-745-600; www.orangutantravel.com) Run by the excellent Ahmad Yani, head of the Guide Association, and the first official guide in Pangkalan Bun. He's honest and can sort your trip to Tanjung Puting and beyond.

Borneo Holidays   ADVENTURE
(🕿29673, 081-2500-0508; borneoholidays@planet-save.com) Owner, Harry Purwanto offers personalised tours of Tanjung Puting and the interior. Harry's slick, English-speaking and a nice guy.

UK-based, eco-responsible tour companies, **Steppes Discovery** (www.steppesdiscovery.co.uk) and **Audley Travel** (www.audleytravel.com) both run well-oiled tours into Tanjung Puting, though it's much cheaper to organise your own trip with the above.

🛏 Sleeping

TOP CHOICE **Yayorin Homestay**   HOME STAY **$$**
(🕿29057; www.yayorin.org; Jln Bhayangkara, Km 1; r incl breakfast 300,000Rp; ✳) Yayorin's (see p242) inspiring headquarters has two new cabins set in lush gardens about 4km east of town. Learn about wildlife and their groundbreaking endeavours, knowing your money is directly helping preserve Kalimantan's forests.

Pangkalan Bun

Hotel Blue Kecubung   HOTEL $$
(☏21211; www.bluekecubunghotel.com; Jln Domba
1; s incl breakfast & taxes 400,000-500,000Rp, d
incl breakfast & taxes 550,000-620,000Rp; ❋☂)
The town's most comfortable accommoda-
tion sits on a hill 10 minutes' walk from the
centre up Jln Abdullah Muhammad. Rooms
have en suites and TVs and are decorated
with an international flair.

Hotel Andika   HOTEL $
(☏21218; Jln Hasanudin 20A; r incl breakfast
70,000-110,000Rp; ❋) Just down the road
from Kal-Star, Andika has 17 en suite rooms
fronting a verdant courtyard. Friendly staff
can organise cars to take you to neigh-
bouring attractions. Its restaurant (mains
15,000Rp; open 8am to 9pm), features Indo-
nesian favourites.

Hotel Bahagia   HOTEL $
(☏21226; Jln P Antasari 100; r 65,000-180,000Rp;
❋) Bahagia has house-proud rooms with
fresh linen, Western loos, TVs, and fridges
for those beers you can't find.

Hotel Avilla   HOTEL $$
(☏27710; Jln Pangeran Diponegoro 81; r incl
breakfast 250,000-300,000Rp; ❋) A kilometre
east of town, Avilla's best rooms are on
the ground floor but all are clean with
TVs, fans, Western en suites and fresh

linen. As close to luxury as you'll get after
the Blue Kecubung.

Hotel Mahkota   HOTEL $$
(☏27002; Jln P Antasari 303; r incl breakfast
190,000-260,000Rp; ❋) Located a few min-
utes east on the main riverfront road of
Jln P Antasari, Mahkota's fragrant, spot-
less rooms are bigger than they should be
given the price. Afternoon tea, armchairs
and a communal seating area upstairs
with swallow-you-up sofas.

Hotel Tiara   HOTEL $
(☏22717; Jln P Antasari; r with fan 70-85,000Rp,
r with air-con 130,000-140,000Rp; ❋) These
mint-fresh rooms in a quiet hotel on the
main drag have tiled floors, Western-style
WC and TV as standard.

✖ Eating

TOP / CHOICE **Pranaban Fish Restaurant** SEAFOOD $
(Jln Hasanudin; mains from 5000Rp;
☺8am-10pm) Down the road from Kal-Star
this semi-alfresco resto is a real gem re-
nowned by locals and expats for its grilled
and fried *bakar* (fish), chicken and duck.
Low-key, friendly vibe.

Meranti   INDONESIAN, CHINESE $$
(☏27487; Jln Kasumayuda; mains 40,000-
50,000Rp; ☺8am-10pm) Fairy-lit Meranti is
roomy with traditional wooden decor and
decent service. Choice swings from ge-
neric Chinese dishes to Indo staples such
as Asam Jakarta Soup, pigeon, steak and
seafood.

Warung Amara Ini   INDONESIAN $
(cnr Gang Addullah Machmud & Jln Kasumayuda;
meals 3000-7000Rp; ☺7am-2pm; ✐) Vegetarians' delight with at least four home-cooked
varieties, plus fish and chicken choices
dished out cafeteria style. Take away or join
the family at a low table.

Iduna Bakery & Café   WESTERN $$
(☏24007; Jln Rangga Santrek 5; mains 15,000-
32,000Rp; ☺9am-9pm) Ambiently lit Iduna's is
perfect for a fix of cappuccinos, beef burgers,
chicken sandwiches, not to mention great
doughnuts, brownies and cakes next door at
its sister bakery. Tempted? Just don't be in
a hurry – the service is dipped in codeine.

Café Quizas   INDONESIAN $$
(Jln Iskandar 635; mains 20,000-50,000Rp; ☺noon-
10pm) Three kilometres east of town, Quizas
occupies a handsome, traditional building
set off the road amid lush gardens. Its menu

is packed with steaks and tasty Indonesian food. Karaoke in the evening!

Find more *warung* on Jln Kasumayuda and Jln P Antasari, supplemented by nightly food stalls. The leading supermarket, **Pelangi** (Jln Kasumayuda), has ATMs.

ℹ️ Information

Many businesses close late afternoons and reopen after dark. Banks around town have ATMs; there's a cluster of them on Jln P Antasari. Internet cafes are happy for you to bring your own laptop and click into their wi-fi.

Apotik Antasari (☑21033; Jln P Antasari 148) Stock up on malaria pills here if you haven't already done so.

Apotik Pondok Sehat (☑21276; Jln P Antasari 86) Well-stocked pharmacy with doctor's offices.

BNI bank (Jln P Antasari) Exchanges travellers cheques and cash.

Pahala Internet Café (Jln Kasumayuda; per hr 5000Rp) Quick connection, no smoking and cool.

Post office (Jln Kasumayuda 29)

RS Sultan Imanudin (Jln Sutlan Syahrir) Hospital.

Tirta Internet Café (Jln Domba 23; per hr 4000Rp) Also sends faxes.

Yessoe Travel (☑21276; Jln Kasumayuda) Books air tickets and runs buses, which leave from its other office on the outskirts of town.

ℹ️ Getting There & Away

Air

Kal-Star (☑28765; Jln Hasanudin 39) has daily flights to Banjarmasin (from where you can pick up flights to Jakarta, Pontianak, Retaping and Semarang), while **Avian Star** (☑25144; Jln Dahl Hamah 2) offers the same as well as flights to the capital, Palangka Raya, on Monday and Thursday (book well ahead or suffer a 15-hour bus journey as penance), and Sampit (three times a week).

Boat

Public speedboats leave from the end of Jln Rangga Santrek for Kotawaringin Lama (50,000Rp, two hours) on Sungai Lamandau.

For ferry services to Java, see p245.

Bus

Buses to Palangka Raya (80,000Rp to 120,000Rp, 11 to 13 hours) continue on to Banjarmasin (125,000Rp to 165,000Rp, 16 to 18 hours) and are run by Yessoe Travel, departing from its office. Avoid arriving in Palangka Raya after midnight – where hotels are mysteriously 'full' – by catching the 7am bus (that said the

night bus spares you the horror of witnessing an endless sea of palm oil plantations). **Maduratna Perdana** (☑22129; Jln P Antasari 17) and **Logos** (☑27275; Jln P Antasari) offer the same routes, as well as Sampit (50,000Rp, six hours).

ℹ️ Getting Around

Taxis to/from the airport (5km) cost 40,000Rp. *Opelet* (motorbike taxis) around town cost 3000Rp. Minibuses to Kumai (20,000Rp, 20 minutes) and *ojek* (motorcycle taxis) leave from the roundabout at the end of Jln Kasumayuda. Taxis to Kumai cost 150,000Rp.

Kumai

☑0532 / POP 23,000

The departure point for Tanjung Puting National Park; come here to choose your *klotok* (boat) and acquire a permit from the PHKA Office (National Park Office) – conveniently situated next to your departure point. A handful of guest houses line the main street, Jln HM Idris. It's also possible to catch a ferry to Surabaya or Semarang. Note: there are no ATMs here so stock up on cash in Pangkalan Bun, 20 minutes away.

🛏️ Sleeping & Eating

Losmen Aloha   LOSMEN $
(☑61210; Jln HM Idris 465; s/d 40,000/60,000Rp) Caribbean-hued Aloha has a restaurant with chequered tables and local fare. Upstairs, there are boxlike, airless rooms with shared *mandi* (dip and pour shower). Laundry service available.

Losmen Permata Hijau   LOSMEN $
(☑61325; Jln HM Idris; r with fan/air-con 70,000/100,000Rp; ❄️) Relatively new, pink-walled PH is still fresh, with a decent cafe and shop selling essentials. Budget rooms have shared *mandi*; the rest have en suites.

At *warung* along Jln HM Idris, try the fresh fish caught a fly-cast away. Open from 6am till 9pm.

ℹ️ Getting There & Away

Reach Kumai by minibus from Pangkalan Bun (1000Rp, 20 minutes). Taxis from Pangkalan Bun airport to Kumai cost 150,000Rp, including all stops for visiting Tanjung Puting National Park (see p248).

Boats run by Pelni connect Kumai with Semarang (160,000Rp, 24 hours) and Surabaya (160,000Rp, 26 hours) three times weekly. The **Pelni office** (Jln HM Idris) is opposite the market. **Dharma Lautan Utama** (☑61008, 081-3483-33444; Jln Gerilya 265) runs boats to Semarang (economy/1st class 140,000/205,000Rp, 19 to 22 hours) weekly and Surabaya (economy/1st class 150,000/275,000Rp, 23 to 26 hours) every four to five days.

Aloha Travel, attached to Losmen Aloha, sells ferry tickets to Surabaya and Serabang as well as onward bus tickets to Banjarmasin (local/VIP 125,000/165,000Rp, 15 hours) and Palangka Raya (local/VIP 80,000/120,000Rp, 10 hours).

Tanjung Puting National Park

Possibly *the* major highlight of Borneo, this unforgettable adventure takes you upriver on a journey reminiscent of Conrad's *Heart of Darkness*. But instead of Kurtz at the end of the trail, you'll be up close and personal with Borneo's great ape in one of the world's last great refuges of the orangutan. To some primatologists the feeding platforms you visit are unnatural and demeaning, but Camp Leakey orangutan foundation has generated global awareness for the apes and provides a sanctuary in a country that does little to protect them.

The only way to experience 4150-sq-km Tanjung Puting National Park is by slow boat (speedboats are noisy and scare the animals); puttering up Sungai Sekonyer.

Tanjung Puting National Park

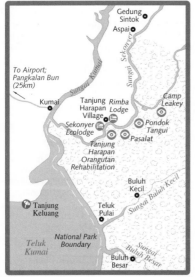

you can see macaques, pot-bellied proboscis monkeys, darting kingfishers, majestic hornbills and – if you're lucky – false gharial crocodiles (best seen at low tide). You're also likely to spot an orangutan hanging silently from a branch hoping for a lift back to **Camp Leakey**, your final stop (they may be cute but don't encourage it).

The reason you'll be gifted such personal interactions with these orangutans is down to one woman and her constant battle to protect the national park from incessant logging and poaching. Dr Biruté Galdikas arrived here in a canoe back in 1971, as a bright-eyed acolyte of famous primatologist, Lewis Leakey (also mentor to gorilla expert Diane Fossey). For the last four decades she's been studying and protecting 'her' orangutans, sometimes drawing criticism from the academic establishment who once lionised her, for over-humanising them. Camp Leakey was her first base, where she made such seminal discoveries as the orangutan's eight-year birth cycle, which makes the species highly vulnerable to extinction. On-site you can still see the decrepit shack she lived in, like some Indonesian rendition of the Munsters house.

Aside from orangutans you may also spot sun bears, porcupines, gibbons and Sambar deer. As you putter upriver keep your eyes peeled for orangutan nests built nightly up in the branches of dipterocarp trees. Ninja-quiet and brilliantly camouflaged, an orangutan's fluorescent-orange aura only lights up when there's sun behind it; as such you may find yourself a few feet away from one without even realising.

The park was Indonesia's first site for the now-controversial practice of orangutan rehabilitation: training orphaned or former captive orangutans to live in the wild (sometimes known as referalisation). Part of the rehabilitation process are the daily feedings to released orangutans at jungle platforms, where you'll go and view them. Feedings last about an hour and take place at three camps: **Tanjung Harapan** at 3pm (orangutans here are semi-wild and less interactive), **Pondok Tangui** at 9am, and Camp Leakey at 2pm (check for schedule changes). Reaching feeding-stations requires a short walk (about 15 minutes) from the dock. Trails can be slippery so wear boots, bring rain protection and vats of insect repellent.

Camp Leakey gets the lion's share of orangutans as most were released around

ℹ ARRANGING A GUIDE

Recommended guides can either meet you in town to take you to your *klotok*, or if requested, wait for your arrival at the airport. It's worth emailing them in advance to check their availability and double-check their rates are similar to figures listed in this title.

there; they're also the most relaxed around humans. Rangers armed with panniers of bananas whoop to empty trees and gradually our distant cousins appear from the dense forest. If you're lucky enough to see alpha male, Tom, be careful not to engage in a staring match (enlarged cheek pads signify an increased level of aggression).

At the end of the wooden boardwalk leading into Camp Leakey there's an excellent information centre highlighting conservation issues, Tanjung Puting's diversity of wildlife and thumbed copies of *National Geographic*.

Pasalat is a reforestation camp where saplings of sandalwood, ironwood and other native trees are being reintroduced to combat logging, mining and fires.

Guides

Taking a guide is not mandatory, but it is vital for facilitating a smooth trip: they'll purchase food, communicate with your *klotok* driver and get you to the feeding platform at the right time, as well as take you trekking. To acquire a licence each guide has to speak basic English and undergo survival training and wildlife knowledge, and they're also excellent at spotting animals.

Recommended guides:

Ahmad Yani (☑852-4930-9250; email: yaniguideteam2lycos.com)

Purwadi (☑815-215-2876; purwadi2010@gmail.com)

Fery Candra (☑813-4961-6480; ferysclub@yahoo.com)

Rustam Efendy (☑856-511-07442; rusty2010@gmail.com)

Andy Arysad (☑813-529-50891; andi-jaka2010@gmail.com)

Guide fees range from 150,000Rp to 250,000Rp per day.

Disreputable boat operators will try to press-gang you at the airport into using their *klotok* and favoured guides; by contacting the above you can ensure this no longer happens.

Rules & Conduct

Avoid travelling park trails without a ranger or guide. Many orangutans are ex-captives and unafraid of humans, so under no circumstances should you approach them physically; they're still semi-wild and certain apes are prone to bag-snatching and occasionally biting visitors. If a female is with her baby be especially vigilant. No matter what boat crew or rangers do, don't feed orangutans or initiate contact with them. Young ones especially are hard to resist, but are highly susceptible to human diseases and you can inflict great harm.

Resist the temptation to swim in rivers – very large saltwater crocodiles still lurk; several years ago a British volunteer was killed swimming just off the dock at Camp Leakey. Water may also be polluted due to mining activities upstream, so wash safely at the river pool or on your boat.

Klotok Hire

Klotok travel is the most romantic way to visit Tanjung Puting. These 8m-to-10m two-tiered wooden boats serve as your restaurant, watchtower and home, and can accommodate up to four adults (two is preferable). Come twilight, you moor on the outskirts of the jungle, your *klotok* flickering in candlelight as your cook dishes up dinner on deck. You bed down early, the upper deck transformed with mattress and mozzie net, reclining on your barge like a Raja. At dawn you wake to the mellow call of the gibbon and myriad animal sounds stirring in a jungle symphony.

Three days, two nights is the average stay, giving you ample time to explore the park beyond the feeding platforms. Boat demand peaks in July and August, but outside these times hiring a *klotok* independently in Kumai is a simple matter. Basic boat designs are similar though all vary in refinement levels, so shop around.

At the time of research, daily rates were 400,000Rp to 450,000Rp for a boat and captain, including fuel. Cooks and food generally cost 100,000Rp per person per day. It's considered normal to provide

THE PEOPLE OF THE FOREST: A FEW FACTS

The average male orangutan is eight times stronger than a human. Semi-solitary in nature, to ascend to alpha status they undergo vicious battles, often losing teeth and fingers in the process. Little love is lost between fathers and sons; Tom, the present regent at Camp Leakey, deposed father, Kusasi, after a long reign, vanquishing him to the jungle. Accession to dominance sees growth in a male's cheek pads, yet after being demoted these soon wither.

Mothers rear their young for seven years – the longest nursery time in the animal kingdom. During this intensely intimate period, they teach them everything from how to climb through the canopy by brachiation (travelling from branch to branch), to the medicinal qualities of plants; which nuts are poisonous, which critters they should avoid and how to mentally map the forest. Rehabilitation of orphans involves as close an approximation to this as possible.

Sumatran and Bornean orangutans differ in a number of ways: the former is smaller, with fairer, softer hair, and chooses to sleep in trees to avoid predators like tigers, while Bornean orangutans often sleep on the forest floor with no such concerns (tigers are long extinct here). Sumatran males also have smaller cheek pads and sport long goatee beards.

the crew's food. So when you add up your guide, food and boat you shouldn't be shelling out more than around 900,000Rp for two people (per day).

Advance book a *klotok* with tour agencies in Pangkalan Bun (see p243) and throughout Kalimantan. Hotels in Kumai can also assist.

🛏 Sleeping

Sleeping on a *klotok* is as much a part of the Tanjung Puting experience as viewing its primates. Only visitors who absolutely must bed down on terra firma should miss it. Some visitors alternate nights on *klotok* and land.

Rimba Lodge HOTEL **$$$**
(☑0532-671-0589; www.ecolodgesindoensia.com; r incl breakfast 500,000-1,500,000Rp; ❇) Riverside Rimba comprises a complex of stilted, comfortable cabanas, enjoying en suites, warm showers and traditional decor. Its restaurant (mains 20,000Rp to 40,000Rp, set menus 80,000Rp to 95,000Rp; open 7am to 9pm) serves Chinese and Indonesian food.

Flora Homestay HOME STAY **$$**
(☑0812-516-4727; r 400,000Rp; Tanjung Harapan) Flora's three rooms are houseproud with fan and en suite. Check out owner Arbana's nearby shop selling locally made handicrafts. Both are located at the entrance to Tanjung Harapan village. Arbana is the man for overnight treks sleeping under the stars.

In Tanjung Harapan village (Tegari Lestari), a few families offer simple **home stays** (r incl dinner 150,000Rp), so ask around. Villag-

ers here used to be loggers until they were recruited by Dr Galdikas to become rangers.

ℹ Information

Visiting Tanjung Puting starts with registration at Pangkalan Bun police station. Bring photocopies of your passport and visa. (Airport taxi drivers know the steps.) This can also be organised by your guide.

Next stop is the **PHKA office** (national parks office; ☑/fax 23832; Jln HM Rafi'l Km 1.5; ◷7am-2pm Mon-Thu, 7am-11am Fri, 7am-1pm Sat) on the way into Pangkalan Bun from the airport. Registration costs 50,000Rp per day per person, and 5000Rp per day for a *klotok* (15,000Rp for a speedboat). Provide a copy of your police letter from Pangkalan Bun and another photocopy of your passport. Then head to Kumai. When the park office is closed, it may be possible to arrange entry at the park's entry checkpoint. Ask your boat captain or guide.

Contact the following organisations for additional information about the region's orangutans, conservation efforts and volunteer opportunities:

Friends of the National Parks Foundation (FNPF; www.fnpf.org) Based in Bali, FNPF runs Tanjung Harapan, Pasalat, plus community education and ecofriendly enterprise initiatives.

☑**Orangutan Foundation International** (OFI; www.orangutan.org; 4201 Wilshire Blvd, Ste 407, Los Angeles, CA, USA 90010) Runs Camp Leakey and publishes *A Guidebook to Tanjung Puting National Park* by Dr Biruté Galdikas and Dr Gary Shapiro.

☑**Orangutan Foundation UK** (www.orangutan. org.uk; 7 Kent Tce, London, NW1 4RP) Works

The dry season runs May to September, when reduced rainfall makes journeys more enjoyable. That said, higher water during the wet season expands boat access. Tanjung Puting's 200 varieties of wild orchid bloom mainly January to March, though in March there is an abundance of fruit in the forest so orangutans may be absent from the feeding platforms.

tirelessly to secure safe 'reintroduction' for orangutans in the Lamandau Reserve (close to Tanjung Puting), as well as supporting conservation groups like Yayorin.

ℹ️ Getting There & Around

Wooden canoes, a quiet alternative to a *klotok* for exploring Sungai Sekonyer's shallow tributaries, can be rented at some camps for 30,000Rp per day. Bring an umbrella or hat and lots of drinking water.

Speedboats from Kumai cost about 400,000Rp, but they're a last resort. It takes less than two hours to reach Camp Leakey, but the trip is uncomfortable, motor noise chases away wildlife, and propellers wreak havoc on river dwellers.

Palangka Raya

☎️ 0536 / POP 213,000

Built in 1957 and once considered as a new capital for Kalimantan, Palangka Raya, its name meaning 'great and holy place', certainly is holy. Mosques and quaint little churches are scattered between wide boulevards, and there are glimmers of greatness with its cantilevered Kahayan Bridge. However, but for the market near Rambang pier and stilted, riverside walkways around Jln Kalimantan, there's little to keep you here.

◉ Sights & Activities

Longhouse-style **Mandala Wisata** (Jln Panjaitan), 2km east of the heart of town, is an arts centre and venue for traditional performances. Shows generally take place on Sunday at 7pm; check the posted schedule for updates.

 Nyaru Menteng Orangutan Education Centre (☎️ 330-8414; Jln Tjinik Riwut Km 29; admission by donation; ⊙9am-3pm Sun), founded by Lone Droscher-Nielsen and run by the Borneo Orangutan Survival Foundation, opens to visitors on Sunday. Special care is taken here to ensure your contact with orangutans is limited and human sicknesses are not transmitted. Normally, a dozen or so orangutans are visible through floor-to-ceiling windows in this sophisticated facility simulating the forest floor. Nyaru Menteng

Arboretum also has a tea-toned peat swamp, with monkeys, birds (best viewed early morning), towering trees, butterflies and mosquitoes, accessible via a patchy boardwalk. Use taxi route A to Jln Tjinik Riwut Km 8 station and take a minibus.

Central Kalimantan is renowned for rattan and bamboo crafts. Souvenir shops along Jln Batam (formerly Jln Madura) sell 'export quality' Japanese-style mats with *kanji* labels.

☞ Tours

Kalimantan Tour Destinations

WILDLIFE CRUISES

(☎️ 323-2099; www.wowborneo.com; Jln Milono Km 1.5) This eco-award-winning business operates romantic, high-luxe river cruises on a beautiful *klotok,* where chances are you'll see wild orangutans. It can also organise home stays and facilitate visits to Nyaru Menteng Orangutan Education Centre, as well as bespoke trips with guides into the interior. Aussie owner Gaye is charming. Head 1.5km south on Jln Milono (taxi route E) to find the office.

Kevin Maulana Tours TRAVEL AGENT

(☎️ 323-4735; kevinmaulana@telkom.net; Jln Milono Km 1.5) Just below Kalimantan Tour Destinations, friendly KM can sort out air tickets, taxi charters and Kijang.

Mulio Angkasa Raya Tour & Travel

TRAVEL AGENT

(☎️ 322-1031; mulio_angkasa@yahoo.com; Jln A Yani 55) Offers booking for flights, car rental and Kijang. Not many staff speak English, though.

At the time of research, the Palangka Raya Guide Association had shut down.

🛏️ Sleeping

Hotel Lampang HOTEL **$$**

(☎️ 322-0033; Jln Irian 2; r incl breakfast 252,000-330,000Rp; ❄️🛜) Nicely maintained hotel with a Western feel (toilets and furniture) by the market. There's also a laundry service and a charming restaurant for breakfast.

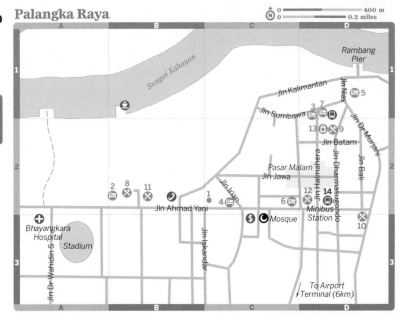

Palangka Raya

Activities, Courses & Tours

Sleeping

Eating

Shopping

Transport

Dandang Tingang HOTEL **$$**
(322-1805; www.dandangtingang.com; Jln Yos
Sudarso 13; r incl breakfast 250,000-415,000Rp, ste

600,000Rp plus 21% tax;) Palatial and cool,
Dandang has comfy rooms with TV, air-con,
coffee-making facilities and hot showers,
looking out onto manicured lawns. Pleas-
antly out of the buzz of town. About 3.5km
east of the town centre.

Hotel Sakura HOTEL **$$**
(322-1680; Jln A Yani 87; r incl breakfast
225,000-375,000Rp, plus 21% tax;) The delightful courtyard and sparkling lobby set
the tone for fresh rooms, some of which
have baths (a rare thing), TVs and generally
springy beds. Opt for ones away from the
noisy road.

Hotel Halmahera HOTEL **$**
(322-1993; Jln Halmahera 24; r incl breakfast
160,000-250,000Rp;) This large, central
hotel by the market offers rooms with TV,
air-con and Western-style bathrooms. It
has some nice little batik decals, fresh linen
and, despite its busy location, the place is
quiet.

Hotel Mahkota HOTEL **$**
(322-1672; Jln Nias 5; r incl breakfast 50,000-
155,000Rp;) Bookended between the market and river, flag-festooned Mahkota has
cool, basic rooms and decent bathrooms
with hot showers.

Hotel Dian Wisata
HOTEL **$**

(☑322-1241; Jln A Yani 68; r incl breakfast 100,000-220,000Rp; ❉) Generously sized, fresh linen rooms, some with oblique river views. There's also an old-fashioned lobby and airy atrium. Be warned, though, you're next to a mosque (as ever) so bring earplugs!

Losmen Cantik
LOSMEN **$**

(☑322-2399; Jln Halmahera 22; r 80,000-133,000Rp; ❉) Basic yet clean digs – standard rooms have shared *mandi* and fan, while superior rooms have en suites, TV and air-con.

✗ Eating

Warung Laris 90
INDONESIAN **$**

(cnr Jln Sumatra & Jln A Yani; mains 20,000Rp; ⊘6-9pm) Lively eatery with vibrant ochre and pink walls, serving up tasty local fare, and despite its proximity to the dusty road it's fresh and clean.

Rumah Makan Melati
INDONESIAN **$**

(Jln Batam; mains 10,000-18,000Rp; ⊘noon-8pm) Bapak Arila grills up the catch of the day – select it yourself – and local vegetables. This breezy, central corner is a spot to watch market life unfold before your eyes.

Telaga Biru
MINIMART **$**

(Jln A Yani) Sells everything from cheese crackers and biscuits, to diapers, chocolate and even eggs. Something for everyone!

Lirissa
BAKERY **$**

(Jln A Yani) It's as though the contents of a patisserie have been airlifted from Paris' Left Bank. This no-frills bakery alchemises frosted doughnuts, custard cakes, chocolate gateaux and homemade biscuits; plus brownies and mouth-watering dumplings. Next to Telaga Biru.

For self-catering, cavernous **Sendy Supermarket** (cnr Jln Ahmad Yani & Jln Dr Murjani) at Palma Mall is your best bet. The food stalls at the **Pasar Malam** (market) run day and night around Jln Halmahera and Jln Jawa.

❶ Information

Several bank ATMs along eastern Jln A Yani accept international cards.

Bank Mandiri (Jln A Yani; ⊘7.30am-2.30pm Mon-Fri) Currency exchange.

Bhayangkara Hospital (☑322-1520; Jln A Yani)

Dinas Pariwisata regional tourist office (Jln Tjilik Riwut Km 5; ⊘7am-2pm Mon-Thu, 7-10.30am Fri) On taxi route A. Has maps and language-hampered help for travel into the interior – it's better to speak to Kalimantan Tour Destinations (see p249).

Main post office (Jln Imam Bonjol; ⊘7.30am-2.15pm) On taxi route D.

Plasa Telkom (Jln A Yani 45; per hr 4500Rp; ⊘7am-midnight) Fast internet, plus telephone, fax, and groceries next door.

❶ Getting There & Away

Air

Garuda (www.garuda-indonesia.com), **Sriwijaya Air** (www.sriwijayaaironline.com) and **Batavia Air** (www.batavia-air.co.id) fly to Jakarta and Surabaya, all with fares from around 360,000Rp.

Kijang go direct to/from the airport (25,000Rp).

Boat

Sungai Kahayan speedboats head to Tewah (300,000Rp, five hours) daily from Gang Flamboyan (Flamboyant Pier), off Jln A Yani. For Banjarmasin, catch the boat off Rambang Pier; the quick option takes six hours, the slow boat, 18 hours.

Bus & Kijang

Morning and evening buses depart for Pangkalan Bun (economy/air-con 80,000/120,000Rp, 14 hours) and Banjarmasin (70,000Rp, five hours) from Milono bus terminal (5km) on taxi route E.

Yessoe Travel (☑322-3466; Jln Banda 7) runs buses from its in-town terminal just north of the market area at comparable fares.

A scheduled Kijang service to Banjarmasin (90,000Rp, five hours) is well organised and comfortable, with a pick-up and drop-off at your designated location.

❶ Getting Around

Minibuses here are called 'taxis' (3000Rp) and ply major thoroughfares. *Ojek* hire costs

---

WANT MORE?

For in-depth information, reviews and recommendations at your fingertips, head to the Apple App Store to purchase Lonely Planet's *Indonesia* iPhone app.

Alternatively, head to Lonely Planet (www.lonelyplanet.com/indonesia, or www.lonelyplanet.com/asia) for planning advice, author recommendations, traveller reviews and insider tips.

30,000Rp per hour. *Becak* (bicycle-rickshaws) congregate on Jln A Yani around the petrol station near Jln Halmahera.

Taxis to/from the airport (6km, 15 minutes) cost 60,000Rp.

Sebangau National Park

This national park was once subject to illegal logging. Canals dug to transport felled timber dried the underlying peatlands, making them more susceptible to burning, as was the case with the severe 1997–98 fires. Researchers estimate the 5687-sq-km park is home to 6900 wild orangutans, among the world's largest populations. Other animals include the Malayan sun bear, gibbons, hornbills, Brahminy kites and clouded leopard. Sebangau's biodiversity includes more than 100 bird species, 35 mammal species and several forest types, most now recovered from the fires of the late '90s. **Tumbang Bulan** is one of the places orangutans can be viewed in their natural habitat.

WWF-Indonesia (www.wwf.or.id) campaigned to establish the park and is at the forefront of plans to involve local groups in low-impact logging, home industry and ecotourism. Its **Palangka Raya office** (☑0536-36997; Jln Pangrango 59) has details on these efforts, and travelling independently to Sebangau. Visitors must gain a permit from the WWF office, which normally takes three days to process, and an English-speaking guide is also essential as you must be accompanied by rangers. All this can be organised by **Kalimantan Tour Destinations** (☑322 2099; www.wowborneo.com); which also runs day trips tracking wild orangutans.

On Sungai Katingan head to **Keruing Village** for very basic WWF accommodation at the field station on Lake Panggualas. You'll need to bring a sleeping bag and recruit a cook or supplies from the nearby village. Local guide **Surakhamansyah** (☑085-252-801 658) can help, and charges around 85,000Rp per day.

SOUTH KALIMANTAN

Covering some 37,000 sq km, KalSel (South Kalimantan) is a province of contrasts, from glimmering rice paddies to the surging Pegunungan Meratus. Despite being Kalimantan's most populated province, 40% of its land mass is heavily forested and dissected by rivers, offering rich pickings for trekking and rafting. Whether it's Banjarmasin's floating markets that beguile you, the swimming buffalo of Negara, or rich Dayak experiences in the misty Meratus range, Kalsel is not to be missed.

Banjarmasin

☑0511 / POP 611,000

Old-timers playing chess on sidewalks, vendors nourishing sleepy cyclo drivers with delicious *bakso;* vast, mazelike markets and creaking timbered houses jostling for space with swank hotels and shopping malls. This is a city where past and present collide. KalSel's 'Venice of the East', with its four rivers interconnected by canals, bustles with life and a colourful Banjarese culture little changed despite contemporary incursions. Banjarmasin is also the base from which to find a guide and head for the dramatic Pegunungan Meratus.

Banjarmasin's main activity bustles around the bend of Sungai Martapura. Most

---

PALM OIL: A DOUBLE-EDGED SWORD

Kalimantan's environment is being stretched to bursting with developed nations offering lucrative returns for mining, logging and the establishment of oil-palm plantations. Palm oil is found in hundreds of products in Western supermarkets and is an important component for biofuel. But this high-yield crop – a boon to the economy and a valuable form of employment for many Indonesians – is the single biggest threat to Kalimantan's forests. Swaths of rainforest have been destroyed, critically endangering Kalimantan's unique biodiversity, for short-term fiscal returns.

The start of 2011 sees a two-year moratorium on clearing forests and peatlands, giving conservationists a chance to establish the argument for 'REDD+ programs', where standing, preserved forests can be monetised and local people financially rewarded for preserving their vital function as global carbon silos. Perhaps then carbon sequestration can finally compete economically with palm oil.

banks are along Jln Lambung Mangkurat. *Angkot* (minibus) routes run outward into the urban sprawl. The *belauran* (night market) around Jln Katamso is a focus of evening activity and a good place for local cuisine.

◉ Sights & Activities

Mesjid Raya Sabilal Muhtadin MOSQUE
(Jln Sudirman) This massive mosque resembles a landed spaceship. During Ramadan, the famous **Pasar Wadai** (Cake Fair) runs along the adjacent riverfront.

Floating Markets CULTURAL TOUR
An evocative reminder of the past, Banjarmasin's floating markets (4am to 9am) shouldn't be missed. Catch a dawn boat (around 5.30am under Hasanudin Bridge) and wend your way through mist-laced tributaries to where traders, their *jukung* (canoes) packed to the gunwales with produce, converge for a morning's business. Taking tea and a cake from a floating *sampan* (small boat) cafe, as this timeless scene unravels before you, is unforgettable.

Pasar Kuin, the best-known floating market, has recently diminished in scale; **Pasar Lokbaintan** (45 minutes from Hasanudin Bridge) is busier, while **Pasar Terapung** is largely uncommercial and much more authentic. Expect to see *tanggui*, the famous broad-rimmed hat favoured by Banjarese, making an appearance as the sun comes up.

Canal Trips CULTURAL TOUR
A trip through people's bathrooms during wash time sounds unappealing, but as water-villagers wash, paddle or swim alongside your boat, you get a glimpse of a lifestyle dating back at least 350 years. Charter a boat with a guide from under Hasanudin Bridge (200,000Rp).

Pulau Kembang ISLAND TOUR
This island is home to noisy long-tailed macaques who'll be waiting for you at the dock. Charter a boat (from 100,000Rp). Caution: macaques can be aggressive.

☞ Tours

With few Western visitors to Banjarmasin, word of your arrival gets around quick among custom-hungry guides, and you may find yourself accosted (pleasantly) in the street.

We worked with **Yasin Mulyadi** (☑0813-5193-6200; yadi_yasin@yahoo.co.id; Jln Hasanudin 33) and found him an excellent guide in the Meratus, with respectful relationships with local Dayak people. **Sarkani Gambi** (☑0813-5187-7858) is friendly, fully licensed and runs tours for large foreign groups as well as bespoke trips for individuals. **Borneo Homestay** (☑436-6545; borneo@banjarmasin.wasantara.net.id), just off Jln Pos and run by trekking expert Joe Yas, has been going strong for years, while **Tailah** (☑436-6100, 327-1685) is another guide who gets consistently glowing reviews. All of the above speak excellent English.

Going rates run from 100,000Rp for canal tours and 150,000Rp for floating markets, including a guide and all transport. Combination tours with Pulau Kaget (home to proboscis monkeys) cost more.

Guide fees for forest trekking start from 300,000Rp per day, plus food, accommodation and transport (usually around 300,000Rp per day for a car and driver, plus 150,000Rp for gas). Rafting costs between 200,000Rp to 250,000Rp depending on your guide.

🛏 Sleeping

Come the weekend, it seems half of Kalimantan descends on Banjarmasin to shop, and it can be a nightmare trying to find digs on a Friday night. To avoid frustration, book ahead.

Swiss-Belhotel Borneo HOTEL **$$**
(☑327-1111; www.swiss-belhotel.com; Jln Pangeran Antasari 86A; s/d incl breakfast from 700,000/760,000Rp; ❈🛜) Upscale, riverside option and ideal for catching a boat to the floating markets. Swiss has a delightful restaurant and a cafe dishing up great sandwiches, Western breakfasts and coffees. The rooms are large and luxurious with cable TV.

Hotel Mentari HOTEL **$$**
(☑436-8944; fax 335-3350; Jln Lambung Mangkurat 32; r incl breakfast 300,000-500,000Rp; ❈🛜) Large, salubrious monolith. An open alcohol policy at the bar makes Mentari something of an oasis. Rooms are comfortable with all the Western trimmings. There's also a spa. Ask for a 25% discount.

Hotel Midoo HOTEL **$**
(☑325-8918; fax 325-0626; Jln Nasution 8; r incl breakfast 150,000-175,000Rp; ❈🛜) A breath of fresh air over the river in Chinatown, this place has friendly staff and 20 sparkling, contemporary rooms. Hot showers, cable TV and very comfy beds. Immaculate.

Hotel Perdana HOTEL **$**
(☑335-2376; hotelperdana@plasa.com; Jln Katamso 8; r 80,000-150,000Rp; ❈) Forty Caribbean-

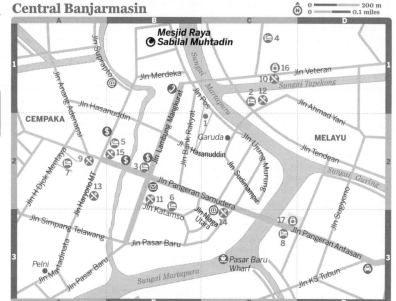

hued rooms around an inner atrium, many of them with air-con and en suites. This quirky, gently ageing hotel is staffed by English speakers and offers a decent breakfast in its cafe.

Hotel SAS   HOTEL **$**
(📞335-3054; fax 336-5967; Jln Kacapiring Besar 2; r incl breakfast 125,000-245,000Rp; ste/f 175,000/195,000Rp; ❄) Attractive, traditional wood decor. The rooms on the east side, with air-con and TVs, are nicer. Ask for a discount, and observe the eccentric staff!

Hotel Mira   HOTEL **$**
(📞336-3955; fax 335-2465; Jln Haryono MT 49; r incl breakfast 175,000-225,000Rp; ❄🛜) Stylish Mira has cable TV in every room, as well as hot showers and Western-style loos. The rooms upstairs with flat-screen TVs and bureaus facing the street are the best.

Hotel Cahaya   HOTEL **$**
(📞325-3508; fax 326-6748; Jln Tendean 22/64; r incl breakfast 175,000-250,000Rp; ❄) Nice rooms with a modern, minimalist feel, free coffee-making facilities and pleasant staff make this an OK choice. Right by the Chinese Temple.

🍴 Eating

Banjarese are crazy about their food. While you're here seek out the local speciality *soto*

banjar, a delicious soup found across the city. Roadside *warung* are the best places to get a real feel for local cuisine. Also, try *belauran* stalls along Jln Niaga Utara.

Depot Kalimantan   BAKERY **$**
(📞325-8286; Jln Veteran 19; mains 15,000Rp; ⏰7am-4pm) Exuding wonderful doughy smells, this homely bakery dishes up armies of pink sponge cakes, croissants, buns and brownies, plus great fruit drinks.

Rumah Makan Abdullah   CAFE **$**
(Jln A Yani Km 1; mains 15,000-20,000Rp; ⏰noon-9pm) Locals say *nasi kuning* (saffron rice) at this unassuming place, next to Hotel Rahmat, is Banjarmasin's best.

Cendrawasih   SEAFOOD **$$**
(Jln Pangeran Samudera; mains 12,000-44,000Rp; ⏰noon-9pm) Delve deeper into Banjar cuisine at this renowned spot. Pick fish, seafood or chicken to cook on the outside grill and enjoy inside with a cornucopia of sauces.

Sate Kijang   INDONESIAN **$**
(📞770-8440; Jln Pangeran Samudera; mains 10,000-20,000Rp; ⏰noon-9pm) Just down from Cendrawasih, this satay cafe/soup kitchen has braziers crackling in the background. The owner's a friendly old guy, as informal as the atmosphere.

Central Banjarmasin

Rumah Makan Jayakarta CHINESE $$
(☎335-8827; Jln Haryono MT 7; mains 20,000-
40,000Rp; ☺7am-9pm) All-day Chinese cafe
selling *kepitang* (crab), *ikan* (fish), *kodok*
(frogs) and excellent *ayam* (chicken) dishes.
Food is cooked on the outside range and –
wait for it – it also sells macaque-sized bot-
tles of Bintang beer!

Pos Indo Plaza FAST FOOD $$
(Jln Lambung Mangkurat) American fast-food
outlets, KFC and Swensen's (ice cream)
here.

Hero Supermarket SUPERMARKET $
(Mitra Plaza, Jln Pangeran Antasari)

🛍 Shopping

Buy maps of the area at **Gramedia** (Jln Veteran 55-61).

Interesting Dayak handicrafts are sold
along Jln Pangeran Antasari (opposite Mitra Plaza); be it woven baskets, beautifully
carved *parang* (knives), as well as Banjarese
batik sarongs (*kain sasirangan*). Stores at

Jln A Yani Km 3.7 sell batik clothes, but large
sizes are hard to find.

There are night stalls around Antasari
Centre and along Jln Anang Andenansi, out-
side the city centre, while **Pasar Belitung**
(Jln Belitung) is on the north side of town.

Mitra Plaza has ATMs, fast-food outlets and Western-style shops in an air-con
environment.

Information

Internet Access

1899 Exclusive Net (Jln R Suprapto; per hr
4,000Rp; ☺24hr) The fastest broadband in
town.

Warnet Kyagi (Jln Pangeran Samudera 94-96;
upstairs/downstairs per hr 4500/5200Rp;
☺24hr) Upstairs level is air-con and smoke free.

Medical Services

Rumah Sakit Ulin (Jln A Yani Km 2)

Money

Major streets and malls have ATMs, plus there's
a cluster at Hotel Istana Barito. For foreign
exchange:

BNI bank (Bank Negara Indonesia; Jln Lambung Mangkurat)

Lippo Bank (Jln Pangeran Samudera; ☺8am-
3pm Mon-Fri)

Post

Main post office (cnr Jln Pangeran Samudera
& Jln Lambung Mangkurat)

Tourist Information

South Kalimantan regional tourist office
(☎327-4252; fax 326-4512; Jln Pramuka 4;
☺7.30am-2.30pm Mon-Thu, 7.30-11.30am Fri)
Even though the staff try hard, tour operators
and guides are more helpful.

Travel Agencies

Adi Angkasa Travel (☎436-6100; fax 436-
6200; Jln Hasanudin 27) Flight bookings via a
few members of staff who speak English.

Arjuna Satrya Wisata Putra (☎335-8150;
ground fl, Arjuna Plaza, Jln Lambung Mangkurat)
Books domestic flights and regional tours. Operates Amandit River Lodge in Loksado (p257).

Carrita Wisata Travel (☎327-4567; Jln Veteran 35) Run by Ricky, who speaks reasonable
English, this solid tour agency is the place to
organise flights and bus tickets if you're based
in Chinatown.

Family Tour & Travel (☎326-8923; familytour-
travel@yahoo.com; Komp Aspol Bina Brata 1E,
Jln A Yani Km 4.5) Books flights and buses to
Pangkalan Bun as well as Balikpapan. Speak to
owner Sam. Closed Sundays.

⊕ Getting There & Away

Air

Garuda (☑335-9065; Jln Hasanudin 31) flies to Jakarta, three times daily (900,000Rp) as well as Palangka Raya (1,620,000Rp). **Sriwijaya Air** (☑327-2377; Jln A Yani Km 2.5) and Lion Air fly to Jakarta (580,000Rp) and Surabaya (400,000Rp). **Batavia Air** (☑335-8996) flies to Surabaya, Jakarta, plus Balikpapan (400,000Rp). **Mandala Air** (☑325-1947; Jln A Yani Km 3) goes to Yogyakarta (350,000Rp).

Taxis to/from Syamsuddin Noor Airport (26km) cost 100,000Rp. Alternatively, take a yellow *angkot* to Km 6 terminal (3000Rp), then a green Martapura-bound Colt. Get off at the airport approach road, and walk 1.5km to the terminal. From the airport, walk to the Banjarmasin–Martapura highway for a Colt to Km 6 (7000Rp). In the mornings roads are very congested, so give yourself a clear hour for the journey.

Boat

Pelni (☑335-3077; Jln Martadinata 10) sails every other day to Surabaya (233,500Rp, 24 hours) and twice monthly to Jakarta (359,000Rp, 20 hours) from Trisakti Pinisi Harbour (3km). **Dharma Lautan Utama** (☑441-4833; Jln Yos Sudarso 8) ferries depart for Surabaya (165,000Rp, 18 hours) every other day.

River boats from Pasar Baru wharf leave five times weekly to Marabahan (15,000Rp, six hours), continuing twice weekly to Negara (20,000Rp, 18 hours).

Bus

The main bus terminal is at Jln A Yani Km 6, southeast of downtown. Colts depart frequently for Banjarbaru (16,000Rp, 25 minutes), Martapura (16,000Rp, 35 minutes), Kandangan (40,000Rp, three hours), Negara (45,000Rp, four hours) and other Pegunungan Meratus destinations.

Several companies run day and night buses to Balikpapan (economy/air-con 110,000/165,000Rp, 10 hours), Samarinda (economy/air-con 135,000/190,000Rp, 13 hours), Muara Teweh (economy/air-con 125,000/150,000Rp, 12 hours), Palangka Raya (35,000Rp, six hours), and Pangkalan Bun (105,000Rp, 20 hours).

One bus leaves daily to Marabahan from Km 6, but it's easier to go to Kayu Tani Ujung in northern Banjarmasin for a Colt (25,000Rp, three hours). There's an extra 500Rp charge for the short ferry crossing. Take an *angkot* to Kayu Tani Ujung (1000Rp) from Antasari terminal.

⊕ Getting Around

Angkot routes (3000Rp) fan out from terminals at Jln Pangeran Samudera circle in the city core and Antasari Centre to the east. *Becak* and *ojek* for hire gather around market areas.

Charter boats (from 25,000Rp per hour) near Jln Hasanudin bridge for canal cruising.

Around Banjarmasin

Three towns southeast of Banjarmasin make worthy day trips, either visited separately or combined.

BANJARBARU

Amid ancient banyan and lontar trees, **Museum Lambung Mangkurat** (☑0511-92453; Jln A Yani 36; admission 750Rp; ⊘9.30am-2.30pm Tue-Thu, Sat & Sun, 9.30-11am Fri) exhibits relics from pre-Islamic Hindu temples, Dayak artefacts, and *halat*, Banjar carved-wood walls and doors. The museum is on the Banjarmasin–Martapura Colt route 30km out of Banjarmasin.

MARTAPURA

Martapura means 'eye of the diamond' and that's exactly what this is – a rough and ready market of precious stones. For US$150 you can pick up a polished and cut, mid-grade diamond from **Bumislamat Central market**, as well as sapphires, rubies and many more. Eat your heart out Jack Sparrow.

Avoid visiting on Fridays, though, when the market swells with workers from Cempaka. Martapura can be visited en route to the Meratus (you pass directly through it).

CEMPAKA

Cempaka's **diamond fields** (⊘closed Fri) illustrate how unglamorous pursuing precious rocks can be. Prospectors work up to their necks in water, hoisting silt to be sifted for gold specks, diamonds or agate. From 1846, 20-carat diamonds have been found in this area – and largest of all, the 167.5-carat Tri Sakti (Thrice Sacred) in August 1965.

To reach Cempaka, take a Banjarmasin–Martapura Colt to the huge roundabout just past Banjarbaru. Switch to a green taxi to Alur (2000Rp) and walk 1km from the main road. Touts aplenty show the way. It's customary to tip these 'guides' 2000Rp.

Kandangan

☑0517

Your final stop before heading off into the interior, Kandangan offers a clutch of decent guest houses, *warung* and a colonial-style market to stock up on ponchos (it rains a lot in the Meratus), comfort grub and torches. There's also a bank with an ATM.

Losmen Loksado (☎21352; Jln Suprapto 8; r fan/air-con 90,000/150,000Rp; ❉), around the corner from the minibus terminal, has fan-cooled rooms with squat toilet and *mandi*. Easily the most atmospheric losmen in town, located on a quiet street with an elegantly faded lobby, **Wisma Duta** (☎21073; Jln Permuda 9; r fan/air-con 90,000/100,000Rp; ❉), has comfortable rooms with *mandi* and squat loos. The management are lovely. You might try **Hotel Mutia** (☎21270; Jln Suprapto; r 175,000-250,000Rp; ❉) whose 12 fragrant, new rooms all come with TV and bouncy beds.

Kandangan's speciality is *ketupat*, sticky rice triangles enjoyed across Indonesia, and served with broiled *harawan*, a river fish, with coconut sauce and a squeeze of lime. Try this at Warung Ketupat Kandangan, 1km northwest of the minibus terminal on the road to Barabai.

The government **tourism office** (☎21363; Jln Jend Sudirman 26), on the main road, 2km south of the town centre, can suggest trek guides.

Colts run frequently to/from Banjarmasin's Km 6 terminal (40,000Rp, three hours) until mid-afternoon. Night buses stop en route from Banjarmasin to Balikpapan and Samarinda around 7pm at a terminal 2km east of town. Catch a Negara-bound minibus (11,000Rp) there, or take an *ojek* (30,000Rp). Pick-up trucks leave Kandangan terminal for Loksado in the morning (12,000Rp, 1½ hours).

Negara

Northwest of Kandangan, wetland Negara is home to some of the world's most spectacular swimmers – water buffalo. The village's buildings are on stilts, the only land above water is the road, and even that can disappear – in floods of mosquitoes, if not rain (so bring vats of Deet).

Farmers rear Negara's water buffalo on wooden platforms known as *kalang*, releasing them daily for grazing and drinking. They can swim up to 5km until 'canoe cowboys' herd them home in the late afternoon.

The wetlands are also remarkable for prolific fish- and bird-life, while the town is noted for forging swords and *kris* (daggers). Surprisingly, Negara has no hotel. You might find a home stay, but Kandangan is a better bet. A few *warung* serve *ketupat* and grilled chicken. Touring Negara by boat costs around 150,000Rp.

Colts from Banjarmasin to Negara (80,000Rp, four hours) leave from Km 6 terminal. From Kandangan to Negara choose among public minibus (7000Rp, one hour), shared Japanese sedan with four people (15,000Rp per person, charter 60,000Rp), or *ojek* (40,000Rp). Twice-weekly boats leave from Pasar Baru pier in Banjarmasin (20,000Rp, 18 hours).

Loksado

Riverside Loksado is hidden in forests and mist-cowled karsts straight from a child's imagination. It's the end of the road (40km east of Kandangan) but gateway to a series of treks through the Pegunungan Meratus, a 2500-sq-km mountain range that brings you into contact with about 20 Dayak villages and a rural way of life recalling halcyon days before industrial logging. Imagine walking through dark, forested jungle to your evening home stay in a former head-hunting village; the drum of the shaman in the distance; damp toadstools glowing with phosphorescence like some weird spectral funhouse; bats and fireflies wheeling around you. Spend a night in Loksado while finding a guide or, if you already have one, head off with plenty of food, a torch and sturdy pair of boots.

A new visitor-information kiosk sets standard prices for services. **Amat** (☎081-3487-66573), a personable Dayak who speaks good English, is Loksado's tourism source.

As ever, we recommend a home stay – you're supporting a village with your visit as well as doing something memorable:

Hotel Wisma HOTEL
(r 200,000Rp) Offers cosy rooms with en suites in a riverside location. To reach it cross the wobbly suspension bridge in the centre of the village.

Mr Alut's Guest House LOSMEN
(☎081-3493-46147; r 130,000Rp) Alut, who's also the person you should see to organise rafting, has accommodation on the shores of the river. Rooms are simple but inviting, with warm blankets and wood walls. Shared *mandi*.

Amandit River Lodge LODGE
(r 200,000Rp) Lies in lush gardens presided over by a misty karst, 3km west of Loksado; no-frills, comfortable rooms with wooden floors and Western toilets. Bring your own food, which can be cooked by the staff. Amandit opens by appointment; give

two days' notice to **Arjuna Satrya Wisata Putra** (☏0511-335-8150) in Banjarmasin.

Muara Tanuhi's **hot springs** (adult/child 3000/2000Rp), 2km west of Loksado, have **Hot Springs Holiday cottages** (☏081-2508-6913; r 110,000-150,000Rp) with two pools and a tennis court. The suburban aesthetic targets Banjarmasin weekenders, but rooms are mildewed and stairways perilously slippery after rain.

Pick-up trucks leave Kandangan terminal for Loksado (12,000Rp, 1½ hours) afternoons, and leave Loksado for Kandangan early mornings.

After treks to the villages listed below, many travellers go **rafting** down Sungai Amandit. The usual drop-off point is Muara Tanuhi, two hours downstream (200,000Rp for up to three passengers). Continuing further downstream to Muara Bubuhi crosses some exciting rapids when the river is high, but costs a lot more. From the nearby road at Muara Bubuhi, minibuses and *ojek* return to Kandangan. Rafting Loksado to Kandangan takes a full day.

Around Loksado

A maze of paths snakes from Loksado through jungle and mountain, taking you across rivers on wobbly suspension bridges, past skeletal longhouses and often bemused villagers who, given the low density of Western visitors, find you fascinating to behold. Mountain paths can be treacherously slippery after rainfall.

Trekking
In order to best absorb the Meratus without getting lost, we strongly recommend you hire a guide in Loksado or Banjarmasin (critical for English speakers). In the event of an emergency you've got someone to watch your back. Guides have solid relationships with villagers – having known them for years. Excellent guide, **Yasin Mulyadi** (☏0813-5193-6200; yadi_yasin@yahoo.co.id; Jln Hasanudin 33), can organise for you to live among Dayak villagers at harvest time, working with them in the rice paddies.

Remember to give your guide an idea of what you want before casting off into virgin jungle – fail to mention a low fitness level and you may find yourself climbing a treacherous waterfall. Ecotourism is still in its infancy and some guides can be cavalier in their approach to potentially dangerous situations.

Guides cost 250,000Rp to 300,000Rp per day; to hire a car from Banjarmasin costs 500,000Rp each way. To reduce costs, make your own way to Kandangan, hop on the local bus to Loksado and find a guide on arrival.

To sample the falls, follow the path from Loksado upstream along Sungai Amandit for three hours (8km) to a series of **air terjun** (waterfalls) past Balai Haratai. Finding the first waterfall is easy, but the middle and top falls and nearby cavern require assistance. Ask for help at Haratai.

Longer treks begin from Loksado or 2km west in **Tanuhi**. The combination of mountains and rivers means plenty of waterfalls and bamboo suspension bridges. The primary forest is a tranquil yet awe-inspiring spectacle. Accommodation is at *balai* (longhouse) along the way, including friendly **Haruyan**, about four hours steep climb from Tanuhi, where villagers farm rice, nutmeg and rubber.

Around Loksado

SHAMAN'S BLUES

In the Pegunungan Meratus the pivotal figure in every village is the *pembeliatn* (shaman). His/her job is to identify bad spirits attaching themselves to the *juus* (soul) of a person, and through invocations and placing himself/herself in a trance, the afflicted soul is purified. Also sought in times of marital distress and for blessings, the shaman is the link between the tangible and those mysterious forces lurking in the forest.

Our home stay in Haruyan village near Loksado brought us in contact with the *pembeliatn;* his drums were rolling as a mute lady led us to their source. A boy lay dying, his family gathered around him in a humble hut. His face daubed in white, the shaman danced around the youth's body rattling bones and bangles, invoking the spirits all night. Despite the presence of mobile phones and satellite dishes in the Meratus, the Dayak spirit world is alive and kicking.

Barabai, renowned for its scenic views, is another terminus for treks. The **Fusfa Hotel** (☎0517-41136; Jln Hasan 144; r 200,000-350,000Rp; ❄) has clean rooms and a restaurant. Barabai minibuses go to Kandangan (8000Rp, one hour).

It's also possible to trek from Loksado to the coast. Reaching **Kota Baru** on Pulau Laut takes three or four days by foot, minibus and boat, crossing Gunung Besar (1892m), KalSel's highest peak. Return to Banjarmasin by bus (55,000Rp, six hours) or take the coast road north to Balikpapan.

MALARIS

A 30-minute walk (1.5km) or 10-minute *ojek* ride through bamboo forest southeast of Loksado leads to Malaris. Its aged *balai* once housed 32 families. Ask the *kepala balai* (village head) about **home stays** (30,000Rp).

UPAU

One of the smallest Dayak groups, Upau's Islam-resistant Deah Dayaks still perform traditional ceremonies, including: the *balian* ceremony to expel evil spirits from the sick, and the *aru*, preparing warriors for head-hunting. Some local families take in guests for home stays. Bring food from Tanjung or Upau's Friday market, and offer a modest sum of money.

There's prime trekking in Pegunungan Meratus, 2km away. Villagers Aman and Dudang know the mountains and act as guides. Take a moderate one-day trek into the foothills, or more strenuous two- or three-day adventures. Terrain can be rough, demanding trekking experience.

To reach Upau, go to Tanjung by minibus from Negara (40,000Rp, two hours) or Colt from Banjarmasin's Km 6 (70,000Rp, six hours). From Tanjung, take a red and yellow *angkot* to Upau (6000Rp, 1½ hours).

EAST KALIMANTAN

KalTim, Indonesia's second-largest province, is home to a colourful mix of peoples including Dayaks, Javanese, Chinese, Banjarese, Bugis and Malays. Sadly for its landscape, it's equally rich in minerals; main cities, Samarinda (long exposed to logging), and Balikpapan (Kalimantan's centre for petroleum extraction), have been major sources of income since the country opened its doors to foreign investment back in the '70s. However, all is not lost, for KalTim boasts dense, unpenetrated jungle, the mighty Sungai Mahakam and some of the best off-coast diving in Borneo.

There is current talk of splitting up KalTim to create a new 'North Kalimantan province', so by the time you read this it may well have lost a few of its northerly towns.

Balikpapan

☑0542 / POP 459,000

Cell phones, swish 4WDs, monolithic hotels and a palpable economic buzz; there's an immediately different vibe in Balikpapan. Offshore oil rigs pipe flames into the night while grey waves roll in along its empty beaches. It's also one of the few places you'll come across children begging, the result of a head-on collision between extreme wealth and poverty. By night, though, the inequities are hidden, the streets aglow with roadside *warung* and a population that loves to hang in the mall.

Shopping mall **Balikpapan Plaza** (cnr Jln Sudirman & Jln A Yani) anchors the town centre.

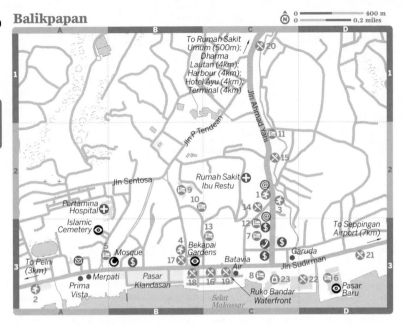

East along Jln Sudirman leads to the airport, west to government offices, plus Pasar Klandasan, which specialises in clothing. Jln Sudirman also parallels the recently revived waterfront with its vibrant fish restaurants. Buy maps from **Gramedia** (2nd fl, Balikpapan Plaza).

Courses

Suprioso BAHASA INDONESIA
(☎081-5455-28484; per hr 135,000Rp) Offers Bahasa Indonesia lessons.

Sleeping

Balikpapan has a wide range of digs, from international shagpile to threadbare traveller trusty. Discount is offered on demand in most upscale places.

Hotel Gran Senyiur HOTEL $$$
(☎080-0122-6677, 820-211; hgs@senyiurhotels. com; Jln ARS Muhammad 7; r incl breakfast from US$120; ✻🛜🛋) Hilltop Senyiur faces off rivals with Louis XV–style pomp; UFO-sized chandeliers, stucco ceilings, piano bar and sumptuous lobby complete with indoor banyan tree. Rooms are predictably lavish and come with every convenience. The number one 'grand' hotel in Kalimantan.

Hotel Gajah Mada HOTEL $$
(☎734-634; fax 734-636; Jln Sudirman 328; s 95,000-235,000Rp, d 135,000-285,000Rp plus 10% tax; ✻) Imposing midrange hotel with great-value rooms enjoying TV, en suite *mandi,* and if you can get one at the back, peaceful sea views. Friendly staff but beware – married couples only if you're travelling as a pair.

Novotel Balikpapan HOTEL $$$
(☎080-7177-7777, 733-111; www.novotel.com/asia; Jln Brigjen Ery Suparjan 2; r incl breakfast 915,000-1,040,000Rp; ✻🛜🛋) World-class hotel, with an ubermodern interior and ambiently lit ceiling, plus a lobby so vast it could rival that of the Overlook Hotel in *The Shining.* There's a patisserie, gym, boutique, excellent pool and numerous cafes.

Mirama Hotel HOTEL $$
(☎412-442; mirama@indonet.net.id; Jln Pranoto 16; r incl breakfast 265,000-500,000Rp plus 21% tax; ✻) Stylish and typically Western, rooms here are tan-walled with deep carpets, tasteful furniture and, in some cases, baths. There's a great cafe selling comfort snacks like hot dogs and sandwiches. Remember to ask for a discount.

Hotel Pacific HOTEL $$
(☎750-888, 750-345; www.hotelpacificbalik papan.com; Jln A Yani 33; s incl breakfast 395,000-

Balikpapan

450,000Rp, d 410,000-520,000Rp; ❄️🛜) This high-luxe businessmen's favourite has a great gym, restaurant with an Asian fusion menu, an imposing lobby and very comfortable rooms with baths, wi-fi and swallow-you-up-beds. You could be anywhere, though.

Hotel Buana Lestari HOTEL **$$**
(📞737-175; buana_lestari_hotel@yahoo.com; Jln Sudirman 418; r incl breakfast 300,000-530,000Rp; ❄️🛜) Eclectic *par accident* with its marble floors, Chinese murals and French paintings, this immaculately clean hotel has elegant rooms, Western en suites, a decent restaurant, massage service and helpful staff.

City Hotel HOTEL **$$**
(📞427-500; www.cityhotel.co.id; Jln Sudirman 45; r incl breakfast 250,000-300,000Rp; ❄️🛜) While it has chic grey walls and minimalist furnishings, this place looks as if it's been

'Tangoed' – everything from the staff's uniform to the couches is bright orange! Comfortable rooms have Western toilets.

Hotel Grand Tiga Mustika HOTEL **$$**
(📞733-788; fax 733-288; Jln ARS Muhammad 51; r incl breakfast from 515,000-610,000Rp, plus 21% tax; ❄️🛜🏊) This heavily Chinese-themed hotel drips with kitsch; be it the lobby's faux waterfall and rosewood chairs or sentinel dragons poolside. Rooms are pristine-white, with cable TV and en suites. The 7th floor cafe offers great city views.

Hotel Ayu HOTEL **$**
(📞425-290; Jln P Antasari, Gunung Kawi 18; r with fan/air-con 140,000/180,000Rp; ❄️) Hidden delight with spotless en suite rooms up a flight of stairs. The cheapest rooms require climbing more stairs.

Hotel Citra Nusantara LOSMEN **$**
(📞425-366; fax 410-311; Jln Gajahmada 76; r with fan/air-con incl breakfast 190,000/250,000Rp; ❄️) Just off the main road, this guest house's shared *mandi* budget rooms are basic – the higher ranks are surprisingly modern – all with a fresh scent. Again, it's a case of married couples only – passport proof required.

✕ Eating & Drinking

Given its expat demographic, Balikpapan caters to a Western palate – be it steaks, fast food and the ubiquity of alcohol. There are some great seafood restaurants on the beach and cheap eats are to be had at all-night *warung* on Jln Pranoto, as well as in pretty Bekapai Gardens (off Jln Sudirman), which set up around 6pm.

TOP CHOICE **Ocean's Resto** SEAFOOD **$$**
(📞739-439; Ruko Bandar waterfront, Jln Sudirman; mains from 18,000Rp; ⏰noon-3pm, 6-10pm) The waterfront has evolved with a colony of decent restaurant-cafe bars, none more so than trendy Ocean's, with its vast display of ice-bound fish waiting to be cooked on the open range.

De Cafe FUSION **$$**
(📞739-439; Jln Sudirman; mains from 18,000Rp; ⏰11am-2pm, 6-11pm) This bakery-cafe is a real gem; chocolate cakes, brownies, pralines, fresh baguettes and eclairs. Its Asian fusion menu makes a nod to Western tastes, with homely snacks and decent salads. Exposed brickwork, comfy sofas and wi-fi might have you coming back for more.

Wisma Ikan Bakar SEAFOOD $$
(Jln Sudirman 16; mains 30,000Rp; ⊘11am-9.30pm) With its colourful aquatic murals (easy to point and order what you want), there's a wealth of *cumi-cumi* (squid) *kepitang*, as well as chicken and fish dished up fresh and daily from the nearby sea.

Restoran Shangrilla CHINESE $$
(Jln A Yani 29; mains 14,000-25,000Rp; ⊘11am-3pm, 6-10pm) This popular, family-run restaurant serves meek and daring Indonesian-Chinese versions of seafood (pages of it!), duck, beef, frog and chicken.

Dapeen Cafe FUSION $
(☎739-140; Ruko Bandar waterfront, Jln Sudirman; mains from 20,000Rp; ⊘noon-3pm, 6-10pm) Close to Ocean's Resto, this chic beachfront joint boasts water features, scarlet-topped tables and low-level lighting. Outside, a decked balcony catches the breeze. Snacks, Japanese and Indo cuisine.

Shang Hai Restaurant CHINESE $$
(☎422-951; Jln Sudirman; mains 30,000-40,000Rp; ⊘noon-3pm, 6-10pm) This Chinese palace of a joint has an encyclopaedic menu offering everything from fried frog and pigeon to a range of Szechuan dishes. Regally lavish, and great sea views.

Bondy's WESTERN $$
(☎424-285; Jln A Yani; mains 30,000-50,000Rp; ⊘noon-3pm, 6-10pm) An expat's institution, offering steaks, homemade ice cream, cakes and terrific seafood picked fresh from beds of ice. There's an alfresco balcony overlooking a courtyard with manicured lawns. Oasis.

D'Cal Rose Cafe INDONESIAN $$
(☎707-911; Bekapai Gardens, Jln Sudirman; mains 20,000Rp; ⊘11am-9pm) Overlooking pleasant gardens, this welcoming cafe cooks terrific *nasi goreng* as well as other Indo staples. The eponymous owner and her impossibly well-travelled husband are great fun.

Warung Rejeki STREET FOOD $
(Jln Sudirman 15; mains 10,000Rp; ⊘breakfast, lunch & dinner) Late-night option for Indonesian mainstays.

Hero Supermarket SUPERMARKET $
(Balikpapan Plaza, Jln Sudirman) Commendable food court here, too.

ⓘ Information

Internet Access
Most upscale hotels have lobby wi-fi if you need somewhere comfortable to work on a laptop. Otherwise try:

Rebel Net (Jln A Yani 26; per hr 5000Rp) Quick connections.

Speedy Internet (Jln A Yani 7; per hr 7000Rp) Air-con, moderately speedy and no smoking rarity.

Medical Services
Pertamina Hospital (☎734-020; www.rspb.co.id; Jln Sudirman 1)

Rumah Sakit Ibu Restu (☎422-304; Jln A Yani 85) Opposite Bondy's.

Rumah Sakit Umum (☎734-181; Jln A Yani)

Money
Banks along Jln Sudirman have ATMs. Many handle foreign exchange:

BNI (cnr Jln A Yani & Jln Sudirman)

BRI (Jln Sudirman 37)

Haji La Tunrung Star Group (Jln A Yani 51; ⊘7.30am-9pm) Moneychanger with several branches.

Travel Agencies
Aerotravel (☎443-350; jony_satriavi@yahoo.com, rivertours@borneokalimantan.com; Jln A Yani 19) Newly established Aero organises specialist river trips up Sungai Mahakam. Also books flights and can help you get to Derawan Island. Ask for English-speaking Jony.

Agung Sedayu (☎420-601; fax 420-447; Jln Sudirman 28) Best source for Pelni schedule and all boat tickets. Also books domestic flights.

Bayu Buana Travel (☎422-751; www.bayubuanatravel.com; Jln A Yani) Very helpful English-speaking staff for flights, Sungai Mahakam tours.

Gelora Equatorial Travel (☎423-251; getbpp@yahoo.com; Jln ARS Muhammad 7) Five of the staff speak good English and can assist with domestic and international flights, tours up Sungai Mahakam, and any travel enquiry.

ⓘ Getting There & Away

Air
SilkAir (☎730-800; Hotel Gran Senyiur, Jln ARS Muhammad 7) flies daily to Singapore (US$330). **Merpati** (☎424-452; Jln Sudirman 32) flies daily to Makassar (370,000Rp). **Kal-Star** (☎737-473; Jln Sudirman 80) flies to Berau (500,000Rp), with connections to Tarakan (761,000Rp), Nunukan (893,000Rp) and Tanjung Selor (761,000Rp). **Batavia** (☎739-225, 766-886; www.batavia-air.co.id; Jln Sudirman 15C) flies to Banjarmasin (395,000Rp), Tarakan (367,000Rp), Jakarta (450,000Rp), Surabaya, Yogyakarta (545,000Rp) and Manado (797,000Rp). **Lion Air** (☎0804-177-8899, 707-3761; www.lionair.co.id; airport) flies to Jakarta (580,000Rp) and Surabaya (305,000Rp). Mandala flies to Tarakan (530,000Rp). **Garuda** (☎422301; Adika Hotel

Bahtera, Jln Sudirman 2) flies to Surabaya (310,000Rp), Denpasar (663,000Rp) and Tarakan (327,000Rp).

Boat

Agung Sedayu (☑420-601) is the best source for all nautical transport information and tickets. See p262.

Dharma Lautan (☑422-194; Kampung Baru dock) runs daily ferries to Mamuju (96,000Rp, 14 hours) and twice a week to Surabaya (350,000Rp) and Makassar (150,000Rp).

Pelni (☑424-171; Jln Yos Sudarso 76) sails to Makassar (economy/1st class 122,000/377,000Rp, 36 hours), Pantoloan (150,000Rp), Pare Pare, Surabaya and beyond.

Prima Vista (☑732-607; Jln Sudirman 138) sells tickets for Pare Pare (125,000Rp, 20 hours), Makassar (150,000Rp, 24 hours), and Surabaya (350,000, 36 hours).

Bus

Buses to Samarinda (economy/air-con 30,000/40,000Rp, two hours) leave from Batu Ampar bus terminal at the north end of town. Buses to Banjarmasin (from 200,000Rp, 12 hours) leave from the terminal across the harbour. Take a route 6 *angkot* to Jln Monginsidi and hop on a speedboat (8000Rp, 10 minutes) to the other side.

❶ Getting Around

Taxis to/from Sepinggan Airport cost 45,000Rp. Or catch a route 7 *angkot* on the highway outside the airport to Damai minibus terminal. Transfer to a route 1 or 3 *angkot* downtown.

Balikpapan Plaza is a focal point for *angkot* (3000Rp). Drivers frequently equip their rides with vast speakers, cranked to ear-splitting levels.

Ojek drivers congregate near Balikpapan Plaza, Gunung Kawi and other strategic spots. Bargaining begins at around 10,000Rp.

Samboja Lodge

▨ **Borneo Orangutan Survival Foundation** (BOS; www.orangutan.or.id) started buying swaths of drought- and fire-devastated land in 2001. The foundation's ambitious plan was to regenerate forests around Samboja; by the middle of 2006, the **Samboja Lestari Land Rehabilitation Program** was in full flow and more than 740 different tree species had been planted. Within this 18.5-sq-km oasis is the **Sun Bear Sanctuary**, home to 52 sun bears from all over Indonesia, some of which had been confiscated by illegal traders. Also here is the inspiring **Orangutan Reintroduction Program**, which has

developed forest schools for young disenfranchised orangutans, providing them with educational playgrounds to learn essential arboreal skills before release to six man-made islands.

Samboja Lodge (☑081-153-7630; www.sambojalodge.com; r with meals US$100, ste with meals US$150-200; ❄) offers accommodation for overnighters and long-term volunteers. Visitors can observe, from a suitable distance, BOS projects, assist and savour 18.5 splendid sq km of regenerating forest.

Samboja Lestari is open on Saturday morning by appointment – other times by special arrangement – for **day visits** (☑0542-702-3600; fax 0542-413-069; admission by donation US$50 Sat, other times US$70). Samboja Lestari is located 90 minutes from Balikpapan and the unpaved approach road requires 4WD during the rainy season.

Two lookout towers and self-guided nature trails facilitate observing three species of eagle, deer, butterfly and occasional wild primates.

Overnight visitors can assist with projects through the **Helping Hands program** (US$20 per day). Tasks include enclosure cleaning, organic farming and wildlife behaviour observation.

BOS also arranges limited visits to orangutan release areas. At **Meratus Forest Camp** (US$50 per person per day), about five hours from Samboja, humans are caged to prevent interaction with released orangutans. Guides lead forest treks to spot orangutans in trees. The price includes meals and accommodation, but not 4WD transport, which is approximately US$100 per day.

During the 1990s, BOS released 75 orangutans into **Sungai Wain**, less than an hour from Samboja. Day-trekking there costs US$37, excluding transport. Plans include a camp for overnight stays too.

If you want to get involved on a volunteer basis, BOS welcomes full-board residents (US$2000 per person per month including accommodation) to help with the animals, building duties and planting primary rainforest trees. Contact volunteer@w-o-x.com to get involved.

Samarinda

☑0541 / POP 350,000

Despite its romantic-sounding name, Samarinda's cracked pavements are overrun with thumb-sized cockroaches, and poverty is acutely visible – particularly in the riverside slums. But don't let us put you off – if you're heading for the natural treasures of Sungai Mahakam, Samarinda makes an excellent base to source a guide. And what the town lacks in cosmetic charm it compensates with friendly urbanites, vivid markets, delicious roadside *warung* and a musical atmosphere courtesy of Indonesian buskers, brightening the polluted air with guitar and song.

The town centres around Pasar Pagi (morning market) and Mesra Indah Mall just opposite. *Angkot* (3000Rp) congregate here. Hotels also cluster here, running north towards Tumendung Airport. The town centre spreads east through Citra Niaga traditional market and west to Jln Awang Long. River boats leave from docks 3km west of the main mosque. Long-distance bus terminals are dispersed around town.

◉ Sights

The striking main mosque, **Mesjid Raya Darussalam** (Jln Niaga Selatan), with its missile-like minarets, is situated between the town's markets, Pasar Pagi and Citra Niaga.

On the south side of Sungai Mahakam, Samarinda-style sarongs are woven in **Samarinda Seberang**. Take a yellow *angkot* from Pasar Pagi.

Every Sunday at 2pm, **Pampang**, 26km west of Samarinda, has authentic Kenyah Dayak ceremonies at its longhouse. Offer a donation for taking photographs. Public minibuses to Pampang leave from Segiri terminal (7000Rp, one hour). Chartering a taxi or Kijang with other travellers for 100,000Rp is an alternative.

⌲ Tours

Samarinda, gateway to Borneo's interior, and an unforgettable *Heart of Darkness* experience up the Mahakam River. Getting the right guide at the right price is essential – there are tragic stories of travellers breaking limbs and being left to die in the jungle by inept guides. Ask for guide certification and a clear itinerary. Recommended guides:

Junaid Nawawi (☑085-2502-49370; junaid.nawawi@plasa.com; Hotel Pirus; ☺2-5pm) Veteran guide.

Abdullah (☑0813-4727-2817; doe21@yahoo.com) Friendly and ever resourceful (even in a sinking boat).

Fajri Deny (☑0852-5009-8887; fajri.denyborneo@yahoo.com)

Suriyadi (☑081-6450-8263)

Rustam (☑735-641, 081-2585-4915)

Jaliani (☑0813-4633-8343)

Tour companies:

Mesra Tours ADVENTURE
(☑738-787; www.mesra.com/tour; Hotel Mesra, Jln Pahlawan 1) Runs full service Sungai Mahakam tours, treks to West Kalimantan, Apokayan Highlands and beyond, and books flights.

De'Gigant Tours ADVENTURE
(☑777-8648, 0812-584-6578; www.borneotourgigant.com; Jln Martadinata 21) In our opinion the best tour company in Kalimantan, offering trips into the interior and up Sungai Mahakam. Owner Lucas will come to your hotel.

⌖ Sleeping

Budget digs are gloomy and should be avoided if possible; midrange options are brighter with fresh rooms, Western bathrooms and cable TV; while top end are world class. In anything but the latter you're likely to encounter the 'we're full' story on arrival. This is because the management must declare a Western guest to the police and often can't be bothered!

Hotel MJ HOTEL $$
TOP CHOICE (☑747-689; www.mjhotel.com; Jln Khalid 1; r incl breakfast 275,000-495,000Rp, ste incl breakfast 465,000-575,000Rp, plus 21% tax; ✲) All 74 fragrant rooms at this contemporary hotel have air-con, en suites, TVs, comfortable beds and Dayak artwork on the walls. Downstairs is a decent cafe, lobby wi-fi and a useful travel agent.

Hotel Mesra HOTEL $$$
(☑732-772; www.mesra.com/hotel; Jln Pahlawan 1; r incl breakfast 320,000-630,000Rp, cottages 850,000Rp, ste 1,648,000Rp; ✲☎☇) On its lush hilltop eyrie on the outskirts of the city, Mesra successfully mixes modern luxury with authentic decor. There's a fitness centre, decent restaurant and travel info service, as well as two pools open for public use (30,000Rp).

Hotel Bumi Senyiur HOTEL $$$
(☑741-443; www.senyiurhotels.com; Jln Diponegoro 17-19; r incl breakfast 720,000-980,000Rp plus 21% tax; ✲@☎☇) This 'Lego' beauty is a breath of elegance, with polished marble floors, spacious rooms with rattan furniture

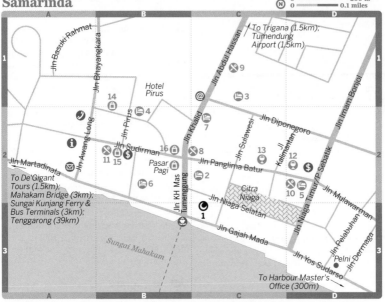

Samarinda

◉ Sights
1 Mesjid Raya Darussalam C3

Activities, Courses & Tours
Hotel Pirus ....(see 16)

⬛ Sleeping
2 Aida C2
3 Hotel Bumi Senyiur C1
4 Hotel Grand Jamrud B2
5 Hotel Grand Jamrud 2 ....D2
6 Hotel Mega Sentosa............................B2
7 Hotel MJ...C2

⊗ Eating
8 Bakso Surabaya C2
Hero Supermarket ....(see 16)

9 Rumah Makan Darmo C1
10 Sari Pacific Restaurant........................D2
11 Sweet Roti Modern B2

🍷 Drinking
12 Déja Vu Bar.......................................D2
13 Platinum Bar C2

🛍 Shopping
14 Alaydrus Souvenirs..............................B1
Bullet Batik ....(see 16)
15 Fitriah Souvenir Shop...........................B2
Gramedia.....................................(see 16)
16 Mesra Indah Shopping Centre..............B2

Information
Internet Café ....(see 7)

and trimmings like flat-screen and cable TV. There's a lovely swimming pool, restaurant and alcohol-friendly bar.

Hotel Grand Jamrud　　　　HOTEL **$$**
(☏743-828; fax 743-837; jamrudhotel@gmail.com; Jln Jamrud 34; r incl breakfast 260,000-450,000Rp; ❄🛜) Hidden down a quiet street, this state-

ly hotel has comfy, nicely furnished rooms, with en suites, cable TV and air-con. It also takes credit and debit cards. A 10% discount is available on request.

Hotel Grand Jamrud 2　　　　HOTEL **$$**
(☏731-233; Jln Panglima Batur 45; r incl breakfast 260,000-450,000Rp; ❄🛜) Lesser sibling to

Jamrud 1, this midrange joint has wood floors, nondescript decor and generally comfy, spotless rooms. There's also an all-day cafe. Curiously, some rooms look out onto next door's outside corridor!

Hotel Mega Sentosa   HOTEL $$
(☎747-015; fax 749219; Jln Veteran 88; r incl breakfast 260,000-375,000Rp; ste incl breakfast 300,000-375,000Rp; ❄) Superior rooms are much more cosy than 'sub-standard' standards, with TVs, Western en suites and comfy beds. The restaurant (mains 15,000Rp to 30,000Rp) offers buffet breakfast and 24-hour room service.

JB Hotel   HOTEL $$
(☎737-688; jbhotel_samarinda@yahoo.com; Jln Agus Salim 16; r 195,000-300,000Rp; ❄🛜) Another 'we're full' offender, banana-hued JB is a schizophrenic muddle of a place, seemingly undecided if it's art deco or Moorish kitsch. Air-con rooms are large and clean. Five minutes north of Pasar Pagi on Jln Khalid.

Aida   HOTEL $
(☎742-572; Jln KH Mas Tumenggung; r incl breakfast from 155,000Rp; ❄) Welcoming you with fairy lights and friendly staff, rooms here are clean with the odd piece of art on the wall to brighten proceedings. Nondescript but central.

✖ Eating

Night cafes proliferate opposite Mesra Indah Mall, with tasty *warung* and unpretentious seafood restaurants further up Jln Abdul Hassan.

TOP CHOICE Bakso Surabaya   INDONESIAN $
(☎732-452; Jln Khalid 4; mains 15,000Rp; ⏰8am-10pm) Directly opposite Mesra Indah Mall, this local, simple cafe is easily the best joint in *el centro* for tasty *bakso*, washed down with a vegetable broth and noodles. Mischievous staff!

Rumah Makan Darmo   CHINESE $$
(☎737-287; Jln Abdul Hassan 38; mains 28,000Rp; ⏰11am-2pm, 6-10pm) This superior but earthy Chinese restaurant with sea-blue walls excels with fresh fish, prawns and squid. Service is friendly and if you're (un)lucky there's often a busker howling outside.

Sari Laut Rumah Makan   INDONESIAN $$
(☎735-848; Jln Pahlawan; mains 30,000-40,000Rp; ⏰6-10pm) The name 'Seafood' is its claim to fame. *Udang galah,* served fragrant, spicy or Padang-style, nets Samarindans and Javanese tourists.

Sari Pacific Restaurant   WESTERN $$
(☎743-289; Jln Panglima Batur; mains 30,000Rp; ⏰8am-9pm) Plush dining, with a menu featuring tenderloin and T-bone steaks as well as beef burgers. Perfect for a carb injection before the basic fare you'll be eating up the Mahakam.

Citra Niaga's many *warung* serve local specialities and Indonesian standards.

Self-catering and snacks:

Sweet Roti Modern   BAKERY $
(Jln Sudirman 8) A cool oasis of scrumptious, calorific sin; this lovely bakery dishes up fresh doughnuts galore, pretzels, sugar buns, brownies and peanut butter!

Hero Supermarket   SUPERMARKET $
(Mesra Indah Mall) Selling everything from fresh fruit to snacky food as well as a deli counter. Good place to stock up on chocolate goodies before heading upriver.

🍷 Drinking

Catering to energy expats, Samarinda's clubs range from hostesses in school uniforms and karaoke booths to high luxe watering holes selling alcohol. Bars open around 7pm and shut between 1am and 3am.

Déja Vu   BAR $$
(Jln Panglima Batur; mains 40,000-55,000Rp; ⏰dinner) Super-slick, low-lit bar and restaurant hidden behind a glazed facade. The menu includes Japanese, Indo and Western cuisine plus a spectrum of cocktails. Upstairs, cool collapses with kitsch karaoke.

Platinum   BAR
(Jln Panglima Batur) Hostess-style bar over-dosing on chrome, darkness and a decent selection of spirits hovering over the bar. Oh, and *more* discordant karaoke.

🛍 Shopping

Mesra Indah Shopping Centre (cnr Jln Khalid & Jln Sudirman) has a mix of local and chain stores, plus a food court; Bullet Batik on the second floor has an impressive range of batik clothes. Citra Niaga shops sell Dayak rattan, carvings and other souvenirs. **Fitriah Souvenir Shop** (Jln Sudirman 10) sells the best range of batik in the city, with finished items as well as rolls of material to choose from.

Keep an eye out for hidden **Alaydrus Souvenirs** (Jln Merah Dehina 58) with its great

Run by Lucas, a Dutchman in Kalimantan for the last 20 years, De'Gigant is hands-down the most professional tour company in Indonesian Borneo. His attention to detail is what counts, with bespoke excursions, licensed guides fluent in English (and a few other languages), and the ability to make things happen in a country where bureaucracy and language are often excruciating barriers. De'Gigant's three-day, two-night trips (5,000,000Rp) up the Mahakam are fascinating, with home stays, Dayak village visits, trekking and wildlife spotting en route. Other adventures penetrate *much* deeper into the interior and last up to 14 days. De'Gigant might not be cheap, but their guides are trust-worthy and Lucas' regional knowledge is unrivalled.

selection of batik sarongs, shirts and semi-precious gems.

For maps, head to Gramedia (Mesra Indah, Jln KH Khalid).

Information

Internet Access
Internet Cafe (Hotel MJ, Jln KH Khalid 1; per hr 10,000Rp; ☺24hr) Free wi-fi in MJ Hotel's lobby, but slow connection.

Sumangkat Internet (Jln Agus Salim 35; per hr 7000Rp; ☺8am-midnight) Plus postal services and wartel.

Warnet Mesra Indah (Mesra Indah Shopping Centre, 2nd fl; per hr 7000Rp; ☺9am-9pm) Free internet use on old console tables provided you eat or drink something from the cafe.

Medical Services
RS Bhakti Nguraha (☎741-363; Jln Basuki Rahmat 150) Clinic.
Rumah Sakit Haji Darjad (☎732-698; Jln Dahlia) Modern, massive hospital. Off Jln Basuki Rahmat.

Money
There are plenty of ATMs in town particularly around **Mesra Indah Shopping Centre**. For foreign exchange:
Bank Central Asia (BCA; Jln Sudirman)
Bank Negara Indonesia (BNI; cnr Jln P Sebatik & Jln Panglima Batur)

Post
Main post office (cnr Jln Gajah Mada & Jln Awang Long)

Tourist Information
Tourist office (☎736-850; cnr Jln Sudirman & Jln Awang Long) Contact English-speaking Dennys for general advice (though pay no heed to his offer of your joining him to hunt wild pigs – would you want to!?).

Travel Agencies
Angkasa Express (☎200-281; aexsri@telkom.net; Plaza Lembuswana) Air tickets.
Prima Tour & Travel (☎737-777; prima_sriol@yahoo.co.id; Hotel MJ, Jln Khalid 1) Air tickets.

ℹ Getting There & Away

Air
Kal-Star (☎742-110; Jln Gatot Subroto 80) flies to Tarakan (960,000Rp), Berau (800,000Rp), Nunukan (1,060,000Rp) and Balikpapan (350,000Rp). For similar rates **Trigana** (☎741-387; Tumendung Airport, Samarinda) flies to Tarakan and Berau every day, Data Dawai three times a week and Long Ampung (800,000Rp) five times weekly. **Lion Air** (www2.lionair.co.id) flies regularly to Balikpapan (730,000Rp). If you're heading to Jakarta fly via Balikpapan.

Boat
Pelni (☎741-402; Jln Yos Sudarso 76) routes visit Pare Pare (170,000Rp, 24 hours), Surabaya (385,000Rp, 24 hours), Toli Toli (134,000Rp, 24 hours), Tarakan (259,000Rp, 24 hours) and Nunukan (225,000Rp, 24 hours).

In addition, there's a twice-weekly private service to Pare Pare (125,000Rp, 24 hours). Just ask the **harbour master** (Jln Yos Sudarso 2) for details.

Mahakam River ferries (*kapal biasa*) leave at 7am from Sungai Kunjang (3km via *angkot*) for Tenggarong (20,000Rp, two hours), Melak (100,000Rp, 16 hours), Long Iram (120,000Rp, 18 hours) and – sometimes – Long Bagun (350,000Rp, 36 hours).

Bus
Samarinda has multiple bus terminals: Sungai Kunjang terminal serves Kota Bangun (23,000Rp, three hours) and Balikpapan (27,000Rp, two hours). Use Lempake terminal at the north end of town for Bontang (25,000Rp, three hours), Sangatta (20,000Rp, four hours) and Berau (150,000Rp, 16 hours). Buses leave when filled from 7am until early afternoon. Minibuses to Tenggarong (10,000Rp, one hour)

depart Harapan Baru terminal on the south bank of Sungai Makaham, reached via *angkot* route G. Minibuses for Sunday afternoon Dayak rituals at Pampang (7000Rp, one hour) leave from Segiri terminal at the north end of Jln Pahlawan.

❶ Getting Around

Minibuses, called *angkot* or taxis (3000Rp), converge at Pasar Pagi.

Taxis from Tumendung Airport (3km) cost 35,000Rp. Alternatively, walk 100m to Jln Gatot Subroto, turn left and catch *angkot* B into town. To charter a car to Kota Bangun costs around 250,000Rp.

Kutai National Park

Under the shade of 300-year-old hardwood trees, 1980-sq-km Kutai National Park teems with sun bears, giant centipedes, monitor lizards, slow loris, giant squirrels and 250 species of birds, including stork-billed kingfishers and rhinoceros hornbills. More immediately you'll come across giant tiger-striped beetles, web-spun tarantula holes and humungous leaves that make you think you've disappeared into *Gulliver's Travels*.

It's a conveniently accessible place to spot orangutans, and **National Park Office** (PHKA; ☑0548-27218; Jln Mularman 236; ◷7.30am-4pm Mon-Thu, 8am-noon Fri) guides work hard to find them; for unlike at Camp Leakey they don't simply arrive at the promise of free bananas. As well, towering banyan trees make for excellent cover – so spotting them requires patience! Early morning is the best time, and if you're here in June, February, March and August, when the forest is replete with fruit, your chances are excellent – you may not have to trek any further than the fruit trees by the veranda of the PHKA lodge, as orangutans come here to feed. It's also possible to spot crocs along the park's mangrove waterways.

By bus from Samarinda's Lempake Terminal (20,000Rp, three hours) head to **San-**gatta, getting off at **Bontang** to register at the National Park office. Registration is free, but a passport photocopy is required. Alternatively, call a day ahead to book a room at the **PHKA headquarters** (r 100,000Rp) in the northern tip of the park, and a trek with head ranger, **Mr Supliani** (☑0813-4643-8803), who can organise your permit so you don't have to waste time at Bontang.

Once in Sangatta the bus drops you at the terminus 3km out of town where you meet rangers Udin or Mr Supliani who take you to the boatman on Sungai Sangatta (stock up on food at the shop by the bridge, to cook at the lodge). The river ride (400,000Rp, one hour) goes to the PHKA headquarters at **Camp Kakap**, the best place in the park to spot orangutans. You'll also need to pay 15,000Rp for a permit into the park. Half-day treks cost 100,000Rp, full-day treks, 200,000Rp (taking you much deeper into the jungle). Avoid the unnecessarily expensive boat ride by taking an *ojek* (30,000Rp each way) from the bus terminal in Sangatta to **Abo Jaya Village**, where Mr Supliani can pick you up.

From Samarinda, Bontang and Sangatta-bound buses run regularly from early in the morning until after lunch to Bontang. From Sangatta, Samarinda-bound buses leave regularly until the last departure at 4pm.

Accommodation at Camp Kakap comprises a basic room at the PHKA Headquarters or identically priced rooms next door at the University of Kyoto research facilities (100,000Rp), complete with jungle noises included in the tariff.

Alternatively, after a morning/afternoon trek in Kutai, retire to a hotel with more comfort but considerably less atmosphere. **Kristal Hotel** (☑0549-550-5292; Jln Pinang Raya 2; r incl breakfast 190,000-300,000Rp; ❄), close to the bus drop, has clean rooms with hot showers and Western en suites. In Sangatta, **Kutai Permai Hotel** (☑0549-550-5292; Jln Yos Sudarso; r incl breakfast 198,000-448,000Rp; ❄) is the businessman's choice.

HANGING BY A THREAD – THE KUTAI DILEMMA

Kutai National Park is a victim at the heart of the country's myriad environmental issues. If the fires of 1997–98 (ravaging some 30% of the park) were not enough, Kutai finds itself host to Borneo's largest open-pit coal mine, oil and gas extraction and a huge population of illegal prospectors. Despite the plaintive cry of conservationists its fate hangs daily in the balance while ministers deliberate whether to sell off land for extraction or preserve the ancient forests and see little financial return.

KALIMANTAN EAST KALIMANTAN

Tenggarong

☎ 0541 / POP 75,000

Once capital of the mighty Kutai sultanate, Tenggarong remembers its past in the **Mulawarman Museum** (Jln Diponegoro; admission 2500Rp; ☺9am-4pm, closed Mon & Fri), which honours the Kutai sultanate that ruled for 19 generations. Notables include a lavish recreation of the royal bedchamber and the hornbill-topped Dayak totem pole out front.

If you're here late September you'll share the city with thousands of Dayaks converging for the colourful **Erau Festival**; a chance to see traditional dances and ritual ceremonies and join a vast intertribal party. Events take place at the *kedaton* (walled city palace) and around town. The Tenggarong **tourist office** (☎661042; Jln A Yani 12) can provide upcoming dates.

For overnights, **Hotel Anda Dua** (☎661-409; Jln Sudirman 65; r 120,000-160,000Rp; ❄) has basic, fan-cooled rooms with shared *mandi,* and out back, comfortable air-con rooms with private bathroom and breakfast included. **Hotel Karya Tapin** (☎661-258; Jln Maduningrat 29; r incl breakfast 175,000-200,000Rp plus 10% tax; ❄) is good value; spotless rooms in an intimate hotel with TV, and showers. It's well placed on a bustling side street with many *warung.*

For food try **Resto Paralayang** (☎665-005; Jln Pahawan, Bukit Biru; mains from 20,000Rp; ☺lunch & dinner), Tenggarong's classiest restaurant, in a house with woven rattan walls and an open courtyard. The menu features Indonesian-style seafood. Meanwhile, **Rumah Makan Tepian Pandan** (Jln Diponegoro 23; mains 10,000-20,000Rp; ☺breakfast, lunch & dinner) is a relaxed, open-air *warung* serving Kutai cuisine and a local spin on Indonesian standards, with a side dish of river views. Find *warung* along Jln Maduningrat and Jln Cut Nya Din, near Jln Sudirman.

Kijang to/from Samarinda (10,000Rp, 1¼ hours) wait at Petugas bus terminal, 5km south of Tenggarong's centre. From here, take an *angkot* into town (2500Rp). *Ojek* cost 5000Rp. Kijang from Petugas terminal also serve Kota Bangun (20,000Rp, two hours). In Samarinda, Tenggaraong Kijang terminate at the end of *angkot* route G, on Sungai Mahakam's south bank.

Mahakam *kapal biasa* (passenger boats) from Samarinda (20,000Rp, two hours) stop 2km north of town, with *angkot* (2500Rp)

to the town centre. Next stop upriver is Kota Bangun (40,000Rp, eight hours).

Sungai Mahakam

The 920km-long Sungai Mahakam is a journey into Borneo's past. Much of the riverbank, especially near Samarinda, bears scars of industrialisation – witness barge upon colossal barge heading downstream, packed with coal – but the deeper you go, the greater the reward, as you pass through gorges and soaring rainforest. Take a detour across lakes dotted with fish eagles; putter down tributaries to old head-hunter villages, beneath screens of tree roots resembling shrunken heads. This is a trip you won't forget.

Double-decked passenger boats leave Samarinda daily at 7am. These *kapal biasa* are comfortable, with an open lower deck for sitting. Remember to bring a good book and something to snack on, for river travel is slow. On the upper level, simple mattresses are laid across the floor for sleeping. If you're making an overnight journey, head directly upstairs to stake a claim (20,000Rp per night).

Much of the year, *kapal biasa* terminate at Long Iram (155,000Rp, 18 hours), 409km from Samarinda. When the river is right, boats continue to Long Bagun, 523km upstream (350,000Rp, 36 hours), where rapids stop them and shelter this section of the river from exploitation.

To explore further, charter a motorised canoe, usually called a *ces* (pronounced 'chess'). It's an 18-hour trip from Long Bagun to **Long Pahangai** through some of the most volatile portions of the river. Only attempt this stretch with seasoned local boaters. Running with the current back to Long Bagun takes six or seven hours.

Ces continue upriver to Long Apari, a focal point for cross-Borneo trips. From there it's about a three-day walk to the West Kalimantan headwaters of Sungai Kapuas at Tanjung Lokan. As ever in Kalimantan, we recommend engaging the services of a guide or tour company.

On the lower Mahakam, it's easy to travel by *kapal biasa*. In the upper reaches, Bahasa Indonesia and/or guides are essential. Some travellers hire guides along the river, others take them from the start (see p264 for information about guides and tour operators). We travelled the

Mahakam with trustworthy **De'Gigant Tours** see p264 and found them to be excellent all rounders.

Expect to pay guides at least 150,000Rp daily (plus food, transport and accommodation). Even without a guide, Mahakam travel gets expensive beyond the *kapal biasa*, with charter rates from 100,000Rp per hour for a *ces* and 1,000,000Rp per hour for a speedboat. The cost of a guide may be offset by his ability to negotiate better deals on boat hires and other transport.

Some travellers complain of disappointing trips so discuss your exact expectations with a prospective guide or tour company before handing over any money. And be prepared to haggle.

KOTA BANGUN

This busy riverside town, a transport hub for the mighty Mahakam, marks the start of many upriver adventures. Most travellers avoid the eight-hour trip by boat from Samarinda, favouring instead the journey by bus (20,000Rp, three hours). From Kota Bangun, bargain for a *ces* to ride the watery 'backroads' via Muara Muntai (300,000Rp, 1½ hours), Tanjung Isuy (350,000Rp, three hours) and Mancong (550,000Rp, six hours). **Maskur** (☑085-250-529-7777), a schoolteacher in Kota Bangun, speaks good English and will work as a guide.

To try spotting the critically endangered Irawaddy dolphin (*Orcaella brevirostris*; *pesut* in Bahasa Indonesia), take a *ces* – never a speedboat for dolphins – to Muara Muntai via Danau Semayang and Sungai Pela. Dolphins are sometimes seen in these waters, but better dolphin-watching lies ahead at Muara Pahu (p271).

In Kota Bangun, **Losmen Muzirat** (☑081-2553-2287; Jln Mesjid Raya 46; r 40,000Rp) is colourfully painted, its rooms simple, fan-cooled affairs with shared *mandi*. There's a decent veranda to watch spectacular sunsets. Directly next door is the best *nasi goreng* in town served up nightly at a roadside *warung*. Further down the road there's an internet cafe and ATM.

MUARA MUNTAI

Built on ironwood stilts and connected by boardwalks, riverside Muara Muntai is charmingly low-key; children rattle over the mudflats on oversized bikes (no such thing as a kid's bike in Kalimantan), while vendors haggle over exotic-looking fruit down the rainbow-coloured street. A decent place to overnight if you're heading to Mancong or Tanjung Isuy (two to three hours away), it comes into its own with the atmospheric night market.

Penginapan Adi Guna (☑0541-205-871, 081-5451-46578; r 50,000Rp) has basic fan-cooled rooms and large, shared *mandi*. There's free flowing coffee and tea and a welcome breeze best enjoyed on the balcony. To find it, follow the boardwalk from the dock and turn right. To the left of the docks around the bend of the river, **Penginapan Tiara** (☑081-3473-76794; r 50,000Rp) has pleasant owners who are happy to cook for you. Their fan-cooled rooms are basic but houseproud.

Reach Muara Muntai from Samarinda by *kapal biasa* (70,000Rp, 10 hours) or bus to Kota Bangun (20,000Rp, three hours) and *ces* from there (200,000Rp, two hours). Chartering a *ces* here for lake cruising costs about 500,000Rp per day.

TANJUNG ISUY

Tanjung Isuy is the Mahakam's first Dayak village. While there are no elongated earlobes, you're equally likely to hear a shaman chanting as a mobile phone chirruping, for the reach of 21st-century culture, though manifest, is only skin deep here.

Tour groups arrive by speedboat for an 'authentic' Dayak experience, mobbing its longhouse for souvenirs, watching pay-by-the-hour Dayak dancing, and zooming away. Activity focuses on **Louu Taman Jamrout**, a longhouse vacated in the 1970s, and rebuilt by provincial authorities as a craft centre and tourist hostel. Independent travellers can commission a dance there for 500,000Rp. There's also an older, decrepit longhouse down the road towards the jetty. Be careful, its floorboards are lethally fragile.

The cruise between Muara Muntai and Tanjung Isuy crosses lush wetlands (keep a vigilant eye out for fish eagle and ibis), shallow lakes and **Jantur**, a Banjar village built on a flooded mudflat.

Tanjung Isuy has two good losmen. About 500m from the jetty, **Losmen Wisata** (Jln Indonesia Australia; s/d 35,000/50,000Rp) offers rooms with double beds off a central dining area. The airy common space has wall-to-wall windows for superior views, and a long, conversation-inducing table. Just next door is **Louu Taman Jamrout** (Jln Indonesia Australia; per person 60,000Rp), where Dayak performances are held. Rooms here are box-like and clean, with warm showers in shared bathrooms and a great communal dinner table. Both losmen have mosquito nets, basic facilities and can suggest the best of nearby *warung*.

Doyo weavings are available at reasonable prices at the craft centre next to Louu Taman Jamrout. Down the road towards the dock, a house across from the first intersection sells carvings and weavings.

Tanjung Isuy is not on the *kapal biasa* route from Samarinda. Chartering a *ces* from Muara Muntai (200,000Rp, 1½ to two hours) is the easiest way to get here. A public *ces* to Muara Muntai leaves daily in the early evening (from 60,000Rp, depending on the number of passengers). You can charter a *ces* direct to Kota Bangun (450,000Rp, three hours), then catch a bus and be in Samarinda or Balikpapan that night. In dry season, Tanjung Isuy is 30 minutes by Kijang or *ojek* from Mancong.

MUARA PAHU

The top spot along the river to view *pesut*, the critically endangered Irawaddy dolphin. An estimated 55 to 75 of these shy cetaceans remain, mainly in this small section of wetland from Danau Semayang through the various tributaries to Muara Pahu.

In the 1980s, *pesut* were common all along the Mahakam to Samarinda. Despite protected status under Indonesian law since 1990, and being a provincial symbol for Kal-Tim, they suffer high mortality rates due to gill-net entanglement and, to a lesser extent, boat collisions and electric fishing. More long term, their habitat is threatened by pollution from speedboats and coal-carrying tugboats, chemical waste from mining, depletion of their prey through unsustainable fishing techniques, and sedimentation in lakes.

Yayasan Konservasi RASI (YK-RASI; Conservation Foundation for Rare Aquatic Species of Indonesia; www.geocities.com/yayasan_konservasi_rasi) fights to save the *pesut,* hoping to create a 70km conservation area along the Mahakam and tributaries, centred on Muara

Pahu. YK-RASI has opened the **Mahakam Information Centre** here, with a riverside veranda for dolphin-watching. It's seldom open, so if it's closed you need to seek out Antok.

The centre arranges *ces* charters around Muara Pahu lasting from one hour to all day (150,000Rp to 600,000Rp), starting with Sungai Bolowan to the Kedang Pahu. Alternatively, Jintan is a black-water river leading into peat swamp. For long trips, bring lunch and plenty of water.

It's also possible to combine dolphin-watching with transport to Maura Muntai or Tanjung Isuy (400,000Rp) via Sungai Baroh, rich with birds and monkeys; to Melak (500,000Rp); and south to Dayak villages Damai or Lambing (600,000Rp). Trained boatmen go slow for wildlife viewing, so travel times vary.

Kapal biasa to/from Samarinda (80,000Rp, 12 hours) pass Muara Pahu in the early evening. **Pension Anna** (r 100,000Rp) has decent rooms.

MANCONG

For optimum jungle drama Mancong is best reached by boat on the Ohong river, meandering past monitor lizards, sapphire-hued kingfishers, bulb-nosed proboscis monkeys and marauding macaques. The journey beneath towering banyan trees, their roots foraging like witches' fingers in the dark river, is as much a part of the Mancong experience as your arrival.

The centrepiece of the village is an exquisitely restored 1930s **longhouse** surrounded by wood-carved sentinels. The locals oblige with welcome dances (available on request for 500,000Rp), which see young and old troop out in traditional attire to enact a 'greatest hits' medley, covering hunting, warrior and incantation rituals and culminating with you being spattered with ceremonial white paint and allowed some target practice on the chief's blowpipe.

There's a souvenir shop with some interesting artefacts. Overnight guests are welcome in the longhouse (60,000Rp per person; no bedding, food or electricity).

To visit Mancong, charter a *ces* from Tanjung Isuy (250,000Rp return) early in the morning, about three to four hours each way. In the dry season, it's possible to travel to/from Tanjung Isuy by *ojek* (100,000Rp, 30 minutes).

Upper Mahakam

MELAK & AROUND

Melak's inhabitants are here to benefit from its rich natural resources; namely coal extracted via open-pit mining, and the town has a rough and ready aspect. While here you may stumble on a *kwangkay* Dayak funeral ritual, cue gambling, brutal cockfights, inebriation and, curiously, the bones and skull of the dead being given a macabre public disco dance.

If you get excited about flowers (and only if), visit the **orchid reserve** at Kersik Luway (16km southwest), noted for its black orchids. Badly damaged in the fires of 1997–98, prime bloom-time is around February.

Eheng (30km southwest), with its 50-year-old Banauq longhouse housing a population of some 30 families, remains a bastion of traditional tattoos and a few pensioners with elongated ear lobes. Residents welcome visitors to spend the night (rates vary), but you'll have to provide your own bedding and food, plus gifts. Reach Eheng from Melak by minibus (12,000Rp, one hour) via Barong Tongkok. Chartering an *ojek* in Melak costs about 100,000Rp a day; a 4WD costs 300,000Rp.

Near Eheng, **Mencimai** has an excellent **museum** (admission by donation; ⊙8am-2pm Mon-Fri) illustrating (in English) local farming practices such as 'slash and burn' (swidden) agriculture.

From Barong Tongkok, minibuses run south to Damai and Muara Lawa (22,000Rp, two to three hours), with an old rattan longhouse. Both villages have losmen.

There's a 24-hour BRI ATM on Jln Tendean. Souvenir shops around town sell rattan and *doyo* (hand-beaten tree bark) bags, hats, baskets and more for 25,000Rp to 50,000Rp, depending on size and quality, plus occasional *mandau* and other relics.

Boats leave daily to Samarinda between 11am and 2pm (120,000Rp, 15 hours, 325km). To/from Tanjung Isuy, charter a *ces* (600,000Rp, four hours).

The daily bus to Samarinda (100,000Rp, nine hours) is an exceedingly uncomfortable ride, much of it on unsealed roads. Minibuses operate between Melak and Tering (15,000Rp, one hour).

🛏 Sleeping & Eating

Most guest houses here are pretty spartan. Melak's food scene is more promising, with riverside restaurants selling great seafood.

Penginapan Rahmat Abadi LOSMEN $
(☑0545-41007; Jln Tendean; r 50,000Rp) Clean, fan-only rooms in this losmen close to the pier, with shared bathrooms.

Hotel Flamboyant HOTEL $
(☑081-253-231-994; Jln A Yani; r with fan/air-con 80,000/130,000Rp; ❀) With its lemon coloured walls, immaculate tiled floors and smart lobby, Flamboyant lives up to its moniker. Western toilets and private *mandi*.

Penginapan Musdayani LOSMEN $
(☑0545-41367; Jln A Yani 2; r with fan/air-con 40,000/125,000Rp; ❀) Standard rooms with fan and shared *mandi*. For a little more you can enjoy en suites and air-con. There's free coffee and a pleasant communal area.

Rumah Makan Jawah Indah SEAFOOD $$
(☑0545-41367; Jln A Yani; mains 20,000Rp; ⊙7am-9pm) Fastidiously clean and cool seafood joint by the river.

Ketapang INDONESIAN $$
(Jln A Yani; mains 30,000Rp; ⊙6-9pm) Opposite the boat landing, Caribbean-coloured Ketapang casts an inviting aroma on to the street – sizzling fried prawns, chicken and fish dishes.

TERING & LONG IRAM

In Sungai Mahakam's gold-mining country, **Long Iram** (140,000Rp, 24 hours from Samarinda) is often the last stop for boats and travellers. There's a handful of colonial buildings on a bend in the river, below rapids rendered impassable when water gets too high or too low.

From the village centre it's a stroll through market gardens or a short *ces* (60,000Rp, 40 minutes) to **Tering**, three settlements straddling the Mahakam. Walk north along Jln Soewondo, turn right at the path to the police station and cross scenic bridges to **Danau Gap** (3km). Some residents of **Tering Lama**, a Bahau Dayak village on the northern bank, still sport traditional tattoos. The village also has four traditional wooden statues and a magnificent church at its eastern end.

To stay overnight in Long Iram, get dropped at the floating cafe on the east bank, climb to the main road, turn right and look for the tiny sign (opposite the two-storey shops) for **Penginapan Wahyu** (Jln Soewondo 57; r per person incl breakfast 70,000Rp).

Down the road, Warung Lestari has the best food on the Mahakam. Order whatever's on the stove.

DATAH BILANG

Datah Bilang is a Protestant community of Kenyah and Bahau Dayaks, who moved from the Apokayan Highlands in the 1970s. Only two older women here still have traditional elongated ear lobes and charge 15,000Rp to 20,000Rp per photograph. **Long Hubung** (100,000Rp, 45 minutes) is another Bahau Dayak village with a basic **losmen** (r 50,000Rp).

Travellers with a thirst for back roads can tackle Sungai Merah northeast into the highlands then cross to Tabang, a rare route that takes around six days. Trekking experience, equipment, food and a Kenyah or Punan guide are *essential*; ask around in Datah Bilang and expect to pay at least 250,000Rp per day for a guide and 200,000Rp for a porter.

LONG BAGUN TO LONG APARI

When conditions allow, *kapal biasa* from Samarinda reach **Long Bagun** (250,000Rp, 36 hours), a small settlement with an abandoned longhouse, a decent shop for supplies, and basic lodgings at **Penginapan Artomorow** (r 70,000Rp). Rapids and shallows have restricted access for large vessels and thankfully protected forests to the east and dampened the impact of modernisation.

From Long Bagun, travellers can charter boats or trek through the forests. River rapids between Long Bagun and the next major settlement, **Long Pahangai**, are treacherous. When conditions allow, it's a four-hour longboat trip from Long Bagun to Long Pahangai, then another day to Long Apari. **Long Lunuk**, between Long Pahangai and Long Apari, is a good base to visit Kenyah villages. Alternatively, stay at **Tiong Ohang**, two hours upstream from Long Lunuk. **Long Apari**, the uppermost longhouse village on the Mahakam, is spectacularly scenic. A boat from Long Lunuk takes five to six hours. From here, cross-Borneo trekkers veer towards West Kalimantan.

To see Sungai Mahakam from the top, fly to Data Dawai, an airstrip near Long Lunuk, with **Sabang Merauke Air** (Teminndung airport, Samarinda) from Samarinda (400,000Rp to 500,000Rp). Their eight-seater, twin prop planes need to be reserved at least a month ahead of flight times.

Berau

☎0554 / POP 52,000

Riverbound Berau comes into its own at night with a slightly carnivalesque atmosphere on Jln Yani; flashing kids rides (operated by pedi-power), fairy-lit *warung*, fruit glowing under paraffin lamps and bobbing Krishna balloons pointing you towards the busy night market on Jln Soetomo.

Berau's international terminal is currently being completed (future flights from Kuala Lumpur, Singapore and Jakarta), so by

---

CASTAWAY ISLANDS OF SANGALAKI

Uninhabited **Pulau Sangalaki** is arguably the prettiest in the Sangalaki archipelago, boasting deserted beaches, turquoise water and washing-powder-white sand-spits. Plankton-rich waters attract giant manta rays; there's a couple of their 'cleaning stations' north of the island. Amid underwater coral formations resembling Venusian landscapes you may see them, though more likely you'll bump into giant green turtles who lay their eggs on Sangalaki's beaches. **Turtle Foundation** (www.turtle-foundation.org) has more information.

Nearby **Pulau Kakaban** is a bizarre evolutionary phenomenon. When geological forces pushed up the atoll, isolating its lagoon, the jellyfish within lost their sting. Swimming among thousands of them in murky waters is eerie and unforgettable. But the real high is back at the jetty where your boatman moors, where the most preserved 'upper reef' in the Celebes Sea drops vertiginously into the abyss. Free-dive past colonies of parrot, bat and clown fish. Passing deep-water itinerants like stingray, barracuda and shark make regular appearances.

the time you read this the exquisite islands of Derawan and the Sangalaki archipelago should be much more accessible.

Sights & Activities

Museum Batiwakkal MUSEUM
(Gunung Tabur Kraton; admission by donation; ⊗8am-1pm Mon-Thu & Sat, 8-11am Fri) Across Sungai Segah, this museum recounts the local sultanate's complex history with rival Sambaliung.

Sleeping

Clean basic digs and upscale luxe giants give you a cross section of choice.

TOP CHOICE Hotel Derawan Indah HOTEL $$
(✆24255; Jln Pangalang Batur 396; r incl buffet breakfast 300,000-400,000Rp plus 21% tax; ❄❋) This huge edifice has the best rooms in Berau, with cavernous bathrooms, plus elegant stained-glass stairwells. The restaurant has an Indo menu. They can also do airport pick-ups. A 10% discount on request.

Hotel Sederhana HOTEL $$
(✆24041; fax 21534; Jln P Antasari 471; r incl breakfast 280,000-365,000Rp; ❄❋) Close to the river, Sederhana has large, well-appointed rooms with granite-grey bathrooms (and baths!), set around a riad-style inner courtyard. There's free wi-fi in the eternally empty cafe. Also attached to the hotel is useful LIA Tours (✆270-7879), who can help with booking flights and taxis to reach Derawan.

Hotel Kartika HOTEL $
(✆21379; Jln P Antasari; r 110,000-165,000Rp; ❄) Spotless midrange option with decent upstairs rooms, with shared *mandi* and air-con as standard. Ground floor gets better and cosier with TVs and Western en suites.

Hotel Rahayu HOTEL $
(✆21142; cnr Jln Pangalang Batur & Jln Gajah Mada; r 100,000-180,000Rp; ❄) Gloomy from the outside, though inside things are brighter, with pleasant rooms enjoying Western bathrooms. Well placed for the night market and riverside.

Hotel Berau Plaza HOTEL $$
(✆23111; Jln P Antasari; r incl breakfast 180,000-250,000Rp; ❄) Despite its proud neon light outside and chandeliered hallway, this is a no-frills hotel. Western en suites, TV and air-con in high-ceilinged rooms. There's a nightclub out back that could be a hostess bar – or maybe they're pleased to see you.

Eating & Drinking

De Boenda Cafe BAKERY $
(✆21305; Jln Antasari 5; mains 10,000Rp; ⊗7am-8pm) Chocolate and sponge cakes, iced coffees, fruit shakes and fresh spring rolls. Watch the morning rush hour alfresco from under an umbrella.

Sari Ponti Restaurant CHINESE $$
(✆21388; Jln Durian 2, 35; mains from 20,000Rp; ⊗8am-9pm) This popular Chinese restaurant has a seafood-leaning menu featuring squid, *tiram* (oysters), frog and *kepitang*, served up in myriad ways.

Marco Polo Cafe WESTERN $$
(Jln Gajah Mada; mains 20,000Rp; ⊗8am-8pm) This new backstreet cafe has alfresco seating and serves up the usual suspects – chicken fried rice and barbecued fish, as well as a number of Western dishes.

Warung Asri INDONESIAN $$
(Jln A Yani; mains 15,000-20,000Rp; ⊗7am-9pm) Overlooking the riverfront, this friendly nook serves fresh eats from *ikan bakar* (fried chicken) to delicious *nasi goreng*. They also do heavenly chicken satay glazed in peanut sauce. Good spot for lunch.

For self-catering, use **Solo SWA** (Jln Sudirman).

Information

Find **ATMs** along Jln P Antasari and Jln Maulana.

BNI bank (Jln Maulana) Foreign exchange.

H2O Net Palace (Jln A Yani 4; per hr 6000Rp; ⊗24hr) No smoking, riverfront internet, with private cubicles and quick connection. Often sporadically closed.

LIA Tours (✆270-7879; fax 270-7283; Hotel Sederhana, Jln P Antasari) Flight bookings.

Primanet (Jln Mangga II; per hr 7000Rp; ⊗24hr) Internet access with comfy pillows on the floor and air-con. Tell the *angkot* driver 'Jln Mangga Dua'. Head down Jln Durian 2 to reach it.

THM Travel (✆21238; Jln Niaga II) English-speaking staff here can help you with flights and advice regarding getting to Derawan and Sangalaki archipelago by boat and taxi.

Getting There & Away

Air

Trigana (✆2027885; fax 2027877; Jln H Isa 2) flies to Samarinda (580,000Rp), Balikpapan (749,000Rp) and Tarakan (330,000Rp).
Kal-Star (✆21007; fax 20279; Jln Maulana

Berau

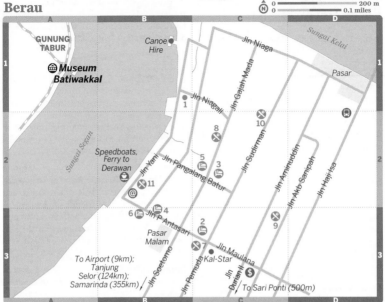

KALIMANTAN BERAU

45) offers daily flights (except Sunday) to Tarakan (379,500Rp), Nunukan (479,000Rp), Balikpapan (699,000Rp) and Samarinda (600,000Rp). **Riau Airlines** (761-855-333; www.riau-airlines.com) flies daily to Balikpapan (500,000Rp).

Boat

Speedboats (*sepit*) to Pulau Derawan (three hours) wait off Jln A Yani. Negotiations may start at 2,000,000Rp one-way, but 1,500,000Rp is more realistic. Far cheaper Derawan transport goes via Kijang (75,000Rp, minimum five persons), to Tanjung Batu, or KM Tasmania I, from where it's a short trip by speedboat to the islands; see p277 for more detailed information.

Bus

The convenient **bus terminal** (Jln H Isa) is just south of the market on *angkot* routes. Buses over good roads to Tanjung Selor (50,000Rp, 3½ hours) are scheduled hourly from 7.30am to 10.30am but won't roll with fewer than 15 passengers. Buses to Samarinda (135,000Rp, 16 hours), over atrocious roads, are scheduled 14 times daily, from 10am to 5pm, subject to the same rule. Kijang (Tanjung Selor 60,000Rp to 75,000Rp; Samarinda 175,000Rp) gather across from the terminal and demand a minimum of four passengers. Buy multiple seats to leave faster.

Berau

Top Sights

Museum Batiwakkal A1

Activities, Courses & Tours

Lia Tours .... (see 6)
1 THM Travel B1

Sleeping

2 Hotel Berau Plaza C3
3 Hotel Derawan Indah C2
4 Hotel Kartika B3
5 Hotel Rahayu C2
6 Hotel Sederhana B3

Eating

7 De Boenda Cafe C3
8 Marco Polo Cafe C2
9 Sari Ponti Restaurant C3
10 Solo SWA C2
11 Warung Astri B2

Getting Around

Taxis to the airport (9km) cost 40,000Rp. Berau *angkot* (3000Rp) drivers are Kalimantan's most compliant, breaking routes to reach your destination. River crossings by fan-tail canoe cost 3000Rp; charters cost 50,000Rp per hour.

Pulau Derawan

📞 0551

Fringed by coral-blue water and powder-fine beaches, this friendly, tear-shaped island is a traveller's dream. It's also one of the richest dive spots in Southeast Asia. Where else can you step off your losmen jetty and be gliding with giant green turtles a moment later? Squid hangs drying in the breeze on sandy Main St and kids gather around you excitedly. By night it's a sleepy affair; braziers glowing on street corners, *bakso* cafes bubbling as the Celebes Sea incandesces with fishing boats.

Among the 30-odd islands in the archipelago, **Nabucco** and **Maratua** have accommodation, however booking is essential and digs are much more expensive if classy (see the boxed text, p277 for more detailed information).

🏊 Activities

Pulau Derawan's underwater activities are conducted from upmarket **Derawan Dive Resort** (📞081-257-411-988; www.divederawan.com; Pulau Derawan) and earthy **Losmen Danakan** (📞086-8121-6143; Pulau Derawan). Individual local dives cost around 250,000Rp, including tank and equipment hire; snorkelling gear costs 55,000Rp to hire per day. Dive trips to Pulau Sangalaki and Kakaban cost around 800,000Rp. Village boats to dive sites cost around 700,000Rp per boat, exclusive of equipment. If you're staying at **Pelangi Guesthouse** speak to Tony about borrowing snorkelling equipment and sourcing a boat and driver. Manta ray sightings are down at the moment; however, the best place to see them is off Pulau Sangalaki.

🛏 Sleeping & Eating

Losmen here are unique, with the sea as your neighbour, their balconies your back garden. There's an absence of luxuries like refrigerated drinks and fruit due to limited electricity (6pm to 6am). Cafes along Main St serve up fresh seafood.

TOP CHOICE **Pelangi Guesthouse**　　LOSMEN $
(📞081-347-807-078; Pulau Derawan; r 150,000-250,000Rp; ❄) Crayola-coloured Pelangi (rainbow) is unfailingly fresh, with stilted cabanas jutting out to sea. A basic cafe, free snorkel gear, private verandas and en suites seal its pole position. Look out for giant green turtles that pop up like periscopes by their jetty.

Losmen Danakan　　LOSMEN $
(📞086-8121-6143; Pulau Derawan; r with fan/air-con 150,000-250,000Rp; ❄) This stilted, fan-cooled accommodation has friendly management and clean cabanas, some with en suites and air-con. Danakan also operates a turtle conservation program with the WWF. Join one of its rangers on a night-time beach vigil.

Derawan Dive Resort　　RESORT $$
(📞081-257-411-988; www.divederawan.com; Pulau Derawan; r 300,000-450,000Rp; ❄) Patronised by divers, its high luxe cabana rooms have wood floors, Western en suites and fresh linen but are somewhat overpriced. The restaurant serves beer, and its burgers and hot dogs are a welcome alternative to fish (mains 20,000Rp).

Losmen Eliana　　LOSMEN $
(📞0812-536-2114; Pulau Derawan; r 100,000Rp) Spotlessly clean, with cool-tiled floors, Eliana sits on the main street, Jln Iskandar. Rooms, which are a little dark, are fan-only with shared *mandi*.

Penginapan Derawan Lestari I　　LOSMEN $
(📞081-347-229-636; Pulau Derawan; r with fan/air-con 75,000-150,000Rp; ❄) Delightful losmen with colourful verandas and air-con. Owner Mr Ismail has a boat that can take you to the neighbouring islands for 700,000Rp.

A FISH CALLED WONDER!

You don't have to be a PADI-certified diver to get the best out of diving on Derawan; an ordinary snorkel trip unveils octopus, hawksbill turtle, lionfish, mandarin fish, spider crab, parrot fish, cuttlefish, pygmy sea horse, scorpionfish, clown fish and moray eel...to name a few! Chances are you'll also get to swim alongside giant green turtles. To see barracuda, shark and manta ray, you'll need to leave the shallow waters of Derawan and hire a local boatman to take you by speedboat to Sangalaki and Kakaban islands. Note that if you aren't a formally trained diver we recommend against busking it here, even though some outfits are happy for you to do so; strong currents, panic attacks and coral cuts are a few things that could endanger your life.

WORTH A TRIP

NABUCCO ISLAND RESORT: PARADISE BOTTLED

Nabucco Island Resort (☏0542-593-635; www.nabuccoislandresort.com; info@nabuccoisland resort.com; Nabucco Island, Maratua atoll; r per person incl breakfast s/d 1,140,000/800,000Rp) is as close to a Robinson Crusoe island as imaginably possible. Its Asian fusion cuisine and beautiful Dayak-Bagao inspired cabanas are well worth the journey, but it's the situation that takes your breath away; within the protective clutches of crescent-shaped Maratua atoll, the water in between, occasionally broken by trippy sandbars, is so perfectly turquoise you feel as if it's been 'Photoshopped'. Guests come to dive with reef shark, giant green turtle, barracuda, tuna, eagle ray and manta. The dive school is world class, and charming traveller-centric managers Evelyne and Rainer may give you a more favourable rate. From Derawan Island, charter a speedboat (850,000Rp) to get here or catch the hotel's speedy taxi boat from Berau (140km).

April's Restaurant INDONESIAN **$$**
(☏081-350-582-483; Pulau Derawan; mains 25,000Rp; ⊗7am-8pm) Wedged between guest houses Danakan and Lestari 1, guacamole-green April's dishes up mouth-watering *ikan bakar* (BBQ fish), as well as fried rice and chicken. We were greeted by a 4ft-long monitor lizard on arrival.

ℹ Getting There & Away

From Berau, the economy route to Derawan is by Kijang (75,000Rp, at least two hours) to Tanjung Batu, and a boat from there. Kijang wait along the riverfront from 9am, but won't leave with fewer than five passengers, which often means departing mid-afternoon while you wait in a cafe on Jln A Yani. Don't be surprised if a different driver appears with your bag in his trunk – your original driver may have failed to find sufficient passengers and handed over your business. At Tanjung Batu, hire a speedboat (400,000Rp to 600,000Rp depending on number of passengers, one hour) to Pulau Derawan. Be prepared to haggle.

A direct speedboat from Berau can cost up to 2,000,000Rp (three hours, 140km). From Derawan, losmen can arrange a village boat to Tanjung Batu (400,000Rp, 2½ hours). Leave early: Kijang depart for Berau at 8am sharp.

Tarakan

☏0551 / POP 103,000

Visited by Japanese and Australian descendants of combatants who clashed on the island during WWII, Tarakan is largely non-descript. If you're overnighting from Tawau in East Sabah en route to Derawan Island and beyond, check out the macaque-rich **mangrove forest** (Jln Gajah Mada; ⊗8am-5pm), 300m from the town centre and an **Australian memorial** (*kuburan Australia*) at the Indonesian military barracks. A

Japanese gravesite (*kuburan Jepang*) is in nearby hills, amid old bunkers.

⌕ Sleeping & Eating

Swiss Bel Hotel Tarakan HOTEL **$$**
(☏21133; www.swiss-belhotel.com; Jln Mulawarman 15; r incl breakfast 400,000-540,000Rp plus 10% tax; ❋❀) For overnights, this hotel has the best international-style accommodation on the island, with a lovely pool and Asian fusion restaurant.

Hotel Bunga Muda HOTEL **$**
(☏21349; Jln Yos Sudarso 7; r 55,000-132,000Rp; ❋☎) This hotel, between the harbours, has wartel (telephone exchange), travel bookings and plenty of smiles. VIP rooms, the only ones with air-con, sleep up to four.

Hotel Paradise HOTEL **$**
(☏22999; fax 32668; Jln Mulawarman 21; r incl breakfast from 100,000-155,000Rp, ste 275,000Rp; ❋) Has midrange comfortable rooms, en suites and a decent Chinese restaurant. Ask for a discount.

Hotel Tarakan Plaza HOTEL **$**
(☏21870; fax 21029; Jln Yos Sudarso 1; r incl breakfast 280,000Rp; ❋) The oldest hotel in the city has revamped rooms already showing signs of wear. The **Angkasa Express** travel office is here.

Warung blossom nightly on Jln Seroja, at **THM Plaza** and **Jln Sudirman**, frying up fresh fish (15,000Rp to 20,000Rp). Also try **Turi Ikan Bakar** or **Bagi Alam I** on Jln Yos Sudarso.

ℹ Information

There are **ATMs** along streets Sudarso, Sudirman and Gusher.

Angkasa Express (☎30288; fax 24848; Hotel Tarakan Plaza, Jln Yos Sudarso) Flights and Pelni tickets.

BNI bank (Bank Negara Indonesia; Jln Yos Sudarso) Foreign Exchange.

Derawan Travel (☎35599; fax 35799; Hotel Paradise, Jln Mulawarman 21) Flights and Pelni tickets.

Immigration office (☎21242; Jln Sumatra) Information on visas and crossing into Malaysia.

ⓘ Getting There & Away

Air

Batavia Air (350,000Rp), **Mandala Airlines** (350,000Rp) and **Sriwijaya Air** (350,000Rp) fly to Balikpapan, connecting to Jakarta, Surabaya and beyond.

Kal-Star (☎51578, 25840; Jln Sudirman 9) flies twice daily except Sunday to Nunukan (250,000Rp), Berau (320,000Rp)and Samarinda (761,000Rp).

Susi Air (☎081-1211-3091) flies to Malinau (250,000Rp), Long Ampung (500,000Rp), Nunukan (200,000Rp) and Long Bawan (450,000Rp), Berau and Balikpapan.

Mission Aviation Fellowship (MAF; ☎22904) offers limited scheduled and charter flights into the interior.

Boat

Pelni (☎51169; Jln Yos Sudarso) ships steam to Makassar (250,000Rp), Pantaloan (110,000Rp), Pare Pare (221,500Rp), Surabaya (365,000Rp) and beyond from Pelabuhan

Malundung, the main harbour at the south end of Jln Yos Sudarso. Travel agents are generally more helpful than Pelni's office.

Morning ferries to Tawau in Sabah (390,000Rp, 3½ hours) depart daily except Sunday from Pelabuhan Malundung. *Indomaya* and *Tawindo Express* run on alternate days and are very similar; choose the day, not the boat. Immigration formalities are at the ferry terminal. Officials take your passport and return it, stamped for Malaysian entry, upon arrival in Tawau. It's also possible to cross into Sabah daily via Nunukan (250,000Rp, 2½ hours, Nunukan-Tawau 75,000Rp, 1¼ hours).

Eight boats run daily to Tanjung Selor (200,000Rp, 1½ hours) from Pelabuhan Tengkayu on Jln Yos Sudarso, opposite the post office.

ⓘ Getting Around

A taxi to/from Juwata Airport (6km) costs 35,000Rp. Alternatively, walk about 200m to the highway and catch an *angkot* (3000Rp). *Angkot* routes follow Jln Yos Sudarso, Jln Sudirman and Jln Gajah Mada. *Ojeks* gather on Jln Sudirman above THM Plaza and across from Gusher.

Understand
Borneo

population per sq km

BORNEO   USA   UK

≈ 30 people

Borneo Today

Deforestation

For information on threats to Borneo's forests, see p293.

Corruption in High Places

Sarawak and Sabah are likely to be key battlegrounds in Malaysia's next general election, which must be held by mid 2013.

Nothing rankles with Borneans more than senior politicians who line their pockets at the expense of the public purse, the island's dwindling rainforests and the land rights of indigenous people. Such matters are almost never reported in the local print and electronic media. In cyberspace, however, there are accounts of state politicians growing rich from deals with favoured companies, including logging conglomerates.

Popular anger at the behaviour of the political elite is likely to bolster electoral support for candidates running against Malaysia's Barisan Nasional coalition, led by the United Malays National Organization (UMNO) of former prime minister Mahathir Mohamad. In a 2010 by-election in Sibu, the opposition candidate won a narrow victory, which may explain why the government has recently been investing a great deal of money in Sarawak's infrastructure.

Inter-Ethnic Relations

When two Borneans meet, the first thing they want to know about each other is their ethnicity. Intermarriage between Borneo's varied ethnic groups, including the Chinese, has been going on for thousands of years, so a person's outward appearance provides few clues about their background. But without this vital bit of biographical information, Borneans don't know quite where to place each other in the island's complicated ethnic and legal patchwork.

Relations between the dozens of ethnic groups in Sarawak and Sabah tend to be more relaxed and open than in Peninsular Malaysia but the

Courtesy Call

If you show up unannounced at a Dayak longhouse, etiquette requires that you present yourself to the head man straight away. When you say, 'take me to your leader', you may feel like an alien in a 1950s sci-fi flick!

It's Rude to Point

Pointing with your index finger, especially towards anything sacred, is a no-no. If you must indicate something in a particular direction, do as the locals do and use your thumb.

Leech Etiquette

If you pluck off a leech (see p29), don't just flick it onto the ground, where it might rebound to attack your friends. Follow jungle best practice and chop it in two with your *parang* (Dayak machete).

belief systems
(% of population)

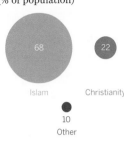

68
Islam

22
Christianity

10
Other

if Borneo were 100 people

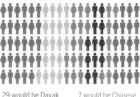

29 would be Dayak
19 would be Banjarese
14 would be Malay
12 would be Javanese

7 would be Chinese
19 would be other

states are not quite the multicultural paradise portrayed in Tourism Malaysia's 'Malaysia – Truly Asia!' campaign. Malays form the majority in a country based on *ketuanan Melayu* (Malay supremacy) but are a minority in Sabah and Sarawak; ethnic Chinese wonder about their place in a society that treats them as outsiders generations after their ancestors put down roots; and members of indigenous groups (Dayaks) juggle tribal identity and religious affiliation (the vast majority are Christian) in a Muslim-majority society that knows little about them.

Marriages are common between Dayak groups that hunted each other's heads just a few generations back, and between Dayaks and Chinese. Some Dayak parents, seeking the best education for their children, send them to academically rigorous Chinese schools, further blurring cultural lines. There are fewer intermarriages with Malays, in part because a non-Muslim must convert to Islam to marry a Muslim.

Ethnic Preferences

Following the race riots of 1969, the Malaysian government implemented a policy of 'affirmative action', ie positive discrimination, to give the majority Malays a more equitable share of the economic pie. The result was a range of subsidies and preferences designed to benefit a category of people called Bumiputra ('sons of the soil') that encompasses Malays and, in Sabah and Sarawak, indigenous groups (Dayaks) – that is, virtually everyone except the Chinese (and, on the mainland, Indians).

As a result of these policies, ethnic Chinese have found themselves facing quotas and discrimination in housing, higher education and public-sector jobs. Critics say the system has created incentives in which individual merit counts less than your background; wealthy, powerful Malays grow ever richer at the expense of poor Malays; and Malaysia's

For the opposition's take on Sarawak's ruling elite, check out http://moc sarawak.word press.com.

Colonialism

While Dutch colonialism is still resented in Kalimantan, most people in Sarawak view the rule of the White Rajahs as having been well-intentioned and, overall, benevolent and beneficial.

1Malaysia

The campaign for Malaysian national unity and ethnic harmony, '1Malaysia', is supposed to promote eight values: perseverance, a culture of excellence, acceptance, loyalty, education, humility, integrity and meritocracy.

MIB

Malay Islamic Monarchy, or MIB, is the 'national philosophy' of Brunei. It emphasises Malay language, culture and customs, Islamic laws and values, and the legitimacy of the sultan.

global competitiveness is sapped. Some Chinese have become frustrated and alienated, causing a brain drain the country can ill afford. Reform, however, is difficult as entrenched Malay interest groups oppose reforms with populist passion.

Some Dayaks jokingly refer to themselves as 'third-class Bumiputra' because while they are supposed to be among the beneficiaries of affirmative action, most advantages seem to accrue to ethnic Malays.

Inter-Religious Relations

In Brunei, the government offers financial incentives to convert to Islam. Baha'ism is banned.

Muslim-Christian relations in Malaysia were clouded in 2010 as the result of a campaign by Muslim fundamentalists to forbid Christians from referring to God as 'Allah' in Bahasa Malaysia. Intra-religious relations in Sabah and Sarawak are less fraught than on the mainland, but Christians and Chinese (these groups overlap to a certain degree) as well as Muslim moderates often express concern that the island – especially Sabah – is not immune from the Islamist winds blowing in other parts of the country.

Anecdotal evidence indicates that whereas in the past Muslims and Christians often participated in each other's communal festivities (Ramadan, Chinese New Year), such easy mingling is becoming less frequent these days, especially among younger people.

Malaysian law, parts of which are based on sharia (Islamic law) and, for Muslims, handled by sharia (Syariah) courts, all but prohibits Muslims from converting to another religion but allows Muslims to proselytise among non-Muslims. Shia Islam is restricted in Malaysia, which follows the Sunni tradition, as is the Baha'i faith.

Head-hunting

Don't be taken aback if your Dayak hosts make self-deprecating jokes about head-hunting. Most Dayaks accept matter-of-factly that taking heads used to be part of their culture – and are glad colonial authorities put an end to the practice.

Colonial Life

If you'd like to get a sense of life in colonial-era Borneo, read *Land Below the Wind* by Agnes Newton Keith and *My Life in Sarawak* by Margaret Brooke, the wife of White Rajah Charles Brooke.

Borneo in Film

» *Three Came Home* (1950) Portrays survival in a Japanese prisoner-of-war camp. Based on a book by Agnes Newton Keith.

» *Survivor* (2000) The first season of the US TV show was filmed on the island of Pulau Tiga in Sabah.

History

Borneo was connected to mainland Southeast Asia – as part of a land mass known as Sundaland – from about 2.5 million years ago until rising sea levels turned it back into an island about 10,000 years ago. Archaeological evidence suggests that human beings arrived in Sarawak – overland – at least 40,000 years ago. More migrants arrived some 3000 years ago, probably from southern China, mixing with earlier inhabitants to form some of Borneo's indigenous groups.

Traders from India and China began stopping by Borneo – as a sideshow to their bilateral commerce – around the 1st century AD, introducing Hinduism and Buddhism. From about 500 AD, Chinese traders started settling along Borneo's coasts. It is believed that the influence of the Sumatra-based kingdom of Srivijaya (7th to 13th centuries) extended to Borneo. During this time, Brunei emerged as a centre for trade with China, and some historians believe that the first Muslims to visit Borneo came from China in the 10th century.

Islam was brought to present-day Peninsular Malaysia, including Melaka, by traders from South India in the early 15th century. Through diplomacy, often cemented by marriage, Borneo's coastal sultanates turned towards Melaka and Islam. Brunei's sultan married a Melaka princess and Sharif Ali, a descendant of the Prophet Mohammed, married a Brunei royal and became sultan, introducing a legal system based on Islamic law.

In the late 15th century, Europeans began to seek a direct role in the rich Asian trade. Christopher Columbus failed to reach India by sailing west, but Portugal's Vasco da Gama found the way around Africa in 1498. In 1511 Portugal conquered Melaka in its bid to control the lucrative spice trade. As a result, Muslim merchants moved much of their custom to Borneo's sultanates, and Brunei succeeded Melaka as the regional Islamic trading centre.

> Archaeological finds in western Borneo include glass beads from the Roman Empire.

> The name Borneo comes from foreigners, and is either a mispronunciation of Brunei or *buah nyior*, Malay for coconut; Malays and Indonesians call the island Kalimantan.

TIMELINE	2.5 million BC	1st century AD	600s-1200s
	Borneo is attached to mainland Southeast Asia as part of Sundaland. Rising seas transform Borneo into the world's third-largest island about 10,000 years ago.	Chinese and Indian traders detour to Borneo. By AD 500, Chinese are settling in coastal present-day West Kalimantan.	Sumatra's Hindu-Buddhist Srivijaya kingdom dominates Southeast Asia's sea trade. Under Srivijaya, ethnic Malays immigrate to Borneo.

Under Sultan Bolkiah in the 16th century, Brunei was Borneo's most powerful kingdom, its influence extending from Kuching all the way to the island of Luzon, now in the Philippines. In subsequent centuries, however, facing a succession of rebellions, Brunei's rulers repeatedly turned to foreigners for help. In exchange for assistance in suppressing an uprising in 1701, Brunei ceded Sabah to the Sultan of Sulu (an archipelago between Borneo and Mindanao). That cession is the basis for ongoing Philippine claims to Sabah.

The British and Dutch began sparring over Borneo in the 17th century, extending a regional rivalry that began in Java and spread to the Malay Peninsula. The Anglo-Dutch Treaty of 1824 carved the region into spheres of interest that were to become 20th-century national boundaries. The Dutch got what became Indonesia; Britain got the Malay Peninsula and Singapore.

Brunei's decline in the late 18th century led Sarawak to assert its independence, emboldened by a flourishing trade in antimony (*sarawak* means 'antimony' in Malay). In 1839 Brunei's sultan dispatched his uncle Raja Muda Hashim, but he failed to quell the separatists. Seeing a chance to rid itself of Bruneian rule, the rebels looked south for Dutch aid.

In a case of impeccable timing, James Brooke, an independently wealthy, India-born son of a British magistrate, moored his armed schooner at Kuching. Raja Muda offered to make the Englishman the rajah of Sungai Sarawak if he helped suppress the worsening revolt. Brooke, confident London would support any move to counter Dutch influence, accepted the deal. Backed by superior firepower, Brooke quashed the rebellion, held a reluctant Raja Muda to his word, and in 1841 Sarawak became his personal fiefdom. The White Rajahs would rule Sarawak for the next 100 years.

Unlike British colonial administrators, Brooke and his successors included tribal leaders in their ruling council and honoured local customs (except head-hunting). They battled pirates, were disinclined towards European immigration, and discouraged European companies from destroying native jungle for huge rubber plantations. They also invited Chinese, many from Fujian and Guandong, to work in Sarawak as miners, farmers and traders. Despite a rebellion by Hakka immigrants in 1857, Chinese came to dominate Sarawak's economy.

When James Brooke died in 1868 he was succeeded by his nephew, Charles Johnson, who changed his surname to Brooke. During his long reign, which lasted until his death in 1917, he extended the borders of his kingdom (at the expense of the sultan of Brunei), developed Sarawak's economy and slashed government debt.

In 1865, Brunei's ailing sultan leased Sabah to – of all people – Claude Lee Moses, the American consul in Brunei. The rights eventually passed

The Venetian Antonio Pigafetta, who sailed with Ferdinand Magellan on his last voyage, visited Brunei in 1521 and dubbed Kampung Ayer the 'Venice of the East'.

As part of the resistance to Japan's occupation, Australian commandos encouraged a head-hunting revival, offering 'ten bob a nob' for Japanese heads.

1445	1511	1610	1824
Islam becomes the state religion of Melaka, Srivijaya's successor as Southeast Asia's trading power. Merchants spread a predominantly tolerant, mild form of Islam that accommodates existing traditions.	Portugal conquers Melaka in a bid to control the spice trade. Brunei succeeds Melaka as Southeast Asia's leading Islamic kingdom and trading centre.	The Dutch build a diamond-trading post in Sambas, West Kalimantan, beginning more than 300 years of Dutch interest in Kalimantan and its natural resources.	The Anglo-Dutch Treaty divides the region into spheres of influence. The Dutch are granted Kalimantan but are preoccupied with Sumatra and Java .

Borders established in the 1800s ended up having a profound impact on the fate of Borneo's rainforests in the 21st century. The vast majority of the territory that Brunei managed to retain is now pristine and protected wilderness, whereas huge swaths of the forest land pried away from the sultan by the White Rajahs and the British North Borneo Company ended up being clear-cut – and, in many cases, turned over to oil-palm mono-culture – in the decades after Malaysian independence.

to an Englishman, Alfred Dent, who also received Sulu's blessing. In 1881, with London's support, Dent formed the British North Borneo Company (later called the North Borneo Chartered Company) to administer the territory. Britain bagged a second Bornean territory, again on the cheap.

The prospect of further fragmentation led the nearly ruined sultanate of Brunei to become a British protectorate in 1888. Despite this, it lost Limbang to Sarawak in 1890, absurdly chopping the sultanate into two discontiguous parts (Brunei still claims the Limbang area). Ironically, Brunei's colonial status in the 19th century paved the way to its becoming Borneo's only independent state a century later.

The presence of the British along Borneo's northern coast spurred the Dutch to beef up their presence in Kalimantan. Dutch commercial exploitation of the archipelago reached its peak at the end of the 19th century with thriving rubber, pepper, copra, tin, coal and coffee exports, plus oil drilling in East Kalimantan. Assertiveness bred disputes with indigenous groups, culminating in 1859 in a four-year war between the Dutch and the Banjarmasin sultanate; resistance persisted until 1905.

In 1917 Charles Vyner Brooke, son of Charles Brooke, ascended to the throne of Sarawak. A veteran of government service, he professionalised Sarawak's administration, preparing it for a modern form of rule.

Imperial Japan, in need of Borneo's natural resources to power its war machine, seized Sarawak's Miri oilfields on 16 December 1941; other targets in the poorly defended region quickly fell. Oil rigs and other key Miri installations were sabotaged to prevent their use by the Japanese but were soon pumping again.

As elsewhere in Asia, Japanese forces in Borneo acquired a reputation for the most horrific brutality. In Sabah, the infamous labour camp at Sandakan's Agricultural Experimental Station housed Allied captives from across Southeast Asia. Of 2400 Australian and British POWs, only six survived. At Mandor, Kalimantan's killing fields, 21,037 people were murdered.

1841	**1881**	**1888**
After helping Brunei's Kuching governor suppress an uprising, Englishman James Brooke becomes first White Rajah of Sarawak.	The British North Borneo Company is established in Sandakan to administer Sabah. It is the state's governing authority until Sabah and Sarawak become Crown colonies after WWII.	Once Southeast Asia's pre-eminent Islamic trading centre, Brunei slumps into British arms as a protectorate, giving Westminster three territories in northern Borneo.

LUCA TETTONI/CORBIS

» Sir James Brooke (1803–1868)

In 1944 a primarily British and Australian force parachuted into Bario in the Kelabit Highlands and allied with indigenous Kelabits against the Japanese. In 1945, Australian troops landed in East Kalimantan, fighting bloody battles in Tarakan and Balikpapan.

After the war, which left many of Borneo's cities in ruins (mainly from Allied bombing), the North Borneo Chartered Company ceded authority over what is now Sabah to the British Crown. In Sarawak, the White Rajah returned briefly under Australian military administration, then handed over control to the British government.

In 1949, after a four-year war, the Dutch withdrew from the Dutch East Indies, and Indonesia, including Kalimantan – which had remained on the sidelines during the conflict – gained independence.

When Malaya gained its independence in 1957, Sarawak, Sabah (then North Borneo) and Brunei remained under British rule. In 1962 the British proposed incorporating their Bornean territories into the Federation of Malaya. At the last minute, Brunei pulled out of the deal, as the sultan (and, one suspects, Shell Oil) didn't want to see the revenue from its vast oil reserves channelled to the peninsula. In September 1963 the Federation of Malaysia – made up of the Malay Peninsula, Singapore, Sabah and Sarawak – was born (Singapore withdrew in 1965).

In the early 1960s, Indonesia's increasingly radicalised, left-leaning President Soekarno laid claim to all of Borneo. His response to Malaysia's 'annexation' of northern Borneo was a military campaign, dubbed the Konfrontasi (1962–66). Soviet-equipped Indonesian armed forces crossed into Sabah and Sarawak from Kalimantan. At the height of the conflict, 50,000 troops from Britain, Australia and New Zealand patrolled Sabah and Sarawak's borders with Indonesia.

Soekarno's successor, President Soeharto (ruled 1967–98), expanded the *transmigrasi* (internal migration) polices initiated under the Dutch, which moved millions of people from overpopulated islands such as Java, Bali and Madura to more remote areas, with East Kalimantan a particular target. Violent clashes – including incidents of head-hunting – occasionally make headlines, but the more insidious effect of this policy has been to marginalise Kalimantan's indigenous communities.

Brunei achieved self-government except in matters of defence and foreign affairs in 1971. In 1984 Sultan Haji Hassanal Bolkiah, a graduate of the Royal Military Academy Sandhurst, reluctantly led his country to complete independence from Britain but continues to maintain very close ties with the UK.

Allied bombing raids in 1945 left Sandakan in ruins, and authorities moved Sabah's capital to Jesseltown, now Kota Kinabalu.

1941–45	1946	1963	1984
Imperial Japan occupies Borneo. Early resistance by local Chinese is brutally repressed. Nascent nationalists greet the Japanese as liberators, but the occupiers' cruelty turns opinion.	Britain acquires two new Crown colonies when the last White Rajah, Charles Vyner Brooke, and the North Borneo Chartered Company cede control of Sarawak and Sabah to Westminster.	Sarawak and Sabah join union of Malaya and Singapore. Their role: to maintain a non-Chinese majority. Indonesia claims all of Borneo and declares Konfrontasi against Malaysia.	Brunei achieves full independence but continues close ties with Great Britain. The last British military base in eastern Asia, home to a Gurkha battalion, is at Seria.

Environment & Wildlife

Borneo is one of the most geologically complex and biologically diverse places on the planet. Situated at the convergence of three great tectonic plates, the island owes much of its astounding biological range to the fact that as recently as 10,000 years ago it was connected to mainland Southeast Asia.

Within the lifetimes of many people alive today, almost the entirety of Borneo's land mass was covered with old-growth forests. Today, the rainforests of Borneo, a biodiversity hotspot of global importance, are critically imperilled – a quick look at Google Earth will illustrate what has been wrought over the last few decades. Fortunately, vast areas of the interior are still relatively untouched, presenting humanity with one last opportunity to preserve Borneo's incredible natural riches.

> Borneo lies within what is known as the 'ever-wet zone' – it gets at least 60mm of rain every month of the year, with rainfall in most months averaging about 200mm.

The Land

At 740,000 sq km, Borneo is the third-largest island in the world after Greenland and New Guinea. It is about one-third larger than France, and almost exactly the same size as Texas.

Bisected by the equator, Borneo is remarkably flat, with over 50% of the landscape less than 150m above sea level. Lowland areas tend to be swampy, with serpentine rivers and poor drainage. Malaysia's longest river is the Batang Rejang (563km) in Sarawak, while Indonesia's three longest rivers are all in Kalimantan: the Kapuas (1143km), the Barito (900km) and the Mahakam (775km).

Mountains dominate much of the centre of the island, running on a diagonal axis from Mt Kinabalu in the northeast, southwestward into West Kalimantan. Unlike many islands in Indonesia and the Philippines, Borneo does not have any active volcanoes because it is part of a very stable continental shelf.

Extensive deposits of limestone in northern Borneo show where ancient coral reefs were buried under thousands of metres of sediment, then lifted to form ranges of hills and mountains. In some areas, water has dissolved the limestone to form vast caves. Sarawak's Gunung Mulu National Park is one of the world's premier limestone landscapes, boasting towering rock pinnacles and the world's second-largest cave chamber. Niah National Park is also famous for its huge caves.

Borneo's most celebrated peak is 4095m Mt Kinabalu in Sabah, the highest mountain between the Himalayas and New Guinea and arguably the epicentre of Borneo's fabulous biodiversity. This colossal dome of granite, forced through the earth's crust as molten rock 10 to 15 million years ago, continues to rise about 5mm a year. Despite its location just north of the equator, Mt Kinabalu was high enough to be exquisitely sculpted by glaciers during the ice ages.

> For an excellent, colourful introduction to Borneo's environment, check out *Wild Borneo* by Nick Garbutt.

Habitats

Borneo has dozens of highly specialised ecosystems. Following are the main ones you're likely to encounter.

There is no record of any human entering Sabah's Maliau Basin until the 1980s.

Coral Reef

Borneo's fabled coral reefs are part of the 'Coral Triangle', a fantastically rich portion of the South China Sea that's home to 75% of the world's coral species and over 3000 types of marine fish. Reefs are in the best shape along the northeast coast of Borneo, where the water is clear and free of sediment. The island of Sipadan in Sabah and Pulau Derawan in East Kalimantan have the greatest concentrations of reefs, while protected areas include Tun Sakaran Marine Park in Sabah and Talang-Satang National Park in Sarawak.

Kerangas (Heath Forest)

Sandy soils that are highly acidic and drain quickly support a highly specialised habitat known as *kerangas,* an Iban word meaning 'land that cannot grow rice'. This forest type is composed of small, densely packed trees that seldom top 20m in height. Due to difficult growing conditions, plants of the *kerangas* have developed extraordinary ways to protect their leaves from the blazing sun and acquire needed minerals. Some, for example, obtain nutrients by providing a home for ant colonies that bring food to the plant.

Kerangas has the world's greatest diversity of pitcher plants (nepenthes), which trap insects in chambers full of enzyme-rich fluids and then digest them.

Found mainly near the coast and inland on sandstone plateaus, *kerangas* is increasingly restricted to protected coastal areas like Sarawak's Bako National Park and remote mountain tops like those in Sabah's Maliau Basin Conservation Area.

Lowland Dipterocarp Forest

Found up to an altitude of about 900m or 1000m, Borneo's lowland forests are dominated by trees belonging to the dipterocarp family. More than 250 species of these magnificent trees, which can reach a height of 60m, anchor Borneo's most ecologically important ecosystem, the lowland dipterocarp forest, which has more species of flora than any other rainforest habitat in the world – a single hectare may shelter 240 different plant species!

Of the countless animals found in a dipterocarp forest, few are as captivating as the many types of gliding animals. In addition to birds and bats, there are frogs, lizards, snakes, squirrels and lemurs that 'fly' between trees.

Dipterocarps, including Borneo's 155 endemic species, produce some of most valuable tropical hardwoods, which is why this type of forest is endangered. Some fine patches can be found at a variety of national parks, including Sarawak's Niah National Park and Sabah's Danum Valley Conservation Area.

HEART OF BORNEO

An initiative of the WWF (www.panda.org), Heart of Borneo (www.heartofborneo.org) has a hugely ambitious goal: to safeguard Borneo's biodiversity for future generations and to ensure indigenous peoples' cultural survival by protecting 240,000 sq km of interconnected forest land in Sabah, Sarawak, Brunei and Indonesia. That's almost a third of the island's land!

Montane Forest

On mountains above 900m, dipterocarp forest gives way to a magical world of stunted oaks, myrtle and laurel trees. Cloud drenched and dripping, montane forest – often with a canopy height of just 10m – is full of ferns, rhododendrons, lichens and thick moss. It also provides a home for a stunning wealth of orchids.

Visitors from around the world travel to the lower reaches of Sabah's montane forests in the hope of seeing some species of the legendary Rafflesia flower.

Mangrove

Flourishing in a tidal world where land meets sea, mangroves have developed extraordinary ways to deal with an ever-changing mix of salt and fresh water, all the while anchored happily in suffocating mud. Not only do these remarkable trees fix the loose coastal soil, they also protect against erosion and even tsunamis.

Uncounted marine organisms and nearly every commercially important seafood species find sanctuary and nursery sites among mangrove roots. The forests' more endearing species include the proboscis monkey and the mudskipper, a fish that spends much of its time skipping along the muddy shore in search of food.

Mangroves once ringed virtually the entire island, especially around river deltas, but are increasingly limited to places like Bako National Park and Kuching Wetlands National Park, both in Sarawak, and Brunei's Temburong District.

Some species of tropical hardwood are so valuable that a single tree can be worth US$50,000. Such trees are sometimes selectively logged using heavy-duty helicopters.

ENVIRONMENT & WILDLIFE JUNGLE LIFE

Jungle Life

From breathtaking coral reefs to luxuriant rainforest, Borneo is one of the greatest showcases of life anywhere on the planet.

Borneo sits at the junction of Asian and Australian biomes, but its strongest affinity is with the Asian mainland because when sea levels drop, Borneo hooks up with Peninsular Malaysia. This has happened on several occasions, once about 50 million years ago, and more recently during the ice ages that lasted from about 2.5 million years ago until 10,000 years ago. Such connections allowed vast amounts of genetic material to migrate onto the island, making it a kind of steamy, tropical Noah's ark. When the seas submerged the land bridges, life on the islands was left on its own to evolve into fantastic new forms. The result is one of the world's great biodiversity hotspots, one in which new species are discovered all the time.

Animals

Borneo's 222 species of mammal – 44 of them endemic – include 13 primates and over 100 kinds of rodents and bats. Snake species number 166, amphibians 100.

If you head into the rainforest, bear in mind that most animals wisely keep their distance from humans and are thus nearly impossible to see. Even researchers with years of field experience have never seen creatures such as the Western tarsier, a tiny mammal that appeared on the cover of the 1st edition of this guide.

Orangutan

Borneo's most captivating animal may be the orangutan, or 'man of the forest' (in Bahasa, *orang* means 'person' and *hutan* means 'forest'). At the top of many visitors' to-see list, Asia's only great ape – endemic to Borneo and Sumatra – is a wonder to behold in its native environment, and even the most seasoned traveller will feel a rush of awe if they cross paths with

'The orangutan's future is dependent on the forests. As more are cleared and converted to agricultural plantations orangutan populations will continue to decline.' Ashley Leiman, OBE, Director of The Orangutan Foundation UK

NATIONAL PARKS & NATURE RESERVES

Borneo's national parks and nature reserves protect some of the island's most luxuriant and ecologically important habitats. Many are easy to get to, and some offer convenient overnight accommodation.

Sabah

Sabah's national parks (www.sabahparks.org) and conservation areas (www.searrp.org) are among the main reasons tourists visit the state. They include the following:

» Crocker Range National Park (139 sq km; no facilities) preserves a huge swath of forested escarpment overlooking the coast.

» Danum Valley Conservation Area (440 sq km; run by the Sabah Foundation and visited mostly by scientists) consists of pristine old-growth rainforest and has a superabundance of wildlife.

» Kinabalu National Park (754 sq km), easily accessible from Kota Kinabalu (KK), is the state's largest and most popular national park. It offers mountain trekking up Mt Kinabalu, forest walks at the headquarters and Mesilau, and the hot springs at Poring.

» Maliau Basin Conservation Area (588 sq km; run by the Sabah Foundation) is a pocket of truly untouched wilderness, protected by mountains, altitude and sheer remoteness.

» Pulau Tiga National Park (15 sq km) consists of three islands 50km southwest of KK: one formed by volcanic mud eruptions, one famous for sea snakes and the third virtually washed away by wave action.

» Tabin Wildlife Reserve (1205 sq km; managed by both the Forestry and Wildlife Departments) – made up of lowland dipterocarp forest and mangroves, much of it technically secondary – shelters elephants and primates.

» Tawau Hills Park (29 sq km), near Tawau in the state's southeast, has forested volcanic hills, waterfalls and hot springs.

» Tun Sakaran Marine Park (325 sq km) protects some of the best reef-dive sites in the world.

» Tunku Abdul Rahman National Park (49 sq km) is a group of five islands, one quite large, a few kilometres from KK. Features include beaches, snorkelling and hiking.

» Turtle Islands National Park (17 sq km) is composed of three tiny islands 40km north of Sandakan, protecting the nesting ground of green and hawksbill sea turtles.

Sarawak

Many of Sarawak's national parks (www.sarawakforestry.com) can be visited on a day trip from Kuching or Miri.

» Bako National Park (27 sq km) has 17 trails leading to coves, *kerangas* and beaches.

» Batang Ai National Park (240 sq km; no facilities), deep in Iban country, is home to lots of wild orangutans.

a wild orangutan. It's almost impossible to deny the appeal of a 90kg animal whose physique, facial expressions and obvious intelligence are so eerily similar to our own.

About 55,000 orangutans live in Borneo, 40,000 of them in Kalimantan and 13,000 in Sabah. Scientists estimate that before human encroachment, the world's orangutan population was roughly 100 times what it is today.

Ranging over large areas of rainforest in search of fruiting trees and insects (a fine source of protein), the orangutan has suffered greatly due to hunting and, especially, habitat loss from logging, oil-palm plantations and fire. Also contributing to their numerical decline is the fact that the interval between a female's pregnancies is usually about eight

» Gunung Gading National Park (54 sq km) features giant Rafflesia flowers as its major attraction.

» Gunung Mulu National Park (529 sq km), Sarawak's most popular national park, is east of Marudi near the Brunei border.

» Kubah National Park (22 sq km) has pristine rainforest, hiking trails and clear rivers you can swim in.

» Kuching Wetlands National Park (66 sq km), a mangrove reserve, is home to proboscis monkeys, crocs and Irrawaddy dolphins.

» Lambir Hills National Park (69 sq km) is famous for its diverse plant species.

» Matang Wildlife Centre (1.8 sq km) has a very active wildlife rehabilitation program, especially for orangutans and sun bears.

» Niah National Park (32 sq km) has massive caves that once sheltered prehistoric humans.

» Pulong Tau National Park (598 sq km), Sarawak's newest park, was gazetted in 2005 to preserve the rich jungle of the Kelabit Highlands.

» Semenggoh Nature Reserve (6.8 sq km) is one of the best places in the world to see semi-wild orangutans.

» Similajau National Park (75 sq km) is a coastal park with hiking trails, beaches and rivers – and estuarine crocodiles.

» Talang-Satang National Park (194 sq km) is a marine park that protects the waters off four offshore islands used by sea turtles to lay their eggs.

» Tanjung Datu National Park (13.8 sq km) has beautiful beaches, clear rivers and coral reefs.

Brunei

Brunei has one major national park and several forest reserves, including:

» Peradayan Forest Reserve (10.7 sq km),which has a trail leading through the jungle to the summit of Bukit Patoi (310m).

» Ulu Temburong National Park (500 sq km), an untouched expanse of pristine forest accessible only by longboat.

Kalimantan

Kalimantan's national parks include the following:

» Kutai National Park (1980 sq km) is a great place to spot wild orangutans under the shade of 300-year-old hardwood trees.

» Tanjung Puting National Park (4150 sq km) is one of the world's last great refuges of the orangutan.

» Sebangau National Park (5687 sq km) is home to one of the world's largest populations of wild orangutans, estimated at 6900, as well as Malayan sun bears and gibbons.

years. The good news is that orangutans seem capable of adapting to new circumstances – in Sabah, for instance, some now live in commercial forest reserves.

Wild orangutans are now difficult to find except in places like Sabah's Danum Valley Conservation Area and Sarawak's Batang Ai region, but semi-wild animals can be seen at the Semenggoh Nature Reserve in Sarawak and the Sepilok Orang-utan Rehabilitation Centre in Sabah.

Proboscis Monkey

Borneo's most peculiar primate, named for the male's pendulous nose, lives mainly in coastal areas, including mangrove forests. It is strictly herbivorous, which is why both sexes need prodigious quantities of cellulose-digesting bacteria – stored in their distinctive pot bellies – to turn their food into useable energy.

Proboscis monkeys are relatively easy to spot as they perform incredible leaps from tree to tree, often at great heights, and then settle down to dine on choice young leaves, the males' noses flopping as they chew.

Proboscis monkeys can often be seen in Sabah at the Labuk Bay Proboscis Monkey Sanctuary and in Sarawak at Bako National Park and Kuching Wetlands National Park.

Gibbons swing by their hands, a unique mode of travel called brachiation that isn't fail-safe: most gibbons have bone fractures from falling.

Gibbon

Swinging effortlessly from branch to branch, gibbons move with such speed and agility that it seems as if they are falling sideways. Unfortunately for primate lovers, gibbons are much easier to hear than see, so like most visitors you'll probably have to make do with scanning the canopy as their whooping songs echo through the rainforest. National parks with gibbon populations include Brunei's Ulu Temburong National Park.

Elephant

Of the 2000 Borneo pygmy elephants (a subspecies of the Asian elephant) estimated to live in northeastern Borneo, the largest population is thought to roam the forests around Sungai Kinabatangan, where they've come into conflict with the owners of vast oil-palm plantations.

New genetic evidence puts to rest the theory that humans introduced the creatures to the island in the mid-1700s. It turns out that they've been on the island for at least 18,000 years.

Rhinoceros

Very little is known about the elusive and critically endangered Borneo rhinoceros, a subspecies of the Sumatran rhino. The world's smallest rhinoceros, its global population is estimated to be less than 50, all of them in Sabah.

A wild Borneo rhino was briefly caught on film for the first time ever, by a camera trap, in 2007 – the captivating clip can be found on YouTube.

Bearded Pig

Bearded pigs are encountered in nearly every type of forested area on the island. Following well-worn paths, these rotund animals, which can weigh up to 150kg, sometimes gather into large herds and migrate incredible distances in search of nuts and seeds. Although they are an extremely popular game animal, they are one creature that hunters and predators truly fear. Except for the tame boar who lives at the headquarters of Bako National Park, be wary of these unpredictable animals and their sharp tusks – they are capable of goring a human in the flash of a whisker.

Mouse Deer

To see the first-ever camera-trap video of a wild Borneo rhinoceros, go to YouTube and search for 'Borneo rhino'.

Few Bornean mammals are more surprising than the 2kg lesser mouse deer, the world's smallest hoofed animal, which is the size of a rabbit but looks like a miniature deer. Males defend themselves and their mates using protruding canines instead of antlers. Skittish and generally nocturnal, they can sometimes be seen during the day by quiet hikers.

Leech

If you'd like to give something back to the rainforest ecosystem, the humble leech – slimy, squiggly and fond of taking up residence in uncomfortable places – can arrange an involuntary donation of blood. For details, see p29.

Birds

A fantastic assortment of birds belonging to 420 species, 37 of them endemic, fill the forests of Borneo with flashes of feather and ethereal calls. The most famous are the hornbills, some of whose eight species have an oversized 'helmet' or 'horn' perched on their beak. The 105cm-long rhinoceros hornbill, with its orange-red horn and loud whooping calls, serves as Sarawak's state emblem. When the 125cm-long helmeted hornbill swoops across the sky, you might think you're seeing a pterodactyl. Revered and hunted by Borneo's indigenous peoples, hornbills are highly threatened by habitat loss.

The rainforests of Borneo are exposed to twice as much sunlight as temperate forests, but just 2% penetrates all the way to the forest floor. That's why so much jungle biodiversity is up in the canopy.

Plants

Borneo has as many species of flowering plants as the entire continent of Africa, which is 40 times larger. The island is also home to over 1000 species of fern. In Lambir Hills National Park, scientists found an astounding 1200 species of tree in a single 52-hectare research plot! Of Borneo's 2000 species of orchid, over 1000 live on Mt Kinabalu.

Many of Borneo's plants struggle to survive in thin, nutrient-poor soils. Some trees hold themselves upright with wide, flaring buttresses rather than deep root systems.

Strangler figs start life as tiny seeds that are defecated by birds in the rainforest canopy, where they sprout and then send spindly roots downward in search of the forest floor. Eventually, some figs grow large enough to embrace their host tree in a death grip. Once the host tree dies and rots away, the giant fig stands upright on a fantastic hollow latticework of its own woven roots. Orangutans, wild pigs and birds are only some of the creatures that rely on the fruit of the strangler fig for their survival.

For details on the extraordinary Rafflesia flower, see p179.

Environmental Issues

Borneo is a land in ecological crisis. If used sustainably, the vast forests of Borneo could provide valuable resources for countless generations. When the forest is logged and fragmented, however, the entire ecosystem falls apart: soils become degraded, peat dries out and may catch fire, rivers silt up, plants and animals disappear, and indigenous human communities suffer grave ills.

Despite the best efforts of local and international environmental groups, the governments of Borneo have a dismal environmental record. Far too frequently, rainforests are viewed as an impediment to 'progress' or as political spoils, with a handful of well-connected people deriving profits from logging concessions granted without public oversight.

Visit the website of the UN Environment Programme (www.grida.no) and search for 'Borneo deforestation' and you will be directed to maps tracing the disappearance of the island's forest cover from 1950 to the present and on to 2020.

Deforestation

Borneo suffers from one of the highest rates of deforestation on earth. In the mid-1980s, about 75% of the island still had its original forest cover; by 2005, the figure was just 50%. Unless something is done, less than a third of the island will retain its forests by 2020. The WWF calculated that in 2005, Borneo was losing 2.5 hectares of rainforest per minute – that comes to 1.5 sq km every hour. The main markets for Bornean wood are China and Japan.

Only a tiny fraction of Borneo's land is protected by law, and even less is subject to laws that are systematically enforced. Sabah and Sarawak

Borneo has about 15,000 species of flowering plant. All of North America – from the Panama Canal to the Arctic – only has about 20,000.

ENVIRONMENT & WILDLIFE ENVIRONMENTAL ISSUES

have been paying lip service to sustainability in recent years, in part because of international pressure, in part because there's not all that much left to chop, but supposedly 'selective' logging continues in formerly pristine areas such as the Kelabit Highlands. Malaysian Borneo is also used as a conduit for illegal timber logged across the border in Kalimantan.

In Kalimantan, which suffers from an almost complete lack of enforcement, illegal logging extends into national park lands. Some ostensibly protected areas, such as much of Kutai National Park in East Kalimantan, are considered by scientists to be 'lost'.

> In 1997 and 1998, catastrophic forest fires in Kalimantan burnt 65,000 sq km of rainforest, killing untold numbers of animals and carpeting much of Southeast Asia with haze.

Oil-Palm Plantations

Alongside logging, the greatest single threat to Borneo's biodiversity comes from the vast oil-palm plantations that are replacing huge swaths of primary and secondary forest in Sabah, Sarawak and Kalimantan – with the encouragement of the governments of Malaysia and Indonesia, the world's two largest palm-oil producers. Originally brought from Africa in 1848, oil palms produce more edible oil per hectare (about 250kg) than any other crop, especially in the ideal growing conditions provided by Borneo.

Palm-oil plantations may appear green – after all, they are covered with living plants – but from an ecological point of view they are dead zones. Even clear-cut areas can recover much of their biodiversity if left alone, but palm-oil plantations convert land into permanent monoculture, reducing the number of plant species by 80% and resident mammal, reptile and bird species by 80% to 90%. Oil palms require large quantities of herbicides and pesticides that can seep into rivers; drainage may lower water tables, drying out nearby peat forests; and the plantations fragment the natural habitats that are especially important to large mammals.

Palm oil is often presented falsely as a 'green' alternative to fossil fuels – see below.

BIOFUELLING FOREST DESTRUCTION

Replacing fossil fuels with renewable biofuels such as palm oil sounds like a great way to mitigate global warming. Unfortunately, immeasurable ecological damage is done when rainforests are converted to oil-palm plantations, something that's happening across Borneo at an ever greater rate.

For starters, creating a plantation means logging the plantation area, destroying plant and animal habitats and displacing indigenous people. Because young oil palms take five years to produce their first crop, timber sales subsidise the preproduction phase. In some cases, unscrupulous operators get a plantation concession – easier to get than a timber concession – fell all the trees and then leave the land denuded.

While palm oil is an extraordinarily versatile food product, it's remarkably lousy as a 'sustainable' fuel. Studies show that the conversion of forests to palm plantations releases far more carbon than all the biofuel they'll ever produce could possibly save. The equation is especially unbalanced when the plantation replaces a peat-swamp forest, which releases huge quantities of greenhouse gases as it dries out, and off the charts when burning is the final step in clearing branches and underbrush.

Plantation monoculture creates a 'green dead zone', robbing wildlife of native food sources, increasing conflicts between wildlife and humans – plantations consider orangutans pests – and pushing indigenous shifting cultivators towards marginal habitats such as peat swamps, where slash-and-burn methods release vast quantities of greenhouse gases and sometimes trigger massive fires.

For more information on the impact of oil-palm plantations on orangutans, see p252.

Hydroelectric Dams

Hydroelectric dams are touted as a source of carbon-free energy, but these huge projects often have serious environmental impacts. In addition, indigenous people are often forcibly relocated to areas where they have difficulty earning a living or maintaining their traditions.

For details on Sarawak's highly controversial Bakun Dam, see p193.

A number of other hydro mega-projects are being planned without public access to feasibility studies, without public feedback and without proper environmental-impact assessments.

Wildlife Trade

Although theoretically illegal, the hugely lucrative trade in wild animals continues. Baby orangutans are captured for sale as pets (see p193), sun bears are butchered so body parts such as gall bladders can be used in traditional Chinese medicine, and clouded leopards are killed for their teeth, bones and pelts.

What You Can Do

Every time a traveller visits a nature site, hires a trekking guide, pays a boatman for transport to a remote longhouse, or provides custom for a local ecotourism initiative, they are casting a vote – by putting cash in local pockets – for the economic (as opposed to purely ecological) value of sustainability and habitat conservation.

Travellers might also check out the website of Wild Asia (www.wild asia.net) to learn more about responsible tourism in the region. Wherever you go, tread lightly, buy locally, support responsible tourism and give respectful, constructive feedback to local operators.

To keep abreast of the campaign to save Borneo's jungles, visit the website of Mongabay (www.mongabay.com), which has worldwide news on rainforest conservation.

Some of the best conservation work in Borneo is being carried out by the WWF (www.panda.org) and its Malaysian affiliate, WWF Malaysia (www.wwfmalaysia.org). Recent WWF achievements include launching the cross-border Heart of Borneo initiative (p288).

Borneo has two Unesco World Heritage Sites: Gunung Mulu National Park in Sarawak and Kinabalu National Park in Sabah.

About 14% of Sabah's land enjoys some form of environmental protection, national parks cover 7% of Sarawak's territory, and about a quarter of Brunei's land is inside a national park, wildlife sanctuary or conservation area.

ENVIRONMENT & WILDLIFE WHAT YOU CAN DO

Dayak Peoples & Culture

Borneo's indigenous peoples, known collectively as Dayaks, belong to scores of different tribal groups that speak about 140 languages and dialects. Some live on the coast, others along the remote upland tributaries of great rivers. A few generations ago, some tribes still practiced head-hunting; today, many Dayaks are well integrated into 21st-century economic life, and it's not unusual to meet university professors, lawyers, government officials and airline pilots who grew up in longhouses.

Among the ancestors of today's Dayaks were migrants from southern China who came to Borneo about 3000 years ago, bringing with them elements of the Dongson culture, including irrigated rice cultivation, buffalo-sacrifice rituals and *ikat* (fabric patterned by tie-dying the yarn before weaving). These newcomers mixed with native groups – people like the cave dwellers of Niah – and eventually developed into more than 200 distinct tribes.

Who's a Dayak?

Not all of Borneo's indigenous tribes refer to themselves as Dayaks, but the term usefully groups together peoples who have a great deal in common – and not just from an outsider's point of view.

Traceable back to about 1840, the term 'Dayak' gained currency thanks to its use by colonial authorities. It appears to be derived from the last two syllables of 'Bidayuh', but few Bidayuh give this much thought. While the Bidayuh of Sarawak are quite happy identifying themselves as Dayaks, Sarawak's Iban, when they talk about Dayaks, are much more likely to be referring to the Bidayuh than to themselves. But shared cultural practices, values and interests – and several generations of Christian faith and inter-group marriages – make it a no-brainer for different groups to work together. The only term that embraces everyone is 'Dayak'.

None of Sabah's indigenous ethnicities are particularly keen on using the term 'Dayak'. Not so in Kalimantan, where native groups have rallied around the Dayak banner and the term has become a focus for political unity across tribal lines.

For the purposes of affirmative action in Malaysia, Dayaks are considered Bumiputra (see p281).

Sabah

More than 30 indigenous groups make Sabah a medley of traditions and cultures. The state's largest ethnic group, known as the Kadazan–Dusun, make up 18% of the population. Mainly Roman Catholic, the Kadazan and the Dusun share a common language and have similar customs; the former originally lived mainly in the state's western coastal areas and river deltas, while the latter inhabited the interior highlands.

The Murut (3.2% of the population) traditionally lived in the southwestern hills bordering Kalimantan and Brunei, growing hill-rice and hunting with spears and blowpipes. Soldiers for Brunei's sultans, they were the last group in Sabah to abandon head-hunting.

Sarawak

Dayak culture and lifestyles are probably easiest to observe and experience in Sarawak, where Dayaks make up about 48% of the population.

About 29% of Sarawakians are Iban, a group that migrated from West Kalimantan's Kapuas River starting five to eight centuries ago. Also known as Sea Dayaks for their exploits as pirates, the Iban are traditionally rice growers and longhouse dwellers. A reluctance to renounce head-hunting enhanced the Ibans' ferocious reputation.

The Bidayuh (8% of the population), many of whom also trace their roots to what is now West Kalimantan, are concentrated in the hills south and southwest of Kuching, near the Kalimantan border. Adjacent villages sometimes speak different dialects. Few Bidayuh still live in longhouses.

Upland groups such as the Kelabit, Kayan and Kenyah (ie everyone except the Bidayuh, Iban and coastal-dwelling Melanau) are often grouped together under the term Orang Ulu ('upriver peoples').

Brunei

Indigenous non-Malays, mainly Iban and Kelabit, account for less than 10% of Brunei's population.

Kalimantan

In Central Kalimantan, the largest indigenous group is the Ngaju Dayak, who live along major rivers and do more fishing than hunting. The Ot Danum Dayaks, who live further upriver, raise fruit, collect natural rubber and make dugout canoes that they sell to downriver tribes.

Along East Kalimantan's Mahakam River, the Kutai are the main indigenous group in the lower reaches, hosting the annual Erau Festival at their capital Tenggarong.

The Kayan and the closely related Kenyah are found in the Apo Kayan Highlands, as well as in Sarawak and Brunei. They are known for building the most elaborately decorated longhouses and for having a strict social hierarchy.

The White Rajahs of Sarawak allowed the Dayaks to live according to their age-old traditions and beliefs except in one area, head-hunting, which they made great efforts to suppress.

DAYAK PEOPLES & CULTURE WHO'S A DAYAK?

THE PENAN

The least integrated – and most economically disadvantaged – aboriginal group in Sarawak and Brunei is the Penan, nomadic hunter-gatherers known for never taking more than they require from the jungle. Because of their distinct culture and lifestyle, some people do not consider the Penan to be Dayaks.

Christian missionaries and the Sarawak government have long pressured the Penan to settle in longhouses, and today many live sedentary lives in northern Sarawak's Baram and Bukit Mas districts; only a few hundred are believed to remain true nomads. Settled Penan may plant rice, but they continue to rely on the jungle for clothing, medicine and food, including sago from palm trees and game that they hunt with blowpipes.

With their lands and way of life under severe threat from timber concessions, the Penan have launched a series of civil-disobedience campaigns that have included blocking logging roads. While many sympathisers – such as the celebrated Bruno Manser (www.brunomanser.ch), an environmental activist who disappeared near Bario in 2000 – seek to protect the Penan's unique way of life, Malaysian authorities insist that they should be assimilated into mainstream society, whether they like it or not.

The unique Punan cave dwellers live between the headwaters of the Mahakam and Kapuas rivers, spanning East and West Kalimantan. Today, most have given up troglodytic living.

West Kalimantan is home to a large population of Bidayuh, most of whom are Catholic (many of the Sarawak Bidayuh are Anglican). Many identify strongly with the locality they're from, eg 'Dayak Terebung' (the name used by Bidayuh from Terebung to refer to themselves).

At the Sarawak Cultural Village near Kuching, you can visit four Dayak longhouses – including the only remaining Melanau longhouse – constructed using just traditional materials and techniques. No tin roofs or satellite dishes!

The Longhouse

One of the most distinctive features of Dayak life is the longhouse (*rumah batang* or *rumah panjai*), which is essentially an entire village under one seemingly interminable roof. Longhouses take a variety of shapes and styles, but all are raised above the damp jungle floor on hardwood stilts and most are built on or near river banks. For reasons of geography, traditional Dayak societies did not develop a government structure beyond that of the longhouse.

The focus of longhouse life is the covered common veranda, known as a *ruai* to the Iban, an *awah* to the Bidayuh and a *dapur* to the Kelabits (other groups use other terms). Residents use this communal space to socialise, engage in economic activities, cook and eat meals and hold communal celebrations.

One wall of the veranda, which can be up to 250m long, is pierced by doors to individual families' *bilik* (apartments), where there's space for sleeping and storage. If you ask about the size of a longhouse, you will usually be told how many doors, ie family units, it has.

Like the rest of us, Dayaks love their mod-cons, so longhouses where people actually live fuse age-old forms with modern conveniences - the resulting mash-up frequently mixes traditional materials (bamboo slat floors) with highly functional features such as corrugated iron, linoleum, satellite dishes and, out the front, a car park. The new longhouses built by the government for resettled Dayak villages usually follow the old floor-plan but use unremarkable modern construction techniques.

Most young Dayaks move away from the longhouse for greener pastures, seeking higher education and good jobs in the cities. But almost all keep close ties to their home longhouse, returning for major family and community celebrations. Some families that choose to remain in the longhouse community build a private house nearby, in part to escape the fire hazard inherent in living in a flammable structure with so many other people.

Dayak Religions

Traditional Dayak animism focuses on the spirits associated with virtually all places and things. It varies from tribe to tribe but is known collectively as Kaharingan.

PERSONAL DECOR

The most striking fashion feature of many older Dayak women (and, in some groups such as the Kelabit, men) is their elongated, pierced earlobes, stretched over the years by the weight of heavy gold or brass rings. Young people rarely follow this custom, and older Dayaks sometimes trim their ear lobes as a sign of conversion to Christianity.

In some tribes, women once tattooed their forearms and calves with bird and spirit designs, but this custom has almost disappeared except deep in the interior. Men still get tattoos (see p162) and, in a few cases, even the infamous *palang* (see p182), which in its extreme form involves placing a *palang* (a metal rod or bone) horizontally through the penis. The result is believed to emulate the natural endowment of the Sumatran rhino.

Carvings, totems, tattoos, and other objects (including, in earlier times, head-hunted skulls) are used to repel bad spirits, attract good spirits and soothe spirits that may be upset. Totems at entrances to villages and longhouses are markers for spirits. The hornbill is considered a powerful spirit, and is honoured in dance and ceremony, its feathers treasured. Black is widely considered a godly colour, so it features in traditional outfits. In some tribes, women have special roles – for instance, a female priestess, called a *bobohizan,* presides over many key Kadazan-Dusun traditional rituals.

Ancestor worship plays a large part in Kaharingan. After death, Dayaks join their ancestors in the spirit world. For some groups, spirits may reside in a particular mountain or other natural shrine. Burial customs include elaborately carved mausoleums, memorial monoliths, or internment in ceramic jars.

Most Dayaks now belong to mainstream Protestant groups (eg the Anglican Church), evangelical denominations (especially the Borneo Evangelical Church, also known as the SIB) and the Roman Catholic Church. Some evangelicals insist on purging all vestiges of previous beliefs, but in most instances Christianity overlays traditional cultural practices. Very, very few Dayaks still follow traditional religious practices.

Festivities such as the harvest ceremony known as Gawai Dayak in Sarawak are usually considered to be an expression of Dayak culture rather than pre-Christian religious beliefs.

Land of the Head-hunters

Head-hunting *(ngoyu)* has been relegated to the realm of Dayaks' self-deprecating witticisms, but for over 500 years it was an important element of Borneo's indigenous culture.

Many of the rites, rituals and beliefs surrounding this gruesome tradition remain shrouded in mystery but one aspect was unchanging: the act of taking heads was always treated with the utmost seriousness. Warriors practised two types of premeditated expeditions: *kayo bala,* a group raid involving several warriors; and *kayo anak,* performed by a lone brave, or *bujang berani.* The hunters of heads bore no personal animosity to their victims.

In the upper regions of the Batang Rejang, the *kayo anak* was a common method of wooing a prospective bride. The most valuable heads were those belonging to women and children because only the savviest and stealthiest warrior could ambush a child or woman as they bathed or picked berries. Such heads were usually hidden away from marauders near the longhouse hearth.

After a successful hunt, the warrior would wander the jungle, wrestling with the taken spirit rather than letting down his guard for a nap. In the morning, he would return to his longhouse where the head would be smoked and strung up for the others to see and honour. Heads were worshipped and revered, and food offerings were not uncommon. A longhouse with many heads was feared and respected by the neighbouring clans.

The tradition began its gradual decline in 1841 when James Brooke, at the behest of Brunei's sultan, started quashing the hunt for heads, in part to attract foreign traders, who had tended to keep their distance due to the island's fearsome reputation for harbouring ferocious cranium-nabbing natives. A nasty skirmish involving a knife-wielding pirate and a Chinese merchant's noodle gave Brooke the opportunity to show the Dayaks that he meant business – he promptly executed the criminal.

Head-hunting, to the extent that it continued, flew under the government's radar until WWII, when British commandos found the practice

Many Dayaks take their Christian faith very seriously, so much so that some communities have banned alcohol – including *tuak* (rice wine) – entirely.

The Iban traditionally kept head-hunted skulls outside the head-taker's family apartment, on the longhouse veranda (*ruai*), while the Bidayuh exhibited theirs in a communal headhouse (*baruk* or *panggah*).

DAYAK PEOPLES & CULTURE LAND OF THE HEAD-HUNTERS

Dayak slash-and-burn (swidden) agriculture is sometimes blamed for deforestation and forest fires, but in fact indigenous farmers are responsible for only a tiny fraction of the island's habitat loss.

useful for the war effort – so long as the victims were Japanese troops. Many of the heads that now adorn longhouses date from this period.

These days, murmurs about head-hunting are usually sensationalised efforts to drum up foreign intrigue – and touristic interest. The last '*tête offensive*' (so to speak) took place in Kalimantan in the early years of the 21st century, when immigrants from the island of Madura, resettled in Dayak areas by the Indonesian government, were the victims.

As Borneo's indigenous people embraced Christianity and rejected traditional animistic superstitions, many longhouses dismantled their dangling skulls. Though if you ask around, you'll quickly learn that the heads haven't actually been tossed away – that would just be bad luck!

Native Land Rights

When a tract of forest is cut down for timber or to make way for a dam or oil-palm plantation, animals are not the only ones who lose their homes – Borneo's forest-dwelling indigenous peoples are also displaced.

The Penan have been especially hard hit by logging and forced relocations. In Sarawak, the government has quashed Penan protests and responded to any sign of civil disobedience with arrests

Some 10,000 Orang Ulu people, most of them Kayan and Kenyah, were forcibly relocated in order to construct Sarawak's controversial Bakun Hydroelectric Dam (p193).

In Kalimantan, immigrants from other parts of Indonesia have encroached upon the Dayaks' traditional lands, producing a sometimes violent backlash.

Visiting a Longhouse

According to longstanding Dayak tradition, anyone who shows up at a longhouse must be welcomed and given accommodation. Since almost all longhouses were, until quite recently, a considerable jungle trek or longboat ride from the nearest human settlement, this custom made a great deal of sense.

Generations of jungle travellers knew the routine: upon arrival they would present themselves to the headman (known as a *ketua kaum* in Malay, a *tuai rumah* in Iban and *maren uma* in Kayan), who would arrange for very basic sleeping quarters. But in the last decade or two, as transport has become easier and tourist numbers have soared, this tradition has come under strain, and these days turning up at a longhouse unannounced may be an unwelcome imposition on longhouse residents – in short, bad manners.

The upshot is that in many areas of Borneo, the days when anyone could turn up unannounced at a longhouse and stay the night are largely over. And even if you make your own way to a longhouse that's happy to have you, you are likely to face significant communication and cultural barriers. Interacting spontaneously with locals isn't always easy as the elders usually don't speak English, and the younger people are often out working the fields or have moved to the 'big city' to pursue careers.

Stranger in the Forest tells the extraordinary tale of Eric Hansen's solo trek across Borneo and his encounters with various Dayak groups, including the Penan.

Finding a Guide

The way to avoid these pitfalls is to hire a guide who can coordinate your visit with longhouse residents and make introductions.

When considering a tour operator or freelance guide, it's best to keep an open mind – they're the experts, after all – but do not hesitate to be upfront about your preferences and concerns. Do you require a certain level of sleeping comfort? Do you have any dietary restrictions? How important is it that you be able to communicate with your hosts in English? Will you be disappointed if you see a satellite dish dangling off the side of the structure? Do you want to be the only traveller at the longhouse, or would you prefer it if there were others? Finding the right guide – and, through them, the right longhouse – can mean the difference between spending a sleepless night with other sweaty, bored tourists, or having a spirited evening (double entendre intended) swapping smiles, stories and shots of *tuak* with the locals.

Sarawak has plenty of tour operators and guides eager to take you (and your money) on Borneo's ultimate cultural adventure. From Kuching, it's easy to arrange day trips and overnights to Annah Rais Longhouse. For something off the beaten track, Kuching-based tour agencies and guides can take you to the remote Sri Aman Division, to rivers such as the Batang Skrang, Batang Lemanak and Batang Ai. The upper Batang Rejang has lots of longhouses but in the last few years we've heard tales of dubious guiding activity in Kapit and Belaga (we've also heard from travellers who've had a great time). Trekkers interested in walking from longhouse to longhouse in the Kelabit Highlands should head to Bario and plan their adventure from there.

In this book, reliable tour agencies are mentioned under Tours in city and town sections, but these lists are by no means exhaustive. The Sarawak Tourism Board (STB; www.sarawaktourism.com) has an online listing of about 100 registered tour operators (click 'Directory'). Some of the best guides work for tour operators, which saves them from having to go through the rigmarole of getting their own STB licence. Some freelance guides are friendly and knowledgeable but, alas, some are not; in any case, neither type can be held accountable if something goes wrong.

Up the Notched-Log Ladder is Sydwell Mouw Flynn's memoir of her parents' missionary work among Sarawak's Dayaks from 1933 to 1950, and her return to the land where she was raised half a century later.

What to Expect

When you arrive at a longhouse, don't be surprised to find that it wouldn't make a very good film set for a period drama about head-hunters. The Dayaks have moved – for the most part willingly – into the 21st century and so have their dwellings. Remember, though, that a longhouse, more than being a building, is a way of life embodying a communal lifestyle and a very real sense of mutual reliance and responsibility. It is this spirit rather than the physical building that makes a visit special.

Every longhouse is led by a headman. Depending on the tribe, he (or in a handful of cases she) may be appointed by his predecessor or elected; either way, heredity often plays a key role in selection. In many areas, longhouses are known by the name of the headman, so if you know the name of your destination you'll already know the name of the chief.

GIFTS

Gift giving has become rather controversial over the last few years, with locals, tourists and tour operators offering a wide variety of advice on the subject. Longhouse communities do not traditionally require gifts from guests; in fact, some say that the tradition of gift giving actually began when travellers started visiting.

To avoid any awkward cultural miscommunications, your best bet is to ask your guide. Longhouses set far off the beaten track may appreciate bulk bags of rice or sugar, while communities that are a bit more in touch with the modern world might appreciate items such as pencils, toothbrushes or fishing line. Some travellers bring something edible that can be shared over glasses of *tuak*. Any way you do it, gifts are never a must, nor are they expected.

Many tourists prefer contributing to the longhouse economy by taking a local longboat trip or buying one of the craft items offered for sale.

If you are visiting independently, it's polite to bring a small gift for the family of the person who invited you.

GAWAI DAYAK

In Sarawak and Brunei, the main pan-Dayak event of the year is Gawai Dayak (literally, 'Dayak festival'), which begins on the night of 31 May and lasts for two days (1 and 2 June are public holidays in Sarawak). Coinciding with the rice harvest, it brings Dayaks who live in the city back to their longhouses for round after round of socialising, eating and the consumption of tuak. Many Dayak communities also hold community events such as dances, sports competitions and beauty contests. Ceremonies marking the rice harvest are age-old, but Gawai Dayak, as a festival celebrated simultaneously by once-rival Dayak tribes all across Sarawak, only dates from the late 1950s.

Depending on the various goings-on at the longhouse you're visiting, you may or may not spend time with the headman, although he will usually 'show face' as it is impolite for him not to do so. Your guide will usually be the one showing you where to sleep, which is likely to be on the longhouse veranda, in a resident's living room, or in a specially built hut next door to the longhouse.

Do your best to engage with the inhabitants of any community you are allowed to enter, rather than just wandering around snapping photographs. A good guide can act as a translator when you strike up conversations, and he or she will keep you abreast of any cultural norms – like when and where to take off your shoes – so you won't have to worry too much about saying or doing the wrong thing.

Eat, Drink & Be Merry

If you are travelling with your own guide, he or she will be in charge of organising your meals – whether it's a separately prepared repast, or a feast with some of the longhouse residents.

The Borneo Project's documentary film *Rumah Nor*, about an Iban community's fight for its land, can be viewed online at http://borneo project.org.

The Iban, in particular, like to honour their guests by offering meat on special occasions. Vegetarians and vegans should be clear about their dietary restrictions as vegetable dishes are often served in a chicken sauce. Meals will be plentiful no matter what, and it is not considered rude or disrespectful to bring your own food, too. Two important things to remember when eating with longhouse residents: don't put your feet near the food (which is always served in a 'family-style' communal fashion); and don't step over anyone's plate if you need to excuse yourself from the eating area.

After dinner, when the generators start clicking off, it may be time to hunker down with the evening's bottle of milky-white spirits: *tuak*. The ceremonial shot glass will be passed from person to person amid chit-chat and belly laughter. Drink the shot when it's your turn (you won't really have a choice) and pass the glass along. *Tuak* may taste mild but many types are pretty potent, and you can expect a stunning hangover the next day. When you reach your limit, simply press the rim of the glass with your finger like you're pushing an eject button. If you don't want to drink, you can claim a medical condition – but make sure you don't get caught sneaking a drink later on! Smiles, big hand gestures and dirty jokes go a long way, even in your native language (and it'll all be second nature when you're nice and lubricated!).

Dayak ceremonies feature a variety of traditional dances and often entail consumption of *tuak*. Accepting an invitation to join the dance and making a fool of yourself are sure crowd-pleasers.

Survival
Guide

Directory A-Z

Accommodation

Accommodation in Borneo runs the gamut from international-standard hotels to upland Dayak longhouses, which themselves range from mod-con central to wood-and-palm structures deep in the jungle. In smaller towns, on outlying islands, and in the hinterlands, your options may be limited to very simple lodgings. Sabah and Sarawak have the best range of accommodation, particularly in the upper brackets, while Kalimantan has fewer top-end hotels and resorts. Brunei boasts one of the world's most opulent hotels.

When scanning accommodation reviews in this book, you can easily spot budget, midrange and top-end options by looking for the symbols $, $$ or $$$ next to the name of the establishment. In the table below, prices are for a double room with private bathroom, except in some budget places.

International-Standard Hotels

All of Borneo's major cities have hotels with the full range of mod-cons and amenities, but standards vary, from topnotch in Kuching, Kota Kinabalu (KK) and Bandar Seri Begawan (BSB) to close-but-no-cigar in places like Miri and Sibu. All but a few are run by local companies rather than the worldwide chains, and many are oriented primarily towards intra-regional business travellers. Booking online is the way to go at most of these places, and you'll often find offers well below rack rates – excellent rooms can be found for less than US$100 per night, sometimes half that.

In Malaysia and Brunei, most room prices you hear quoted include the 10% service charge. If you're unsure if your room rate is all-inclusive, ask if the quote is 'plus-plus' – a 'yes' means that the service charge and taxes have *not* been factored in.

Local Hotels

Often run by people of Chinese ancestry, the island's small hotels are the mainstay of the domestic hospitality market. The more salubrious ones are a decent option for budget travellers (some that we don't mention double as brothels). Starting at about US$17 for a double, they're generally fairly spartan: bare floors, no-frills furniture and absolutely no style. The showers and toilets are usually en suite, but may be down the hall for cheaper rooms. Before you check in, make sure the room you're being offered is properly ventilated, ideally with windows, and hasn't taken on that dank tropical fug.

Resorts

Some places that style themselves as 'resorts' have plenty of seaside (or jungle) activities and impeccable service, but others go mainly for the domestic business-conference market.

For a relaxing, resort-style holiday in Sabah, you can choose among several excellent seaside resorts in and near KK, or head to an offshore island such as Pulau Mantanani, Pulau Manukan, Pulau Tiga or Layang Layang, or the islands of the Semporna Archipelago.

Sarawak's best-known resort area is the Santubong Peninsula but, to be frank, this is not southern Thailand. For a rainforest resort with a Dayak-meets-Bali vibe, head to the Hilton Batang Ai Longhouse Resort or the Borneo Highlands Resort.

Brunei will blow you away with the over-the-top Empire Hotel & Country Club, or you can relax in the jungle lodge in Ulu Temburong National Park.

BOOK YOUR STAY ONLINE

For more accommodation reviews by Lonely Planet authors, check out hotels.lonelyplanet.com/Borneo. You'll find independent reviews, as well as recommendations on the best places to stay. Best of all, you can book online.

SLEEPING PRICE CATEGORIES

	SABAH & SARAWAK	BRUNEI	KALIMANTAN	KUALA LUMPUR	SINGAPORE	JAKARTA
Budget ($)	under RM60 (RM80 in KK & Kuching)	under B$60	under 180,000Rp	under RM60	under S$100	under 225,000Rp
Midrange ($$)	RM60-300	B$60-150	180,000-870,000Rp	RM60-300	S$100-200	225,000-540,000Rp
Top End ($$$)	over RM300	over B$150	over 870,000Rp	over RM300	over S$200	over 540,000Rp

Kalimantan has several seaside and island resorts, including on quaint Pulau Derawan.

Guest Houses & Backpacker Accommodation

Borneo's main tourist cities offer accommodation specifically designed for foreign travellers on a budget. Ideal for meeting fellow travellers, these places generally offer a choice of dorm beds or small private rooms (usually with common bathrooms), and also have a common area, an internet terminal or two, a basic kitchen and, if you're lucky, a washing machine and a rooftop garden for hanging out in the evening. Some rent bicycles and conduct tours of local sights, and for many it's a point of pride to provide up-to-the-minute travel information (eg regarding transport options). Dorm beds start at about US$5 per night, while private rooms go for US$17 and up. If you want your own room, cheap hotels often offer better value.

Because many guest houses (especially in Kuching) are situated in converted commercial buildings and old shophouses, not all the rooms come with windows. This might work with proper ventilation, but in some establishments the rooms are musty enough to choke

a horse – check before you check in!

Longhouses

According to tradition, passers-by are always welcome to overnight at longhouses, the age-old dwellings of many (but not all) of the indigenous peoples of Borneo. For details on Dayak culture and the etiquette of staying over, see p296.

Home Stays

Sabah and Kalimantan have plenty of welcoming home stays offering good value and a local vibe; many of them are listed in this book. Brunei's home stays tend to cater to tour groups and domestic tourists with their own cars.

Sarawak's tourism authorities have been encouraging the residents of far-flung *kampung* (villages) to open home stays but haven't quite nailed the right mix of training, infrastructure and quality control. Some of the home stays they publicise are just fine, while others are guest-ready only on paper, with rundown facilities, hosts who speak no English, and nothing to do.

Camping

In many national parks, camping is permitted only near park HQ; in Sarawak, the per-person charge is RM5.

If you pitch your tent in the vicinity of a longhouse, it

may look like you're spurning residents' hospitality. Some travellers compromise by erecting their tent on the longhouse's covered veranda.

As for equipment, a two-season tent with mosquito netting is ideal, and a summer-weight sleeping bag or just a bag liner will usually suffice unless you intend to do some climbing (the mountains get colder than you'd imagine).

Business Hours

Opening hours for eateries vary widely. *Kopitiam* and *kedai kopi* (Borneo's ubiquitous 'coffee shops', ie restaurants) that cater to the breakfast crowd, open very early – well before dawn – but may close before lunch. Others (generally the newer ones) will start service later in the morning and stay open until 9pm or 10pm. Bars usually open around dinnertime and close at around 2am.

Bank hours are generally 10am to 3pm or 4pm on weekdays and 9.30am to 11.30am on Saturday.

Shop hours are variable, although a good rule of thumb for small shops is that they're open Monday to Saturday from 9am to 6pm. Major department stores, shopping malls, Chinese emporiums and some large stores are open from around 10am until 9pm or 10pm seven days a week.

Government offices are usually open Monday to Friday from 8am to 4.15pm, and on Saturday from 8am to 12.45pm. Most close for lunch from 12.45 to 2pm; on Friday the lunch break is from 12.15pm to 2.45pm to accommodate Friday prayers at the mosque. (Note: in Brunei government offices are closed on Friday and Sunday.)

During Ramadan, business and office hours are often shortened and Muslim-owned restaurants may close during daylight hours. In Brunei, many offices end the day at 2pm from Monday to Thursday and at 11.30am on Friday and Saturday.

Children

Borneo is a great place for family travel, especially if the kiddies like monkeys, flowers, bugs and vibrant colours. Babies will attract a lot of attention.

Children receive discounts for both attractions and transport. Chinese hotels are a good bargain as they charge by the room rather than the number of people. However, cots are not widely available in cheap accommodation. Some top-end places allow two children under 12 to stay with their parents at no extra charge.

Baby formula and nappies (diapers) are widely available in Borneo, as is baby food. However, it makes sense to stock up on these items before heading to remote destinations or islands.

Customs Regulations

Tourists to Malaysia and Indonesia can bring with them up to 1L of liquor and 200 cigarettes duty free.

Signs at Malaysian airports inform visitors that

Climate

Kota Kinabalu

Kuching

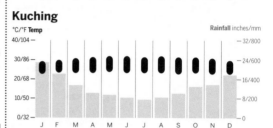

Bandar Seri Begawan

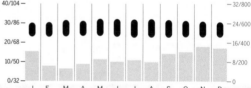

Balikpapan

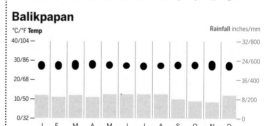

items not allowed into the country include daggers, cloth decorated with verses from the Koran, piranha fish and anything made in Israel.

Non-Muslim visitors to Brunei, provided they're over age 17, are allowed to import 12 cans of beer and two bottles of wine or spirits for personal consumption. Also permitted: 200 cigarettes.

Singapore's duty-free liquor allowance for travellers coming from Malaysia is...zero. Travellers, whatever their port of embarkation, must declare any cigarettes they are carrying. Theoretically, failing to declare even one pack of smokes can incur a S$200 fine. Chewing gum, of course, is also a no-no.

Electricity

The electricity supply is 220V AC, 50 Hz. Sarawak and Sabah (Malaysia) and Brunei use UK-style plugs with three massive square pins. Kalimantan (Indonesia) uses European-style plugs with two round prongs.

240v/50hz

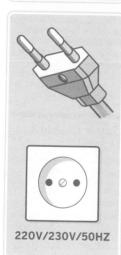

220V/230V/50HZ

Embassies & Consulates

Sabah

Australia (✆in KL during office hours 03-2146-5575, after hours 03-2146-5555, in Kota Kinabalu 088-267-151; www.malaysia.embassy.gov.au; suite 10.1, level 10, Wisma Great Eastern Life, 65 Jln Gaya, Kota Kinabalu) Honorary consul; report emergencies to the embassy in Kuala Lumpur.

Indonesia Kota Kinabalu (✆088-218-600; indocon@indocon.po.my; Lg Kemajuan, Karamunsing; ⊙9am-5pm Mon-Fri); Tawau (✆089-772052; ✆089-752969; Jln Sinn Onn; ⊙9am-noon, 1-3pm)

UK (✆in Kota Kinabalu 088-251-775, 24hr in KL 03-2170-2200; http://ukinmalaysia.fco.gov.uk; Kota Kinabalu) Honorary consul; contact the High Commission in KL for emergency travel documents. The honorary consul can visit UK citizens who are in hospital or in prison.

Sarawak

Australia (✆in KL during office hours 03-2146-5575, after hours 03-2146-5555; www.malaysia.embassy.gov.au; Kuching) Honorary consul; in case of emergency, the KL embassy will contact the consul in Kuching.

Indonesia (Konsulat Jenderal Republik Indonesia; ✆085-460-734; kjri-kuching@hotmail.com; Jln Stutong, Kuching; ⊙visa applications 9am-noon Mon-Fri, visa collections 3-5pm Mon-Fri, closed Malaysian & Indonesian holidays) To get here from Saujana Bus Station (RM2), take City Public Link bus K8 (every 30 to 45 minutes) to 'Jln Song/Friendship Park' or Sarawak Transport Company's buses 8G1, 8G2 or 8G3. A taxi from the centre costs RM25 one way.

UK (✆in Kuching 082-250-950, in Miri 085-452-415, 24-hr in KL 03-2170-2200;

Kuching) Honorary consul; contact the high commission in KL for emergency travel documents. The honorary consul can visit UK citizens who are in hospital or in prison.

Brunei

Australia (✆222-9435; www.bruneidarussalam.embassy.gov.au; 6th fl, Dar Takaful IBB Utama, Jln Pemancha)

Canada (✆222-0043; www.canadainternational.gc.ca/brunei_darussalam; 5th fl, Jln McArthur Bldg, 1 Jln McArthur)

France (✆222-0960; www.ambafrance-bn.org; units 301-306, Kompleks Jln Sultan, Jln Sultan)

Germany (✆222-5547; www.bandar-seri-begawan.diplo.de; 2nd fl, unit 2.01, block A, Yayasan Complex, Jln Pretty)

Indonesia (✆233-0180; www.indonesia.org.bn; 4498 Simpang 528, Jln Muara, Kampung Sungai Hanching)

Malaysia (✆238-1095/6/7; www.kln.gov.my/web/brn_begawan; 61 Simpang 336, Jln Kebangsaan)

Netherlands (✆337-3201; gerbert.schoonman@shell.com; Brunei Shell Petroleum, Seria) Honorary consul.

New Zealand (✆222-2422, 222-5880; c/o Deloitte & Touche, 5th Floor, Wisma Hajjah Fatimah, 22-23 Jln Sultan) Honorary consul.

Philippines (✆224-1465/6; www.philippineembassybrunei.net; 17 Simpang 126, km 2, Jln Tutong)

Singapore (✆226-2741; www.mfa.gov.sg/brunei; 8 Simpang 74, Jln Subok)

UK (✆222-2231, 222-6001; http://ukinbrunei.fco.gov.uk/en; 2nd fl, Unit 2.01, Block D, Yayasan Complex, Jln Pretty)

USA (✆238-4616; http://brunei.usembassy.gov; Simpang 336-52-16-9, Diplomatic Enclave, Jln Kebangsaan) The new US embassy complex is about 5km northeast of the Terrace Hotel.

Malaysia (☎0561-732-986, 0561-736-061; www.kln.gov. my/perwakilan/pontianak; Jln Sultan Syahrir 21, Pontianak; ⏱8am-4pm Mon-Fri)

Kuala Lumpur

Australia (☎03-2146-5555; www.malaysia.embassy.gov.au; 6 Jln Yap Kwan Seng)

Brunei (☎03-2161-2800; No 19-01 Tingkat 19, Menara Tan & Tan, Jln Tun Razak)

Canada (☎03-2718-3333; www.malaysia.gc.ca; 17th fl, Menara Tan & Tan, 207 Jln Tun Razak)

France (☎03-2053-5500; www.ambafrance-my.org; 192-196 Jln Ampang)

Germany (☎03-2170-9666; www.kuala-lumpur.diplo.de; 26th fl, Menara Tan & Tan, 207 Jln Tun Razak)

Indonesia (☎03-2116-4000; www.kbrikualalumpur.org; 233 Jln Tun Razak)

Ireland (☎03-2161-3427; www.embassyofireland.my; 218 Jln Ampang)

Netherlands (☎03-2168-6200, emergency 012-235-3210; www.netherlands.org. my; 7th fl, South Block, 218 Jln Ampang)

New Zealand (☎03-2078-2533; www.nzembassy.com/ malaysia; level 21, Menara IMC, 8 Jln Sultan Ismail)

Philippines (☎03-2148-9989; www.philembassykl.org. my; 1 Changkat Kia Peng)

UK (☎03-2170-2200; http:// ukinmalaysia.fco.gov.uk; 185 Jln Ampang)

USA (☎03-2168-5000; http:// malaysia.usembassy.gov; 376 Jln Tun Razak)

Jakarta

Australia (☎021-2550-5555; www.indonesia.embassy.gov. au; Jln HR Rasuna Said Kav C 15-16, Jakarta Selatan)

Brunei (☎021-3190-6080; www.mofat.gov.bn; Jln Teuku Umar No 9, Menteng)

Canada (☎021-2550-7800; www.canadainternational. gc.ca; World Trade Centre, 6th

fl, Jln Jenderal Sudirman Kav No 29-31)

France (☎021-2355-7600; www.ambafrance-id.org; Jln MH Thamrin No 20)

Germany (☎021-3985-5000; www.jakarta.diplo.de; Jln MH Thamrin No 1)

Malaysia (☎021-522-4974; www.kln.gov.my/web/idn_ja-karta; Jln H. Rasuna Said Kav X/6, No 1-3, Kuningan)

Netherlands (☎021-524-8200; http://www.mfa.nl/ jak-en; Jln HR Rasuna Said Kav S-3)

New Zealand (☎021-2995-5800; www.nzembassy.com/ indonesia; Sentral Senayan 2, 10th fl, Jln Asia Afrika No 8, Gelora Bung Karno, Jakarta Pusat)

UK (☎021-2356-5200; http:// ukinindonesia.fco.gov.uk; Jln MH Thamrin No 75)

USA (☎021-3435-9000; http:// jakarta.usembassy.gov; Jln Medan Merdeka Selatan No 3-5)

Singapore

Australia (☎6836-4100; www. australia.org.sg; 25 Napier Rd)

Brunei (☎6733-9055; www. mofat.gov.bn; 325 Tanglin Rd)

Canada (☎6854-5900; www. canadainternational.gc.ca; 1 George St, No 11-01)

France (☎6880-7800; www. ambafrance-sg.org; ☎101-103 Cluny Park Rd)

Germany (☎6533-6002, emergency 9817-0414; www. singapur.diplo.de; No 12-00 Singapore Land Tower, 50 Raffles Pl)

Indonesia (☎6737-5037; www.kbrisingapura.com; 7 Chatsworth Rd)

Ireland (☎6238-7616; www. embassyofireland.sg; No 08-00 Liat Towers, 541 Orchard Rd)

Malaysia (☎6733-6135; www. kln.gov.my/web/sgp_singapore; 301 Jervois Rd)

Netherlands (☎6737-1155; http://singapore.nlambassade. org; No 13-01 Liat Towers, 541 Orchard Rd)

New Zealand (☎6235-9966; www.nzembassy.com/ singapore; Ngee Ann City, Tower

A, No 15-06/10, 391A Orchard Rd)

UK (☎6424-4200; http:// ukinsingapore.fco.gov.uk; 100 Tanglin Rd)

USA (☎6476-9100; http:// singapore.usembassy.gov; 27 Napier Rd)

Food

A panoply of cuisines are cooked up by each of the three main ethnic groups in Borneo:

» Malays and Indonesians

» ethnic Chinese from a variety of dialect groups

» over 30 indigenous (Dayak) groups

There are also small communities of ethnic Indians.

During the month of Ramadan – which through 2014 falls between very late June and the end of August – Muslims are forbidden by Sharia law to eat or drink from dawn to sunset. But even in conservative Brunei, some restaurants continue to serve food to non-Muslims.

When looking through our recommendations under Eating, budget, midrange and top-end options are indicated by the symbols $, $$ or $$$ next to the name of the establishment. In the table on the next page, prices are for the cheapest non-vegetarian main dish on the menu.

Gay & Lesbian Travellers

Malaysia is by and large a socially conservative society and 'out' behaviour is looked upon disapprovingly; we strongly suggest discretion. According to the Australian government website www. smartraveller.gov.au, 'homosexual acts between males are illegal and penalties include corporal punishment and long prison sentences. Homosexual acts between women may be considered

EATING PRICE CATEGORIES

	SABAH & SARAWAK	BRUNEI	KALIMANTAN	KUALA LUMPUR	SINGAPORE	JAKARTA
Budget ($)	under RM5	under B$3	under 9000Rp	under RM5	under S$6	under 20,000Rp
Midrange ($$)	RM5-RM20	B$3-8	9000-54,000Rp	RM5-20	S$6-25	20,000-50,000Rp
Top End ($$$)	over RM20	over B$8	over 54,000Rp	over RM20	over S$25	over 50,000Rp

an "act of gross indecency with another" and penalties include imprisonment'.

Brunei, a devoutly Muslim country, has an even sterner outlook. According to www.smartraveller.gov.au, 'consensual homosexual acts between adults (of either sex) are illegal and penalties include prison sentences'.

Homosexuality is not a crime in Indonesia (Kalimantan), but the state is fairly conservative in these matters, so obviously 'out' behaviour is a very bad idea.

Insurance

Do not travel without travel insurance. Before you buy a policy, check the fine print to see if it excludes risky activities like scuba diving, mountain climbing or caving. If you want to visit remote areas such as Sabah's Maliau Basin Conservation Area, you'll need a plan that covers helicopter evacuation.

Internet Access

Most top-end hotels and backpackers' guest houses, and an increasing number of midrange places, offer wi-fi, at least in the lobby. Many places, including guest houses, also have internet computers, often for a nominal charge. Western-style coffee shops are usually wired for wi-fi.

Internet cafes can be found in the main towns and cities of the coast and, increasingly, even in the smaller towns of the interior. Access is usually quite cheap, averaging around US$1 per hour.

Areas without internet access of any sort include many of the offshore islands and huge swaths of the interior.

Legal Matters

In Malaysia, certain drug crimes carry a 'mandatory death sentence', and when entering Brunei you'll see signs reading 'Warning: Death for drug traffickers under Brunei law'. Indonesia also has harsh penalties for the smuggling or possession of drugs.

Gambling and the possession of pornography are punishable by severe penalties in these countries. It is illegal to work without a proper working visa.

The sale and public consumption of alcohol is forbidden in Brunei.

Under Indonesian law, you must carry identification (eg a passport) at all times.

Maps

Getting a hold of accurate, up-to-date maps of Borneo is a real problem. Malaysia still keeps most maps classified, partly as a holdover from the Konfrontasi with Indonesia

(way back in the 1960s!), and partly to make it difficult for indigenous groups to pursue land claims against logging companies. Brunei doesn't officially release any of its maps to non-Bruneians, and accurate maps of Kalimantan are simply impossible to get.

The best road maps available for Sabah (1:800,000) and Sarawak (1:1,000,000), including the main cities, are produced by **Periplus** (www.periplus.com); if you're driving, these are the least confusing maps to use. A map covering both Sabah and Sarawak (1:1,300,000) is published by **Globetrotter** (www.newhollandpublishers.com). These maps can usually be found at major bookshops in KK and Kuching, but it's a good idea to buy them online before you arrive.

Periplus does not publish a Kalimantan map, so you'll have to make do with its Indonesia map if you want something beyond the maps in this book.

The only commercially produced map of Brunei is the almost useless 1:20,000-scale *Street Directory* (B$14.95). Much more user-friendly is the free *Official Map of Brunei Darussalam*, available at tourist offices.

Google Earth (http://earth.google.com) is a very useful resource, providing a fairly clear overview of river and road networks, particularly along the northern coast. For those planning a trek into the sticks, it is the best way to check the extent of remaining jungle cover. Google Earth has especially clear images of many of Borneo's cities. For Brunei, Google Earth is easily the best supplement to the maps in this book.

The coverage of Borneo by **Google Maps** (http://maps. google.com) is spotty at best.

Media

Malaysia's print media are pretty much owned or controlled by pro-government factions. For the opposition perspective, look online.

The Kuching-based *Borneo Post* (RM1; www. theborneopost.com) is the main English-language newspaper in Sabah and Sarawak. The *New Sarawak Tribune* (RM1; http://tribune.my), Borneo's second English-language daily, reappeared in 2010. The original *Sarawak Tribune* ceased publication in 2006 following its decision to reprint a controversial Danish cartoon depicting the Prophet Mohammed (the editor wanted to illustrate a news story entitled 'Cartoon No Big Impact Here').

Also available in Malaysian Borneo is the Kuala Lumpur–based *New Straits Times* (RM1.80; www.nst.com. my). This is yet another pro-government paper – not the place to look for trenchant commentary or explosive exposés.

In Brunei, the *Borneo Bulletin* (B\$0.80; www. borneobulletin.com.bn) is filled with local and international news, most of it from news agencies, none of it locally controversial. News stories refer to the sultan as 'the benevolent ruler' so no prizes for guessing that the paper does not do hard-hitting investigative reporting.

Top-end hotels usually have satellite-TV relays of CNN, BBC, Star and other English-language stations.

Money

Tipping is not practised much in Borneo.

Sabah & Sarawak

Malaysia's currency is the ringgit (RM, for Ringgit Malaysia, or MYR), which is divided into 100 sen. Banknote denominations are RM1, RM5, RM10, RM50 and RM100.

The ringgit used to be known as the Malaysian dollar (M\$) and Malaysians sometimes still refer to a ringgit as a *dolar*. To further confuse things, in Bahasa Malaysia Singapore and Brunei dollars are known as ringgit.

The amount of Malaysian currency you are allowed to bring into or take out of the country is limited to RM1000, a legacy of the 1997 Asian financial crisis. As a result, outside of Malaysia the exchange rates for ringgit are often poor.

ATMs are widely available in cities, towns and urban airports but not in rural areas. However, some ATMs do not take international cards. Many banks also do cash advances at the counter.

The easiest banknotes to change are those in US, Australian and Singapore dollars and pounds sterling. Some banks aren't keen on exchanging any foreign currency, and small-town branches may not handle exchange transactions at all. Cities and large towns have moneychangers, and even smaller towns often have a shop that handles foreign currency.

To change travellers cheques in US, Australian or Singapore dollars or in pounds sterling (other currencies may be harder to cash), banks generally charge RM5 or RM10 per cheque, or RM20 per transaction plus RM0.15 per cheque.

Brunei

The Brunei dollar (B\$) is available in denominations of B\$1, B\$5, B\$10, B\$50, B\$100, B\$500 and B\$1000 and, believe it or not, B\$10,000. Thanks to the 1967 Currency Interchangeability Agreement between Brunei and Singapore, the two countries' dollars are worth exactly the same and can be used in both countries. Singaporean banknotes (with the possible exception of S\$2, which has no Bruneian counterpart) are universally accepted in Brunei, and Brunei banknotes can be used almost everywhere in Singapore. To celebrate the pact's 40th anniversary, a commemorative B\$20/S\$20 note was issued in 2007.

For currency exchange, moneychangers are generally a better bet than banks, though some places in BSB have a pretty hefty spread between their buy and sell rates.

ATMs are widely available, though not all take international credit/debit cards. Major credit cards (Visa, MasterCard and American Express) are widely accepted.

Kalimantan

Indonesia's currency is the rupiah (Rp). Banknotes come in denominations of 1000Rp, 2000Rp, 5000Rp, 10,000Rp, 20,000Rp, 50,000Rp and 100,000Rp (sounds like a lot, but it's worth just US$11). Coins you may see include 50Rp, 100Rp, 200Rp, 500Rp and 1000Rp; newer ones are lightweight aluminium, older ones are either bronze-coloured or bi-metal.

Public Holidays

The online events calendars produced by **Sabah Tourism** (www.sabahtourism.com) and **Brunei Tourism** (www.bruneitourism.travel) and the RSS 'Events' web feed on the website of **Sarawak Tourism** (www.sarawaktourism.com) have details on public and religious holidays.

Sabah & Sarawak

New Year's Day 1 January
Chinese New Year January or February
Federal Territory Day (Pulau Labuan only) 1 February
Maulidur Rasul (Prophet's Birthday) Varies, but between mid-January and mid-February through 2014
Good Friday Late March or April
Labour Day 1 May
Wesak Day (Buddha's Birthday) Sometime in May
Harvest Festival (Sabah only) 30 and 31 May
Gawai Dayak (Sarawak only) Evening of 31 May to 2 June
Birthday of Yang di-Pertuan Agong First Saturday in June

Hari Raya Puasa (Eid al-Fitr; end of Ramadan) Varies, but in very late July or August through 2014
Independence Day 31 August
Sabah Chief Minister's Birthday (Sabah only) 16 September
Sarawak Chief Minister's Birthday (Sarawak only) 23 October
Malaysia Day 23 October
Hari Raya Aidiladha (Eid al-Adha) Varies, but in October or early November through 2014
Deepavali (not in Sarawak or Pulau Labuan) Late October or first half of November
Awal Muharram (Muslim New Year) Varies, but in November through 2013
Christmas Day 25 December

Brunei

New Year's Day 1 January
Chinese New Year January or February
Maulidur Rasul (Prophet's Birthday) Varies, but between mid-January and mid-February through 2014.
Brunei National Day 23 February
Royal Brunei Armed Forces Day 31 May
Gawai Dayak (Ibans only) Evening of 31 May to 2 June
Isra Mikraj (Prophet's Ascension) Varies, but in June through 2014
Sultan of Brunei's Birthday 15 July
Nuzul Quraan (Koran Revelation Day) Varies, but in July or August through 2014
First Day of Ramadan Varies, but in July or very early August through 2014
Hari Raya Aidil Fitri (end of Ramadan) Varies, but in very late July or August through 2014.
Hari Raya Aidil Adha Varies, but in October or early November through 2014

Islamic New Year Varies, but in November through 2013
Christmas Day 25 December

Kalimantan

Tahun Baru Masehi (New Year's Day) 1 January
Tahun Baru Imlek (Chinese New Year) January or February
Maulid Nabi Muhammed (Prophet's Birthday) Varies, but between mid-January and mid-February through 2014
Hari Raya Nyepi (Balinese Day of Silence) Sometime in March
Wafat Yesus Kristus (Good Friday) Late March or April
Waisak (Buddha's Birthday) Sometime in May
Kenaikan Yesus Kristus (Ascension Day) Sometime in May
Isra' Mi'raj Nabi Muhammed (Prophet's Ascension) Varies, but in June through 2014
Idul Fitri (end of Ramadan) Varies, but in very late July or August through 2014
Hari Proklamasi Kemerdekaan (Independence Day) 17 August
Idul Adha Varies, but in October or early November through 2014
Tahun Baru Hijriyah (Islamic New Year) Varies, but in November through 2013
Hari Natal (Christmas Day) 25 December

Safe Travel

The Australian government (www.smartraveller.gov.au) warns travellers of a 'high threat of kidnapping by terrorists and criminals' in 'the islands, dive sites and coastal areas of eastern Sabah', including Sipadan, Mataking and Pandanan. Concern about the area dates from the abduction of 21 hostages from Sipadan by Philippines-based Abu Sayyaf terrorists in 2000.

Borneo is generally very safe for travellers of both sexes, but in villages and logging camps things can get dodgy when alcohol enters the picture.

Saltwater (estuarine) crocodiles, the world's largest living reptiles, are a very real danger in waterways, especially in muddy estuaries. Exercise caution when swimming in rivers, even far inland, and never swim near river mouths.

Telephone

Cheap prepaid SIM cards make it easy and remarkably inexpensive to keep in touch, both with local contacts and with family and friends around the world. If you bring along your own gadget, make sure it can handle 900/1800MHz and is not locked. In Borneo, the cheapest Nokia cell phones start at about US$40.

Some electronic devices (eg iPods) let you make Skype calls anywhere there's a wi-fi signal (eg hotel lobbies, guest houses and many cafes).

Sabah & Sarawak

The country code for Malaysia is ☏60. When calling Malaysia from overseas, dial:

» ☏60

» the area code or the three-digit cell-phone access code, minus the initial zero (in this book, area codes are indicated under city names)

» the local number (six or seven digits)

Within Malaysia, the access code for making international calls is ☏00. Useful numbers:

» Ambulance ☏999
» Police ☏999
» Fire ☏999
» Directory enquiries ☏103

Many shops sell prepaid calling cards, but these are going the way of the dial-up modem as mobile phones become ubiquitous.

Sabah and Sarawak have three cell-phone networks on which various companies buy air time. **Celcom** (www.celcom.com.my) generally has the best coverage, making it possible to phone home from places like Bario (in the Kelabit Highlands) and the slopes of Mt Kinabalu. There's 3G coverage, but certain packages require that you pay a per-day rate. The other two mobile companies are **DiGi** (www.digi.com.my) and **Hotlink** (www.hotlink.com.my).

All three companies' prepaid SIM cards, available at shops and kiosks in all but the tiniest villages, cost just RM8.50 (the equivalent of just a minute or two of international roaming charges) and take about 10 minutes to activate (you'll have to show your passport). With Celcom, recharge cards come in denominations from RM5 to RM50. Local calls cost RM0.12 to RM0.15 per minute; international direct dialling costs just RM0.18 per minute to North America and to land-line numbers in Australia and the UK (mobile lines cost RM0.88 a minute). SMSs (text messages; RM0.06 or less each) are hugely popular and are a great way to communicate with locals and expats.

Brunei

Brunei's country code is ☏673. Within Brunei, the access code for making international calls is ☏00. Brunei does not have area codes. **TelBru** (www.telbru.com.bn) is the national phone company. Useful numbers:

» Ambulance ☏991
» Police ☏993
» Fire ☏995
» Search & Rescue ☏998
» Directory enquiries ☏113

Bruneian prepaid SIM cards cost B$30 (including a B$25 annual license fee) and must be registered within a week of activation (after that the number will be blocked). The cheapest and easiest way to buy one is to go to the office of **DST Communications** (www.dst-group.com; ground fl, western building, Yayasan Complex, Jln McArthur) in central BSB; bring your passport. Various shops also sell DST SIM cards but they often charge a premium and neglect to handle registration. For international calls, using the access code ☏095 ('IDD 095') is cheaper than ☏00; calls to Australia, the UK and the USA cost B$0.30 to B$0.50 a minute.

The sultanate's other cell-phone service provider, **b.mobile** (www.bmobile.com.bn) sells SIM-card starter packs for B$36.

If you have a Malaysian SIM card, it will not work in Brunei unless you pay astronomical roaming charges or climb to the top of Ulu Temburong National Park's canopy walk.

Kalimantan

The country code for Indonesia is ☏62. When calling Indonesia from overseas, dial:

» ☏62

» the area code minus the first zero (in this book, area codes are indicated under city names)

» the local number

Pulsa prepaid SIM cards can be bought in cities and towns for about 10,000Rp and need to be activated by the shop owner. **Telcomsel** (www.telkomsel.com) SIM cards are good for cheap overseas calls. Telcomsel is fine along the coast of East Kalimantan but in the interior **Indosat** (www.indosat.com) has better coverage.

Time

Sabah, Sarawak and Brunei are all eight hours ahead of Greenwich Mean Time. Thus, all three are:

» two hours behind Melbourne and Sydney

» the same time as Singapore

» seven hours ahead of Paris

» eight hours ahead of London

» 13 hours ahead of New York

» 16 hours ahead of San Francisco

Sabah, Sarawak and Brunei do not have daylight-saving time (DST), so these figures shift by an hour when DST is in effect in Australia, Europe or North America.

Kalimantan is divided into two time zones: Indonesian Western Standard Time (UTC +7), which is observed in West and Central Kalimantan; and Indonesian Central Standard Time (UTC +8), which is observed in East and South Kalimantan.

Toilets

You'll find a lot of squat-style ('Turkish') toilets in Borneo, particularly in public places. Western-style seated toilets are the norm in hotels and guest houses. You may be expected to flush using a plastic bucket.

Toilet paper is often unavailable in public toilets, including those with a fee, so keep a stash handy. In urban areas, you can usually discard used toilet paper into the bowl without causing clogging, but if there is a wastepaper basket – as there often is in rural bogs – it's meant to be used.

Tourist Information

Your best sources of information are often guest house owners, guides, tour agencies and your fellow travellers.

Brunei

Brunei's national tourist body, **Brunei Tourism** (www. bruneitourism.travel), has a very useful website. By the time you read this, it should have three offices, including one at the airport.

KH Soon Resthouse in BSB can supply information on land transport to Miri (Sarawak) and Sabah.

Kalimantan

Kalimantan is only one of the many islands under the purview of Indonesia's **Ministry of Culture & Tourism** (www. indonesia.travel). Local tourist offices can be found in many of Kalimantan's bigger cities but they range from very helpful to well-meaning but hopeless.

Sabah & Sarawak

The two state tourism authorities, **Sabah Tourism** (www.sabahtourism.com) and **Sarawak Tourism** (www. sarawaktourism.com), have useful websites with details on festivals and other current events. The tourist information offices in larger cities generally have helpful staff and entire walls filled with up-to-date travel information.

Sarawak Forestry (www. sarawakforestry.com), which is responsible for the state's national parks (as well as 'sustainable logging'), has an especially informative website, publishes useful brochures (RM1.50) and runs very helpful offices in Kuching and Miri. Staff even answer the phone! Accommodation at certain national parks can be booked at its offices, through its website or via http://ebooking.com.my.

Sabah's national parks are run by **Sabah Parks** (www. sabahparks.org), which has an information office in KK.

Travellers with Disabilities

Borneo has a long way to go in this regard. Most buildings, public transport and tourist destinations are not wheelchair accessible, and navigating Malaysian cities in a

---

MALAYSIA'S STAR, STRIPES & CRESCENT

It's no coincidence that the Malaysian flag, based on a 1947 design, looks so much like its American counterpart. For a while after WWII, the US was popular in Malaya, in part for having helped get rid of the Japanese, and the US flag was seen as an excellent way to represent a federal system of government.

The Malaysian flag has 14 horizontal red-and-white stripes (one more than the American flag) representing the country's 13 states and either its federal government or, collectively, its three federal districts (the 14th stripe originally represented Singapore, which left the federation in 1965). In the upper left-hand corner is a field whose dark blue, taken from the Union Jack, was once seen as representing the Commonwealth but is now interpreted as signifying national unity. The crescent (representing Islam) and the 14-point star (representing the unity of the federation) are both yellow, the traditional royal colour.

wheelchair can be a very trying experience due to varying pavement heights and other infrastructure shortcomings. Most tour companies that operate in the interior do not accommodate people with physical disabilities.

Visas

Make sure your passport is valid for at least six months beyond your date of entry and, if you'll be travelling overland through Brunei, that you have enough pages for lots of entry stamps (no fewer than 10 if you travel by road from Sabah to Sarawak!).

Sabah & Sarawak

Visas valid for three months are issued upon arrival to citizens of:

» the US
» the EU (except Bulgaria, Estonia, Greece, Latvia, Lithuania, Monaco and Portugal, whose nationals get one month)
» the Commonwealth (except Bangladesh, India, Pakistan, Sri Lanka, Cameroon, Ghana, Mozambique and Nigeria, whose nationals require advance-issue visas)
» most wealthier Arab states, including North Africa (except Libya)
» Switzerland, Japan, South Korea and Lebanon

One-month visas are issued on arrival to citizens of:

» most countries in Latin America
» most countries in the former Soviet Union
» non-Commonwealth ASEAN countries (except Myanmar)
» certain African countries

Advance-issue visas are required for citizens of Bangladesh, China, Colombia, India, Montenegro, Pakistan, Serbia, Sri Lanka, Taiwan and most countries in sub-Saharan Africa. Israeli passport holders are issued Malaysian visas only in exceptional circumstances.

The website of Malaysia's Ministry of Home Affairs' **Immigration Department** (www.imi.gov.my) has complete information on visa types, who needs them and how to get them.

Visa Extensions

Malaysian visas can be extended in the Sarawak towns of Kuching, Bintulu, Kapit, Lawas, Limbang, Miri and Sibu; and, in Sabah, in KK, Keningau, Kudat, Lahad Datu, Sandakan, Semporna, Sipitang, Tawau and Tenom.

In general, Malaysian visas can be extended for 60 days. Bring your departure ticket and be ready to explain why you would like to

stay longer and where you'll be staying; a photo is not required. Approval is usually same day.

Extensions take effect on the day they're issued, so the best time to extend a visa is right before the old one expires. If your visa still has a month of validity left, that time will not be added to the period covered by the extension.

Some travellers report that they've been able to extend their Malaysian visas by going through Malaysian border control at the Brunei border and then, without officially entering Brunei, turning around and re-entering Malaysia.

Overstaying your visa by a few days is not usually a big deal, especially if you're a genuine tourist and have no prior offences. However, at the discretion of immigration officers, any violation of Malaysia's visa rules can result in your being turned over to the Immigration Department's enforcement section, if you're in Sarawak, and taken to Serian, 60km southeast of Kuching, for questioning. Bummer of a way to miss your flight.

Brunei

When it comes to getting into Brunei, Americans are luckiest (they get a free 90-day visa on arrival) and Israelis

---

SARAWAK & SABAH PASSPORT STAMPS

Under the terms of Sabah and Sarawak's entry into Malaysia, both states retain a certain degree of state-level control of their borders. Malaysian citizens from Peninsular Malaysia (West Malaysia) cannot work in Malaysian Borneo (East Malaysia) without special permits, and tourists must go through passport control and have their passports stamped whenever they:

» arrive in Sabah or Sarawak from Peninsular Malaysia or the federal district of Pulau Labuan
» exit Sabah or Sarawak on their way to Peninsular Malaysia or Pulau Labuan
» travel between Sabah and Sarawak

When entering Sabah or Sarawak from another part of Malaysia, your new visa stamp will be valid only for the remainder of the period left on your original Malaysian visa.

the unluckiest (they can't visit at all). Travellers from Western Europe, New Zealand, Singapore, Malaysia and a few other countries score 30 days at the border, while Canadians, Swiss and Japanese get 14 days. Because of a recent spat between Brunei and Australia, Aussies don't need to apply for a visa in advance but do have to ante up B$5 (payable only in Brunei or Singapore dollars) for a three-day transit visa (you need to show a ticket out), B$20 for a single-entry visa valid for two weeks, or B$30 for a multiple-entry visa valid for a month (this is the one to get if you'll be going overland between Sarawak and Sabah).

People of most other nationalities must obtain a visa (single/multiple entry B$20/30) in advance from a Brunei Darussalam diplomatic mission – unless, that is, they'll just be transiting through Brunei (ie arriving from one place and continuing on to a different place), in which case a 72-hour visa is available upon arrival. For more information, see:

» www.mofat.gov.bn/visa information/visaarrange ments.htm

» www.immigration.gov. bn/002/html/melawat.html

Kalimantan

As of 2010, tourists from 64 countries – including Australia, Canada, the EU, India, Japan, New Zealand, South Africa and the US – receive a 30-day Indonesian visa-on-arrival (VOA) at three entry points to Kalimantan:

» Tebedu–Entikong land crossing, between Kuching (Sarawak) and Pontianak (West Kalimantan)

» Balikpapan (Sepinggan Airport)

» Pontianak (Supadio Airport)

The cost is US$25, payable only in US dollars (at the Tebedu–Entikong crossing,

at least, ringgit and rupiah are not accepted!). Once in the country, a VOA can be extended by another 30 days for US$25.

If you arrive in Kalimantan – by land, sea or air – from outside Indonesia at any other entry point, or if your passport is not from one of the 64 designated VOA countries, you must obtain a visa in advance. You might also want to apply for a visa ahead of time if you know that you'll be staying in Kalimantan (especially in remote areas) for more than 30 days.

In Sabah, Indonesia has consulates in KK and Tawau, and in Sarawak there's a shiny new consulate in Kuching. A 60-day visa costs RM170; bring a photo, your ticket out of Indonesia, and a credit card or cash to show that you've got funds. Visas are generally issued the same day.

For a full list of the countries whose nationals score a VOA and a full list of the entry points at which they are issued, see www.embas syofindonesia.org/consular/voa.htm.

Volunteering

Pay-to-volunteer programs are available at the **Sepilok Orang-Utan Rehabilitation Centre** (see www.travellersworldwide.com) in Sabah; and in Sarawak at the

Matang Wildlife Centre (www.orangutanproject.com) and through Talang-Satang National Park's Sea Turtle Volunteer Programme (contact the National Park Booking Office in Kuching).

Women Travellers

Borneo is a relatively easy and pleasant place for women travellers. Although local women (especially ethnic Chinese) wear shorts and tank tops in the cities, it's a good idea to dress fairly conservatively in Muslim areas and to cover up when visiting a mosque (robes and headscarves are sometimes provided). Overall, things are considerably more laid-back and liberal in Borneo than, say, in northeastern Peninsular Malaysia.

Brunei is more conservative than Sabah or Sarawak. Some women have reported being the object of catcalls and come-ons, especially from passing motorists.

As with anywhere else, it pays to use common sense and caution. Do not get lulled into a false sense of security just because everyone seems so relaxed and easygoing. Solo hitchhiking is a bad idea anywhere, and Borneo is no exception. Do not walk alone at night if possible, lock the door to your hotel room, and do not accept drinks or food from strangers.

Transport

GETTING THERE & AWAY

Almost all travellers arrive in Borneo by air, most of them from the 'gateway cities' of Singapore, Kuala Lumpur (KL) and Jakarta. However, there are ferries to Sabah from the southern Philippines, and Kalimantan has ferry links to Java and Sulawesi.

Flights and tours can be booked online at www.lonely planet.com/bookings.

Air

Sabah

For information on flights from KL and Singapore, see p41 and p49.

AirAsia (www.airasia.com) Can get you to Kota Kinabalu (KK) from Peninsular Malaysia (KL, Johor Bahru and Penang), Singapore, Jakarta, Clark (Philippines), Taipei, Shenzhen and Hong Kong.

JetStar (www.jetstar.com) Links Singapore with KK.

Malaysia Airlines (www. malaysiaairlines.com) Has direct flights to KK from Peninsular Malaysia (KL, Johor Bahru and Penang), Hong Kong, Kaohsiung (Taiwan), Seoul and Tokyo (Haneda).

Tiger Airways (www.tiger airways.com) Flies from Singapore to KK.

Sarawak

For information on flights from KL and Singapore, see p41 and p49.

AirAsia (www.airasia.com) Has direct flights to Kuching, Sibu and Miri from both KL and Johor Bahru. Also links Singapore with Kuching and Miri, and Penang with Kuching.

Malaysia Airlines (www.mal aysiaairlines.com) Has flights to Kuching from Singapore and KL.

Brunei

Royal Brunei Airlines (www.bruneiair.com) Brunei's national carrier links Bandar Seri Begawan (BSB) with London, Dubai, Auckland, Melbourne, Brisbane, Hong Kong, Shanghai, Surabaya, Jakarta and Bangkok (code share with Thai Airways International). Shorter flights (eg to Singapore) tend to be pricey, but the company sometimes offers good long-haul deals.

AirAsia (www.airasia.com) Serves KL.

Cebu Pacific Air (www. cebupacificair.com) Flights to Manila.

Malaysia Airlines (www. malaysiaairlines.com) Goes to KL.

Singapore Airlines (www. singaporeair.com) Flies to Singapore.

Kalimantan

Following a spate of tragic air disasters due to old planes and safety failures, a number of airlines operating in Kalimantan were shut down, while an EU ban forced other airlines to have a hasty rethink and renew their fleets. The air is a much safer place to travel now.

Berau airport is in the process of getting international connections.

For details on flights from Jakarta, see p54.

AirAsia (www.airasia.com) Flies from KL to Balikpapan.

Batavia Air (www.batavia-air. com) Has flights from Singapore, Batam (near Singapore), Yogyakarta, Jakarta, Tarakan, Surabaya, Manado and Palu to Balikpapan and/ or Pontianak. Palangkaraya and Banjarmasin can be reached from Jakarta and Surabaya.

Garuda (www.garuda -indonesia.com) Has flights from Jakarta and Yogyakarta to Balikpapan. Banjarmasin and Pontianak can be reached from Jakarta; Pontianak is also accessible from Surabaya.

Kal Star (www.kalstaronline. com) Has regular flights from Jakarta to Kalimantan and lots of intra-Kalimantan connections.

Lion Air (www2.lionair.co.id) Flies from Jakarta to Banjarmasin, Balikpapan and Palangkaraya, with onward flights to all major cities in Kalimantan.

Silk Air (www.silkair.net) Links Singapore with Balikpapan.

Sea

Sabah

Ferries link Sandakan with Zamboanga, on the Philippine island of Mindanao, twice a week.

Kalimantan

Ferries connect Kalimantan with Jakarta, Semarang and Surabaya on Java, and with Makassar, Pare Pare, Mamuju and Toli Toli on Sulawesi.

To/From Java

Pelni (www.pelni.co.id) Has routes that include: Balikpapan to Makassar and Surabaya, with connections to Jakarta and Medan; Samarinda to Pare Pare and Makassar; Batu Licin (Banjarmasin) to Surabaya; and Pontianak to Surabaya and Jakarta.

To/From Sulawesi

Pelni (www.pelni.co.id) Has a route from Makassar (Sulawesi) to Balikpapan.

Prima Vista (✆0542-732-607; Jln Sudirman 138, Balikpapan) Has ferries to Surabaya from Balikpapan, Sampit, Kumai, Banjarmasin and Makassar.

GETTING AROUND

Air

Borneo is covered by a surprisingly extensive network of flights, and it's often remarkably cheap to hop around the island by air. Air travel is the only practical way to reach some destinations, such as Sarawak's Kelabit Highlands and Gunung Mulu National Park.

There's something incredibly exciting and romantic about buzzing over the jungle in an 18-seat DeHavilland Twin Otter turboprop – or bouncing around in a cloudburst, raindrops crashing furiously on the pilots' windshield, which passengers can see out of because the cockpit doesn't have a door. Note: on some Twin Otter routes (eg up to Bario) there are strict limits on both carry-on and checked baggage – they even weigh the passengers!

In most cases, you can buy air tickets on relatively short notice, but for a few destinations, including Gunung Mulu National Park, Bario and Ba Kelalan (all in Sarawak), it's a good idea to book ahead, especially in July and August and around holidays. Tickets for most flights can be purchased online.

Sabah & Sarawak

AirAsia (www.airasia.com) Links Kuching with Sibu, Bintulu, Miri and KK; and KK with Tawau, Sandakan, Pulau Labuan, Miri and Kuching.

Batavia Air (www.batavia-air.co.id) Can get you from Kuching to Pontianak three times a week.

Malaysia Airlines (www.malaysiaairlines.com.my) Has flights from KK to Kuching and BSB (Brunei).

MASwings (www.maswings.com.my) Serves 16 destinations in Sabah (including Sandakan, Lahad Datu and Tawau) and Sarawak (including Lawas, Limbang, Bario, Miri, Gunung Mulu National Park, Bintulu and Sibu). Has hubs in KK, Kuching and Miri.

Brunei

Malaysia Airlines (www.malaysiaairlines.com) Goes to KK.

MASwings (www.maswings.com.my) Flies from Miri (Sarawak) to three destinations that are just a boat and/or bus ride away from BSB: Lawas, Limbang and Pulau Labuan.

Kalimantan

Kalimantan has a comprehensive network of air links handled by:

Batavia Air (✆inside Kalimantan 0536-323-8882, outside Indonesia +62-21-389-99888; www.batavia-air.com) Serves Samarinda, Pontianak, Banjarmasin, Balikpapan and Palangkaraya, and also has flights from Kuching to Pontianak.

IAT (Indonesia Air Transport; ✆inside Kalimantan 0561-736-603, outside Indonesia +62-21-808-70666; www.iat.co.id)

Kal-Star (✆inside Kalimantan 0561-737-473, outside Indonesia +62-0561-73747; www.kalstaronline.com) Destinations include Pangkalan Bun

---

CLIMATE CHANGE & TRAVEL

Every form of transport that relies on carbon-based fuel generates CO_2, the main cause of human-induced climate change. Modern travel is dependent on aeroplanes, which might use less fuel per kilometre per person than most cars but travel much greater distances. The altitude at which aircraft emit gases (including CO_2) and particles also contributes to their climate change impact. Many websites offer 'carbon calculators' that allow people to estimate the carbon emissions generated by their journey and, for those who wish to do so, to offset the impact of the greenhouse gases emitted with contributions to portfolios of climate-friendly initiatives throughout the world. Lonely Planet offsets the carbon footprint of all staff and author travel.

Border Crossings

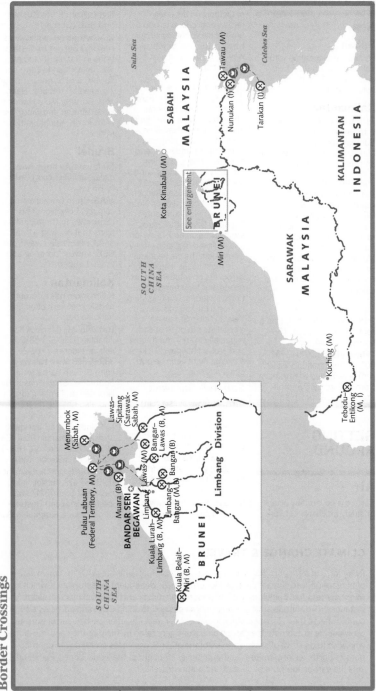

(Tanjung Puting National Park) from Banjarmasin and Pontianak.

Lion Air (☐inside Kalimantan 0511-747-480, outside Indonesia +62-0274-7831919; www2.lionair.co.id)

Bicycle

It's unlikely that Borneo will take off as a popular bike-touring destination anytime soon. Few roads have shoulders/verges, many are in varying states of disrepair, and heavy lorries often drive quite fast. There's also the climate – Borneo straddles the equator and the combination of heat, humidity, torrential rains and sun can be merciless. If you choose to ride, take extreme caution with traffic: drivers are not used to seeing bicycles and will give you precious little leeway. Remember to bring a helmet, a reflective vest, high-power lights and a wealth of inner tubes and spare parts.

Boat

Until the advent of planes and roads, boats were the only way to cover long distances in Borneo, both along the coast and in the interior. Rivers still play a major transport role, and in some trackless areas – such as Sarawak's Batang Rejang – they're the only ride in town.

On wider rivers, 60-seat 'flying coffins' – long, narrow speedboats often mistakenly believed to have been made from used aeroplane fuselages – are the norm. Upstream, the only craft that can make headway against the rapids and dodge submerged rocks are motorised wooden long-boats, expertly manoeuvred by local boatmen and boat-women.

Rates vary tremendously for water travel, the crucial factor being whether locals use the vessels for daily transport or if the boat is exclusively for tourists.

Sabah

Nature sites accessible by boat include Tunku Abdul Rahman National Park, the Semporna Archipelago and Pulau Tiga National Park.

In the west, sea ferries link Menumbok with Muara in Brunei; KK with Pulau Labuan; and Pulau Labuan with Muara. In Sabah's southeast corner, ferries link Tawau with Tarakan and Nunukan in Kalimantan.

Sarawak

Sarawak's Batang Rejang is sometimes called the 'Amazon of Borneo' and a journey upriver is still very romantic, despite the lack of intact forest en route.

Along the coast, speedboats link Limbang and Lawas with Pulau Labuan and Brunei. In western Sarawak, motorboats are the only way to get to Baku, Tanjung Datu and Talang-Satang National Parks.

Brunei

Speedboats link BSB with Bangar (in Brunei's Temburong District) and Lawas and Limbang (in Sarawak's Limbang Division), and car ferries go from the Serasa Ferry Terminal in Muara, 25km northeast of BSB, to Pulau Labuan and the Sabah port of Menumbok. The only way to get to Ulu Temburong National Park is by longboat.

Kalimantan

Ferries link Tarakan and Nunukan (East Kalimantan) with Tawau (Sabah). A visa-on-arrival is available if you're entering Sabah but not if you're travelling in the other direction, ie into Kalimantan.

To get around Kalimantan, the only scheduled public boats are found on the Mahakam River and go as far as Long Bagun if the water is high enough, otherwise they stop at Data Bilang, Long Iram or Tering. For other rivers, it's necessary to charter, or else wait for a local boat to fill up.

Bus, Van & Taxi

Borneo's coastal cities are connected by a network of cheap and relatively comfortable buses.

Intercity buses generally depart from a long-distance bus terminal on the outskirts of town, linked to the city centre by bus and taxi. There's usually no need to purchase bus tickets in advance – just show up and shop around for the next departure (large clocks posted at bus-company counters make this easy). For many destinations, departures are most frequent in the mornings, but on some routes (eg Miri to Kuching) there are also afternoon and overnight buses.

Around most cities, including Kuching, short-haul bus services have been decimated by the proliferation

BORDER CROSSINGS

Details on visa requirements for Malaysia, Brunei and Indonesia appear on p314.

Information on overland travel to and through Brunei can be found on p234 and p237. For information on travelling overland from Sarawak to Kalimantan, see p164, p242 and p220.

Details on ferry links from Sabah to Kalimantan appear on p123 and p278.

of private cars and chaotic, privately operated minivans.

Sabah

An arc of excellent paved roads extends from KK southeast to Tawau, passing Mt Kinabalu, Sepilok, Sandakan, Lahad Datu and Semporna (gateway to Sipadan) along the way. Large buses ply this route on a daily basis, while even more frequent minivans and shared taxis and jeeps connect both the main cities and secondary towns. Getting from KK to any towns north, all the way to Kudat, and southwest to the Brunei border, is easily done by share-taxi or jeep. The same applies if going from Sandakan to any towns south to Tawau. Just keep in mind it's always hard to find any kind of public transport after 5pm.

The southern road that connects Tawau to Sapulot is not entirely paved yet, nor is it serviced by public transport, but you can arrange private transport down this way, and occasional (very occasional) minibuses ply the route. Getting to very remote villages by public transport is tougher – in these situations you need to hope shared taxis and jeeps have enough passengers. These vehicles typically leave very early in the morning.

Sarawak

Frequent buses run by a clutch of companies ply the Pan Borneo Hwy from Kuching to Miri, stopping along the way in Sibu and Bintulu, near Niah Caves National Park, and at Lambir Hills National Park. From Miri, frequent buses head via Brunei to Sabah.

Long-haul buses link Sarawak's coastal cities, including Kuching, with Pontianak (West Kalimantan) via the Tebedu-Entikong border crossing.

Bus service from Kuching to destinations in Western Sarawak is very limited or nonexistent, except to Lundu, Bako Bazaar and the Semenggoh Nature Reserve, and minivan services, recently deregulated (de facto if not de jure), are in a state of total chaos. For many destinations, the only transport options are hiring a taxi or joining a tour group.

Brunei

Only one company, known as Jesselton Express (for services heading from BSB towards KK) and PHLS (for services from BSB towards Miri), is allowed to pick up and drop off passengers inside the sultanate. One or two buses a day go from BSB southwest to Miri (via Seria and Kuala Belait) and northeast to KK (via Limbang, Lawas and various destinations in Sabah).

Kalimantan

Buses in Kalimantan are a mixed affair, ranging from comfy to purgatorial. The same can also be said of its highways and minor roads, which vary from silk-smooth asphalt to a muddy, potholed pumpkin soup during the rainy season (when you may have to disembark and push). VIP-style buses with air-con operate between Balikpapan and Samarinda, and from Samarinda to Banjarmasin and Bontang. The rest of the country involves patchy roads, inhumanly quick drivers and, often, overcrowding on woefully smoky, dilapidated buses. Bring with you patience, an inflatable neck cushion, an iPod and anything else to ease the journey.

The only official land crossing between Kalimantan and Malaysian Borneo is at Tebedu-Entikong, in western Sarawak between Kuching and Pontianak. Long-haul buses link Pontianak with Kuching, the cities of Sarawak's central coast and Brunei.

Car & Motorcycle

Driving is on the left in all three countries that share Borneo. The nicely paved Pan Borneo Hwy runs all along Borneo's northern coast, from Sematan in Sarawak's far west via Brunei (and its many border crossings) to Tawau in the southeast corner of Sabah. Kalimantan's road network is limited, with lots of sections yet to be paved.

Road signage is often haphazard, with many junctions – including T-junctions – lacking any indication of where to go. Yogi Berra may have advised, 'when you get to a fork in the road, take it', but that's easier said than done.

Car Rental

Driving a rental car gives you maximum flexibility but can involve major hassles – in Borneo, these are likely to include poor or nonexistent road signage, a dearth of proper road maps, dilapidated vehicles, and small rental companies that try to foist repair charges onto you. In Kalimantan you may have trouble asking for directions unless you speak Bahasa Indonesia.

Car-hire companies have desks in the arrivals halls of larger airports; in city centres, hotels and guest houses can help find an agency. We've heard reports that some local companies try to take advantage of tourists by furnishing them with 10-year-old cars whose tyres are bald and boots (trunks) leak. Before you sign anything or hand over any cash, check out your vehicle very carefully, especially if it's an older Malaysian-made model such as a tiny Kancil or Wira, and verify the insurance excess (deductible).

In Sabah and Sarawak, prices for a Kancil start at an absolute minimum of RM100/560 per day/week at the cheapest outfits. Renting through an international company such as **Hertz** (www.hertz.com) costs about double that, but your vehicle is likely to be newer, safer and better maintained. In Brunei, prices start at about B$80 a day, in Kalimantan – where available – at about 1,500,000Rp per day.

With some companies you can drive from Sabah or Sarawak into Brunei, or vice versa, for no extra charge, while others demand a fee of RM50 or RM100. Renting a car in one city and returning it in another can be expensive – count on paying RM500 extra to pick up a vehicle in Miri and drop it off in Kuching.

A valid overseas licence is needed to rent a car. An International Driving Permit (a translation of your license and its provisions) is usually not required by local car-hire companies, but it's recommended that you bring one. Minimum age limits (eg 21) may apply.

Taxi Hire

For transport to places within a 50km or 70km radius of where you're staying, hiring a taxi on a per-trip, half-day or per-day basis may be your best option, especially if there's no public transport. For day trips from public transport–challenged Kuching, for instance, count on paying about RM200 for an eight-hour excursion. When you factor in fuel, this often works out only slightly more expensive than renting. Bonuses: you bear no liability in case the car is damaged, and you've got the driver to take care of navigation and

mechanical problems and find places to eat.

In Kalimantan, the norm is to hire a Kijang (taxi), agreeing on remuneration for the driver in addition to paying for fuel.

Hitching

Hitching is certainly possible in most parts of Borneo. It's usually quite safe for male travellers, but we don't recommend it for female travellers. Some drivers will expect a small 'tip' or assistance with petrol costs for driving you. At the very least, if you stop for food, you should offer to pay for their meal.

Local Transport

Bicycle

Within cities, bicycles are becoming a very rare sight, as increased prosperity has brought the creature comforts of gas guzzling to Malaysia and Brunei. However, some guest houses rent or lend bicycles to their guests. Out in the country, locals still use bicycles to get around small *kampung* (villages), and if you can get hold of a bicycle – rental options are rare – this can be a very pleasant way to spend a day or two.

Boat

Small motorboats and motorised longboats are often used for short river, bay and sea journeys. Examples include the trip across Sungai Sarawak in Kuching and transport from central BSB (Brunei) to the water village of Kampung Ayer.

Taxi

Taxis are common in Borneo's larger cities; meters, drivers who use them and fixed rates are not – except, as of July 2010, in Kuching. Luckily, you'll find that most drivers in Borneo are quite honest. Just be sure to set the price before starting out and only pay upon arrival.

Tours

One way to get the most out of a national park visit, jungle trek or longhouse sojourn is to go with a guide who knows the territory (and, in the case of longhouses, the headman). Indeed, it's the only way to see some things – the summits of Gunung Mulu or Mt Kinabalu, for instance.

For details on reputable Brunei-based tour companies and guides, many with extensive websites, see Tours in city and town listings. Most guest houses and hotels have relationships with at least one local tour operator, and some run their own in-house travel agencies. It's best to ask other travellers about their experiences with these before plunking down any money.

Train

The only railway line on Borneo, run by the Sabah State Railway, runs from Tanjung Aru, near KK, south to Tenom, a distance of 134km. At press time this scenic line, which began operations in 1896, was about to reopen after several years of renovations.

Health

Travellers tend to worry about contracting infectious diseases when travelling in Borneo, but infections are not nearly as common as you might think and rarely cause serious illness. Malaria does exist but is usually limited to isolated upland areas.

The following advice is a general guide only and does not replace the advice of a doctor trained in travel medicine.

BEFORE YOU GO

If you take any regular medication, bring double your needs in case of loss or theft, and carry these extra supplies separately. You may be able to buy some medications over the counter in Borneo without a doctor's prescription, but it can be difficult to find some of the newer drugs, particularly the latest antidepressants, blood-pressure medications and contraceptive pills.

Insurance

Even if you are fit and healthy, don't travel without health insurance. Extra cover may be required for adventure activities such as rock climbing or scuba diving. Remember: if you're uninsured, emergency evacuation can be expensive, and bills of over US$100,000 are not uncommon.

Insurance is available online from www.lonelyplanet.com.

Recommended Vaccinations

Most vaccines don't produce immunity until at least two weeks after they're given, so visit a doctor four to eight weeks before departure. Ask your doctor for an International Certificate of Vaccination (otherwise known as the 'yellow booklet'), which will list all the vaccinations you've received.

Proof of vaccination against yellow fever will be required only if you have visited a country in the yellow-fever zone (parts of Africa and South America) within six days prior to entering Malaysia, Brunei or Indonesia. If you're coming from Africa or South America, check to see if you require proof of vaccination.

Websites

There's a wealth of travel-health advice on the internet. For further information:

Centers for Disease Control & Prevention (www.cdc.gov) Excellent general information.

World Health Organization (www.who.int/ith) Publishes a superb book – *International Travel and Health* (downloadable) – and has authoritative information on disease distribution.

Further Reading

Lonely Planet's pocket size *Asia & India: Healthy Travel* is packed with useful information, including pre-trip planning, emergency first aid, immunisation and disease information, and what to do if you get sick on the road. *Travel with Children* from Lonely Planet includes advice on travel health for young children. Other recommended references include *Traveller's Health* by Dr Richard Dawood (Oxford University Press), and *Travelling Well* by Dr Deborah Mills (available at www.travellingwell.com.au).

IN BORNEO

Availability & Cost of Health Care

There are good medical facilities – with reasonable rates – in Borneo's larger cities; this is especially true in Sabah, Sarawak and Brunei. As you head into the hinterlands, however, you will find few if any medical facilities.

You will have no problem communicating with doctors in English, and almost all nurses know at least some English. Pharmacists also tend to speak reasonable English – this can be important, as many medications are available under a variety of names in different parts of the world.

Infectious Diseases

Dengue Fever

This mosquito-borne disease is present in Borneo. As there's no vaccine available, it can only be prevented by avoiding mosquito bites. The mosquito that carries dengue fever bites during both day and night, so use insect-avoidance measures at all times. Symptoms include high fever, severe headache and body ache (dengue was once known as 'break-bone fever'). Some people develop a rash and experience diarrhoea. There's no specific treatment, just rest and paracetamol – don't take aspirin as it increases the likelihood of haemorrhaging. Some forms can be dangerous, so see a doctor to be diagnosed and monitored.

Leptospirosis

Leptospirosis is a bacterial disease that's most commonly contracted after river rafting, canyoning or caving, sometimes as a result of contact with rat urine or faeces. Early symptoms are very similar to the flu and include headache and fever. It can vary from a very mild to a fatal disease. Diagnosis is through blood tests and it is easily treated with Doxycycline.

Malaria

Malaria is not common but is present in Borneo, particularly in parts of Kalimantan. Brunei is malaria-free; in Sabah and Sarawak, the disease is absent from coastal areas and only occasionally found in or around remote lumber camps. One reason for the relative rarity of malaria is the relatively low mosquito population in much of Borneo (thanks in part to the island's millions of cave-dwelling, insectivorous bats). Get up-to-date information on infected areas before your trip and as soon as you arrive in the country.

In areas with minimal to no risk of malaria, the potential side effects from antimalarial tablets may outweigh the risk of getting the disease. For some rural and upland areas, however, the risk of contracting the disease outweighs any tablet side effects. Remember that malaria can be fatal. Before you travel, seek medical advice on the right medication and dosage for you.

Malaria is caused by a parasite transmitted through the bite of an infected mosquito. The most important symptom of malaria is fever, but general symptoms such as headache, diarrhoea, cough or chills may also occur. Diagnosis can be made only by taking a blood sample.

Two strategies should be combined to prevent malaria – mosquito avoidance and antimalarial medications. Most people who catch malaria are taking inadequate or no antimalarial medication.

Travellers in malarial areas are advised to prevent mosquito bites by taking these steps:

» Use a DEET-containing insect repellent on exposed skin. Wash this off at night (if you're sleeping under a mosquito net treated with permethrin). Natural repellents such as citronella can be effective but must be applied more frequently than products containing DEET.

» Choose accommodation with screens and fans (if not air-con).

» Sleep under a mosquito net impregnated with permethrin.

» Wear long sleeves and trousers in light colours.

» Impregnate clothing with permethrin (in high-risk areas).

» Use mosquito coils.

Rabies

Rabies is present in Kalimantan but is much less common in Sabah, Sarawak and Brunei. This fatal disease is spread by the bite or lick of an infected animal, most commonly a dog or monkey. Seek medical advice immediately after any animal bite.

REQUIRED & RECOMMENDED VACCINATIONS

The World Health Organization recommends the following vaccinations for travellers to Borneo:

» Adult diphtheria and tetanus
» Hepatitis A
» Hepatitis B
» Measles, mumps and rubella
» Polio
» Typhoid
» Varicella

Recommended for longer-term travellers (more than one month) or those at special risk:

» Japanese B Encephalitis
» Meningitis
» Rabies
» Tuberculosis

MEDICAL CHECKLIST

» **Antibiotics** – consider including these if you're travelling well off the beaten track; see your doctor and carry the prescription with you.

» **Antifungal cream or powder** – for fungal skin infections and thrush.

» **Antihistamine** – for allergies such as hay fever; to ease the itch from insect bites or stings; and to prevent motion sickness.

» **Antiseptic (such as povidone-iodine or betadine)** – for cuts and grazes.

» **Antispasmodic** – for stomach cramps, eg Buscopan.

» **Aspirin or paracetamol (acetaminophen in the USA)** – for pain or fever.

» **Bandages, Band-Aids (plasters) and other wound dressings**

» **Calamine lotion, sting relief spray or aloe vera** – to ease irritation from sunburn and insect bites or stings.

» **Cold and flu tablets, throat lozenges and nasal decongestant**

» **Contraceptives**

» **DEET-based insect repellent**

» **Ibuprofen** – or another anti-inflammatory.

» **Iodine tablets** (unless you are pregnant or have a thyroid problem) – to purify water.

» **Loperamide or diphenoxylate** – 'blockers' for diarrhoea.

» **Multivitamins** – consider for long trips, when dietary vitamin intake may be inadequate.

» **Permethrin** – to impregnate clothing and mosquito nets.

» **Prochlorperazine or metaclopramide** – for nausea and vomiting.

» **Rehydration mixture** – to prevent dehydration, which may occur, for example, during bouts of diarrhoea; particularly important when travelling with children.

» **Scissors, tweezers and a thermometer** – note that mercury thermometers are prohibited by airlines.

» **Sterile kit** – in case you need injections in a country with medical-hygiene problems; discuss with your doctor.

» **Sunscreen, lip balm and eye drops**

» **Water purification tablets**

Having pre-travel vaccination means the post-bite treatment is greatly simplified. If you are not pre-vaccinated, you will need to receive rabies immunoglobulin as soon as possible.

Environmental Hazards

Diving

Divers and surfers should seek specialised advice before they travel, to ensure their medical kit contains treatment for coral cuts and tropical ear infections. Divers should ensure their insurance covers them for decompression illness – specialised dive insurance is available through **DAN Asia-Pacific** (Divers Alert Network; www.danasiapacific.org). Have a dive medical before you leave your home country.

Heat

Borneo is hot and humid throughout the year. Most people take at least two weeks to adapt to the climate. Swelling of the feet and ankles is common, as are muscle cramps caused by excessive sweating. Prevent these by avoiding dehydration and too much activity in the heat. Take it easy when you first arrive. Don't eat salt tablets (they aggravate the gut), but drinking rehydration solution or eating salty food helps. Treat cramps by stopping activity, resting, rehydrating with double-strength rehydration solution and gently stretching.

Dehydration is the main contributor to heat exhaustion. Symptoms include feeling weak, headache, irritability, nausea or vomiting, sweaty skin, a fast, weak pulse and a slightly increased body temperature. Treatment involves getting the sufferer out of the heat and/or sun, fanning them and applying cool wet cloths to the skin, laying the victim flat with their legs raised and rehydrating with water containing a quarter of a teaspoon of salt per litre. Recovery is usually rapid, although it's common to feel weak for some days afterwards.

Heatstroke is a serious medical emergency. Symptoms come on suddenly and include weakness, nausea, a hot, dry body with a body temperature of over 41°C, dizziness, confusion, fits, and eventual collapse and loss of consciousness. Seek medical help and commence cooling by getting the sufferer out of the heat, removing their clothes, fanning them and applying cool, wet cloths or ice to their body, especially to the groin and armpits.

Prickly heat is a common skin rash in the tropics, caused by sweat being trapped under the skin. The result is an itchy rash of tiny lumps. If you develop prickly heat, treat it by moving out of the heat and into an air-conditioned area for a few hours and by having cool showers. Creams and ointments clog the skin, so they should be avoided. Locally bought prickly-heat powder can be helpful for relief.

Insect Bites & Stings

Ticks are contracted after walking in the bush and are commonly found behind the ears, on the belly and in armpits. If you have had a tick bite and experience symptoms such as a rash at the site of the bite or elsewhere, a fever or muscle aches, you should see a doctor.

Leeches are found in humid rainforest areas. They do not transmit any disease but their bites are often intensely itchy for weeks afterwards and can easily become infected. Apply iodine-based antiseptic to any leech bite to help prevent infection (see also p29).

Bee and wasp stings mainly cause problems for people who are allergic to them.

Anyone with a serious bee or wasp allergy should carry an injection of adrenaline (eg an EpiPen) for emergency treatment. For others, pain is the main problem – apply ice to the sting and take painkillers.

Most jellyfish in Southeast Asian waters are not dangerous, just irritating. First aid for jellyfish stings involves pouring vinegar onto the affected area to neutralise the poison. Don't rub sand or water onto the stings. Take painkillers, and anyone who feels ill in any way after being stung should seek medical advice. Take local advice if there are dangerous jellyfish around and keep out of the water.

Skin Problems

Fungal rashes are common in humid climates. There are two common fungal rashes that affect travellers. The first occurs in moist areas that get less air such as the groin, armpits and between the toes. It starts as a red patch that slowly spreads and is usually itchy. Treatment involves keeping the skin dry, avoiding chafing and using an antifungal cream such as Clotrimazole or Lamisil. Tinea versicolour is also common – this fungus causes small, light-coloured patches, most commonly on the back, chest and shoulders. Consult a doctor.

Cuts and scratches become easily infected in humid climates. Take meticulous care of any cuts and scratches to prevent complications such as abscesses. Immediately wash all wounds in clean water and apply antiseptic. If you develop signs of infection (increasing pain and redness), see a doctor. Divers and surfers should be particularly careful with coral cuts as they become easily infected.

Traveller's Diarrhoea

Traveller's diarrhoea is by far the most common problem affecting travellers – between 30% to 50% of people will suffer from it within two weeks of starting their trip. In over 80% of cases, traveller's diarrhoea is caused by a bacteria (there are numerous potential culprits), and therefore responds promptly to treatment with antibiotics. Treatment will depend on your situation – how sick you are, how quickly you need to get better, where you are, etc. Traveller's diarrhoea is

TAP WATER

» Never drink tap water unless you've verified that it's safe (many parts of Sabah, Sarawak and Brunei have modern treatment plants).

» Bottled water is generally safe – check that the seal is intact at purchase.

» Avoid ice in eateries that look dubious, especially in Kalimantan.

» Avoid fruit juices if they're not freshly squeezed or you suspect they may have been watered down.

» Boiling water is the most efficient method of purifying it.

» The best chemical purifier is iodine. It should not be used by pregnant women or those with thyroid problems.

» Water filters should also filter out viruses. Ensure your filter has a chemical barrier such as iodine and a small pore size, ie less than 4 microns.

HEALTH ADVISORIES

Many governments' travel websites include health information:

Australia www.smartraveller.gov.au
Canada www.travelhealth.gc.ca
New Zealand www.safetravel.govt.nz
South Africa www.dfa.gov.za/consular/travel_advice.htm
United Kingdom www.dh.gov.uk
United States www.cdc.gov/travel

defined as the passage of more than three watery bowel actions within 24 hours, plus at least one other symptom such as fever, cramps, nausea, vomiting or feeling generally unwell. Treatment consists of staying well hydrated; rehydration solutions such as Gastrolyte are the best for this.

Always seek reliable medical care if you have blood in your diarrhoea.

Loperamide is just a 'stopper' and doesn't get to the cause of the problem. It can be helpful, for example if you have to go on a long bus ride. Don't take Loperamide if you have a fever, or blood in your stools.

Ways to avoid traveller's diarrhoea include eating only freshly cooked food and avoiding shellfish and food that has been sitting around in buffets. Peel all fruit, cook vegetables, and soak salads in iodine water for at least 20 minutes. Eat in busy restaurants with a high turnover of customers.

Travelling with Children

Borneo is a great place to travel with children. However, there are specific health issues you should consider before travelling with your child.

All your children's routine vaccinations should be up to date, as many of the common childhood diseases that have been eliminated in the West are still present in parts of Borneo. A travel-health clinic can advise you on specific vaccines, but think seriously about rabies vaccination if you're visiting rural areas or travelling for more than a month, as children are more vulnerable to severe animal bites.

Children are more prone to getting serious forms of mosquito-borne diseases such as malaria, Japanese B encephalitis and dengue fever. In particular, malaria is very serious in children and can rapidly lead to death – you should think seriously before taking your child into a malaria risk area. Permethrin-impregnated clothing is safe to use, and insect repellents should contain between 10% and 20% DEET.

Diarrhoea can cause rapid dehydration and you should pay particular attention to keeping your child well hydrated. The best antibiotic for children with diarrhoea is Azithromycin.

Women's Health

In urban areas, supplies of sanitary products are readily available. Birth-control options may be limited, so bring adequate supplies of your own form of contraception.

Language

WANT MORE?

For in-depth language information and handy phrases, check out Lonely Planet's *Indonesian Phrasebook* and *Malay Phrasebook*. You'll find them at **shop.lonelyplanet.com**, or you can buy Lonely Planet's iPhone phrasebooks at the Apple App Store.

Malay, or Bahasa Malaysia, is the official language of Malaysian Borneo (Sabah and Sarawak) and Brunei; it's the native language of people of Malay descent there. Indonesian, or Bahasa Indonesia, is the official language of Kalimantan and the mother tongue of most people of non-Chinese descent living there. The two languages are very similar, and if you can speak a little of either you'll be able to use it across the island. We've avoided duplication in this language guide by providing translations in both languages – indicated by (I) and (M) – only where the differences are significant enough to cause confusion.

Each of Borneo's indigenous groups has its own language, but their members all speak Bahasa Malaysia or Bahasa Indonesia. Various dialects of Chinese are spoken by those of Chinese ancestry in Borneo, although Mandarin is fairly widely spoken and understood.

You'll find it easy to get by with only English in Borneo, particularly in Sabah, Sarawak and Brunei. English is the most common second language for Borneo's ethnic groups and is often used by people of different backgrounds, like ethnic Chinese and ethnic Malays, to communicate with one another.

In both Bahasa Malaysia and Bahasa Indonesia, most letters are pronounced more or less the same as their English counterparts, except for the letter *c* which is always pronounced as the 'ch' in 'chair'. Nearly all syllables carry equal emphasis, but a good approximation is to lightly stress the second-last syllable. The main exception to the rule is the unstressed *e* in words such as *besar* (big), which sounds like the 'a' in 'ago'.

Pronouns, particularly 'you', are rarely used in both Bahasa Malaysia and Bahasa Indonesia. *Anda* (in Indonesian) and *kamu* (in Malay) are the egalitarian forms designed to overcome the plethora of terms relating to a person's age and gender that are used for the second person.

BASICS

Hello.	*Salam./Helo.* (I/M)
Goodbye.	*Selamat tinggal/jalan.* (by person leaving/staying)
How are you?	*Apa kabar?*
I'm fine.	*Kabar baik.*
Excuse me.	*Maaf.*
Sorry.	*Maaf.*
Yes.	*Ya.*
No.	*Tidak.*
Please.	*Silakan.*
Thank you.	*Terima kasih.*
You're welcome.	*Kembali.* (I) *Sama-sama.* (M)

My name is ...
Nama saya ...

What's your name?
Siapa nama anda/kamu? (I/M)

Do you speak English?
Anda bisa Bahasa Inggris? (I)
Adakah anda berbahasa Inggeris? (M)

I (don't) understand.
Saya (tidak) mengerti. (I)
Saya (tidak) faham. (M)

ACCOMMODATION

Do you have any rooms available?
Ada kamar/bilik kosongkah? (I/M)

How much is it per day/person?
Berapa harga satu malam/orang?

Is breakfast included?
Makan pagi termasukkah?

campsite	*tempat kemah* (I)
	tempat perkhemahan (M)
guesthouse	*rumah yang disewakan* (I)
	rumah tetamu (M)
hotel	*hotel*
youth hostel	*losmen pemuda* (I)
	asrama belia (M)
single room	*kamar untuk seorang* (I)
	bilik untuk seorang (M)
room with a double bed	*tempat tidur besar satu kamar* (I)
	bilik untuk dua orang (M)
room with two beds	*kamar dengan dua tempat tidur* (I)
	bilik yang ada dua katil (M)
air-con	*AC (pronounced 'a-se')* (I)
	pendingin udara (M)
bathroom	*kamar mandi* (I)
	bilik air (M)
mosquito coil	*obat nyamuk*
window	*jendela/tingkap* (I/M)

KEY PATTERNS

To get by in Indonesian, mix and match these simple patterns with words of your choice:

When's (the next bus)?
Jam berapa (bis yang berikutnya)?

Where's (the station)?
Di mana (stasiun)?

How much is it (per night)?
Berapa (satu malam)?

I'm looking for (a hotel).
Saya cari (hotel).

Do you have (a local map)?
Ada (peta daerah)?

Is there a (lift)?
Ada (lift)?

Can I (enter)?
Boleh saya (masuk)?

Do I need (a visa)?
Saya harus pakai (visa)?

I have (a reservation).
Saya (sudah punya booking).

I need (assistance).
Saya perlu (dibantu).

I'd like (the menu).
Saya minta (daftar makanan).

I'd like (to hire a car).
Saya mau (sewa mobil).

Could you (help me)?
Bisa Anda (bantu) saya?

DIRECTIONS

Where is ...?
Di mana ...?

What's the address?
Apa alamatnya?

Could you write it down, please?
Anda bisa tolong tuliskan? (I)
Tolong tuliskan alamat itu? (M)

Can you show me (on the map)?
Bisa tunjukkan kepada saya (di peta)? (I)
Tolong tunjukkan (di peta)? (M)

at the corner	*di sudut/simpang* (I/M)
at the traffic lights	*di lampu lalu-lintas* (I)
	di tempat lampu isyarat (M)
behind	*di belakang*
far (from)	*jauh (dari)*
in front of	*di depan*
near (to)	*dekat (dengan)*
opposite	*di seberang* (I)
	berhadapan dengan (M)

Turn left/right.	*Belok kiri/kanan.*
Go straight ahead.	*Jalan terus.*

EATING & DRINKING

A table for (two), please.
Meja untuk (dua) orang.

What's in that dish?
Hidangan itu isinya apa? (I)
Ada apa dalam masakan itu? (M)

Bring the bill/check, please.
Tolong bawa kuitansi/bil. (I/M)

I don't eat ...	*Saya tidak mau makan ...* (I)
	Saya tak suka makan ... (M)
chicken	*ayam*
fish	*ikan*
(red) meat	*daging (merah)*
nuts	*biji-bijian/kacang* (I/M)

Signs

Buka	Open
Dilarang	Prohibited
Kamar Kecil (I)	Toilets
Keluar	Exit
Lelaki (M)	Men
Masuk	Entrance
Perempuan (M)	Women
Pria (I)	Men
Tandas (M)	Toilets
Tutup	Closed
Wanita (I)	Women

Key Words

bottle	botol
breakfast	sarapan pagi
cold	dingin/sejuk (I/M)
cup	cangkir/cawan (I/M)
dinner	makan malam
food	makanan
fork	garpu/garfu (I/M)
glass	gelas
hot	panas
knife	pisau
lunch	makan siang/tengahari (I/M)
market	pasar
menu	daftar makanan (I) menu (M)
plate	piring/pinggan (I/M)
restaurant	restoran
spicy	pedas
spoon	sendok/sedu (I/M)
vegetarian	makanan tanpa daging (I) sayuran saja (M)
with	dengan
without	tanpa

Meat & Fish

beef	daging sapi/lembu (I/M)
chicken	ayam
crab	kepiting/ketam (I/M)
fish	ikan
lamb	daging anak domba (I) anak biri-biri (M)
mussels	remis/kepah (I/M)
pork	babi
shrimp	udang

Fruit & Vegetables

apple	apel/epal (I/M)
banana	pisang
carrot	wortel/lobak (I/M)
cucumber	ketimun/timun (I/M)
jackfruit	nangka
mango	mangga
orange	jeruk manis/oren (I/M)
peanut	kacang
starfruit	belimbing
tomato	tomat/tomato (I/M)
watermelon	semangka/tembikai (I/M)

Other

bread	roti
cheese	keju
egg	telur
ice	es/ais (I/M)
rice	nasi
salt	garam
sugar	gula

Drinks

beer	bir
bottled water	air botol
citrus juice	air jeruk/limau (I/M)
coffee	kopi
milk	susu
tea	teh
water	air
wine	anggur/wain (I/M)

EMERGENCIES

Help!	Tolong!
Stop!	Berhenti!
I'm lost.	Saya sesat.
Go away!	Pergi!

There's been an accident.
Ada kecelakaan/kemalangan. (I/M)

Call the doctor/police!
Panggil doktor/polis!

I'm ill.
Saya sakit.

It hurts here.
Sakitnya di sini. (I)
Sini sakit. (M)

I'm allergic to (nuts).
Saya alergi terhadap (biji-bijian). (I)
Saya alergik kepada (kacang). (M)

SHOPPING & SERVICES

I'd like to buy ...
Saya mau/nak beli ... (I/M)

I'm just looking.
Saya lihat-lihat saja. (I)
Saya nak tengok saja. (M)

May I look at it?
Boleh saya lihat? (I)
Boleh saya tengok barang itu? (M)

How much is it?
Berapa harganya?

It's too expensive.
Itu terlalu mahal. (I)
Mahalnya. (M)

Can you lower the price?
Boleh kurang?

There's a mistake in the bill.
Ada kesalahan dalam kuitansi ini. (I)
Bil ini salah. (M)

ATM	*ATM* (pronounced 'a-te-em')
credit card	*kartu/kad kredit* (I/M)
internet cafe	*warnet* (I)
	cyber cafe (M)
post office	*kantor/pejabat pos* (I/M)
public phone	*telpon umum/awam* (I/M)
tourist office	*kantor pariwisata* (I)
	pejabat pelancong (M)

TIME & DATES

What time is it?
Jam berapa sekarang? (I)
Pukul berapa? (M)

It's (seven) o'clock.
Jam/Pukul (tujuh). (I/M)

It's half past (one).
Setengah (dua). (I)
  (lit: half two)
Pukul (satu) setengah. (M)

Question Words	
How?	*Bagaimana?*
What?	*Apa?*
When?	*Kapan?* (I)
	Bila? (M)
Where?	*Di mana?*
Who?	*Siapa?*
Why?	*Mengapa?*

in the morning	*pagi*
in the afternoon	*siang/tengahari* (I/M)
in the evening	*malam/petang* (I/M)
yesterday	*kemarin/semalam* (I/M)
today	*hari ini*
tomorrow	*besok/esok* (I/M)
Monday	*hari Senin/Isnin* (I/M)
Tuesday	*hari Selasa*
Wednesday	*hari Rabu*
Thursday	*hari Kamis*
Friday	*hari Jumat/Jumaat* (I/M)
Saturday	*hari Sabtu*
Sunday	*hari Minggu*
January	*Januari*
February	*Februari*
March	*Maret/Mac* (I/M)
April	*April*
May	*Mei*
June	*Juni/Jun* (I/M)
July	*Juli/Julai* (I/M)
August	*Agustus/Ogos* (I/M)
September	*September*
October	*Oktober*
November	*November*
December	*Desember*

TRANSPORT

Public Transport

What time does the ... leave?	*Jam/Pukul berapa ... berangkat?* (I/M)
boat	*kapal*
bus	*bis/bas* (I/M)
plane	*pesawat* (I)
	kapal terbang (M)
train	*kereta api*

I want to go to ...
Saya mau/nak ke ... (I/M)

Does it stop at ... ?
Berhenti di ...?

How long will it be delayed?
Berapa lama keterlambatannya? (I)
Berapa lambatnya? (M)

I'd like to get off at ...
Saya mau/nak turun di ... (I/M)

Numbers

1	satu
2	dua
3	tiga
4	empat
5	lima
6	enam
7	tujuh
8	delapan (I)
	lapan (M)
9	sembilan
10	sepuluh
20	dua puluh
30	tiga puluh
40	empat puluh
50	lima puluh
60	enam puluh
70	tujuh puluh
80	delapan puluh (I)
	lapan puluh (M)
90	sembilan puluh
100	seratus
1000	seribu

Please put the meter on.
Tolong pakai argo/meter. (I/M)

Please stop here.
Tolong berhenti di sini.

I'd like a ... ticket.	Saya mau/nak tiket ... (I/M)
1st-class	kelas satu (I)
	kelas pertama (M)
2nd-class	kelas dua (I)
	kelas kedua (M)
one-way	sekali jalan (I)
	sehala (M)
return	pulang pergi (I)
	pergi balik (M)

the first	pertama
the last	terakhir
the next	berikutnya

bus station	terminal bis (I)
	stesen bas (M)
bus stop	halte bis (I)
	perhentian bas (M)
cancelled	dibatalkan
delayed	terlambat/lambat (I/M)
platform	peron/landasan (I/M)
ticket office	loket/pejabat tiket (I/M)
timetable	jadwal/jadual waktu (I/M)

Driving & Cycling

I'd like to hire a ...	Saya mau sewa ... (I)
	Saya nak menyewa ... (M)
bicycle	sepeda/basikal (I/M)
car	mobil/kereta (I/M)
jeep	jip
motorbike	sepeda motor (I)
	motosikal (M)

diesel	solar/disel (I/M)
helmet	helem (I)
	topi keledar (M)
petrol	bensin/petrol (I/M)
pump	pompa/pam (I/M)

Is this the road to ...?
Ini jalan ke ...?

Where's a service station?
Di mana pompa bensin? (I)
Stesen minyak di mana? (M)

(How long) Can I park here?
(Berapa lama) Saya boleh parkir di sini? (I)
(Beberapa lama) Boleh saya letak kereta di sini? (M)

I need a mechanic.
Saya perlu montir. (I)
Kami memerlukan mekanik. (M)

The car has broken down at ...
Mobil mogok di ... (I)
Kereta saya telah rosak di ... (M)

I have a flat tyre.
Ban saya kempes. (I)
Tayarnya kempis. (M)

I've run out of petrol/gas.
Saya kehabisan bensin. (I)
Minyak sudah habis. (M)

(m) indicates masculine gender, (f) feminine gender and (pl) plural

ABC – ais kacang, a shaved-ice treat

adat – Malay customary law

agama – religion

air – water

air terjun – waterfall

alor – groove; furrow; main channel of a river

ampang – dam

APEC – Asia-Pacific Economic Cooperation

arak – Malay local alcohol

arrack – see *arak*

Asean – Association of Southeast Asian Nations

atap – roof thatching

ayam – chicken

balai – house or longhouse (Kalimantan)

balian – shaman (Kalimantan)

bandar – seaport; town

bandaraya – city council

batang – stem; tree trunk; the main branch of a river

batik – technique of imprinting cloth with dye to produce multicoloured patterns

batu – stone; rock; milepost

belacan – fermented shrimp paste

belauran – night markets (Kalimantan)

belian – ironwood

bandung – floating general stores (Kalimantan)

bis kota – intercity bus (Kalimantan)

bobihizan – female priestess in Dayak communities (Sabah)

bomoh – spiritual healer

bukit – hill

bumboat – motorised sampan (small boat)

Bumiputra – literally, 'sons of the soil'; indigenous Malaysians, including Malays and Dayaks

bunga raya – hibiscus flower (national flower of Malaysia)

ces – motorised canoes

dadah – drugs

dagang – beef

daging – see *dagang*

daerah – district

dato', datuk – literally, 'grandfather'; general male non-royal title of distinction

Dayak – indigenous peoples of Borneo (used mostly in Kalimantan and Sarawak)

dipterocarp – family of commercially valuable rainforest trees

dolmen – stone burial markers found in Kelabit areas

dusun – small town; orchard; fruit grove

genting – mountain pass

godown – river warehouse

goreng – fried, as in 'nasi goreng' (fried rice)

gua – cave

gunung – mountain

hilir – lower reaches of a river

hutan – jungle; forest

imam – keeper of Islamic knowledge and leader of prayer

ikan – fish

ikat – woven cloth

istana – palace

jalan – road (abbreviated 'jln')

jong sarat – hand-woven cloth made with gold and silver threads

kain sasirangan – tie-dyed batik

kain songket – traditional Malay hand-woven fabric with gold threads

kampong – village

kampung – see *kampong*

kangkar – Chinese village

kapal biasa – river boats (Kalimantan term)

karst – characteristic scenery of a limestone region, including features such as underground streams and caverns

kedai kopi – eatery, often with several food stalls; literally, 'coffee shop' (Bahasa term)

kerangas – heath forest; in Iban, means 'land that cannot grow rice'

khalwat – literally, close proximity; exhibition of public affection between the sexes which is prohibited for unmarried Muslim couples

Kijang – Indonesian brand name of a Toyota minibus or pick-up

klotok – Kalimantan houseboat

kongsi – Chinese clan organisations, also known as ritual brotherhoods, heavenman-earth societies, triads or secret societies; meeting house for Chinese of the same clan

kopitiam – eatery, often with several food stalls; literally, 'coffee shop' (Chinese term)

kota – fort; city

kramat – Malay shrine

KTM – Keretapi Tanah Melayu (Malaysian Railways System)

kuala – river mouth; place where a tributary joins a larger river

kueh – cakes, often made with coconut

kuih – see *kueh*

kway teow – thick white Chinese noodles

laksa – noodle soup

laksamana – admiral

lalapan – raw vegetables (Kalimantan)

langur – small, usually treedwelling monkey

laut – sea

lebuh – street
lorong – narrow street; alley (abbreviated 'lg')
lubuk – deep pool

macaque – any of several small species of monkey
mandau – machete (Kalimantan) **mandi** – bathe; Southeast Asian wash basin
masjid – mosque
mee – noodles
Melayu Islam Beraja – 'Malay Islamic Monarchy', Brunei's national ideology, known as MIB
merdeka – independence
midin – Sarawak edible jungle fern
Molong – Penang hunter-gatherer lifestyle
muara – river mouth
muezzin – mosque official who calls the faithful to prayer

nasi – rice
nasi campur – rice buffet (pronounced 'nah-see champoor')
negara – country
negeri – state

ojek – motorcycle taxi (Kalimantan)
opelet – minibus (Kalimantan)
orang asing – foreigner
Orang Asli – literally, 'original people'; Malaysian aborigines
Orang Laut – literally, 'coastal people'
Orang Ulu – literally, 'up-river people'

padang – grassy area; field; also the city square
pantai – beach

pao – Chinese steamed buns (sometimes filled with meat or sweet bean paste)
parang – long jungle knife
pasar – market
pasar malam – night market
pegunungan – mountain (Kalimantan)
Pejabat Residen – Resident's Office
pekan – marketplace; town
pelabuhan – port
penghulu – chief or village head
pengkalan – quay
permuda – youth militias active in Indonesia during WWII
pondok – hut or shelter
pua kumbu – traditional finely woven cloth
pulau – island
puteri – princess

raja – prince; ruler
rakyat – common people
ranee – princess or raja's wife
rantau – straight coastline
rattan – stems from climbing palms used for wickerwork and canes
rimba – jungle
rotan – see *rattan*
roti – bread
rumah – house
rumah betang – longhouse (Kalimantan)
rumah panjai – longhouse
rumah panjang – see *rumah panjai*
rumah walet – Kalimantan birdhouse

sambal – curry sauce or paste
sampan – small boat
sarong – all-purpose cloth, often sewn into a tube, and worn by women, men and children

sarung – see *sarong*
seberang – opposite side of road; far bank of a river
selat – strait
semenanjung – peninsula
simpang – crossing; junction
songkok – traditional Malay men's hat
sungai – river
sharia – Islamic system of law
syriah – see *sharia*

tambang – river ferry; fare
tamu – market
tanah – land
tanjung – headland
tasik – lake
teksi – taxi
telok – see *teluk*
teluk – bay
temenggong – Malay administrator
towkang – Chinese junk
transmigrasi – transmigration (Indonesian government policy)
tuai rumah – longhouse chief (Sarawak)
tuak – rice wine drunk in indigenous communities
tudong – headscarf
tunku – prince

ujung – cape
UMNO – United Malays National Organisation (Malaysia's ruling party)

wartel – public phone office (Kalimantan)
warung – small eating stalls
warung kopi – coffee stall (Kalimantan)
wayang – Chinese opera
wayang kulit – shadow-puppet theatre
wisma – office block or shopping centre

behind the scenes

SEND US YOUR FEEDBACK

We love to hear from travellers – your comments keep us on our toes and help make our books better. Our well-travelled team reads every word on what you loved or loathed about this book. Although we cannot reply individually to postal submissions, we always guarantee that your feedback goes straight to the appropriate authors, in time for the next edition. Each person who sends us information is thanked in the next edition – and the most useful submissions are rewarded with a free book.

Visit **lonelyplanet.com/contact** to submit your updates and suggestions or to ask for help. Our award-winning website also features inspirational travel stories, news and discussions.

Note: We may edit, reproduce and incorporate your comments in Lonely Planet products such as guidebooks, websites and digital products, so let us know if you don't want your comments reproduced or your name acknowledged. For a copy of our privacy policy visit lonelyplanet.com/privacy.

OUR READERS

Many thanks to the travellers who used the last edition and wrote to us with helpful hints, useful advice and interesting anecdotes:

Emma Binfield, Charlotte Blencowe, Maja Browne Adams, Joanna Burger, Sarah Chang, Anne Dauert, Philip Eaves, Johann Essl, Ellen Fleer, Laura Græns, Elisabeth Haase, Matt Hahnewald, Mathew Hemming, Fiona Holmes, Daniel I Smith, Ewan Johnston, Jenney Kaz, Elizabeth Koenig, Nadège Lanau, Francis MacDonnell, Tony McDonald, Jerry Moes, Jock and Janice Moilliet, Gavin Mooney, Tanja Nijhoff, Akane Nishimura, Jon Pearson, Rhys Peters, Carla Rodrigues, Lucy Roller, Lauren Rudick, Candice Sala-Gasperini, Richard Storey, Angie Teasdale, Monika Trojan, Hak van der Sijp, Patrick Westenhoff, Kevin White, John Whiteing, Johan Wiklund

AUTHOR THANKS

Daniel Robinson

Literally hundreds of people went out of their way to make this a better book, but I'm especially indebted to Abol Hassan Johari, Ashfa Harris, Brandon Presser, Brian Clark, Mr Chua (Eng Hin), Donald and Marina Tan, Emong Tisang, Eric and Annie Yap, Eric Thompson, Folker Silge, Glenn and Kat van Zutphen, James Relf, Jayall Langub, Jessie from the Sibu tourist office, Kelvin Egay, Mrs Lee of Miri, Leo Biddle, Leslie Chiang, Louise Teo, Matthew Amster, Murtadza Othman, Philip Yong, Robert Basiuk, Ross Atack, Rudy Chong, Stephen Ley, Susan Pulut, Verdi (for writing Aida) and the whole Bario gang, including Al Davies, Captain David (Bennet), Douglas Munney, Garawak Nulun, Jaman, Joanna Joy, John Tarawe, Rebita and Seluma.

I am indebted to this volume's great team of editors and cartographers – Ilaria Walker, Bruce Evans, Sarah Bailey, David Connolly and Jacqueline Nguyen – for their support and understanding during the write-up and, finally, to my wife, Rachel, for backstopping me at every turn – I dedicate my parts of this book to her.

Adam Karlin

Terimah kasih: Ed Chin, Kat, Howard, Mr Ong, Joel, Howard, the Kudat crew, Kevin, Catherine, the countless smiling Sabah citizens who make their state my favourite in Malaysia, Ilaria for getting me on this title, Daniel and Richard for being such a great team to work with, my folks for the usual, and Rachel, who helps me see the world with fresh eyes.

Richard Waters

I couldn't have written this chapter without Lucas at De'Gigant Tours lighting my way. Ashley Leiman, head of the Orangutan Foundation

UK; Lone Droscher-Nielsen; and Togu at Yayorin were vital to my understanding of some of the region's complex conservation issues. Special thanks to guides Purwadi in Tanjung Puting, Yasin Mulyadi in the Meratus, and Abdullah in our adventures up the Mahakam. My friends Richard and Jason should also be mentioned for their iron, English stoicism as our boat sank (twice) in dark water and darker jungle. My thanks to Evelyne and Rainer for their company and generosity, to commissioning ed Ilaria Walker, and to the editors and cartographers at Lonley Planet.

Simon Richmond

Cheers to Ilaria for her support from Lonely Planet HQ. In KL, many thanks to Alex Yong, Eli Wong, Steven Gan, Andrew Sebastian, Elizabeth Cardosa, Pam Currie, Sueann Chong, Narelle McMurtrie, Chris and Eddy and Adline binti Abdul Ghani. For great shared meals and allowing me to tap into their foodie knowledge, Robyn Eckardt, David Hagerman, Adly Rizal and Honey Ahmad are all stars.

Iain Stewart

Thanks to Ilaria, my editor Sarah Bailey, and all the Lonely Planet team in Melbourne. On the ground, to Mei for memorable nights out and Yudi for his friendship and company.

Joshua Samuel Brown

Thanks to Tony Tan at Betel Box, Ruqxana Vasanwala at Cookery Magic, Ginny and Kieran, Asako and Jonathan and everyone else who helped keep me sane (or tried) during multiple Singapore projects in 2010. And to all the chilli crabs: you did not die in vain.

ACKNOWLEDGMENTS

Climate map data adapted from Peel MC, Finlayson BL & McMahon TA (2007) 'Updated World Map of the Köppen-Geiger Climate Classification', Hydrology and Earth System Sciences, 11, 1633–44.
Cover photograph: Young Orangutan, Sabah, Ernest Manewal. Many of the images in this guide are available for licensing from Lonely Planet Images: www.lonelyplanetimages.com

THIS BOOK

This 2nd edition of Lonely Planet's Borneo guidebook was coordinated by Daniel Robinson, who researched Sarawak and Brunei. Richard Waters researched Kalimantan, and Adam Karlin researched Sabah. The gateway chapters were compiled by Joshua Samuel Brown, Iain Stewart and Simon Richmond, and Dr Trish Batchelor wrote the Health chapter, which was then revised by Daniel Robinson. This guidebook was commissioned in Lonely Planet's Melbourne office, and produced by the following:

Commissioning Editors
Ilaria Walker, Kalya Ryan

Coordinating Editors
Sarah Bailey, Bella Li
Coordinating Cartographer Jacqueline Nguyen
Coordinating Layout Designer Lauren Egan
Managing Editor Bruce Evans
Senior Editors Anna Metcalfe, Susan Paterson
Managing Cartographers David Connolly, Adrian Persoglia, Anthony Phelan
Managing Layout Designers Celia Wood, Jane Hart
Assisting Editors Elisa Arduca, Jackey Coyle

Assisting Cartographers Diana Duggan, Marc Milinkovic
Cover Research Naomi Parker
Internal Image Research Sabrina Dalbesio
Language Content Branislava Vladisavljevic, Chelsea Eaw
Talk2Us Coordinator Lisa Knights

Thanks to Melanie Dankel, Ryan Evans Laura Jane, Yvonne Kirk, Nic Lehman, Gerard Walker

index

how to use this book

These symbols will help you find the listings you want:

◉	Sights	🎎	Festivals & Events	☆	Entertainment
🏃	Activities	🛏	Sleeping	🛍	Shopping
🍃	Courses	✗	Eating	❶	Information/Transport
☞	Tours	🍷	Drinking		

These symbols give you the vital information for each listing:

☎	Telephone Numbers	🛜	Wi-Fi Access	🚌	Bus
⊙	Opening Hours	🏊	Swimming Pool	⬇	Ferry
🅿	Parking	🥗	Vegetarian Selection	Ⓜ	Metro
⊖	Nonsmoking	📖	English-Language Menu	Ⓢ	Subway
❄	Air-Conditioning	👪	Family-Friendly	⊖	London Tube
@	Internet Access	🐾	Pet-Friendly	🚋	Tram
				🚆	Train

Reviews are organised by author preference.

Look out for these icons:

TOP CHOICE — Our author's recommendation

FREE — No payment required

🍃 — A green or sustainable option

Our authors have nominated these places as demonstrating a strong commitment to sustainability – for example by supporting local communities and producers, operating in an environmentally friendly way, or supporting conservation projects.

Map Legend

Sights
- ◉ Beach
- ◉ Buddhist
- ◉ Castle
- ◉ Christian
- ◉ Hindu
- ◉ Islamic
- ◉ Jewish
- ◉ Monument
- ◉ Museum/Gallery
- ◉ Ruin
- ◉ Winery/Vineyard
- ◉ Zoo
- ◉ Other Sight

Activities, Courses & Tours
- ◎ Diving/Snorkelling
- ◎ Canoeing/Kayaking
- ◎ Skiing
- ◎ Surfing
- ◎ Swimming/Pool
- ◎ Walking
- ◎ Windsurfing
- • Other Activity/Course/Tour

Sleeping
- ◎ Sleeping
- ◎ Camping

Eating
- ✗ Eating

Drinking
- ◎ Drinking
- ◎ Cafe

Entertainment
- ⊙ Entertainment

Shopping
- ⊙ Shopping

Information
- ◉ Bank
- ◉ Embassy/Consulate
- ◉ Hospital/Medical
- ◉ Internet
- ◉ Police
- ◉ Post Office
- ◉ Telephone
- ◉ Toilet
- ◉ Tourist Information
- • Other Information

Transport
- ◉ Airport
- ◉ Border Crossing
- ◉ Bus
- ┼◉┼ Cable Car/Funicular
- -◉- Cycling
- -◉- Ferry
- Ⓜ Metro
- ═◉═ Monorail
- 🅿 Parking
- ◉ Petrol Station
- ◎ Taxi
- ┼◉┼ Train/Railway
- ═◉═ Tram
- • Other Transport

Routes
- Tollway
- Freeway
- Primary
- Secondary
- Tertiary
- Lane
- Unsealed Road
- Plaza/Mall
- Steps
- Tunnel
- Pedestrian Overpass
- Walking Tour
- Walking Tour Detour
- Path

Geographic
- ◉ Hut/Shelter
- ◉ Lighthouse
- ◉ Lookout
- ▲ Mountain/Volcano
- ◉ Oasis
- ◉ Park
-)(Pass
- ◉ Picnic Area
- ◎ Waterfall

Population
- ◉ Capital (National)
- ◉ Capital (State/Province)
- ◉ City/Large Town
- ◦ Town/Village

Boundaries
- –––– International
- ----- State/Province
- ---- Disputed
- – – – Regional/Suburb
- —— Marine Park
- ⌐⌐ Cliff
- ▬▬ Wall

Hydrography
- River, Creek
- Intermittent River
- Swamp/Mangrove
- Reef
- Canal
- Water
- Dry/Salt/Intermittent Lake
- Glacier

Areas
- Beach/Desert
- +++ Cemetery (Christian)
- ××× Cemetery (Other)
- Park/Forest
- Sportsground
- Sight (Building)
- Top Sight (Building)

Simon Richmond

Gateway Kuala Lumpur Simon first visited Kuala Lumpur, Melaka and Penang in 1996. Entranced by the brilliant blend of cultures and fantastic food, he has been a frequent visitor to Malaysia ever since. The award-winning travel writer and photographer has helmed Lonely Planet's *Malaysia, Singapore & Brunei* guide for the past three editions, one of the many titles he has researched for the company and other publishers in the past decade or so; find out more at www.simonrichmond.com.

Read more about Simon at:
lonelyplanet.com/members/simonrichmond

Iain Stewart

Gateway Jakarta Iain first visited Jakarta in 1992, and has returned to the Big Durian many times since. He always seems to find a new corner of this giant, challenging yet fascinating city on each trip. Iain's covered Jakarta for Lonely Planet and several newspapers and magazines.

Read more about Iain at:
lonelyplanet.com/members/iainstewart

Joshua Samuel Brown

Gateway Singapore Joshua is an American-born expatriate currently living a professionally nomadic lifestyle in an undisclosed Central American Nation. A prolific traveller and writer, his features have appeared in an eclectic variety of publications around the globe, including the *South China Morning Post*, *Business Traveller Asia*, *Clamor Magazine* and *Cat Fancy*. Follow his strange adventures at his blog Snarky Tofu (http://josambro.blogspot.com).

Read more about Joshua at:
lonelyplanet.com/members/joshuasamuelbrown

OUR STORY

A beat-up old car, a few dollars in the pocket and a sense of adventure. In 1972 that's all Tony and Maureen Wheeler needed for the trip of a lifetime – across Europe and Asia overland to Australia. It took several months, and at the end – broke but inspired – they sat at their kitchen table writing and stapling together their first travel guide, *Across Asia on the Cheap*. Within a week they'd sold 1500 copies. Lonely Planet was born.

Today, Lonely Planet has offices in Melbourne, London and Oakland, with more than 600 staff and writers. We share Tony's belief that 'a great guidebook should do three things: inform, educate and amuse'.

OUR WRITERS

Daniel Robinson

Coordinating Author, 20 Top Experiences, Welcome to Borneo, Need to Know, If You Like..., Month by Month, Itineraries, Adventure Borneo, Regions at a Glance, Sarawak, Brunei, Borneo Today, History, Environment & Wildlife, Dayak Peoples & Culture, Directory A-Z, Transport Daniel has been writing about Southeast Asia since 1989, when he researched the award-winning 1st edition of Lonely Planet's guides to Vietnam and Cambodia. Since then he has taken a special interest in tropical rainforest habitats and the role that sustainable tourism can play in their conservation. In Borneo, Daniel is especially fond of strolling the Kuching waterfront at sunset, slurping Sarawak *laksa*, tramping through Gunung Gading National Park in search of giant Rafflesia flowers, watching orangutans cavort in Semenggoh's jungle canopy and taking longboat rides up remote rivers. Daniel, who holds a BA in Near Eastern Studies from Princeton University, writes for a variety of magazines and newspapers, including the *New York Times*.

Read more about Daniel at:
lonelyplanet.com/members/danielrobinson

Adam Karlin

Sabah Adam has previously researched mainland Malaysia for Lonely Planet's *Malaysia, Singapore & Brunei* guide and jumped at the chance to head to Borneo for some wild jungle fun. And oh what fun. In the course of his research he hitched a ride on a jeep into the Maliau Basin, burbled happily at cuttlefish in the Semporna Archipelago, tossed a fish head to a water monitor, got ankle deep in bat shit in caves and wasted on Johnny Walker in KK and came close to a perfect travel moment when he witnessed a wild orangutan swing over his head – with baby attached. Adam has researched and written over 20 Lonely Planet guides.

Read more about Adam at:
lonelyplanet.com/members/adamkarlin

Richard Waters

Kalimantan Richard was born in the north of England and seems to have spent most of his life escaping it. His first travels were around Europe as a teenager, then Central America and US by camper van during the last days of the Guatemalan civil war. These days he satisfies his itchy feet writing for newspapers such as the *Sunday Times*, *Independent*, *Telegraph* and *Daily Mail*, and magazines *Elle* and *CNN Traveller*. Lonely Planet seems to send him to jungles rather a lot – if it's not watching hornbills in Borneo it's listening for tigers in Laos. To read more of his work and articles visit www.richardwaters.co.uk. He lives with his fiancée and two kids in the Cotswolds.

Read more about Richard at:
lonelyplanet.com/members/richardwaters

OVER PAGE MORE WRITERS

Published by Lonely Planet Publications Pty Ltd
ABN 36 005 607 983
2nd edition – July 2011
ISBN 978 1 74179 215 7
© Lonely Planet 2011   Photographs © as indicated 2011
10 9 8 7 6 5 4 3 2 1
Printed in China

Although the authors and Lonely Planet have taken all reasonable care in preparing this book, we make no warranty about the accuracy or completeness of its content and, to the maximum extent permitted, disclaim all liability arising from its use.